TERRIBLE VICTORY

TERRIBLE

MARK ZUEHLKE

VICTORY

FIRST CANADIAN ARMY AND THE

SCHELDT ESTUARY CAMPAIGN:

SEPTEMBER 13–NOVEMBER 6, 1944

Douglas & McIntyre

VANCOUVER/TORONTO

Copyright © 2007 by Mark Zuehlke
First paperback edition 2008

08 09 10 11 12   5 4 3 2 1

All rights reserved. No part of this book may be reproduced, stored in a retrieval system or transmitted, in any form or by any means, without the prior written consent of the publisher or a licence from The Canadian Copyright Licensing Agency (Access Copyright). For a copyright licence, visit www.accesscopyright.ca or call toll free to 1-800-893-5777.

Douglas & McIntyre Ltd.
2323 Quebec Street, Suite 201
Vancouver, British Columbia
Canada V5T 4S7
www.douglas-mcintyre.com

Library and Archives Canada Cataloguing in Publication
Zuehlke, Mark
Terrible victory : First Canadian Army and the Scheldt Estuary campaign, Sept. 13–Nov. 6, 1944 / by Mark Zuehlke.
Includes bibliographical references and index.
ISBN 978-1-55365-227-4 (cloth) · 978-1-55365-404-9 (paper)
1. Scheldt River Estuary, Battle of, 1944.
2. Canada. Canadian Army—History—World War, 1939-1945.
3. World War, 1939–1945—Campaigns—Netherlands.
4. World War, 1939-1945—Campaigns—Belgium. I. Title
D756.5.S34Z84 2007   940.54′21   C2007-901955-2

Editing by Elizabeth McLean
Jacket design by Naomi MacDougall & Peter Cocking
Interior design by Peter Cocking
Jacket photographs: top: photographer unknown, LAC E004665470
bottom: Daniel Guravich, LAC PA-138284
Maps by C. Stuart Daniel/Starshell Maps
Printed and bound in Canada by Friesens
Printed on forest-friendly paper

We gratefully acknowledge the financial support of the Canada Council for the Arts, the British Columbia Arts Council, the Province of British Columbia through the Book Publishing Tax Credit, and the Government of Canada through the Book Publishing Industry Development Program (BPIDP) for our publishing activities.

OTHER MILITARY HISTORY BY MARK ZUEHLKE

*Holding Juno: Canada's Heroic Defence of the
D-Day Beaches: June 7–12, 1944* *

Juno Beach: Canada's D-Day Victory: June 6, 1944 *

The Gothic Line: Canada's Month of Hell in World War II Italy *

The Liri Valley: Canada's World War II Breakthrough to Rome *

Ortona: Canada's Epic World War II Battle *

*The Canadian Military Atlas: Four Centuries of Conflict from
New France to Kosovo (with C. Stuart Daniel)* *

*The Gallant Cause: Canadians in the
Spanish Civil War, 1936–1939*

*For Honour's Sake: The War of 1812
and the Brokering of an Uneasy Peace*

*Available from Douglas & McIntyre

War is a crime. Ask the infantry, ask the dead.
ERNEST HEMINGWAY

To most soldiers who fought from the beaches through to Germany, the fighting in the Scheldt was the worst and most ferocious.
CAPTAIN E.C. LUXTON, REGINA RIFLES

That Scheldt was hell on earth.
LIEUTENANT BILL HAYWARD,
NORTH SHORE (NEW BRUNSWICK) REGIMENT

[CONTENTS]

Preface *1*
Acknowledgements *4*
Maps *6*

INTRODUCTION　A Simple Plan *12*

PART ONE　THE FALL OF DREAMS *29*
1　Beginning of the End *31*
2　The Jewel *43*
3　The Streetcar War *58*
4　A Very Heavy Program *71*
5　Illusion of Victory *85*
6　Poor Devils *101*
7　Simonds Takes Command *120*

PART TWO　THE CINDERELLA DAYS *137*
8　Off Our Backsides *139*
9　Close to the Danger Line *155*
10　A Hard Fight *171*
11　With Devastating Effect *188*
12　Did Our Best *204*
13　A Hell of a Way to Go *221*
14　In the Back Door *235*

PART THREE　TIGHTENING THE RING *251*
15　Of First Importance *253*
16　The Toughest Yet *270*
17　A Godsend *288*
18　Black Friday *301*

19	Dominate the Situation *316*
20	To the Last Cartridge *335*
21	Foot-Slogging Jobs *351*

PART FOUR   FIGHT TO THE FINISH *369*

22	Troops on the Ground *371*
23	The South Beveland Race *390*
24	Let's Take the Damned Place *407*
25	The Damned Causeway *427*
26	A Fine Performance *442*

EPILOGUE   The Scheldt in Memory *461*

APPENDIX A   Canadians in the Scheldt: September 13 – November 6, 1944 *467*
APPENDIX B   Canadian Infantry Battalion *472*
APPENDIX C   Canadian and German Army Order of Ranks *473*
APPENDIX D   The Decorations *475*

Notes *477*
Bibliography *518*
General Index *529*
Index of Formations, Units, and Corps *541*

PREFACE

AFTER COMPLETING the two-volume series—*Juno Beach* and *Holding Juno,* which detailed the opening seven days of the invasion of Normandy, I paused to consider what part of Canada's World War II military experience should come next. Certainly, my resolve to continue this work was strong, and there remained many significant battles fought by the Canadian Army to write about. During conversations with Major Michael Boire and others who have helped me immensely over the years since I embarked on a road that has now yielded six books on the war, I broached the idea of a book on First Canadian Army's battle to open the Scheldt estuary in the late summer and early fall of 1944. "Little glory in that one," Michael opined. "And damned complicated and hard to tell," he cautioned.

Preliminary research confirmed his opinion, but it also left me determined to tell the story. Initially, I worried that perhaps this battle had already been extensively covered, but—as had been true with Canada's role in D-Day, this proved not the case. There was Denis and Shelagh Whitaker's *Tug of War,* but, as Denis Whitaker was the commander of the Royal Hamilton Light Infantry, it concentrated mostly on operations of 2nd Canadian Infantry Division north of Antwerp. Then there were several books about Canada's role in Allied operations in northwest Europe that hustled through the

Scheldt in a chapter or two. Even C.P. Stacey's official history, *The Victory Campaign,* treated the Scheldt campaign curiously—giving the events of September scant coverage, and rushing through 4th Canadian Armoured Division's operations from mid-October to early November to the east of 2 CID in a few paragraphs. Undoubtedly, the motivation here was conservation of pages in what was necessarily a large volume.

But something else about Stacey's treatment caught my eye. A "Cinderella Operation," he called it, meaning that the Canadians had to do much with the leavings of supplies not allocated to other Allied armies. As the vital port of Antwerp remained closed to Allied shipping until the campaign was concluded, he seemed unduly apologetic about how long it took to finish the job. Stacey tends to undervalue the contribution of the army he was detailed to write about as its official historian, but regarding the Scheldt he seemed even more extreme.

Digging deep into the records, gathering veteran accounts, and conducting an extensive, detailed tour of the battleground itself, I came away with the opinion that First Canadian Army's conduct of the Battle of the Scheldt had, given the resources provided, been exemplary. I was also struck by the incredibly difficult conditions in which this battle was fought. Repeatedly, veterans referred to it as the worst fighting they saw in the war, and it was easy to see the truth of this.

Was there glory there? In today's world, the word rings as almost archaic. Curiously, I have never heard a veteran use the word. But they do unhesitatingly mention related terms, such as pride and honour. They honour their comrades, are proud of their regiment, and respect the role that Canada played in this titanic struggle for freedom. As has been the case with my past books, *Terrible Victory* is ultimately a tribute to the many thousands of young—often painfully so—Canadians who put their lives at risk in the service of their country. No one in this volunteer army had to go overseas.

In the style of my other books, the story is told by interlacing personal accounts of veterans with material drawn from official records, regimental histories, and many other sources. Hundreds of documents were consulted to ensure that the events are portrayed as accurately as possible. Often, of course, accounts of events from one source differ with those from another. And veteran memory sometimes conflicts with the official record. In such cases, I have consulted as many sources as possible in an attempt to arrive at a reasonable conclusion as to where the truth likely lies.

A WORD ABOUT spelling of place names is in order. Anyone who has travelled in Flemish Belgium will have encountered the problem. You drive towards a village marked on the map as, say, St. Leonard. But you never find it. Instead, you realize the village just passed, identified by signs as Sint-Lenaarts, was the place you sought. The maps Canadians used in World War II Belgium were based on Belgian Army maps, which translated Flemish place names into French ones. Out of respect to the Flemish, who suffered heavily in the fighting to open Antwerp, I have used the Flemish spellings—except for the commonly Anglicized place names of Antwerp (Antwerpen) and Ghent (Gent). Where the Belgian border meets the Netherlands, another difficulty arises, for the two nationalities often disagree on the spelling of places close by. In these cases, I have used the Flemish spelling when in Belgium and Dutch when in the Netherlands. British readers will particularly note that the city of Vlissingen on Walcheren Island is not referred to as Flushing—habitually the case in British works.

Although the number of veteran accounts and recollections of this battle is fewer than has been the case in my past books, I was struck by how closely their memories coincided with the "official" record. Seldom was there any significant contradiction beyond the occasional inability to place an event on the correct date. Our World War II veterans are aging, but the memories of most can still be trusted, regarding these weeks when First Canadian Army underwent its most gruelling test of arms.

ACKNOWLEDGEMENTS

A SPECIAL DEBT OF thanks is owed to the many veterans whose experiences of the Scheldt Campaign appear here. This time out, fewer were available to be personally interviewed or corresponded with, but fortunately many had contributed reminiscences to regimental histories, various archives, or been interviewed previously by other sources. Particularly, I must thank Professor Cecil Law for his enthusiastic correspondence with me about his personal experiences as a young lieutenant in the South Saskatchewan Regiment and for helping piece that regiment's role in the battle together so well. He also spent many hours photocopying and taping together topographic maps of the Scheldt battlefield from his collection that were invaluable in tracing the ebb and flow of the battle. Once again, Ken MacLeod of Langley, B.C. made interviews of veterans in the Vancouver area available, and John Gregory Thompson did the same in southern Ontario. The Royal Winnipeg Rifles Association (British Columbia Association) provided a copy of their veteran account collection entitled *Perspectives*. And, yet again, to Johan, Francis, Luc, and many others for working out civilian casualties.

Ottawa translator and very good friend Alex MacQuarrie provided frequent and extensive translations of both Dutch and French sources. Colonel Tony Poulin translated Le Régiment de la Chaudière's war diary and regimental history for me. A World War II and Korean War veteran, he is dearly missed.

In Holland, I could not have done without the immense contribution of time and wisdom made by Johan van Doorn. Happening upon my website and seeing that I was working on a book about the Scheldt, he contacted me, and from this a friendship has flourished. His extensive knowledge of World War II operations in Holland was invaluable. He also put me in touch with other Dutch and Belgian historians who went out of their way to share what knowledge they could. In Belgium, they are Francis Huijbrechts, Luc Cox, and Wally Schoofs; in Holland, Tom Goossens and Rene Hoebeke. Rene's 928-page *Slagveld Sloedam* is undoubtedly the ultimate work on the Walcheren Causeway fighting. Additional thanks to Francis for assistance in getting the Belgian name places correct, and to Luc for checking these twice.

At the Directorate of Heritage and History, Department of National Defence, Dr. Steve Harris spent time discussing the Scheldt Campaign and ensuring that I was able to access every relevant document in the collection. Michel Litalien was also helpful here. Jane Naisbitt and Carol Reid did similar service at the Canadian War Museum Library and Archives. Staff at Library and Archives Canada went out of their way to enable a researcher from out of town to make best use of extremely limited time. Chris Petter and staff at the University of Victoria's Special Collections were their usual pleasure to deal with.

Writing of this book was greatly assisted by a grant from Canada Council for the Arts. Also on the professional front, my agent Carolyn Swayze continues to do wonders at helping to keep this writer's career solvent and advancing in the right direction.

Scott McIntyre's enthusiasm as the publisher of Douglas & McIntyre for more Canadian battle books is laudable, and also makes continuation of this work possible. Once again, Elizabeth McLean stepped into the breach to edit the manuscript, an act for which I am very grateful. And C. Stuart Daniel was there once more to draw the maps that are so vital in enabling readers to follow the action.

On the home front, Frances Backhouse patiently listened yet again to endless war stories, and was always supportive. That two writers can thrive and live under the same roof remains a source of special wonder to me, but I am very glad this has proved to be so.

6 / TERRIBLE VICTORY

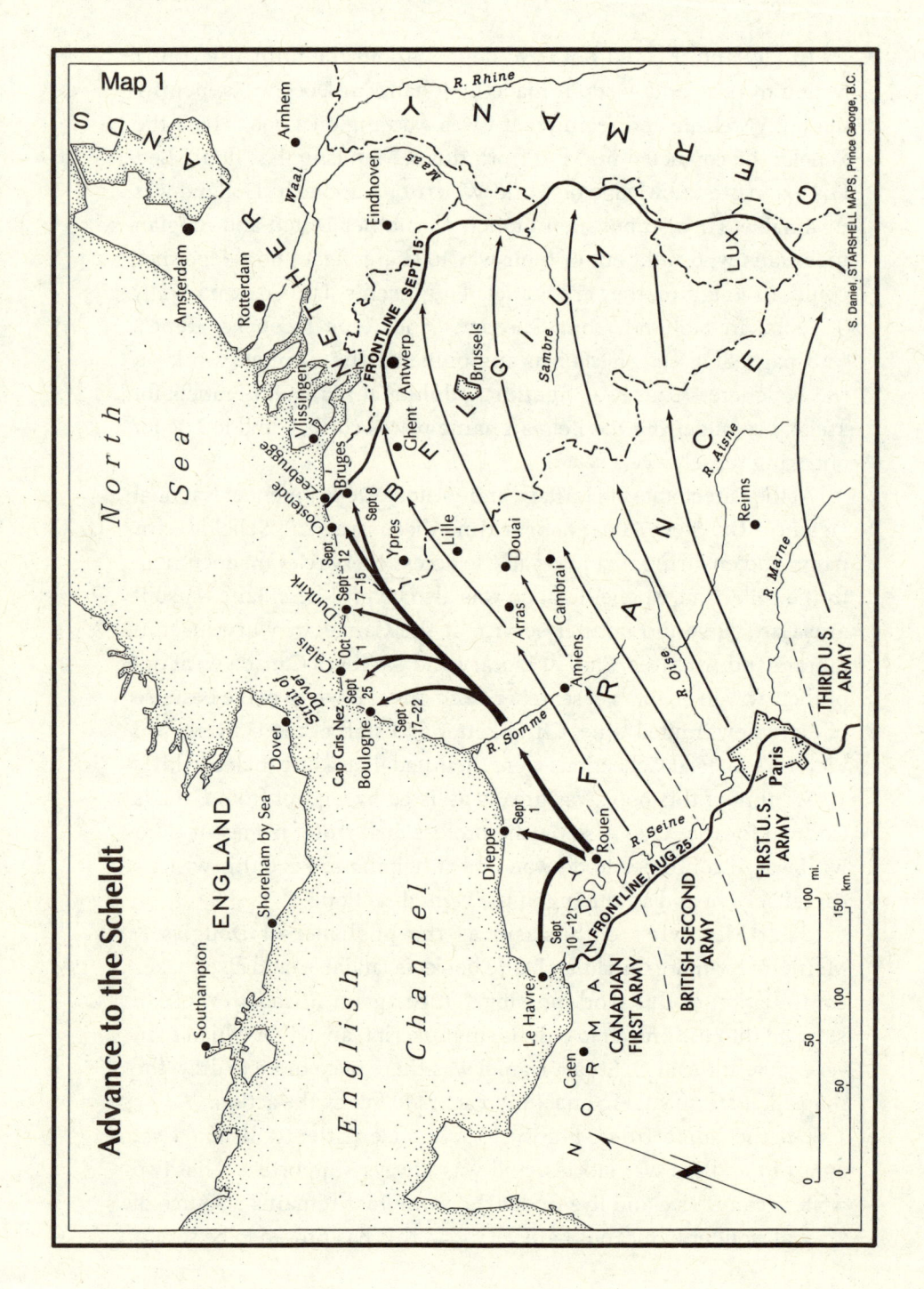

MAPS / 7

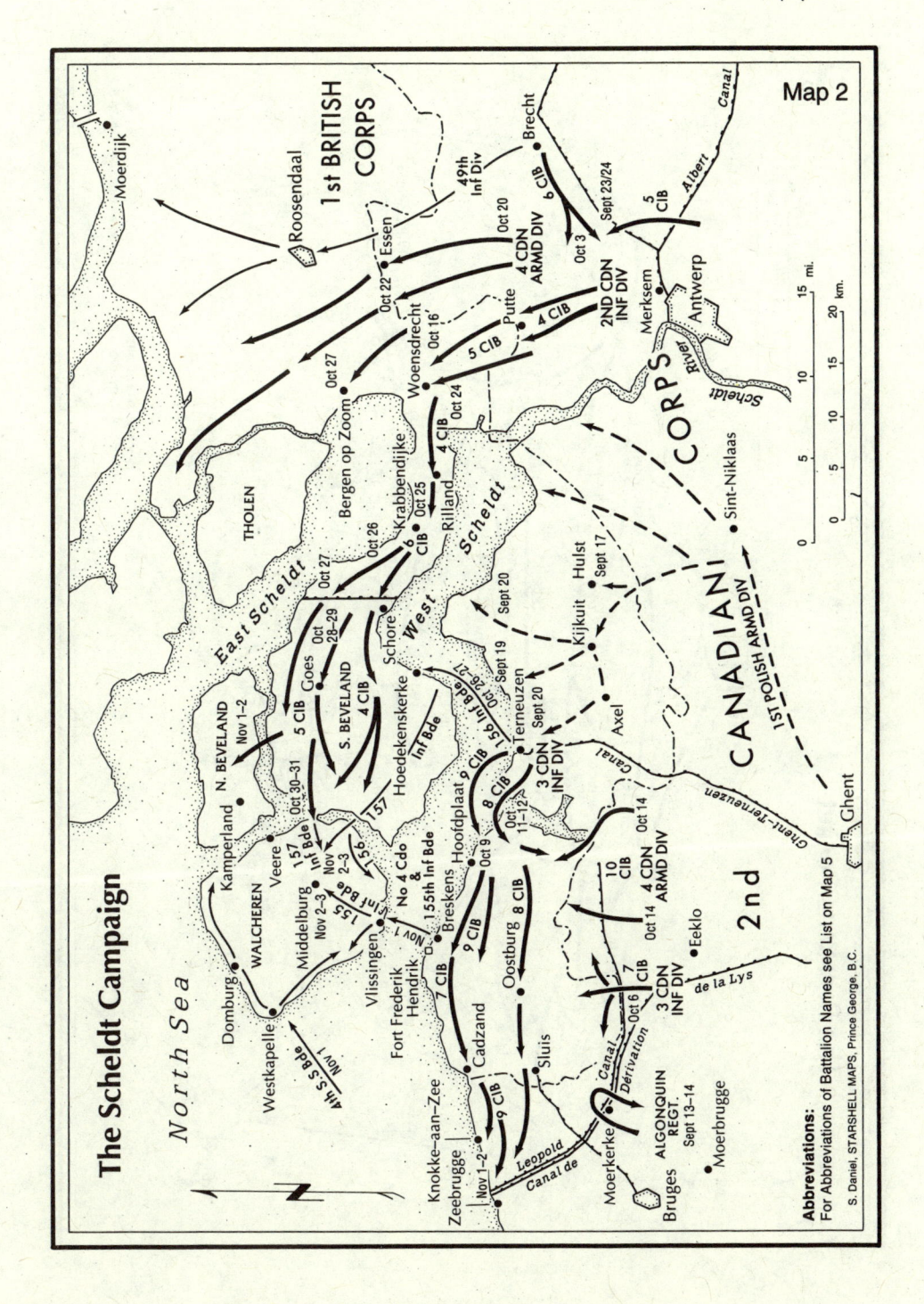

Map 2

The Scheldt Campaign

8 / TERRIBLE VICTORY

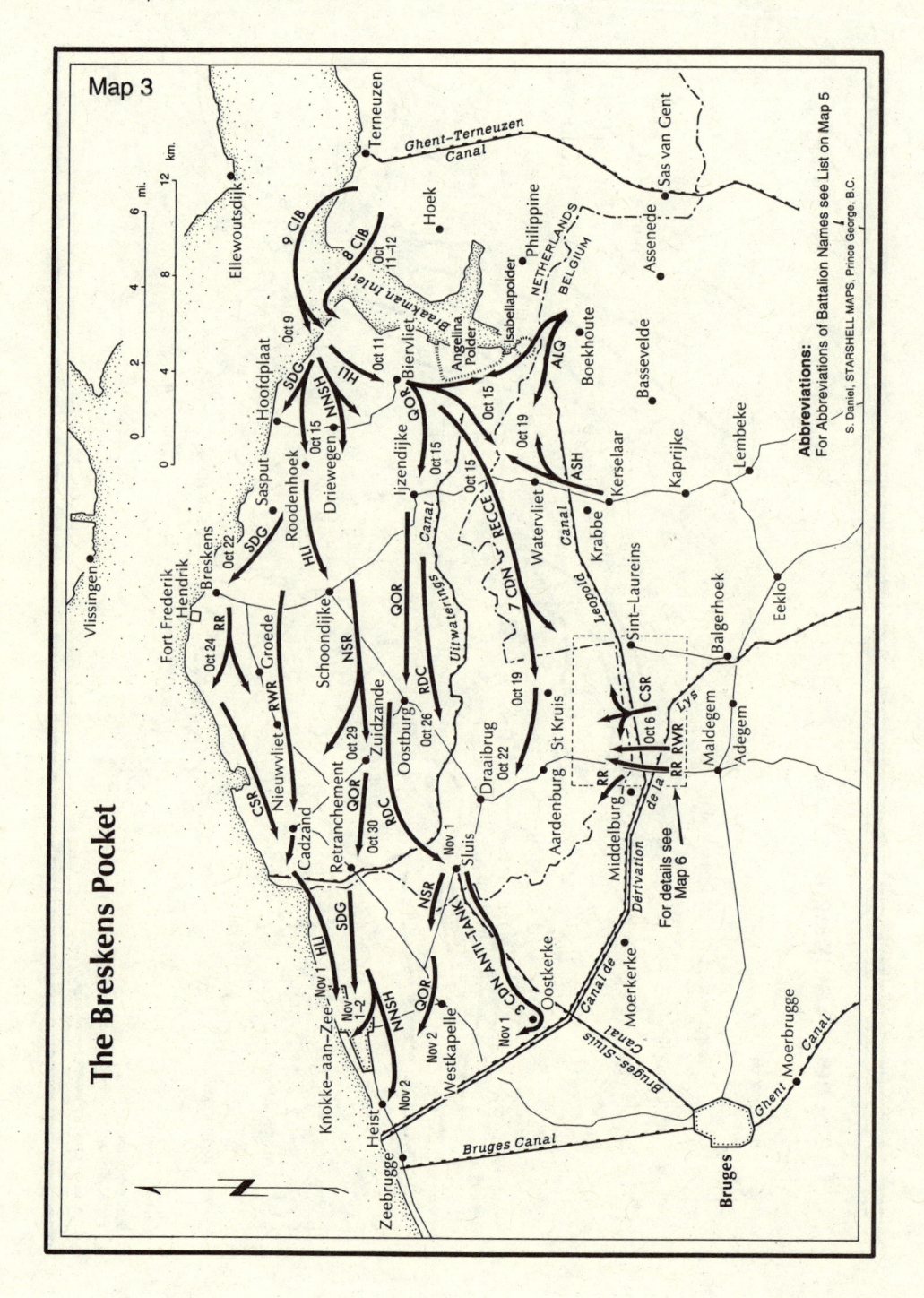

Map 3: The Breskens Pocket

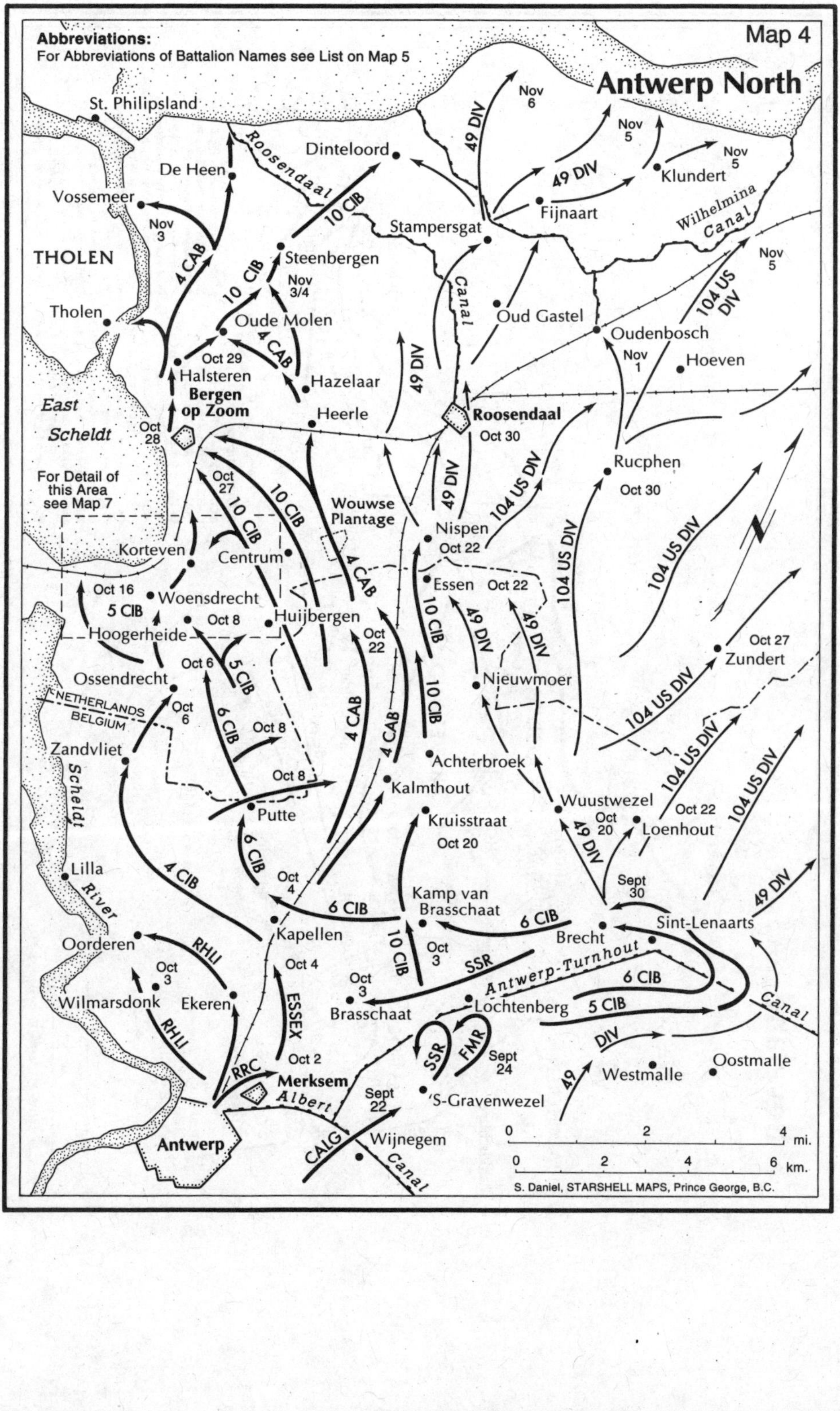
Map 4
Antwerp North
Abbreviations:
For Abbreviations of Battalion Names see List on Map 5
St. Philipsland
Roosendaal
Dinteloord
De Heen
Vossemeer
Nov 3
4 CAB
THOLEN
Tholen
10 CIB
Steenbergen
Nov 3/4
Oude Molen
Oct 29
Halsteren
Hazelaar
Bergen op Zoom
East Scheldt
Oct 28
Heerle
For Detail of this Area see Map 7
Oct 27
Wouwse Plantage
Korteven
Centrum
Oct 16
Woensdrecht
5 CIB
Oct 8
Huijbergen
Hoogerheide
Oct 6
Ossendrecht
NETHERLANDS
BELGIUM
6 CIB
Zandvliet
Scheldt River
Putte
Lilla
4 CIB
Oorderen
RHLI
Wilmarsdonk
Ekeren
Oct 3
Kapellen
Oct 4
ESSEX
Oct 2
RRC
Merksem
Albert Canal
Antwerp
CALG
Wijnegem
Sept 22
'S-Gravenwezel
SSR
FMR
Sept 24
Brasschaat
Lochtenberg
Antwerp-Turnhout Canal
Kamp van Brasschaat
Kalmthout
Kruisstraat
Oct 20
Achterbroek
Nispen
Oct 22
Essen
49 DIV
Roosendaal
Oct 30
Canal
Stampersgat
Oud Gastel
Fijnaart
Klundert
Nov 5
Nov 6
Wilhelmina Canal
Oudenbosch
Nov 1
Hoeven
104 US DIV
Rucphen
Nieuwmoer
Wuustwezel
Loenhout
Zundert
Oct 27
Sept 30
Brecht
Sint-Lenaarts
Westmalle
Oostmalle
49 DIV
0 2 4 mi.
0 2 4 6 km.
S. Daniel, STARSHELL MAPS, Prince George, B.C.

10 / TERRIBLE VICTORY

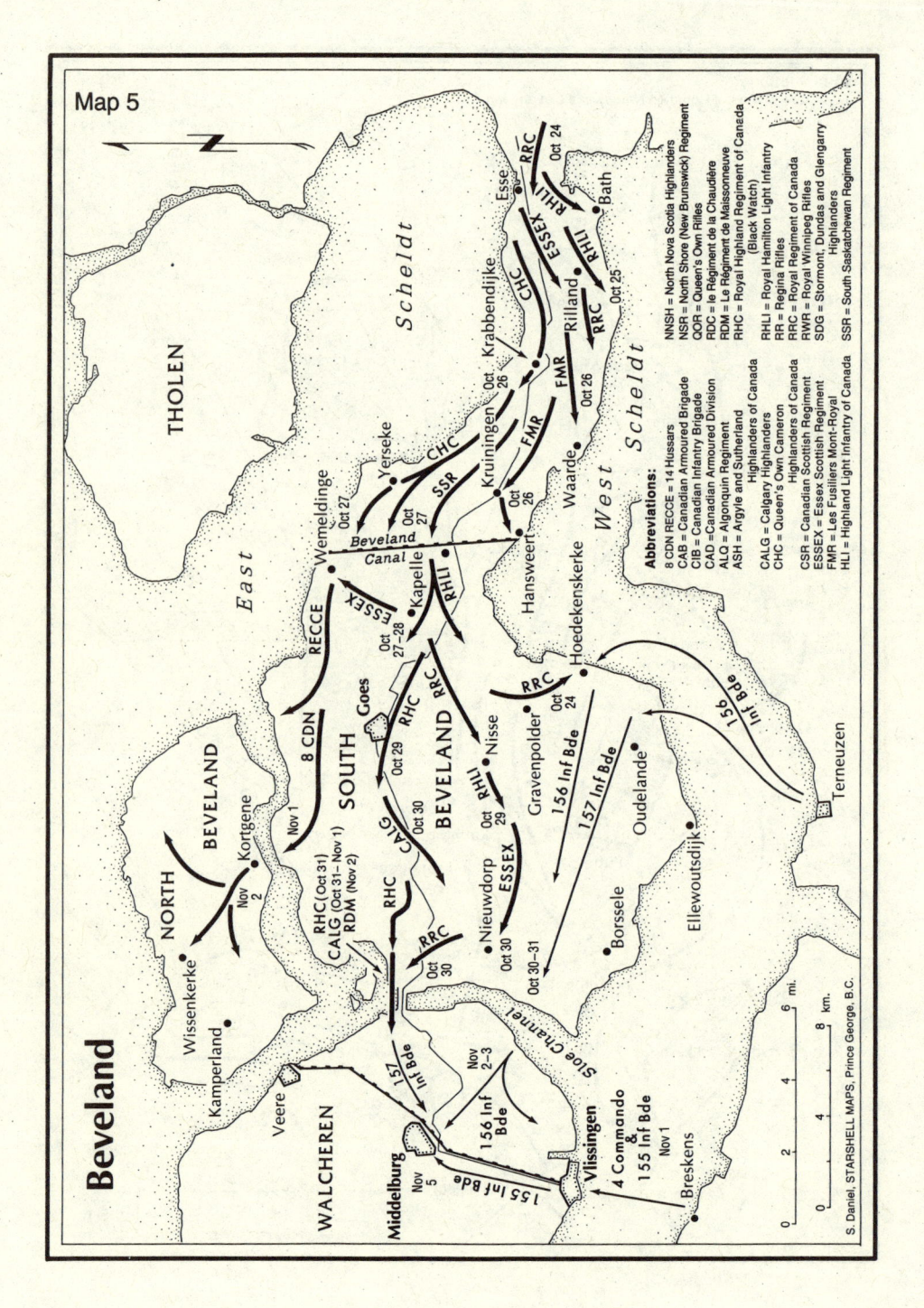

MAPS / II

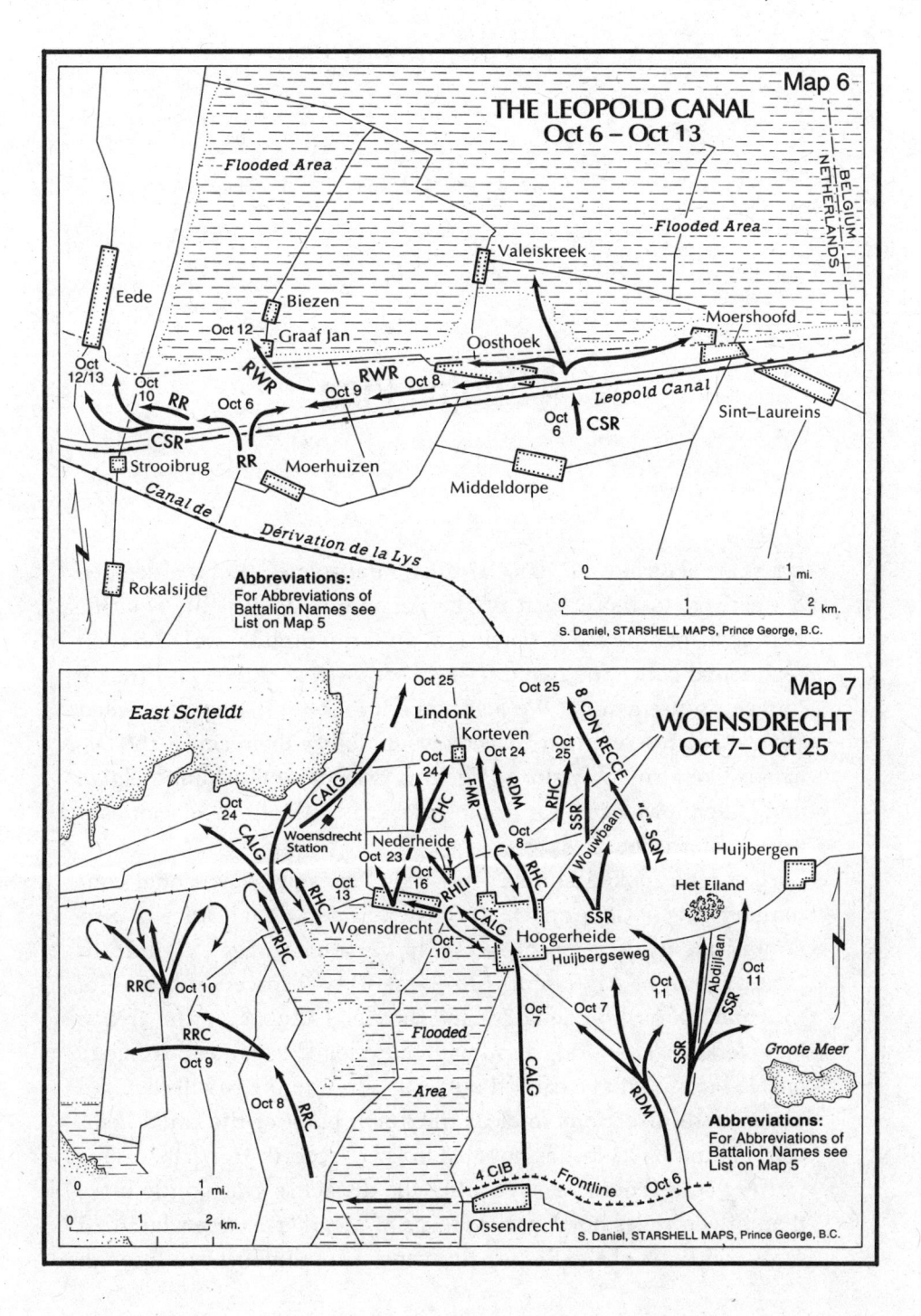

[INTRODUCTION]

A Simple Plan

IT ALL DEPENDED on 360 Canadian infantrymen. But that seemed natural to these men of the Algonquin Regiment. For this regiment, hailing from North Bay, Ontario, proudly wore on their regimental badge the motto NE-KAH-NE-TAH, an Algonquin Indian phrase pronouncing: "We lead, others follow." If they succeeded, 4th Canadian Armoured Division would follow them across the two canals like a runaway storm, flooding over the intervening Belgian and Dutch lowlands clear to the southern bank of the Scheldt estuary's western arm.

The plan looked simple, even tidy, on paper. Divisional commander Major General Harry Foster's operational order of September 13, 1944 set it out in crisp, terse language: "At zero hr [2200] tonight Alg[onquin] R[egiment] will force a crossing of the canal Dérivation de la Lys and the canal Leopold in the area of Moerkerke...This bridgehead will be exploited as far as possible to enable bridging to be carried out... 4 Cdn Armd Div will then fan out in both directions to clear the north bank of the canal Leopold pushing on as fast as possible to Fort Frederik Hendrik."[1] This fortress ruin seemed easily within the division's grasp, little more than fifteen miles north of the village of Moerkerke. A few hundred yards southeast of the fort lay Breskens, a small port town through which the Germans were frantically ferrying men and equipment across the estuary's three-mile-wide mouth to the port of Vlissingen on Walcheren Island.

With Breskens in Canadian hands, Fifteenth German Army would be denied this last-ditch avenue of escape. Nearly 100,000 troops still on the southern shore would be trapped—their only choice to surrender or to be destroyed piecemeal at First Canadian Army's leisure. The loss of such a great number of men would deal Germany a catastrophic blow certain to shorten the war. Additionally, the first major step in opening the Scheldt estuary to enable ships to reach the giant port of Antwerp, already in Allied hands, would be complete. With its miles of undamaged docks available to offload desperately needed supplies, a final nail would be driven into Hitler's coffin.

Nobody expected the Algonquin attack to come off as smoothly as Foster's order implied, but the prevailing belief emanating from First Canadian Army's headquarters was that "a sudden surprise crossing would keep the enemy on the move." Strung out along the twelve-mile stretch where the two canals ran tightly parallel to each other were reportedly no more than five thousand men—all that remained of the badly mauled 245th Infantry Division. Caught off guard, they should have no opportunity to launch an effective counterattack. "There were," army intelligence officers stated, "no indications of the enemy being in strength on the opposite side of the canals."[2] If the attack was put in quickly, boldly, and with minimal advance reconnaissance in order to prevent tipping the Germans off, success should be assured. Dissenting voices, such as that of 4th Division's Captain Ernie Sirluck, who suspected that the Germans lurked behind the canal in far greater strength, were dismissed as alarmist and further proof that reports by division and brigade intelligence officers were seldom credible.[3]

Studying the intelligence appreciation handed down to the Algonquins on the morning of September 13, Major George L. Cassidy assumed "the enemy was thoroughly disorganized, had scarcely any equipment, and was taking refuge behind the canal in a sort of desperation. In any case, it was felt he would show little or no fight if attacked in force. With these soothing words in our ears, we were told that we had been elected to make the initial crossing... It was also made known that reinforcements would arrive in the afternoon. Some of these were the result of another 'comb-out' of specialist people, such as carpenters, shoemakers, etc. Each company was to be built up to a strength of ninety all ranks, and, upon the arrival of the assault boats, each company would carry out a short training period on the erection and carrying of these."[4]

The thirty-five-year-old officer, who commanded 'A' Company, and prior to the war had eked out a living as a teacher in Cobalt, Ontario, was more worried that the promised reinforcements would have long forgotten whatever infantry combat training they had received. Providing enough replacements to keep First Canadian Army's fighting battalions fully manned was proving a chronic problem. As it was, the 90 men promised to each company fell well below the mandated strength of 126 officers and men.

But there was no time to brood. Cassidy had to rush to join Algonquin commander Lieutenant Colonel Robert Bradburn and the rest of the battalion's officers for a hasty reconnaissance of Moerkerke. Everyone crowded into five jeeps for the short trip from their current base in the village of Sijsele. The three-mile stretch of road having been swept earlier by the scout platoon, there was no need for caution. At least, not until everyone was piling out of the jeeps in the village square and a sniper round cracked overhead, causing a disorderly scramble for cover. Any time one of the Canadians ventured into the open, a shot rang out.

Unable to determine the sniper's position, Bradburn decided that only the company commanders would join him on the reconnaissance, while the platoon commanders were directed to an inn that was open for business despite the sniper. Noting that the platoon lieutenants settled into the challenging duty of drinking Belgian beer "with visible reluctance," Cassidy and the other company commanders followed Bradburn into a three-storey building where a corporal from the scout platoon had set up a telescope that, because of intervening groves and lines of trees, provided a limited view of the canals.[5]

None of the men liked what he saw. The crossing was to be made immediately to the east of a blown bridge, with each company forcing its way over at different points. Gaining the south bank of the Canal de Dérivation de la Lys (known to the Flemish as Afleidingskanaal van de Leie) without being detected should be relatively easy under cover of darkness. Roads lined by trees and farmhouses extended out of the centre of Moerkerke all the way to each jumping-off point. But the canals constituted a damnable obstacle. Each was ninety feet wide, and separating them was a flat-topped dyke of the same width. The Leopold had been dug in 1842 to drain the low-lying ground to the northeast, whereas the Dérivation was constructed a few years later to drain a wide swath of marshy, sandy country to the north of Ghent. About seven miles east of Moerkerke, the canals parted ways to enter their respective drainage grounds.[6]

It was going to be necessary to drag the boats over one dyke to gain the Dérivation and then hoist them up and across the intervening dyke in order to cross the Leopold. Most likely, they would be under fire the whole way. If the Germans were thicker on the ground than promised, the regiment would be slaughtered, but there was neither the time nor sufficient ground cover to permit a small patrol to try and determine what opposition was in place. "So, with some misgivings, the party returned to Sysseele [known by the Flemish as Sijsele]."[7]

At 1700 hours, Bradburn convened a final Orders Group and presented the full plan of attack to his officers. The operation had been tightly scripted by 10th Canadian Infantry Brigade's headquarters staff, with division giving it final approval. Cassidy's 'A' Company would cross on the far left quite close to the blown bridge. Crossing to the right would be first 'B' Company, then 'C' Company, and lastly 'D' Company, with a seventy-five yard separation between each. The boats were to be delivered to the square by Moerkerke's church and carried from there to the launching points. Bradburn cheered his officers up considerably when he set out the fire support they could expect. The entire divisional artillery would provide covering fire, along with the brigade's mortars and the medium machine guns of the New Brunswick Rangers. Forty collapsible wood and canvas assault boats, fourteen reconnaissance boats, and a few civilian craft would carry them over. Special ladders to which grappling hooks were attached would aid the men in climbing the steep dykes. So that the Algonquins could concentrate on the attack, eighty men from the Lincoln and Welland Battalion—the Lincs—would act as paddlers and help manhandle the boats over the dykes.[8]

Once across the canals, 'A' and 'B' Companies would clear the hamlet of Molentje, which consisted of about fifteen farmhouses straddling the road just north of the blown bridge, while 'C' and 'D' Companies advanced four hundred yards across open fields to secure a road that extended east out of Molentje, parallel to the Leopold Canal. Intelligence reported that 'A' Company would not need to guard its left flank, as the ground to the west was flooded. Once the Algonquins established a firm bridgehead, engineering units would throw up a bridge on the site of the destroyed one. When the bridge was serviceable, 10 CIB, amply supported by armour, would push out towards the towns of Sluis and Aardenburg as the first stage of the advance to Breskens. The attack would go in at 2200 hours.

Thinking the plan over, Cassidy decided it "had obvious advantages. It was simple and control would not be difficult. The crossing place was not a too-obvious one, yet it had suitable off-loading points for boats and bridging, and the route to the crossing points was fairly sheltered...there were few questions."[9]

WORRISOMELY, THOUGH, the reinforcements arrived late. "It was barely possible to take down their names, assign them to companies, give them the briefest of briefings, and show them what an assault boat looked like, and then it was time to move off." The Algonquins marched quickly to Moerkerke, where the boats were found next to the ruins of the church and the Lincs' eighty-man ferrying party under command of Lieutenant R.F. Dickie joined them.[10] Each company was met by a member of the scout platoon, who would guide it to the designated launch point.

As the men shouldered the boats and headed in darkness towards the canals, artillery and mortar rounds thundered down on both shores. A stiff breeze caused the smoke from the explosions to drift like a dense fog around the Canadians, so it was hard to find their way. Following his guide, who was having trouble locating the route, Cassidy led his men "between some stone garden walls, through an alleyway so narrow that the erected boats had to be carried sideways on the men's heads. Arms and paddles kept slipping out and crashing on the pavement, and there were a good many spluttering curses flying about."[11]

It took thirty minutes for the companies to grope by circuitous routes over a distance that, as a crow flew, was barely more than five hundred yards. By the time the men started heaving the boats up the bank of the first dyke, the artillery program had run its course and the guns ceased firing. As the boats were being launched, German infantry on the opposite shore opened fire with machine guns, rifles, and mortars. But the Algonquins and Lincs—eighteen men to a boat—dug their paddles hard into the icy water and drove into the deadly hail.

'A' Company was lucky, the fire on its front relatively light. In minutes, it gained the middle dyke. The riflemen leading the scramble up its bank overran several Germans stunned by the artillery fire. Dragging the boats over the dyke, the platoons piled back into them and quickly paddled across the Leopold. Only as they landed did Cassidy realize that just two of the Lincs who were to ferry the boats back had actually joined his party. The rest had either been diverted unintentionally to the other companies or had got lost. As the boats were too large and heavy for two men to manhandle back over the centre dyke, Cassidy decided they would have to stay where they were until it was possible to delegate men to return them. A quick reorganization in the lee of the dyke revealed that only one man in the company had been wounded in the crossing. 'A' Company's attack was going pretty well according to script.

Not so for 'B' Company. The boats carrying Lieutenant Thomas Clair Dutcher's platoon paddled straight into the line of a 20-millimetre gun's fire that "raised complete havoc." Many of the men, including the twenty-five-year-old officer from Elmvale, Ontario, were wounded. Those left unscathed were unable to reorganize for the next crossing because of the gun's persistent fire. Dutcher's wounds proved fatal; he died on September 17.

The same gun blasted away at 'B' Company's two remaining platoons, but they managed to cross the first canal and launch into the Leopold. Crossfire from MG 42 light machine guns punched holes in the boats and kicked up waterspouts all around them as the men paddled frantically for the other shore. Overhead, flares popped and illuminated the scene for the German gunners. Tracers flashed past. When the boats touched the dyke, Captain A.R. Herbert's platoon took cover in its lee and crept close to the 20-millimetre gun position. Then Herbert and several other men knocked it out with well-thrown grenades. Gun silenced, Major J.S. McLeod was able to reorganize his company. Grimly, he determined that an entire platoon's worth of men had already been either killed or wounded in less than thirty minutes.

Well to the right of 'B' Company, Major A.K. Stirling's 'C' Company crossed fairly easily despite encountering some heavy small-arms fire. But the men landed at a point where the canal was densely lined by tall alders that blocked Stirling's field of view. He was also blinded by the lingering smoke from the artillery bombardment. Gazing about, Stirling saw through the haze a line of trees to his left that extended inland. He mistook these for ones that had been identified earlier as useful markers to guide his company to its assigned position. Cursing the fact that his radio had stopped working, Stirling led his men to the trees and beyond. He would have liked to establish contact with the other company commanders to confirm his position relative to theirs.

'D' Company, meanwhile, had launched directly in front of a second 20-millimetre gun. To escape the deadly fire, Major W.A. Johnston ordered his men to paddle well to the right of their assigned landing point. After landing, the company marched about five hundred yards inland and then hooked to the left to gain a position astride the road parallelling the canals, near to where the operational plan called for them to dig in. Scouts soon made contact with 'C' Company, which was found to be far off its intended course and almost to the immediate rear of Johnston's men. Stirling and Johnston met for a quick conference and decided that 'C' Company, still close to the canal, should anchor itself in the line of trees and secure the battalion's right flank from the beachhead up to the road. Once they were in position, Johnston would move through the forward elements of 'C' Company at the road and take up the position that had been Stirling's original objective.

As 'C' Company moved towards the tree line, a flare arced out of it and starkly illuminated the infantrymen. In the distance, several mortars thumped and seconds later the rounds exploded in their midst. Some men fell wounded, but the rest charged recklessly into the trees and overran the Germans who had fired the flares. Equipped with a radio, they had been directing the mortar fire.

It was now about 2300, and a relative calm descended over the battlefield. Everyone was worn out from dragging the heavy boats across the centre dyke. Nerves were on edge. In Molentje, Cassidy's 'A' Company was clearing the buildings on the west side of the main road. In the darkness, ensuring that every stairwell, room, and cellar held no enemy was difficult. Where the road intersected the one parallelling the canal, Cassidy called a halt. He placed one platoon in buildings covering the road, another in a group of buildings to the northwest that provided good observation out to the left flank, and the third platoon extended along the left flank of the hamlet back to the canal. His headquarters was set up in a large grain mill. Cassidy now discovered that the supposedly flooded area to the west was dry, providing a perfect avenue of approach. Cassidy told everyone to keep a sharp eye turned that direction. So far, his company seemed blessed with only one early casualty.

To 'A' Company's right, McLeod's men were progressing more slowly in clearing buildings, due to their earlier losses. Hoping to get an assessment of 'B' Company's advance, Cassidy crossed into its sector and joined McLeod in the street. The two men were just beginning to speak when a Schmeisser machine pistol to the left of the road let out a long burst that sent them dodging for cover. By the time the German handling the gun was driven off, the two majors decided it would be unwise for the weakened company to attempt a renewed advance. Instead, it was to tuck in to the right of 'A' Company and then extend feelers out to establish a link with 'C' Company. The officers didn't know that 'C' Company was not in its assigned position or that 'D' Company was on the rightward edge of that area. A serious gap in the Canadian line had opened. As well, the entire position was now only about 250 yards wide instead of 450, as originally planned.

Around midnight, the calm was shattered as the Germans opened up with heavy artillery and mortar fire that rained down throughout the bridgehead. Clearly, the Germans had recovered from their initial surprise. It was equally obvious that they knew precisely what the Canadians intended, and any attempt to approach the old bridge site was met by accurate shelling. Despite this, the engineers of 9th Canadian Field Squadron, with elements of 8th Canadian Field Squadron in support, were able to mark the building line for the bridge with white tape, and a bulldozer began grading approaches on the southern bank while under fire.[12] Cassidy considered that the setbacks suffered so far were relatively minor. With the morning, the operation should enable 4th Canadian Armoured Division to bridge the canals and begin the breakout to Breskens.[13]

NEWS THAT THE Canadians had forced a crossing of the canals greatly alarmed the Germans. The Algonquins had barely clambered out of their assault boats when General der Infanterie Werner Freiherr von und zu Gilsa, commander of LXXXIX Corps, was alerted to their presence. Summoning his driver, the officer hurried to Lapscheure to meet Generalleutnant Erwin Sander, who commanded 245th Infantry Division, responsible for defending the canals. On September 4, Oberkommando der Wehrmacht (OKW) in Berlin had emphasized the importance of preventing any breach of the Leopold Canal when it formally designated the Breskens area as "Scheldt Fortress South" and ordered its defenders to "hold out to the last."[14]

The Belgian village of Lapscheure was less than three miles northeast of Moerkerke, so as the two men conferred, the sounds of fighting could be plainly heard. Fifty-five years of age, von Gilsa had entered the army immediately after his nineteenth birthday, served through the Great War, and risen steadily up the command chain since 1939. He was no alarmist, but it was plain that German control of the approaches to Antwerp and Fifteenth Army's escape route at Breskens could be lost unless immediate countermeasures were taken. Von Gilsa gave Sander "the strictest instructions that the bridgehead must at all costs be eliminated." If necessary, the corps reserve would be thrown into the battle.[15]

Sander was already aggressively unleashing his infantry and artillery against the Algonquins. Patrols carried out by the 936th Grenadier Regiment soon discovered the gap between the two Algonquin companies to the east and those inside Molentje. Using the cover of darkness, the Germans crept up close to 'C' Company's perimeter and hit it hard all along the line. Soon they succeeded in infiltrating between the two forward platoons and the one holding a base position at the canal. With Stirling's already weakened company strung out among the trees in a line that stretched about 180 yards from the canal inland, the men were unable to hunt down and eliminate the infiltrators.[16] When some closed to within twenty feet of the slit trenches that housed Stirling's headquarters section near the bank, only rapid fire thrown out by Privates George Arthur Wright and A.G. McGuffin manning a Bren gun prevented the position being overrun.

All contact with Lieutenant Geoffrey John Hunter's platoon—holding the middle of the line—was lost. Lieutenant K.E. Butler, whose platoon was farthest inland, was wounded and only with difficulty carried safely back to the canal. As the first predawn light began to touch the horizon, Stirling realized his company had been shredded—with casualties upwards of 75 per cent.[17]

The Germans were equally focused on destroying the battalion's headquarters and the engineers vainly trying to bridge the canals. Shortly after the attack had gone in, Moerkerke became subject to heavy, continuous shelling. Moerkerke was a typical Flemish village, a scatter of red brick houses—some with adjoining pastures and large gardens—and shops loosely clustered around a square where a large church, whose belfry had soared to a height of more than one hundred feet, stood. The tower no longer existed. At about 1430 hours on September 13, knowing the tower would provide the advancing Canadians with a dominating observation post, the Germans had set up an 88-millimetre gun on the edge of Molentje.

Nine shells had been fired, each scoring a direct hit, and the tower had collapsed onto the church itself. Tons of bricks and supporting beams penetrated the roof to cause extensive damage within.[18] Now the village itself was being slowly battered to pieces.

At first, the barrage seemed randomly directed, but by 0100 hours the Algonquins realized that the fire was zeroing in on their headquarters in some buildings deliberately selected for their unassuming size and position. The Regimental Aid Post, which had so far taken in only a few casualties, took a direct hit. Roman Catholic Padre Tom Mooney died instantly. Protestant Padre W. Valentine, Medical Officer Captain W.F. Mackenzie, and several attendants were wounded. Walking wounded and uninjured alike hastily evacuated the seriously injured from the RAP into the shelter of battalion headquarters. But when this building suffered a series of direct hits, Lieutenant Colonel Bradburn ordered a general evacuation to another building. No sooner had everyone started setting up the new headquarters than it "became the centre of a well-aimed barrage," prompting another move.[19] The German artillery's uncanny and precise targeting of the battalion command centre through successive moves seriously disrupted attempts to support operations in the bridgehead.[20]

In the bridgehead, the situation was increasingly confused. From 0300 to dawn, 'A' and 'B' Companies occupied a quiet place in the middle of a storm. Shells bound for Moerkerke screamed overhead, while constant gunfire to the east told Major Cassidy that the other two companies were hotly engaged. But he was unable to establish radio contact with the embattled companies, and reports coming from a battalion command on the run were scanty. Still, Cassidy and 'B' Company's McLeod remained optimistic that daylight would clear the situation up and enable the Algonquins to drive the enemy off.

Instead, dawn revealed that Germans had used the darkness and mist to press in all around the Algonquins. Suddenly, "every man on the bridgehead [was] fighting for his life," Cassidy later wrote. Snipers cropped up in houses throughout Molentje and had to be cleared out one by one. No sooner were some houses swept clean than new snipers infiltrated into them. Lieutenant Dan McDonald found himself pinned down in a chicken coop with an egg two inches from his nose, pondering whether to eat it there or take it along when he had a chance to escape.

Germans had managed to cross back onto the central dyke and were firing into the Algonquin's rear. The persistent morning mist made it difficult to locate the Germans, who filtered about like ghosts within its grey cloak. From the top storey of the grain mill that housed 'A' Company's headquarters section, Private T. Hansen spotted five enemy soldiers setting up in a concrete dugout on the southern bank of the Dérivation de la Lys. Over open sights at a range of almost five hundred yards, Hansen killed each of the men with his Lee Enfield. Cassidy was disquieted to realize "that even the 'home' side of the canal was not clear."

Scanning the small Canadian perimeter with binoculars, Cassidy "could see Algonquins in slits, then Germans, then more Algonquins, but it was not possible to identify which company they belonged to."[21] A runner from 'D' Company reported that it was in dire straits.

This was no overstatement. The most forward sections of the lead platoon had been forced to retreat under fire to avoid being cut off. Tying in with the rest of the platoon farther back, the men had just begun frantically digging new slits when a shell landed in their midst and mortally wounded their section commander, Corporal Ernest Freve. "Never mind me, dig in and get under cover," he shouted to prevent his men trying to carry him to safety. Lying in the open, Freve called encouragement to his men until he died.[22]

NO AMOUNT OF heroism could enable the Algonquins to prevail this day. By mid-morning the Germans were throwing in well-organized, battalion-strength attacks. Ammunition was running short. Cassidy bitterly realized that in "our inexperience, or because we were confident of uninterrupted supply, we had brought only normal extra ammunition with us." A dozen ammo parties were formed to ferry supplies into the bridgehead, but each was broken up by the Germans dug in on the dyke between the canals. Matters were further complicated by a lack of boats. Five of the original forty assault craft had been sunk in the attack, and many of the others were beached on the wrong side of the canals for lack of crews to paddle them back. One error after another was tipping the odds against the Algonquins.

Cassidy and the artillery forward observation officer, Captain Davies, were able to keep the Germans somewhat at bay by calling in artillery fire on suspected forming-up areas. But the situation was precarious, as the enemy pressed in from all sides. At 1030 hours, a small German artillery piece opened up on 'A' Company's rear from inside a house at the foot of the blown bridge, where the engineers were supposed to have been constructing the Canadian crossing. Lieutenant N.R.F. Steenberg and Lance Corporal Vernon Everett Spiers rushed the building, but as Spiers opened a cellar door, a Schmeisser shrieked out a burst and the twenty-six-year-old from Etwell, Ontario, fell dead. Steenberg withdrew, teed up another attack covered by a Bren gun, and knocked the gun out with two grenades. The action garnered him a Military Cross.

Throughout the perimeter, casualties were mounting and ammunition was nearly exhausted. When Cassidy rounded up some grenades to distribute to Lieutenant Edward Roberts's platoon up the road, he learned that the young Ottawa-born officer had been killed by a shell and all the sergeants and senior corporals debilitated by wounds. Lance Corporal E.F. Brady had taken charge, but he had only twelve men left. Brady "was cool and efficient, completely confident of the outcome, and his only worry was to get enough ammunition to go on." The men were searching Germans taken prisoner for ammunition, for by now they were primarily using captured weapons. Brady's steady leadership would earn him a Military Medal.

The young soldier's optimism was misplaced. At 1100 hours, the tempo of German attacks attained a new fury. Fifty per cent of 'B' Company's men were casualties, and Major McLeod had ordered a fighting withdrawal back through Molentje to the centre of the hamlet, where he hoped to regroup. To the right, 'C' Company's Major Stirling was trying to get his wounded back to the canal in the desperate hope that they might be evacuated to safety. He and Private Wright tried to move one of the boats on the canal bank to a position of cover, but were driven back by shellfire. When Wright tried again alone, he was killed.

With the Germans in among the Canadians, it was impossible for Cassidy and Davies to bring artillery fire to bear. An attempt to direct three-inch mortars onto a German position only resulted in the fire falling onto the Algonquins. Davies turned to Cassidy and said he wanted to prepare a smoke artillery plan to cover the battalion in the event it was ordered to withdraw across the canals. The German shelling was increasingly accurate, enabling the enemy to overrun all of 'A' and 'B' Companies' forward positions. Those men who survived "crawled back through ditches and through houses, finally concentrating in a narrow semicircle just north of the bridge."[23]

At noon, the order came for the Algonquins to break out from the closing trap to the home side of the canal. Bradburn had been desperately trying to get relief to his embattled battalion, to no avail. Unable to ferry ammunition across the canals, he had requested a parachute drop, only to be told no planes were available. A hasty plan to throw the Argyll and Sutherland Highlanders in to reinforce the bridgehead was abandoned for lack of boats. Facing the inevitable, Major General Foster authorized the withdrawal.

No time was wasted. Within minutes of receiving the order, Davies was calling down the planned smokescreen. A barrage was laid down by artillery, mortars, and the main guns of the nearby South Alberta Regiment's Sherman tanks. The fire was maintained until the companies all escaped piecemeal across the canals. In twos and threes, the Algonquins fought their way back to the bank of the Leopold Canal. German shelling had intensified, the enemy soldiers pressing in as they smelled victory. Providing the artillery with coordinate corrections, Davies tightened the smokescreen around the retreating men. Across the canal, the gunners were chucking out a terrific rate of fire. In the batteries of 15th Canadian Field Artillery, the order was given to "fire until ammunition expended."[24] Nobody could remember such instructions being given before, but they set to fulfilling the task despite muscles that cried out for a rest from hefting the 25-pound shells and powder charges. When it was over, the gunners had unleashed 11,000 rounds in a twenty-four-hour period.[25]

The firing had the desired result, holding the Germans sufficiently at bay to enable most of the Algonquins to escape. Generalleutnant

Sander was awed by "the most incredible artillery barrage that [he] had ever seen." The 245th Infantry Division commander expected that it foretold an attempt to reinforce the current bridgehead and was surprised to learn "the enemy had retired and used this form of cover to evacuate his troops."[26] Although the Germans had repulsed the crossing attempt, they paid a heavy price, with 166 men being killed outright or later succumbing to wounds. Among these was the commander of 936th Grenadier Regiment, Major Herman Drill. Hundreds of other wounded Germans flooded the hospitals in Sluis and Oostburg in the battle's aftermath.[27]

Not all the Canadians managed to get out, despite men attempting to drag or carry the wounded while others protected them with covering fire. A number of the more badly injured had to be left. Stretcher-bearer Private Albert Joseph Coté volunteered to remain with three tourniquet cases. Soon after the other Algonquins headed off, shellfire wrecked the building where he and the wounded men sheltered. Coté was fatally wounded. When Sergeant L.J. Marshall learned that 'A' Company's Sergeant James Henry Speck had been inadvertently left behind in Molentje, he turned back from the canal bank and with nineteen-year-old Private Gerald Reginald Kelly went back to get him. The two men found the house and Kelly hoisted the wounded Speck over his shoulder. They were running towards the canal when a mortar round landed just four feet away. The blast killed Kelly and Speck instantly. Injured by the explosion, Marshall managed to drag himself to the canal.

There were few boats, so the men had to hold the perimeter in ever lessening numbers as those that went before them escaped. Each trip was made through a rain of shellfire, but the heavy smokescreen concealed the withdrawal from the German infantry sufficiently to prevent them bringing their small arms to bear. The remnants of 'C' Company trickled in, but they had been unable to get word through to the most forward platoon. Lieutenant Hunter and his men had been cut off. The thirty-two-year-old from Fort William, Ontario and his handful of surviving men fought on until Hunter was killed. Then the few remaining men surrendered.

By this time, the withdrawal was over, ending when a final group of men reached the canal to find that the boats were all gone. Casting aside their weapons and most of their clothing, they swam across the Leopold Canal, crawled over the intervening dyke, and then swam the Dérivation de la Lys to safety. The Algonquins had suffered terribly. Casualties totalled eight officers and 145 other ranks. Three officers were dead, along with 26 other ranks. Five officers had been wounded, as had 53 other ranks, and 66 men were missing and presumed taken prisoner.

Cassidy and many of the other Algonquins straggled up the grass-covered road from the canal into Moerkerke. Some were near naked, all desperately tired. Passing the corner by the ruined church, Cassidy encountered a large sergeant from the engineering unit that had been prevented from building the bridge that might have saved their attack. The man had liberated a large box of Dutch cigars from a shell-shattered storefront and "was calmly handing one to each survivor, while the shells whistled overhead and crumped into the buildings. It was almost like receiving one's diploma on graduation day... It was a sober, but not a depressed, group of men who were reorganized in farmyards about a mile from the canal. There was an air of regret and sadness certainly, but also a feeling of what can only be called 'battle elation.' The tension had been terrific; men had carried themselves along with a sort of superiority complex; and though we had been beaten, and soundly, no one felt that it was because of any individual failing, but only that we had met far superior forces."[28] By 1500, the Algonquins had withdrawn entirely to Sijsele and Moerkerke was once again contested ground.

High command hinted darkly that the failure could be attributed to Belgian spies betraying the Algonquin preparations. How else to account for the rapidity of the counterattacks?[29] But the only forthcoming evidence was the discovery of a Belgian in Moerkerke possessing a hidden radio, and it was later determined that he had directed the deadly fire on the battalion command post during the morning of September 14.[30] It was unlikely that he could have divined the Canadian intention before the attack.

Regardless, the optimistic plan set down by Major General Foster was in tatters. There would be no immediate attempt to force a crossing. In fact, II Canadian Corps commander, Lieutenant General Guy Simonds, issued an edict later that afternoon stating, "we will now maintain contact, and exert some pressure without sacrificing our forces in driving out an enemy who may be retreating."[31] The evident wishful thinking was that Fifteenth Army would do the work for the Allies by fleeing north of the Scheldt estuary, thus sparing First Canadian Army a grim and likely protracted campaign to evict it. This proved a pipe dream. The Algonquin failure at the canals became the opening round in what became Canada's bloodiest test of arms in World War II—The Battle of the Scheldt.

PART ONE

THE FALL OF DREAMS

[1]

Beginning of the End

THEY CALLED IT "The Pursuit," and everyone from supreme command generals to the lowliest private had wanted to believe it would finally end in Berlin—the war finished before Christmas. "The Pursuit" seemed the Allied reward for tenaciously enduring the gruelling battle to break out of the Normandy beachhead. During those terrible weeks from D-Day to August, it had seemed that the ring of German steel pinning the Canadian, British, Polish, and American divisions inside that murderous land of hedgerows and shattered cities and towns might never break. But when the German hold had been broken and the Allied armoured cars and tanks were suddenly on the loose, barrelling into the heart of France with the infantry and artillery racing behind, the dream of an early end was embraced.

Supreme Headquarters Allied Expeditionary Force (SHAEF) intelligence summaries resonated with optimism. "The August battles have done it and the enemy in the West has had it," one declared. "Two and a half months of bitter fighting have brought the end of the war in Europe within sight, almost within reach." The Germans were fleeing in disarray, their strategic situation deteriorated so "that no recovery is possible" and the chance of "organized resistance under the control of the German High Command is unlikely to continue beyond 1 December 1944, and... it may end even sooner."[1]

Every day, the great Allied divisions rolled from sunrise to sunset, easily swatting aside sporadic German roadblocks. The Germans in France were reeling after Normandy. More than fifty thousand had been slaughtered or captured east of Caen in the Falaise Gap meat grinder. Barely eighteen thousand had slipped through the narrow gap before First Canadian Army slammed it shut on August 21. Those who eluded destruction did so only by abandoning most of their tanks, artillery, and transport.

Army Group B—the massive German force that had fought relentlessly at first to drive the Allies back into the sea from which they had come on June 6 and then, when such a decisive victory proved impossible, had attempted to bottle up the Allies in Normandy—had been shredded. Fleeing north across the Seine was nothing more than its tattered remnants—lacking cohesion, demoralized, on the run. On August 29, then Army Group B commander Generalfeldmarschall Walter Model told Adolf Hitler that, of the eleven Panzer and Panzer Grenadier divisions in Normandy, each had fled across the Seine with no more than five to ten tanks. These divisions could reform as no more than eleven regimental-sized battle groups, and only if promptly re-equipped with weapons and reinforcements. The survivors from the sixteen infantry divisions might be sufficient to field just four divisions, but the caveat here was that they had "only a few heavy weapons and for the most part are equipped with nothing more than small arms...The supply of replacements in men and material is utterly inadequate... There is no reserve whatever of assault guns and other anti-tank equipment." To hold the Allies, Model urgently required reinforcement in the form of twelve Panzer divisions and thirty to thirty-five infantry divisions.[2] It was a prescription that Hitler was incapable of fulfilling.

Total German losses in Normandy had been staggering—about 200,000 dead or wounded, another 200,000 taken prisoner. Added to that was the loss of 1,300 tanks, 20,000 vehicles, 500 assault guns, and 1,500 field guns and heavier artillery pieces. The disaster was matched only by Stalingrad. One division, heavily engaged by the Canadians throughout the Normandy campaign, was the 12th ss (Hitlerjugend) Panzer Division. This division, largely comprised of fanatical Hitler Youth, had been slaughtered. On D-Day, it had numbered 20,540 men and 175 tanks.[3] Only 300 escaped Normandy, and every tank was either abandoned or destroyed.[4]

But the Allied victory carried a heavy price. Casualties totalled 206,703, of which the United States lost 124,394 and the British, Poles, and Canadians 82,309. Canada's losses were disproportional to the smaller numbers it fielded. From D-Day when 3rd Canadian Infantry Division surged onto Juno Beach through to August 23, there had been 18,444 Canadian casualties—5,021 of those fatal—out of about 60,000 men who had begun. Every Canadian infantry regiment had gone through the grinder. The Canadian Scottish Regiment landed at Juno on D-Day with a total strength of 800 officers and men. By August 21, it had taken 627 casualties, of which 198 were fatal. Although it arrived in Normandy only in late July, the Algonquin Regiment reported 67 dead, 53 missing, and 125 wounded—a total of 245—of its original strength of 800.[5] Field Marshal Viscount Bernard Law Montgomery reported that of all the British, Canadian, and Polish divisions forming his Twenty-First Army Group, 3 CID had suffered the heaviest losses. Running close second was 2nd Canadian Infantry Division.[6] A sobering fact, considering the Canadians had landed just three divisions since June 6, compared to the twelve British and one Polish division that comprised the rest of Montgomery's force. Consequently, First Canadian Army ended the Normandy campaign greatly weakened.

Indeed, First Canadian Army was somewhat of a misnomer. In reality, the Canadian contingent was little more than a single corps supported by ancillary units attached to army headquarters. The three divisions and one armoured brigade that provided the majority of the army's fighting teeth generally fought under immediate direction of II Canadian Corps's commanding officer, Lieutenant General Guy Simonds. On July 23, I British Corps had been attached to First Canadian Army, bringing under its command the British 3rd, 49th, 51st (Highland), and 6th Airborne divisions.[7] Three days earlier, the newly arrived 1st Polish Armoured Division had joined II Canadian Corps—the beginning of a long relationship between the Canadians and Poles. First Canadian Army retained this structure throughout the rest of the Normandy campaign.

Such ad hoc divisional attachments to First Canadian Army were necessitated by a lack of Canadian troops in western Europe, resulting from the decision made in two stages during 1943 to transfer Canadian units from Britain to the newly opened Italian front. First Canadian Infantry Division and 1st Canadian Armoured Brigade had gone to participate in Operation Husky, the July 10 invasion of Sicily. Attached to British Eighth Army, this division had fought through the Sicilian campaign and then joined the march up the Italian boot. Later that year, 1 Canadian Corps headquarters with 5th Canadian Armoured Division had also transferred to Italy to serve as part of Eighth Army, and 1 CID had come under its command. Ostensibly, the intention of this carving away of almost half of First Canadian Army's manpower was to provide a core of combat-experienced Canadians for the future invasion of northwest Europe.

The decision, however, had been equally motivated by political considerations. Public sentiment at home, encouraged by the popular press, had clamoured for the Canadian army overseas to do some fighting. Partly this was fuelled by a desire for any kind of victory after the debacles of Hong Kong and Dieppe. In November 1941, the Royal Rifles of Canada and Winnipeg Grenadiers had reinforced Hong Kong colony, only to be included in the general surrender on December 24 after the Japanese invasion. This tragedy was followed by the disaster of Dieppe on August 19, 1942. Out of 5,000 Canadians landed at Dieppe, 807 had been killed and 1,946 taken prisoner.

When Canadians read daily newspaper reports about British, Australian, New Zealand, and other Commonwealth forces fighting major engagements in northern Africa, Burma, and on other fronts, the coverage of the endless training exercises conducted by the Canadian Army overseas paled by comparison. When would Canadian soldiers finally fight and garner battle honours for the nation? Under increasing public pressure, and subject to a noisy campaign by a cabal of Canadian officers in Britain who wanted to see the army blooded, the federal government finally gave in and lobbied the British to include Canadian troops in the forthcoming Mediterranean operation.

The Canadian government expected that prior to the invasion of France, 1 Canadian Corps would return from Italy to join First

Canadian Army, but it soon became apparent that the British had no intention of providing the large flotilla of transport ships necessary to carry out such a transfer or of reorganizing their own commands to facilitate such a complex reshuffling. So i Canadian Corps remained in Italy while First Canadian Army went to battle shorthanded, dependent on Montgomery parsing off other divisions to strengthen it for each assignment.

i British Corps consequently remained under First Canadian Army for its part in "The Pursuit." Montgomery was determined to keep the Germans running. On August 20, he had circulated a directive impressing upon "all commanders the need for speed in getting on with the business. The Allied victory in N.W. Europe will have immense repercussions; it will lead to the end of the German military domination of France; it is the beginning of the end of the war."

"But if these great events are to be brought about, we must hurl ourselves on the enemy while he is still reeling from the blow; we must deal him more blows and ever more blows; he must be allowed no time to recover."[8]

First Canadian Army's immediate task was to have II Canadian Corps close the Falaise Gap while simultaneously marching out of Normandy. I British Corps would push northeastwards along the coastline. Once the Gap was closed, the rest of II Canadian Corps would rush to join the pursuit. First Canadian Army was then to "advance to the Seine...cross the river...and operate to clear the whole Havre peninsula to the west of the Army boundary." The port at Le Havre was to be secured quickly.[9]

So the Canadians had started their run up the French coast, with orders to clear each channel port along the way. Because the Germans had reportedly transformed each port city into a fortress manned by thousands of men ordered to hold out as long as possible, they were not expected to move as quickly as British Second Army or the American armies. These were racing blitzkrieg fashion across France by inland routes that put them well ahead of the Canadian advance. But to the Canadians, even their more measured advance seemed hare-paced after the turtle-like gains made during the weeks of gridlock in Normandy.

ROLLING TOWARDS the Seine in the midst of 2nd Canadian Infantry Division's long train, 4th Canadian Field Regiment Lieutenant George Blackburn thought "this drive to...the Seine was but a victory march with each [artillery] troop acquiring its own endless story of mad incidents, such as advance parties 'liberating' villages miles in front of the most forward infantryman or 'recce car.'"

The regiment's tractors pulling the 25-pound guns, trucks loaded with men and supplies, Bren carriers, and jeeps raised great clouds of dust as they raced along the country roads. A "kaleidoscope" of images passed by: "Madly cheering French civilians lining the streets of villages gay with tri-colours...the refreshing green rich farmland, the apple orchards...the barrels of apple cider... tomatoes, apples and masses of flowers pressed on every vehicle... weak ersatz coffee...all-powerful Calvados and cognac...urchins begging, 'cigarette for papa,'...Maquis with red, white and blue arm bands and the inevitable German rifle slung on their shoulders...laughing women yelling, 'Merci Canadi-ens!'...sullen women with towels wrapped as turbans around their heads to hide the fact they'd been shaved for their affairs with Germans...and ringing church bells."[10]

The division had been stalled by a hard three-day action required to clear the dense woods of the Forêt de la Londe, which covered the approach to the Seine opposite Rouen. When it was over, 577 men were casualties. The South Saskatchewan Regiment had been particularly hard hit, losing 185 men, including 44 who had died. But 3rd Canadian Infantry Division and 4th Canadian Armoured Division slipped across the Seine near Elbeuf on August 27 to the right of the forest, turned the German rear, and forced those defending the forest to take flight or be trapped.[11]

Major Ronald Shawcross, commanding the Regina Rifles' 'A' Company, was amazed at how fast the advance moved once the Seine was crossed. "We went full speed ahead and damn the horses. We stopped every two hours for the necessary iron rations and bully beef that we had with us. Generally we stopped in orchards that were open and could rest without fear of anybody sneaking up on you." As they passed through one village or town after another, "Prisoners kept showing up... and all we did was take their weapons and send them back along the road... for others to capture. The paymaster's money was coming handy for fowl, rabbit, fruit, etc. We were now well ahead of our rations and kitchens."

In every town, crowds cheered the passing troops. "Kisses, wine and beer all over the lot, it was a good thing there was no lipstick available in France. Everyone welcomed us with open arms. There wasn't enough beer, wine and Calvados or we didn't stop long enough for it to do us much good or harm. We went on to Montreuil, Etaples, le Turne, Hauteville, it was a hell of a trip, forty-five miles in less than one day without a great deal of rest or hot food."[12]

Blackburn noted that the advance became "swift and easy" and because of 2 CID's line of advance "it was obvious to all that the objective... was Dieppe. 2nd Division was to be given the opportunity to revenge August 1942. But when the forward elements of our infantry were feeling their way towards the outskirts, they were welcomed by Royal Marines standing with glasses of beer in their hands in the doorway of a café and informed that they, the marines, had landed the night before at the port in assault fashion to find the Germans gone."[13] Divisional headquarters staff driving into Dieppe on September 1 were met by "hysterical joy on the part of the civilians."[14] First Canadian Army's commander Lieutenant General Harry Crerar ordered the division to stand down for four days to carry out badly needed equipment maintenance and catch its breath. It would then pass through 3 CID, allowing that division a similar maintenance and rest period.

Crerar issued his orders without consulting Montgomery, who took immediate exception. He immediately signalled Crerar: "NOT repeat NOT consider this the time for any div[ision] to halt for maintenance. Push on quickly."[15] Crerar was not to be swayed. He calmly but firmly countered that there was no reason for 2 CID to move until a crossing had been secured over the Somme and that the pause was essential to allow this division, which had lost a third of its infantry strength, to absorb 1,000 reinforcements currently en route from Normandy to Dieppe.[16] Crerar's decision was further influenced by the desire of 2 CID commander Major General Charles Foulkes to hold a religious service and parade on September 3 to honour the men who had fallen during the Dieppe raid. Asked to personally supervise the parade, Crerar willingly consented.

On the afternoon of September 2, Montgomery sent Crerar another signal summoning him to British Second Army headquarters for a meeting the next day at 1300 hours. The wording led Crerar to assume this was to be a one-on-one affair and he suggested rescheduling it to 1700 to permit his attending the Dieppe ceremony. To ensure that no further communication scuttled his plans, as Crerar left his headquarters on the morning of September 3 for Dieppe, he instructed his Chief of Staff, Brigadier General Churchill Mann, that under "no circumstances was he to receive any further communications from Monty until it was too late to cancel his role in the Dieppe ceremonies."[17]

During the service at the cemetery, Crerar read a message from William Lyon Mackenzie King. "I am sharing your joy upon the entry of Canadian troops into Dieppe today," the prime minister said. "Nothing has so stirred Canada as the rapid series of victories achieved by our forces in recent weeks. My warmest congratulations to you all."[18] Whereas Mann had forwarded this message immediately upon its receipt, he withheld a note from Montgomery until the ceremony concluded at 1440 hours. Montgomery tersely insisted upon Crerar's attendance at a meeting that had by then started almost two hours earlier. In the note, Montgomery clarified that this was a high level event to be attended by his American counterpart, General Omar N. Bradley, and all theatre Allied army commanders.

Realizing that his failure to attend smacked of cavalier disobedience, Crerar flew immediately to Second Army headquarters, only to find the meeting long over and all but General Miles Dempsey departed. The Second Army commander consoled Crerar that his attendance had probably been unnecessary, as the meeting had entirely concerned future cooperation between his army and that of First U.S. Army. Both men knew, however, that rebuffing Montgomery was not lightly done.

Hastening to Montgomery's headquarters, Crerar was greeted with icy rage. The field marshal brushed aside Crerar's argument that the Dieppe ceremony and his attendance there were necessary. As the exchange became increasingly heated, Crerar declared that there "was a powerful Canadian reason why I should have been present... at Dieppe. In fact, there were eight hundred reasons—the Canadian dead buried at Dieppe cemetery." Crerar's failure to obey instructions, Montgomery retorted, meant that "our ways must part." Shaken but unbowed Crerar said that he expected Montgomery would now take the matter to higher channels of authority, while he would seek instructions from his government—the only body that could relieve him of command. As if suddenly realizing the dispute had escalated out of proportion, Montgomery abruptly backed down and declared the matter closed. A few days later, he even apologized by letter.[19] But the years of growing antipathy between the two men could not be erased.

FIFTY-SIX YEARS OLD, Henry Duncan Graham Crerar was a World War I veteran and graduate of Royal Military College, who had been appointed Chief of the Canadian General Staff in December 1941, then given command of 1 Canadian Corps in Britain. A fervent nationalist who wanted Canada's army to play a significant role in the Allied war effort, he had convinced Prime Minister King to accede to the British request that Canadians be sent to reinforce Hong Kong. He had also lobbied relentlessly for Canada to play the major role in the Dieppe raid. As 1 Canadian Corps commander, Crerar had headed up the cabal of officers that succeeded in having Canada included in the Sicily and Italian campaigns.

It soon became clear that Montgomery, who commanded British Eighth Army in Italy, thought little of Crerar's ability. Montgomery had reached this conclusion in February 1943, when he had led a study group in Tripoli that analyzed traditional Allied battle doctrine in relationship to the lessons learned during the African desert battles. While disillusioned with the performance of all the commanders present, he singled out only Crerar for written condemnation. "I don't think he has any idea of how to handle Corps in battle," Montgomery wrote. When Crerar headed up 1 Canadian Corps, Montgomery tried to ease him into the task by first having him temporarily command 1st Canadian Infantry Division. Crerar haughtily declined the suggestion as beneath his rank.

He quickly ran afoul of Eighth Army practices of keeping things simple and paperwork at a minimum by issuing a stream of lengthy written orders backed by sheaves of intelligence summaries, reports, and staff analyses. In an army where Montgomery's casual approach to uniforms and adherence to military protocol set an informal tone, Crerar was also a stickler for proper dress and behaviour. On March 9, 1944, when Crerar returned to Britain to take the reins of First Canadian Army, his departure was greeted with general relief throughout Eighth Army. But Montgomery considered the Canadian government mistaken in giving Crerar such a critical command.

Crerar was equally disliked by his two corps commanders—II Canadian Corps's Lieutenant General Guy Simonds and I British Corps's Lieutenant General John Crocker. No sooner had Crocker come under Crerar's command than the two had a nasty falling-out when the British general refused to obey to the letter a series of highly detailed orders. Crerar had immediately asked Montgomery to relieve the experienced officer, who had been in either divisional or corps command since 1940. While noting that the egos of both men contributed, Montgomery believed Crerar the main problem: "I fear he thinks he is a great soldier and he was determined to show it the very moment he took over command at 1200 hrs on 23 July. He made his first mistake at 1205 hrs; and his second after lunch." Because the chain of command had to be maintained even if the man at the top was wrong, Montgomery gave Crocker a harsh dressing-down. But he also warned Crerar not to meddle overly in corps level battle planning. An army commander, he counselled, "must stand back from the detailed tactical battle; that part is the province of his corps commanders." Over time, Crocker and Crerar learned to work fairly well together, but there was little mutual respect.[20]

Simonds's opinion of Crerar had soured long before he took command of II Canadian Corps. The forty-one-year-old had enjoyed a meteoric career since the war's outbreak. He advanced from the rank of major to major general in just three and a half years—becoming the youngest corps commander in the Commonwealth forces. It was while serving a stint as Crerar's Brigadier General, Staff that Simonds witnessed the man's backroom politicking that led to the Dieppe raid. Had it not been for Crerar, Simonds came to believe, the raid never would have been carried out and a Canadian tragedy averted. Simonds left Crerar's staff not only disliking the man, but deeply distrusting him.[21]

Montgomery and Simonds both considered Crerar severely handicapped by the fact that he had never held a battlefield command. Simonds had gained such experience leading 1st Canadian Infantry Division across Sicily and into Italy before contracting jaundice. Montgomery thought his handling of the division had been exemplary, and considered the young general a protégé and the perfect candidate for First Canadian Army command. Simonds had returned to command 5th Canadian Armoured Division in Italy shortly before Crerar's arrival. The two had soon become embroiled in an increasingly vitriolic dispute over nothing more than Crerar's envy of a sumptuous and efficient caravan that Simonds had designed as his sleeping quarters and headquarters when the division was on the move. After an exchange of heated letters, both had questioned the other's sanity in notes to Montgomery. Although Crerar eventually recommended Simonds for corps command, he did so reluctantly, harbouring the suspicion that the young officer was unbalanced.

From the sidelines, Simonds had observed the dispute with Montgomery over the Dieppe ceremony and considered it more evidence that Crerar increasingly "was just not minding the shop." Since the breakout from Normandy, Simonds had urged Crerar to step up the pace of First Canadian Army's advance. Simonds knew from intelligence reports that the German Fifteenth Army was evacuating hundreds of men a day from Breskens. Instead of methodically isolating each port and laying siege until the garrison surrendered, Simonds wanted to leave only sufficient forces to "mask them," condemning the trapped garrison to wither on the vine for lack of supplies. Meanwhile, the army could press on to Breskens and cut off the German escape route.[22] A strategic thinker, Simonds grasped the importance of not only securing Antwerp but equally of clearing the sixty-mile-long West Scheldt estuary that linked the port city to the North Sea.

He also recognized that Fifteenth Army was on the brink of escaping an encirclement that should have assured its destruction. An opportunity was slipping through Allied hands, and Simonds worried that its loss would cost them dearly in time lost and casualties suffered.

Devoted to Montgomery, Simonds chose to ignore the fact that Crerar had not been ordered to make haste to Breskens. In his methodical way, the Canadian army commander was implementing Montgomery's instructions to quickly open each port so that it could be used to bring in supplies from Britain, desperately needed to fuel the rapid advance of the Allied armies. With each passing day, the supply trail running all the way back to the Normandy beachhead lengthened, and a crisis threatened that could only be alleviated by bringing supplies to points closer to the head of the advance.

"The Pursuit" was in jeopardy, the tanks, armoured cars, and thousands of trucks rushing across France literally beginning to run out of fuel. The supply situation made it logical that the early opening of Antwerp—Europe's largest port—should be the highest Allied priority. Coupled with the opportunity to snare and eliminate Fifteenth Army, directing the Canadian thrust towards the Belgian port and strategic parts of Holland immediately to its north seemed obvious. Yet Montgomery's attention was turned elsewhere and his distraction would condemn First Canadian Army to a forthcoming campaign that was both unnecessary and of tragic consequence.

[2]

The Jewel

On September 4, less than twenty-four hours after the Dieppe Memorial ceremony, the tanks of 11th British Armoured Division growled into the outskirts of Antwerp. This was the crowning moment in the division's spectacular dash ordered by xxx Corps commander Lieutenant General Sir Brian Horrocks on August 30, to capitalize on that day's winning of a crossing over the Seine. "A tall, lithe figure, with white hair, angular features, penetrating eyes and eloquent hands, [who] moved among his troops more like a prophet than a general," the forty-nine-year-old Horrocks had distinguished himself at El Alamein, only to be critically wounded a short time later. Despite being warned that his injuries were so severe he would never again hold field command, Horrocks had responded to a call in early August from Montgomery to take over xxx Corps.[1]

Both Horrocks and Montgomery had recognized the opportunity presented as xxx Corps—and indeed all Twenty-First Army Group—moved north of the river hot on the heels of a thoroughly disorganized adversary. "All risks are justified," Montgomery had told Horrocks. "I intend to get a bridgehead over the Rhine before they have time to recover."[2] In the specially modified Sherman from which the gun had been removed to make room for additional radios and a small table that served as his mobile command post, Horrocks had rushed to 11th Armoured Division's headquarters and personally briefed Major General G.P.B. "Pip" Roberts. The tank division commander happily reported that the day before his division had advanced twenty-one miles, a gain Horrocks brushed aside as insufficient. Countermanding orders for the division to harbour for the night, he instructed Roberts to keep moving by moonlight to seize Amiens and the Somme River bridge crossings before the Germans could destroy them.[3] Once across the Somme, it would push through to Antwerp.

Horrocks assured Roberts that his division would not be driving into the blue alone. Close behind, 50th Infantry Division would clear out German pockets of resistance that the tankers should bypass rather than fight. On its left, 7th Armoured Division would push towards Ghent, while to the right the Guards Armoured Division headed for Brussels.[4] In one hard strike, xxx Corps would end the battle for Belgium before the Germans could organize a defence.

Despite the fact that the division's tankers had been on the move for thirty-six hours and fought a sharp engagement for the Seine crossing, the tanks had plowed into the gathering darkness. There was no moon, only a torrent of rain that reduced the roads to muddy lanes that crumbled into ruin under the great weight of the tanks and their chewing tracks. Despite the harsh weather, the lead tanks—having driven fifty-five miles during the night—reached Amiens shortly after dawn and found three of the four bridges in the hands of French resistance fighters who had seized them just hours before to prevent their destruction. Barely pausing, the tanks crossed over. "The race for the Rhine was now on," Horrocks later recalled, "and the next few days were the most exhilarating of my military career."[5]

On September 2, the British tankers entered Belgium southeast of Lille. The same day, two American corps—xix and vii—also broke into Belgium to the east of the British. When the Guards Armoured Division entered Brussels the following afternoon, it bogged down in the face of a euphoric citizenry that clogged the streets and showered the tankers with flowers. There was no thought of pausing. Antwerp lay within easy grasp of 11th Armoured Division, prompting Roberts to ask Horrocks for a "definite objective" because the entire city was far too large to be secured by tanks only lightly supported by infantry.

"Go straight for the docks and prevent the Germans destroying the port installations," the corps commander responded.[6]

Accordingly, at noon on September 4, 11th Armoured Division rolled into Antwerp and was met by elements of the Belgian resistance who already controlled or were fighting to secure many of the port facilities, city services, and, most importantly, several key bridges that spanned the Albert Canal directly to the south of Merksem. From radio reports, the Belgians had known the British tanks were coming and had raised 3,500 fighters the day before. Although lightly armed, the Belgians had surprised the German occupation force.

Fully realizing their importance to the Allied cause, the Belgians concentrated on seizing key transportation links and isolating or securing as much of the vital dockyard infrastructure as possible. Only three miles of the docks fronted the Scheldt proper, the remaining twenty-seven miles snaking into and around a complex network of inlets to the north. Behind this maze, a community and industrial complex existed that was largely separate physically, socially, and economically from Antwerp. In its midst, thousands of seamen and dockyard workers lived in tightly clustered villages complete with bars and churches. Large warehouses, sheds, machine shops, and ship repair plants were strung along the quays, behind which sprawling railroad marshalling yards teemed with trains waiting for cargo to carry throughout Europe. The docks had grown so rapidly that areas of flat, scrubby grassland lay just beyond the industrial complexes and villages.

Running east from the port area was the eighty-mile-long Albert Canal, dug between 1930 and 1939 to provide a transportation link for heavy shipping to travel inland from Antwerp to Liège. From there, the canal tied into a spiderlike rail and waterway hub that extended its threads into the heartlands of Germany and France. With a minimum bottom width of eighty feet, it could be navigated by two-thousand-ton vessels.

A series of lift bridges at Merksem provided vital canal crossing points. The resistance commanders had long appreciated the strategic importance of these bridges to enabling the Allied advance to pass quickly into Holland. Equally important was the electrical plant on the Merksem side of the canal that supplied power to the cranes and other dockyard machinery. To the north of the Scheldt were two locks the Belgians considered strategic keys to securing the port intact. The Kruisschanssluis controlled the Scheldt tidal flows in and out of the port, while No. 12 Sluiskens, about a mile north of Kruisschanssluis, prevented flooding of the low ground to the north and east of the port.

Through the night of September 3–4, hundreds of Belgian fighters led by sea captain Eugene Colson had gone into action to wrest these vital objectives from German hands. Colson had been born in Merksem, so he was intimately familiar with every nook and cranny. Striking quickly, the Belgians won two of the bridges. A well-placed 88-millimetre gun prevented their capturing the larger Groenendaallaan crossing. Unable to defeat the gun with their light weapons, the Belgians were pinned down on the bridge's south side. But their fire prevented the Germans detonating explosives to destroy the span. To ensure they were ready for immediate use by the British, the other bridges were lowered and fixed in position. By dawn, the tanks had not appeared and the Germans had used the time to reorganize. They launched a series of relentless counterattacks against the outnumbered and outgunned Belgian fighters. Throughout that day and on into the morning of September 5, the Belgians clung to their gains while looking over their shoulder in hopes that the tankers would appear.

At the Merksem power plant, the fighters were driven off with heavy casualties. Then the two captured bridges fell and were blown by the Germans. That left only the unsecured Groenendaallaan Bridge. No. 12 Sluiskens was also overrun, and the Germans opened its floodgates to inundate large areas of low ground in the northern suburbs. Although reportedly in Antwerp, still the tanks did not come.

Colson was frantic and angered at seeing his brave fighters slowly butchered. If all the bridges were lost, there would be no rapid advance into Holland. Not twenty miles north of Antwerp were the Zeeland islands of North Beveland and Walcheren and the South

Beveland peninsula. The latter, which had also once been an island, was connected to the Dutch mainland via a mile-wide isthmus. If the Allies crossed the Albert Canal and gained control of the isthmus near the town of Woensdrecht, the German Fifteenth Army's escape route from Breskens through Walcheren and South Beveland to the mainland would be capped. Colson believed the entire army could be eliminated in one coup de grâce. Yet with every passing minute, this priceless opportunity was slipping away.[7]

Meanwhile, the tanks had begun pushing through Antwerp shortly after noon on September 4 and met solid opposition in the form of thousands of Belgians who thronged the streets in welcome. One of the division's battalion commanders later described the scene in a letter to his wife. "The difficulties... amongst this mass of populace crowding round still cheering, still flag waving, still thrusting plums at you, still kissing you, asking you to post a letter to America, to give them some petrol, some more arms for the White Brigade [part of the Belgian resistance], holding baby under your nose to be kissed, trying to give you a drink, inviting you into their house, trying to carry you away, offering information about the enemy... had to be seen to be understood."[8]

The tankers, exhausted from a drive that had carried them 230 miles from the Seine to Antwerp in just six days, failed to exploit the opportunity that lay within easy grasp. Their orders had been to capture the docks at Antwerp intact and that job appeared done. "Had any indication been given that a further advance north was envisaged," the regimental historian later wrote, the bridges "might have been seized within a few hours of our entry into the city."[9] But Major General Roberts believed any further advance of "secondary importance" to securing the dockyards fronting Antwerp proper. "No one mentioned the canal," the division's diarist noted. "All that Army and Army Group kept saying was, 'You must get the docks, you must get the docks.'"[10]

Consequently, on September 5, when British tankers approached Groenendaallaan Bridge and Colson urged them to take on the 88-millimetre gun to win the crossing, he was rebuffed with the simple explanation that the tankers had no orders to advance. Colson stormed to Roberts's headquarters, four miles to the south at Lier, and pressed his case, only to have the British officer politely thank him for his concern before dismissing him like some errant schoolboy. Returning to the docks, Colson watched the British tankers withdrawing. "Goddamn you Britishers," he shouted. "Goddamn you." He vowed to continue the bitter contest for control of the bridge until the British came to their senses.[11]

The British decision to allow the initiative the Belgians had handed them on a platter to pass by was largely the result of a failure of Twenty-First Army Group to provide the corps commanders with vital intelligence. "If I had ordered Roberts to bypass Antwerp and advance only fifteen miles north-west," Horrocks later wrote, "in order to cut off the Beveland isthmus, [Fifteenth Army] might have been destroyed or forced to surrender."[12] But Horrocks had not been informed that the Germans were conducting a desperate withdrawal to the north bank of the Scheldt that left them vulnerable to being bottled up on Walcheren and South Beveland if he corked the isthmus. And so, having accomplished the amazing feat of breaking through to Antwerp, and considering the port largely secure, he ordered the corps to stand down for a rest and equipment maintenance. Despite intelligence from the Belgian resistance that the Germans were building their strength there, Horrocks "did not anticipate at that time any serious resistance on the Albert Canal. It seemed to us that the Germans were seriously disorganized."[13] There would be no effort to renew the advance until September 7.

Horrocks soon realized his mistake, later declaring September 4 as "the key day in the battle for the Rhine. Had we been able to advance that day we could have smashed through and advanced northward with little or nothing to stop us... but we halted and even by that same evening the situation was worsening."[14] The short, heady days of "The Pursuit" were at an end.

ALTHOUGH HORROCKS assumed responsibility for failing to continue the advance on September 4, the decision was understandable in light of the lack of direction from his superiors. Fixated on reaching Germany by the fastest possible means, the Allied army commanders and Supreme Headquarters Allied Expeditionary Force head General Dwight G. Eisenhower entirely overlooked the strategic and tactical opportunity that had developed in western Belgium. On the very day Antwerp fell, Eisenhower sent Montgomery a dispatch that directed Twenty-First Army Group and First U.S. Army, both operating northwest of the Ardennes, "to secure Antwerp, breach the Siegfried Line covering the Ruhr and seize the Ruhr." This, he said, would be part of a "broad front" extending from the coast virtually to the Swiss border that assumed the "best opportunity for defeating the enemy in the West is to strike at the Ruhr and Saar." These two regions provided the industrial backbone for Germany's war effort.

Eisenhower believed their capture would cripple the country's ability to continue. German forces facing the Allies were thought to be no more than twenty weak and disorganized divisions. Hit hard, before reinforcements could be brought from the Eastern Front, the Germans would be unable to prevent a "quick crossing of the Rhine and a rapid conquest of one (or both) of the enemy's all-important industrial areas." Eisenhower was fixated on the Rhine, his mention of Antwerp seemingly nothing more than a casual aside. And he gave no attention to securing the Scheldt estuary or closing the trap on Fifteenth Army.[15]

Vehemently opposed to Eisenhower's broad-front strategy, which he believed the Allies were incapable of supplying from the existing port facilities, Montgomery was no less focused on getting to the Rhine. Everything else was secondary. He argued that all Allied resources should be dedicated to crossing the Rhine "at the expense of any other undertaking."[16] Rather than continuing to hit the Germans everywhere at once, though, Montgomery sought to launch a single "full-blooded" thrust, with British Second Army serving as the rapier that would pierce the Rhine at Arnhem.[17] Three airborne divisions would be dropped to seize vital bridges at Grave, Nijmegen, and Arnhem so that the armoured divisions spearheading the offensive could gain the north bank of the Rhine before the Germans organized a coherent defence.

On September 7, in order to prepare for this operation—soon codenamed Market Garden—Montgomery ordered Second Army to begin concentrating northeast of Antwerp. Three days later, while arguing that Market Garden should be adopted as the sole offensive to the Rhine, Montgomery explained to Eisenhower that this concentration of force on the Allied left flank was the "quickest way to open up Antwerp...which...would not only help our logistic and maintenance situation but would also keep up the pressure on the stricken Germans in the area of greatest importance, thus helping to end the war quickly." Antwerp, he declared, would then be "behind the thrust." As for the "approaches to the port, which we had not yet got," Montgomery seemed to consider that they would fall automatically to the Allies once Second Army broke through to the Rhine.[18]

Only one voice in the Allied high command warned that failing to open Antwerp before all else was a grave mistake. Admiral Sir Bertram Ramsay, the Supreme Commander's Naval Commander-in-Chief, had advised Eisenhower and Montgomery by telegraph on September 4 that opening Antwerp and Rotterdam to Allied shipping should be their highest priority. Both ports, he said, were "highly vulnerable to mining and blocking. If enemy succeeds in these operations the time it will take to open ports cannot be estimated." He also warned that it "will be necessary for coastal batteries to be captured before approach channels to the river routes can be established."[19] Antwerp, Ramsay emphasized, was "useless" unless the Scheldt estuary was freed. It was plain that, until the harbour was opened, the Allies would be hobbled by their inability to adequately supply the advancing armies.

Supplying such a huge force from the ports of Great Britain constituted a titanic logistical challenge. Initially, all supplies, except for fuel, had been unloaded from ships onto the beaches at Normandy, and two large artificial harbours—called Mulberries—had been constructed to speed the process. For fuel supply, the Allies had laid a "pipeline under the ocean" (PLUTO) that ran from Britain to Normandy. No sooner had the two Mulberries been set in place, however, than a massive storm that began on June 19 and raged for two days extensively damaged the American Mulberry off Omaha Beach. The Americans were forced back to relying on over-the-beach supply. Once the Allies broke out of Normandy, the supplies landed outpaced the availability of transport to keep the advancing armies adequately supplied. The French railroad system south of the Seine had been heavily damaged by aerial bombardment, so the majority of supplies had to be moved by road, a slow, cumbersome process.

Eisenhower sought to address the problem by assigning most of the supplies coming in to Market Garden, but his subordinate American generals gave only lip service to this instruction—hoarding supplies for their own forces at every opportunity. Only about 650 tons of supplies daily were redirected by them to Montgomery's Twenty-First Army Group.[20]

Montgomery was left to rely on his own resources to supply Market Garden. It soon became apparent that trying to move both troops and stores from Normandy would not be possible if the offensive was to begin as scheduled on September 17. So British Second Army's VIII Corps, which was to have come forward to attack on the right of XXX Corps to protect that flank of the advance, was grounded west of the Seine and its trucks given over to the movement of supplies.[21]

To increase the daily tonnage of supplies reaching British Second Army, Montgomery's staff reduced the normal allotment for First Canadian Army.[22] As I Corps was engaged in a relatively static operation at Le Havre, the majority of its transport was also stripped off to move supplies up for Market Garden. When 3rd Canadian Infantry Division concentrated on Boulogne, much of its transport was appropriated by the Royal Canadian Army Service Corps to move supplies forward to the rest of First Canadian Army.[23]

As 4th Canadian Armoured Division, like all the other Allied divisions, drew farther away from Normandy, the supply convoys faced an increasingly difficult task. "We were having a terrific time to supply them with petrol," Lieutenant Colonel M.L. Brennan, 4 CAD's Commander Royal Canadian Army Service Corps, recalled. The trucks shuttled daily back to a designated location between the beaches and the forward elements of the division, which served as an intermediate supply dump. "The source was getting farther behind us every day. It got behind about one hundred miles. That means a drag of two hundred, and with all the *cul de sacs,* one-way bridges, darkness, weather, running without lights, and so on, that's a hell of a pull."[24]

Brennan spent each day racing in a jeep from the source of supply to the point of delivery, urging the convoy drivers to greater haste. One night, his worst fear materialized when a convoy stopped moving. "It was raining—a terrible night—when my units got bogged down... I came along in my Jeep to the end of a line—oh, hell, there must have been 150 vehicles on the road. I couldn't get my jeep past, so I got out and walked." A mile later, Brennan opened the door of the lead truck and found the driver and convoy officer sound asleep. In fact, everyone was asleep. Not a soul in any of the trucks had wakened from where each slumped over the steering wheel during his entire trek forward. Waking the officer, he ordered all the drivers assembled. Brennan glared at the weary, rain-soaked drivers. "According to the Army," he growled, "I run a bloody transport unit. But I doubt it. In my opinion it consists of the most useless bunch I've ever had the misfortune to come into contact with. I'm quite certain you couldn't supply anything. The troops are up forward fighting, but don't mind that. Don't let that worry you. Sit down and rest."

From the darkness, Brennan heard someone mumble, "The miserable old so-and-so. He never lets us off the bloody road." But in a few minutes the convoy was roaring towards the front again. Brennan knew, however, that eventually the drivers and trucks they drove would reach the end of their endurance. When that happened, the entire supply chain would freeze up.[25]

It was to ease this supply crisis plaguing all the Allied forces that First Canadian Army's priority mission was to advance up the coastline to clear the channel ports. Equally, the German decision to order the port garrisons to hold out to the bitter end was intended to deny the Allies their use for as long as possible. This defensive effort largely succeeded. Even at Dieppe, where the German garrison decamped without a fight, port facilities were sufficiently damaged beforehand to prevent their opening to any shipping until September 7, and its full potential of 6,000 to 7,000 tons a day would not be realized until month's end.[26]

On the same day Dieppe had fallen, September 2, 1 British Corps had come up against the formidable German defences at Le Havre—with a daily shipping capacity of 20,000 tons—but the defenders were ensconced in heavy fortifications that forced Lieutenant General John Crocker to methodically prepare an attack not scheduled to begin until September 10. Intelligence also showed that the docks and approaches had been severely damaged, which would greatly delay its opening to shipping. When Oostende fell to 4th Canadian Infantry Brigade on September 9, the story repeated itself. Fourteen ships had been sunk to block the entrance and both channel and harbour had been heavily mined. Many of the quays had been destroyed and those that survived suffered extensive damage.[27]

Meanwhile, 3rd Canadian Infantry Division had reached Boulogne on September 5 to find ten thousand Germans ready to fight. 11 Canadian Corps commander Lieutenant General Guy Simonds soon realized that a meticulously planned full-scale assault would be required. Dubbed Operation Wellhit, this attack could not be put in before September 17. Everywhere along the coast, First Canadian Army had besieged one port after another, but none was immediately available for use by Allied shipping. Until Antwerp was secure, the Allied supply situation would remain perilous.

With each passing day during the week following September 4, Eisenhower—belatedly recognizing the truth of Ramsay's warning—emphasized the importance of opening Antwerp to Allied shipping a little more strongly. But he never directly ordered Montgomery to detail part of Twenty-First Army Group to carry this out. "Antwerp," one U.S. Army official historian wrote, "was a jewel that could not be worn for want of a setting."[28]

YET, IF EISENHOWER and Montgomery failed initially to recognize the strategic importance of the Scheldt estuary, the same could not be said of their opponents. The sudden appearance of 11th Armoured Division in Antwerp on September 4 had sent a shudder of panic throughout the German command chain. Generalfeldmarschall Walter Model, Oberbefehlshaber (OB) West, noted in his diary that "by the advance to Antwerp the enemy have closed the ring round Fifteenth Army." He ordered the army's more southerly situated elements to "withdraw, fighting, on the coastal 'fortresses'" (Boulogne, Calais, Dunkirk, and Oostende) while a last-ditch effort would be made to evacuate as many men via Vlissingen on Walcheren Island to the mainland, where they could escape along the highway running inland from Bergen op Zoom to Breda.[29] Expectation was that few would get away.

Hitler fully appreciated Antwerp's importance to the Allied supply effort and determined to deny the use of the port captured so easily. Emphasizing the need to continue holding onto the coastal fortresses to the last bullet, he also ordered every effort made to defend Walcheren Island, whatever parts of Antwerp were still in German hands, and the "Albert Canal... as far as Maastricht." The commander in Calais and his counterpart on Walcheren Island were designated fortress commanders, so they could act on individual initiative without prior clearance from their superiors. Hitler also placed First Parachute Army under Army Group B's command, with orders for it to establish a strong blocking position north of Antwerp and along the north bank of the Albert Canal. To strengthen the western command structure, Hitler reinstated Generalfeldmarschall Gerd von Rundstedt as OB West while Model retained command of Army Group B.[30] The sixty-nine-year-old von Rundstedt had been dismissed from this position on July 6 for failing to stem the Allied advance in Normandy, but now Hitler needed his organizational skill to respond to the calamity developing across the Western Front. Model was to focus on averting disaster in western Belgium by denying the Allies the use of Antwerp and blocking the gateway to the Ruhr. As for Fifteenth Army, the consensus held that the "situation was now hopeless."[31]

The order to use First Parachute Army to prevent the British breaking out to the north of Antwerp was largely wishful thinking, for this was not an operational force. It was "merely a nucleus of parachute troops being organized and trained in various locations under the over-all direction of Generaloberst Kurt Student." The charismatic Student, who had commanded the airborne force that conquered Crete in 1941, happened to be at the Führer's headquarters—known as the Wolfsschanze, near Rastenburg in East Prussia—on September 2 when news arrived that Antwerp was imperilled. The immediate reaction was one of "utmost surprise and consternation." Returning to his small headquarters in Berlin, Student considered there was nothing he could personally do, until his phone rang on the afternoon of September 4. "I was ordered to form a new defence front along the Albert Canal immediately. Its right wing was to extend to the mouth of the Scheldt, where this river flows into the West Scheldt."[32]

Lacking an army but possessed of a small headquarters staff, Student immediately flew from Berlin to Holland. By the evening of September 5, he had arrived at the headquarters of LXXXVIII Corps in the village of Moergestel, just east of Tilburg, to take control of a grab bag of units and establish a line along the Albert Canal. This corps came under Student's command and Hitler promised the rapid deployment of 3rd and 5th Parachute Divisions. A further ten battalions would be culled from another military district and sent to his aid.[33]

Hitler also received some unexpectedly welcome news from Reichsmarschall Hermann Göring on September 4. Completely unknown to Oberkommando der Wehrmacht (OKW), Göring had been quietly rebuilding the Luftwaffe's paratroop arm. Learning of the crisis at Antwerp and that Student had been sent to stem the tide, Göring offered six parachute regiments in various stages of training. By culling convalescent depots, another two regiments could be formed. This would provide Student with 20,000 men. A further 10,000 could be raised by reassigning Luftwaffe air and ground crews that were idling for lack of fuel for their squadrons. While the paratroops were not yet trained to the elite standards normal to such troops, they at least had basic infantry training. Although the same could not be said of the air force personnel, they, like the paratroops, were thoroughly indoctrinated Nazis. "Young, ardent and loyal, they could be relied upon to fight for Hitler to the end."[34] Hitler grabbed the offer, and these units were soon streaming towards the Albert Canal by whatever transport could be cobbled together.

Everywhere, the Germans were improvising in a similar manner, trying to stem the Allied tide with divisions hurriedly transferred with the urgency of fire brigades. Nowhere were they more surprised by the success of these efforts than to the north of Antwerp. When the British failed to immediately advance and cut the Beveland isthmus, Student gained the breathing space to receive reinforcements and tie them into the ever-strengthening defensive line behind the Albert Canal. By September 6, he saw that disaster had been averted not through his actions but through the inexplicable lack of action by the British. There would be no second chance. He would make them fight hard from here on for any gains along his sector.

Hitler had been so heartened that he decided it was now possible to form a "bridgehead south of the Scheldt Estuary and to organize a strong defence of Walcheren Island" rather than just evacuating whatever elements of Fifteenth Army could be brought out by the ferry link between Breskens and Vlissingen. Consequently, each ferry shuttling Fifteenth Army troops across the three-and-a-half-mile-wide channel to Vlissingen returned to Breskens loaded to the gunnels with men and equipment of 70th Infantry Division. Battalions from this division soon held defensive positions around the bridges in the area of Ghent, with orders to keep them open for use by the withdrawing Fifteenth Army.

Still, the retreat had the air of an all-out rout. Close to 100,000 men were on the move and little unit cohesion remained. Fifteenth Army had been retreating hard from the Pas de Calais coast, desperately trying to keep ahead of the Allied advance until opportunity to pause and regroup presented itself. There had been little available transport. Most of the troops had walked the entire distance. All along the way, they had been harried by the British and American fighter-bombers and strafed by Spitfires and Mustangs. The roads were strewn with dead horses, wrecked trucks and wagons, corpses of comrades. By the time they entered Belgium, many of the men were barefoot, weaponless, uniforms in tatters, bodies grimed with filth. Hunger gnawed their guts and demoralization weakened their resolve. It was not uncommon for men to slip off the roads into nearby woods, and when the rest of the column had passed by, to walk south and surrender to the advancing Allies.

As these units crossed the bridges held by 70th Infantry Division, they were intercepted by officers and non-commissioned officers intent on turning this rabble back into soldiers. Orders were shouted, fists and clubs swung, guns drawn and occasionally fired. Men were herded into ad hoc squads, then into platoons, then into companies and even battalions. Order began to emerge out of the chaos. If Fifteenth Army could succeed in getting across the West Scheldt intact, it would quickly be reformed into a viable fighting force.

Meanwhile, a line had been drawn by the Germans in western Belgium from Zeebrugge on the coast through Bruges and Ghent. The Bruges–Ghent Canal that ran between the latter two ancient cities provided a strong obstacle. There would be no escape for the garrisons in the coastal fortresses to the south, however. These elements of Fifteenth Army could only fight on until they were inevitably eliminated by First Canadian Army.

No sooner had the Germans fully manned the defensive line than First Canadian Army began punching holes in it. While it soon became apparent that Ghent and Bruges could not be held, the defenders were buying vital time for Fifteenth Army to continue the evacuation, not only from Breskens but now also the more easterly port of Terneuzen. The evacuation was not allowed to proceed unmolested. Each day, dozens of Allied bombers and fighter-bombers attacked the port facilities and sought to sink the ferries and other vessels commandeered by the Germans.[35]

When the Bruges–Ghent line crumbled under persistent pressure from the Canadians on September 10, the Germans quickly fell back on a new line behind the Leopold Canal and had in place a solid defensive line by September 13. At any moment, the defenders expected the Canadians to try to win a crossing, but their orders were clear. The canal must not be breached, for—stretching as it did from the North Sea coast almost to the Braakman Inlet, immediately west of Terneuzen—it was the best remaining physical obstacle south of the Scheldt estuary.

[3]

The Streetcar War

O**N SEPTEMBER** 6, Field Marshal Montgomery turned his back on Antwerp. This was the same day that 11th British Armoured Division made a belated and half-hearted attempt to establish a bridgehead over the Albert Canal immediately to the north of the city. The attack was easily thwarted by determined German counterattacks. Two days after this failure, the division was ordered out of Antwerp and sent forty miles eastwards in support of the Guards Armoured Division, which had won a crossing over the canal at the village of Beringen. Montgomery had no intention of using this bridgehead or another secured on September 7 in front of Geel, thirty miles east of Antwerp, for operations to free up Antwerp. These crossings were a vital first step for Market Garden that would enable his divisions to reach the operation's planned start line at Neerpelt, fifteen miles northeast of Beringen on the south bank of the canal.

British Second Army's efforts were now entirely directed towards carrying out this ambitious offensive. As part of the general move eastwards, XII Corps replaced XXX Corps in the bridgehead area on September 12, permitting Lieutenant General Horrocks to rest and prepare his divisions for their starring role in the drive to Arnhem. VIII Corps was brought up to the east of XII Corps. Although XII Corps was nominally responsible for Antwerp, its divisions were extended across too wide a front to do more than protect the parts of the harbour already under Allied control.[1]

Despite the fact, that as early as September 10, Eisenhower let it be known he now recognized the vital importance of opening the port, Montgomery summarily "put the Antwerp matter at the bottom of his agenda."[2] The Twenty-First Army Group commander had convinced himself that Market Garden could be adequately supplied without its use. In a token effort to mollify Eisenhower and free himself from further thought about Antwerp, Montgomery decided that responsibility for securing the city and port and clearing the Scheldt approaches would be handed to First Canadian Army. But his instructions to Lieutenant General Harry Crerar decreed these tasks to be the army's "last priority," only to be undertaken after the channel ports of Boulogne, Dunkirk, Calais, and Le Havre were all captured.

Crerar accordingly notified his corps commanders that "in view of the necessity to give first priority to the capture of the Channel ports... the capture, or destruction, of the enemy remaining North and East of the Ghent–Bruges Canal becomes secondary in importance. While constant pressure and close contact with the enemy, now withdrawing North of R[iver] Scheld[t], will be maintained, important forces will not be committed to offensive action."[3]

II Canadian Corps now had responsibility for a front running about sixty miles eastwards from the coast to Antwerp, but it also was heavily engaged in operations extending all the way south to Boulogne. Here, 3rd Canadian Infantry Division was teeing up its major assault planned for September 17. Knowing that the defenders were ensconced inside heavy fortifications, Lieutenant General Guy Simonds intended to subject them to major aerial and artillery bombardment before sending in his troops. The operation was sure to require several days to complete, and consequently, this division and most of II Canadian Corps's heavy artillery would be tied down here until the battle was concluded. After Boulogne, 3 CID was to advance north and lay siege to Calais. Meanwhile, 2nd Canadian Infantry Division was farther north, having closed on Dunkirk on September 6.

Only 4th Canadian Armoured Division and the 1st Polish Armoured Division were positioned for operations that could begin to loosen the German hold on the approaches to Antwerp. 4 CAD was working its way up the Belgian coast north of Dunkirk, with orders to push the Germans out of Bruges and gain a crossing over the Dérivation de la Lys near Eeklo. About thirty-five miles inland, Eeklo formed the boundary between the Canadians and their Polish counterparts, who had taken over from XII British Corps the task of pushing the Germans out of the area between Ghent and Antwerp. 1 British Corps was far to the south besieging Le Havre, and would not complete that city's liberation until September 12.

First Canadian Army was thus so extended that it could not undertake major offensive action against the retreating Fifteenth Army or prevent the Germans hardening a series of defensive lines. Major General Harry Foster's 4th Armoured Division had first bumped into these defensive works three miles south of Bruges on September 8, where the Germans were dug in behind the Bruges–Ghent Canal.

Despite stiff resistance, the Canadians gained a narrow bridgehead over the canal near Moerbrugge two days later. Roughly halfway between Ghent and Bruges, the Poles attempted to win a similar crossing on the night of September 10–11 to the northwest of Aalter, but were thrown back.[4] The morning brought new orders for the Poles to replace the 7th British Armoured Division in Ghent, as part of the shifting of responsibility for this front from XII British Corps to II Canadian Corps. In a series of fierce small actions, the 4th Canadian and 1st Polish divisions managed to completely crack the line on the Bruges–Ghent Canal, sending the Germans racing back to their next defensive position behind the Leopold Canal. Having grown used to the Germans offering little more than token resistance to delay their advance, the Canadians and Poles were taken aback by the stubborn defence the Germans offered from this new position. That this was a foretaste of the fight to come, however, was not recognized by either Crerar or Montgomery. Both generals dismissed the fighting along the Leopold Canal as of slight consequence, and the divisions clearing the channel ports retained First Canadian Army's priority in terms of attention and resource allocation.

Undoubtedly, operations to free up the approaches to Antwerp would have remained at the bottom of Montgomery's list despite Eisenhower's increasingly strident notes had not a stern directive from the Combined Chiefs of Staff—the joint American and British high command—added its weight on September 12. Meeting in Ottawa, the Combined Chiefs had reviewed and despite reservations had endorsed Market Garden. But with deliberate emphasis, they also stressed to Montgomery the "necessity for opening up the north-west ports, Antwerp and Rotterdam in particular, before the bad weather sets in."[5]

Immediately upon receipt of this directive, Montgomery signalled Crerar fresh instructions. While capturing Boulogne remained the highest priority, Montgomery added that the "early opening of Antwerp is daily becoming of increasing importance and this cannot take place until Walcheren has been captured and the mouth of the river opened for navigation. Before you can do this you will obviously have to remove all the enemy from the mainland in that part where they [are] holding up north east of Bruges. Airborne army considers not possible use airborne troops in this business. Grateful for your views as to when you think you can tackle this problem."[6]

The following day, as 4th Canadian Armoured Division's Algonquin Regiment assembled at Moerkerke for its doomed attempt to win a bridgehead across the Dérivation de la Lys and the Leopold Canal, Montgomery shifted gears entirely. "Early use of Antwerp so urgent that I am prepared to give up operations against Calais and Dunkirk and be content with Boulogne. If we do this will it enable you to speed up the Antwerp business? Discuss this with me tomorrow when you come here for conference." Immediately after the September 14 conference, Montgomery issued fresh instructions that outlined the plan for Market Garden and his expectations for First Canadian Army.

"*Our real objective, therefore, is the Ruhr,*" he said, but "on the way to it we want the ports of Antwerp and Rotterdam, since the capture of the Ruhr is merely the first step on the northern route into Germany." While, upon further reflection, he had decided that Crerar should still capture Boulogne and Calais, the "whole energies of the

[First Canadian] Army will be directed towards operations designed to enable full use of the port of Antwerp." He promised airborne troops could participate in an assault on Walcheren Island once the Canadians had cleared the shore of the Scheldt estuary. Responsibility for Antwerp would devolve entirely to the Canadians on September 17. Once the approaches to Antwerp were opened, the Canadians were "to destroy all enemy to the west of [British Second Army's left flank], and open up the port of Rotterdam." To free 2nd Canadian Infantry Division, Dunkirk would merely be surrounded by 4th British Special Services Brigade, and the German garrison cajoled into surrender by bombarding it with both propaganda leaflets and bombs. The 3rd Canadian Infantry Division, however, would finish the capture of Boulogne and Calais, and so would not be available to participate in clearing the Scheldt for some weeks.[7]

SECOND CANADIAN INFANTRY DIVISION started pulling up stakes around Dunkirk on the morning of September 16. It numbered about 15,000 men, less than its authorized strength of just over 17,000 due to casualties outpacing replacements. Aboard more than 8,600 vehicles—almost 1,000 motorcycles, 600 Bren carriers, 880 15-cwt trucks, more than 1,000 three-ton trucks, and other odds and sods, the division moved out by brigades—each departing in a single convoy that included its assigned supporting artillery regiment.[8] The 4th Canadian Infantry Brigade led, followed by the 5th, and finally the 6th on September 19. "Our route for this hundred mile march," noted the Royal Regiment of Canada's intelligence officer, "lay through many places reminiscent of the Great War, including Poperinghe, Ypres, St. Julien, Thielt, Langemarke, Roulers, and Ghent. The weather was clear and bright, ideal for 'sightseeing.' All along the way, we were cheered by the people who showered apples, pears, plums, tomatoes on us at every opportunity."[9]

Passage through the Great War battlefields proved an evocative experience for most of the young Canadians. "The fresh green countryside around Ypres and St. Julien showed no signs of an earlier and more bitter war," wrote the Essex Scottish war diarist. "Memory is short, it is true, but most of the troops, many of them unborn when these names were on all tongues, knew well of these places and took a keen interest in all that they saw. Of particular interest was the magnificent war memorial near St. Julien past which the column rolled at high speed to testify to our fathers that we still sought the foe."[10]

It was early evening on the 16th when 4 CIB entered Antwerp. Lieutenant George Blackburn of the 4th Field Regiment was struck by the fact that even though "twelve days had passed since the four British tanks had nosed into this the biggest port in the continent making it allied territory... the people [still] thronged the beautiful wide Grand Boulevard, colourful with hundreds of their red, orange, and black flags, to cheer the passing vehicles and fill any that happened to stop with cigars, fruit and drinks."

Resistance fighters also swarmed the Canadians, peppering them with questions and offering information about the enemy across the Albert Canal. The Germans, some of the fighters told Blackburn, had orders "to destroy the harbour." Looking at the largely unscathed port facilities, he found it "inexplicable" that "the Germans who had been defending the port had pulled out... without taking time to destroy the port although tons of dynamite were available for that purpose. But now they seemed to appreciate their error and all indications were that they intended to rectify it if possible."[11]

The infantry regiments stopped inside the city, and, "after ridding themselves of enthusiastic admirers... cooked a meal on the street, while waiting for their reconnaissance units to return from the port area to guide them into the lines they were taking over from 53rd British Infantry Division."[12] Meanwhile, the 4th Field Regiment carefully manoeuvred guns and munition trailers through the crowds and was soon, Bombardier Ken Hossack of 'A' Troop noted, setting up inside "excellent German-build dugouts at Noordkasteel, just north of Antwerp's dock area. The fine defences here were constructed and ready for occupation if an Allied landing had been attempted near the city. The cooks situate in a nice clubhouse by the side of a large swimming pool, where the Supermen and collaborators once made merry with their wives and sweethearts."[13]

It was well after dark when the infantry regiments began taking over the front lines from their British counterparts. The Essex Scottish made the switch with the Highland Light Infantry under harassing shellfire from Germans dug into positions in and around the northern suburb of Merksem. Three men from the reconnaissance party were wounded.[14]

Scuttlebutt held that the division was going to be here for some time, its role to guard the docks and port facilities. Divisional headquarters soon confirmed the rumour with instructions that the infantry were to aggressively patrol beyond the front line to keep the Germans off balance and collect intelligence. No immediate plans were afoot to gain control of more of the port facilities or Albert Canal crossings, which frustrated the Belgian resistance fighters still trying to wrest the northern docks and villages from German hands. But in the absence of tank support, 2 CID was too weak to mount a strong attack against the well-entrenched German forces.

Canadians and Belgians established a mutually supportive relationship that differed sharply from the standoffish approach adopted by the British during their short occupation of Antwerp. The British had little trusted the resistance units commanded by Eugene Colson because they were mostly comprised of Flemish Belgians who were members of the Nationale Kongsgezinde Beweging (National Movement for the King). That meant their loyalty was pledged to King Leopold III rather than the British-backed government-in-exile. King Leopold, who had been both head of the government and army commander-in-chief, had surrendered his forces on May 28, 1940, just ten days after the Germans invaded. Although the decision was immediately repudiated by the Belgian government, it was unable to prevent the soldiers laying down arms. While the government had fled to exile in London, Leopold had surrendered alongside his troops and was imprisoned by the Germans until 1944 at his royal château near Brussels. As the Allies moved north from Normandy, he was unwillingly evacuated to Austria. Despite the fact that Leopold's personal intervention in 1942 was credited with saving about 500,000 Belgian women and children from deportation to work in munitions factories in Germany, the British government and Belgian government-in-exile—comprised primarily of French Belgians—were determined to force his abdication in favour of his brother Charles. Consequently, neither the British nor the government-in-exile endorsed cooperation between Twenty-First Army Group and the NKB resistance fighters.[15]

None of these political machinations much concerned Major General Charles Foulkes or his staff at 2 CID headquarters. By September 19, they reported being awash in intelligence reports from the "Belgian secret army who are working in close liaison with us."[16] Nobody bothered sorting out whether the resistance fighters they dealt with from one moment to another were members of the NKB, the Belgian National Movement, Group G, Independence Front, Liberation Army of Belgium, Secret Army, or the formal Witte Brigade (White Brigade) that became the informal designation Canadians used to identify any resistance unit. That each of these movements had its own political and military agenda ranging from Flemish independence to creating a communist state, to re-establishing the monarchy of King Leopold III meant nothing to the Canadians.

The resistance organizations operating in the Antwerp area were largely of similar mind. The immediate task was to defeat the Germans and, as Colson's resistance fighters had swelled to almost 3,000 as more men stepped up to volunteer, they could play a key role in stemming German attempts to regain control of the dock areas in Allied hands.[17] Brigadier Fred Cabeldu, commanding 4th Canadian Infantry Brigade, had been met upon arrival in Antwerp on September 16 by NKB and White Brigade fighters and was impressed that they "had already organized themselves and offered their whole-hearted cooperation." Soon his brigade and Colson's fighters were carrying out joint patrols and beginning to plan more aggressive operations intended to gain control of some of the villages north of the Albert Canal.[18]

The Canadians became immersed in the surreal Antwerp-area battlefront. Never had they fought inside a thriving, fully inhabited city. Antwerp bore no resemblance to the ruins of Caen in Normandy. "Ordinary urban life went on in Antwerp much as in peacetime. The trams continued to run; night clubs remained open; and the shops sold a reasonable assortment of goods. Two bands played each night at the Century Hotel... and the Belgian girls in their elegant evening dresses were certainly (or did it, after all, only seem so?) the most beautiful in the world," the Royal Regiment of Canada's regimental historian later wrote.[19]

Because of the battlefront's static nature, each regimental commander was permitted to give 7.5 per cent of his men leave for five hours at a time, with everyone required to be back with his unit by 2230 hours each night. Initially, the men's pockets bulged with Belgian francs.[20] Although a private's pay was only $1.30 a day with an augmentation of $35.00 per month for men who were married that went directly to their wives, the soldiers in Antwerp had not had many pay parades since landing in Normandy, and deployment in Antwerp provided opportunity for each regiment to distribute a hefty amount of back wages.[21]

BOMBARDIER HOSSACK DECLARED Antwerp "a veritable UTOPIA, with wine, women and song in abundance, and [it] is visited often and well with and without the official passes."[22] Blackburn, who was promoted to captain while in Antwerp, thought the city "had a fantastic unreality about it... normal civilian activity was being carried on as though the war was miles away instead of a few short blocks. The sidewalks were packed with well-dressed shoppers going to and from shops offering an amazing array of luxuries. Civilian cars moved unconcernedly about the streets and cafés and hotels, each with some form of orchestra, according to their size, gave forth music and laughter and all the other sounds of a people in a festive mood. To those occupying an [Observation Post] this period seemed even more amazing. To them it meant leaving a building from where the Germans could be seen and 'shot up' and where because of hostile shells and snipers they had to 'keep their heads down,' catching a street car and riding up town to have tea in one of the most famous hotels in Europe among fashionably dressed people listening quietly to the hotel orchestra. After the life of filth and slit trenches of the [Normandy] bridgehead, Antwerp seemed a paradise."[23]

"The cost of high living is telling on the boys," Hossack gloomily reported a few days into the deployment. "Our extra cigarettes, soap and chocolate disappear for francs but still we're poor. In the end everything from jeeps to dirty underwear claims its price."[24] Officers fretted about the fact that the men were going to seed, hard drinking was prevalent throughout the ranks, and it was not uncommon for soldiers to return from the city too drunk to stand watch. Yet the officers also knew that these men had been facing constant danger for months, and few were put on charge. Even those absent without leave for days went mostly undisciplined. The war was still there, right on the Albert Canal within a short streetcar ride of the city. And each day the patrols went out, skirmishes were fought, shells exploded in the positions, and men who had been enjoying drink and fine food only hours earlier died or were maimed. They called it the "Streetcar War" and declared it craziness, and knew that when the inevitable orders came to move out from Antwerp they would do so with a measure of relief at getting back to a war that was more real and easily understood.

Despite its festive air, Antwerp was a city where danger lurked for unwary soldiers. While many known fascists had been rounded up by the resistance, some eluded the sweeps. Germans wearing civilian clothing regularly infiltrated the city to gather intelligence and kidnap soldiers for interrogation. Snipers operated frequently behind the Canadian lines. Most of the roads leading from the rear areas to the front lines were under German observation from heights of ground, tall buildings, and port structures located north of the Albert Canal, so any movement generally drew mortar or artillery fire. Men occasionally went missing while on leave only to turn up later dead in a ditch. Such a fate befell Gunner James Carson of the 4th Field, whose corpse was found in one of the canal locks. "Accident or foul play?" Hossack wondered. "We'll never know." [25]

According to the Royal Regiment's historian, officers and men alike went into Antwerp "fully armed, the pistols in their pockets and the knives strapped to their persons providing a strange contrast to the plush and gilt *décor,* the sweet music, and the soft lights of the cabarets." [26]

Even no man's land presented, in the words of the division's war diarist, "a very curious situation. Merksem, a suburb of Antwerp, lies north of the Albert Canal and is in enemy hands. Yet civilians pass to and from Merksem via the tram line to the canal, where they alight, cross the canal on foot and resume their journey in a tram operating on the other side of the canal." Despite the "field security problem" this created, the Canadians proved "unable to put a stop to this traffic."[27]

While civilians came and went from Merksem at will, the same was not true for the Canadians. Repeated attempts to penetrate the town were blocked by "what seemed to be a... screen of well-placed MG posts supported by mortars and light guns."[28] Slowly, however, the aggressive fighting patrols sent out by the Canadians and Belgians gained control over the port facilities to the north of the Albert Canal. But Merksem and the other communities of Ekeren, Oorderen, and Wilmarsdonk which arced around the outer edges of the port to its immediate north and east were sufficiently in dispute that the Canadian hold remained tenuous.

Between September 18 and 21, control of Oorderen and Wilmarsdonk, hamlets surrounded by fields that had been partially flooded when the Germans opened nearby locks, seesawed back and forth. During the fight, a pattern developed whereby Oorderen changed hands daily. Daylight hours saw the Royal Hamilton Light Infantry in control of its streets, but with sunset they were forced out by the Germans. In keeping with the bizarre nature of the Streetcar War, both sides frequented the same small tavern—the Germans taking over the seats around the inkeeper's tables after darkness. "The innkeeper thought it was a great joke," Sergeant Gordon Booker later recalled.[29]

Patrols on both sides were lost; their fate known only to the opposing side. On September 18, a two-man patrol guided by a resistance fighter "never returned and it is suspected that they were taken prisoner." Early the next morning, a patrol from 'A' Company led by Lieutenant Donald Trumpour Knight walked into an ambush while groping its way through heavy fog. An MG 42 hidden in a house ripped off a burst that cut down the thirty-two-year-old officer from Toronto. Six hours later, Captain C.D. MacKay rolled his carrier platoon into the north end of Oorderen and shot up several German patrols trying to infiltrate the town partially as an act of vengeance.[30] In the absence of tanks, 4 CIB's infantry regiments had taken to using their carrier platoons as quasi-armoured units that could quickly deliver concentrated machine-gun fire. On September 20, an Essex Scottish reconnaissance patrol crept across ground being rapidly flooded by an unusual rising tide caused by the autumnal equinox and caught a six-man German patrol literally napping. Four were taken prisoner and another shot and killed.

Obvious to everyone that day was that the contest between the Germans and Canadians was coming to a decision point as sharp firefights crackled all along the frontage of 4 CIB's lines. No sooner had night fallen than a strong German fighting force erupted out of Merksem and struck directly at the Essex Scottish front. The battalion had just taken in sufficient reinforcements to beef its rifle companies up from three to the mandated four and everyone "was expecting a peaceful night, when suddenly a vicious attack burst upon the ['D' Company] area."

The Germans got across the Albert Canal undetected, moved over an intervening railway embankment, and then charged across the open pastures lying between the railroad and the company's position. In minutes, the Germans had men setting charges on a main bridge crossing the canal. A fierce firefight ensued. When the carrier platoon went to the aid of the beleaguered 'D' Company, it ran into heavy fire. Every man in one section was killed or wounded, but the survivors in the other section broke through. The fire from the carrier-mounted Bren guns covered 'D' Company's forward platoons as they pulled back through a hail of German bullets in order to clear the area for counter mortar and artillery fire.[31] The 4th Field Regiment hammered out "2,400 rounds... in a flurry of firing" that broke the German attack.[32] As the Germans retreated, the Essex snapped hard on their heels to keep them running and prevent their setting off any of the charges laid on the bridge. When the fight was over, the news passed through the ranks that the regiment's commander, Lieutenant Colonel Paul Bennett, had been wounded in the leg by a sliver of shrapnel but refused to be evacuated until the fight was decided.[33] By 2300 hours, the charges had been removed from the bridge and the situation declared "restored."[34]

The determined nature of this attack so concerned Major General Foulkes that he personally visited 4 CIB headquarters the following morning and "stressed the importance of the docks and [that he] appreciated that the enemy would make every effort to infiltrate and blow up the docks." Clearly this was the case, for dawn came in Oorderen with an attack by two platoons against a small Royal Hamilton Light Infantry patrol. A "sharp skirmish ensued in the centre of the town," reported the regiment's war diarist. The patrol was saved from being wiped out when the carrier platoon rushed to the hamlet to cover its withdrawal. Heavy mortar and artillery fire later in the morning drove the Belgian resistance out of Wilmersdonk.

Cabeldu considered trying to gain a permanent hold over Oorderen, but rejected the idea because "our forces were too spread out to include occupying the town. So fighting patrol [would continue] to deny the town to the enemy." While a necessary compromise, it did nothing to advance securing the ports. Then, at 1950 hours on September 21, a massive explosion was heard from the vicinity of the critical Kruisschanssluis—the outermost one controlling the water levels within the northern port area. Racing to the site, Cabeldu learned that the Germans had floated a mine down the river in an attempt to breach its gates. Although damaged, the lock continued to function, capable of moving water in and out as needed to provide ship access into the port facility. But the sabotage attempt underscored the vulnerability of their tenuous protective screen as long as the Germans were entrenched so close to the port.

[4]

A Very Heavy Program

BRIGADIER FRED CABELDU's inability to force the Germans back from the northern edges of Antwerp was symptomatic of Lieutenant General Harry Crerar's difficulties in developing a full operational battle plan. Badly overextended by conflicting priorities that left its divisions straggled along a line running from Le Havre up the coast to near Bruges and then inland to Antwerp, First Canadian Army could only take on the Germans defending the Scheldt estuary in piecemeal fashion.

Although his planning staff had begun trying to bring some order to the operation, the Algonquin Regiment's September 13 attempt to force the Leopold Canal at Moerkerke, 2nd Canadian Infantry Division's move to Antwerp, and a Polish drive into the gap between Antwerp and the Ghent–Terneuzen Canal on September 17 did not result from any formal battle plan.[1] They aimed either to capitalize on perceived enemy weaknesses or, as was true for 2 CID's move to Antwerp, to accord with instructions from Twenty-First Army Group.

While the Algonquin assault had ended in disaster, the Polish offensive proved a stunning success. After two days of hard fighting, the Poles had swept the Germans out of Ghent's northern suburbs on September 14. When an attempt to continue this drive directly north to Terneuzen was blocked by stiff opposition, a deft sidestep almost thirty miles eastwards enabled the Poles to slip out of the German grip. From two miles north of where Sint-Niklaas stood astride the main Ghent–Antwerp highway, the Poles kicked off a five-pronged thrust on September 15 to seize Terneuzen and sweep the Germans away from the shores of the Scheldt estuary lying between this small port town and Antwerp.[2] Assured by First Canadian Army headquarters that the operation would merely entail "mopping up" Germans already on the run towards Terneuzen, General Stanislaw Maczek expected to achieve his objectives easily.[3]

The first day of the attack confirmed this impression, as his Polish troops slammed across the Dutch border and threw the Germans behind the Hulst Canal—a navigable waterway that linked Hulst to the Ghent–Terneuzen Canal. By day's end, the 10th Dragoon Regiment had breached the canal near Axel, about five miles south of Terneuzen. Shortly after dawn on September 17, however, the Germans struck back with a combined infantry and tank counterattack that eliminated the bridgehead. The following day Maczek threw the 3rd Polish Infantry Brigade over the canal in front of the village of Kijkuit. Despite immediate encirclement by strong German forces, the brigade clung to its beachhead through a long night. Their defiant stance covered Polish engineers, who managed to erect a bridge over which several tanks rushed to bolster the brigade on the morning of September 19. Seventy-six Germans were quickly taken prisoner as the enemy beat a hurried retreat.[4]

The Poles were soon across the canal in strength, a combined infantry and armour column rushing west to seize Axel, and the other prongs breaking out towards the coastal objectives. They pushed through a low, flat landscape of fields separated by hundreds of small canals. The connecting dykes had been breached by explosives to impede the Allied advance by flooding all the land below sea level. This confined the Polish infantry and tanks to dangerously constricted routes on top of the dykes or on the few main roads that had been constructed on raised beds. Believing they had denied the Poles freedom of movement, the Germans deployed only small platoon-strength fighting squads to cover each available line of advance.[5] But the Poles met these blocking parties with massed tank fire that demoralized the Germans and shattered their defensive positions.

With about two hundred tanks prowling along close to the infantry, the Poles were able to move steadily forward—rapidly overwhelming any German defenders who got in their way. By evening, Axel was taken, putting the Polish column within five miles of Terneuzen.

Realizing that the port must soon fall, the Germans began a general evacuation. The ferry operation running from Terneuzen to Vlissingen on Walcheren Island ran nonstop that night. Columns of troops and equipment fled west across two bridges that crossed the Ghent–Terneuzen Canal, then on towards Breskens. All bridges over the canal to the south of these crossings were destroyed to prevent the Poles getting across with their tanks and striking the withdrawing forces from the flank. With the dawn on September 20, Polish artillery brought the port facilities of Terneuzen under fire and the ferry operation was ordered abandoned.[6] But at 1700 hours, when the leading Polish troops reached the docks, they caught several barges crammed with German troops being towed out of the harbour. The tanks opened fire, sinking the barges. Five officers and 176 men of 712th Infantry Division were fished out of the water. How many men had been killed by the shellfire or drowned was unknown. With Terneuzen taken, the Poles only needed to round up any Germans trapped between the Ghent–Terneuzen Canal and the west bank of the Scheldt River to complete their operation.[7]

General Maczek told Crerar this task would require only two days. The swiftly conducted advance from Ghent had cost the Poles 71 killed, 191 wounded, and 63 missing—a rate of casualties that seemed disproportionately high to Maczek despite having taken 1,173 prisoners and killed many more Germans—undoubtedly seriously weakening the already reduced strength of 712th Infantry Division.[8] The Polish general attributed the heavy casualty rate to the "very difficult conditions of the ground. Numerous canals, inundation areas, a great number of wooded dykes, and narrow roads on those dykes." Another contributing factor was his limited access to artillery support and the fact that the ammunition dumps for those guns lay 125 miles to the rear.[9]

The Polish experience underscored the conclusion reached after the briefest of glances by Crerar and his planning staff that clearing the Scheldt approaches would be difficult. Replying to Montgomery's

September 14 instruction that he was to capture Boulogne, Dunkirk, and Calais while also rendering Antwerp usable, Crerar noted that the "capture of Walcheren and Beveland islands look like very tough propositions to me—at this stage—and to require a lot of 'doing.' I certainly will want to secure the mainland end of the peninsula leading from Zuid Beveland before launching a final assault, but my studies have not yet proceeded sufficiently to indicate how I would propose to conduct that operation as a whole."[10]

Crerar's instincts were sound. Just nine days after Montgomery and XXX Corps's Lieutenant General Horrocks had failed to take advantage of the golden opportunity that would have achieved precisely this result, he recognized that it was essential to secure the isthmus that linked South Beveland and Walcheren to the mainland. He also understood that First Canadian Army faced a major campaign that would have to be fought across a broad, asymmetrical front, which would be greatly extended on September 17 when British Second Army "set out on its narrowly concentrated thrust towards Arnhem." This eastwards move by Lieutenant General Dempsey's army would create a gap between First Canadian Army and his XII Corps that Crerar could only plug by deploying I British Corps about fifteen miles east of Antwerp. Clearing of the Scheldt would consequently fall almost entirely on the shoulders of II Canadian Corps.

Compared to the almost needlelike thrust Second Army would make with Market Garden, the British official historian later noted, the Canadians faced "widely extended tasks... Not only had they first to capture two of the defended Channel ports and to 'mask' a third; they must also drive the Germans from their strong bridgehead south of the Scheldt and from their dominating positions north of the estuary in Walcheren and South Beveland. All this would be necessary to secure 'full use of the port of Antwerp.' It was a very heavy program for an army which consisted of two armoured and four infantry divisions..."[11] But the historian failed to note that half of these divisions would effectively be engaged in the drive to the Maas, so it came down to three divisions undertaking the listed tasks. Further, the meandering nature of the estuary and the chokepoint presented by the peninsula also meant that II Canadian Corps's divisions would each operate independent of the others, so that any concentration of force against specific German weakpoints would be difficult to achieve.

Montgomery's September 14 reversal that made opening Antwerp a priority while removing Dunkirk from the army's immediate to-do list, and also the possibility of airborne troops, little bolstered Crerar's increasingly sagging spirits. Life in the field, even with the relative comforts enjoyed by those living at army headquarters, was exacting a personal toll. The fifty-six-year-old general was dogged by persistent dysentery stubbornly resistant to normal medical treatments. Each day, Crerar awoke weaker than before.[12]

Given his penchant for detail, Crerar set to developing an extensive analysis of the problem. Thousands of aerial photographs along with masses of intelligence reports on German strength, fortifications, and apparent intentions were examined in microscopic detail and then developed by his headquarters staff into a series of long reports. Staring at the photographs and consulting dozens of marine and topographic maps collected from every possible source confirmed what Crerar and his planners had suspected—the topography was as formidable as the expected German opposition.

"God created the world, but the Dutch created the Netherlands" was a popular saying in Holland. Nowhere was this truer than in Zeeland. Dutch efforts to manage their relationship with the sea extend back to 500 B.C. when the first artificial dykes were erected to enable settlement below sea level. As technology improved, the Dutch had slowly prevailed in this centuries-long seesaw battle with the sea for domination over lands drained that all too often were later lost to renewed flooding. By the beginning of the twentieth century, about 25 per cent of the Netherlands was reclaimed land lying below sea level—known as polders. The southwest corner of the Netherlands constituted Zeeland, a region of islands separated by estuaries, one of the nation's most concentrated polder areas. Virtually all of Holland south of the West Scheldt was polder, as was most of South Beveland and Walcheren. The smaller North Beveland had been entirely reclaimed.[13]

"Polder," stated one Canadian Army report, "is extremely flat with a striking abundance of water in a neat pattern of parallel ditches. The horizon is often formed by a dyke, and broken only by occasional windmills... Land drainage is [essential] for both polders and canals. The water level is so near the ground level that failure of artificial drainage would cause the level to rise, creating saturated ground and sheet flooding."

Another report noted that the "soil of polders is almost universally very heavy clay designated by the Dutch as sea clay [lacking intermixed fine sand]. It is the type of heavy ground which often needs two to three horses to plough." Ground water lurked under the clay at depths of two to four feet in September, but in dry weather would still support wheeled and tracked traffic. Given a little rain, however, "the surface [became] very slippery—immediately so on the cultivated land and as soon as the grass is worn off the pasture." Wheeled vehicles could not operate on such ground, the report concluded, and tanks would do so with difficulty and risk bogging down. Setting up artillery on polders was also difficult because of the closeness of groundwater to the surface. The weight of the guns and their firing recoil might sink them in a mire of muck. This meant it would be preferable to situate artillery on top of dykes, but that made them more vulnerable to German detection and counterbattery fire.[14]

While Crerar and his staff were sure the worst fighting would occur when they attempted to clear the north bank of the West Scheldt, the army had first to liberate the south shore. An examination of the ground in the twenty-two-mile by ten-mile rectangle of country they dubbed the Breskens Pocket was sobering. A greater obstacle than the flooded polders was presented by canals, particularly the Leopold Canal, which ran in tandem much of the way with the Dérivation de la Lys from Zeebrugge on the coast to the Isabellapolder, just south of the Braakman Inlet. Forming a barrier to the immediate east of the sprawling Isabellapolder was the Ghent–Terneuzen Canal.[15] The twenty-five-mile-wide gap between this canal and the termination of the Leopold Canal offered the only point where the German front line was not dug in behind a deep water barrier, but it was known to be heavily fortified.[16]

Between this defensive canal line and the West Scheldt coast lay "a honeycomb of polders fringed on the coast by dunes and dykes, throughout its entire area liable to saturation or flooding. Except along the edges of embankment or canal, or in occasional wooded depressions, trees were few, ditches took the place of hedges and a sparse population had scattered its farmhouses wherever the soil was firm and dry, or strung its cottages along the roads or on the brink of the polders. It was not a country for armour, and amphibians were the only sort of vehicle likely to flourish there. A few villages like Eede, Oostburg, Sluis and Cadzand, and places on the coast, like Knocke and the port of Breskens, offered the prospect of resistance behind rubble and concrete."[17]

CRERAR AND HIS STAFF were just beginning to appreciate the difficulty of rooting the Germans out of the Breskens Pocket when Second Army launched its drive towards the Rhine on September 17. Simultaneously, II Canadian Corps's 3rd Canadian Infantry Division kicked off Operation Wellhit against the German garrison defending Boulogne. These major operations temporarily overrode all other concerns.

Market Garden had the potential of bringing the war to a speedy conclusion if the XXX Corps managed to gain the Arnhem crossing of the Neder Rijn. (Just east of Arnhem and Nijmegen, the Rhine divided into two branches, with the Neder Rijn or Northern Rhine passing through Arnhem and the Waal through Nijmegen.) To accomplish their first task, the British tanks and supporting infantry had to dash up a narrow sixty-mile stretch of highway, fifty miles of which were to be secured by airborne forces dropped earlier. Success depended on XXX Corps shattering the "hard but brittle" defensive crust of the German front line facing the Albert Canal start line and advancing so quickly that there would be no time to rally the scant reserves believed to be in the area. Not even the presence of two SS Panzer divisions was believed a threat, as intelligence reported them so reduced by the summer fighting, that together they could muster no more than two brigades.[18]

September 17 dawned as a perfect day for airborne operations, with little wind and only high overcast well above the paratroopers' jump altitudes. By noon, the greatest airborne armada in history—4,600 aircraft carrying three airborne divisions—was over

Holland. The 101st U.S. Airborne dropped closest to xxx Corps to secure the area between Veghel and Zon, the 82nd U.S. Airborne landed between the Maas and Waal rivers to seize a crossing at Nijmegen, while the 1st British Airborne landed west of Arnhem and then moved to take the town and the major road and rail bridges that spanned the Neder Rijn. At 1435 hours, having learned the airborne troops were safely landed, Horrocks ordered his leading Irish Guards Armoured Division to break the German line.

Market Garden was an intricate plan that relied on each entwined thread weaving together to form a perfect pattern. Almost from the outset, it began to unravel as setbacks piled one atop the other. Although the initial airborne troops gained many key objectives, fog in Great Britain critically delayed or prevented the landing of reinforcements the following day. At Arnhem, the British paratroopers gained a toehold in the town, only to face the fury of ss Panzer troops and tanks present in far greater numbers than predicted. Lacking armour of their own, the British were not only outnumbered but outgunned. Unless Horrocks broke through quickly, their fate was set.

Hope of early relief died on the afternoon of September 19 when the armour arrived at Nijmegen to find the vital rail and road bridges still in German hands despite the best efforts of the American paratroops. These crossings were not won until late the next day. When the Irish Guards attempted to move out from this bridgehead the following morning, they were quickly blocked by heavily dug-in German forces. With that, Market Garden was in tatters. Despite heroic efforts by the divisions involved, which managed to establish a narrow link through to the Neder Rijn on September 24, it was obvious that relieving the paratroops in Arnhem was impossible. The Germans north of the river were too strong, the Allies too weakened by losses incurred in the advance, and they had yet to fully secure the road from German counterattacks. On September 25, the order was given for the paratroops to pull out. Only about 2,500 of the 10,000 that had dropped nine days earlier remained—the rest either killed or taken prisoner. They slipped silently into the darkness, screened by an artillery barrage. During a long, grim night, 2,163 men were safely brought over the river.[19]

Market Garden was over. "Had good weather obtained, there was no doubt that we should have obtained full success," Montgomery blustered afterwards.[20] Whether the offensive could have succeeded, the failure to gain a crossing at Arnhem meant he "could not position the Second Army... to be able to develop operations against the north face of the Ruhr. But the possession of the crossings over the Meuse at Grave, and over the Lower Rhine (or Waal as it is called in Holland) at Nijmegen, were to prove of immense value later on; we had liberated a large part of Holland; we had the stepping stone we needed for the successful battles of the Rhineland that were to follow."[21]

Montgomery was "bitterly disappointed." This was his second attempt "to capture the Ruhr quickly... But we still hadn't got it." And having failed to achieve that, Montgomery looked over his left shoulder more carefully than he had in weeks and realized that he also had failed to open the approaches to Antwerp "so that we could get the free use of that port. I reckoned that the Canadian Army could do it *while* we were going for the Ruhr. I was wrong."[22] How he could have thought this might happen with First Canadian Army strung out and engaged in a multitude of operations in compliance with his orders was not something Montgomery cared to elaborate.

While Market Garden had been underway, 3rd Canadian Infantry Division's 8th and 9th Infantry Brigades had fought for control of Boulogne—an operation that did not end until September 22 after six hard days of battle. That day, despite overwhelmingly outnumbering the Canadians, 9,517 German defenders surrendered. It was a surprising achievement, but one that came at a price of 634 killed, wounded, and missing. This was a significantly higher rate of casualties than the 388 suffered by 1 British Corps at Le Havre, where two divisions had forced the surrender of a garrison little larger than that of Boulogne.[23]

The fall of Boulogne did not mean that 3 CID could now turn to operations on the Scheldt. Calais remained. Nor did it mean any relief soon to the critical Allied supply problem—Boulogne's port was blocked by sunken ships and so damaged that it would not open for traffic until October 12.

Waiting behind the Calais defences were 7,500 Germans. Again, two infantry brigades—the 7th and 8th Canadian—undertook the operation on September 24. A tough fight ensued that cost about 300 casualties and ended with the German surrender on October 1. The port was badly damaged, not predicted to open until sometime in November.[24] During this engagement, 9 CIB had eliminated German cross-channel batteries at Cap Gris Nez that had long harassed Dover with intermittent shelling. The batteries were captured on September 29, and another 1,600 Germans bagged as prisoners in exchange for 42 casualties.[25]

ALTHOUGH THESE OPERATIONS did much to complete the coastal port clearing, they ensured that II Canadian Corps could not begin seriously trying to clear the Scheldt approaches during September for simple lack of strength. After the Algonquin Regiment had been repulsed on September 13–14 in front of Moerkerke, the 4th Canadian Armoured Division had shifted its strength east with the Lake Superior Regiment (Motor) leading the way across the Dérivation de la Lys near Eeklo, about six miles from where this canal broke away from the Leopold Canal to follow a southerly route. With the Germans retreating quickly before it, the division spread out to clear the ground bordered to the north by the Leopold Canal and to the east by the Ghent–Terneuzen Canal. By September 22, the division's 10th Canadian Infantry Brigade was preparing to test the defences guarding the twenty-five-mile-wide gap between these two major water obstacles.[26]

Meanwhile, east of Antwerp, the 2nd Canadian Infantry Division had completed deploying its 5th and 6th Infantry Brigades in front of the Albert Canal by September 19 and the 5th was planning to try and gain a crossing on the night of September 20–21.[27] As with the previous actions by divisions of II Canadian Corps, these offensive moves were not part of the army's formal battle plan. That was still being crafted, the senior commanders and their staffs beginning to pin down the details based on an "elaborate appreciation of the problem of capturing Walcheren and South Beveland" that Crerar's Plans Section tabled on September 19.

The crux of the problem rested on the inaccessibility of both islands. Only the narrow—barely 2,000-yard-wide—isthmus of salt flats and polders connected South Beveland to the mainland. Forced back upon it, the Germans would enjoy a particularly narrow defensive front. Running about twenty-five miles from east to west, the peninsula itself was bisected at the ten-mile point by the South Beveland Canal, over which a double bridge provided the only rail and road crossing. The canal was a vital Dutch transportation link used before the war by barges carrying goods from the West Scheldt to northern parts of the country. Four and a half miles long, 21 feet deep, and averaging a breadth of 130 to 160 feet, of the many canals parsing the peninsula into sections this was "the most formidable as a military obstacle." While a couple of secondary roads existed, the main road was the only one that spanned the peninsula's length. "Given the difficulties of deployment over sodden country on either hand," any attacker would be channelled onto this road, which would perfectly suit the defender.

Walcheren was even more formidably isolated. Separating it from South Beveland was the Sloe Channel, "a shallow, treacherous, partially silted gap, shining with ooze, runnels and water, forbidding to boat or beast, but crossed by the causeway bearing the road and railway line from South Beveland. The island is about nine miles from north to south and roughly the same distance at its widest part from east to west. The same landscape of polders and intricate system of drainage prevails as elsewhere throughout the region, though with rather more rough pasture and with the attendant hindrances to movement across country, especially after rain... the level of saturation is never deep and towards the end of September a very slippery surface laced with ditches would slacken and hinder the passage even of tracked vehicles off the roads, and the pace of infantry would be slow." Walcheren was home to two large towns. Vlissingen, known to the British as Flushing, was a thriving small port and industrial centre through which many English tourists had passed by ferry for prewar vacations. Middelburg was the provincial capital and before the war a thriving market town. Except for the medieval part of Middelburg, still surrounded by a fortress wall, most of the island lay well below sea level and would, "but for its ancient dykes and dunes... be lost to the sea."

North Beveland, the smaller island that stood midway between South Beveland and Walcheren, had "much the same configuration" and would have to be attacked in much the same manner as its neighbours.[28]

Simply bulling from the mainland onto South Beveland and then across the narrow Sloedam linking it to Walcheren begged disastrous losses. So the planners proposed a multifaceted operation that would see not only an attack from the mainland, but also the landing of amphibious and airborne forces. They envisaged a major drive onto South Beveland from the mainland that would push through to the canal while a parachute brigade was dropped to the west of it to "disorganize the enemy and secure the small harbour of Hoedekenskerke." Once this harbour was secure, waterborne forces could come to the aid of the paratroops.

Having won South Beveland, another parachute brigade would drop on Walcheren directly behind the Sloe and quickly gain control of it. This bridgehead would then be built up by forces brought in by boat and over the causeway. With Montgomery waffling about whether airborne troops would be put at First Canadian Army's disposal, the planners also drafted various schemes that resembled the first except that only waterborne forces would assist on South Beveland and Walcheren. But they considered airborne troops "a most important adjunct of this operation" and pressed Crerar to advocate strongly for them.

As both islands were protected by powerful coastal gun positions, the planners also called for Bomber Command and 2nd Tactical Air Force to carry out extensive air operations against the guns and other known German defensive positions. Once the south shore of the Scheldt had been cleared, they recommended deploying all available artillery to the coast to fire upon the enemy defences.[29]

Those defences were considered formidable, but the planners found it "no simple matter... to make any accurate assessment of the forces defending the islands or of their dispositions." Fifteenth Army was still being evacuated from Breskens, and thousands of troops were moving daily from Walcheren's Vlissingen to gain the mainland via the South Beveland isthmus. How many would be held back to defend the north bank of the Scheldt estuary could only be speculated.

As Market Garden played out, Allied intelligence gained a better appreciation of the disposition of enemy divisions. The 64th and 70th Infantry Divisions appeared to have been retained for defending the Scheldt, particularly after two Grenadier Regiments from the 64th were identified as stationed behind the Leopold Canal with "orders to fight to the last man." This division was believed to number only about 4,000 men and it was expected that despite these orders they intended to merely hold here until the canal was breached and would then give up the Breskens Pocket and escape by ferry to Walcheren, where they would continue the fight.

The 70th was believed responsible for defending Walcheren and South Beveland. Consisting of between 6,000 and 6,500 men, the division was considered a poor one, largely composed of "men suffering from chronic stomach ailments." Added to the strength of both the 64th and 70th divisions, they believed, were stragglers from the 226th and 712th Infantry Divisions and a catch-all assortment of "naval and artillery battalions, engineers, gunners and harbour guards" that boosted the entire Scheldt defence force to about 20,000 men. Of these, some 4,000 were thought to be defending the two Beveland islands, 11,500 Walcheren, and 4,400 the Scheldt's southern shore.

Walcheren bristled with pillboxes and gun positions situated densely along its shoreline of dykes and sand dunes. Underwater obstacles, vast networks of barbed-wire barriers, and minefields added to its defence system. About twenty-five artillery batteries were emplaced on the island. All the large coastal batteries—one 220-millimetre, five 150-millimetre, one 120-millimetre, thirteen 105-millimetre, two 94-millimetre, and three 75-millimetre—were capable of an all-round traverse. The bigger guns could range at will over much of the Scheldt's coastline. There was no doubting that Walcheren would be a tough nut to crack.[30]

One intriguing possibility considered in detail was to deliberately breach the dykes and flood the entire island. This idea was based on the realization that, as advantageous as the topography of the islands was to the defence, once "the isthmus into Beveland had been closed, the German garrison would be cut off from all contact with their own military hinterland except by sea to the northern islands. Thus imprisoned, they would share the vulnerability of Zeelanders...to the hazards of tide and flood. Deliberate inundation," freely utilized by the Germans elsewhere, the planners declared, could thus become "a two-edged sword. Were it not for the dunes and dykes which surround [Walcheren] island as rim to a saucer, raised up with arduous ingenuity by countless generations of Dutchmen in their own unending war against the sea, its cultivated fields and thriving communities...would be reduced to the banks of mud from which they were reclaimed. All that would be left above high tide would be some of the roads, irrelevant on their dykes, the remnants of the sea defences and the dunes on the perimeter, tree-tops, the roofs of farm buildings, the port of Flushing, and the town of Middelburg, itself an uncertain and dwindling island. Such a calamity faced through the centuries of their tireless engineering, now overhung the helpless Dutch."

The Germans might well resort to flooding Walcheren on their own, the planners thought, by causing the drainage system to cease operation. This would flood the polders and greatly restrict the attackers' freedom of movement. But if the Allies breached the outer dykes by bombardment and "letting in the sea...the menace and destructive potentiality would grow with the tide: were it to be full and the gap wide, our Intelligence expected that a deluge from eight to ten feet deep would rush in and that, in the shape of a huge tidal wave, the sea would begin a relentless re-conquest of the land. In about three days Walcheren would be covered."

On September 16, however, still confident that Market Garden would succeed and bring "imminent victory in the west," they had dismissed the proposal for "reasons of morality. Apart from the physical difficulties involved," they wrote, "are the moral questions. At this stage of the war, and for purposes so fleeting, it is unlikely that even exponents of total war would bring down on their nearest neighbours a calamity equal to an earthquake or volcanic eruption. It is possible but improbable."[31]

[5]

Illusion of Victory

WHEN FIRST CANADIAN ARMY'S planning staff tabled an appreciation on September 19 that rejected deliberate flooding of Walcheren Island and set out a tentative plan for the campaign, they immediately drew fire from Lieutenant General Guy Simonds. "It is my opinion that the Plans Section appreciation is based upon too many hypothetical considerations," he wrote caustically on September 21, "which may differ very considerably from actualities." First and foremost was the assumption that the south bank of the Scheldt estuary must be cleared before any operations against South Beveland and Walcheren were undertaken. Clearing this area, Simonds contended, "may be a major operation and... it may be so saturated [by deliberate German flooding] that it would be useless to us for gun positions from which Walcheren defences may be commanded." He predicted that operations to clear the Scheldt's north bank might have to proceed before the south bank was freed from the German grip.

Simonds also thought the planners far too sanguine in their discussion of the problems his divisions would face breaking into South Beveland via the narrow isthmus connecting it to the mainland. This "may well turn out to be an approach down a single stretch of road some five miles in length, bordered by impassable ground on either side. It would be equivalent to an assault landing on a 'one craft front' on a coast where it was only possible to beach one craft at a single pre-known point on which the whole fire power of the defence could be concentrated."

An amphibious assault on Walcheren, unsupported by airborne troops, "cannot be ruled out... It may be the only way of taking it," he argued. "Though it would be a last resort and a most uninviting task, I consider it would be quite wrong to make no preparations for it, and to be faced at some later time with the necessity of having to improvise at very short notice. I am strongly of the opinion that the necessary military and naval forces should now be earmarked, married up and trained against the contingency that they may be required."

Simonds still hoped airborne troops could assault Walcheren and he knit their deployment into his proposed combined forces offensive plan. It would develop in five stages. First, and surely most controversial, Simonds embraced the idea that aerial bombing "should be undertaken to break the dykes and completely flood all parts of the island below high water level." Stage two would see the few remaining unflooded areas "systematically attacked by heavy air bombardment, day and night, to destroy defences and wear out the garrison by attrition." To add to the psychological stress, as many heavy bombers en route or returning from raiding targets in western Germany "should be routed over Walcheren so that the garrison can never tell whether the approach of large aircraft indicates attack or not. This combined with heavy bombing attacks will drive the enemy to cover on approach of large aircraft formations and will help to 'cover' the eventual airborne landing." Once "the morale of the garrison has sufficiently deteriorated, waterborne patrols may be sent to determine the situation. If found to be ripe, airborne, followed by waterborne, troops should be landed immediately following a bomber raid (when defenders have been driven to ground) and mop up and take the surrender."

Having stated his general plan for Walcheren, Simonds presented his campaign to open the Scheldt. From Antwerp, 2nd Canadian Infantry Division would push northwards to cut off South Beveland and, if possible, advance across the isthmus. Meanwhile, 4th Canadian Armoured Division would continue operations in the Breskens Pocket until it could be relieved by 3rd Canadian Infantry Division. Simonds considered this an unfortunate compromise as such fighting ill-suited an armoured division, "but I have nothing else available within the present constitution and tasks of [11 Canadian Corps.]" Once 3 CID was freed from its operations against Boulogne and Calais, it would relieve 4 CAD and "complete the clearing of the area north of Leopold Canal if this has not been completed by that time." One 3 CID brigade, however, would be held back and "earmarked with necessary Naval counterpart to train... for seaborne operations against Walcheren." At the same time, airborne forces would be selected and trained "for landings on those parts of Walcheren Island which cannot be 'sunk' by flooding. Bombing should be instituted immediately to "break dykes and flood Walcheren Island" and to eliminate "defences and break morale of defenders of 'unsinkable' portions of the island."[1]

Lieutenant General Harry Crerar was already in the midst of preparing for a critical conference of staff officers representing First Canadian Army, Twenty-First Army Group, the First Allied Airborne Army, Royal Navy, and Royal Air force to agree on how to clear the Scheldt estuary when Simonds's report hit his desk. Although Crerar quibbled with some points, there was much in Simonds's proposal that meshed with his own thoughts on clearing the north bank of the Scheldt. On the day Simonds drafted his commentary, Crerar had been explaining his script for what had been codenamed Operation Infatuate to Allied Naval Commander-in-Chief Admiral Sir Bertram Ramsay and Montgomery's Chief of Staff, Major General Sir Francis "Freddie" de Guingand.

In contrast to Simonds, Crerar accepted that the south bank of the Scheldt estuary had to be taken before a final plan for clearing the north bank could be decided. He also wanted the area extending from Bergen op Zoom on the East Scheldt coastline about seven miles east to Roosendaal brought firmly into Allied hands in order to protect the forces crossing the isthmus onto South Beveland from German counterattack. Once these two conditions were met, Crerar thought the isthmus could be attacked in coordination with an amphibious assault on South Beveland at Hoedekenskerke. He also envisioned "a minor combined operation designed to land infantry only on the south-west coast of Walcheren." To support this, "from a purely military point of view... sustained and heavy bomber attacks" should target the German defences "on the basis of complete destruction" and this might include deliberate breaching of the dykes.

Agreeing that an assault landing might be required, Ramsay promised sufficient landing craft and fire support from two 15-inch-gun monitors and the battleship HMS *Warspite*. Royal Navy Captain A.F. Pugsley, an experienced destroyer commander who had commanded a naval assault group on D-Day and had his headquarters ship sunk under him during the invasion, was assigned to work with II Canadian Corps planners on the naval contribution. As for flooding the island, de Guingand would solicit "the views of higher authority," and connect II Canadian Corps with No. 84 Group so that a plan for bombing Walcheren could be developed.[2]

On September 22, while preparing for the forthcoming day's major conference on Operation Infatuate, Crerar more closely analyzed Simonds's report, using a pencil to tick off each point that accorded with his own thinking. The proposed movements of II Canadian Corps divisions were checked off, but in his marginal notes he substituted 4th British Special Services Brigade—currently masking Dunkirk—for the 3 CID brigade that Simonds had intended to assault Walcheren. The demand that Walcheren be flooded was not commented upon, but he checked off the use of bombing to destroy defences and break the German garrison's morale.[3]

Once the south bank of the West Scheldt was cleared and the isthmus sealed off, "then the difficult assault and capture of Zuid [South] Beveland and Walcheren will be successively carried out." Rejecting Simonds's notion that an operational plan could be detailed at this point, Crerar offered only a tentative one that would most likely entail an assault across the isthmus and a waterborne landing from near Terneuzen onto South Beveland at Hoedekenskerke. These two operations might occur "concurrently or successively. Finally, once South Beveland was taken, a "seaborne combined operation, involving, from this Army, 4 SS B[rigade] launched against the SW coast of Walcheren Island or possibly the NE coast if North Beveland in

[Canadian] possession." This attack would be "in conjunction with an attack launched from Zuid Beveland."

While in the midst of drafting his notes, Crerar received the discouraging news that Eisenhower had personally scotched deployment of airborne troops for clearing either South Beveland or Walcheren. In doing so, Eisenhower confirmed an earlier refusal by Lieutenant General Lewis H. Brereton, the Allied Airborne Army commander. Brereton defended his decision "because of intense flak on Walcheren, difficult terrain which would prevent glider landings, excessive losses likely because of drowning... and the fact that the operation is an improper employment of airborne forces."[4] The reasoning behind the last point was not explained and was certainly open for debate, as others believed this kind of drop onto a concentrated objective or to break a strong defensive line by assaulting its rear fit precisely with the correct use of airborne forces.

Eisenhower tried to soften the obvious blow to First Canadian Army's plans by arguing that the allocation of aircraft to mount such an airborne operation would "divert aircraft from the direct support of the Canadian assaulting forces. My decision is therefore *not* to launch an airborne operation but to make a priority demand on Bomber Command, and Eighth Air Force for the complete saturation of the targets you select. All medium bombers will also be made available to assist."[5]

Crerar was little impressed. "Until yesterday," he wrote, "I was promised the additional assistance of two [parachute brigades] of an Airborne Division. While dropping conditions are undoubtedly poor in the Dutch Islands, so are other conditions which concern these particular offensive operations. I consider, therefore, that the decision to withhold Airborne forces from Operation 'Infatuate' may well have made its accomplishment still more difficult."

The Canadian commander fully intended to hold Eisenhower to his promise. He would seek "large scale heavy bomber attacks by Bomber Command, and if possible Eighth USAAF be carried out against known enemy defences" on Walcheren and South Beveland or the southern bank of the West Scheldt. Crerar now entirely embraced the concept of flooding Walcheren. "If technically feasible, and no restrictions imposed on grounds of higher policy, air effort should also be designed to destroy locks and flood Walcheren Island—thus isolating the enemy to high ground," he entered as his concluding remark.[6]

Thirty-six staff officers were crowded into a stuffy room at First Canadian Headquarters the next day when Crerar walked them through his operational plan, ending with the proposal that, if SHAEF sanctioned it and Bomber Command deemed it possible, Walcheren be flooded. Simonds then took the floor and "stressed the favourable situation that would develop if Walcheren could be flooded by breaching the dykes in the vicinity of Westkapelle. The enemy would be forced to the unfloodable parts of the island, principally the sand dunes and an assault landing could be made on these positions from the rear. LCTS [Landing Craft, Tanks] might disgorge LVTS [Landing Vehicles, Tanks] near the breached dyke and the LVTS could then proceed through the gaps and be used to assault the rear of the positions." Simonds wanted heavy bombing of Walcheren to begin as soon as possible. But he also noted that no matter how quickly the south bank of the Scheldt was cleared or the Bergen op Zoom to Roosendaal line attained, the attack on the peninsula and Walcheren Island would not be possible for about twenty-one days due to a shortage of heavy ammunition for the Canadian artillery regiments. These were now dependent on receiving munitions through Dieppe, and until a rate of 1,500 tons daily was attained, the gunners would quickly exhaust their ammunition.[7]

When Simonds returned to his seat, a general discussion ensued. To the surprise of both Crerar and Simonds, their desire to have Walcheren flooded met unexpected opposition from Brigadier Geoffrey Walsh, II Canadian Corps's chief engineer. Walsh declared the plan to breach the Walcheren dykes "impracticable."[8] Air Vice-Marshal R.D. Oxland demurred that he could not say it was possible or not. He stressed that his role was simply that of an air adviser to the Canadians, "and that the decision to engage targets in Walcheren rests with C-in-C Bomber Command and the Supreme Allied Commander."[9]

Despite Walsh's and Oxland's reticence, the general mood of the room slowly drifted towards adopting the flooding idea. "The advantages seemed to outweigh all doubts about the efficacy of the plan," noted one RAF commentator. "Flooding would completely disorganize the enemy's communications, immobilize his reinforcements and at the same time put out of action a number of defence works. Furthermore the assault forces would be able to take advantage of the floods by swimming through the breach in armoured vehicles and operating behind the enemy's forward positions." It was decided that Bomber Command and Walsh's engineers should seriously scrutinize the idea.[10]

When Captain Pugsley's turn to address the naval issues surrounding an operation against Walcheren came, he said the most immediate problem was that the North Sea approaches to the Scheldt as well as the estuary itself were heavily mined. The good news, though, was that minesweepers were already working to clear the sea to the west of the island. Within a few days, it should be possible for the monitors and perhaps even *Warspite*—were it committed to the operation—to come within an offshore bombardment range of ten miles. Pugsley's pronouncement garnered the navy a round of applause for its energy because "clearing a way through the German mine fields—the first major hazard in the seaward approaches—was a source of encouragement to all." The navy captain, however, followed the good news with bad. As "the combined operation would probably take place in October," he cautioned, "about four days out of six could be counted as being unsuitable [to amphibious landings] owing to heavy swells."[11]

The conference ended with most questions unresolved and many points still to be studied and referred to higher command for approval or rejection. But Crerar was able to immediately direct 4th Canadian Armoured Division and 2nd Canadian Infantry Division to carry out the first two phases of the campaign that he considered prerequisites to the launch of Operation Infatuate—clearing the Scheldt's south bank and advancing northwards from Antwerp towards Bergen op Zoom and Roosendaal. Both were sure to be difficult tasks, facing strong defensive lines dug in behind a major canal.

ON SEPTEMBER 18, 5th Canadian Infantry Brigade had deployed to the east of Antwerp along the south bank of the Albert Canal. As the 53rd Welsh Division, which had been manning this line, had pulled out before the Canadians arrived, neither Brigadier W.J. "Bill"

Megill nor his battalion commanders were able to glean any useful intelligence from their British counterparts.[12] Glaring across the canal's ninety-foot span from the opposing bank were remnants of the 719th Infantry Division cobbled into company-sized fighting units. These Germans acknowledged the brigade's arrival with desultory sniper, mortar, and artillery fire that did little to dampen the spirit of optimism that pervaded throughout 2nd Canadian Infantry Division's ranks as news travelled that Market Garden had been launched.

When the sound of hundreds of aircraft overhead on September 19 caused everyone at divisional headquarters to spill outside to see great formations of gliders, rumours that this operation was underway were confirmed. A few hours later, BBC Radio announced that airborne troops had landed at Nijmegen and Arnhem.[13] The war might be over sooner than expected.

Megill told his battalion commanders that their immediate task was to "prevent the enemy from blowing [the canal's] locks, as this would result in the inundation of a large tract of land."[14] To prevent German sabotage, 5 CIB would carry out aggressive patrolling along the banks of the canal while absorbing badly needed reinforcements. Even though the brigade was stationed outside Antwerp, it was exposed to many of the surreal aspects of the Streetcar War. The Calgary Highlanders set about cleaning themselves up and carrying out basic training exercises. They had "many 'green' men and if they can be taught the fundamental principles of battle drill it will be a much easier task for us in our next battle. Every available moment will be utilized in this manner," noted the battalion's war diarist. Across the street from battalion headquarters, however, a bar was open that was drawing a lot of uniformed troops. The war diarist soon commented that its proprietor had "given some of the lads a 'ribbing'" on the night of September 18. "The price of beer had been raised three times during the evening and worst of all there appeared to be no particular closing hours." It was promptly blacklisted with nobody allowed to "frequent the spot during the day."[15]

Despite this initially festive attitude, Megill quickly impressed on his battalion commanders that they were not there to relax. The brigade's purpose extended beyond merely keeping the Germans at bay, it was to win a bridgehead over the Albert Canal.

Megill's army career differed sharply from that of most Permanent Force officers. He had enlisted in the signal corps in 1923 as a private when just sixteen years old. After six years' service, Megill left to study engineering at Queen's University. Two years later, he returned to army life with a commission. The year before the war started, he attended imperial staff college at Quetta, India, and garnered praise from its instructors for both tactical and administrative skill. This was followed by a series of staff postings on return to Canada that culminated in appointment to senior staff officer of 1 Canadian Corps under Crerar. The two men failed to hit it off, Crerar thinking Megill professional enough but lacking in imagination and handicapped by not having any field command experience. Perhaps recognizing this weakness, Megill asked for and received a reversion from acting Brigadier to Lieutenant Colonel so that he could take command of the Algonquin Regiment in October 1943. This posting lasted only until February 1944, however, when Megill was promoted to command of 5 CIB as part of a major housecleaning by 2nd Canadian Infantry Division's new commander, Major General Charles Foulkes, who got rid of all three of his brigadiers in favour of younger officers.[16]

Now that his other brigades had reached the Antwerp front, Foulkes was determined to win a crossing over the Albert Canal and then quickly establish a bridgehead across the Antwerp–Turnhout Canal— known by the Flemish as Kanaal Schoten–Turnhout–Dessel—to the north. Breaching both these defensive lines would well position the division to drive through to the South Beveland isthmus. Accordingly, he ordered Megill on September 20 to gain a bridgehead across the canal in the area of Wijnegem, about three miles east of Merksem and the Antwerp dockyards.[17]

Megill held an O Group at his headquarters at 2130 hours to explain his plan to the battalion commanders. In the early morning hours, he said, the Black Watch would send two scouts across the water to check the German strength. This would be followed by a fighting patrol "to find out if the Hun had withdrawn." If "the fighting patrol could successfully cross, then the Calgary Highlanders would also cross. It was specifically laid down that it was NOT to be an assault crossing. Bridging would commence as soon as a bridge-head was established. Three Coys were to be pushed over the canal and make the bridge-head fairly wide. While Coys were pushing and consolidating, patrols would be out front to maintain contact with the enemy." As no vehicles could be used, everything would have to be manhandled across and wounded evacuated "by hand initially across the locks" to points where the first aid men would "nest" them until they could be loaded safely onto Jeep ambulances.[18]

Shortly after midnight, two Black Watch scouts—Privates Wilkinson and Sharpe—slipped across the canal in a small boat. Crouched on the shore behind them, scout platoon leader Lieutenant Joe Nixon "was paying out... line, letting the boat across." But he soon "found that the line would not reach to the other bank so he took off his belt and tied it to the rope. This was still not long enough so he quickly and silently took off his boots and used the laces to extend the line. The boat was now near enough to the far bank for the Scouts to jump out, but in so doing the lace was pulled out of Lt. Nixon's hand and he was unable to pull the boat back. As a result, when the patrol returned to the bank, after penetrating the enemy's lines for about 2,000 yards, they found the boat still on their side and were able to effect the return trip in the swirling mists before dawn, unobserved. They report that the enemy are holding this area in strength."[19]

Despite the patrol's findings, Megill ordered the Black Watch's Lieutenant Colonel Frank Mitchell to send a fighting patrol across one of the locks per the original plan. It was still dark when the fourteen men crawled out onto the lock only to be pinned down immediately by machine-gun fire. Unable to make any forward progress, Mitchell eventually called the men back.

Megill turned up shortly afterwards, and began to criticize the Black Watch's performance to Mitchell's face. The relationship between these two officers had been increasingly combative since the Black Watch had been badly mauled in Normandy during attacks that Mitchell believed Megill should never have ordered. Facing more criticism that he believed warranted, the lieutenant colonel's temper snapped and a bitter argument ensued. Mitchell was unceremoniously relieved of command and sent into purgatory as commander of the 10th Canadian Base Reinforcement Group. His replacement, Lieutenant Colonel Bruce R. Ritchie, had served as the Black Watch second-in-command before being promoted to command of the South Saskatchewan Regiment. Lieutenant Colonel Vern Stott, second-in-command of the Calgary Highlanders, took over command of the South Saskatchewans. Although Megill instigated Mitchell's firing, the decision to give the battalion to Ritchie was made by Foulkes over the brigadier's opposition. Megill felt that the Black Watch needed a strong controlling hand and that either Stott or young Denis Whitaker, who commanded the Royal Hamilton Light Infantry, would be the better choice.[20] But Ritchie had deep roots in the regiment, having served with it before the war and during active service until his promotion to battalion command, and Foulkes felt he would be the best man for the job.[21]

As this command shakeup was underway, the Calgary regiment replaced the Black Watch, with orders to cross the canal via a damaged lock gate to the west of Wijnegem on the night of September 21–22. Lieutenant Colonel Donald MacLauchlan decided to first slip a small fighting patrol drawn from 'C' Company over, to clear a row of houses standing to the north of a road that parallelled the canal. The rest of the company would then reinforce it and expand the bridgehead to the west, while 'D' Company did the same to the east. As these two companies widened the bridgehead, 'A' Company would push its perimeter northwards.[22]

MAJOR FREDERICK "FRANCO" BAKER, 'C' Company's commander, knew precisely who he wanted to lead the fighting patrol—Sergeant Ken Crockett. The twenty-four-year-old Nanton, Alberta native had entered the army in March 1941 and had been an instructor at British Columbia's Camp Vernon Battle Drill School before finally turning down an offered commission in order to go overseas in May 1944 with some of the men he had trained. Joining the regiment in mid-July, Crockett had a reputation as "one of those ideal wartime NCOs... bright, very strong physically and aggressive."[23]

It was about 1930 hours when the Highlanders finished establishing their presence in front of the canal, already too dark for Crockett to look over the canal and opposite shore. But Baker had been well briefed and could tell the sergeant that the southern lock gate had a two-foot-wide catwalk with a handrail running along its top. In the middle of the canal between the two gates was a small, bare island. The northern gate's catwalk was intact for just half its length. For the last seven feet, only a six-inch water pipe provided footing, but a portion of the handrail remained to help the men keep their balance.

Besides the cluster of houses, the ground north of the canal consisted of fields broken by patches of brush and small stands of trees. Getting onto the gates undetected would be difficult because open fields bordered the south bank of the canal.

Although suffering from dysentery, Crockett never considered ducking the assignment. His entire platoon wanted to go, but he decided to take only nine men. Crockett expected a fight, so he took two Bren gunners and armed the other seven with Sten guns. One man also carried a PIAT anti-tank gun, another a two-inch mortar, and a third the platoon's 22-pound No. 38 wireless. Everyone had two to three bandoliers of ammunition slung over their shoulders and every pouch on their web belts crammed with magazines. After exchanging their boots—which had steel hobnails and toe and heel plates—for sneakers, Crockett gathered the men around him. "If the flare goes up," he said, "no matter where we are at, you get as low as you can and don't move. Nobody fires until I tell you." Everything depended on silence, and even then Crockett knew it was likely they would "get caught on the lock gates." At 0130 hours, Crockett led his men into the inky darkness. It was drizzling, the ground underfoot slick with mud.[24]

Reaching the canal undetected, Crockett crept across the southern gate to the island and peered into the blackness beyond. Whether there were Germans there or not, he couldn't tell. Returning to his men, the sergeant led them forward, with Corporal R.A. Harold directly behind him. Once on the island, Crockett whispered for the others to stay put while he checked the feasibility of crossing the north gate. The pipe was greasy from the rain and the promised handrail nothing more than a wire strand. Slinging his Sten across his back, Crockett slid one hand along the wire as he carefully placed one foot in front of the other on the slippery pipe. At the other end, a barbed-wire barrier blocked the way off the gate, but the Germans had failed to anchor it.

Again, Crockett returned to his men and led them out onto the pipe. Reaching its end, Crockett and Harold carefully lifted the wire barrier aside. Suddenly, a sentry yelled a challenge and a machine gun ripped off a burst. Most of the patrol was still on the pipe, and one of the men was hit. Dragging the wounded man, the others quickly gained the northern bank, where Crockett and Harold shouted at them to take cover in the tall grass. By now, three machine guns were throwing out searching fire. Yelling, "Give them shit!" Crockett killed the sentry with a well-aimed burst and then charged the nearest machine gun. Firing his Sten from the hip, he eliminated the gun crew.

Private I.P. MacDonald, who was carrying the PIAT, joined Crockett at the overrun gun position, and the two men crawled to where they could fire the anti-tank weapon at a second machine gun set up inside one of the houses facing the canal. MacDonald fired two rounds, destroying the German gun with the second. The third machine gun fell to fire from the two-inch mortar that Crockett and another man put into action.[25]

While Crockett led the fight, Harold tended the wounded. Crawling to the wounded man who had been left sprawled on the pavement beside the canal, he dragged him to cover despite machine-gun slugs chipping at the concrete all around. By the time Harold patched the man up, three more wounded Highlanders had fallen back on his position. He and Private Myers guided the men back to the lock gate and across the pipe before leaving them to make the rest of the way on their own.

With the remaining six men putting out a furious rate of fire to keep the rapidly gathering number of Germans at bay, ammunition was beginning to run low. Crockett rushed to the man with the wireless and told him to call for reinforcements, only to hear that the aerial had been lost and the set was useless. The sergeant roughly shook the man, shouting that their lives depended on finding the aerial. Together, the two men crawled on hands and knees through the grass under heavy fire until the aerial was retrieved. Minutes later, at 0420 hours, the rest of 'C' Company poured over the lock gates in single file and the German resistance slackened.[26] Brigadier Megill recommended Crockett for the Victoria Cross for his bravery, but he received a Distinguished Conduct Medal instead, because someone up the command chain deemed the engagement insufficiently important to "warrant such a decoration."[27]

By 0600 hours, three rifle companies were across the canal. Low black clouds, creating a twilight effect, hung over the battlefield and the men moved in and out of thick patches of ground fog that made it difficult to see either friend or foe. In this confused landscape, a bitter battle raged through the morning. The Highlanders knew that to win the day they must expand the bridgehead sufficiently to render it safe for the engineers to build a bridge next to the lock, and the Germans knew that a bridge would render their line along the Albert Canal untenable. Shell and mortar fire pounded the small Canadian toehold, frustrating attempts by the engineers to begin work. Slowly 'C' Company pushed westward, 'A' Company northward, and 'D' Company eastward.

On the eastern flank, Major Bruce MacKenzie put two platoons forward into a line of buildings that stood about two hundred yards from the lock gates. Once this position was secured, he ordered the platoons to move out across a field to clear some woods beyond. As the men moved into the open, a German machine gun in the woods ripped into their ranks. Screams cut the air. Some men were killed outright, many more wounded. Rather than continue head on into the escalating and increasingly deadly fire, the platoons began shrinking back towards the locks. MacKenzie frantically tried to rally them to renew the charge while throwing out a steady rate of fire with his Sten gun, but the situation became hopeless and a withdrawal was ordered.

As the men went back, Corporal William Fedun—a twenty-three-year-old from Springside, Saskatchewan—grabbed a Bren gun and covered their withdrawal until he was shot down. MacKenzie hoisted a badly wounded sergeant and carried him back to the locks. He then rallied 'D' Company and led them in a renewed drive that quickly evicted some German soldiers who had reoccupied the buildings. By 1215, the situation in the bridgehead seemed desperate, but the Highlanders were determined to prevail. A wireless message to brigade reported 'D' Company "practically wiped out on right flank... [heavy] hand to hand fighting. Cal[gary] High[landers] confident of holding."[28] The war diarist at 5 CIB headquarters, closely following the fight from the incoming wireless reports, noted "this was the first time our troops had met the enemy using bayonets."[29]

All might have been lost had the Highlanders not managed to set up a ferry operation using makeshift rafts, which shuttled badly needed ammunition across the canal to the rifle companies and brought their wounded back. This steady resupply, combined with some close-in mortar and artillery fire accurately directed by Captain Mark Tennant on positions inside a cement factory, prevented the Germans mounting a concerted counterattack.

Then, at 1330 hours, as the sun burned through the clouds for the first time and the fog abruptly lifted, the German mortar and shellfire ceased. Fearful that the respite might be short-lived, the engineers hurriedly unloaded the equipment needed to build the bridge. Work began at 1645 and still the German guns were silent. By 1900, the canal was spanned, and at 2115 hours, le Régiment de Maisonneuve moved its first company across. Three hours later, the entire regiment was over and moving north into the night to expand the bridgehead.

The bridgehead operation cost the Highlanders fewer casualties than initially feared in the confusion of the day, but the final tally was bad enough—fifteen dead and thirty-four wounded.[30] They could take heart, though, in the fact that the action proved decisive. When the Germans realized at about noon that the bridgehead would hold, a general withdrawal to the north bank of the Antwerp–Turnhout Canal had been ordered. No estimate of German casualties was compiled, but they had thrown two and a half companies and a platoon of engineers all from 1st Battalion, 743rd Grenadier Regiment into the fight, and among the many dead suffered was the regimental commander, who had taken personal command.[31]

WHILE THE CALGARY HIGHLANDERS had been winning the bridgehead over the Albert Canal, 4th Canadian Armoured Division's Algonquin Regiment had again gone into action to force its way into the Breskens Pocket. This time it attempted to break in via the gap at the Isabellapolder along the southern tip of Braakman Inlet. The objective was Maagd-van-Gent, a small village about two miles west of the inlet. 'D' Company kicked off the drive with No. 16 Platoon forward, but it was quickly pinned down by heavy fire the moment the men entered the polder. The company's other platoons made it through to the dyke overlooking the polder area, but were unable to go farther. When a 'C' Company platoon tried to reach the stranded platoon, it was cut to pieces, only nine men managing to crawl back after night fell.

September 23 dawned with 'D' Company still trying to relieve the lost platoon, which had been out of contact since it was first cut off. Finally, "due to lack of activity and fire on the enemy side" from where the platoon had been forced to ground, it was written off as overrun and taken prisoner. Ten men were reported dead, the lost platoon's strength of twenty noted as missing, and another thirteen men wounded for nothing gained. It was evident to the regiment that "this place was going to be a grim battleground." A thought made even grimmer by the news that the Algonquins were to hold their positions, but that no immediate renewal of the attack was planned.[32] Instead, knowing 4 CAD was not going to be on this front much longer, Major General Harry Foster instructed his brigadiers to avoid unnecessary casualties. 10 CIB Brigadier Jim Jefferson directed the Algonquins at the end of the day that "in view of the heavy opposition in the gap their task would now be to contain the enemy and harass him with fire and by active patrolling but NO major effort would be made to dislodge him."[33]

This was the beginning of "a nightmare period for the Algonquin Regiment," noted its historian. "There was not even to be the illusion of victory or success—but simply the dismal succession of patrol after patrol."[34]

[6]

Poor Devils

WHETHER WINNING OR losing localized fights with the Canadians, September 23 proved a benchmark day for the Germans operating around the Scheldt estuary, for this was the day Fifteenth Army completed its escape through Breskens to Walcheren Island and then to the mainland. In a coded message promptly decrypted by Ultra, OB West Generalfeldmarschall Gerd von Rundstedt "expressed his thanks to the naval headquarters and units who had played a role in moving 82,000 men, 530 guns, 4,600 vehicles, over 4,000 horses and much valuable material across the West Scheldt." The actual figures were even better than von Rundstedt believed. Naval Special Staff Knuth, the ad hoc ferry command that had carried out the evacuation, reported between September 4 and 23 moving through the ports of Breskens and Terneuzen 86,100 men, 616 guns, 6,200 horses, 6,200 vehicles, and 6,500 bicycles.[1]

About 10,000 men, comprising Generalmajor Knut Eberding's 64th Infantry Division, remained in the Breskens Pocket with orders to hold out as long as possible. This was the only division deemed by Fifteenth Army commander General der Infanterie Gustav von Zangen as "still maintaining its full fighting power, both as to its strength and equipment." Above all, he noted, Eberding "controlled [it] in a very efficient way...The fighting quality of this division was increased considerably by the fact that formations of the other divisions, which were taken across the river, left behind a considerable quantity of war material of all kind, including artillery guns, anti-tank artillery guns, ammunition and also food supplies... Equipped in such a way, the division—compared with other formations, which had been engaged south of the Scheldt—represented a unit of special fighting power for its present task of forming an efficient line of barricade."[2]

On the other shore of the West Scheldt, the 70th Infantry Division under Generalleutnant Wilhelm Daser was tasked with defending Walcheren Island and the South Beveland peninsula. This area was designated Northern Scheldt Fortress; Eberding's Breskens Pocket was Southern Scheldt Fortress. Given that it was manned mostly by men with "gastric complaints," the 70th was rated as only capable of "defensive actions." During the fighting around Ghent, the division had "suffered heavy losses both by actions and by diseases, up to almost one third of its entire strength." It had also been stripped of one regiment and an artillery battalion to reinforce the defence of the canal line north of Antwerp and then stripped of two pioneer companies sent to the 64th Infantry Division. "Nevertheless," von Zangen wrote, "its 'fighting quality' had to be rated very high, as now it was again committed in a territory well known to and improved by its men (who had been stationed here prior to being sent to fight at Ghent)... Besides, the control of the division was in the hands of a quiet, reliable commander, who succeeded in welding together all the different branches of armed forces, specially on the island Walcheren, for the purpose of effective defence."[3]

Neither division was expected to conduct offensive actions. Their mission was to prevent Antwerp's use by the Allies for as long as possible. So long as these divisions held out, von Zangen impressed upon their commanders, they would play a vital role in "the defense of the German frontier" by buying time to organize, because the Allies would continue to face crippling supply shortages.[4]

To the north and east of Antwerp, where the Germans had carried out a hasty withdrawal to behind the Antwerp–Turnhout Canal, General der Infanterie Otto Sponheimer's LXVII Corps of the Fifteenth Army held the line. Responsibility for this area had passed to Sponheimer from Generaloberst Kurt Student's hastily cobbled-together First Parachute Army on September 14.[5] Sponheimer had three divisions—the 346th Infantry bolstered by the 70th Infantry's 1018th Grenadier Regiment, the 711th Infantry, and the 719th Infantry. An armoured and antitank gun component was added by the 280th Assault Gun Brigade and elements of the 559th GHQ Heavy Anti-tank Battalion.[6]

Both the 346th and 711th divisions were "in extremely bad shape, having just been patched up by the addition of supply troops in the area. They numbered 6,000 to 8,000 each."[7] On September 23–24, the 719th Infantry Division was transferred from LXXXVIII Corps to Sponheimer just after its withdrawal to the Antwerp–Turnhout Canal. Sponheimer expected that a major Canadian offensive out of Antwerp would at any moment drive him out of the defensive line centred on Merksem that ringed in the city's northern docks. With his weak divisions badly overextended, Sponheimer had little confidence in his ability to hold. His 711th was dug into a line that ran from the main road onto the Beveland isthmus down to the village of Lilla on the Scheldt River, facing the 1st Polish Armoured Division on the opposite shore. The 346th held the ground between Lilla and Merksem. Left of the 346th, the 719th had been strung along the Albert Canal before its withdrawal. When the 719th pulled back, the 346th was forced to also retire on its eastern flank to positions behind the canal extending all the way to Sint-Lenaarts (which the Canadians called St. Leonard), while retaining responsibility for the line from Lilla to Merksem—a total distance of about fifteen miles. It was the need to defend such an extended line that resulted in 70th division's 1018th Grenadier Regiment being shifted to support the 346th by taking over the Lilla–Merksem section.[8]

Generalleutnant Erich Diestel, who commanded the 346th, considered his division barely fit for duty, let alone such an important tasking. After escaping to Walcheren Island, it had marched off the Beveland peninsula and assembled about four miles northeast of Antwerp for what was to have been a long overdue rest and rebuilding period. The division was barely five thousand strong, and over the next four to five days was only brought up to a strength of eight thousand by infusions from two divisions that had been shattered in the flight out of France—the 331st and 344th infantry divisions. In the same area, the 711th had also been reforming when orders came on September 18 for both to go back into the fighting lines alongside the 719th.[9]

Although the divisions charged with denying Allied use of Antwerp's port were weak in numbers and quality, the combination of defensible terrain and limited numbers that First Canadian Army could put into the field made them a formidable opponent. Repeatedly, German divisions had shown themselves capable of rapidly rising from the ashes to offer another stubborn fight. In Normandy, they had proven masters of the defensive battle, and it was clear they would bring this skill to the forthcoming struggle.

JUST HOW POTENT an opponent the Germans remained was rammed home to the battalions of 6th Canadian Infantry Brigade on September 24 during an attempt to force a crossing of the Antwerp–Turnhout Canal in front of Lochtenberg, about seven miles northeast of Antwerp. All the bridges here had been demolished, and reconnaissance patrols reported the canal line heavily defended. Intelligence reports stated that the Germans were set on "retaining as long as possible the landward approaches to Beveland," and the canal provided the best remaining defensive position. Consequently, "it was apparent that a well-prepared assault would be necessary."

The plan called for the Calgary Highlanders, immediately southwest of 6 CIB, to put in a feint attack just before dawn.[10] Once the feint drew off some of the defenders facing its portion of the line, Les Fusiliers Mont-Royal would cross in assault boats to the right of a blown bridge in front of Lochtenberg, while the South Saskatchewan Regiment did the same on its left. Each battalion would be supplied with six folding assault boats that could carry eighteen men each. Plentiful fire support would be provided by the 5th and 6th Canadian Field Regiments and two platoons of heavy mortars. Once the bridgehead was established, the engineers would throw a bridge over. A squadron of 8th Canadian Reconnaissance Regiment (14th

Canadian Hussars) would then precede the Queen's Own Cameron Highlanders of Canada in a two-and-a-half-mile drive out of the bridgehead to Kamp van Brasschaat—a former Belgian military base where the Germans were believed to have a headquarters. The crossing was set for 0700 hours.[11]

It was a dirty morning, heavily overcast with sporadic showers and dense fog at ground level. Major Armand Brochu's 'C' Company led Les Fusiliers Mont-Royal towards the canal at 0500, followed by Major Fernand Beaudoin's 'B' Company. Once both companies were over, Major Georges White's 'A' Company would cross and consolidate the immediate bridgehead, while the first two companies pushed towards Lochtenberg. 'D' Company, the support platoons, battalion headquarters, and vehicles would remain on the south bank until the engineers put a bridge over.

The French-Canadian troops advanced quietly through a wood that masked their approach to the canal from the Germans on the other side. Right on schedule, Brochu's men slid the boats down into the canal, clambered aboard, and paddled hard for the opposite shore. They had feared going straight into a hornet's nest of enemy fire, but neither a shout of alarm nor a gunshot rang out. Within minutes, 'C' Company was out of the boats and scrambling up the opposite bank to take up firing positions, while the two engineers manning each boat paddled back to fetch the next lift.[12]

To the west, it was an altogether different story for the South Saskatchewan Regiment. At 0615, the pioneer platoon commander returned from the wood where they were to concentrate for the launch and reported the place crawling with Germans. As no opposing forces were supposed to be south of the canal, the South Saskatchewans' attack plan was completely disrupted. Rather than enter into a firefight to win the canal launching point, Lieutenant Colonel Vern Stott hurriedly shifted the battalion a short distance westward, hoping an unmolested crossing could be made there.[13] 'A' Company, with Lieutenant Cecil Law's No. 9 Platoon leading, moved out along what his 1/25,000 map showed as a narrow track. When the track turned out to be a small water-filled canal, Law's men were forced to advance on top of a low dyke that formed the canal's left bank.[14]

Having been posted to the regiment on September 15, Law was a newcomer. But that was true for most everyone that morning. The mauling the South Saskatchewans had suffered in the Forêt de la Londe at the end of August had depleted the ranks almost completely of men who had gone ashore in Normandy. Only six officers who landed in Normandy had remained. To bring the regiment back to strength, it had received about five hundred reinforcements during the short rest in Dieppe. All twenty-four lieutenants had joined since the forest battle.[15]

Law had deep military roots. His father had served in the Seaforth Highlanders of Canada in the Great War and was again overseas with that regiment. At thirteen, Law had jiggled his age in order to join the Vancouver regiment in 1936. In 1940, upon graduating from Duke of Connaught High School in New Westminster—where he had commanded the cadets—Law enlisted in Victoria's Canadian Scottish Regiment because the Seaforths were already overseas. After being shipped to Britain as a reinforcement in 1942, Law's father intervened to bring him back into the Seaforth fold. Law was shortly sent to Canada for officer training and commissioned in May 1943. Just before D-Day, he again returned to Britain, and in September was assigned to the South Saskatchewans in France.[16]

If the officers were inexperienced, the men they commanded were generally even more so. Most had been dredged up from rear-area duties, and whatever basic training they had received was long forgotten. About 90 per cent of Law's platoon was completely green. Only his platoon sergeant and five other men were survivors from Normandy. "These poor lads had no idea of infantry," he later commented. "They couldn't properly load a Bren magazine, knew nothing whatsoever about grenades... some of them had thrown exactly one No. 36 grenade without ever learning how to clean, arm, or worse, disarm, or really make them ready for throwing. The PIAT was a complete mystery. Only a couple had ever seen a two-inch mortar. They gave me heart failure ten times a day, but I couldn't really blame them. Yet I had almost no chance to train them at all, before going in."[17]

The surrounding sugar beet fields were sectioned by ditches that either cut across the canal with only a narrow lock providing a crossing point or were diverted away by an equally narrow dyke. On the canal bank opposite, the ditches proved impassable for No. 7 Platoon, preventing it from keeping step with Law's platoon. Still well short of the Antwerp–Turnhout Canal, No. 9 Platoon found itself alone when No. 7 Platoon was forced to turn back.

Minutes later, machine-gun and rifle fire started cracking past Law and he shouted for his platoon to hit the dirt. The intervening locks they could cross on their stomachs, but the intersecting dykes were slightly higher than the surrounding terrain, so they had to dash madly over them and then flop down prone on the other side. After one such sprint, Law looked back to see how his men were doing and saw that the soldier behind was on his hands and knees, "head down... dragging his rifle alongside him on the ground." Its barrel was pointed directly at Law. The lieutenant asked if the man had ever been taught how to crawl correctly. No, he replied. Under sporadic fire, Law demonstrated "how to leopard-crawl with head up, and then the thought struck me that he might have limited knowledge of his rifle too. 'Is your safety on?' I asked. 'No Sir,' he answered proudly, while I had a short heart failure. 'Well put it on until you're ready to fire,' I said rather too fiercely. He looked hurt. 'You might catch the trigger on a branch and shoot me,' I explained. 'Now keep your head up when you crawl so you can see what you're getting into.' Alas, only a short distance further on, he was crawling with his head held very high indeed and took a bullet right through the head. I really felt sick for that poor lad."[18]

Eventually, Law could see the main canal. On the opposite bank was a cluster of houses, and it was from these that the majority of the German fire was coming. "Section leaders," Law shouted, "get some fire on those houses so we can get up to the bank for a look." To his dismay, Law realized his section leaders had no idea how to organize their men. Like some sergeant on a training shoot, Law started crawling from one man in a section to another to personally indicate where each should direct his fire and at what rate. Soon this section was firing, but it was the only one doing so, and the Germans responded with furious MG 42 bursts. Two of the men were ripped by slugs.

Law was desperate, realizing that his inexperienced platoon was going to have to break off the action and escape to the cover of a nearby dyke. He ordered the two-inch mortar team to fire a couple of high-explosive rounds on the houses, followed by three or four smoke bombs to cover the withdrawal. The first round left the tube and promptly exploded about eight feet overhead, badly wounding the two men manning it and the platoon PIAT man. With Law and his sergeant throwing smoke grenades for cover, the platoon finally extracted itself. It was 0900 and the South Saskatchewans were far behind schedule.[19]

As 'A' Company came back, Stott headed off to brigade headquarters to tee up a new plan with 6 CIB commander Brigadier J.G. "Guy" Gauvreau. Until his promotion on August 30, Gauvreau had commanded the Fusiliers and it was at that battalion's headquarters that Stott finally found him. Although the Fusiliers had an unopposed crossing, the leading 'A' Company had been blocked by heavy machine-gun fire after gaining a crossroads about one hundred yards south of Lochtenberg village. The Fusiliers were caught in the open, while the Germans were dug into thick woods immediately north of the road parallelling the canal and several houses grouped around the crossroads. Planning to personally direct the developing fight, Major Joseph-Mignault-Paul Sauvé had taken his tactical command section across the canal.[20] Gauvreau had set up at battalion headquarters to support Sauvé, for although the thirty-seven-year-old was a veteran of Normandy and more recent battles, this was his first as battalion commander.

After Stott tersely briefed Gauvreau, the brigadier ordered the battalion to cross at the original site. The two artillery regiments would smother both the woods held by the Germans and the opposite bank of the canal with high explosives. They would also fire extensive smoke to conceal the men going over in boats. The new assault would kick off at 1300 hours. As the South Saskatchewans manhandled the boats to the initial crossing point, the gunners of the 5th and 6th Field Regiments alternated between shelling the woods, the north bank of the canal, and blasting the woods and houses where the Germans were holding up the Fusiliers. The fire on the Germans south of the canal proved effective, for when the South Saskatchewans reached the concentration point they found the woods abandoned.

'A' Company, dragging the boats forward, headed towards the canal on schedule. Five minutes later, the battalion's three-inch mortars started dropping smoke rounds to cover the move. At 1310, the artillery weighed in with fire that "caused terrific damage to buildings in enemy territory and effectively silenced the majority of the enemy weapons."[21] Twenty minutes after the artillery opened fire, Lieutenant Cecil Law and his No. 9 Platoon came out of the woods and headed to the canal with three assault boats.

Things started well enough, with Law's platoon quickly making the crossing under the smoke cover. The company's other two platoons soon joined it and established a solid base on the bank. At 1330, company commander Major Ken Williams relayed the signal "Whippet" to battalion, signifying that 'A' Company was tight on the opposite shore. Major Harry Williams started feeding 'B' Company over. By 1425, his men were across.[22]

Law ran over to Major Harry Williams and explained that he was taking his platoon east along the right side of the road, and 'B' Company should move up the left side in accordance with the battalion plan.[23] 'D' Company would then cross over and defend the landing site, while the two lead companies pushed to a crossroads that led to their final objective of Lochtenberg about a half-mile to the east.[24] Unable to locate his own company commander, Law set out with No. 9 Platoon. He expected the rest of 'A' Company would come up behind as soon as 'D' Company was firm on the canal bank.[25]

Dogging close behind 'B' Company's Williams was eighteen-year-old Private Charles "Chic" Goodman carrying the wireless set. Relatively speaking, despite his youth, Goodman was a South Saskatchewan veteran—having gone up from 'B' Echelon reinforcement status to the battalion's fighting units after Bourgébus Ridge on July 20. He had seen a lot of combat since. The St. John, New Brunswick native had joined the cadet corps in grade six. With his mother's permission, Goodman had lied about his age to enlist in the regular army when he was only sixteen. The older soldiers had quickly nicknamed the scrawny kid Chic, short for chicken, and referring to his skinny arms and legs. But Goodman had thrown himself into soldiering, enjoying the challenges. He was soon rated a crack shot. Having an uncle who had been a signaller in the Great War and had taught him Morse code and other signalling methods, Goodman qualified for the Royal Canadian Signals Corps. After Bourgébus, he had served as a platoon rifleman until the reorganization at Dieppe resulted in his being made a company signaller.

Ahead of Goodman and the rest of Williams's company headquarters section, Lieutenant Ernest Arlond Toole's platoon was on point. The twenty-nine-year-old officer, who also hailed from St. John, had only joined the battalion on September 12 and had made Goodman's acquaintance the night before. Toole had left their hometown just weeks earlier and the two had agreed to catch up on local news after the current action.

'B' Company was advancing rapidly up a ditch bordering the road—too quickly so far as Williams and Goodman were concerned. They were darting past houses that nobody from Toole's platoon had bothered clearing. Any number of Germans could be inside. Turning to Goodman, Williams said he was going to catch up to the lieutenant and rein him in. "Do you want me to come?" Goodman asked. "No, you stay here with the company section." Taking his runner, Williams sprinted off towards the front of the advancing column. Moments later, the forward platoon was cut to ribbons in a crossfire coming from positions to its front and left flank. Toole was among the men killed in seconds.[26] Suddenly, a small tank rolled out from behind one of the buildings about a hundred yards ahead, and its machine gun ripped off a long burst that killed Williams.

Both 'B' Company and 'A' Company's No. 9 Platoon came under intense fire from their front and were driven to ground inside the ditches. The tank growled back and forth, snapping off rounds from its small main gun and bursts from the machine gun. Unlike most infantrymen, who tended to identify any tank as the mastodon Tiger with its powerful 88-millimetre, Law realized this one was much smaller, lightly skinned, mounting only a 37-millimetre cannon. That meant a well-placed PIAT round could knock it out. Trouble was that Law's PIAT gunner had been wounded and his assistant confessed he had no idea how to fire the weapon.[27]

Across the road, Goodman heard someone from 'A' Company shouting about whether anyone knew how to fire a PIAT. Goodman had paid attention during his PIAT training and figured he was as skilled as anyone. Dashing across the road, he crawled up the ditch to Law, loaded one of the two-and-a-half-pound hollow-charge explosive bombs, and shouldered the thirty-two-pound launcher. The first round was a clean miss.[28] Goodman fired another round and scored a hit that Law thought knocked one of the tank's track guards off, causing it to skew into a tree.[29] Reaching into the bomb carrier for the third and final round, Goodman pulled out a stash of bully beef and cheese instead. "Guess someone figured there was a better chance of being hungry than encountering a tank," Goodman ruefully muttered.[30] Law sent the assistant gunner running back to 'A' Company to fetch more ammunition, while Goodman dodged back across the road to rejoin his unit.[31]

Knowing that 'B' Company was badly exposed to the fire coming from the houses and that it was only a matter of minutes before his platoon was cut to pieces, Law decided the only thing to do was to cross the road and take the fight to the Germans inside the houses. Having earlier lost his mortar to the prematurely exploding round, Law and his sergeant covered the move with smoke grenades. None of his green troops were "keen to brave the tracers, which seemed like a solid wall of fire." But when he yelled, "Go," everyone "pelted across the road and into the alleyway between the houses." Amazingly, nobody was hit.

When they tried getting into the backyards to take the houses from the rear, Law discovered that the thin cement walls bordering the grounds had been topped with broken glass meant to deter thieves, but proving a hellish impediment to the movement of troops. Finally managing to get into the backyards, the platoon discovered that the Germans had fled. A farmhouse to the north, however, posed a new threat that Law decided had to be secured. The platoon rushed across open ground and gained the house unscathed. But when a section moved to check a root cellar about twenty yards north of the building, it was caught by machine-gun fire. One man died and another two were wounded.

Law began fortifying the house by setting up two of his Bren guns at the corners facing north, and the third on the farmhouse's top floor. In the cellar, the Canadians found the farmer, his wife, and three children hiding. Joining the Bren gunner upstairs, Law looked out a window as a half-track drove out into the field about thirty yards away. It was headed north, the crew sitting down rather than manning the 15-millimetre machine gun and its driver clearly exposed to their fire. Realizing that the Germans could easily be killed before they could retaliate, Law yelled at the men to open fire. "But they were just too scared to do so." Watching the half-track trundle off to the safety of nearby woods, Law "practically sobbed." He later reflected that the men might have been right, for the farmhouse could have easily been ripped apart by the powerful machine gun, capable of putting out armour-piercing rounds at a velocity of 2,715 feet per second, which would have cut through the walls like a knife through hot butter.

By now, the platoon leader was feeling out on a limb. The rest of the company should have caught up, but there was no sign of it. Lacking a radio, he sent a runner to find the company headquarters and report his location. It was beginning to get dark, and he feared that if the Germans in the woods realized how weak the farmhouse position was they would counterattack. The farmwife emerged from the cellar to offer Law and his men bowls of potato soup. "We hated to take their food, but we were literally weak from hunger and the stress of the day." Law had just finished gulping down his serving when the runner came back with instructions for them to withdraw across the canal. The Fusiliers had been thrown back, and brigade had ordered the South Saskatchewans to pull back as well.[32]

A FEW HUNDRED yards to the east of the South Saskatchewans, Les Fusiliers Mont-Royal had stepped into a hornet's nest at the crossroads in front of Lochtenberg. By 1430, fire was hitting the battalion from the front, the right, and the rear. They could hear German reinforcements unloading from trucks on their right where a wood obscured their view. From the same direction, the creaking tracks of many tanks could be heard.

Sauvé dashed from one company to another, pulling the men tightly together to prevent their lines from being infiltrated. Moving between 'B' and 'C' Companies, he spotted a cluster of men in the nearby forest. "Don't bunch up," he yelled at them. One of the men fired his rifle at the officer. "Take it easy. Pipe down. It's your c.o.," Sauvé shouted. This time, the response was a flurry of machine-gun and rifle fire. "They're Jerries, Sir," cried the forward observation officer (FOO) from the 6th Field Regiment, supporting the Fusiliers, and the two men hurried to cover.[33]

At 1700 hours, the perimeter was hit by about two hundred German infantry supported by a dozen captured French Renault light tanks. Lacking any anti-tank weapons but a couple of PIATs, there was nothing the French-Canadian troops could do. With their lines being infiltrated all over, Sauvé ordered a fighting withdrawal to the canal.[34] The FOO called in one "Mike" target after another, trying to break up the counterattack by having 6th Field Regiment fire all two dozen 24-pounders at once, but to no avail. Germans and Canadians became badly intermingled, men exchanging fire at close range. Finding himself separated, and almost encircled by Germans, the FOO only escaped by ditching his No. 19 wireless set and swimming the canal.[35] About 150 men were either missing or killed.[36] An operation that had started so promisingly for the Fusiliers had ended in disaster.

Meanwhile, the South Saskatchewan Regiment still clung to its precarious position. Lieutenant R. Kitching had taken over 'B' Company and was trying to direct artillery fire against the Germans. But neither he, nor the company sergeant major, nor Goodman and the other signaller knew how to properly direct artillery fire—a sign of their inexperience. They were reduced to giving their map position and leaving it to the gunnery officers on the other end of the wireless to figure out where to drop the shells. As a result, a good many rounds were landing closer to the company than to the German positions. But the fire did seem to keep the enemy at bay.[37]

Soon after the Fusiliers retreated to the south bank of the canal, Major General Foulkes arrived at 6 CIB headquarters to discuss the situation with Brigadier Gauvreau. The two men "decided to withdraw the S. Sask. R. to the south side of the canal as it was impossible to get [antitank guns] across before first [light]."[38] At 1910, the order came for an immediate withdrawal. Stott decided to wait an hour for darkness, so that the men might slip back without being detected by the Germans. The withdrawal proved the mirror opposite of the crossing attempt, as everything proceeded like clockwork.

Law's isolated platoon came last. Before pulling out from the farmhouse, the lieutenant sent Private Henry Stadelmier to see if any of the section at the root cellar were still alive. Stadelmier brought back one wounded man and then went back to recover the identity disks of the dead soldiers. When the private failed to return, Law shouted that the platoon had to leave and he was to catch up. A muffled reply from that direction led the lieutenant to think that Stadelmier had understood and would soon be along. On the way to the canal, the platoon passed "numerous 'B' Coy dead at the crossroads." Stadelmier still had not caught up when Law crossed the canal. He was posted as missing.[39]* Casualties for the day totalled four officers and thirty-five other ranks. Law filled out a casualty report for his platoon, wrote letters to the relatives of those who had died or were missing, and, after midnight, "crawled into my slit trench just as it began to rain."[40] Considering that most of his men "barely knew which end of the rifle to point and nothing of the other weapons," he thought, sending those "poor devils" into battle "was a crime. I wept over some of those poor kids."[41]

THE CANADIAN ATTEMPT to cross the Antwerp–Turnhout Canal at Lochtenberg had greatly alarmed LXVII's General der Infanterie Otto Sponheimer. Had the attack succeeded, the Canadians would have been positioned to drive a wedge between his corps and the rightmost division of First Parachute Army. Responding to the gravity of this threat, Generalleutnant Erich Diestel had ordered an immediate full-out counterattack by his 346th Infantry Division. If the Cana-

---

* On October 2, Private Stadelmier's corpse was found near the canal. It appeared that he had been hanged. Only then did Law pause to think that Stadelmier "could not only speak German, but might have been a Jew, poor man! How stupid I was not to think of it. But then, we had not yet realized how vulnerable Jews were." (Law correspondence with author, 24 July 2006)

dians managed to put a bridge in place, Diestel knew the canal line would be rendered indefensible. A bridgehead anywhere along the canal's length that allowed the movement of tanks and artillery to the north side would make a German retreat inevitable.

Generalfeldmarschall Walter Model at Army Group B preferred to retreat at his discretion rather than having the moment imposed by the Allies. In a detailed estimate of the situation written in the late afternoon of September 24, Model suggested "that in order to obtain reserves and save strength," Fifteenth Army withdraw behind the Waal River. LXVII Corps would remain south of the river, but pull back to a line running from Bergen op Zoom through Roosendaal to Moerdijk. Model passed his assessment up to OB West Generalfeldmarschall Gerd von Rundstedt and to OKW in Berlin. Still locked in the final phases of capping the Market Garden Operation at Arnhem, von Rundstedt readily concurred with Model's proposal. He "believed the proposed sacrifice [of ground] was justified by the necessity of gaining reserves for the expected large-scale operations between Arnhem and Aachen."

All that Model needed was agreement from Berlin, but within a few hours of sending the signal he received a call from OKW. The Führer had personally "rejected the proposals." At 0140 hours, the morning of September 25, a terse Führer directive arrived that underscored the earlier refusal. "Few things were more abhorrent to the Führer than suggestions of withdrawal. His reaction was immediate and precise," noted a later report. He ordered "Fifteenth Army and First Parachute Army to stand fast in their present lines."[42]

But even as Hitler hobbled LXVII Corps to the canal, First Canadian Army was beginning to crack this defensive line. I British Corps had started its long move from the area of Le Havre on September 20 to form the army's extreme right flank and relieve XII British Corps of responsibility for this part of the Antwerp–Turnhout Canal. To strengthen and provide this corps with armoured teeth, Lieutenant General Harry Crerar attached 1st Polish Armoured Division to it. Still regrouping, taking in reinforcements, and refitting their tanks after the fighting between Ghent and Terneuzen, the Poles would not join the British divisions until September 27.[43]

1 British Corps was not to wait on the Poles. The same day 6 CIB was repulsed in front of Lochtenberg, the 49th (West Riding) Division's 146th Infantry Brigade prepared to attempt a crossing about six miles west of Turnhout near the town of Rijkevorsel. Divisional reconnaissance had determined that the Germans had withdrawn from the ancient medieval city to spare it being damaged, but the immediate surroundings were so heavily mined that any thought of crossing the canal there was abandoned. The British would resort to an assault by boat, with the 4th Lincolns carrying out the attack.

This section of canal was defended by 719th Infantry Division, which had been "thoroughly battered from the previous battles and, besides, was no longer made up entirely of units belonging organically to it after it had to give up one of its two infantry regiments as corps reserve for LXXXVIII Corps." Dredged up to replace this regiment was a unit thrown together from non-German volunteers, prisoners of war from East European countries, "railway security detachments, Labor Service units, and Luftwaffe training units, which was under the command of a regimental staff of an air-force pre-flight training regiment." The division was still finding its footing behind the canal, having only finished withdrawing the last of its units back from the unsuccessful attempt to hold the Albert Canal line.[44]

The Lincolns had no idea that the Germans across the canal were still disorganized and of relatively poor quality. Before them, the ground leading to a blown canal bridge stretched flat and open. A large cement plant across the road parallelling the canal offered prime observation sites and defensive fire positions, so a night attack was set for one minute past midnight on September 25. Groping through the pitch darkness, the lead company launched its assault boats and paddled silently for the other side. Any second, German fire was expected. But the Lincolns reached the other side undiscovered. On one flank, a few shots rang out as 'C' Company moved into position, but no general alarm followed and no Germans moved to investigate whatever had triggered the fire of the sentries. Dawn found the Lincolns well ensconced, the Germans completely surprised to discover British soldiers in their midst, and Royal Engineers already well along the way to having a Bailey bridge across the canal.[45]

Within hours of the Lincolns establishing their bridgehead, the South Wales Borderers of 56th Infantry Brigade gained a second crossing immediately west of their position. 'D' Company was just beginning to dig in when a man followed by a large body of troops shouted in perfect English: "Stop firing, you bloody fools." Fearing the approaching troops were from another British battalion, the Welsh soldiers hesitated, and the two forward platoons were overrun by a strong German force and forced to withdraw. Left behind were the forward sections of each platoon, but they stood firm in their slit trenches and repulsed each attack. Meanwhile, 'B' Company had also crossed the canal and despite the confused fighting in 'D' Company's sector managed to secure several farmhouses and knock out a pillbox guarding the road parallelling the canal. These clearing actions, however, badly separated the platoons from each other, and at 0600 hours the Germans counterattacked each in force. For three and a half hours the battle raged until Sherman tanks from 'B' Squadron of the Canadian Sherbrooke Fusiliers, which was supporting the 49th Division, arrived and drove off the attackers with its 75-millimetre main guns and raking machine-gun fire. Fifty Germans were killed in the action and another seventy taken prisoner.[46] A light German tank was also wrecked by fire from the Sherbrooke tanks.

The Sherbrookes had crossed on one of two Bailey bridges—designated Plum 1 and Plum 2—that the Royal Engineers had thrown over the canal. Each was capable of bearing heavy vehicle traffic, enabling the Sherbrookes to get two squadrons of Shermans into the bridgehead in the knick of time to prevent the British infantry being overwhelmed by the determined German counterattacks. While 'B' Squadron had rushed to the aid of the 56th Brigade, 'A' Squadron moved out alongside the infantry of the 146th Brigade.

In the 146th's sector, the initial sluggish German response allowed a hard push towards Rijkevorsel that continued despite the counterattacks to the west aimed at eliminating the bridgehead. 'A' Squadron's supporting fire cut apart the German units trying to muster a defence of the town and two hundred prisoners were taken in exchange for only one Sherman knocked out.[47] By evening, the 146th had taken Rijkevorsel.

This gain, concluded one German report, put 719th Division "in a most precarious position."⁴⁸ Accordingly, LXVII Corps's Sponheimer decided to pull 711th Division "out of its sector at the mouth of the Scheld[t] and to commit it for a counterattack on Rijkevorsel and the cement plant. All available artillery was concentrated under the corps artillery commander and subordinated to the division for this attack." Sponheimer also shifted his corps headquarters closer to his left flank in "order to exert greater influence than previously on the left wing."

Before day's end on the 26th, the 711th Division began a heavy assault on Rijkevorsel that at first threatened to drive the British out. Violent fighting developed in the streets, but the counterattack was soon blunted by the infantry and Canadian tanks.⁴⁹ The following morning, the bridgehead was strengthened, with the Sherbrookes' 'C' Squadron advancing alongside the 49th British Reconnaissance Regiment to clear areas to the southwest. 'A' Squadron was in Rijkevorsel supporting the 56th's Essex Regiment while 'B' Squadron was operating alongside the Gloucestershire Regiment.

It remained tough slogging, but by the end of the day the Germans had been pushed completely out of Rijkevorsel. 'A' Squadron had helped in forcing the surrender of eighty Germans, knocked out a self-propelled gun, and overrun an 18-centimetre mortar that had caused the infantry much grief. Intelligence officers from the Sherbrookes were soon scurrying about the divisional prisoner cages trying to gain some insight into the organization of the foe the tankers faced, but came away perplexed. "These prisoners originally belonged to many different units," they reported, "and so the difficulty of estimating the strength and organization of the opposing enemy reliably was great. The units had become of such mixed composition that enemy platoon commanders now did not even know the units to which they belonged. The designations of units were apt to vary from day to day as commanders became a casualty, and no one had any clear idea who was on his flanks or in reserve. In the past three days many bodies had been collected from various localities and formed into battle groups, at least a dozen being identified."⁵⁰

Despite a concerted effort by the remnants of the 711th and 719th divisions, the Germans were recognizing that saving the Antwerp–

Turnhout Canal line was impossible. On September 28, its fate was sealed when 1st Polish Armoured Division struck out from west of Turnhout towards Merksplas, about two miles north of the canal, and 5th Canadian Infantry Brigade crossed into the 49th Division's bridgehead to begin a hard drive westwards along the north bank of the canal to roll up the 346th Infantry Division's positions there.

The Polish drive particularly panicked the LXVII Corps command. "This thrust," stated one report, "tore the front open on the right wing of 719 Inf Div in the Merksplas area and made useless any further effort by 711 Inf Div to regain the Antwerp–Turnhout Canal." That night, the 711th moved into defensive positions north of Rijkevorsel, its intention now merely to stem the breakout by 1 British Corps towards the vital lifeline connecting the Germans in the Breskens Pocket, Walcheren Island, and the South Beveland Peninsula to mainland Holland.[51]

[7]

Simonds Takes Command

AT FIRST CANADIAN Army headquarters, final plans were being nailed down for the formal campaign to free up Antwerp. Complicating matters was Field Marshal Montgomery's obstinate refusal to consider the operation as more than an inconvenient sideshow. Despite the failure of Market Garden, the Twenty-First Army Group commander's attention remained fixated on that offensive's area of operations. When Eisenhower politely reminded Montgomery on September 24 that "We need Antwerp," the field marshal's response two days later was to concur that this was an important business, then to stridently advocate another all-out push to the Rhine. While opening Antwerp was essential, he said, the opportunity remained to destroy the Germans barring the way into the Ruhr industrial area. While First Canadian Army opened Antwerp, Montgomery wanted to send British Second Army charging out from Nijmegen to gain the northwest corner of the Ruhr, with First U.S. Army driving up to the right towards Cologne. Montgomery envisioned these armies respectively gaining bridgeheads over the Rhine to the north and south of the Ruhr and then converging to control the entire western part of the region.[1]

It was an ambitious and impractical proposal. The Allies had insufficient munitions and fuel to undertake three full-scale army operations. Yet Montgomery was not one to abandon plans of his own making. And the drive to the Ruhr would also salvage something positive from Market Garden's failure, which had left Second Army holding a thumb-shaped fifty-mile-long by fifteen-mile-wide salient exposed to German counterattack from both its flanks and tip. Nijmegen was close to the eastern flank. If Second Army jumped off from here on a southeastwards drive towards the Ruhr, the Germans would be forced to try and stop it. With First U.S. Army coming up from the south, the two armies could crush the enemy between them and win a large part of the Ruhr valley.

Yet Second Army could hardly strike out from Nijmegen without exposing itself to attack by the German forces arrayed on the western flank of the salient. There was only one way to neutralize this threat without Montgomery being forced to leave several divisions in place. First Canadian Army, Montgomery decided on September 27, would have to not only free the approaches to Antwerp but also "thrust strongly northwards on the general axis Tilburg-S'Hertogenbosch, and so free the Second Army from its present commitment of a long left flank facing west." The Dutch town of s'Hertogenbosch lay about fifty miles northeast of Antwerp, well east of where Lieutenant General Harry Crerar had planned to have 1 British Corps advance to form a blocking line running from Roosendaal to Bergen op Zoom, in order to isolate the Germans on the South Beveland peninsula and Walcheren Island. Montgomery's directive forced him instead to move this corps northeast to clear the Germans off the salient's western flank.[2] Once again, Montgomery was deliberately denying First Canadian Army the ability to use all its strength to open Antwerp.

Crerar might well have balked at this new directive from Montgomery, but the general's deteriorating health had finally reached a critical juncture on September 25, when doctors at No. 16 Canadian General Hospital in Saint-Omer decided he must be returned to England to be treated for dysentery and tested for a possible blood disorder. Crerar had flown the next day to Montgomery's headquarters to recommend that temporary army command go to Lieutenant General Guy Simonds.[3] Montgomery enthusiastically endorsed having his protégé take the helm of First Canadian Army, believing the young general would tackle the job with a vigour and competence beyond Crerar's capacity. He also knew that, unlike Crerar, Simonds would be less likely to question or drag his feet over orders issued by Montgomery.

The elevation of Simonds to army command caused a ripple effect throughout the command chain of 11 Canadian Corps. Major General Charles Foulkes of 2nd Canadian Infantry Division moved up to head the corps, while Brigadier R.H. "Holly" Keefler, the commander of 2 CID's artillery regiments, took divisional command.[4]

The transition was carried out quickly. By early evening, Simonds had his office at corps headquarters tidied up, his papers and personal effects packed, and carried out the formal handover to Foulkes. The Corps Chief of Staff, Brigadier Elliot Rodgers, watched this process abjectly, confiding to his infrequently updated personal diary: "It will be a let down to have him leave. For our own sake I hope most sincerely that it is not permanent but I fear it may be. He took his corps flag 'for a souvenir' and took his caravan [modelled on the one that Crerar had so envied in Italy and which had soured their relationship]... Never have I worked for anyone with such a precise and clear & far reaching mind. He was always working to a plan with a clear cut objective which he took care to let us all know in simple and direct terms, thus we were able to help him achieve that object. He reduced problems in a flash to basic facts and variables, picked out those that mattered, ignored those that were side-issues and made up his mind and got on with it. No temporizing or bad decisions either... Simonds will command the Army with a facility which will surprise some people—but it will be a sad day for us when he goes for good."[5]

His successor was far less popular, and considered by many to be nowhere near as competent. The same age as Simonds and also born in Britain, Foulkes had joined the Royal Canadian Regiment in 1926. A major when the war began, his career advanced at a pace that only slightly trailed Simonds's meteoric rise. Rivals, the two men cared little for each other. During the Normandy campaign, Simonds had almost fired Foulkes from command for what he considered incompetent handling of 2nd Canadian Infantry Division during Operation Spring. His counterpart at 4th Canadian Armoured Division, Major General Harry Foster, despised Foulkes—considering him "mean and narrow" with "a sneering supercilious attitude towards anyone over the rank of major." A short, pudgy man, he was noted for a dour and unapproachable countenance. His orders often lacked clarity and he was not seen as a take-charge kind of general. But he enjoyed the backing of Crerar, who had carefully helped smooth the man's promotional advancement. Unlike almost everyone else in the Canadian command chain, Crerar considered Foulkes to possess "exceptional ability, sound tactical knowledge, a great capacity for quick, sound, decisions, energy and driving power." As a corps commander, Crerar had personally asked for Foulkes to be assigned as his Brigadier, General Staff. It had been from this post that Crerar had successfully recommended him for divisional command.[6]

Despite his dislike, Simonds had gone along with Crerar in selecting Foulkes to command II Canadian Corps. Arguably, there was nobody else more suitably qualified who possessed equal seniority. Harry Foster had only attained divisional command in mid-August, and this was also true of 3rd Canadian Infantry Division's Major General Dan Spry.

To some degree, the corps commander mattered less than might have been expected, because Simonds intended to closely control the forthcoming campaign. From army headquarters, he would direct the movement of the corps and its divisions, and provide the support necessary for it to carry out its mission. Crerar's illness had come at a timely moment for the ambitious young general. Simonds's debut as an army commander—only the third general to hold the position—would entail fighting what might prove to be the hardest and most complex operation the army had yet faced. And because Crerar's planning had barely advanced beyond general principles, Simonds had a golden opportunity to demonstrate his ability both as a strategist and tactician. Simonds lost no time establishing his presence at army headquarters in Ghent. At mid-morning on Wednesday, September 27, he strode into headquarters and immediately announced a major planning session for that Friday. Staff scrambled to ensure the relevant senior officers would be in attendance. Besides his corps commanders and senior staff officers, the attendance list required representatives from 2nd Tactical Air Force, Bomber Command, the Royal Navy, SHAEF, and Twenty-First Army Group. Where Crerar's love of paperwork and consultation required thick, detailed planning briefs laden with analysis that led to drawn-out meetings, Simonds knew what he wanted and made it clear that everyone was to march in step. Chief clerk Oscar Lange, who had worked for Simonds elsewhere, recognized the pattern. "A strict disciplinarian, he expected no less than excellence from everyone under his command. He looked like a soldier; he acted like a soldier. He was stern and clever. He stood for no nonsense."[7]

For too long, First Canadian Army had been pushing into action guided only by a general plan. While it was true that Crerar had been hobbled by the need to clear the channel ports and the fact that Market Garden had dominated the attention of his superiors, most of September had been allowed to pass with each division of II Canadian Corps operating without any overall coordination. Simonds was determined to change that by implementing a clear operational timetable.

The Friday meeting would end with that goal achieved, and on Monday, October 2, Simonds planned for the battle to begin in earnest. But there would be no pause on the frontlines while he reorganized. On the Antwerp–Turnhout Canal, 2 CID would immediately win a bridgehead as a vital preliminary step towards enabling the launch of the northwards drive to cut off the Germans holding the South Beveland peninsula and Walcheren Island. Simonds announced that this bridgehead was to be in place before the Friday meeting convened.

THE BRIDGEHEAD ASSAULT was conceived as a two-pronged operation, with 5th Canadian Infantry Brigade crossing to the north side of the canal via the bridgehead won on September 25 south of Rijkevorsel by the 49th (West Riding) Infantry Division. Early on September 28, Le Régiment de Maisonneuve would lead the brigade's drive westwards by capturing the village of Oostbrecht, about two and a half miles northwest of the bridgehead. Once the Maisies gained this objective, the Black Watch would advance straight alongside the canal to Sint-Lenaarts, and the Calgary Highlanders would then leapfrog through to seize Brecht, about a mile and a half farther west.[8] This would put the brigade's forward battalion midway between Rijkevorsel and Lochtenberg, where 6th Canadian Infantry Brigade was to again try winning a bridgehead in the operation's second prong. The next morning, the two brigades could link up and the canal would be in hand.

6 CIB's Brigadier Guy Gauvreau and the commander of the 11th Field Company, Royal Canadian Engineers had decided that if an infantry platoon crossed the canal in front of Lochtenberg and held the Germans at bay, a bridge capable of supporting antitank guns could be built in just forty-five minutes. Gauvreau gave the infantry task to South Saskatchewan Regiment. Once the bridge was in place, the antitank guns would be rushed over, with the rest of the infantry battalion close behind. Supported by the guns, the South Saskatchewans would not be vulnerable—as had happened to Les Fusiliers Mont-Royal—to being overrun by German armour. Gauvreau was insistent that unless the South Saskatchewans succeeded in shielding the sappers so that the bridge could be built, the operation would be cancelled. He "was not prepared to suffer any serious casualties" to win the bridgehead.[9] With 5 CIB crossing to the east on a well-secured bridge, Gauvreau saw no point in throwing his understrength battalions into another meat grinder. If the crossing failed, 6 CIB would simply cross over on the heels of 5 CIB and pass through to take Lochtenberg from the east.[10]

Since the repulse on September 24, the brigade had been battering the Germans on the opposite shore with mortar, artillery, and air strikes by Royal Air Force rocket-firing Typhoons. While the mass of exploding ordnance provided a fireworks display for the South Saskatchewans, there was no indication that it made any real dent in the German defences concentrated inside concrete pillboxes dug close to the canal bank. These pillboxes enjoyed excellent fields of fire on the waterway and the opposite shore, where any movement attracted immediate enemy rifle and machine-gun fire. The battalion's positions were also subjected to random shelling. All this enemy fire had a deadly effect. On September 27, the battalion suffered ten casualties, two fatal.[11]

Lieutenant Cecil Law, who had received a welcome transfer from No. 9 Platoon to command the battalion's mortar platoon, and now figured he had some chance of surviving the war intact, was in a small concrete building that day with Lieutenant Colonel Vern Stott and other members of the battalion headquarters staff, which housed the controls for one of the canal's locks. Suddenly, a heavy machine gun began raking its exterior. "I was fascinated at one instant to be looking up at the steel bars of the little window in the lock house we were in, when an armour-piercing MG bullet passed right through the centre of one of the bars... Stott was cut in the face with some of the fragments."[12] With much to do to ready the battalion for its assault the next morning, Stott refused to report to the Regimental Aid Post for treatment.

The battalions of 5 CIB had meanwhile concentrated around the village of Oostmalle, two miles south of the 49th Division's bridgehead, on the night of September 27. At 0630 the next morning, the rifle companies of Le Régiment de Maisonneuve marched to the bridgehead and began to organize north of the canal for the attack.[13] As Les Fusiliers Mont-Royal had been overrun because the Germans struck with about fifteen light tanks and a larger number of half-tracks mounting 15-millimetre machineguns, 5 CIB's attack was to be well supported by armour. Joining the Maisies was 'A' Squadron of the Fort Garry Horse Regiment drawn from 2nd Canadian Armoured Brigade and a troop of armoured cars from the 14th Canadian Hussars (8th Reconnaissance Regiment). The Hussars were to lead, followed by Lieutenant Arthur Thompson's Fort Garry troop of four Shermans, then two companies of infantry, then the Maisonneuve battalion headquarters, with the rest of the infantry and 'A' Squadron close behind. Artillery support would be provided by 5th Field Regiment, Royal Canadian Artillery.[14]

As far as the tankers were concerned, the operation was poorly conceived. They had been forced to scramble twenty miles from a concentration area at Contich, directly south of Antwerp, to reach the bridgehead in time to go into action. Then, despite strong objections by Fort Garry's Lieutenant Colonel Eric Mackay Wilson to Brigadier Holly Keefler—now commanding 2 CID—that regulations forbid "placing of Armoured Regiments under command of any formation lower than a division," they were put under the command of 5 CIB's Brigadier Bill Megill. In recent weeks, this unusual divisional policy had been a running sore to Wilson and the other tank commanders of 2 CAB tasked with working alongside the 2nd Division. But nothing they said could get the policy, introduced by Major General Foulkes, reversed. That the 5 CIB infantry battalions the tankers were to serve had little experience working directly with tanks further salted Wilson's injured sense of propriety.[15]

The Canadians advanced at 1230 hours under a bright sunny sky, increasingly a rarity, and for awhile it seemed that Wilson's anxieties were baseless. The little German resistance met was easily brushed aside by Thompson's tanks. But when the column was within six hundred yards of Oostbrecht, an 88-millimetre gun opened fire from "a corner of the village churchyard." Thompson's Sherman was hit and began to burn.[16] The twenty-six-year-old officer from Winnipeg and twenty-four-year-old Trooper Robert Blake of Campbellford, Ontario were killed, but the other three crewmen managed to escape. Within minutes, the rest of 'A' Squadron had rushed to back up the embattled troop. Soon the Shermans were exchanging volleys of main-gun fire with several antitank guns. When the infantry lagged in coming up in support, the tankers launched "a frontal assault, with the infantry bumbling in behind."[17]

A sharp action ensued as the tankers and infantry tangled with Germans for control of the village. The Maisonneuves' historian remarked later that his regiment's soldiers were "obliged to engage in combat with a well-trained enemy." In the fray, Lieutenant Roger Valois received three wounds—succumbing to his injuries the next day.[18] Finally, at 2100 hours, the Germans were driven from the village.[19]

Although 'A' Squadron had no other men killed in the bitter fight, it paid dearly in tanks. Only five tanks from the four troops and the three tanks of headquarters section remained operational. Furious at the needless waste, which mostly occurred during the squadron's frontal assault on the German guns, Wilson burst into Megill's brigade tactical headquarters, and, noted a war diarist gleefully, stood "up on his hind legs and 'talk[ed] tank' to the red tab officers and everyone else on the proper employment of the tank arm. [He] recalls that artillery had to fight for years to be recognized as a separate arm with special abilities and limitation. [He] pleads for more battle-wise tactic of shooting in the infantry from the flank, rather than fronting 88-mm guns head-on."[20]

Oostbrecht had taken far longer to clear than expected, which resulted in the rest of the brigade's planned action being thrown well off schedule. The intention had been for the Black Watch to move on Sint-Lenaarts once the Maisonneuve had secured their objective. Darkness found the regiment only entering Rijkevorsel, its march up from Oostmalle having been slowed to a crawl because the road was clogged with Maisonneuve transport and support vehicles. In Rijkevorsel's narrow streets, the Black Watch advance completely stalled, and they were left sitting under "heavy shell and mortar fire while waiting for the [Maisonneuves] to 'pull its tail up.'" Several casualties and a destroyed Bren carrier later, the regiment was again on the move. When it finally halted on a crossroads south of Oostbrecht about a mile east of Sint-Lenaarts, Lieutenant Colonel Bruce Ritchie "was not disposed to make preparations for a night attack upon what was apparently a very strongly held position, but the Brigadier left him no alternative, and ordered him to attack with the least possible delay."

Ritchie convened an immediate O Group in a farmhouse beside the road. 'B' Company, he said, would march almost to Oostbrecht and then take a road running from there into Sint-Lenaarts from the northeast, while 'A' and 'C' Companies approached on a road bearing straight from the crossroads into the village, and 'D' Company pushed in on a road that parallelled this one several hundred yards to the south. It was midnight before the companies started moving.[21] 'B' Squadron of the Fort Garry Horse was ordered by brigade to support the Black Watch attack, but its role was limited to establishing a position overlooking the open ground in order to provide close gun support. As the tankers moved into position, they were presented with the sobering sight of Thompson's tank burning fitfully to the north.[22]

The two companies advancing down the centre road ran into heavy crossfire, but pressed into the outskirts of the village and established a strongpoint centred on a large house opposite the church, which gave them command of the main road and the village centre. No sooner had the two companies set up shop here than the Germans counterattacked in force, even manhandling a 75-millimetre anti-tank gun "around the corner of the church in full view of our troops on the lawn before the large house they were occupying. All the enemy were killed before they had a chance to fire a shot." The night fighting was chaotic in the extreme, neither side sure where the other was located. In the midst of the fighting around the church, a German officer strolled into the street, nonchalantly carrying his briefcase as if on the way to a nocturnal staff meeting. Lieutenant Clements called for him to halt. The officer "did so, smartly, and received a burst of Sten gun, leaving one less German officer to prepare for the war," the Black Watch war diarist wryly noted.

Meanwhile, Major Slater's 'B' Company had come up on the village from the north, but was unable to break through to the companies near the church. His radio knocked out, the major relied on sending runners to and from battalion headquarters to keep Ritchie apprised of his situation. 'D' Company was also unable to link up with the two companies holding the centre, but succeeded in establishing itself alongside the canal.

Fighting remained heavy around the church square throughout the night, but just before dawn, at 0600 hours, the Germans shifted their attention to 'D' Company. A hard attack supported by mortar and machine-gun fire inflicted heavy casualties on the company, and all its officers were "either killed, wounded, or taken prisoner." Captain Douglas Chapman rushed from battalion headquarters to take over command, and "the situation was gradually restored."

Despite support from the Fort Garry Horse's 'B' Squadron, the Black Watch remained hard-pressed. To relieve the situation, Ritchie ordered the Bren carrier platoon to open up the streets that would link 'D' Company to those by the church. Captain Selby Stewart led the carriers forward and "very boldly and brilliantly executed" the operation by charging "down the street, firing their [light machine guns] at all positions, and possible positions, and the enemy with bazookas in the lanes and side streets were incapacitated before they could do much damage. The boys went in with such verve that it is thought that the enemy felt himself attacked by a much larger force than that employed. One of our carriers was knocked out by a bazooka [Panzerschreck], but we suffered no casualties." By midmorning, the battalion was largely in control of Sint-Lenaarts, but still engaged in clearing out pockets of resistance and fending off faint-hearted counterattacks.[23]

At noon, Brigadier Megill re-evaluated the situation to best exploit it with the Calgary Highlanders. Originally, the Calgarians were to have passed through Sint-Lenaarts to secure Brecht, but Megill was leery to push this battalion that far out in light of the heavy German resistance so far encountered. Also, the original hope that 5 CIB would be able to link up with 6th Brigade between Brecht and Lochtenberg had been dashed when the South Saskatchewan Regiment had failed in its attempt the previous afternoon to win a bridgehead.

Although a South Saskatchewan platoon led by thirty-two-year-old Lieutenant Iler Lacey had managed to get across the canal in front of Lochtenberg, it had been unable to suppress the German fire from a pillbox about three hundred yards from the crossing point where the sappers were to push across their prefabricated bridge. When Lacey led two of his platoon sections against the pillbox, the Nova Scotia native was killed after getting his men only halfway to the position. The attack crumbled. Repeated attempts to destroy the pillbox with antitank fire from across the canal also failed, and at 1800 hours, Lieutenant Colonel Vern Stott ordered a barrage of artillery fire laid on to cover the withdrawal of the men from the north bank. At this point, a German machine gun opened up on the antitank gun that had been positioned next to Stott's command post inside a house, and the battalion commander was hit in the leg by bullet splinters. This time, he was evacuated to the Regimental Aid Post for treatment, but soon set off to personally report the situation to Brigadier Gauvreau.[24]

With this in mind, Megill decided it would suffice if the Calgary Highlanders managed to occupy the stretch of canal between Sint-

Lenaarts and Eindhoven, a village about a mile and a half due west. Midway between the two villages, a road spanned the canal, and here the brigade's engineers thought they could quickly put a bridge over. Getting a bridge across the canal in this area accorded with Brigadier Keefler's rejigged divisional plan, which now called for 6th Canadian Infantry Brigade to cross there and then drive westwards to occupy Lochtenberg and Kamp van Brasschaat. A bridge would then be put across at Lochtenberg. Together with the one between Eindhoven and Sint-Lenaarts, the two crossings would provide 4th Canadian Armoured Division easy access to the north bank, from which it could advance to begin clearing the mainland east of South Beveland, while the 5th and 6th brigades of 2 CID continued to drive west along the canal to break the tenacious German grip on Merksem and the northern sections of the port of Antwerp.[25]

The remaining tanks of the Fort Garry's 'B' Squadron formed behind the two Calgary companies that were to lead the attack. At 1615 hours, the "fireworks began," the Calgary war diarist recorded, when "a vicious, vigorous, crackle rent the air as the supporting tanks opened fire." Five minutes later, Major Bruce MacKenzie led 'D' Company across the start line alongside the canal. 'A' Company, commanded by Major Del Kearns, followed a parallelling road a few hundred yards to the north. The other two companies were close behind, ready to pass through if the lead companies faced stiff opposition. 'D' Company met little German opposition, but was fired upon several times by elements of Les Fusiliers Mont-Royal holding the south bank of the canal, which had been unaware that friendly units were mounting an operation. Fortunately, no casualties resulted before Private W.C. Alexander was able to paddle across in a purloined boat and inform the Fusiliers of the Calgarians' presence.

While 'D' Company was dodging friendly fire, 'A' Company ran into heavy opposition at 1800 hours and was pinned down by an 88-millimetre gun. Private Robert E. Bingham and two other men were ordered to knock it out with the company's two-inch mortar. Bingham led the team into the courtyard of a nearby house. He and one of the others had just stepped through a doorway when an 88-millimetre shell exploded outside. The blast picked Bingham "up like I was a feather and threw me about ten feet inside the house." Momentarily dazed, Bingham regained his senses to find the third man lying in the doorway, riddled with shrapnel. "His leg was opened as if by a meat cleaver and the foot was hanging by a piece of skin." Ignoring his own wounds, Bingham tended the badly wounded soldier until the stretcher-bearers arrived to evacuate them.

The attack bogged down as night fell and the companies faced increasing volumes of machine-gun, mortar, and artillery fire. Lieutenant Colonel Donald MacLauchlan ordered everyone to dig in tight for the night and to send out patrols to try and determine the strength of the German defenders. 'A' Company continued to take the worst of things, having to stave off several counterattacks. In the early morning hours, however, the tempo of German fire slackened. As dawn broke on September 30, 'D' Company sent a patrol forward that trekked through heavy rain right through to Eindhoven where it was informed by relieved citizens emerging from their cellars that the Germans had withdrawn.[26]

By midday, the Calgarians had patrols out on all sides of Eindhoven and were finding that the Germans had broken off the action. Fort Garry's 'B' Squadron had only eight tanks remaining operational when it withdrew from the front. Having seen two of his squadrons reduced by half, due to their being sent pell-mell into fights with no infantry to protect them from ambush by antitank rocket launchers, Lieutenant Colonel Wilson decided enough was enough. Demanding a personal meeting with Keefler at his divisional headquarters, Wilson detailed the "spendthrift manner in which [brigades and battalions]... have been employing tanks. It has been normal," he pointed out, "during the past week for [his] tanks... to be sent into frontal attacks on fortified villages with inf[antry] following 1000 [yards] in their rear."[27] Wilson considered this nothing more than the infantry using the tankers as "decoys." Then, if no immediate resistance was met, the brigadiers or battalion commanders would insist the tanks "charge straight ahead regardless of considerations affecting their security or usefulness."[28]

An artilleryman by specialty, Keefler patiently heard the tanker out and acknowledged that the special operational issues that armoured regiments faced were probably not fully recognized by the infantry commanders. He agreed to adhere to the principle that the tanks of 2nd Canadian Armoured Brigade would be under, and responsible to, divisional command rather than either brigades or battalions. While they would continue to support these formations, Wilson had won the right for his commanders to seek divisional permission to reject any requested missions that would produce unnecessary tank casualties.[29]

While this wrangling was going on, the tired Calgarians had finished mopping up the area around Eindhoven and were just beginning to think about a well-deserved rest when they learned more fighting lay ahead. Brigadier Megill, encouraged by the reports of weakening German resistance, had decided to advance as far as Brecht. They were to open the first day of October by pushing about one-third of a mile north from the canal to secure a crossroads. The Black Watch would use that as the start point for an advance up two roads that led to Brecht, a half-mile farther on.

THE GAINS WON by 5th Canadian Infantry Brigade were short of what had been hoped at the end of September. Still, the fact that 2nd Canadian Infantry Division had battalions on the north bank of the Antwerp–Turnhout Canal, marking its end as a major defensive barrier, was welcome news to everyone at First Canadian Army Headquarters. Turning the eastern flank of the Germans north of Antwerp was one of several steps Lieutenant General Guy Simonds had identified during his September 29 briefing as essential precursors to the overall campaign to clear the approaches to the city's port.

Simonds had addressed a crowded room that Friday. Besides his senior staff, the corps commanders and their key personnel had been present. Captain P.B. Lucas representing the Allied Expeditionary Air Force, Air Commodore L.W. Dickens of Bomber Command, and Royal Navy Captain A.F. Pugsley, along with some of their staff people, had also attended.[30] Simonds made it clear from the outset that he was in charge. "My intention is," were the first words spoken, and from there Simonds launched into a concise and clear explanation of how the operation would unfold. It was almost precisely the same plan that he had submitted to Crerar on September 21 in response to the operation proposed by the army's Plans Section.

The bold strokes set out during this meeting were that 2nd Canadian Infantry Division would push north from Antwerp to cut off the South Beveland peninsula; 4th Canadian Armoured Division would move up alongside 2 CID to the east and establish a blocking position running from Bergen op Zoom across to Roosendaal, to the north of the isthmus that connected the peninsula to the mainland; and 3rd Canadian Infantry Division would clear the Breskens Pocket. As a finishing touch, Walcheren Island would first be flooded by aerial bombardment breaching its dykes in key places and then invaded by amphibious forces. While 11 Canadian Corps carried out these tasks, 1 British Corps would move north into Holland to guard the left flank of British Second Army, in accordance with Field Marshal Montgomery's recent directive.

All but one aspect of this plan had been expected by everyone in the room. Stunning many of the officers, however, was the adamance with which Simonds insisted that Walcheren Island be flooded. Both his chief army engineer and the representatives of Bomber Command immediately raised objections. Brigadier Geoff Walsh had studied the feasibility of breaching the dykes in detail and concluded it was "not practicable" in a detailed written report tabled on September 24. Flooding the island, Walsh believed, would only be possible if a hundred-foot-long breach was blasted in the Westkapelle dyke, which protected the island's seaward side. The largest dyke on Walcheren and one of the oldest in Holland, this dyke was constructed of heavy clay compacted over centuries. Breaching it would mean blasting "some 10,000 tons of clay" out of the way. Walsh could not envision bombers being able to accurately deliver sufficient tonnage of explosives to achieve this. Neither could the representatives of Bomber Command.

When everyone had finished, Simonds fixed his steel-blue eyes on the air force officers. "Well, gentlemen, that's pretty disappointing," he said. "Had you been able to take that on as a task it would have undoubtedly saved many lives in the assault."[31] He then invited the bombers and engineers to take another look, for he had studied the same aerial photos, charts, and reports gathered from locals, seamen, and hydrographic engineers and concluded the opposite. Having a stereoscope set up, Simonds had the flyers "scrutinize a series of air photographs, taken in pairs... that supported his contention that if the dyke were breached, the land on the inside was low enough to be inundated, a conclusion borne out by the testimony of Dutch civilians who said that if the dyke were broken the island would sink. He used other air photographs of bomb patterns caused in previous operations by the R.A.F. to show that... similar tasks had been carried out with a degree of accuracy commensurate with that required for the target now proposed."[32]

That Simonds had personally studied the matter in detail was nothing unusual, for he was a proven innovator. When planning Operation Totalize—the breakout from Caen to Falaise in the beginning of August—Simonds had been watching some self-propelled 105-millimetre artillery pieces while pondering how to move his troops rapidly into battle aboard vehicles, without having them all killed by German defensive fire. Suddenly, he imagined converting these Priests, as they were designated—which had thick armour plating—into armoured personnel carriers.[33] Stripped of its gun and related equipment, each Priest would have sufficient room to carry about ten men plus its crew. That inspiration led to the creation of the Kangaroo, and the Canadian lead assault units had gone into Totalize protected inside their hulls.

After a prolonged discussion, Lucas asked whether Simonds was worried that if the breaching attempt failed, the bombing might jeopardize other means of attacking the island. Simonds "replied that no disadvantage would follow, since the situation would simply remain as it existed already." Looking at the photos of the Westkapelle dyke, Lucas remarked that it was larger than he had expected and breaching "it would prove to be a long and difficult business." While Lucas's skepticism was clear, Simonds received unexpected support from Dickens of Bomber Command.

The bombers, he said, could be brought to bear on the dyke and he was willing to give it a go. But he could not guarantee success. Simonds said all he was asking was that they try. Dickens agreed that if Simonds was able to get permission from SHAEF, Bomber Command would attempt to make the breach.

Convinced that the flooding would save the lives of many soldiers who would otherwise die trying to invade the heavily defended island, Simonds immediately signalled SHAEF for permission. General Dwight Eisenhower, anxious to get Antwerp open, did not ponder the matter long. It was made clear to him that the breach was possible and so it was a matter of the "grim calculus of cost for cost determined on behalf of the men who would soon be ordered to make the assault by land or water, in the teeth of the enemy's fire. Considerations of strategy prevailed over those of economics; the saving of life had a stronger case than the avoidance of dire hardship and of the loss of land and stock for our helpless friends, the Dutch. Too much depended on silencing the German guns for these unhappy alternatives to be avoided and Walcheren's rich acres were condemned to the spoliation of the sea," stated one report compiled after the meeting. When the argument was presented to Marshal of the Royal Air Force Sir Arthur Harris, his response was curt and to the point. "The wholesale destruction of property is, in my view, always justified if it is calculated to save casualties."[34]

Eisenhower agreed. On October 1, a deceptively simple coded signal was passed on by Twenty-First Army Group to Simonds. It read: "The Supreme Commander has approved the project to flood the island of Walcheren."[35] Simonds had prevailed. The battle would be fought according to his design.

PART TWO

THE CINDERELLA DAYS

[8]

Off Our Backsides

FIRST LIGHT on October 1 saw 5th Canadian Infantry Brigade fighting to expand its bridgehead at Sint-Lenaarts on the Antwerp–Turnhout Canal with an attack towards Brecht and Eindhoven. The Calgary Highlanders were to lead off with a push one-third of a mile north on the road linking Sint-Lenaarts and Brecht, to secure a crossroads that would become the start point for the Black Watch's advance on Brecht. As soon as the Black Watch was on its way, the Calgarians would head west along the canal to Eindhoven. With Brecht and Eindhoven taken, the ground would be prepared for 6th Canadian Infantry Brigade to sally out from this bridgehead on October 2 to gain Lochtenberg, and then march west alongside the canal to Brasschaat and marry up with 4th Canadian Infantry Brigade, which was to simultaneously be seizing Merksem and other port facilities north of Antwerp. This three-brigade operation by 2nd Canadian Infantry Division was a necessary precursor to the ultimate goal of cutting the South Beveland isthmus.

It was still dark when two Calgary Highlander companies groped their way through heavy rain that made identifying landmarks all but impossible. Their orders were to secure the crossroads for the Black Watch before dawn. 'A' Company was on the left, 'D' Company the right, with the carrier platoon creeping along behind. The impenetrable darkness combined with unreliable maps made it hard for the company commanders to maintain a proper bearing.

About halfway to the crossroads, 'A' Company came under machine-gun fire. Rather than get tangled in a firefight, Major Del Kearns bypassed the position. Disoriented by the change in direction, he led the company past the crossroads and into Brecht's outskirts. Minutes later, he was on the wireless reporting being locked in a fight requiring his men "to clear houses to get out of town and fight their way back to their objective!"[1] Extracting 'A' Company from Brecht took several hours, but Kearns declared that he was back at the crossroads and snug near 'D' Company shortly before dawn. The Calgarians' commander, Lieutenant Colonel Donald MacLauchlan, phoned Brigadier Bill Megill at 0639 hours to say that the Black Watch could advance.[2]

The Black Watch's Lieutenant Colonel Bruce Ritchie called shortly thereafter questioning whether the Calgarians were actually in control of the start line, and insisted that a line of buildings near 'A' Company's position be reinspected to ensure "that they were absolutely unoccupied."[3] Ritchie's unease stemmed from a previous Calgary failure to secure a start line at May-sur-Orne during Operation Spring on July 25 that had forced the Black Watch to advance with a completely exposed right flank. Only fifteen of the three hundred men sent into that attack had returned. The rest were either killed or captured.[4] Anticipating Ritchie's distrust, MacLauchlan had promised the task would be properly executed and he was infuriated to have his word and competency questioned. It little helped that MacLauchlan knew his command ability was shaky. "Completely out of his depth as a battalion commander," Montgomery had declared after MacLauchlan assumed command of the Calgarians in 1942. He "knows practically nothing about how to command... is so completely at sea that he inspires no confidence at all. He is a very decent chap; but I am sorry for him as he just knows nothing whatever about it."

Megill had agreed, but decided to give MacLauchlan the chance to prove himself in combat. After a dubious initial start in Normandy, the lieutenant colonel had handled an August 13 assault of Clair Tizon so competently he was awarded a Distinguished Service

Order. Not that MacLauchlan had placed himself in harm's way. He was a commander who led from the rear, insisting on headquarters situated in deep bunkers and wearing an American steel helmet that he felt offered superior protection to the standard Canadian issue. Aloof, intolerant, and quick to criticize, the thirty-seven-year-old was unpopular despite having roots in the regiment that dated back to 1921.[5]

Ritchie couldn't care less whether he provoked MacLauchlan. Once the buildings near 'A' Company's position were reported clear, he demanded that 'D' Company check some near its position. Then, at 0700, Ritchie requested that the two Calgary company commanders come back to discuss the situation. That proved the last straw. MacLauchlan called Megill and demanded that he "rely on his assurance and order the [Black Watch] on to the start line."[6]

Megill intervened and the Black Watch pushed off at 0800. The evening before, he and his company commanders had carefully observed the ground they were to advance across and targeted any apparent defensible positions for artillery and mortar bombardment.[7] A fire plan had been devised based on 6th Canadian Field Regiment bringing seventy rounds per gun to bear, with added fire from the brigade's heavy mortar platoon and a medium artillery regiment.[8]

With the Fort Garry Horse's 'B' Squadron close behind, the Black Watch advanced quickly while Brecht was shattered by explosions. "Such was the accuracy of the barrage," the battalion's war diarist recorded, "that when the riflemen reached the point where... enemy mortars had been sited, they found all six of his mortars out of commission, and in the area over forty craters from our Medium and Field Artillery shells."[9] A bloody fight ensued. Fire from antitank guns knocked out two of the eight Fort Garry Shermans, but the remaining six pushed on with the infantry and soon were helping to clear the town.[10] By noon, the Germans had been pushed out.

The "stacks of ammunition" the Germans had been forced to abandon served as evidence that they had not been expecting to lose the town. No sooner was Brecht reported taken than the Germans subjected it to heavy shelling and mortaring that further reduced the place to a ruin while snipers picked away from the outskirts.[11] In the fighting at Sint-Lenaarts and Brecht, the Black Watch's casualties numbered 119, with 26 killed. Reinforcements—11 officers and 55 other ranks—lagged badly behind this rate of loss, and the battalion would go into its next battle critically understrength.[12]

With Brecht taken, the Calgary Highlanders started advancing west along the canal towards Eindhoven, about two-thirds of a mile away. If the village fell easily, they would carry on a few hundred yards to a local crossroads that would become the start line for 6th Canadian Infantry Brigade's Queen's Own Cameron Highlanders of Canada. When 'A' and 'C' Companies moved out with six Shermans from the Fort Garry's 'A' Squadron, the squadron tank commander announced cheerfully over the wireless: "Little men now moving forward and Rattler [the tanks] right behind."[13]

One of the "little men" out front was Private Don Muir, who was walking point. Normally, the section corporal did this, but had been too sick. Muir was nervous, worried about snipers, and sure "the first guy" would be the certain target.[14]

With the fields along the canal bordered by hedgerows, the likelihood of snipers or hidden machine-gun positions was high. But Muir and the other Calgarians were fortunate. The advance was little more than a walk in the park, although made noisy as the tanks stopped at the edge of each new field to shell the facing hedgerow, while the infantry advanced across the open. "It was beautiful to watch," recorded the squadron tank commander, "you could observe the trace of our shells, passing in between [the infantry] and over their heads... As soon as they started forward numerous white flags appeared on our front and when we raised our fire, thirty-two scared Jerries came running to our position."[15]

The Calgary Highlander war diarist praised MacLauchlan's "carefully thought-out plan... unfold[ing] itself slowly and semi-magically. Arty and the tanks had a field day and shoots and manoeuvres were clicking like book-drills." Soon the leading troops entered Eindhoven and headed for the tower of a distillery on the opposite side. Eindhoven was secure at 1530 hours and the Highlanders pushed on for the crossroads. With things going so well, however, one company kept right on going—"clearing the village of Locht, securing not only what was to have been the start line for the Camerons of Canada but also their objective!"[16]

Taking advantage of the unexpected gains won by the Calgarians, the Cameron Highlanders started their advance at 1715 hours, marched rapidly to a crossroads near Locht—about one and a half miles southwest of Brecht and two miles short of Lochtenberg—and turned hard north to drive towards Sternhoven, about a mile away. Meeting only light resistance, the two leading companies reported they were in the village at 1850 hours and considered the "objective clear."

This capped a day of welcome progress after the earlier failures in front of the Antwerp–Turnhout Canal. 5 CIB had established a triangle-shaped bridgehead that put 6 CIB on a firm footing for its operations. The security of the bridgehead was evidenced when No. 2 Platoon of 11th Field Company, Royal Canadian Engineers started work at 1600 hours on an eighty-foot-long bridge. This was the second attempt to push a bridge across the canal at the former Westmalle–Brecht road crossing. At 2300 hours the night before, an engineering party had been driven to cover by intense shelling. Five men had been caught by the blast of a single shell. Sappers Roger Charles Dionne and Robert Strahan Milne died instantly. Lance Corporal Arthur Emil Winters succumbed to wounds in an ambulance racing him and several other sappers to the nearest field hospital. Soon after the wounded were taken into the hospital, Sappers Cecil Amos Bell and Frank Arnold Lowe died. During this second bridging attempt, however, the job was completed in less than six hours "without mishap." The bridge was named Keefler Bridge, after 2 CID's acting commander, Brigadier Holly Keefler.[17]

Still, it remained to be seen if 6 CIB could drive the Germans off the rest of the canal and link up with 4th Canadian Infantry Brigade coming out of Antwerp, if that brigade could fight its way north from the city.

ON OCTOBER 2, 4 CIB was to advance on Merksem, the port town that sprawled for a mile along the Albert Canal's northern bank, immediately east of where it met the Scheldt River. Its many port facilities were considered vital, but the town's labyrinth of built-up streets provided ideal defensive positions from which the Germans were able to raid the Canadian lines.

Never one to expose men to unnecessary casualties, Brigadier Fred Cabeldu decided on a cautious approach. First, he instructed Lieutenant Colonel R.M. Lendrum commanding the Royal Regiment of Canada to send a strong patrol under cover of early morning darkness into Merksem. If the Germans were not in strength, the regiment was to advance one company after another into the town and gain control of its centre.[18] This was Lendrum's first battalion command combat test. But Cabeldu believed Lendrum more than competent, for the officer had commanded 'B' Company of the Canadian Scottish Regiment when Cabeldu had led that battalion ashore on D-Day.

When Lendrum had assumed command a couple of weeks earlier, the Royals were in poor shape. The battalion "had been badly depleted by casualties, exhausted with the fighting and movement of the Normandy campaign and the pursuit across France, and more than a little shaken by the hard knocks it had received," the regimental historian judged. Officers and men alike, however, quickly "responded to the sure touch of the new Commanding Officer. A quiet, thoughtful man who was utterly unruffled in action, Lieutenant Colonel Lendrum proved himself a thorough and efficient leader. He hated casualties, and although willing to accept them when necessary, he always tried to minimize them by flexible planning and intelligent tactics."[19] Cabeldu's approach meshed perfectly with Lendrum's instincts.

Not content to limit the attack on Merksem to just one regiment, Cabeldu also ordered the Essex Scottish to enter the town from the west at first light by crossing the Groenendaallaan Bridge. A stiff fight might be required here, as the bridge was overlooked by Groenendaal kasteel, a large château the Germans had heavily fortified. Cabeldu hoped that the later timing of this attack would see most of Merksem already taken by the Royals and convince the Germans not to contest the crossing.

The Royals received welcome reinforcements in the form of a full battalion's worth of Belgian resistance fighters. Merksem was home to many, so they were anxious to participate in its liberation. Lendrum adjusted the order of his battalion's attack to put the Belgians in line behind his first company. Shortly after midnight on October 2, 'C' Company moved out from a stadium near the canal. Following right behind were the Belgians, voluntarily carrying the collapsible assault boats. Many wore white butchers' coats to identify themselves as members of the White Brigade, and 'C' Company's Major E.J.H. "Paddy" Ryall was grateful that there was only a ghost of a moon, for the coats "were more conspicuous than could be wished."[20]

The canal crossing went well and by 0420 hours, 'C' Company was moving towards the heart of Merksem still undetected.[21] As the Belgians began crossing, however, 'C' Company bumped several pockets of Germans and sharp firefights broke out as the Canadians overran these troops. Realizing Merksem was threatened, the Germans immediately began mortaring both sides of the canal.[22] Not used to night fighting, the resistance fighters bunched up. Thirteen were killed and ten seriously wounded, including one man who lost both an arm and a leg.[23] When a party of Belgian stretcher-bearers rushed to gather up the wounded, the Canadians were horrified to see they were all female nurses. "These girls," noted the regiment's historian, "behaved with considerable heroism, but it was nerve-wracking to see women in such a position and becoming casualties. Finally the Belgians were persuaded to leave the fighting to the Canadian soldiers, and most of them reluctantly departed, except for a few who remained to act as guides."

By 0700, 'C' Company controlled the southwestern outskirts of Merksem, and 'D' Company passed through to seize the main square. This was the key to controlling the town, for its five major streets all converged there. Meeting scant resistance, Major R.T. "Bob" Suckling led his company headquarters section and No. 18 Platoon to the square and established firing positions in several of its buildings. The company's other two platoons moved about six hundred yards past the square, along the main highway running from Antwerp on a northeastward axis through the heart of Merksem, and established a strong blocking position to meet any counterattack.

Having set up his wireless in the tramway office overlooking the square, Suckling discovered that the many buildings between his position and the school across the Albert Canal that served as battalion headquarters prevented any communications. In the school principal's office, Lendrum sat helplessly, wondering what was happening in Merksem and how he might help 'D' Company. Suddenly, the principal's telephone jangled on the desk. Reflexively, Lendrum answered and was astonished to hear Suckling's voice. The Belgian scouts had spliced a phone in the tramway office to a strand of telephone wire that the resistance had managed to run across the canal undetected by the Germans. Suckling's voice kept softening, until Lendrum could hardly hear and was afraid the connection was about to be lost.[24] "Bob, why are you whispering?"

"The frigging Germans are just outside the door," Suckling replied.[25] The major estimated his men "were in the midst of over 200 enemy who were marching around the street with a small [antitank] gun looking for the house in which they were located." The Canadians lay doggo, holding their fire until a large group of Germans was concentrated on the street immediately beneath the building in which most of No. 18 Platoon was stationed. From the second-storey windows, the Canadians showered a deadly rain of Type 36 grenades and captured German stick grenades onto the soldiers milling below. The square erupted with explosions and shrapnel that left dozens of Germans screaming and bleeding on the brown cobblestones while the rest scattered.[26]

Soon another large German force began congregating in a nearby park. From the tramway office's second storey, Captain Bill Dunning, the 4th Field Regiment's Forward Observation Officer, shouted his firing instructions downstairs to the Belgian scout, who relayed them to battalion headquarters via the spliced telephone line.[27] Caught in the open by the shellfire, the Germans panicked and fled.[28]

That put an end to serious German contention for Merksem's centre. 'A' Company moved into the town, and that evening the Royals marched forty-four prisoners from the 1018th Grenadier Regiment towards the canal.[29] The resistance fighters had also rounded up twenty-five Belgian ss volunteers, fanatical Nazis who had been left behind and surrendered only after a stiff fight between the two Flemish forces.[30] For the Royals, the operation was an unquestionable success. Casualties were unexpectedly light, just three dead and two wounded. In the early part of the contest, however, one of 'D' Company's platoon commanders, Lieutenant R.W. Davies, had become separated from his men and taken prisoner.[31]

While the Royals had fought for control of the town square, the Essex Scottish attack on Merksem's eastern flank had gone in. 'C' Company, under Major J.W. Burgess, quickly gained control of Groenendaallaan Bridge. All buildings between the bridge and the towering Groenendaal kasteel had been levelled by earlier artillery fire and the ground badly cratered, providing the Germans an ideal position within the three-storey château with its two towers to rake the open ground with fire. Burgess had no option but to lead his men into this killing zone at the run. To their surprise, the Germans offered only fitful resistance and the Essex quickly broke into the building and rounded up fifty-three prisoners. The Essex war diarist described them "as a uniformly miserable type... only too glad to give in when rooted out of their positions."

Lieutenant Colonel John Pangman threw two more companies into the attack on either side of 'C' Company, and the Essex began sweeping through the town on a broad front. The men moved slowly, picking their way up streets strewn with mines. As the soldiers advanced, they were greeted by civilians, "who were extremely glad to see us as they had been short of food and under stress for weeks." When they reached an antitank ditch on the northern outskirts, the Essex stopped for the night. The war diarist cheerfully depicted October 2 as a "lovely day and one on which the crazy battle for Merksem was to reach a culminating point... On the whole, it was a most satisfactory day for the [battalion]... finally succeeded in getting off our backsides and pushing the enemy out of a strong position—one which... he had defended quite well."[32]

But every victory carries its price, and this time the Belgian resistance had paid the most. Captain George Blackburn, a 4th Field Regiment forward observation officer, ended the night billeted in a Merksem cellar along with a number of "pretty young girls from the best families in Antwerp bravely fighting back tears, sitting in a candlelit cellar as they told what they had seen when they came across the canal that afternoon with the Maquis as 'nurses.'"

Assigned to 'A' Company, Blackburn had entered Merksem that evening. By nightfall, the veteran who believed he had seen just about every aspect of combat in Normandy and the drive up the coastline to Belgium, had to admit to being somewhat disoriented by the confusion that went hand-in-hand with fighting in the built-up outskirts around Antwerp. A "story of weird experiences, crossing the Albert Canal in the dark in storm boats, of targets whispered cautiously into public telephones, of a company cut off, of 20-[millimetre] ack ack guns firing down the street, of company headquarters groups locking the door of the house they occupied in unknown territory and sleeping all night having little idea where the rest of the company or the enemy were."[33] The Streetcar War was taking its psychological toll and almost every man in 4 CIB welcomed the fact that they would now march away from the city.

THERE REMAINED, HOWEVER, a substantial roadblock west of Merksem at Oorderen, about five miles north of Antwerp, where the Royal Hamilton Light Infantry and the Germans had been stalemated since September 21. The Germans held a formidable defensive line amid a major railroad marshalling yard just under a mile beyond the town. Such was its strength that each night the Rileys had been obliged to withdraw from Oorderen to avoid being overrun. At dawn, the Germans obligingly withdrew to their defences and the village again passed into Canadian hands. Hoping the loss of Merksem would disrupt the German forces all along the line, Brigadier Fred Cabeldu instructed Lieutenant Colonel Denis Whitaker to gain control of the marshalling yard on October 3.

Twenty-nine-year-old Whitaker was one of the army's youngest regimental commanders. A star Toronto Tigers quarterback and graduate of Royal Military College, he had heroically led his platoon through a maelstrom of fire to gain its objective at Dieppe—one of few units to do so. His valour earned him a Distinguished Service Order. Whitaker had since led the regiment into Normandy, gaining a reputation as a gifted commander destined for rapid promotion. Despite Whitaker's youth, he was a battle-wise officer whose athletic experience enhanced a keen tactical sense.

Tackling the marshalling yard defences head-on would get his men slaughtered. About twice as long as a football field, the yard stood on a height of ground. A series of pillboxes had been distributed at regular intervals across its length, and in between these strongpoints the Germans had dug machine-gun pits beneath freight cars. Whitaker's scouts had reported the night before that the yard held about two hundred defenders, many manning machine guns.

But Whitaker had also had the scouts probe to the west, where the twin track system merged and hooked sharply southwards to enter the port facilities. The scouts confirmed that this flank was lightly defended. If he could get a company in there quietly, they could catch the Germans by surprise. Whitaker decided that he would conduct a feint with the rest of the battalion against the German front while Major Joe Pigott's 'C' Company came in from the left.

To ensure that the Germans had their heads down, Whitaker intended to smother the marshalling yard with supporting fire. In concert with 4th Field Regiment's Major Jack Drewery, a fire plan was devised that included eight 50-calibre Vickers manned by two platoons of the Toronto Scottish Regiment (MG), the 40-millimetre Bofors anti-aircraft guns of two troops of an anti-aircraft regiment, a troop of 17-pounder antitank guns from 2nd Canadian Anti-Tank Regiment, all twenty-four field guns of the 4th Field, and sixteen additional 3.7-inch anti-aircraft guns. While some of this firepower would be directed at identified strongpoints, the guns of 4th Field would provide an unusual variant of a creeping barrage by moving at right angles from west to east in lifts of one hundred yards every four minutes, directly along 'C' Company's line of advance from the west, across the breadth of the marshalling yard.[34]

Whitaker considered the twenty-three-year-old Pigott a crack company commander who had proven himself both courageous and skillful. Unlike most everyone else in the regiment, Pigott had retained the body armour issued at the beginning of the Normandy campaign and still wore it whenever he went into battle. Over three thousand of the British-made individual light armour protection units had been issued to 2nd Canadian Infantry Division. Weighing about 2.5 pounds, the armour consisted of three sections of canvas-covered, one-millimetre-thick manganese steel plate—the same composition used in Commonwealth helmets—linked by webbing that offered general protection from the shoulders to just above the groin.[35] Although well-padded, because it was designed to be worn under the battle dress tunic rather than over it, the plates tended to chafe and promote heavy perspiration. They also hampered rapid movement. Consequently, most of the troops had quickly abandoned them. Pigott doggedly wore his and on at least one occasion the armour prevented a serious, possibly fatal wound.[36]

When Whitaker outlined his attack plan at 1630 hours on October 2, it was clear that 'C' Company could use any protective armour available.[37] This isn't going to work, Pigott thought. "If Jerry ever looked to his right and saw us coming down between the rows of boxcars...well, he'd have us like pins in a bowling alley."[38]

Keeping his reservations to himself, Pigott assembled his men on the start line before dawn. Faces blackened and in stocking feet for quiet movement, the men waited tensely. Whitaker and Drewery were nearby in a red-brick steeple. At 0545 hours, the quiet night was split asunder as the guns opened up and Pigott led his men into the attack. They stole along a cinder-coated roadbed that ran the length of the marshalling yard, the shells advancing in lifts as planned to their front.[39] Three 17-pounders from 'C' Troop of the 2nd Canadian Anti-Tank Regiment were blasting out rounds as fast as the loaders could slam them into the breech. Two of their guns were targeting freight cars that protected machine-gun pits and the other a mortar position.[40]

From the steeple, Whitaker and Drewery were horrified to see that the fire from one of 4th Field Regiment's 25-pounders was lagging, failing to keep up with the assigned lifts, so that the shot fell right into Pigott's path. Whitaker knew he had seconds to make a decision that might cost the lives of his company—order Pigott to abort to avoid being exposed to the gun's shells or do nothing and hope for the best. Aborting now, he decided, would likely result in 'C' Company suffering just as many casualties trying to break off the action as the shells might inflict. The lieutenant colonel kept quiet, letting events run their course.[41]

The gamble paid out as Pigott's men pressed forward rapidly. As the shells lifted the next hundred yards, 'C' Company was already dashing into the area of the previous concentration to overrun most of the Germans before they could recover. Fortunately, the shot from the errant artillery gun fell wide and caused no casualties. At the head of No. 13 Platoon, Lieutenant A.A.H. Parker was badly wounded in the hip at the attack's outset. "Scarcely able to walk," he hobbled the thousand yards required to bring his men to their final objective before agreeing to be evacuated. His courage and determination earned him a Military Cross.

At 0630 hours, just forty-five minutes after crossing the start line, Pigott signalled Whitaker that the marshalling yards were taken.[42] Although the attack had gone smoothly, it was no cakewalk. Four men were dead, another twenty-one wounded—more than 25 per cent of Pigott's troops.[43] All the casualties had been inflicted by small-arms fire, most from snipers bypassed during the advance who opened up from the rear. These were rooted out of their positions or chased away by a platoon of 'B' Company, which then became entangled in a field of Schützenmines (S-mines) while returning to Oorderen. Several of the spring-loaded canisters were tripped, and unleashed their 350-ball-bearing loads at a height of three feet with deadly effect. The same fate had befallen a patrol from 'B' Company the night before. Taken together, the company lost two men killed and twelve wounded to this deadly form of mine.[44]

When Whitaker and Drewery went forward to Pigott's position at 0700, he reported having killed or wounded about thirty Germans and was holding eighty prisoners—all from the 711th Infantry Division.[45] Whitaker thought the young officer much relieved that, despite its losses, his fears that 'C' Company would be wiped out had not materialized.[46]

EAST OF OORDEREN, 6th Canadian Infantry Brigade had passed through the lines of 5th Canadian Infantry Brigade near Brecht on October 2 and pushed westwards towards 4th Canadian Infantry Brigade. The South Saskatchewan Regiment and Queen's Own Cameron Highlanders of Canada led, with the former moving along the canal to conclude the unfinished business of seizing Lochtenberg, while the latter struck out northwestwards to secure Kamp van Brasschaat. This was an attack in depth, the front extending almost three miles north from the canal to the former Belgian military base.

Under heavy morning cloud, the South Saskatchewans followed two parallelling roads from Locht towards the objective three miles away. Little opposition was encountered until 0730 hours, when 'D' Company on the inland road and 'B' Company next to the canal were within a mile of Lochtenberg. Both companies faced a dense deciduous forest with heavy undergrowth that provided excellent concealment. Suddenly, from its edge "came every type of fire imaginable." Machine guns, at least one antitank gun, a number of small mortars, and light arms spat out fire at close range. A shell struck a Bren carrier bearing 'D' Company's lunch ration, setting it afire. Caught in the open, the infantry hit the dirt and would have been pinned there had the Fort Garry Horse's 'B' Squadron not been grinding along in its wake. Growling up alongside the most forward platoons, the tankers hammered the woods with 75-millimetre gunfire and raking bursts from the machine guns. Captain G. McLean, the 6th Field Regiment FOO, called down a thick rain of artillery fire that shattered tree trunks and sent shards of wood whizzing through the air with the same deadly force as the steel shrapnel released by the exploding rounds.[47]

When the German fire lessened, the infantry dashed into the woods and were soon sending prisoners back. At first, they came by ones and twos, then ten at a time, then almost twenty. By 1200 hours, fifty-four Germans had surrendered—infantry, artillerymen, and anti-aircraft gunners hastily cobbled together to resist the Canadian advance. Thirty minutes later, the lead companies reported in from Lochtenberg, and the "objective that had almost been ours once before, only a few days ago, was finally in our hands," wrote the regiment's war diarist. "There would be no withdrawal over the canal this time."[48]

Villagers came out to meet them and turned over four pay books taken off the bodies of South Saskatchewan men killed in the first two attacks. The villagers had managed to bury these four soldiers where they had fallen. But the corpses of other dead Saskatchewans remained unburied, because the Germans had driven the Belgians off with machine-gun fire whenever they attempted to form a burial party. One of the unburied men was identified as Major Harry Williams, who had led 'B' Company on its ill-fated September 24 assault.[49]

North of Lochtenberg, the advance by the Camerons had ground to a halt in the face of stiff resistance at about 1630 hours, after 'B' Company and supporting tanks from the Fort Garry Horse's 'C' Squadron had gone only a thousand yards beyond the start line. The advance was through dense woods, so the tankers "were road-bound" to a single column and unable to manoeuvre. Sergeant Gerald Jorgenson, commanding the leading troop, noted with concern that the infantry appeared unused to working with tanks—likely because about half their number were recent reinforcements with no combat experience. Most seemed poorly trained. When a German defensive line opened up from some facing woods with heavy machine-gun and antitank fire, the advance stalled despite the tankers being able to rapidly knock out two of what they believed were three 88-millimetre guns.[50] The remaining gun, however, proved too well placed and its fire forced the infantry to ground.

It soon became evident that the position could be taken only with heavy casualties, so Lieutenant Colonel Ernest Payson Thompson—at twenty-three, the youngest battalion commander in the Canadian army—recalled the force to reorganize for a more robust attack the next day. By 2200 hours, infantry and tankers were back at the start line. Casualties had been light, but among the dead was Captain Edward James Reid, the twenty-eight-year-old acting company commander from Manitoba, who held a Military Cross from an earlier engagement.[51]

That night, to everyone's surprise at the Camerons' headquarters, a four-man patrol under Sergeant Andy Rylasdaam made it across ground bathed in bright moonlight into the very heart of Kamp van Brasschaat and its surrounding hamlet without encountering German resistance. Establishing contact with some Belgian civilians, they spent the night comfortably in the hamlet's centre, returning just before dawn with their report. By then the weather had turned dirty, and at 1000 hours the regiment kicked off a renewed attack, advancing through icy drizzle. Against only token resistance, the Camerons made good progress, reporting the camp in their hands at 1230 hours and eighty-two prisoners taken.[52]

October 3 also proved a good day for the South Saskatchewan Regiment, which moved directly east away from where the Antwerp–Turnhout Canal bent south just outside Lochtenberg, and marched on Brasschaat. The two-and-a-half-mile advance proceeded quickly, despite the need to eliminate light pockets of resistance all along the way, and the leading 'A' Company entered the town at 1800 hours. "Rarely have troops been received so warmly with flowers, kisses, apples, kisses, beer, kisses, and much handclasping and smiles. Many Belgians were crying with emotion." During the last two days, the regiment had suffered four dead and twenty-four others wounded.[53]

By the following day, 6 CIB had secured a solid base west from Kamp van Brasschaat to Kapellen and tied in with 4 CIB advancing north from Antwerp, with its left shoulder anchored on the Scheldt River at Oorderen. This put 2nd Canadian Infantry Division in place to advance from Merksem towards Bergen op Zoom and cut off the South Beveland isthmus.[54]

[9]

Close to the Danger Line

Like an unseasonable snow, leaflets released from the bomb bays of two B-17 Flying Fortresses of the United States Air Force's 406th Squadron drifted onto Walcheren Island on October 2. Leave the island or find a "safe place," read the thousands of white notices that farmers gathered in from fields, children chased down in schoolyards, and housewives swept up off brick walks leading to tidy houses and apartments. The same message repeated on Radio Oranje in England, listened to on clandestine radios.

Thirty-six-year-old Willem Gabrielse had been digging potatoes on his farm near Westkapelle when the leaflet snow began. He and others heatedly discussed the warning notice; everyone agreed that a severe, prolonged aerial bombardment must be about to target enemy troops and installations on the Dutch islands in the Scheldt estuary.[1] The leaflet warned that all "roads, canals, transport lines, power stations, railway yards or sheds, warehouses and depots, enemy concentration of all kinds—are the centres of danger. Leave their vicinity immediately." This left few options. Travel only by foot. Stay off roads. Stick to the fields and carry little. Avoid congregating in groups for risk of being mistaken for German forces. Avoid low-lying ground and military objectives until the Allies liberated the islands.[2]

Low places, roads, concentrations—all Walcheren was one or the other. The island was a saucer that would be sea were it not for the great encircling dykes. And how could they get off the island? The Sloedam, that narrow causeway linking it to South Beveland, was guarded by German troops and undoubtedly one of the likeliest "centres of danger." So where to go? And perhaps, despite the island's many coastal batteries that guarded the approaches to the West Scheldt estuary, it would not be targeted anyway. One of those batteries was emplaced immediately north of Westkapelle, dug in behind the dyke on that rare instance of Walcheren ground above sea level. More batteries were nearby, either facing the North Sea or covering the West Scheldt's mouth.

In September, the Royal Air Force had attacked several of these batteries, inflicting little damage. But the bombing had been pinpointed, and consequently, few civilian injuries resulted. Surely the same would be true for any new raids. Stay away from the battery north of town and they should be safe. Fleeing was impossible; even the open fields were strewn with mines. Having watched the German engineers sowing the mines in the fields close to Westkapelle, everyone knew the areas to avoid. But of the fields beyond they knew nothing. In the open, there would also be no protection from the bombs, while at home most had built or identified possible shelters: the cellar of a nearby windmill, an inner room in a stout building down the street, or a trench dug in the garden behind the house. Advising flight was absurd. Even if they reached the Sloedam, the Germans would turn them back unless they had an official pass.[3] Close to 100,000 civilians called Walcheren Island home. About a quarter of these dwelt in Middelburg, but since the bombings of September another 25,000 had sought refuge behind the city's medieval walls. Situated inland, Middelburg was strategically irrelevant.

By grim mischance, hardly a single notice had fallen upon Westkapelle itself, so the imminent danger was less comprehended there than elsewhere on the island. The gun batteries, people agreed, would be the target. Nobody thought of the great dyke that held back the North Sea and made life on Walcheren possible. It had stood since the fifteenth century. Even as they blessed its existence, it had been there all their lives and so seemed immutable.[4]

Consequently, on the morning of October 3, as 252 Lancaster bombers lumbered off landing strips and struggled into formation, the people of Westkapelle went about as normal with only a slightly anxious eye turned westwards for aircraft. Seven Mosquitos of No. 8 (Pathfinder Force) Group RAF preceded Nos. 1, 3, and 5 Bomber Groups.[5] The Mosquitos that would mark the bombing site for the Lancasters arrived over the dyke just south of Westkapelle at 1300 hours.[6] Each of the two-engine planes released phosphorous flares, known as Christmas Trees, to delineate the target for the Lancaster bombardiers.

The anti-aircraft guns that bristled on Walcheren immediately went into action, flinging streams of fire at the bombers slowly droning in waves of thirty Lancasters, flying at about five thousand feet altitude because of the low overcast. For the next two hours, bombs showered down, a total of 1,262 tons of explosives. When the last bombers broke away, their bombardiers reported "the sea pouring through a gap in the wall and spreading about three quarters of a mile inland." The raid's finale was to have involved several bombers dropping massive Tallboy bombs loaded with 12,000 pounds of explosive to penetrate deep into the dyke in order to cause an earthquake-like effect. Because the dyke was already successfully breached, these planes returned home without releasing their loads. Not a single bomber was lost to the "large amount of flak." No. 84 Group soon had reconnaissance aircraft overhead that confirmed "the gap was about 75 yards in width while the sea was rapidly covering the fields south of Westkapelle."[7]

On the ground, chaos reigned. When the Mosquitos dropped their flares, the citizens of Westkapelle realized that a raid was imminent. People ran in every direction to seek shelter, forty-five crowding into the confines of a cellar under the large De Roos Molen (Rose Mill) windmill. Despite the marking flares, there was nothing precise about the bombs' falling patterns. The Lancasters rained explosives all through the town and neighbouring farms. Much of Westkapelle ceased to exist during two hours of hell.

In the windmill's cellar, thirty-eight-year-old Jo Theune huddled in the entranceway. The mill, which stood close to the dyke, was her father's. In the opening moments of the raid, the obstetrical nurse had helped him carry her bedridden mother to its cellar. Accompanying them had been one of Jo's brothers, his wife, and their fourteen-year-old and seven-year-old daughters, as well as the son of another sibling. Seeing the bombers approaching from the west, the dark depths of the cellar before them, the two girls had taken fright and refused to go inside. Running out of time, the one brother led his family away to seek shelter elsewhere.

The concussion of the blasts from the first wave of bombs shook the mill to its foundations. Then an eerie silence descended. It was pitch dark, dust and grain chaff drifting down from the ceiling to coat heads and shoulders. "The bombers are done, gone," someone whispered. Everyone spilled out into the daylight. Jo Theune circled the mill, noting with dismay the large cracks opened in its walls. She was informing her father when the drone of engines warned of another wave. No sooner had they crowded back inside than the ground shook wildly as bombs exploded around the mill. Theune's mother moaned that she was feeling badly and Jo rushed to get water from a bucket by the entrance. Just as she reached the bucket, a bomb struck the mill itself.

"Everything came down, stone, beams, bags of grain and dust, dust everywhere," Theune said later. She was unable to see, barely able to move, trapped in the rubble. Deep in the cellar, people screamed and sobbed. Some had been crushed under great blocks of stone. Most were trapped, separated from others by fallen timbers and stones. Then the water began trickling in. People called to each other in the darkness that it must be flowing in from a ditch behind the mill. But a man tasted it and anxiously announced that it was salty. Realization dawned. The dyke was broken.

Slowly, inexorably, the seawater seeped in, rising higher and higher. Theune was at the top of the cellar stairs by the door—farther from the floor than anyone else. She repeatedly called out to her father and mother, but received no reply. None of the others below knew where they were. People kept talking back and forth, reporting what was happening in their little pockets. Theune tried to recognize voices, to call out names and ask how they were doing. Surely rescuers must be coming, Jo Theune assured them, becoming more frightened by the moment. Slowly the number of voices lessened, one no longer replying, then another.

The water was now closing in on her nephew. They will come soon, Jo assured him. "But it's taking so long, auntie, will the Lord Jesus not help us?" the boy replied. Those were his last words. Then there was only herself and a neighbour—Joost Janisse with his baby Cornelia. He was pinned inside a tight pocket, thrusting his daughter with his arms up into a narrow little gap above his head, the water rising slowly up his body. His wife had been by his side when the mill collapsed. But he could not reach her now, had no idea where she was, or if she lived.

Groping about, Theune found a small opening through interlocked fragments of timbers and stone, began moving slowly up through the tight spaces, gaining precious inches that lifted her above the relentlessly rising water. Wriggling into a crevice, she stuck fast, and could go neither forward nor backward. The water pooled blackly below her, the landing by the door now submerged. If she slipped out of the crevice, the pool would have her. Jo Theune tried not to move.

Then voices came. She heard men exclaim with joy as they freed Janisse and his baby. "Keep calling out," the men urged Jo, as they sawed through timbers, pulled aside stones with bare hands—frantically clearing a path through the ruin, guided by her voice. Soon they carefully extracted her from the dangerously unstable rubble. Jo's body was completely black and blue, she had serious internal bruising, and blood streamed from one arm and leg. Unable to walk, she was carried to safety. She, Janisse, and his baby were the only survivors.[8]

Between the bombing and the immediate flooding, about one-third of Westkapelle was reduced to ruins. More civilians died from the explosions than drowned. Some burned to death when flares from the Mosquitos set houses alight. Some were crushed when trenches dug behind their homes for shelters collapsed from the concussion waves rolling through the ground. Cellars caved in on others. People nearby witnessed the wreckage of Westkapelle buildings thrown hundreds of feet into the air by the explosions. About 160 residents of Westkapelle died on October 3, but the suffering on Walcheren had only begun. Through the deceptively narrow-looking breach the sea continued to flow, spilling outwards from Westkapelle across the fields to engulf other villages and towns.

"RAF SINKS DUTCH island to silence Nazi guns," blared the October 4 London *Daily Herald* front-page banner headline. The guns of Walcheren were all silenced, drowned, their garrisons forced to run for their lives. Both the *Herald* and its competitor, the *Daily Express*, shared the delusion that the Tallboy bombs had been dropped and many gun positions destroyed. The guns had been the objective, the papers asserted. The *Express* also claimed that Vlissingen and Middelburg were flooded.

Radio Oranje offered a more accurate assessment, noting that although Westkapelle was flooded along with about 175 acres of surrounding countryside, the entire island would not be submerged. But as each high tide propelled more waves through the dyke's breach, greater flooding would result. "We had to make this sacrifice," the announcer assured the people of Walcheren. "The German batteries had to be washed away, and this is a great step towards the liberation. The men guilty of this are in one place only, in Berlin."[9]

Quick to capitalize on the deliberateness of the breaching, the German propaganda machine tried to win public opinion by claiming a catastrophe. Five thousand killed, German-controlled Dutch newspapers claimed.[10] "An evil work of destruction, the water... flooding into Zeeland's most beautiful island. Walcheren, treasure house of a centuries-old culture, became a prey to the waves."[11]

The islanders were not misled. While lamenting the loss of life and property damage, few shifted their loyalties to the Nazis or hoped the Allies did not soon liberate them. In the days that followed, Westkapelle gathered its dead out of the ruins, burying 138 in temporary graves. During one of the burial ceremonies, Meester W.F.P. Kurtz, the German-appointed acting mayor, scolded the assembled citizens that they could thank their Allied friends for the deaths. A stony silence greeted this remark, and then the people as one turned and walked from the cemetery without a word. Kurtz was left by the graves, alone, scorned.[12]

The destruction caused to Westkapelle from the bombs and subsequent flooding rendered it largely uninhabitable. By evening of October 3, most people had left, going to villages inland in hopes that the sea would not reach that far. Local experts, who had spent years gauging water volumes as they managed and built the dykes, estimated that two million cubic metres had flowed in prior to the ebb tide and half had then returned to the North Sea. Predictions were that all of Walcheren lying west of a long canal that bisected it from Veere on the north coast to Vlissingen would be inundated within three weeks' time.[13]

Breaching the dyke at Westkapelle had, however, been Bomber Command's feasibility test and the results had surpassed expectations. When several bombs fitted with delayed timing fuses exploded the following day, the added damage combined with the inflowing water to double the gap's width. Based on the success of this first raid, bombing other outer dykes was approved to hasten the flooding. This was expected to "completely disorganize the enemy's communications, immobilize his reinforcements and at the same time put out of action a number of his defence works. Furthermore the assault forces would be able to take advantage of the floods by swimming through the breach in amphibious vehicles and operating behind the enemy's forward positions."[14]

Little damage had been inflicted on military installations, though, and no German casualties resulted. Oberkommando der Wehrmacht reported on October 4 that the defence of Walcheren "was not significantly affected by the flooding. Only a few positions are out of action." South Holland's German naval commander, Captain Aschmann, noted that, while two radar stations near Westkapelle had been disabled, they had not taken direct hits and would soon be repaired. Shortly after the raid, Aschmann arrived from Vlissingen by car to examine the damage first-hand. "Great destruction in the village, so that it is no longer possible to pass through it," he wrote.

"Between Zoutelande [a coastal village three miles south] and Westkapelle the water has risen so high that the car can only be driven through at a walking pace... The whole area around the breach is so ploughed up that it is impossible to approach it with vehicles."[15]

While the October 3 Westkapelle raid proved that breaching the Walcheren dykes was possible, RAF high command remained opposed to diverting bomber squadrons from missions over Germany for operations in support of First Canadian Army. The Canadians, they believed, had become "bomb happy," calling for air support whenever German opposition stiffened. In a strange twist of logic, Chief of Air Staff, Air Chief Marshal Sir Charles Porter declared that "the constant application of heavy bombers to the land battle, when it is not essential and its only purpose is to save casualties, must inevitably lead to the demoralization of the army." Eisenhower's Deputy Supreme Commander, Air Chief Marshal Arthur Tedder, wholeheartedly agreed. "We are now, I am afraid, beginning to see the results in precisely that demoralization of which you speak," he replied. "The repeated calls by the Canadian Army for heavy bomber effort... is in my opinion only too clear an example. It is going to be extremely difficult to get things back on a proper footing."[16]

Even before the bombers flew towards Westkapelle, Tedder and other RAF commanders were obstinately lobbying Eisenhower to reverse his earlier promise that First Canadian Army would receive priority air support in compensation for his decision not to employ airborne troops against South Beveland and Walcheren. Bomber Command and the Eighth Air Force, he had assured Crerar and Simonds, would provide "complete saturation of the targets you select. All medium bombers will also be made available to assist."[17]

This assurance in hand, Simonds had based his plans on the belief that not only could he expect the dykes breached as required to flood the island, but also that bombers would be available for "prolonged air preparation" against the heavily fortified gun batteries guarding it. While RAF had come through with three raids in September against selected batteries—including the one at Westkapelle—their scale had been relatively small, just 616 tons of ordnance dropped, with minimal damage inflicted. RAF thereafter rejected conducting a prolonged campaign to smash the batteries, sheltered in strong concrete bunkers, until immediately prior to Walcheren's actual invasion.

Air Marshal Trafford Leigh-Mallory, in the process of winding down the Allied Expeditionary Air Force he had commanded through its support of the Normandy invasion, argued RAF's case to Eisenhower. "If we have to concentrate what would amount to the major proportion of our bomber forces on Walcheren for so long a period, the enemy would be free to concentrate his fighter effort in the forward areas, his communications and military build up would progress to a large extent unimpeded, and he would be given an opportunity to recuperate his oil and industrial resources which we know are now so seriously depleted. It is, therefore, most important that the maximum bombing effort should be directed against Germany." Leigh-Mallory proposed subjecting Walcheren to limited attacks against selected targets, such as the dykes and a few specific batteries, and then three days prior to the assault and during it implementing a heavy bombing program. Such raids, he argued, would cause as much damage as would a prolonged effort because the Germans would not have time to make repairs. RAF airily dismissed arguments that it took a great bomb tonnage to destroy concrete positions from the air and that, when damaged, such constructions could not be quickly repaired.

Despite his promise, Eisenhower was swayed and offered Leigh-Mallory "general agreement." When the case was put to Montgomery, the Twenty-First Army Group commander wrote, "I agree with you." Limited attacks for now against select targets to flood the island and "generally disturb enemy morale," then three to four days before the assault, "we should fairly let them have everything we have got."[18] Having lost Montgomery's backing, Simonds could do nothing but watch bleakly as First Canadian Army was stripped of its high priority on bomber support. RAF attacks through October, particularly against Walcheren, would be on a limited scale.

The air support cutbacks were symptomatic of a predilection running from Eisenhower down to Montgomery to assert the urgent need for First Canadian Army to open the approaches to Antwerp while simultaneously denying the means to do so. On October 2,

Simonds had learned that the British and American offensives towards the Ruhr would have first call on all supplies. The Canadians could make do with leftovers.[19]

Only one man in high command seemed to grasp the difficulties the Canadians faced and kept his attention firmly fixed on the need to open Antwerp to Allied shipping before the armies ground to a halt for want of supply. Admiral Sir Bertram Ramsay, the Naval Commander-in-Chief, persistently reminded Eisenhower and his staff that nothing should have greater priority. He rode Montgomery equally hard. On October 1, Ramsay personally directed that an assortment of Landing Craft, Tank being used as cross-Channel shuttles be taken off this service so their crews could prepare for the forthcoming assault on Walcheren. Montgomery's headquarters staff at Twenty-First Army Group immediately protested that losing these vessels from the shuttle service would "interfere with operations having a higher priority."

Ramsay shot back that he "knew of no operation with priority" over Infatuate and that the Supreme Commander's Chief of Staff had confirmed this. Two days later, Ramsay visited Simonds at First Canadian Army headquarters in Belgium to make a personal assessment. Beforehand, the Twenty-First Army Group Chief of Staff, Major General Freddie de Guingand, had telephoned Simonds's Chief of Staff, Brigadier General Churchill Mann, and demanded that the Canadians mention nothing that might lead the naval officer to "become concerned as a result of the priorities being given to British Second Army op[erations] within [Twenty-First Army Group.]"[20] Loyal troopers, Simonds and Mann kept their lips zipped—giving no inkling that British Second Army was pushing hard for the Ruhr on a trajectory that required 1 British Corps to direct its operations, not to support 11 Canadian Corps in cutting off and then clearing South Beveland, but instead to support the British forces. Ramsay was not fooled. He knew what Montgomery was doing and loudly decried it, even arguing that the drive towards the Ruhr should be abandoned until the port was opened.

Simonds, however, strengthened the impression that First Canadian Army faced no undo difficulties completing its assignment despite the paucity of manpower, external support, and supplies. He complained neither to Montgomery nor anyone else, and merely pointed out to his corps commanders on October 2 that the Ruhr offensives "have a prior call on administrative resources" and that it was "necessary for First Canadian Army to clear the Western flank of British Second Army by a thrust North Eastwards." The consequence that this left II Canadian Corps to clear the Scheldt alone was accepted without question.[21] Privately, however, some of his staff referred to the campaign to open Antwerp as a Cinderella operation, to which Allied command gave more "lip service than practical priority."[22]

II Canadian Corps was terribly understrength, particularly where it most mattered on the sharp end of the infantry battalions. During the Normandy campaign, the three divisions had suffered heavier casualty rates among infantrymen than Canadian Military Headquarters (CMHQ) had planned for. By September, although there was a 13,000-man reinforcement surplus, the pool was short 2,000 infantry-qualified soldiers. When Market Garden failed and First Canadian Army descended into the bitter fight for the Scheldt, the only way to rectify the deficiency was to commit conscripted Canadians to combat—precisely what the Canadian government had promised would not happen when the National Resources Mobilization Act (NRMA) was imposed in 1940.[23]

The NRMA had divided Canada's military into two tiers, with those Canadians volunteering for regular service designated for General Service (GS) and the conscripts facing other assignments. The GS volunteers could be assigned either for General Service, Overseas (GSO) or retained for home defence duties. Meanwhile, conscripts were liable for service only in the western hemisphere. Generally, that meant assignment within Canada and the certainty of avoiding combat. This was a domestic political strategy to head off a situation like the Great War conscription crisis that had caused unrest, particularly among Quebecois.

By fall of 1944, there were approximately 390,000 GSO-designated army officers and soldiers. Of these, about 254,000 were in northwest Europe, Italy, and the United Kingdom. A majority of

158,000 were already serving in field formations, either with First Canadian Army in northwest Europe or 1 Canadian Corps in Italy, and the rest were allocated to service units. Total strength of the five fighting divisions was about 85,000, of which only about 39,000 were infantry. As Lieutenant General Tommy Burns, who commanded 1 Canadian Corps through the Gothic Line battle of August–September 1944, noted with some consternation, from 390,000 men, the army remarkably "could not find the bodies to reinforce the... infantry." Adapting a metaphor of Winston Churchill's, Burns said that "the tail kept growing vastly, the teeth little."[24]

By October, it was commonplace for infantry battalions to be 25 per cent, or 200 men, understrength. A battalion's four rifle companies routinely fielded only 75 to 80 men instead of the mandated 127. The situation was most desperate among the French-Canadian regiments. On September 1, Les Fusiliers Mont-Royal was short 333 infantrymen and Le Régiment de Maisonneuve 276.[25]

The impact such shortages had on morale among the "old sweats," who had survived the Normandy campaign and still marched northwards with no end in sight, was serious. After the heavy casualties in September's fights for the canals, it was difficult to believe they would not all be killed or wounded. Fatigue, one Maisonneuve officer reported, was a growing problem, and this prompted "first class soldiers" to risk punishment for being Away Without Leave as this "was the only way they could get any rest." This regiment, the officer said, routinely sent rifle companies into attacks with only about forty men.[26] All too often, these badly depleted battalions were incapable of winning the objective assigned.

To alleviate the shortage, rear areas were scoured for excess personnel that could be sent to the infantry units. Cooks, typists, mechanics, electricians, anybody could suddenly be presented with an infantrymen's kit and assigned to a rifle battalion. Most of these soldiers had long forgotten even rudimentary infantry skills, so feeding them into the front lines little bolstered a battalion's fighting ability. The Black Watch diarist lamented "the critical situation now existing in the [battalion,] resulting from the great percentage of our reinforcements being personnel" from rear-area units "who with very little training are sent forward as infantry. This is our greatest problem and the solution is not yet in sight as the necessary training time is evidently not available."[27]

Veteran troops generally considered these men as much a hazard as the Germans, a fact that Captain George Blackburn had realized when he encountered a two-man Royal Regiment of Canada patrol consisting of a sergeant and a private walking along a street in newly liberated Merksem. A Sten gun the private carried awkwardly, slung over his shoulder with the barrel pointed down, suddenly went off. As Blackburn felt something sting the calf of his left leg, the young soldier said, "That's the third time it's done that this morning." Looking at the weapon in puzzlement, he proceeded to point the muzzle directly at Blackburn's stomach. Seeing that the safety was not engaged, Blackburn quickly pushed the barrel away and ordered the private to secure his weapon. The soldier, who admitted to being a cook until sent to the Royals, confessed he had no idea what Blackburn meant. After getting well out of the cook's line of fire, Blackburn determined he had suffered a minor flesh wound that was determined insufficiently serious to warrant a hospital stay.[28]

Even reinforcements drawn from the designated infantry pool were proving poorly trained. The Black Watch war diarist reported that most of the reinforcements it was receiving were "a good lot, with all sorts of confidence and a truly aggressive spirit," but were also "inexperienced and like to dash out to see what is happening if an air burst or shell goes off anywhere in the neighbourhood." Many were soon "throwing grenades and firing the PIAT for the first time."[29]

One Canadian training instructor in the United Kingdom took specific interest in a soldier who, upon arriving at No. 2 Canadian Infantry Reinforcement Unit, failed basic tests on the Bren gun, the Thompson submachine gun, all forms of grenades, and the PIAT. During an interview, the young Torontonian told the instructor he had enlisted on March 7, 1944 and been sent to Brantford, Ontario for eight weeks' training. This he completed on May 26, but during that time the soldier had been assigned light duty and exempted from training for four weeks. He was also excused from all but two of the route marches intended to physically toughen recruits. Sent to the

Advanced Training Centre at Camp Borden for a week, he was again assigned light duty for its duration. Posted next to a Calgary training centre for two months, a gas stove explosion resulted in an injury that had him off duty for three weeks. In all his time in Calgary, the soldier fired one smoke bomb and two high-explosive bombs from a two-inch mortar, but was unable to meet basic rifle and Bren gun standards. Sent overseas on September 1, he was made a hut orderly. Again, he received only the most rudimentary weapons training during this time before being sent to a battalion. Although on paper this soldier had received several months of training, the instructor realized he had acquired only twelve weeks' experience.[30] Nothing about this man's story would have surprised the "old sweats," who were daily encountering such soldiers.

Understrength battalions and almost nonstop operations led Revered Robert Lowder Seaborn, the Canadian Scottish Regiment's Protestant chaplain, to argue in a paper requested by 3rd Canadian Infantry Division's senior divisional chaplain that morale was "close to the danger line." The popular padre, who had won a Military Cross during the Juno Beach fighting for carrying wounded to safety while under fire, plainly stated that "a soldier has nothing pleasant to look forward to except the end of hostilities. He feels there is no nearer goal in sight, when he will be able to relax in safety and comfort. His only other chance of a change from the hard and exacting life is to be wounded and have a spell in hosp[ital], and perhaps thus reach England and have some leave. Another alternative of release is, of course, his death in action... He has gone on from one phase of the campaign to another and is both bitter, discouraged and tired; and still has been given no assurance of a time when, or of conditions under which, he will get leave. This matter of leave is a major factor in this worsening of morale... Periods of rest are not frequent enough to keep the soldier fresh enough to have spirit for fighting. A rest period of seven days after nearly two months, and another beginning after two more months, is not sufficient to keep men up to par. The men are worn out."

Treatment of wounded further lowered morale, he said. "Some men who were wounded and hospitalized in England received no leave before being sent to Reinf[orcement] Units and back to the [battalion.] This is considered to be unjust in the extreme. Further, when a man goes to a RU after a period of action, he is treated 'not (to quote a man) as a hero but as a damned fool.'" The officers and NCOs staffing these units were described as stupid, ignorant, and overbearing. "The soldier returns to his unit with a grudge and with resentment towards the army. He is glad to be back only because he is, in a battalion, treated as a human being and is among friends."[31]

Seriously contributing to the growing resentment of the line troops was the entire NRMA plan. That wounded were being rushed back to units immediately upon recovery because of manpower shortages was not lost on them. Nor was the fact that back in Canada, about 60,000 NRMA troops were sitting out the war in relative comfort and without any great risk. "Zombies" was one of the kinder epithets assigned these soldiers. Observing the troops under his command, listening to their gripes, Lieutenant General Burns had concluded that most "thought that if the Zombies would not go overseas of their own free will, the government should compel them to... They were asking whether the Canadian people realized what it meant to them to face death or wounding, to suffer hardship in a country so far from home. The soldier could not believe that if this were truly understood, the people would fail to support the troops at the front by taking any action required."[32]

From the NRMA's inception, the military had sought without much success to encourage inducted troops to volunteer for General Service, Overseas. Underage Private Charles "Chic" Goodman, a GS volunteer who found his battle training at Camp Vernon involved live firing and field craft that served him well overseas, was present for one choreographed attempt to convert NRMA troops. Goodman had been part of a battalion-sized draft bound from Camp Vernon—British Columbia's largest military camp—for the United Kingdom. Shortly before the troops shipped out, Pacific Command's Major General George Pearkes attended a full camp parade. Three isolated groups were arrayed on the parade ground. Goodman and the other men headed overseas made up one, the other GS soldiers still undergoing battle training a second, and the NRMA men awaiting western hemisphere assignments a third. The fifty-six-year-old Pearkes had risen from the rank of trooper during the Great War to command a battalion and—having earned a DSO, MC, and even the Victoria Cross for heroism during the bloodbath of Passchendaele in 1918—was Canada's most decorated soldier. Like many senior commanders, Pearkes believed reliance on volunteers to be a misguided policy that no longer delivered the numbers needed for First Canadian Army. Under a warm Okanagan sun, from the reviewing stand, the well-spoken Pearkes delivered "an impassioned talk about going to defend your country and so on and then the commander of the camp stepped forward and said: 'These people are now proceeding overseas,' grandly pointing towards Goodman and the others in one formation. 'All those who wish to join their comrades, one step forward, march.' Not a man moved," Goodman observed. Disgusted, Pearkes stormed from the podium. The NRMA men returned to their barracks without a glance over their shoulders as Goodman and the overseas volunteers gathered their kit and went to meet the train.[33]

Napoleon, Lieutenant General Burns observed, had said: "'God is on the side of the bigger battalions.' One of the supreme duties of the military officer, then, is to see that the battalions are kept big...Wastage comes from a few men insufficiently worked or insufficiently cared for...They are lost as fit soldiers, the total mounts up rapidly, and presently the nations' armies find themselves with no fit soldiers to replace casualties. If this happens to us before it happens to the enemy, we have lost the war."[34]

[10]

A Hard Fight

IN OCTOBER 1944, the German LXVII Infantry Corps barring 2nd Canadian Infantry Division's drive northwards was also facing dire manpower shortages. With the full weight of two brigades advancing across a ten-mile-wide front that extended west from Kamp van Brasschaat to the Scheldt River, 346th Infantry Division was hard pressed on October 4 to hold its line. "Far inferior in numbers and in materiel and part of them imperfectly trained, [the troops] gave their best and fought tenaciously," a German after-action report stated. "Especially the men unused to battle, the regional defence troops and members of navy groups—dockyard workers- and festungpionier [fortress engineer] units committed on the dams right east of the mouth of the Scheld[t]—which were considered in less danger—were not equal in the long run to the sensations and the hardships of major combat. Mobile Panzer defence was lacking, blocking measures were not effective, and in close combat with the Panzerfaust the regional defence troops, inexperienced in combat, were not equal to the enemy tanks."

The Canadian advance "caused nervousness and apprehension" at Fifteenth Army headquarters, for it appeared the entire right wing of its defensive front might be dislodged and the Breskens Pocket and West Scheldt lost. To stabilize the Bergen op Zoom to Breda line, "some substantial formation was needed," but Fifteenth Army commander General der Infanterie Gustav von Zangen realized he "could not expect any help from the outside and had to rely entirely on [his] own resources."[1]

His only available reserve was the ad hoc Kampfgruppe (Battle Group) named after its commander, Generalleutnant Kurt Chill.[2] By the time the Canadians pushed northwards on October 4, Chill's men, crammed aboard trucks and a large number of buses commandeered from the Brabant District Railways and Bus Service, were en route from Tilburg to south of Bergen op Zoom.[3]

Canadian intelligence officers rated Chill an officer "of great skill and uncommon energy." On September 2, Chill had cobbled the remnants of the 84th, 85th, and 89th infantry divisions, two reinforced battalions of the Hermann Göring Training Regiment, the crack 1st Battalion of the 2nd Parachute Regiment, and two battalions of the 6th Parachute Regiment into a coherent fighting force that blocked XXX British Corps from crossing the Albert Canal. Since then, the three-thousand-strong Kampfgruppe Chill had served as a mobile fire brigade, moved to wherever Fifteenth Army was most threatened.[4] Kampfgruppe Chill's true bite was provided by the two thousand paratroops commanded by Oberstleutnant Friederich von der Heydte, a daring officer who believed the best defence was an attack. "I had only to attack—and I got everything I wished. If I said, I can't attack without this and this, the next day, I got it."[5]

This day, however, Kampfgruppe Chill was still on the move with plans to reorganize at Korteven, a village midway between Bergen op Zoom and Hoogerheide. Consequently, the immediate fighting fell on 346th Infantry Division, bolstered by several "assault-gun brigades or battalions...with some 50 to 60 assault guns or assault tanks" that could be "hurled as [a] 'fire department' from one point of fierce fighting to another...in defence and counterattack." A "special system of transport, traffic control, and assembly points put into effect by Corps made possible rapid commitment of these Panzer units at all points of heaviest fighting on the corps front."[6]

Fourth Canadian Infantry Brigade's advance from Merksem and Oorderen caught the Germans by surprise, as suddenly, one German report stated, "the skirmishes...expanded...into earnest fighting and the enemy now attacked seriously...via Oorderen towards Berendrecht and tried to take this town."[7] Although 4 CIB had its sights locked on Berendrecht, this was not the primary objective. That honour fell to Woensdrecht, which the Essex Scottish were to reach by advancing well to the east of Berendrecht following a line running north through Ekeren to Putte—astride the Belgian-Dutch border—and then up the No. 11 Highway.

At 0800 hours, the Essex marched in a long line up the verge of a narrow road from Merksem towards Ekeren. Crowding the road itself were the battalion's Bren carriers, those of the artillery forward observation officer, and a squadron of the 14th Canadian Hussars' large Daimler armoured cars. The Germans rapidly gave ground and infantry patrols soon reported Ekeren abandoned and "indications all along the line were that the enemy was withdrawing rapidly," the Essex war diarist recorded. "It was then decided to press on as quickly as possible, bypassing enemy pockets on the way, with a view to seizing a bridgehead over the Opstalbeek River" at Stabroek, about six miles north.[8]

The Canadian force marched, passing through one village after another and meeting no resistance. Optimism soared. This so resembled those heady days after Normandy that it was easy to believe the Germans were again running. The warm, almost summery day added to the pleasant dream—as did the fact that "the route was lined with delighted civilians who produced fruit and beverages and swarmed all over the vehicles wherever they stopped."[9]

Following behind were the gun batteries of 4th Canadian Field Regiment. The large trucks pulling the guns and trailers spanned the road's width, so gunners preceded the column in jeeps, waving rifles to warn the civilians to back off in order to prevent slowing it. So rapid was the advance that the artillery could barely keep the guns within range should they be needed. Bombardier Ken Hossack was unfazed by the sight of many "'good Germans' (dead ones)... sprawled along the sides of the road and the ditches." Periodically, the column stalled, forced to wait while engineers filled "in the huge craters in the road, caused by enemy demolition bombs," that the armoured cars and infantry had been able to dodge around. "We bump through these depressions and continue on."[10] At 1600 hours, the gun batteries pulled into positions on the outskirts of Kapellen, four miles north of Merksem, and dug the guns in.[11] Soon it was "very noisy—the OP's... spotting good targets and we fire regularly. The cooks find shelter about a mile to our rear and we argue whether or not the meals are worth the route march. There is considerable enemy shelling but none falls among us," Hossack wrote.

By this time, three Essex companies had passed through Stabroek two miles ahead and were seeking a river crossing. 'A' Company was "well on the right, 'D' in the centre almost due north... and 'B' wandering in the flooded area to the left." Battalion headquarters was established in a large house in the centre of town and Stabroek declared liberated. An hour later, 'D' Company reported that it controlled an intact bridge and was repulsing counterattacks that soon fizzled out. The Essex settled into the comfort of strong defensive positions for the night. During the day, fifty prisoners had been taken and many other Germans were seen "hot-footing down the road trying to keep ahead of our advance."[12]

Shortly after dawn, on a cool, cloudy Thursday at odds with the previous day's warm weather, "the attack continued relentlessly" with 'B' Company conducting a hard right hook along a narrow track to gain the highway at Putte, while 'A' and 'C' Companies moved cross country on its left flank. About mid-morning, 'B' Company closed on Putte and German resistance suddenly stiffened. The infantry had to root out one machine-gun position after another while being subjected to random shelling and mortaring. By the time the company had fought its way through to the central square of this "long, skinny town," its already badly depleted ranks were down to just forty men not killed or wounded.[13]

No sooner had 4th Field's Forward Observation Officer Captain Ted Adams and his wireless operator, Bombardier Ernie Hodgkinson, installed themselves in a church tower to the immediate rear of the leading Essex platoon than a determined German counterattack began, supported by heavy artillery and mortar fire, the attack forced the surviving members of 'B' Company to pull out of the town to regroup. Stranded, from the height of the tower, Adams could clearly see German troops edging up the streets towards the square. Waiting until they were just 150 yards from his position, he coolly called in coordinates that would catch the closing troops in a Mike target concentration of all twenty-four guns of the 4th Field Regiment. Having moved that morning from Kapellen to Stabroek, the regiment unleashed a devastating bombardment.[14] "The gunners," Hossack reported, "slug much ammunition and sweat a-plenty as we fire continuously, in support of our infantry."[15]

With the battle for Putte in the balance, Lieutenant Colonel John Pangman ordered 'D' Company to pass through 'B' Company and throw the Germans back before they could recover from the artillery fire. Soon the relief company managed to drive the Germans out of town and discovered Adams "among the 'liberated populace' waving" as they set up positions in the town square.[16] Adams was awarded a Military Cross and Hodgkinson a Military Medal.

The Essex Scottish had not advanced alone during these two days. To its left, the Royal Regiment of Canada had crossed the Opstalbeek River on the bridge just north of Stabroek and struck out towards Berendrecht, three miles west of Putte, with 'B' Squadron of 14th Canadian Hussars out front. The Hussars had just recently begun swapping Humber model armoured cars for the much heavier Daimler. The Daimler Mk 1 had a lower, more tanklike profile than the tall-turreted earlier model armoured cars. Its two-pounder (40-millimetre) main gun also provided more punch than the Humber's 37-millimetre gun, although both cars were also equipped with a BESA 7.92-millimetre machine gun. With a fifty-mile-an-hour top speed, it was also five miles an hour faster than the Humber. Although the "Humber had served us well and faithfully throughout France and Belgium," the regiment's historian wrote, "there was no denying the superiority of the car with which we were now being equipped." The troops "were loud in its praise."[17]

Their effectiveness was proved when Lieutenant Colin Ridgway's troop plowed into the streets of Berendrecht with the two-pounder high-velocity guns pounding and machine guns spraying fire at any Germans sighted. The aggressiveness and violence of this assault prompted the hundred men defending the village to surrender—an event that garnered the twenty-eight-year-old a Military Cross.[18]

As 4 CIB's battalions settled in for the night amid the newly liberated towns of Berendrecht and Putte, Brigadier Cabeldu briefed their commanders on the next phase that he hoped would carry them almost to Woensdrecht. First thing in the morning, the Royal Hamilton Light Infantry would jump off from Putte up the No. 11 Highway about four miles to a line of sand dunes on either side of the roadway, while the Royal Regiment of Canada seized Ossendrecht to the west. From these preliminary objectives, it was less than three miles to the prize of Woensdrecht.[19]

THE RILEYS ADVANCED from Putte at 0615 hours on October 6, "bumped into very light opposition and learned that the enemy had withdrawn during the early [hours] of the morning."[20] Hoping to overtake the Germans before a new defensive line was set up, Lieutenant Colonel Denis Whitaker mounted 'A' Company on the hulls of a Fort Garry Horse troop from 'A' Squadron and, with the battalion's Bren carrier platoon leading, the column set off in pursuit.

Outside Putte, the Rileys had entered Holland—but the country little resembled the coffee-table-book stereotype. This was the Brabant Wall area—an anomalous ridge of high ground whose western flank presented a distinct wall that overlooked the polder ground between it and the West Scheldt. The Brabant Wall began rising gently near Ossendrecht and reached its maximum height of about sixty feet at Hoogerheide before gradually declining to merge with the surrounding, almost sea-level countryside near Steenbergen to the northeast of Bergen op Zoom. East of the ridge, the ground varied in height from forty to sixty feet. The Brabant's sandy soil was home to an interwoven mix of dunes, heaths, woods, shallow marshes, small lakes, meadows, and pockets of farm fields. This was Holland's most rugged terrain. Few serviceable roads ran through it, and those that did were little more than narrow dirt tracks. From Hoogerheide, the highway from Antwerp ran west of the Brabant to Bergen op Zoom, while a secondary route cut east from Hoogerheide to Huijbergen before turning north well to the east of the Brabant country.

The advance up the highway from Antwerp towards Hoogerheide progressed smoothly for about two and a half miles.[21] Then, at 0930 hours, with dense woods crowding either side of the highway, the Canadians closed on the Mutse Straat crossroads. Here, "the enemy had felled many large trees across" the highway. No sooner was the roadblock sighted than a 20-millimetre antitank gun and several machine guns opened fire from behind it.

Carrier drivers spun their vehicles off the road to find cover, the infantry spilled off the Shermans, and the tank troop, commanded by Lieutenant Holt, tried to engage the antitank gun. Unable to locate it, Holt drew back. As the tanks pulled clear, Major J.B. Halladay led 'A' Company into an assault that resulted in it being "pinned down by overwhelming fire" and went to ground to avoid unnecessary casualties.[22]

Whitaker came up at 1300 hours and ordered Halladay's men to hammer the roadblock with fire to cover 'B' Company's move along a rugged track, which hooked through the woods to the left to gain the Mutse Straat and outflank the Germans. Supporting the infantry was another troop of Fort Garry tanks. Before leading his men into the attack, however, Major H.A. "Huck" Welch took a section of men and crept out to take a look at the stout defensive works. Closing in, he discovered the Germans had abandoned it.

The advance recommenced with 'C' Company leading, but for the next four hours it had to fight one small firefight after another to keep going. By the time the sand dunes were gained, twenty-four men had been wounded, one mortally.

Meanwhile, the Royal Regiment of Canada had started out at about 0500 hours and, taking the Germans by surprise, 'D' Company was soon astride Middel Straat. This road brought the company to a position atop the Brabant Wall at a hamlet named Hageland. About a mile northwest, Ossendrecht crowded up against the Brabant Wall's flank.

From Hageland, the Royals snaked along a path running close to the edge of the ridge to enter the eastern outskirts of Ossendrecht. 'D' Company held up at the outskirts, providing a firm fire base from the ridge line, while 'A' and 'C' Companies moved into the town supported by armoured cars of the 14th Canadian Hussars. It was 0730 hours. Suddenly, resistance stiffened, particularly as a hidden self-propelled gun began firing on the advancing troops.[23] Captain George Blackburn was the 4th Canadian Field Regiment's forward observation officer. 'D' Company commander Major Bob Suckling and Blackburn set about hunting the hidden gun that was supporting a force of advancing infantry. Having spotted the gun, Suckling broke into a nearby house and guided Blackburn to a window overlooking it. The gun had been concealed on a culvert crossing a tree-choked little creek. Blackburn called in a Mike Target on the gun, but while that was in the works the Germans seemed to sense the presence of the two officers and began smashing rounds into the row of buildings containing their observation post. As the German shells marched from one house to another towards their position, Blackburn feared the artillery fire would come too late. Then, just as it seemed he was staring straight into the German gun barrel, the artillery salvo fell. The German gun disappeared in an inferno of explosions.

But there was no time to relax. The German infantry were still counterattacking, coming at the Royals in an odd v-shaped formation that perhaps indicated the man out front was an officer leading reluctant men forward. Blackburn ordered the guns swung to intercept them. Even though the first salvo fell behind the Germans, they all hit the dirt. Then, before Blackburn could adjust the range to zero a salvo onto them, the Germans retreated right into the line of a second concentration. When the smoke cleared, only the crumpled grey-clad bodies of a few dead remained.[24] The artillery broke the German resistance. Within a few hours, the Royals reported Ossendrecht cleared. By 2130 hours, they were enjoying a hot meal that had been brought forward and receiving the welcome news that 5th Canadian Infantry Brigade would pass through 4 CIB's lines to carry out the morning's advance to Woensdrecht.[25]

Even though 2 CID was making good progress in its push to Woensdrecht, its right flank was growing more acutely exposed with every mile gained. Ostensibly, this flank was covered by 1 British Corps, until 4th Canadian Armoured Division could complete its planned move from the Leopold Canal to join operations here. But

Lieutenant General John Crocker's corps was still marching to Field Marshal Montgomery's orders to secure the left flank of the British Second Army's salient won during Operation Market Garden, by driving the Germans back behind the Maas River to the north of s'Hertogenbosch. So Crocker was advancing on a line north from Turnhout towards the parallel-positioned cities of Breda and Tilburg. That put his divisions about twenty-five miles east of 2 CID, creating a huge gap where the Germans could move with impunity.

The porosity of 2 CID's lines was driven home to the gunners of 4th Canadian Field Regiment on October 6, when they moved to a new firing position just north of Putte. To ensure that two of the three batteries were always available to support the advance on Ossendrecht, the move was carried out in stages. First, an advance party, including 'A' Troop's Gun Position Officer Lieutenant Bob Grout, arrived in the area of sand dunes and scrubby pines. Grout quickly located positions for each of the troop's guns and then "went to sleep in the sun... As far as he was concerned there was not a human anywhere within miles, and the fact did not bother him that the country on the right flank of the position had not been gone through by the infantry," the regimental historian later wrote.[26]

Things seemed far less benign as the gun troop began to arrive in the area just before sunset. Passing through Putte and entering Holland, they were greeted by German shells falling "right and left of the road," Bombardier Ken Hossack recalled. "Rifle bullets sing over the position as we try to get the guns accurately oriented... all work ceases while preparations are made to deal with what may be a fanatical sniper. The firing increases, many more rifles are firing now. Patrols are organized and set out to do battle."

Twenty-nine-year-old Gunner Frederick "Eddie" Edwards of Calgary "fires his Bren gun from the hip at close range but the gun jams, a heavy enemy MG opens up, and Edwards is seriously wounded." Troop Sergeant Major George Phillips "crawls to Edwards and places a shell dressing over the largest wound. Gunner [John] Rawlings catches a rifle bullet in the shoulder and crawls back for aid—a jeep takes him to the MO [Medical Officer]. Tin hats are in vogue now. As the enemy rifle and MG fire increases it is decided to use a 25-pounder, 'open sights,' in an effort to dislodge them." The highly respected thirty-one-year-old Phillips "has worked his way back to the Command Post and, since he knows the enemy's exact location, behind a crest...will direct the gun's fire. No. 3 gun...is selected and several rounds are fired" at a range of about six hundred yards. "The enemy's MG turns onto No. 3 gun and sprays in from right to left. The bullets crash through its protective shield and the gun crew drops flat but not before [Phillips] is hit and instantly killed. The Bofors AA gun also opens up and rains many shots into the enemy's position. Their fire ceases and we presume that they have withdrawn. An armoured car goes out to pick up Edwards but he is dead. Evening brings the end to a sad day and we appoint extra guards for the night but no further small arms fire is forthcoming. Targets are engaged at various ranges during the night; the following day finds us firing frequently—sometimes to our immediate rear, requiring the gun barrels to describe a half-circle in order to aim in the right direction."[27]

MORE OFTEN, THE guns fired in support of 5 CIB's advance on Woensdrecht, which had run into trouble soon after the Calgary Highlanders crossed the start line near Ossendrecht. Reveille had come at 0430 hours. The night had been clear and cold, so the rum ration portioned out after breakfast "helped chase the chill out of many bodies." Dawn found the men on the march towards the front line of the Royal Hamilton Light Infantry, which they passed through at 0800.

About twenty minutes later, Major Ross Ellis's 'B' Company out on point, with five tanks from the Fort Garry Horse's 'C' Squadron grinding along close behind, moved into some deep woods to the east of the road running from Ossendrecht to Hoogerheide and started taking light small-arms fire. The machine guns on the Shermans quickly quelled it with long bursts. The Calgarians made good time, but at 0900 they heard heavy firing off to the right, where Le Régiment de Maisonneuve should have been covering their flank.[28] Both battalions were to converge on Hoogerheide to gain control of the high ground above Woensdrecht. Although also on the Brabant Wall, Woensdrecht was lower than neighbouring Hoogerheide. In fact, the pinnacle of Woensdrecht's Roman Catholic church tower was precisely the same height as the floor of the Roman Catholic church in Hoogerheide.

The plan was to first secure Hoogerheide and secondly Woensdrecht, which would enable the Canadians to effectively sever the link between South Beveland and the mainland. After Woensdrecht fell, the Black Watch would pass through and push a mile north to seize Korteven and establish a blocking position there. This would prevent any German attempts to re-establish a connective link between South Beveland and their mainland units.[29]

But the plan quickly went awry when the Maisonneuve, supported by six Fort Garry Horse tanks, closed on a roadblock of fallen trees and were fired upon by heavy mortars, machine guns, and antitank guns. In less than five minutes, the German fire, coming from positions behind the roadblock and from inside two deep antitank ditches dug along either side of the road to prevent the barrier being easily bypassed, had killed or wounded thirty-seven Maisies. Repeated attempts either to storm the roadblock head on or to outflank it were broken by intense fire, and the tanks were unable to find firing positions that did not expose them to the well-concealed antitank guns.

Realizing that the attack was stonewalled, tank commander Captain Bill Little jumped from his Sherman and ran to find a better position. While he was doing this, Lieutenant Livingstone rolled his tank to within fifty yards of the roadblock and started pounding it with shells and raking the antitank ditch with the machine guns. But this failed to quell the German fire, and when the Maisies fell back to the cover of some nearby bushes, Livingstone—almost out of ammunition—also withdrew. An antitank round had damaged the tank engine, so that it barely limped to cover. Livingstone commandeered one of his sergeant's tanks.[30] By this time, Little had returned from his reconnaissance and quickly described the firing position he had discovered. Deliberately moving his tank so it was badly exposed, Little drew the enemy fire so that the other tanks "could dash to the flank position... Although his tank was hit several times, it was not knocked out." Once the other tanks were set, Little pulled out. Spotting a self-propelled gun hidden in some trees on the way back, he engaged and knocked it out. Little's actions resulted in a Military Cross.[31]

From their new position, the tankers proved still exposed and the Maisonneuves were unable to put in an effective attack. Whenever the tankers slipped out of the trees and brush to zero in on targets, the Germans lashed out with a stunning rate of antitank fire. During one such foray, the tank commanded by Sergeant Williamson took a direct hit on the turret and he was severely wounded in the shoulder.[32] By evening, Lieutenant Colonel Julien Bibeau sought to break the deadlock by sending a company of Maisies out on either flank through the woods to get behind the roadblock. Nightfall caught the troops still deep in their respective woods, so Bibeau ordered them to hunker where they were until dawn.[33]

On the left flank, the Calgary Highlanders had enjoyed easier going until No. 12 Platoon emerged from woods about a thousand feet from where No. 12 Highway intersected the road they were following. At that point, a line of machine guns dug in behind the cover of a slight rise just south of Hoogerheide forced it back. Platoon commander Lieutenant Alexander Keller hurried over to Captain Fraser's tank to get the Fort Garry Horse Shermans to suppress the German position with main gun fire while he led his men in a frontal charge. The tanks quickly deployed and started pumping out shells. Keller stood up, tersely told his men to follow, and walked into the open field directly towards the enemy position without a backward glance. After a moment's hesitation, his men rushed to follow. Fortunately, the tank fire was so heavy and accurate that the Germans were forced to ground and unable to man their guns, so the platoon crossed the killing zone without casualties. As they closed on the rise, the tankers ceased fire at the last moment and Keller led his men over the top into the German position. Caught by surprise, the sixteen troops manning eight deadly MG 42 machine guns surrendered. Keller's dash resulted in a Military Cross.

Pushing on through thickening small-arms fire backed by generous doses of mortar and artillery rounds, 'B' Company on the right and 'C' Company on the left pushed into the outskirts of Hoogerheide. By evening, the two companies were well into the southern

Corporal S. Kormendy sighting for sniper Sergeant H.A. Marshall of the Calgary Highlanders during the fighting near Hoogerheide. Ken Bell photo. LAC PA–131246.

above · Streams of fire ignite a conflagration during a demonstration by 4th Canadian Armoured Division WASPS on October 4, 1944 to test the feasibility of laying down a cross-canal flame attack. Harold G. Aikman photo. LAC PA–131241.

top right · Scouts of the Queen's Own Cameron Highlanders on the prowl near Kamp van Brasschaat on October 9, 1944. Dense thickets such as this were typical of the vegetation found in the Brabant Wall country. Ken Bell photo. LAC PA–131248.

right · Gunner R. Leclerc, Bombardier O. McIntosh, and Gunner J. Koropelniski fire their 25-pounder on German positions two miles away from a position next to the Scheldt River to the north of Antwerp on October 2, 1944. Ken Bell photo. LAC PA–131239.

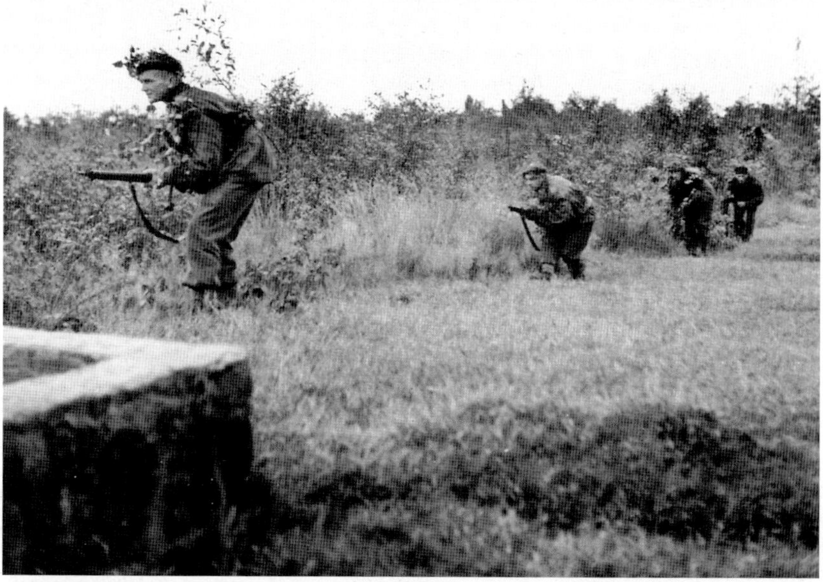

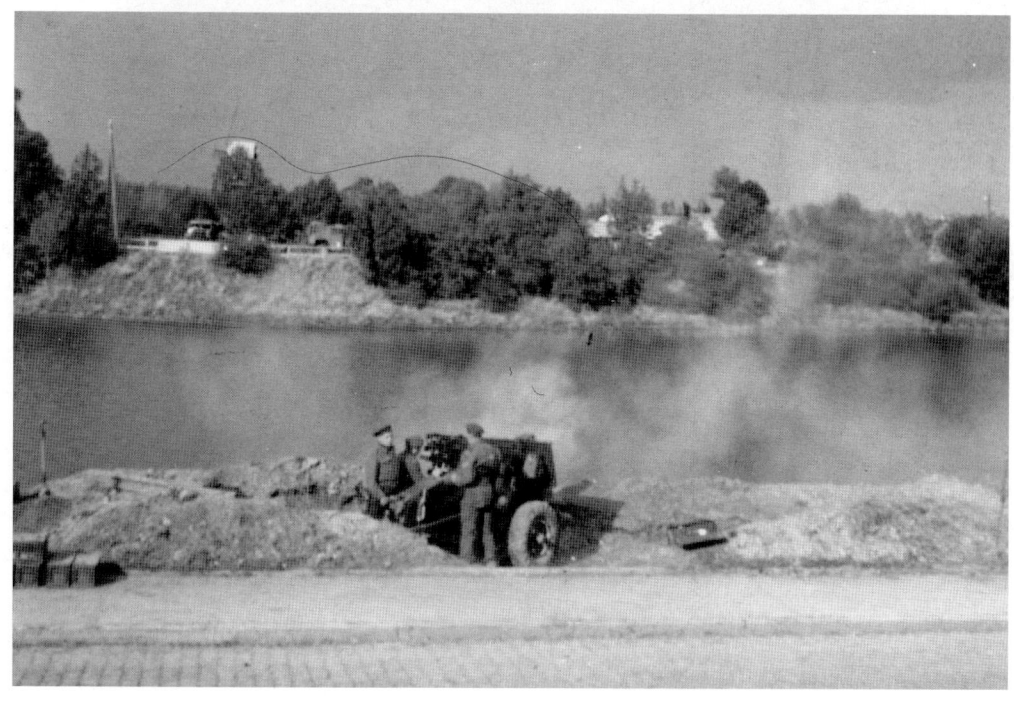

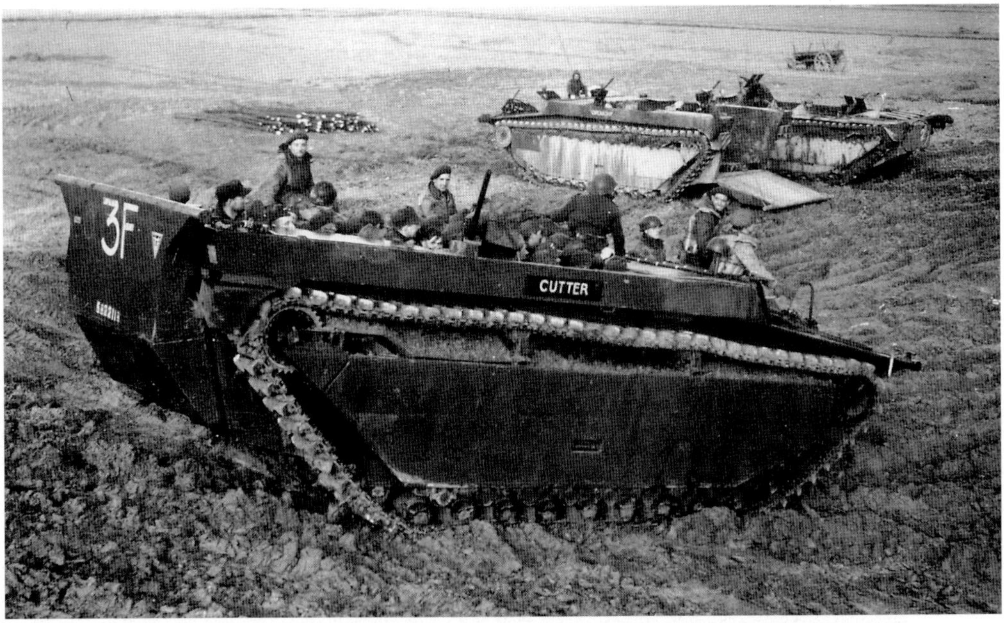
3F
CUTTER

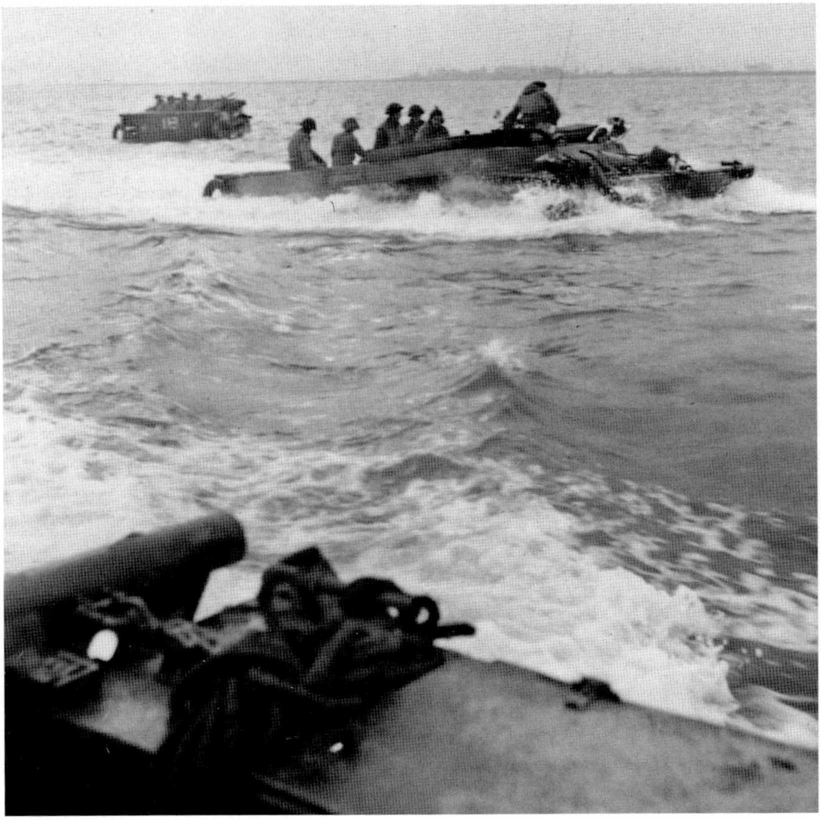

top left · Terrapins bringing German prisoners back to the Terneuzen area from the beachhead near Hoofdplaat on October 13, 1944. Donald I. Grant photo. LAC PA–136823.

left · Buffaloes heading across the Braakman Inlet on October 11 carrying 8th Canadian Infantry Brigade to the beaches taken by 9th Canadian Infantry Brigade during Operation Switchback. Donald I. Grant photo. LAC PA–131249.

above · A group of German paratroops advance past a knocked-out Sherman tank during the fierce fighting on the Brabant Wall. Note the antitank weapons carried by two of the men. Photographer unknown. Photo courtesy of Johan van Doorn.

above · Canadian Scottish Regiment troops attempting to rescue a mired Bren carrier by pulling it free with a second carrier. Deep mud and flooded polders such as the one in the background made clearing the Breskens Pocket a nightmare and earned 3rd Canadian Infantry Division the nickname of the Water Rats. Donald I. Grant photo. LAC PA–138424.

top right · A mine explodes on the shore of the Scheldt estuary. Photographer unknown. LAC E004665470.

right · Corporal Morgan of the Winnipeg Rifles on guard during the advance through the Breskens Pocket. Hugh H. McCaughey photo. LAC PA–142107.

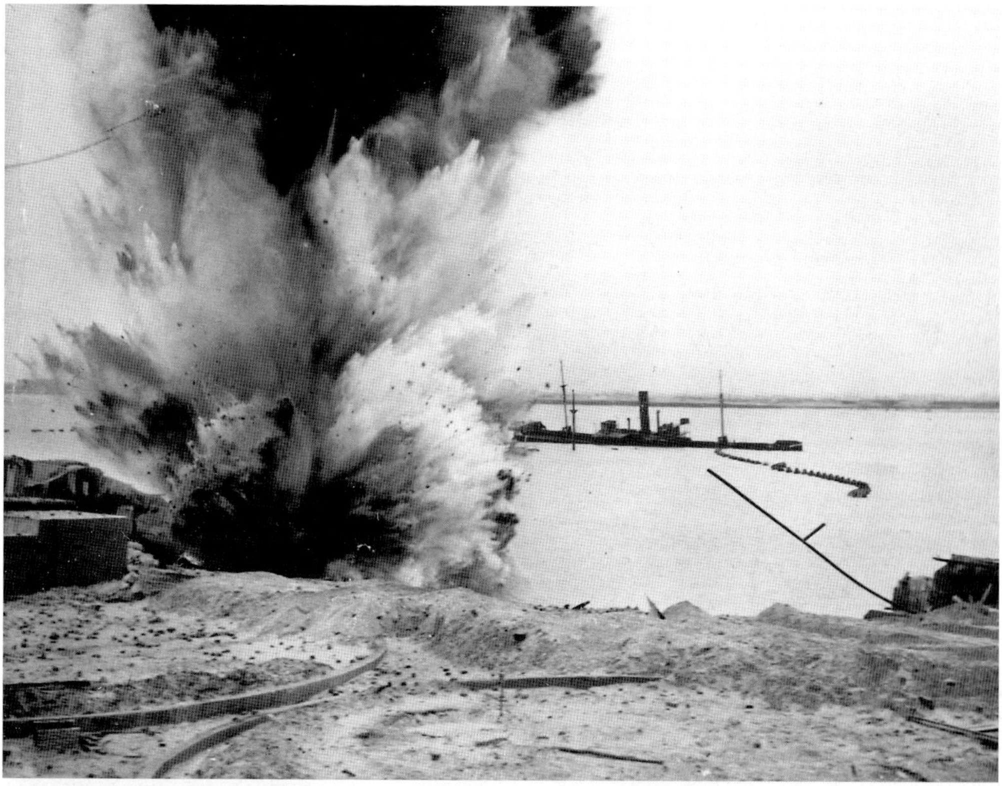

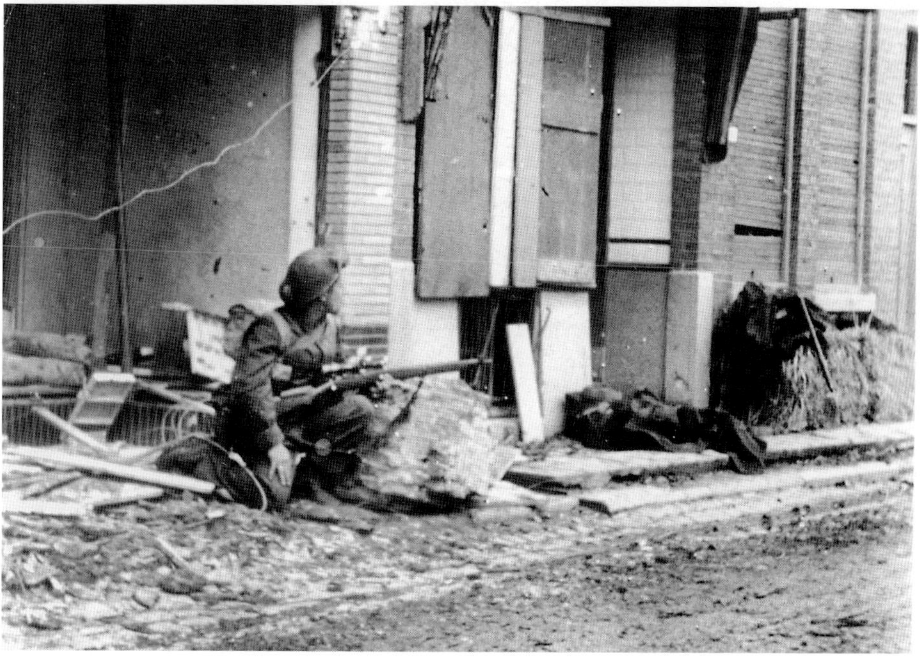

An ambulance crosses an FBE (floating boat equipment) bridge over the Beveland Canal near the village of Schore during 2nd Canadian Infantry Division's advance to cut the South Beveland isthmus. Engineers from the 2nd Field Company, RCE lost several men completing this critical bridge. Ken Bell photo. LAC PA–138427.

half of the village, but resistance remained stiff. Having been subjected to heavy shelling to break the German defences, many of the buildings were in ruins, streets and yards badly cratered. The body of a girl caught in the bombardment lay near a smouldering house. Most of the villagers cowered in cellars, hoping the battle would soon pass.

When 'D' Company pushed two platoons through 'B' Company's lines, fire from three pillboxes stopped the advance in its tracks. Realizing that the infantrymen were helpless to knock out the heavily fortified position, Sergeant T.J. Reed decided to deploy his antitank gun platoon. To do so, he had to get the guns to a good line of fire, and the route was covered by a German self-propelled gun. Reed's six-pounders were towed by Bren carriers, and the sergeant ordered his men to crouch low to gain the protection of the thinly armoured walls. The carriers broke into the open, zigzagging wildly at top speed to elude the SPG's fire. Everyone made it, but no sooner had the guns been unhitched and prepared to fire than another SPG rolled out of the gloom of the gathering night, gun cracking. One antitank gun was disabled and the crews of the others dove for cover. Ignoring the incoming shells, Reed dashed to one gun and started manhandling it around to fire at the SPG. Soon the gun crew rushed to join in and their fire managed to knock out the enemy gun. Reed received a Distinguished Conduct Medal for bravery.[34]

As the approaching darkness shrouded the battered village, the fighting became increasingly chaotic. The five Fort Garry Horse tanks were prowling around, trying to support the infantry and searching for the elusive SPG guns. On the hunt, Sergeant Gregory John Eno turned a corner and was staring directly at what he thought looked like a Panther's silhouette. A battlefield behemoth weighing forty-five tons, protected by 120-millimetre-thick frontal armour, and mounting a high-velocity 75-millimetre gun, a round from a Panther could easily slice through the Sherman's 75-millimetre-thick armour. It also had far longer range than the Canadian tank's less powerful 75-millimetre gun. Range was no issue here, the two tanks just yards apart. But the German was ready and positioned for a shootout. Its gun spoke as Eno began swinging his turret to meet it. The round smashed into the Sherman, disabling it. Despite the risk that the Sherman would live up to its nickname of "Ronson Burner" by bursting into flames, Eno ordered the crew to stay put even as a second shot careered harmlessly past. Eno's first shot punched through a weak point in the tank's armoured hide and set it ablaze. The sergeant, who had distinguished himself often since coming ashore on D-Day, received what his comrades considered a long overdue Military Medal.[35]

A pale moon rose to wash the village and surrounding fields in a cold light. Sporadic gunfire broke out as Canadians and Germans stalked each other. Major Wynn Lasher, another officer, and a Bren gunner spotted a German sitting on the back step of a house calmly plucking a chicken. The Bren gunner raised his weapon to fire a burst into the man, but Lasher reached out and pushed its barrel down. "No, wait until he finishes plucking the chicken," the officer whispered. When the German finished, the three Canadians took him prisoner and confiscated the chicken for their dinner pot.[36]

The battlefield had become so fluid that the advance party for the battalion headquarters had to drive a group of Germans away from the farmhouse about half a mile south of the village that had been selected for the night's base. The day's battle had proven less costly than the intensity of fighting had suggested—four dead and two wounded. Although they had not won all their objectives, the Calgarians were in control of the Hoogerheide crossroads and a route lay open for a westward advance into Woensdrecht. While the number of German dead remained undetermined, the battalion had taken sixty-two prisoners. These "were not," the war diarist recorded, "all old, sickly men but rather young, fairly well-built men. However, some of them spoke English and informed us that it was the first battle for many of them... It was generally accepted that the day had been a hard fight."[37]

"ON THIS DAY Ossendrecht was lost after a battle," LXVII Corps's Chief of Staff, Oberst Elmar Warning, gloomily reported. "The situation was becoming more and more threatening. There were no more reserves available." Until Kampfgruppe Chill entered the fray, the Germans could only delay Woensdrecht's fall. "During the night of

7–8 Oct[ober]...the enemy pushed into Hoogerheide. Violent fighting developed, which led to the loss of the south half of the village." Oberstleutnant Friederich von der Heydte reported that he could not commit Kampfgruppe Chill's three parachute battalions, which were just beginning to arrive, until the afternoon of October 8.[38] Warning told von der Heydte that Hoogerheide must be recovered immediately, "otherwise the overland connection with the Island of Walcheren is in danger."[39] With the front held by a host of ad hoc forces, corps command gave Warning overall command, but Kampfgruppe Chill remained largely independent because the corps Chief of Staff recognized that von der Heydte was the more experienced combat officer.[40]

Corps command's greatest concern was the crumbling state of morale that had led many of its troops to surrender to the rapidly advancing Canadians or to hurriedly retreat after the briefest of fights. There had even been cases where officers abandoned their commands. To stiffen the backbone of officers and troops alike, it ordered that any "commander of a strongpoint [be] shot summarily for cowardice in the presence of the enemy, if he is the first to retire without the order to do so, with the poor excuse that he wants to report the situation."[41] Yet, despite poor morale, the majority of the Germans continued to fight with a dogged determination. One conscript scrawled in his diary, "Am very ill. They left me in a foxhole some 100 metres from my room. I have a high temperature but I do not want to go to hospital, not for all the world. Now every man counts. That's why I, a conscript, shall join the battle again."[42]

This overall tenacity surprised the Canadians, who were repeatedly assured by intelligence reports that the enemy was finished and one more push would see him off. An October 7 11 Canadian Corps intelligence summary declared, "The enemy has been conducting an orderly withdrawal, his rearguards offering stubborn resistance all the way. The causeway to South Beveland and the only road communication with the island is now well within the range of our artillery. It is now clear that he has given up any plan...to stand on the mainland approaches to Walcheren."[43]

Closer to the ground, Brigadier Holly Keefler was less optimistic and increasingly concerned about 2 CID's long, unprotected right flank that became more vulnerable with each advance. On October 6, he consequently diverted 6th Canadian Infantry Brigade and the bulk of the Fort Garry Horse to secure it. At 1100 hours, Keefler outlined his plan to 6 CIB's Brigadier Guy Gauvreau. Until now, the brigade had been conducting limited offensive operations across a line running from Brecht to Kapellen, intended merely to keep the Antwerp–Turnhout Canal's northern bank and the rear of the division safe from counterattack. As all three of the brigade's battalions were badly understrength, Keefler and Gauvreau had been proceeding gingerly to avoid unnecessary casualties, and save 6 CIB for the pivotal role it was to play in the forthcoming drive across South Beveland and over the causeway onto Walcheren Island.[44]

Now, Keefler announced, Les Fusiliers Mont-Royal, concentrated near Kapellen, would be replaced by a "mixed force" consisting of an antitank battery, a troop of anti-aircraft gunners turned into infantry, and some resistance fighters. The Fusiliers would become part of a motorized force—codenamed Saint Force—that would advance from Putte to Kalmthout and Achterbroek, about five miles distant. In addition to the Fusiliers, the force would include the Fort Garry Horse's 'A' and 'B' squadrons, a squadron of 14th Canadian Hussars' armoured cars, a platoon each of Toronto Scottish Regiment's heavy machine-gunners and mortarmen, and a troop of 23rd Canadian Anti-Tank Battery armed with 17-pounders.

As some of the armoured units were supporting the South Saskatchewan Regiment near Brecht, both commanders were anxious that their extraction not be disclosed to the Germans because the South Saskatchewans were "too thin on the ground and any sign of withdrawal might [encourage] the enemy to infiltrate."[45] Keefler had intended to launch the operation on October 7 at 1000 hours, but the Essex Scottish in Putte only received instructions to secure a designated start line one mile north of the town at 0130 hours and met stiff resistance from the 1018th Grenadier Regiment troops, who had to be rooted out from behind several well-positioned roadblocks.

Consequently, it was 1330 hours when the 14th Hussars sent an initial reconnaissance party along the single road connecting Putte to Kalmthout. They quickly encountered a roadblock and started taking antitank fire. Hastily withdrawing, the Hussars attempted to find an alternate route to bypass the position. But each track wending off through the dense woods and marshes either petered out or wandered in the wrong direction. At 1700 hours, an exasperated Keefler called off the operation, planning a fresh attempt on October 8.[46]

This time, the Fusiliers and tankers would lead the drive, despite the fact that the infantry was short 226 men and so less than three-quarters of its normal strength. The Fort Garry Horse officers were briefed on the new plan "dreamed up on the previous night" at 0645 hours, and came away understanding that Saint Force's "hastily improvised" purpose was "to worry the enemy on the right" to take pressure off the thrust on Woensdrecht.[47]

Tankers and infantrymen crossed the start line at 0805 hours. A mist that cut visibility to about 150 feet clung to the ground. After advancing a few hundred yards, the tanks came under fire from hidden 88-millimetre guns, and the road was heavily mined. Several hours were spent bypassing the German strongpoint. The mist having dissipated, the tanks were able to locate and break up pockets of resistance, and the advance began to quicken. By late afternoon, Saint Force had reached Dorp, a mile north of Kalmthout. This armoured thrust greatly alarmed LXVII Corps, which feared the Canadians were making for Essen, about seven and a half miles farther north.[48] A complete breakout was only prevented "in hard, fluctuating fighting" by throwing in "the last reserves [other than those of Kampfgruppe Chill], put together from division trains and alert units."[49]

At Dorp, these reinforcements stiffened the resistance and Saint Force was heavily shelled and mortared. At 1730 hours, Keefler met Gauvreau and told him that the Germans were concentrating in strength north of Hoogerheide to undertake a major counterattack against that village. Therefore, Saint Force's operation was cancelled. While the Fusiliers concentrated at Kalmthout, the tanks were withdrawn and sent west to meet this threat.[50]

[11]

With Devastating Effect

ON THE EARLY MORNING of October 8, Brigadier Holly Keefler had ordered 4th Canadian Infantry Brigade to send a probe from Ossendrecht onto the South Beveland isthmus to sever the communication link between the island and Bergen op Zoom. Assured that resistance would be light, Major D.S. "Tim" Beatty led the Royal Regiment of Canada's 'D' Company directly west along a dyke road bordered by fields covered in eight feet of water as a result of deliberate German flooding. A troop of the 14th Canadian Hussars armoured cars, two antitank gun sections, two Toronto Scottish three-inch mortar sections, and two of this battalion's Vickers machine-gun sections were in support—as were fifty Belgian resistance fighters. About a mile out from Ossendrecht, the fields ceased being flooded. But the force remained in true polder country, wide fields of reclaimed land protected by a grid of dykes with scarcely a tree or bush in sight. Beatty and his men hoped the heavy mist hid them from German eyes.[1]

Beatty kept the advance moving smartly, for the mist might lift at any time. When the lead platoons surprised and drove off about thirty German infantry supported by a 20-millimetre gun, the short bursts of gunfire gave the game away. From the seaside village of Bath on the southern edge of the isthmus, fusiliers from

70th Infantry Division rushed to block the Canadian advance, and were soon joined by a self-propelled gun sent from Bergen op Zoom. This ad hoc force tried to slow 'D' Company's pace with scattered machine-gun fire. But the hastily improvised positions dug into the dykes were easily located and Beatty was able to eliminate them with artillery or mortar fire. By evening, 'D' Company had advanced six thousand yards and, halfway between Ossendrecht and Bath, was dug in along the east side of a north-south–running polder dyke. Under cover of darkness, 'A' Company came forward to provide reinforcement.[2]

In Hoogerheide, meanwhile, the Calgary Highlanders had cleaned out the remaining resistance by mid-morning. To their right, Le Régiment de Maisonneuve had also emerged from its hiding spot in the woods in a renewed advance. Encountering a strong German position, Lieutenant Charles Forbes led his platoon to outflank it, only to have his men driven to ground by heavy fire. Alone, Forbes charged on, firing his Sten gun and shouting for his men to follow. Forbes "rushed two posts, killed two crew members and captured five more."[3] That cleared the way to its objective on the east side of Hoogerheide. With Hoogerheide declared secure, the path was open for the Black Watch to begin its move up the road to Korteven.

Mist wrapped Hoogerheide and the ground north of it as the Black Watch officers gathered next to a windmill outside the village to be briefed by Lieutenant Colonel Bruce Ritchie. Standing on a damp patch of grass, the officers listened glumly as Ritchie told them the rifle companies would have to win their own start line north of the village because 5 CIB's other two battalions were only just finishing clearing the immediate area of Hoogerheide. Given the fog and lack of intelligence regarding possible opposition, Ritchie said "a more cautious advance was called for" than the original mile-long dash straight to Korteven that brigade had planned. With a troop of tanks from the Fort Garry Horse's 'C' Squadron, two companies would push in line up either side of the main highway to its crossing with Dool Straat, about midway between Hoogerheide and Korteven. Here the regiment would concentrate while Ritchie assessed whether it was possible to go farther.[4]

As Ritchie was giving his orders, Oberstleutnant Friederich von der Heydte was setting up his headquarters in the magnificent Mattemburg estate country house to the north of Korteven. In the surrounding woods and small open fields, the paratroops were readying for battle. Considering that the best intelligence was gathered personally, von der Heydte soon jumped into his Kubelwagen and headed for Hoogerheide.[5]

As he raced south, the Black Watch's 'C' Company on the left and 'D' Company on the right started marching up the road at 1030 hours. 'A' Company followed the former, 'B' the latter. Back at a large schoolhouse in Hoogerheide, Ritchie anxiously monitored the wireless. No sooner had the rifle companies and trailing tanks disappeared from view than Ritchie heard the sharp sounds of gunfire and the thud of explosions. Yet it was almost an hour before 'D' Company reported having gained the start line for the attack, and Ritchie realized his men had been "forced to fight every inch of the way up to it."[6]

Pausing by a bakery just north of where the highway intersected a major crossroad named the Raadhuisstraat, von der Heydte peered south and saw through the windows of a house a line of soldiers approaching his position along another street. Suddenly, he recognized the distinctive piss-pot profile of British helmets and lunged back into the Kubelwagen. Reversing at full speed, von der Heydte backed out of range before the startled Black Watch troops could open fire. He arrived back at Mattemburg, "considerably scared but unharmed," and began preparing to counterattack the Canadians as quickly as possible.[7] His aim was simple. The paratroops, supported by 225th Assault Gun Brigade and 70th Artillery Regiment, would advance "without delay" to retake Hoogerheide and then Ossendrecht. This would restore a strong defensive line capable of protecting the isthmus.[8] The paratroop commander was completely confident this could be done, as was Oberst Elmar Warning, who considered the "leadership and troops" of these units "excellent; the cadre personnel consisted of long-experienced, battle-tried, active parachutists, the main body of the troops of very good replacements." The 225th Assault Gun Brigade was likewise "well tested."[9]

Having gained their start line, the Black Watch advanced to Dool Straat. Opposition kept hardening, as paratroops stiffened the defences with heavy machine guns and skillful sniping. Artillery and mortar fire pummelled the Canadians. 'D' Company's No. 17 Platoon, under Lieutenant Lewis, crossed the side road and set up a fighting position inside three houses, only to receive orders from company commander Major Popham to fall back because of heavy casualties and reorganize at the start line. Near Dool Straat, 'C' Company dug in at 1335 hours and the Black Watch went over to the defensive.[10]

WITH EACH PASSING hour, German artillery and mortar fire directed against Hoogerheide increased. When exploding rounds severed the telephone lines linking the Calgary Highlanders headquarters to the forward companies, Captain Mark Tennant drove forward in a Bren carrier. Stopping behind the cover of the village church, Tennant dismounted and jogged around to the cemetery to assess the situation ahead before driving into it. Badly savaged by incoming shells, the cemetery was macabre. Tombs had been shattered and graves broken open so that the bones of corpses were tossed all over. As he trotted up the stairs leading to a church entrance, a shell struck nearby. Badly wounded, the officer fell to the ground. Several soldiers rushed to drag Tennant into a ditch, and when the shelling slackened, had him taken back to headquarters in the carrier.[11] The medical officer applied emergency dressings and sent the officer by ambulance to a field hospital. Hovering close by as Tennant was bandaged, a tearful Lieutenant Colonel Donald MacLauchlan declared in a choked voice as the ambulance drove off, "There goes a stout fellow! Worth three men to us!"[12]

In the mid-afternoon, a group of Dutch civilians slipped through the lines and advised Calgary Highlanders Company Sergeant Major Harold Larson that a large force of German infantry supported by tanks, guns, and various types of fighting vehicles was gathering to the north of Hoogerheide. Larson quickly passed the information to Lieutenant Colonel MacLauchlan, who sent it on to brigade. "There are reports of a strong enemy force forming up between Bergen op Zoom and Korteven composed of 1,000 troops with tanks, guns, and AFVS," the brigade war diarist recorded. "This may possibly be a strong counter-attack force."

An aerial reconnaissance soon confirmed that a major German force was massing north of Korteven.[13] In an attempt to disrupt this buildup, eight Typhoons of 257th Squadron, Royal Air Force strafed the area with rockets. The planes were met by intense anti-aircraft fire from guns von der Heydte had deployed to protect his headquarters and rallying ground. One badly damaged Typhoon crashed in the woods near Mattemburg, killing its twenty-two-year-old pilot, New Zealander J.R. Powell.

In the early evening, Germans began infiltrating the outskirts of Hoogerheide to warn the civilians to clear out, less for humanitarian reasons than because the paratroops feared they might try to disrupt the counterattack or carry intelligence to the Canadians. While some civilians headed north to Bergen op Zoom, more passed through the Canadian lines to find safety in the Belgian border area.

All three 5 CIB battalions braced that evening for certain attack. The Brabant Wall presented a natural barrier that protected the brigade's western flank, so the Calgary Highlanders were able to concentrate to meet a head-on attack from the north. Their defensive area covered the left side of the village, anchored on the Raadhuisstraat, while the Black Watch held the right side. On the village's eastern edge, this battalion's carrier platoon established a blocking position where a road called the Woowbaan came in on a forty-five-degree angle from the northeast. Out on the right flank from the Black Watch position, Le Régiment de Maisonneuve had its outer flank anchored on the edge of an airstrip that until recently had been intermittently used by the Luftwaffe.[14]

Once darkness fell, paratroopers began infiltrating Hoogerheide, probing for weaknesses. With each passing hour, the intensity of shelling and mortaring increased. The exploding shells made sleep impossible, so the soldiers huddled in their fighting positions were alert. Consequently, when two paratroopers crept up, intent on killing or capturing the Black Watch troops in one slit trench, they were immediately shot dead by a Bren gun burst.[15] Several small counterattacks tested the line. First, the Calgarians 'C' Company drove off an attack. Then it was 'D' Company's turn. From all along the perimeter, the grinding sound of tanks, self-propelled guns, and other vehicles could be heard.[16]

A counterattack struck the Black Watch's 'D' Company, and as it was being fought off, a large number of German infantry marched down the Wouwbaan towards the blocking carrier platoon.[17] Attached to headquarters, carrier platoons served as an inherent mobile fighting unit that could pinch-hit as armour when necessary by moving rapidly from one hotspot to another. Normally, a carrier platoon numbered about sixty-five men, twice as strong as a regular rifle platoon. Because the carriers mounted Bren guns, these platoons had far more firepower. They travelled aboard a dozen carriers, the same number of motorcycles, and several jeeps.[18]

Perfectly positioned, the carrier platoon "made no move, and held their fire until the enemy was from 50 to 60 yards away, and then they opened up with everything they had, killing over fifty...Very heavy fighting ensued and it was over two hours before the enemy decided that he had had enough. We lost no ground, and accounted for many Germans in the engagement."[19]

Although the counterattacks on the Calgary line were smaller than those against the Black Watch, Lieutenant Colonel Donald MacLauchlan was growing increasingly alarmed. He urgently requested tank support, but was told by brigade at 2115 to provide his own support with the battalion carrier platoon.[20] At 2205, he asked Brigadier Bill Megill for reinforcement by 4th Canadian Infantry Brigade, a request immediately rejected. When reports from the front indicated that German patrols were probing his far left flank, MacLauchlan feared he was going to be outflanked and pleaded with Megill for two companies of reinforcements to extend his line. Megill had nothing to offer him.[21]

While MacLauchlan fretted, some officers in his headquarters staff were delighted when the farm's owner broke out "several cases of wine, milk and jam" and "presumed upon the farmer's generosity" by sampling the wine. Hearing this, MacLauchlan "announced his displeasure in a scathing blast. These are trying days for our c.o.," noted the battalion war diarist. "He worries about everyone and everything."[22] It was increasingly obvious MacLauchlan was verging on a breakdown, likely a victim of battle exhaustion. Just as apparent—from the increasing racket across the length of the perimeter of German rifle, machine-gun, and mortar fire, the rumbling back and forth of tracked vehicles, the shouts in German as men yelled back and forth to each other in the darkness, the sound of shovels and picks cutting into the earth to carve advanced fighting positions, and the endless infiltration attempts—Hoogerheide was about to be the focus of a terrific attack by a superior force.

AT 0015 HOURS on October 9, two Calgary Highlander scouts lay hidden in a grove of trees west of Hoogerheide watching a gathering of shadowy figures. That patrol from 'C' Company, one suggested, before hearing the guttural sounds of soft German voices. Careful not to be heard, the scouts withdrew and headed for battalion headquarters.[23] As more reports of Germans massing on the outskirts filtered in, the ongoing infiltrations also escalated in size. At 0400 hours, Major Del Kearns's 'A' Company, guarding the vital Raadhuisstraat crossroads on the western flank, was struck so hard that it requested reinforcement. In 'D' Company's position just to the east, Major Bruce MacKenzie radioed: "Will give assistance immediately," only to call again that the "promise could not be kept because... they themselves were busily engaged in breaking up a Jerry infiltrating party." Both companies had to call in artillery close to their fronts to prevent being overrun. At 0515, 'A' Company remained engaged in scattered house-to-house fighting with running groups of Germans, but reported "a perceptible decline in the ferocity of the Hun attack."

Then at 0600 the paratroops struck in force—'A' Company reporting that it "was once again in the throes of another counterattack."[24] Two German battalions, one from Zandvoort to the northeast and the other from Nederheide to the northwest, attempted to break into Hoogerheide.[25] German artillery saturated 'B' Company's position east of the church, while 'C' Company was treated to heavy mortaring. When Major Frederick "Franco" Baker radioed headquarters that he was under mortar fire, the war diarist noted that his "usual cheery voice... was grim and tight."

Although the attack concentrated on the Calgarians, the Black Watch were heavily shelled and harassed by many snipers. Small fighting patrols managed to capture several of the snipers, identified as paratroopers who were "definitely the cream of the crop. They range in age from 20 to 26 years, are fine physical specimens, keen to fight and with excellent morale."[26]

The pressure on Kearns's 'A' Company mounted alarmingly as the morning wore on and about a dozen self-propelled guns began jockeying in the facing woods for firing positions. Had it not been for the fire direction provided by a 5th Canadian Field Regiment forward observation officer, the company would have been overrun. Besides the SPGs, another grave threat was posed by paratroopers who had manned several concrete bunkers studded at regular intervals inside a small wood dominating the village's northern edge. To wipe these out, Major Ross Ellis assembled a fighting patrol consisting of No. 11 Platoon from 'B' Company and a tank troop from the Fort Garry Horse's 'C' Squadron.[27] After the Shermans shelled the wood, No. 11 Platoon rushed it. Still dazed by the fierce shelling, the Germans were just moving towards the bunker firing apertures when the Calgarians started chucking grenades in at them. Thirty-three paratroops immediately poured out with arms raised, calling, "Kamerad."[28] This action provided 'A' Company with a welcome respite, and gave Kearns a chance to hurry back to brief MacLauchlan on the company's vulnerability. At the farmhouse, Kearns dropped into a chair across from the lieutenant colonel just as a shell exploding outside blew in a window, and was struck in the leg by shrapnel and glass.[29] As Kearns was carried to the Regimental Aid Post, headquarters advised Lieutenant Don Munro that he now commanded 'A' Company.[30]

All that morning and into the afternoon, the Raadhuisstraat crossroads was caught in the maw of a fierce artillery and mortar duel, with each side bombarding the section controlled by the other. Virtually every building along its length was reduced to rubble. The rest of Hoogerheide was also carpeted by German shells. In the late afternoon, the shelling only intensified, with all three 5 CIB battalions reporting being smothered by shells.[31] The heightened rate of fire coincided with the three battalion commanders assembling at brigade headquarters for a briefing. Brigadier Bill Megill calmly began explaining division's orders that the brigade "take the next bite to the NW at the neck" to expand its hold on the Brabant Wall.

The three men all jumped to their feet, forcefully arguing as one that "it cannot be done with three [battalions] only and still prevent the Hun from coming in from the NE—it would need at least one more [battalion]."[32]

Megill knew they were right and asked divisional headquarters for reinforcements, which Brigadier Holly Keefler passed up the command chain to 11 Canadian Corps. In short order, Major General Charles Foulkes promised that the 4th Canadian Armoured Division's 29th Armoured Reconnaissance Regiment (South Alberta) and one company of 10th Canadian Infantry Brigade's Algonquin Regiment would be immediately sent from the Breskens Pocket to relieve the South Saskatchewan Regiment and Queen's Own Cameron Highlanders at Brecht and Brasschaat. This would free these battalions to replace the Royal Hamilton Light Infantry and Essex Scottish, currently securing the division's right flank near Putte, so they could take over Hoogerheide and renew the offensive against Woensdrecht. Moving these 4 CAD units constituted the first step in the already agreed plan to bring the entire division east from the Breskens Pocket to cover 2 CID's flank and join the drive on Bergen op Zoom.[33]

While Megill had been getting this reinforcement plan in place, MacLauchlan had been racing back to Hoogerheide in his Bren carrier—having sent a wireless message that his company commanders were to come in for a face-to-face briefing at 1600 hours. He arrived to find the officers displeased at being called away from their commands at such a critical time. Lieutenant Munro curtly reported that 'A' Company faced attacks from three sides. MacLauchlan became "visibly upset," seeming almost in despair when a wireless report came in that the company was in danger of "being overrun." 'A' Company also reported that it, along with 'D' Company, was "under heavy mortar and terrific shelling," but could not counter with artillery because the paratroopers had "moved in swiftly and it would have endangered our own positions."[34]

Realizing the battle had reached a climax, the company commanders rushed back to their units. Lieutenant Munro found the tattered remnants of 'A' Company had already lost control of the crossroads and retreated past 'D' Company into the village. Intent on regaining the crossroads, Munro caught his men up and began reorganizing them. In 'D' Company's perimeter, Major MacKenzie was yelling that there would be no retreat, while pleading with headquarters for tank and artillery support. A shell exploded and he fell severely wounded. Captain Bob Porter took command. Porter had no idea what had happened to 'A' Company. Unable to raise it on the wireless, he phoned headquarters to see if it was still in contact with 'A' Company. Negative, MacLauchlan said.

When the attack on 'A' Company had come in, many of its men were still trying to shake off the effects of the preceding heavy bombardment. A shell blast near Privates Don Muir and John Bowron had knocked Muir unconscious. Bowron had helped Muir into the shelter of a basement already containing two other injured men. With another man, Bowron had gone looking for a stretcher just as the company broke and started retreating. Bowron was swept along with the tide. Back in the basement, Muir awoke to find a German "taking off my watch. I think it was one that I had taken off a German before that. I slipped into unconsciousness again. When I woke up next day, they were all gone and I managed to crawl up the cellar stairs. There was just nothing left of the house." [35]

Scattered along the embattled Raadhuisstraat, much of 'A' Company was fighting in small, isolated pockets within houses where two or three men controlled only the rooftop while paratroops were beneath them on the ground floor. Germans and Canadians squared off with grenades, bayonets, rifle butts, and fists. [36]

Lieutenant Munro and the small number of men he had rounded up used 'D' Company's front as a start line and started up the street towards the crossroads. Munro hoped to gather up the other men as he went, but all he met were Germans, and he could see that they were establishing a strong defence around the crossroads. About forty paratroops were spotted coming across open fields towards it from the north. Munro directed artillery onto them "with devastating effect," but that alerted the Germans on the crossroads to his presence. Realizing that he was about to be surrounded, Munro concentrated his men next to the church on the Raadhuisstraat for a final stand. Among the men with Munro was Private Bowron. "We had eight Bren guns, a few Stens, a six pounder and a seventeen pounder for support. We had roughly six thousand rounds of .303 ammunition...We fired steadily all that night." All around lay the bodies of dead comrades and enemy soldiers.

Lieutenant John Anderson of Vulcan, Alberta, who had signed up as a private when war was declared in 1939 and worked his way up from the ranks, was killed. So, too, was recently promoted Sergeant Raymond A. Harold, who had been Sergeant Ken Crockett's right-hand man on the Antwerp–Turnhout Canal locks. 'A' Company had a staggeringly high fifteen fatal casualties and an equal number wounded.[37]

With night falling, MacLauchlan sent Captains George Stott and Del Harrison to find 'A' Company. They groped through the darkness, dodging parties of paratroopers, before finding Munro and his men still fighting. There was no way his small force could regain the crossroads or break out of the encirclement.[38] MacLauchlan had also lost contact with the Black Watch on his right flank, so had no idea whether they were holding or not.

The Black Watch had been under far less pressure throughout the day. But as night fell, a sixty-eight-ton Ferdinand self-propelled gun that packed an 88-millimetre gun edged in between two of its companies, so unexpectedly that it was in the battalion's midst before artillery could be brought to bear. Menacingly, the behemoth "continued to roll forward, down the street, where our 'C' Co[mpany] was located. As it came close to one of the houses one of our men inched a PIAT over the window sill of an upstairs window, and with one bomb put it out of commission."

Casualties had been relatively light for the Black Watch, but the grim news passed through the ranks that its carrier platoon commander, Captain John Ethelbert Orr, had been killed by a sniper's bullet within thirty yards of battalion headquarters. The twenty-eight-year-old from Moose Jaw was widely regarded as "one of the most courageous officers this unit has ever known."[39] As night tightly wrapped the embattled town, the paratroopers, except for those still trying to eliminate Munro's surrounded troops, pulled away.

During the night, another O Group was convened at the small, cramped farmhouse south of Hoogerheide that served as brigade headquarters. When all the officers had crowded into the stuffy living room, the brigade war diarist thought the place looked more "like Grand Central Station on a Sunday night than the place from where brigade is supposed to be fought."[40] Brigadier Megill and his battalion commanders were all tired and shaken, so there was less incredulity and more outrage when Brigadier Keefler "announced his intention to attack."[41] When Megill calmly outlined the condition of the battalions and the stiffness of opposition, Keefler changed his mind. There would be no attack for at least forty-eight hours and it would be carried out by 4 CIB while 5 CIB moved into reserve.[42] But the Calgary Highlanders were to regain the vital crossroads that 'A' Company had lost before being relieved on the afternoon of October 10.

At the end of the session, Megill took MacLauchlan aside and ordered him temporarily relieved for an obviously needed rest. Major Ross Ellis of 'B' Company would take over the battalion for a few days. MacLauchlan agreed, but returned to battalion headquarters to monitor events until the regiment was pulled out of the line.[43]

Captain Bob Porter's 'D' Company, supported by Ellis's company, moved out at 0500 hours to rescue the isolated remnant of 'A' Company and then push through to the crossroads. Although it managed to raise the siege of Lieutenant Munro's small unit, the attack failed to gain the crossroads. By mid-afternoon, Brigadier Megill decided to leave that job to the Royal Hamilton Light Infantry and pulled the Calgarians out of the line. In the fighting, Porter had been wounded and evacuated.

The Calgary Highlanders had thirty killed and seventy wounded in the Hoogerheide fight—about 25 per cent of their effective fighting strength going into the action.[44] The Black Watch had also suffered heavily, but mostly during its abortive October 8 advance on Korteven. Twelve dead, fifty-three wounded, and sixteen missing.[45] Nonetheless, 5 CIB had fought a larger force of paratroopers to a bloody draw and barely lost any ground. In doing so, they retained the vital jumping-off point for the forthcoming attack on Woensdrecht.

Hoogerheide itself had been martyred to the cause of an Allied victory. Seventy-two houses were destroyed by fire and 355 by shellfire. Another 235 were lightly damaged. By the end of October 10, barely an undamaged structure remained.[46]

IN THE POLDER country to the west of the Brabant Wall, the Royal Regiment of Canada had continued its attempt to gain control of the isthmus linking South Beveland to the mainland. Before advancing on October 8, the men of Major Tim Beatty's 'D' Company had substituted extra ammunition and grenades for their hard rations, so had passed the ensuing night dug into the muddy ground of a dyke on the western flank of a wide polder becoming ever more cold and hungry. "The bleak, mist-shrouded polders had an eerie, unearthly look even by day" that had grown only "grimmer and more menacing" during the hours of darkness. There were constant alarms. At one point, a lance corporal awoke in his slit trench to find a German paratrooper standing over him. Beating the German to the draw, the Royal killed him with a Sten gun burst that alerted the rest of the company in time to drive off an infiltrating enemy patrol.[47]

The dawn did little to raise spirits. Grey cloud hung over the featureless polders. Their uniforms were damp, boots sodden. Beatty intended to seize a sluice gate and pumping works the Germans were using to threaten the company's current position. He would have liked to have gone even farther, but Lieutenant Colonel R.M. Lendrum had cautioned against rashly going too far and getting cut off from the other companies—two still concentrated in Ossendrecht.[48] This instruction, combined with the sudden appearance of a force of German tanks, self-propelled guns, and infantry that began digging in along the road northeast of his position, convinced Beatty to restrain his naturally aggressive instincts.

Just before this German force appeared, 'D' Company had been reinforced by several guns of the British 1st Royal Marines Heavy Anti-Aircraft Regiment. Armed with mobile 3.7-millimetre guns, the Marines opened fire with disappointing effect. The rounds from the guns exploded in air bursts that seemed to do little damage. It was, however, apparently enough to discourage the Germans from attacking.[49]

The day progressed with Beatty directing either the Marines or the Toronto Scottish mortars to break up German attempts to organize a counterattack, while waiting his opportunity to assault the sluice gates. In the mid-afternoon, a force of about fifty Germans materialized from the other side of a dyke facing 'C' Company's position with their hands up. As a platoon went out to gather them in, the Germans suddenly snatched up weapons and opened fire. Falling back under the cover of a quickly laid smokescreen, the platoon managed to escape.

Towards evening, Beatty sent a platoon commanded by Lieutenant L.L. Pleasance against the sluice gate and pumping works. Sprinting across the polders, the platoon surprised the Germans and took fifty prisoners. The action garnered Pleasance a Military Cross and Sergeant H.E. Foster a Military Medal.[50]

That ended 'D' Company's actions for October 9, which the Royals considered one of frustration. The war diarist reported being surprised by the "strong resistance to our attempts to cut off the peninsula. Unfortunately, as long as he is in control of the mouth of the Scheldt, our supply problem will still provide many headaches."[51]

The next morning, Lendrum and Brigadier Fred Cabeldu hammered out a plan for the Royals to put in a two-company attack "to seize the main road through the neck" of the isthmus. Heavy cloud precluded air support, so a major artillery fire plan would precede the infantry as they advanced across the open polders. Much of the morning was spent by the artillery observers identifying German positions between the Royals and the road and parallelling railroad that ran across the northern edge of the isthmus. Once the Royals gained the road, the isthmus would be severed.[52]

By noon, the two companies in Ossendrecht and battalion tactical headquarters had moved out into the polders to form up behind 'A' and 'D' Companies. At 1300 hours, with the artillery, Marine anti-aircraft guns, and Toronto Scottish mortar and machine-gun platoons all firing madly at assigned targets, 'C' Company passed through 'A' Company's lines. Major Paddy Ryall led his men into open ground where they could easily have been slaughtered had the Germans not been forced to ground by the intense and highly accurate supporting fire. Within an hour, Ryall's leading platoon reached a farm less than a quarter-mile from the road.[53] On the dyke behind the farm, the Royals overran and captured a 75-millimetre antitank gun and its crew. From there, 'C' Company was within firing range of both the road and railroad.

Realizing that the link to South Beveland was in jeopardy, two reserve companies of paratroops from the 6th Regiment rushed forward and counterattacked. One company moved to block any Canadian attempt to attack Woensdrecht from the west, while the other sought to eliminate 'C' Company. Supporting the latter operation were two self-propelled guns. Ryall brought artillery fire down on the Germans advancing across the polder, while an antitank gun of 2nd Canadian Anti-Tank Regiment took on the SPGs. When the antitank gun knocked one of the SPGs out of action, the other became mired in mud and immobilized while taking evasive action. The German counterattack collapsed.[54]

'B' Company, meanwhile, had kicked off its advance only to be stopped by a strong German position midway to the railroad. But it was still able to range small-arms fire on the road and railway. The day's fighting cost the Royals three dead and twenty wounded.[55] German casualties were estimated at about fifty dead, approximately twice that wounded, and 156 prisoners.[56]

Both sides spent the night regrouping and preparing respective attacks—the Germans to restore control over the isthmus, the Canadians to sever the link. Each greeted the dawn of October 11 by raining the other with heavy artillery bombardments. The Royals' 'A' Company jumped through 'C' Company's lines at 1530 hours, while the paratroops let them come forward unmolested "until they were making a charge up an embankment then opened up with heavy fire resulting in heavy casualties particularly to 7 [Platoon]. Mortar fire then became intense and a counterattack was made on 'A' Company from their objective with the result that they withdrew through 'C' Company."

The Germans then struck both 'C' and 'B' Companies with a counterattack supported by flamethrowers, which was barely driven off.[57] As the light bled from the sky, both sides were like two punch-drunk fighters, glaring at each other across the mat, neither willing to make the next swing. Remarkably, no Royals had died this day, but thirty-three were wounded.[58] The paratroops entrenched themselves deeply into the railway embankment. Before them lay the open polder, which their many heavy machine guns transformed into a killing zone. From Woensdrecht, the Germans could also saturate the polders with flanking fire. They would wait for the Canadians, who held Hoogerheide and were within several hundred yards of controlling the isthmus itself, to make the next move.[59]

But this would not be for at least two days, as Brigadier Keefler had decided it would take this long for 2 CID to regroup and develop a new offensive plan.

[12]

Did Our Best

WHILE 2ND CANADIAN Infantry Division had been pushing north from Antwerp, on the evening of October 4, two 3rd Canadian Infantry Division brigades had concentrated south of the Leopold Canal near Maldegem. This move to face the Breskens Pocket had only come after the division captured Calais on October 1, freeing 7th Canadian Infantry Brigade to carry out a ninety-mile march to the canal. Major General Dan Spry now prepared to implement a precisely planned four-phase reduction of the pocket as set out by Lieutenant General Guy Simonds. Operation Switchback seemed deceptively simple.

Phase One, to begin the morning of October 6, would see 7 CIB assault the canal dead north of Maldegem across a mile-wide front with Strooibrug and Moerhuizen anchoring the ends. At Strooibrug, the Dérivation de la Lys angled southwards away from the Leopold Canal, so an assault here meant crossing only one waterway rather than two—the situation that had contributed to the Algonquin Regiment's September 13–14 defeat.

The brigade was to establish a bridgehead bounded by Middelburg to the west, Aardenburg to the north, and extending east to Moershoofd. The bridgehead's deepest point of penetration would be at Aardenburg, just under two miles from the canal. From this bridgehead, 8th Canadian Infantry Brigade would kick off Phase Two to capture the town of Sluis, two and a half miles to the northwest, while 7 CIB pushed northwest on its left flank to the Bruges–Sluis Canal.

Phase Three would follow on October 8, but on an entirely different front. While 7 CIB and 8 CIB concentrated at Maldegem, 9th Canadian Infantry Brigade had gathered near Ghent. Here, it was undertaking a hurried refresher course in amphibious landings. On October 8, Simonds planned to send 9 CIB aboard amphibians from Terneuzen, across the mouth of the Braakman Inlet, to land close to Hoofdplaat. Having struck the Germans from behind, the brigade would drive straight along the coast to Breskens. Simultaneously, 7 CIB would be moving northeast from Sluis to seize Oostburg and Schoondijke, while 8 CIB headed west for the coast near Retranchement. As a final touch, 7th Canadian Reconnaissance Regiment (the Duke of York Royal Canadian Hussars) armoured cars would clear the Leopold Canal. Once all this manoeuvring was quickly completed, Phase Four would see 8 CIB close the pocket by moving south along the coast to the city of Knokke-aan-zee, which showed on Canadian maps as Knocke-sur-Mer. The essence of Operation Switchback was to overwhelm the Germans by hitting them hard on so many fronts that their forces could never be concentrated.

Army intelligence reported that the 64th Infantry Division consisted of only seven thousand troops, but had no information regarding the strength of "artillery and coastal defence units or possible battle groups" that might augment this strength.[1] There were, in fact, about fifteen thousand Germans in the pocket.[2] Their backs were against the wall formed by the West Scheldt and they were ordered to fight to the death. Yet Allied intelligence repeatedly dismissed any possibility that the division would make a determined stand. Instead, the concern was the Breskens landscape itself. "The area," intelligence staff wrote, "is completely flat, with a network of minor canals and ditches, and numerous areas which are permanently flooded. It is criss-crossed by dykes which mostly carry roads or tracks. The fields, or 'polders,' are open and afford little or no cover. Church towers and buildings are the only viewpoints."[3]

Because of the exposed landscape, Operation Switchback was to enjoy lavish artillery support. The heavy guns of II Canadian Corps and Ninth British Army Groups Royal Artillery were committed. And 4th Canadian Armoured Division's field regiments would be added to 3 CID's inherent firepower to put six field regiments on the gun lines. This meant that 144 25-pounders, 128 mediums—with calibres of 4.5-inch, 5.5-inch, or 105-millimetre, and 55 heavy 7.2-inch guns capable of ranging a shell weighing more than two hundred pounds onto targets almost ten miles away—were available. "The maximum amount of artillery that can bear will support each operation in turn," Simonds had declared.[4]

Of course, not all of this great weight of artillery could range on every potential target, so the regiments were detailed to support either 7 CIB's assault across the Leopold Canal or 9 CIB's amphibious operation at Hoofdplaat. Although units additional to 3 CID's field regiments were committed, full operational control rested with that division's commander of artillery, Brigadier Stanley Todd, rather than—as was standard—the artillery commander of II Canadian Corps. There were two reasons for this unorthodox decision. First, the gunners were only supporting 3 CID rather than multiple divisions. Second, communications between the gun regiments, the infantry battalions, and the overseer of artillery operations would be too ponderous if all communications had to pass through corps headquarters, which was situated two miles east of Ghent in Destelbergen.

Todd assigned the 15th and 19th Field Regiments and the 10th Medium Regiment to 9 CIB, while 7 CIB would initially be supported by the British Ninth Army Group's medium and heavy gun regiments, from positions to the right, and the batteries of II Canadian Corps's regiments to the left of the Leopold Canal crossing point.[5] Despite the preponderance of artillery, Simonds and his staff knew the German fortifications on the Leopold Canal were unlikely to suffer extensive damage because they were dug in on the north-facing side of the dyke—making them largely immune to all but a chance hit. Still, the intensity of fire should force the Germans to hunker inside these positions until 7 CIB was almost across the canal and the fire had to lift to avoid friendly casualties. Further, to prevent the Germans realizing precisely where the canal was to be crossed and reinforcing that section, the artillery would fire only as the Canadian Scottish Regiment and the Regina Rifles began 7 CIB's attack.

These restrictions served as a serious handicap to the artillery's effectiveness, so an additional weapon was sought to improve the odds. A careful reconnaissance from Strooibrug east to the Isabellapolder had given the Canadians a good understanding of the canal's defensive positions. While this confirmed that artillery bombardment promised to be ineffective, it also revealed that the fortifications were possibly susceptible to a novel form of attack. Flamethrowers had so far seen little use in northwest Europe, but the Canadian arsenal contained both the man-packed Lifebuoy and a modified Bren carrier designated as the Wasp Mk II. Each battalion had a small contingent of these carriers. In September, Wasp crews had tried firing their flame guns across canals similar to the Leopold. "It was discovered that by inclining the carrier part-way up the slope of the bank its flame could be thrown not only against the opposite bank, but beyond it, where enemy slit trenches and dugouts might be expected to be sited."[6]

Consequently, twenty-seven Wasps would support the assault.[7] While most were 3 CID's inherent machines, those of 4th Canadian Armoured Division's 10th Infantry Brigade were also allocated.[8] With an effective range of 120 to 140 yards, the Wasps could easily project streams of flame across the canal. Lieutenant George Bannerman, a flamethrower specialist assigned to First Canadian Army, believed the weapon's main purpose was to cause demoralization rather than physical injury—as few defensive positions could actually be penetrated with fire. But the Leopold Canal fortifications were different, perfectly suited for subjection to "Golden Rain." To cause a Golden Rain, he wrote, the "gun is fired at maximum elevation, in the direction of the enemy, with the result that the rod of fuel breaks up in mid air into small, ignited blobs of fuel. Depending on the wind, this 'Golden Rain' will cover a very large area of ground."

By firing over the dyke, the Golden Rain would shower down on the positions, setting alight any straw or wood covering the slit trenches or spattering into the trenches themselves. "Enemy who were hit by a sizeable 'shot' of the fuel died almost immediately. If only a few blobs of the burning fuel struck a man it was possible for him to smother the flame. But, if he was struck by a large blob, smothering was practically impossible and in this case the fats in the human body were literally burned up."[9] This was the horror Bannerman prepared to visit upon the men defending the Leopold Canal.

In addition to providing its Wasps, 10th Canadian Infantry Brigade would support 7 CIB's assault with an elaborate deception the day before, intended to "draw off much German strength from the real crossing to the westward."[10] Two battalions—the Algonquins and the Argyll and Sutherland Highlanders—were to play the primary role. Since their September 23 failure to force a breach at the Isabellapolder adjacent to the head of the Braakman Inlet, the Algonquins had been locked in a "succession of patrol after patrol. Patrols that didn't start off right, patrols that never came back, patrols that came back at half-strength, with not even a prisoner to show for the cost."[11]

The luckless Algonquins again drew the short end of the straw, receiving orders to assault an enemy "dug in solidly in concrete bunkers underneath the [dykes whose] quality [was] demonstrably high... They were skilled in the use of their weapons, and the defensive belts of fire that they had woven were almost impossible to traverse, even at night," Major George Cassidy lamented. "The machine gun fire, for instance, was laid on so that it would sweep the [dyke] tops at about eight inches height. One could not even crawl under this. Their mortar targets were registered to a matter of feet, rather than yards, and they had plenty of mortars to use. Besides the ubiquitous 88mm. guns, they had the use of the coastal and railroad guns still in the 'pocket' area, and the fire from these could be brought to bear on almost any point on the pocket perimeter. Altogether, it would take Spartan measures to achieve any success here." To date, successes had been entirely absent. The Algonquins greeted the orders grimly, particularly as they were not informed as to its purpose.[12]

The Argylls, meanwhile, were spared the casualties that would inevitably be suffered by actually trying to cross the canal. They would instead stage an elaborately choreographed demonstration to hoodwink the Germans into believing that they and the Algonquins were trying to break into the Breskens Pocket.

Both battalions played their hands on October 5, the Algonquins advancing three companies into the killing field, ostensibly to "test the enemy defences and to take [prisoners] in the vicinity of Isabella," with predictable result. Twenty-eight men were killed or wounded, including thirty-four-year-old Captain Fred Grafton, who died after being evacuated to hospital in England for absolutely no gain. "The above mentioned [operation]," the war diarist bitterly recorded, "though necessary, will probably appear in the papers as 'only patrol activity.' We wonder if the contented readers realize the amount of blood and lives lost under the heading of those three little words."[13]

By contrast, the Argylls were mere bystanders to a surreal attack mounted by nothing more than a troop of sound effects specialists. Equipped with "mobile record-players with an amazing set of records, representing bridge-building activities, complete with typically Canadian dialogue and expression," the specialists broadcast over powerful speakers aimed at the Germans, while a thick smokescreen obscured the canal, artillery and mortar fire saturated the area, and "tanks and carriers" raced "madly back and forth on our side of the canal, 'revving' their motors constantly and making as much noise as possible." The result was a great deal of German fire thrown at the Argyll line, but no casualties.[14] Whether the ruse worked was never determined.

"IN THE WEIRD half-light of the cold October morning...the grimly determined" Canadian Scottish Regiment and Regina Rifles "trudged heavily along the dirt verges of the cobblestone roads" towards forming-up positions near the canal.[15] Much of the dim light that guided their way came from exploding shells fired to cover the sounds made by the troops and machines congregating behind the south canal bank. Teams of engineers had marked out approach lanes with white tape and were now readying the narrow floating kapok bridges. Once a toehold was gained on the other side, these would be unlimbered to span the canal and enable most of the men to cross on foot rather than aboard boats. Preparing and crewing the boats had been tasked to troops from 8 CIB's North Shore (New Brunswick) Regiment's 'C' and 'D' Companies. Also forming behind the high southern canal bank were the Wasp carriers. Despite this hubbub, there was no indication that the Germans suspected anything amiss, the eight- to ten-foot-high canal bank blocking their view.[16]

The Canadian Scottish would cross east of the village of Oosthoek, while the Reginas went over just in front of Moerhuizen. An unusual wrinkle in the Regina plan was the fact that one of the lead companies was not actually part of the battalion. Rather, it comprised First Canadian Army's Headquarters Defence Company drawn from the Royal Montreal Regiment (RMR), which had exchanged duties with the Reginas' 'B' Company just before Calais to gain combat experience. The RMR had performed well during the Calais operation, and Lieutenant Colonel Foster Matheson had decided there was no reason it should not participate in attack. For simplicity, battalion headquarters referred to the RMR as if it were 'B' Company. As Major A.H. Lowe had seen action at Calais, he was designated Left Out of Battle in order to give his second-in-command, Captain Robert Schwob, some command experience. This company would cross on the left and Major Ronald Shawcross's 'A' Company on the right.

Twenty-eight-year-old Shawcross had joined the Reginas in 1936 and risen from the ranks to lead 'A' Company onto the sand on D-Day. A tough soldier, he was bloody unhappy about today's plan. It seemed that every time a hard fight was ensured, 'A' Company got put on the sharp end and the strain on the men was showing. They "were getting very tired and the NCOs were getting worn out, you could see it from looking at them. They were losing weight, getting gaunt, they were turning a yellowish colour and their eyes were just blank."[17]

Even assembling for the attack had been tough. The company had moved across the open fields with mud oozing over boot tops, only to come under German mortar fire. Rifleman Fred Kidd had thrown himself into the mud so only his nose showed until the bombardment ceased. Then he joined the others trudging forward.[18]

Lying on his stomach in the mud on top of the canal, Shawcross looked across to where a machine-gun post in a cement blockhouse enjoyed a clean field of fire precisely where his company was to go over. He had been assured this would pose no problem. The Wasps "would be brought up to us, trained on the far side and we would go over after the flame throwers had played for about five minutes. That would have fried everybody on the far side and we would have gone over with no opposition."[19] He hoped to hell this would prove the case.

At 0525, the Wasps opened up with huge streams of fire. "The sky lit up in a scarlet glow which was visible for miles," reported the Canadian Scottish regimental historian. As the flamethrowers began to run out of fuel, both battalions moved forward. The Can Scots' 'B' Company headed for the water in front of Oosthoek, while 'D' Company started from a point midway between this village and Moershoofd to the east. The last flames fell just as the two companies scrambled into the assault boats. Everyone knew, as Captain E. Fraser later wrote, that "to have success in such a show the infantry must actually go in under the flames or cross when the last flame has left the Wasp and to be able to take up the positions which [the enemy] have vacated or surrendered on the opposite bank of the canal."[20] Getting it right, the Can Scots paddled out while the "liquid fire was still burning whatever it struck, and some houses 30 yards north of the canal were set on fire. Flaming gobs of liquid fire were even burning on the water. Any enemy in the trenches immediately opposite the 'Wasps' was put out of action, and many who escaped were terrified."

While the assault boats crossed, the engineers pushed a kapok bridge over, and it was quickly anchored to enable 'C' Company to cross and reinforce 'B' Company in capturing Oosthoek. 'A' Company would remain on the other side in reserve.[21] Within twelve minutes, the three assaulting companies had gained the opposite bank.[22]

The attack had begun well for the Can Scots, but the Reginas faced an altogether different situation. In front of 'A' Company, the flame mostly fell short and lay burning on the surface as Shawcross's men tried to launch the boats. The fires on the water silhouetted them. As his men and some of the North Shores from Major O. Corbett's 'D' Company manhandled the boats down the bank, machine-gun fire tore into the canvas craft, disabling most. Shawcross pulled his men back to a stone farmhouse on a road running close to the canal. The major hoped to get through to battalion headquarters on his No. 18 wireless for instructions. If the Wasps could be redeployed and new boats found, perhaps he could try again. Setting up behind the house, Shawcross and his headquarters section had just got the radio ready when what he believed must have been one of the powerful German coastal guns scored a direct hit on the building. The back wall disintegrated, burying everyone. Shawcross was dug out. Although his right leg seemed to be dragging a bit and barely able to take weight, he considered himself uninjured. One man had been crushed to death; two others had legs so mangled they had to be amputated. The radio was demolished, so Shawcross limped to battalion headquarters to personally get new orders.[23]

East of 'A' Company, Captain Schwob had ordered his No. 1 and No. 3 Platoons from the Royal Montreal Regiment to launch their boats the moment the Wasps stopped firing. Schwob accompanied No. 3 Platoon, which was commanded by Sergeant W. Craddock. Fires were burning all along the opposite bank and the launch went fine. But as the men took to the water, a number of flares arced into the sky and illuminated them. The machine guns in the pillbox to the right and other isolated gun positions opened up with a storm of fire. Sergeant Harry Thomas Murray's No. 1 Platoon paddled into "the centre of the cone of fire." The lead boat with Murray aboard was shredded, the sergeant and almost everyone aboard killed. Lifting their fire slightly, the machine-gunners tore into the platoon's second boat, causing another slaughter.[24]

No. 3 Platoon, meanwhile, crossed unscathed and the men scrambled to the top of the canal bank. From the opposite shore, twenty-five-year-old Lieutenant William Noel Barclay from Montreal's Westmount led No. 2 Platoon and the company headquarters aboard another flight of boats. All around, bullets kicked up waterspouts, and tracers whipped close overhead as the men paddled frantically, but they seemed blessed by angels as the German gunners failed to find them. Then, just as the lead boat touched the shore, a burst tore into it. Barclay, who the regimental war diarist described as a "very gallant officer and gentleman, fell to the bottom of the boat mortally wounded."[25]

The RMR consolidated on top of the canal bank, digging in and quickly gathering their wounded. Determined to keep the attack from stalling, Schwob ordered Sergeant Craddock's No. 3 Platoon of about twenty-five men to move north 150 yards before hooking to the left to gain the main road that crossed the canal at Strooibrug and led to Aardenburg. Sergeant C.S. Hayward was to go west along the dyke with No. 2 Platoon to clear out the machine-gun positions as far as the bridge crossing.

Craddock's men headed off first, with five survivors from No. 1 Platoon along. It was now light and Schwob and the rest of the company initially watched their progress, but when they moved into some trees the soldiers disappeared from sight. Schwob set up his headquarters in a trench on the bank. With him were Company Sergeant Major D. Page and Forward Observation Officer Lieutenant Gamelin of the 12th Canadian Field Regiment. Gamelin could offer little help, as both the company wireless set and his own had been knocked out by bullets during the crossing. Also crowded into the trench or nearby shelters were the growing number of wounded. Lance Sergeant C.B. Shipley had a bullet hole in the leg, Private R.L. Pugh had a smashed arm, while others were less severely injured, but their numbers increased rapidly as wounded came back from No. 2 Platoon.[26]

Sergeant Craddock's platoon advanced with two sections forward and the third providing fire support. Shortly after the platoon moved beyond the canal bank, a machine-gun burst caught Corporal G.W. Findlay in three places and he collapsed. The platoon's medical orderly, Rifleman Gordon Ashby—loaned to the RMR by the Reginas—rushed to his side, but reported Findlay finished. Leaving him, Craddock double-timed the platoon away from the German gun to a dirt road bordered on either side by ditches. Proceeding along the road, Craddock headed towards a cluster of houses. Before they reached the buildings, however, snipers brought them under fire and the platoon sought cover in one of the ditches. The houses were about five hundred yards distant and the platoon began crawling towards them. Craddock later wrote: "The enemy now had us really pin-pointed and things got pretty hot, with fire coming from our front, from the left, and also the rear." After covering about two hundred yards, the fire worsened. The two Bren guns were useless, jammed with mud.

Craddock realized that there were Germans in the ditch immediately across the road from them just as a grenade landed near him. He was wounded by the explosion. A bullet struck Private Adelard Roger Martin in the head, killing him. Then Private N.S. Taylor was shot in the shoulder. A brisk grenade exchange ended with the Germans in the opposite ditch moving off. But Private W.J. Barrick was seriously injured, one hand almost sheared off. Corporal Raymond Wishart had been shot and killed. "They were picking us off pretty rapidly and the situation was hopeless. I decided we would have to give up. I was in severe pain, but was clear of mind when I made this decision," Craddock wrote. "The platoon put up as good a show as it possibly could...Jerry had us isolated. We did our best." The remnants of No. 3 Platoon, RMR were taken into captivity. Craddock and about fourteen others would, however, be liberated from a German hospital on October 26. Among them was Private Findlay, not as badly wounded as Rifleman Ashby had thought, who had been rescued by a German patrol.[27]

While Craddock's platoon was being overwhelmed, Sergeant Hayward's No. 2 Platoon moving west alongside the canal had been held up by snipers, and a runner was sent to report this to Captain Schwob. Ordering CSM Page to keep the headquarters section put, Schwob ran forward. Jumping into a trench behind where the leading section had taken cover, Schwob arrived just as Private W.P. Cosgrove moved by with a captured German sniper in tow. Seeing the Canadian officer, the German soldier asked for a cigarette. Schwob swore at him instead. A second later, Private L.V. "Shorty" Hughes, who was at his side, was drilled in the helmet by a sniper's bullet and fell to the ground. To Schwob's surprise, the man quickly regained his feet, pulled his helmet off, and found a "neat hole through it. On examining his head, [Schwob] finds that 'Shorty' is uninjured. On satisfying himself that he is alright 'Shorty' raises his eyes to heaven, crosses himself and murmurs, 'They are still with me.'"

Men nursing various bullet wounds were trickling back from the leading section to Schwob's position. Within minutes, "at least eight or nine men had become casualties," the company's war diarist wrote. "The sniping is a menace as it is extremely accurate. [Private] R.M. Thornicroft appears with an extremely bloody arm obviously smashed by a bullet." Schwob slapped a field dressing on the man and sent him and the other more badly wounded back to the landing site for evacuation. En route, "one of Hitler's super-men, seeing an unarmed and obviously wounded man decides he is an ideal target and shoots him dead."[28] The dead soldier was Richard Maurice Thornicroft.

Under fire, Schwob worked his way up to the leading section. Sergeant L.G. Thomson was in command of the eight-man group. Corporal Elwyn Bernard Thomas and Private T.E. Pollari had been severely wounded and were sheltered in a shallow trench. Thomas had a bullet in his stomach; Pollari had been shot in the head and was unconscious. Private Cosgrove asked Schwob for permission to go back for a stretcher to carry the men to safety. The captain immediately agreed, but as Cosgrove began to head off, a bullet grazed his head and knocked him unconscious. Schwob decided further efforts to evacuate Thomas and Pollari would only get more men killed or badly wounded.

The RMR was in dire straits. No. 1 Platoon had been slaughtered. Sergeant Craddock's No. 3 Platoon remained unaccounted for. Schwob and No. 2 Platoon were pinned down, and the captain estimated that at least 50 per cent of the men on the canal were dead or wounded. Thomas was clearly dying. Ammunition was running low, Schwob had no communication with his headquarters section, and he could see Germans creeping in for an assault. Retreat was impossible, so Schwob prepared for a "last stand" he expected none would survive.

AT COMPANY HEADQUARTERS, CSM PAGE was thinking the same thing. He had a handful of men spread along a short, shallow trench on top of the bank. Moving along the line, he checked each man and found them still game for a fight. As he reached the end, Page spotted a German armed with a grenade getting ready to pitch it his way. The CSM shot him dead. More Germans were approaching, and seconds later they launched an assault. Page and his small party met the charge with a furious volley of fire that drove the Germans back. In the aftermath, Page discovered that almost every man with him was now suffering from one wound or another. It was not yet 0900. The company had been shredded in less than four hours.[29]

Just as the survivors braced themselves to die, the sound of voices across the canal drew their attention. On the opposite bank, the Reginas' 'D' Company was preparing to cross about fifty yards to the west of where No. 2 Platoon was pinned down. Gaining the northern shore at 0855 hours, 'D' Company tried to advance beyond the canal bank, but was immediately halted by heavy machine-gun and mortar fire. Captain Mel Douglas's men started frantically digging in, only to hit water when their slit trenches were no more than a foot deep. Lying in the cold, muddy water, they waited for the German fire to slacken.[30]

Across the canal, Lieutenant Colonel Foster Matheson had his battalion tactical headquarters in an abandoned World War I pillbox dug into the south-facing side of the canal embankment. The pillbox had been partially flooded, but by carpeting the floor with brush, the place had been rendered crudely serviceable and the heavy concrete provided welcome cover for the continual rain of mortar and artillery fire. A hole dug into the top of the embankment directly above the pillbox enabled Matheson and his staff to observe the battle.

The position was also used to concentrate Bren gun fire on the enemy pillbox to the right of the crossing area whenever assault boats were sent across with reinforcements and ammunition, bringing back the wounded on the return trip. Rifleman Evert Nordstrom was manning a Bren, shooting long bursts at the German pillbox apertures every time the boats took to the water. Largely, the Germans ignored him, concentrating their fire on the assault boats. But after Nordstrom fired on the pillbox one time, he realized that a gunner was zeroing in on him. "Their machineguns fire at a very rapid rate and this time about every fifth bullet was a tracer and it appeared with the path they were coming at me that I was going to be hit right between the eyes and what a cracking sound as the bullets went by my ear," he later remembered. Whenever he thought of that moment afterward, Nordstrom shuddered.[31]

Recognizing that the two companies on the other side of the canal were in jeopardy of being overwhelmed, Matheson ordered 'C' Company across at 1020 hours. Major Leonard Gass and his men landed immediately behind 'D' Company, then struck out to the east to secure the ground about seven hundred yards distant where 'A' Company was to have originally landed.[32] No. 15 Platoon was on the right, No. 14 in the centre, and No. 13 to the left. Lieutenant Ken Bergin, commanding the centre platoon, had never seen anything like the enemy fire coming his way. "Hell was really breaking loose with very heavy enemy machine gun fire raking the top of the embankment and coming also from our right rear." That puzzled Bergin because it meant there were German gunners on the south bank of the canal. The fire from behind "was causing heavy casualties amongst our men, as there was absolutely no cover on the water side of the embankment. I ordered an advance and led the platoon over the top of the embankment, but the enemy fire was so heavy that those not killed or wounded had to reverse their attack and regroup on the waterside. I managed to reach and drop in on Major Gass, after a short briefing, I returned to the platoon position to rally the few remaining men for another attempt to cross the embankment. Before we could proceed, Major Gass's runner reached me with orders to return to the major's position. Just as he finished uttering these orders, a burst of machinegun bullets struck him killing him instantly. I ran and crawled back to Major Gass's trench again but by the time I got there, he and those with him had been killed. I scrambled back over once again to gather what was left of 14 Platoon. Rifleman Raymond Graves and three or four others went over the top. I angled off to the right and landed in a trench containing Lieutenant [George] Black and four other members of 13 Platoon."[33]

Much of the German fire was coming from a large concrete pillbox bristling with machine guns, and at noon Captain Douglas led 'D' Company against this position. While some of the men hammered the fortification with PIAT guns, the others charged it head on. Many were cut down, but the survivors chucked grenades inside. The pillbox was taken, but at a terrible cost. Only twenty-seven men remained in 'D' Company.[34]

The Reginas were now so cut up all they could hope to do was retain the narrow toehold atop the dyke, as the Germans began counterattacking. In the mid-afternoon, enemy soldiers closed on the trench holding Lieutenant Bergin and men from Nos. 13 and 14 Platoons of 'C' Company. When they lobbed a couple of grenades into the position, Bergin and a rifleman "each grabbed [one] for the return trip, but before we could get them clear, they exploded in our hands wounding five of the six including Lt. Black. The next thing we knew, there was a number of Germans standing above us pointing their Schmeissers at our heads and shouting [in German] hands-up and come out. As there was nothing more we could do, we complied... Everything... had suddenly become quiet, no resistance on our right or left, leading me to believe we had lost our entire company."[35]

After a cursory search for weapons, the six men were detailed to carry stretchers bearing German wounded to the rear. Their route took them across a system of boardwalks that had been slung over flooded fields. While crossing these, Bergin and Black deliberately spilled the soldier on their stretcher into the water. As they dropped into the muck to retrieve the man, the two officers covertly shoved their platoon books, maps, and aerial photographs under the boardwalk to prevent their falling into German hands. Bergin soon became separated from the others, and endured a long captivity that saw him liberated in February from a German camp by Russian troops, only to be transferred as a prisoner to Odessa until being put aboard a British ship for repatriation on March 26, 1945.[36]

'C' Company, meanwhile, having lost most of its officers and many men, was placed under command of the RMR's Captain Schwob, while the eleven men still standing from this unit were added to 'D' Company's strength in an attempt to make it battle-worthy. Even with the added men, it only mustered thirty-eight.[37]

The rate at which the Reginas were burning through ammunition just to hold on was threatening to overwhelm Regimental Sergeant Major Wally Edwards and Lance Corporal Bert Adamoski, who "were going steady, in a jeep with a trailer, bringing up mainly ammo, especially hand grenades, then bringing back the wounded, and Brens that had seized up to clean. Our fellows threw so many grenades it would make your head swim to try to keep track of them—more than they had hairs on their heads!"[38] The battalion's normal daily complement of munitions for combat operations had been quickly exhausted and completely replenished, only to be burned off again. Edwards had never seen anything like it.[39] The number of guns jamming due to the fine sand on the dykes was particularly worrisome. Matheson ordered men from the carrier and antitank platoons to crowd into the headquarters pillbox to take turns stripping and cleaning jammed Brens, Stens, and rifles that had been sent for repair. Everyone was working flat out.[40]

In the late afternoon, 'A' Company was ferried over to the spot where 'D' Company had landed, and Schwob pulled his men back close to Major Ronald Shawcross's position. 'A' Company had arrived bearing cases of grenades in addition to those each man normally carried on his web belt. "The Germans were just on the other side of the high [dyke], so it was a question of whose grenades were the best." Shawcross and the other long-time regimental veterans knew "to pick up a grenade, pull the pin, count to three and throw; by the time it landed it was ready to explode." But the new men "would pull the pin and throw it, they were five-second grenades and Germans would pick them up and throw them back."[41] Many of the German grenades were quickly chucked back as well, but it was a dangerous game, as Lieutenant Bergin had learned earlier.

At last light, the situation was desperate. "The entire battalion now consisted of a single line of men along the southern edge of the dyke. A few steps behind them was the Leopold Canal. 'C' Company was positioned just to the right of the landing spot, 'A' Company was in the centre, and 'D' Company held the left edge. Efforts were made to gain depth, by extending groups to the front, but this was impossible owing to the terrific fire which answered every movement...The enemy, besides being able to work up to the dyke itself, could fire into this confined area from three sides. He was also able to maintain heavy observed fire on the canal, across which supplies were brought. From strongpoints to the west along the dyke he could fire into the position accurately, since he had visual command of both sides of the bank. Every advantage in fact rested with the enemy."[42]

In the narrow perimeter, the riflemen huddled in their slit trenches and waited to be counterattacked. With them were several forward observation officers from the 12th Field Regiment. Throughout the day, they had been able to do little to tip the scales to favour the Canadians because the fighting had been "at such close quarters that it was difficult [for artillery] to do any shooting."[43] But it was clear to the gunners that their services could prove vital at any moment if the Germans tried to bring in reinforcements for massed counterattacks, so they spent the day feverishly building up their shell supplies so that each gun had four hundred more rounds than normally allotted.[44]

At 2000 hours, Matheson called a conference of his battalion staff to plan for the grim night that likely lay ahead and the next day's operations. He took the opportunity to praise the Royal Montreal Regiment, pointing "out that they were the only company of the two leading companies to cross the canal, who had accomplished their task... by doing so they enabled the operation to continue." It was a fifteen-minute tribute peppered with expressions such as "grim determination," "great courage," and "splendid fighting ability." He closed by saying, "I cannot pay too high a tribute to the RMR [Company]. I have only one regret and that is that I must tell you that this company is wiped out. My sympathies go out to the RMRs at the loss of all these good men, but the important thing in war is to accomplish the task given to you. This the RMRs have done and it could not have been done better."[45]

[13]

A Hell of a Way to Go

WHEREAS THE REGINA RIFLES assault had begun to unravel the moment the lead companies began crossing the canal on October 6, the Canadian Scottish Regiment had not run into major opposition until it moved up on top of the dyke and encountered "plenty of small arms fire, but [also an] increasing amount of mortar and shell fire [that] made it clear the enemy was going to fight hard and that he had plenty of support to back him up."[1] This came as a nasty shock to 'C' Company's Lieutenant Royce Marshall, who had understood this was to "be a nice easy attack." Disseminating what army intelligence had assured would be the case, company commander Major Roger Schjelderup had said: "There will be nothing to this. The enemy are white bread troops, so it will be a pushover."[2] Schjelderup's attempt to boost morale belied his deep concern over how hastily the operation had been thrown together. Getting to the launch site alone had required a forced six-mile march carrying full battle gear that meant his men went into action already fatigued. It was not only the march, though. Everyone in 7th Canadian Infantry Brigade was worn out from the Channel port clearing mission and needed a long rest. Instead, it was once again into battle.[3]

'B' and 'D' Companies had been first across the canal, and Lieutenant L. Hobden one of the first men to jump out of an assault boat. Several boats had been set on fire by flamethrower fuel that had landed in the water. But the flamethrowers appeared to have done the trick. There was no immediate opposition, confirming that "anyone in the slits would have fried." While trying to get his bearings, Hobden realized that 'B' Company's No. 12 Platoon had "headed right up for Holland" rather than going west along the canal towards Oosthoek.[4] This had taken them out into the flooded fields and "up to their knees and going deeper when I caught up to them and settled them down," Hobden later wrote. Pointing No. 12 in the right direction, Hobden ran back to his No. 11 Platoon and the two platoons moved in line towards Oosthoek.[5]

While Hobden had been reorganizing the rest of the company, Major Earl English had headed directly for Oosthoek with No. 10 Platoon and his company headquarters section. At first, opposition was "very disorganized," but resistance stiffened as they reached the hamlet's outer edge, and English ordered the men to dig in around one of the outer farms.[6] Oosthoek was not so much a hamlet as a collection of small farms facing a road that angled off from the canal on a gradual northwesterly plane. As Hobden's part of 'B' Company approached a crossroad that ran north to Vuilpan, it was met by heavy mortar fire. Hobden put No. 12 Platoon into a house close to English's position and set No. 11 Platoon into two houses closer to the crossroads.[7] 'B' Company had shifted from offence to defence.

Having crossed the canal on the shaky kapok bridge behind 'B' Company, 'C' Company came under such heavy fire that it was unable to move along the top of the dyke. Instead, Major Schjelderup told Lieutenant Marshall that his No. 15 Platoon should hug the steep and heavily overgrown south side of the bank. Marshall and his men "slithered along the side of the dyke for about 800 yards. This was hard work but finally we arrived at the position...where the company attack was to be launched."[8]

Schjelderup was close behind with the rest of the company. After a 250-yard advance, he "realized that 'B' Company could not have reached its objective and that the far side of the canal bank was still occupied in strength by the enemy. This produced a very unusual and difficult situation," he wrote later. "The top of the dyke was under observation and enemy machine-gun fire and the enemy were in strength in deeply dug trenches on the far side... From these positions they were able to lob quantities of grenades on 'C' Company, which was clinging perilously with their feet literally either in, or a step above, the water of the canal."[9]

Marshall attempted to break the dangerously developing stalemate with a platoon assault across the embankment towards Oosthoek. "As soon as we went over the top of the dyke we were met with enfilade fire from the left and right flanks which forced us to go to ground and orient ourselves."[10] The lieutenant had never seen anything like the ground the platoon was in. Absolutely flat, cut by canals and rivers, and mostly flooded. The areas not flooded were "covered with trees, hedgerows and villages. The water obstacles... made movement by foot or organized military formations extremely difficult. Here the enemy had a major advantage in that he had... flooded certain areas... and knew every inch of ground."[11]

The platoon was using the exposed root systems of a row of poplars parallelling the canal for cover, everyone worming deep into the scant protection in an attempt to escape the incoming fire. Marshall realized "that if we were going to 'get going' it had to be done then or we would never move at all. I posted one Bren gun to protect my left and we made a dash for the closest buildings 500 yards to our front. I am sure that machine gun fire is the best incentive to get men moving. On reaching the house we received fire from other farm buildings about 500 yards further on. This fire was so directed that we could not go to the right or left of the building, in fact, when we attempted to collect wounded Germans who were lying groaning and crying for water we were fired upon. This fire caused a couple casualties."[12]

Schjelderup capitalized on Marshall's toehold within Oosthoek by pushing No. 14 Platoon forward. Soon the two platoons were locked in a "long drawn-out contest in which every weapon the company possessed was employed" to little effect. In an attempt to contact the Regina Rifles, No. 13 Platoon edged along the canal and managed to knock out two machine-gun posts at point-blank range with a PIAT gun before its commander realized he was getting too far out on a limb to continue. Falling back along the canal, the platoon advanced across the road running through Oosthoek to seize a house to the right of No. 15 Platoon.[13]

Back on the canal bank, Schjelderup was becoming overwhelmed by casualties. Dragging badly wounded men back to the crossing point for evacuation was a torturous process, with soldiers continually falling into the water and having to be hauled out before they drowned. When the company second-in-command, Captain Thomas William Lowell Butters, was struck in the neck by a shard of grenade shrapnel, he fell into the canal. Schjelderup was able to pull the bleeding officer out in time to prevent the current sweeping him away. A stretcher-bearer had to lie down beside Butters on the steep bank to prevent his sliding back into the water.[14] Eventually evacuated, his wound proved so serious that Butters was invalided out of the service.[15]

It was late afternoon before Schjelderup got all 'C' Company into the northwest corner of Oosthoek. Only then did 'B' Company also set up in the hamlet. Joining English at his headquarters, the two officers coordinated a defensive plan for the night.[16]

As night fell, 'A' Company joined the rest of the battalion on the north side of the canal to secure the original crossing site. 'B' Company was to its immediate left and 'C' Company farther out along that flank. To the right of 'A' Company, Major David V. Pugh's 'D' Company had been plagued by problems similar to those faced by the other two assault companies. It had taken Lieutenant O.N. Falkins's platoon four separate assaults against well-emplaced machine-gun positions to finally gain a precarious toehold in Moershoofd. The entire battalion front was about 1,000 yards wide with the farthest northerly penetration only about 700 yards, where 'B' and 'C' Companies were dug in. Throughout the night, the quiet was "broken periodically by blazing gunfire as the opposing troops prodded each other's defences."[17]

AT 7 CIB HEADQUARTERS, Brigadier J.G. "Jock" Spragge had anxiously monitored the Leopold Canal battle, frustrated by there being little brigade could do for the battalions beyond ensuring that the

12th Field Regiment's guns kept disrupting German attempts to move in reinforcements. Several Typhoon fighter-bomber sorties had also been directed against identified German artillery positions located near the towns of Aardenburg and Saint Kruis. With nightfall, Spragge realized the two battalions across the canal were too weak to reach one another to create a continuous front. The only option was to commit his reserve battalion, the Royal Winnipeg Rifles, to fill the gap.[18]

At 2100 hours, Spragge ordered Lieutenant Colonel John Meldram to take the Winnipegs across the canal on the kapok bridge behind the Can Scots and be on the move towards the Reginas by 2300 hours. Despite not arriving back at his own headquarters until 2230 hours, Meldram got 'A' and 'B' Companies, under overall command of Major J.T. Carvell, over the bridge on schedule.[19] Only "able to fight their way about 1,000 yards westward along the canal before the enemy's unceasing resistance brought them to a halt," Carvell ordered his men to dig in, and hoped the morning would bring some means to renew the advance. The situation was badly confused, both companies caught in a "swept and coverless lodgement, never more than 200 yards from the bank." Casualties were mounting, and with the position so exposed, evacuating the wounded was extremely dangerous.[20] Both the Reginas to their left and the Can Scots behind were still locked in fierce gun battles.

Increasingly heavy small-arms and machine-gun fire harried the Reginas more with each passing hour. It was a cloudless, moonlit night so the Canadians could see the Germans advancing. Lying in a slit trench next to a couple of Reginas firing their rifles at the shadowy figures darting forward, 12th Field Regiment's Captain John Beer put in yet another call for every gun to spread its fire out in a linear pattern across the front of the narrow bridgehead. Having come across the canal with the Royal Montreal Regiment, Beer was exhausted by the rate of the fire direction he had provided throughout the day, considering the narrow distances separating the Canadians from the Germans. The risk of an inaccurate map reading could mean catastrophe for the troops around him.[21] Throughout the night, Beer called in seven major defensive fire missions to break up attacks before they could gather full steam.[22] Radio reports sent to brigade told the story. At 0145, Captain Mel Douglas reported 'D' Company on the right flank was "Being overrun...want arty task swung to the left." Minutes later, he reported: "Counterattack beaten off once and is coming in again." Beer duly brought down more shells and by 0305, Douglas could say, "Things are quieter now."

An hour later, it was 'A' Company's turn, Major Ronald Shawcross reporting being under small-arms fire and that there "may be something forming up," only to confirm "being counterattacked. Need grenades." At 0435 hours, 'C' Company called for artillery on a position four hundred yards to its right. Then, at 0520 hours, it reported enemy "advancing and firing" on its position and that artillery was "taking action."[23] First light saw no relenting in the German efforts to overrun the Reginas.

But the ferocity of counterattacks against the Canadian Scottish had been even greater. In a house on the south side of the street running through Oosthoek, Lieutenant Royce Marshall and No. 15 Platoon had created a stout fortified position "by piling sacks of salt which we had found in the barn attached to the rear of the house around the doors and windows." As evening had drawn in, the men were grousing about how hungry they were because no rations had been brought forward. "Fortunately, a couple of stray chickens wandered by and within minutes they were plucked, drawn and being boiled in a discarded pot found in the farm house. No chicken ever before tasted so fine," Marshall wrote.

After dark, Marshall checked in with Major Schjelderup, who was set up in the basement of a small, partially destroyed stone house. Schjelderup told him that all the company could do for now was hold its position. Back with his platoon, Marshall posted sentries and the other men bedded down on straw gathered from the barn. Unable to sleep, Marshall lay there listening to the shuffling of his men and realized that everyone was equally on edge. The tension in the air was palpable, the eerie quiet menacing.

Marshall was just beginning to drift off when a sentry shook his shoulder and reported "men were advancing down the road towards our position. Obviously this could only mean one thing! I ordered the sentries to open fire and then I aroused the whole platoon who took their positions in the house. Within minutes the enemy fire became so intense from all sides that we knew...we were surrounded." At least 150 Germans had infiltrated Oosthoek and cut 'C' Company's platoons off from each other. Marshall's men were blazing away with Bren guns, Stens, PIATS, and rifles. Enemy bullets spattered the building, making Marshall grateful for the sacks of salt thickening the walls around windows and doors. It was pitch-black inside the house, making it impossible for the men to see the grenades the Germans tossed inside. Most were potato mashers that caused a lot of concussion but threw little shrapnel. Still, the concussion was causing casualties. Twice, exploding grenades knocked Marshall to the floor, but each time he received nary a scratch. With every passing minute, however, the volume of fire thickened and the number of wounded was mounting alarmingly. Men lay where they dropped, those still on their feet so engaged in fighting for their lives they had no time to move the fallen.[24]

'C' Company was desperate. When the attack came in, Sergeant Armando Gri, commanding No. 14 Platoon, had sprinted over to apprise Schjelderup that his platoon was likely to be overrun, leaving company headquarters vulnerable. He then ran back through a rain of incoming German grenades, firing his Sten from the hip at any sign of movement and killing at least four enemy soldiers. Back with his platoon, Gri led it in a desperate gun battle that raged for over an hour. The platoon was spread out among a couple of buildings and slit trenches interspersed between. Dead and wounded soon sprawled throughout the position. Finally, only Gri remained in the fight "against overwhelming odds. Savagely he moved from house to house and ditch to ditch cutting down all enemy who came within range of his Sten gun. The situation became absolutely impossible as he found his last house set afire and his ammunition almost expended. Finally, with his clothes afire, and all magazines empty, he was forced to surrender." Gri was the only survivor from the platoon. The heroism of the twenty-six-year-old from the little mining village of Phoenix near Trail, British Columbia, garnered a Military Medal.[25]

At company headquarters, the situation was grave. The small headquarters section had done what it could to barricade itself by scrounging timbers, stones, and other materials to strengthen the walls. With a Sten gun in hand, Company Sergeant Major Wilf Barry manned the door leading from the basement into the yard. When a tall soldier walked up within two feet and called something that sounded like, "Ist dat Hans?" Barry shot him dead. That action precipitated a shower of grenades from out of the darkness that tore the dead soldier to pieces. Clutching a Sten, Schjelderup joined Barry at the door and the two men met each German charge with long bursts that left bodies littering the ground in front of them. Meanwhile, Captain Bob Brownridge, the artillery FOO, was trying to direct fire practically onto the company's positions but was unable to establish contact. Nor could the company signaller raise battalion headquarters. Schjelderup told the small group that they could only hold and hope for reinforcement after first light. If they failed, he believed the Germans would break through to the canal and the entire battalion would be wiped out.[26]

The Germans were throwing grenades through various gaps in the basement wall. Shrapnel from one peppered Schjelderup's back. Ignoring repeated calls for them to surrender, the small group of men fought on. Suddenly, smoke grenades exploded all around the basement, making it impossible to see the surrounding grounds. Under this cover, a party of Germans detonated demolition charges in an attempt to collapse the building into the basement. Several fires broke out, but the house still stood. Schjelderup knew "we had no hope now of survival unless a counterattack could be launched by our battalion very quickly."[27]

There was no likelihood of that happening. 'B' Company's Lieutenant L. Hobden's No. 11 Platoon was closest to 'C' Company's position, but the officer considered intervention impossible because he could see Germans lining up and searching prisoners close to their position. There also seemed to be Canadian stretcher-bearers retrieving wounded under a white flag, which left the officer more unsure what to do. He "didn't dare fire... especially as we were worried about what might happen to the prisoners." Then firing broke out from within 'B' Company's lines to his rear. Hobden looked over at his sergeant and the two men agreed: "If all those Jerries come at us, complete with mortars... somebody is kaput." Hobden ordered the platoon's maps, documents, and money hidden, and then the troops "manned our positions and waited."[28] (Hobden was mistaken or misled. There were no Canadian stretcher-bearers at work in 'C' Company's perimeter, and it was never determined whether the Germans had been evacuating men under a false flag.)

Meanwhile, 'C' Company's No. 15 Platoon was still fighting valiantly when, at 0500 hours, the Germans set a heavy machine gun up at the rear of the house and began firing long bursts of tracer fire into their position. The tracers set the straw in the barn afire and that section of the building was soon ablaze. A corporal, who was now commanding a section after its sergeant became a casualty, ran over to Marshall. "What do we do now, Sir?" Marshall felt that this "was the greatest decision that I, at that time, ever made. There were two courses open—one to stay in the house and be burned alive or to rush out and be cut down by German troops whom we supposed to be waiting outside for just that moment. I decided that we should make an attempt to reach the platoon commanded by Lieutenant Peter MacDonnel, which was about 800 yards away. We gathered our wounded together and I went out through the front door first. To my surprise there was not an enemy soldier outside. I quickly called out to what was left of my platoon and carrying our wounded we made a dash to our closest platoon. On the way we passed German officers who must have believed that we were also Germans. As it turned out this withdrawal was most timely for I had only twelve men left in my platoon and each carried an average of ten rounds of ammunition. We did, however, come out with all of our weapons."[29]

Dawn was breaking when Marshall and his men joined No. 13 Platoon, and the two units were immediately subjected to heavy German fire. Until that moment, MacDonnel's men had been little engaged and, lacking a clear line of sight to the other platoons, had not realized that the rest of the company had been virtually wiped out. Now the fire pinned them in position, preventing any attempt to break through and rescue the headquarters section.

In the basement, Schjelderup and his men would be killed if they continued fighting. They could hear the Germans emplacing more demolition charges. It was clear they were going to be soon blown up or buried. Their ammunition was exhausted. So the major ordered the maps and documents burned, then he led the men into captivity.[30]

With the dawn, Marshall and MacDonnel could see Germans and Canadians intermingled. "We could not fire but had to stand and watch our people being marched away." Only those two officers and about 35 to 40 men from 'C' Company's approximately 105 remained. Twenty men were taken prisoner. On October 23, close to half escaped from a train en route to Germany. Schjelderup and Gri were among the escapees, reaching friendly lines after seventy-five harrowing days on the run.[31]

THE ROYAL WINNIPEG REGIMENT tried to retrieve the situation with a counterattack through No. 13 Platoon's position early on October 7 towards the part of Oosthoek that 'C' Company had lost. Fighting was immediately at close quarters. When heavy machine-gun fire from a brick house pinned the leading elements, Privates J. Goodall and L. Blue wriggled forward to blast the building with a PIAT gun. Then the riflemen charged in and cleared the house in hand-to-hand fighting.[32] Despite this, the attack faltered. Canadians and Germans dug in just yards apart to engage in a bitter day-long exchange of bullets. Both sides were hammering the narrow bridgehead area with artillery and mortar fire. Snipers were constantly at work, and the back-and-forth pitching of grenades became a macabre sport. When the skies cleared momentarily, Typhoons rocketed and strafed German rear areas. Smoke from burning buildings drifted over the battlefield and the smell of death hung over everything.

Getting supplies across the canal was a constant ordeal, the two companies of North Shore (New Brunswick) Regiment paddlers suffering heavy casualties until 16th Field Company engineers got a kapok bridge, with its narrow plank deck and cable handrails, installed behind the Reginas. With a bridge in place at both crossing points, supplies could be delivered by heavily burdened men dashing across under enemy fire. The exhausted North Shores were relieved from ferrying duties.[33]

In an attempt to bolster the firepower that 7 CIB could bring to bear on the bridgehead, the Regina and Royal Winnipeg mortar platoons set up immediately south of the Dérivation de la Lys just east of where it parted ways with the Leopold Canal. The position was considered far enough back to be concealed from German observation and retaliatory shelling, but the two platoons quickly drew artillery and mortar fire. The Winnipeg unit's tubes were positioned near an abandoned south-facing World War I pillbox dug into the canal bank, the concrete structure providing good shelter to which the men dashed each time German fire roared in.

When Winnipeg Rifleman Jim Parks and the others had arrived here during the night, they had tried to dig normal mortar firing holes that could double as shelters from enemy fire, but six inches down they hit water. To create a firm firing platform, they filled bags with sand dug out of the dyke and lined the bottom of the hold. Then they "put old ammunition boxes down...to make a firm base for the plate." This proved only marginally satisfactory. "The force of a mortar bomb going out would drive the barrel down into the ground," Parks later recounted. "First ten rounds or so, the barrel would just keep going down until the bottom of the barrel had been driven into the water. So we'd dig down and get the base plate out and put in more sand and empty cases until we got a firm base." Finally, they had enough sandbags and ammunition boxes emplaced to prevent the tube sinking further. But this achievement disinclined them from shifting position, even after the Germans zeroed in with airburst rounds, because they didn't want to have to build a new firing platform.[34]

Both platoons threw out a terrific rate of fire during the day. "Firing was so continuous that the weapons became overheated." The two regiments handled this problem by firing in relays. When the Regina mortars overheated, they would cease fire and the Winnipeg mortar teams would take over and vice versa. Each went through "huge quantities of ammunition." The Reginas alone burned through 1,078 rounds in just three hours.[35]

Much of the mortar and artillery fire, however, was landing too far north to seriously disrupt the Germans because they were so close to the Canadian lines. To enable the mortars to bring their fire in closer, three Regina mortarmen went across the canal to provide wireless guidance. Among them was Rifleman Denis Chisholm. Arriving at the south bank of the Leopold, Chisholm was told that "ammunition and water supplies were in great demand and everyone crossing had to carry as much of these items as possible." In addition to his own equipment, Chisholm loaded up one hundred rounds of .303 ammunition, a number of grenades, and a Jerry can full of water.

The three men were then told the drill. Scramble over the bank, slither down to the kapok bridge, run like hell across, and get into a slit trench as fast as possible. Each man went over the top, followed a beat later by another. Chisholm was third in line. Reaching the bridge, he saw one of the stabilizing floats was out of line so that the thing tipped precariously near the opposite bank. But the first two men made it over, and Chisholm dashed out. "I made it about three quarters of the way across, couldn't keep my balance and fell in. Being a good swimmer I thought I could hit bottom, kick off and come to the top, but this being a canal deep enough for barges, there was no bottom.

"I dropped the Jerry can but still clung to the rifle, I guess the result of the years of training. I broke water, couldn't reach the float and started down again. Now I let the rifle go and fought my way up but was pulled down again by all the weight. I thought, 'What a hell of a way to go after coming so far.

"Just then someone grabbed me and helped me up on the float. Half drowned I lay there until this person yelled at me to get going, and disappeared the way I had come. A shell or mortar bomb landing nearby gave me all the incentive needed and I landed in a slit trench with a fellow crouched in the corner. I asked him for a dry cigarette but he didn't answer. I then realized he was dead... the number of bodies strewn along the bank would break your heart."[36]

The death toll kept mounting. Lieutenant Tom Odette, a platoon leader in the Reginas' 'D' Company, was standing between his two section leaders, looking out over a low wall inside a ruined structure, when a sniper round snapped in, punched through the man on one side, and ricocheted off a wall behind into the other. "I felt a blow on the back of my neck from stone fragments but otherwise I escaped being wounded that time. But the other two were dead!"[37]

Darkness brought more German counterattacks, making the "night of October 7–8... a literal hell." The Regina 'C' and 'D' Companies fended off fierce attacks. Beyond their positions, "wounded Jerries were heard screaming all night."[38] In the Canadian Scottish area, the fighting became so "close at times that several Germans were killed with Commando knives."[39]

At 0200 hours, Lieutenant Bob Gray, a Regina officer returning to the unit, crossed the bridge and entered this hell. He and another officer were to take over 'C' Company. They found it cut down to just the company sergeant major and forty men, who were dug into the canal bank. "The noise and uproar were deafening." The CSM reported repelling the counterattack and then the utterly exhausted man was sent to the other side of the canal for a rest. Gray took command. The area that 'C' Company held "was crowded, vulnerable, wet and quite small... We did not know what to do with our dead. They could not be removed because of enemy sniper fire. All we could do was to push them up on the canal bank in front of us, and leave them there.

"We could light no fires and smoking after dark had to be done under cover... It was dangerous to expose oneself... German rifle grenadiers and snipers were always looking for targets. We were dug in beneath a row of very high poplar trees. A grenade fired from a German rifle at considerable distance from us, could explode by hitting the branches of trees which were over our heads. This sent a shower of shrapnel down on those who were dug in below. Unlike a noisy mortar or a whining artillery shell, these grenades arrived silently and did their deadly work."

This night, the Germans introduced another hazard, which was to become a regular event during 7 CIB's terrible ordeal—shelling by coastal guns. "Trust the Germans to have guns which could fire in any direction—no matter where they were emplaced!" Gray lamented. When these guns fired, the Canadians would see a terrific flash of light far off in the distance. Each time, "there was a flash of light which was followed in a few seconds by the rumble of the explosion as the shell left the gun. After a few more seconds pause, we could hear the shells rushing like express trains through the trees above our heads to land with huge explosions to the rear." By timing the interval between the flash and the first shriek of the massive round coming in, then multiplying the seconds passed by 1100 to account for the speed of sound, they could roughly calculate where the gun was positioned. This night they figured Cadzand, almost ten miles away.

"Each salvo was fired at a lower elevation as the guns were gradually depressed. When we were in the slit trenches each salvo passed closer and closer to our heads. Usually the guns ceased firing when the shells seemed to be six or eight feet above us. Fortunately not one shell hit a tree near us, so no one was hurt. Battalion headquarters behind us were not as lucky, and they got the hell pounded out of them several times. After the first night's shelling we had the men convinced that the Hun could not depress the guns enough to hit us."[40]

Shelling by coastal guns became just another of the grim conditions that 7 CIB endured. Having gained a toehold on the north bank of the Leopold Canal, division was determined to retain it. Retreat was not an option. But the brigade was so badly shot up and hemmed in by an equal or superior German force that maintaining the bridgehead was obviously the best it could manage. Whereas it had been anticipated that 8th Canadian Infantry Brigade would quickly pass through 7 CIB and widen the bridgehead—making the Leopold Canal phase of Operation Switchback the main effort—funnelling in another brigade was no longer feasible.

Those officers in the brigade who were in the know about Operation Switchback's overall plan were all thinking the same thing. "Perhaps the projected 9th [Canadian Infantry Brigade] assault landing will ease this front."[41] That amphibious assault across the Braakman Inlet into the rear of the Breskens Pocket was supposed to be launched on the morning of October 8. What was to have opened a secondary front now had greater significance.[42] It was, in fact, the division's only hope.

[14]

In the Back Door

NOT UNTIL IT CLEARED Boulogne on September 22, and silenced the gun batteries at Cap Gris Nez west of Calais a week later, was 9th Canadian Infantry Brigade able to begin moving on October 3 to Desteldonk, a village three miles northeast of Ghent. The move was conducted in one day-long hop by trucks that carried the brigade "from France, across Belgium, to the borders of the Netherlands by 1830 hours that evening."[1] A move over such a distance and with such haste put the troops on notice that they headed not for a much desired rest but to a new field of battle.

"An inkling of what we may be doing shortly was gained today when the c.o. and party attended a demonstration of a new type of amphibious craft," the Highland Light Infantry of Canada war diarist wrote the next day. "A very high degree of security is being maintained at this time and as yet the c.o. alone knows what our role will be and the type of job we are to do."[2]

The HLI's Lieutenant Colonel Nicol Kingsmill and other senior 9 CIB officers were introduced to three types of amphibians: Landing Vehicle, Tracked (2), Landing Vehicle, Tracked (4), and the Terrapin Mark 1. Generally called Buffaloes, the two LVT models were quite similar. Each was lightly armoured and powered by a radial aircraft engine. On land, they ran on tracks, while on water, retractable scoops extended from the tracks to provide propulsion. Top speed on land was 20 miles per hour, and 7.5 miles per hour on water. Except for a small covered bridge at the very front, both models were open topped. The LVT(2) was principally designed to carry personnel and was accessed by scrambling over its sides, whereas the LVT(4) had a ramp mounted at the rear for loading equipment and vehicles. Its motor had also been shifted from the middle to behind the front cabin in order to create a vehicle bay. Powered by two centre-mounted Ford v8 engines and running on eight wheels, the Terrapin "had a curiously clumsy appearance owing to one pair of wheels being set higher than the rest." These raised front wheels enabled it to gain traction on steep embankments for exiting canals and rivers. Lacking armour or any gun mounts, the Terrapins were designed to carry about four tons of supplies and equipment, and were intended to land on already secured beachheads.[3]

These amphibians were manned by personnel of 5th Assault Regiment, Royal Engineers from the 79th British Armoured Division. Having received the flotilla only a month earlier, their operational training was judged "most limited." While mastering the complexities of handling and maintaining the vehicles, the engineers were also kept busy retrofitting them with additional light armour kits—a task they were unable to complete in time for the operation. Even those vehicles fitted with the additional armour were still vulnerable because it was too thin to stop either bullets or shrapnel. Although the Buffaloes came with four gun mountings, those sent to 5th Assault Regiment lacked weapons. Two .30-calibre Browning machine guns per vehicle were scrounged up to give each some inherent firepower. They also lacked wireless sets, so No. 19 radios were installed. Few spare parts were available for repairs, but the engineers planned to make up this shortage by cannibalizing Buffaloes that became disabled during the operation.[4]

9 CIB was even less prepared for an amphibious operation than the British engineers. Intensively trained for its role in seizing Juno Beach on June 6, one report acknowledged that "few of the original personnel remained." The 5th Assault Regiment's 80th Squadron commander, Major R.T. Wiltshire, also noted that 9 CIB had been the

reserve and had landed after the beaches had been largely secured. Consequently, the "present attack was...its first essay at this technique under battle conditions."[5]

The technique was to be learned quickly. On October 5, the North Nova Scotia Highlander non-commissioned officers were drilled on loading and unloading from Buffaloes. Now experts, each spent the following day training their sections. Most found the Buffaloes "a very striking vehicle" that appeared "to have quite a performance."[6] But the fact remained that each battalion's total training "consisted of roughly half a day."[7]

Riding in a Buffalo was not for the claustrophobic. "For this operation a working figure of 30 'marching' personnel per LVT was adopted (in addition to the crew)...The men, who had to stand, were rather cramped." No seating had been installed and the compartment was jammed with men and battle gear.[8] The target thirty-man load was intended to enable a single Buffalo to carry a full platoon. In many cases, however, platoons were understrength, providing a little more leg room.

5th Assault Regiment's flotilla numbered one hundred Buffaloes and forty Terrapins. Most Buffaloes had the rear drop ramps—because of the many vehicles needing to be delivered to the beach. The North Nova Scotia Highlanders, for example, required only twelve Buffaloes to carry its troops, but another thirty-seven to accommodate its supporting unit's mechanized equipment, such as the medical officer team, the mortar and antitank-gun platoons, the pioneers, and the three Wasps. Each Buffalo could generally carry only a single vehicle.[9]

In a small harbour on Ghent's northern outskirts, the flotilla gathered on October 7. The Buffaloes intended to "swim" the twenty miles north by canal to Terneuzen, with the North Nova Scotia Highlanders and Highland Light Infantry aboard. These two battalions would form the landing's first wave, and it was thought that by travelling on the canal they would reach Terneuzen more quickly than by road. It was to be largely a night move to avoid German detection. Once the Buffaloes reached Terneuzen, they would enter the inlet, and the assault would begin shortly after 0100 hours on

October 8. This way, 9 CIB should be firmly established inside the Breskens Pocket by first light. The rest of the brigade, including the Stormont, Dundas and Glengarry Highlanders, would be trucked to Terneuzen. When the Buffaloes returned from landing the first wave, the Glens and other support units would be ferried over. The Buffaloes would then be withdrawn and subsequent beachhead supply would be by Terrapins.[10]

Loading was completed on schedule by 1730 hours. "Everything," wrote the North Nova war diarist, "went according to plan and it was a very impressing sight to see all the vehicles strung out in a long procession moving up the canal. As it was dark, all the tail lights were put on to act as a guide."[11]

Captain Jock Anderson, the HLI padre, travelled in a Buffalo loaded with a Jeep and a few men from the Regimental Aid Post team. The HLI were strung in a long line of Buffaloes behind an equal number carrying the North Novas. Anderson was surprised how "these things made an awful noise." At first, it was still daylight and civilians "would follow us on their bicycles and yell and cheer and we would shout things to them. I remember thinking: 'Good Heavens, this is a surprise attack?' I felt someone would be bound to get word through to the Germans and they'd be waiting for us."[12]

Anderson was not alone in this fear. As it chugged up the canal and flares burst overhead at 2200 hours, the North Nova headquarters staff "began to wonder if they had discovered our plan."[13] Not only the noise was a concern, but also the bright exhaust flame the engines emitted in the dark. Yet, even as the flotilla passed within four miles of the Germans dug in at the Isabellapolder, the absence of shelling indicated that it had avoided detection.

The canal journey, however, was more difficult than anticipated. All along the way, the convoy had to manoeuvre around "a number of wrecks, broken bridges and floating footbridges." These the engineers had earlier marked with beacons, so there were no collisions. Then, halfway to Terneuzen, the Sas van Gent locks were transited only with much delay. The locks and various lift bridges en route were all manned by armed engineers to guard against saboteurs and ensure that canal authorities did nothing to slow or block the flotilla's passage.[14]

Before the Germans abandoned Terneuzen, they had crippled the lock that enabled boat traffic to pass between the canal and the West Scheldt. The Buffaloes were well behind schedule as they approached this obstacle just before midnight. Because the lock was inoperable, each Buffalo was to claw its way up the "steep bank of the dyke and [move] along the land for a few hundred yards before going into the water again."[15] To help the Buffaloes escape the canal, the engineers had installed two wooden ramps. Tracks clawing the wood, each vehicle in turn fought its way up the ramps. But as each heavily laden Buffalo rolled off the ramp, great gobs of mud were left behind. The ramps also began to splinter and disintegrate under the tremendous weight of the slipping and churning machines. "Very slow progress was made, until bulldozers were employed to winch the LVT up the ramps, but even with the improvement gained thereby, only 30 vehicles were out of the canal at the time scheduled for departure down into the outer harbour."

Twice the operation was delayed, but at 0330 hours it was finally postponed until the early morning of October 9. This was not only because Buffaloes were still being dragged out of the canal, but also it was past low tide, a heavy mist that would hinder navigation had set in, and at least eight Buffaloes were either broken down or stuck on mud banks in the canal.[16] Among the stranded was a Buffalo carrying the Royal Engineer flotilla commander, the North Nova Scotia battalion commander, Lieutenant Colonel Don Forbes, and his entire headquarters section. "The crew worked all night to get it off but it was a hopeless job," complained the North Novas' war diarist.[17]

By dawn, other than for those mired, most of the Buffaloes were out of the canal and concealed within the harbour. The risk of German detection was great. If the element of surprise was lost, the assault would probably fail. In the canal, the men aboard the stranded command Buffalo were bemused when a Dutch civilian approached in a rowboat and offered to pull them off with his motor boat. The flotilla commander eagerly accepted. "In about twenty minutes he arrived back on the scene with a great canal boat about 200 feet long. It was amazing to see...the way he handled the vessel. It certainly did not take him long to get us off the bar, and we proceeded to the point where the rest of the vehicles were in harbour."[18]

Mist having lifted, it was a bright, sunny Sunday morning. Although ordered to remain aboard the Buffaloes to avoid detection, the soldiers were tied up alongside a main thoroughfare used by churchgoers. "Oh boy," Padre Anderson thought, "what a surprise this is going to be," as people gawked down and began chatting with the men.[19]

THE LIKELIHOOD THAT the operation had been compromised was so high, there was some thought to scrubbing it. Yet to do so would do nothing to relieve the pressure bearing down on the embattled 7th Canadian Infantry Brigade bridgehead on the Leopold Canal. At his tactical headquarters inside a school in Sluiskill, a village three miles south of Terneuzen alongside the Ghent–Terneuzen Canal, 9 CIB's Brigadier John "Rocky" Rockingham and 3rd Canadian Infantry Division's Major General Dan Spry worried over the situation. Then, at 1430 hours, II Canadian Corps's acting commander Major General Charles Foulkes appeared, and a formal O Group was convened ninety minutes later. When all the brigade's senior officers were crowded into one of the classrooms, Rockingham announced the operation was on. H-Hour—the actual landing time—would be 0220 hours, October 9, to take advantage of tidal conditions.[20] The passage from Terneuzen to the landing sites near Hoofdplaat would take about thirty minutes.[21]

One unforeseen hazard in the original planning was the fact that the Buffaloes had to move at night through a West Scheldt channel laced with shallows and running with strong tidal currents. Although Dutch pilots familiar with the waters had been drafted into service and were to travel ahead of the flotillas in motorboats operated by Royal Engineers, language differences posed a potential complication. Recognizing the need for a qualified naval navigator, First Canadian Army's naval liaison officer, Royal Navy Lieutenant Commander Robert Franks, volunteered his services.

Franks quickly determined that the compasses on the motorboats were unsuited for the task at hand. "I spent the day in obtaining a suitable compass (from the R.A.F.), in making a careful 'recce' of what I could see of the river from peeping over the dykes, and in studying the chart, assessing the tide and all the usual preparations."[22]

Normally, such an amphibious assault would be supported by naval ships firing from offshore, but the German coastal batteries blocked any naval vessels from entering the West Scheldt. To compensate, the 4th Canadian Armoured Division's field regiments and several medium artillery regiments would begin firing across the Braakman Inlet fifty minutes prior to touchdown. Fifteen minutes before H-Hour, the two landing beaches would be marked by coloured flare shells to serve as reference points for the approaching flotillas, and more markers would then be "fired at random points in enemy territory to put him off the scent. At H-5, as the craft now were standing off, the beaches [would] once again [be] pin-pointed by flare shells."[23]

The Highland Light Infantry were to land on Amber Beach, a small cove the planners described loosely as "a harbour," which was protected by a narrow island that became swamped at high tide. This beach lay about four miles west of Terneuzen. Green Beach, where the North Nova Scotia Highlanders would go ashore, was a mile and a half farther on. It was protected by an artificial breakwater that extended into the channel. Intelligence, particularly accurate reports provided by Dutch resistance fighter Peter de Winde, indicated that the area was lightly defended. Aerial reconnaissance showed "few prepared positions" and that the Germans "considered that the mud flats, which line[d] the shore would effectively defeat any effort to make a landing." But consultations with Dutch engineers had convinced the Canadians "that the mud flats were not impassable, especially since grass covered much of their surface."[24]

Once the assault battalions landed, the Buffaloes would return for the second lift, while First Canadian Army's Chemical Warfare Section hid the Buffaloes with a smokescreen. To stretch from Terneuzen to Hoofdplaat, the smoke should prevent the enemy gunners from ranging on specific targets and would be kept in operation until an overland link between 9 CIB and other elements of First Canadian Army could be established.[25]

At 2300 hours, the flotilla began preparing to set sail. Through the ranks of the HLI, the distressing news passed that its well-liked commander, Lieutenant Colonel Kingsmill, had "been evacuated to hospital due to illness." Second-in-command, Major G.A.M.

Edwards, now to lead the amphibious assault, knew he faced a tough inauguration as battalion commander.[26]

The two flotillas were to cross Braakman Inlet in separate columns, led by the one bearing the North Novas to Green Beach. Each flotilla had three rifle companies up front. Following behind were the Buffaloes carrying vehicles, with the fourth rifle company positioned roughly in the middle. For the beach approach, the Buffaloes would spread out line abreast and advance in waves—the three rifle companies out front.

A motorboat was to guide each flotilla. Because Green Beach was the farthest away, Lieutenant Commander Robert Franks was aboard the motorboat leading the North Novas. "By 0030 hours we were lying off the sea ramp...showing two dim red lights astern. Well on time the first LVT waddled down the ramp and splashed into the water. We led slowly out of the canal entrance as more and more took to the water and formed up astern. It was a nearly ideal night, calm and quiet with a half moon behind light cloud, but a bit of haze which restricted visibility to a mile at the most. We were quite invisible from the north shore of the Scheldt, where all was quiet.

"We soon reached the main part of the river and turned west along the coast, keeping about half a mile off...We went slowly, and as far as could be seen, all our LVTs were formed up and following. I then set course due west across the entrance of [Braakman Inlet]. Just as we cleared the land, our artillery barrage started up, 'plastering' the far beach and other targets. The noise effectively blanketed our sounds and was generally most heartening."

The landing was to "be on either side of a groyne [the breakwater] which proved to be a good landmark and we were able to identify it and then lie off flicking our lamps to guide the LVTs in. They deployed and thundered in past us, looking, and sounding, most impressive. Landing was successful and I could see, through my binoculars, the infantry disembark on dry land and form up and move off. The artillery barrage had by now, of course, ceased and there was silence except for the roar of the engines and an occasional rifle shot."[27]

TOUCHDOWN FOR BOTH flotillas was at 0210 hours, ten minutes ahead of schedule. The Buffaloes carrying the North Nova rifle companies waded onto the beach, then the men tumbled over the sides "into thick, clinging, slippery mud" and waded through the shallows onto the equally mucky shore. The gentle slope of the seaward side of the dyke was quickly surmounted and the infantry slithered down the steep landward bank. Odd strings of tracer flashed over their heads, and a few hundred yards inland a barn or haystack burned. 'B' Company was on the right, 'C' Company in the centre, and 'D' Company to the left. The latter company overran a dugout, rousting nine half-asleep Germans.

Corporal Lee Burch with Lieutenant Tingley in trail stole carefully eastwards along the canal bank towards a sentry seen "swinging his arms to get warm, his rifle lying against a post." Both men were amazed that the soldier appeared oblivious to the invasion. When they got close enough, Tingley dashed forward and wrestled the German to the ground. In English, the man begged for his life. Tingley demanded to know where his officer was, and the prisoner pointed to a small shelter the two Canadians had passed without noticing. They walked the prisoner back and woke the officer and a corporal, still in their bedrolls. The English-speaking prisoner next guided Tingley and Burch to another shelter. When the two men stepped inside, they were face to face with eight Germans sitting on a long plank bench braced against the opposite wall. The Germans lunged for grenades and guns, but Burch cut them all down with his Sten gun in one long burst of fire. The two Novas then marched their three prisoners back to where 'D' Company was digging in.[28]

Behind the infantry, the "beach was a hive of industry. The great motors roaring and these huge amphibious monsters crawling like great reptiles from the sea," wrote the North Novas war diarist, "out over the dyke and spitting flame from their exhausts. Throughout all this noise not a shell fell in our area, although the Highland Light Infantry...were being shelled a little. The companies soon got on their objectives with few casualties. Captain J. Graves of 'B' Company was wounded and evacuated."[29]

On Amber Beach, the HLI met more resistance and a number of the Buffaloes bogged down in mud. "On touch down all of our companies were held up by small arms fire," the HLI war diarist reported. "Mortar and artillery fire was also encountered and progress was limited. Our objectives were not reached."[30] The artillery was from 20-millimetre anti-aircraft guns being fired with fully depressed barrels. While the HLI were able to quickly overrun and silence a gun battery to the right of the beach, they were unable to reach one on the left. The guns there remained free to shell the beach.[31]

HLI Captain Jock Anderson had spent the passage to Amber Beach lying on one of the stretchers aboard the ambulance jeep he was to drive. Rather than lounging comfortably, the padre lay stiffly, gripped with fear, "still worried about it not being a surprise." Any moment, he expected German guns to rip the thinly armoured Buffaloes to bits. "All I could think of was the way the enemy would be waiting and very few of us would land...That was the scaredest I ever was—it registered more."

To his amazement, the Buffalo ground up onto the muddy beach and dumped its ramp without drawing fire. Behind the wheel, Anderson rolled the jeep into "pitch dark with a corporal and some Stretcher Bearers. The next thing I know is we're lying there and whang, whang, a piece of spent shrapnel hit the side of my helmet and gave me a headache, but didn't do any harm." He didn't remember jumping clear of the jeep.

Before them, the dyke rose more steeply than it did at Green Beach. He wondered how "in the dickens do we get off it. I got the fellows on the front of the jeep and I put the four wheel drive in low, and we literally went up almost perpendicularly over it. The Germans were on the next dyke no more than 200 yards away.

"The dyke is grass and people have the wrong idea about it. It is just like a mound of earth with usually a road underneath or above. As soon as I was over, I saw a farm house. It was dark and I ran in and told the fellows this is where we'll set up our Aid Post." He would bury the dead in a temporary cemetery out back alongside the dyke.[32]

Dawn brought intensified German resistance, and the HLI and North Novas struggled to adapt to a battlefield unlike any previously encountered. "Fighting took the form of attacking from one dyke to the next," wrote the HLI's regimental historian. "These dykes carved the ground into squares and the attacking forces, to hold one dyke, had to dislodge the enemy from the entire perimeter of the square.

Even on doing so they still came under fire from the next parallel dyke held by the enemy. The ground itself afforded no cover and was too water-logged to permit the digging of even the shallowest slit trenches... not only did the wet condition of the ground result in a complete absence of cover except in the lee of the dykes or in isolated buildings but also made it impossible to use any supporting armour. In fact, the only vehicles with the landing troops were jeeps and carriers, and all routes being along the top of the dykes, it was hazardous to use even these."[33]

Not just the terrain made fighting in the Breskens Pocket an ordeal. The North Novas discovered that the "Germans in the Scheldt were a different type. They were courageous and had not lost heart. They were determined to fight to the last ditch of the dirty, muddy country, asking no quarter and giving none... The roads seemed to run in squares and the Germans were dug in at every strategic corner. They had had months of time to make preparations and were so cunning in their defences that no wholesale operation could be handled. It had to be instead a slow slugging, one corner at a time, without benefit of tanks... It was cold and wet... There was continual shelling and mortaring and conditions were horrible."[34]

'C' Company was introduced to these realities when it pushed out from the centre of Green Beach alongside a westerly-running dyke. Machine guns opened fire from a distant dyke, as Corporal L.E. Russell's section with the company commander, Major E. Wright, alongside, dashed through some high grass. From this scant cover, they were able to spot eighteen Germans on a dyke lying crosswise to the one they followed. Russell sneaked his section around the corner where the two dykes joined, and jumped the Germans from behind with a mad charge. First to close with the enemy, Russell ripped into them with his Sten gun and almost single-handedly killed sixteen and wounded the other two.

Russell's platoon then firmed up a defensive position along the dyke, only to be bracketed by heavy shelling that killed its officer, Lieutenant Ronnie McNeil, wounded the sergeant, and left only eight men unhurt. Taking command, Russell braced to meet a counterattack visibly forming up behind the opposite dyke. The corporal selected firing positions for each surviving soldier, and then rushed to where Wright had established his company headquarters to tee up artillery fire. He rejoined the platoon just as the Germans charged. The riflemen poured out a steady stream of fire, artillery shells crashed down right on the Germans, and the attack was quickly shredded.[35]

'C' Company's experience was not unique. It was the same for all the North Nova companies and for the HLI. Each attempted advance, whether successful or not, cost heavy casualties. When the Germans counterattacked, it was their turn in the meat grinder. Every advantage lay with the defence.

Neither side able to use armour to any effect, each placed extraordinary call on artillery. That morning, Brigadier Stanley Todd—3rd Canadian Infantry Division's artillery chief—shifted the 13th and 14th Field Regiments to the northeast of Kaprijke to put them in range of the beachhead. This added to the 15th and 19th Field Regiments and 10th Medium Regiment already firing support from the eastern side of the Braakman Inlet.[36] Normally, artillery fired from positions behind the advancing battalions, but here the gunners positioned east of the beachhead were shooting on an oblique angle while those at Kaprijke, due south and behind the Leopold Canal, fired straight at 9 CIB. This meant the forward observation officers had to use extra caution not to overshoot targets, something they had never previously faced.

ALTHOUGH THE FIRST landings had been on schedule, the mud beaches had delayed the unloading of vehicles. Consequently, the flotillas were not returned to Terneuzen and ready to move the second lift until 0815 hours. Now daylight, the services of Lieutenant Commander Franks were no longer required. "I was proud to be the only naval member of yet another successful 'combined operation,'" he observed dryly.[37]

The day was partly cloudy, the seas calm, not a wisp of mist. Had it not been for the Canadian Chemical Warfare Section unit dashing "about with the generators on the back of a motor boat known as 'Smokey Joe,'" the Buffaloes would have been strung out like so many ducks in a row for the German gunners on Walcheren Island. But the smoke thrown out by the generators screened the long flotilla throughout its passage to Green Beach, forcing the Germans to fire blind. So they concentrated on sinking Smokey Joe. The Stormont, Dundas and Glengarry Highlanders aboard the flotilla anxiously watched as "shells dropped in the water around the craft, sending up big water spouts," but none scored a hit.

Not only the Glens and brigade headquarters were being carried to Green Beach. Also present were a Cameron Highlanders of Ottawa machine-gun company and mortar platoon, a platoon of engineers, a company of No. 23 Field Ambulance, and a platoon from the Royal Canadian Army Service Corps detailed to offload and move stores up to the fighting units. Touchdown came at about 0930 hours and, as the Buffaloes growled onto the muddy beach, everything seemed calm. Just as the men and vehicles started unloading, however, "hell broke loose, with heavy artillery, mortar and everything the enemy could muster being poured into the small foothold." The Glens' signal officer, Lieutenant Neil Medhurst, and his signaller, Private Malcolm Elvin Thomas Armstrong, died instantly when a shell hit their jeep as it descended a Buffalo ramp. "The shelling was so bad that some of the men lay flat on the ground and dug with their hands so as not to present a standing target for flying shrapnel; others took shelter in small sheds while their 'buddies' dug. The sheds, however, offered more comfort than cover! Casualties mounted rapidly during the next hour and a half and then orders were received to push out of the bridgehead into the Hoofdplaat objective."[38]

Lieutenant Colonel Roger Rowley was eager to get his men to the fishing village of Hoofdplaat, so ordered 'A' Company to advance along the seaward side of the dyke while 'B' Company would go up the landward side. 'C' Company would be to the left, driving straight up a road that led to the village, with 'D' Company close behind.[39] The plan of attack was typical Rowley, a hard charger always in a hurry and careless of details, but who got the job done whatever the costs.[40]

Sergeant Fred Howarth of 'A' Company was huddling in a trench with Private Jack Tighe when the attack order came. "We got out of the trench... going single file and Jack Tighe was hit by a sniper as he went through a gap in the dyke... we were under direct fire from an enemy 20mm gun. By the time we reached our 'destination' (the gun) we were pinned down and I had three men left in my section—

Snyder, Hall, and myself. We came to a culvert in the ditch and Lt. H.C. Fisher had been hit by a shell on the other side of the culvert and we could hear him over there. Lt. Ted Annable said he had to get over to him. I told him: 'The minute you get up out of this ditch, they're going to shell us and you'll get hit!'... But he decided to try to get over there.

"The moment he stepped up they hit him. The shell tore right through his hip and he was a goner right there, but he was still alive and one of the bravest things I think I ever saw was when a jeep came up with [a Stretcher Bearer] in it and it was Cec Lalonde who was driving. He brought that jeep up, along with another man aboard and the jeep was riddled with bullets. Even the jerry cans on it had fluid running out of them. Lalonde still put Annable on the stretcher and they put him in the jeep and took him back out. But he died shortly after from his wounds."[41]

In addition to the 20-millimetre gun, 'A' Company was blocked two hundred yards short of the village by a large concrete bunker manned by snipers and machine gunners. Rowley ordered one of the antitank platoon's six-pounders to take on the enemy gun and bust the bunker. Corporal "Matty" Matheson's section went up in a carrier, towing the gun behind. As they approached 'A' Company, the Germans sprayed the carrier and bullets hit Matheson in both legs. Privates M.S. MacDonald and Fred Crowe pulled the man into a ditch, but MacDonald was also wounded in the process. They soon reloaded Matheson in the carrier and withdrew.[42]

'C' Company, meanwhile, had managed to push into Hoofdplaat against only scant resistance from snipers. Having gained the village, it moved north along the outskirts in an attempt to reach the Germans pinning down 'A' Company, while 'B' Company swung south into the fields to close off any avenue of escape in that direction. 'A' Company was frantically trying to figure out the precise location of the 20-millimetre gun, but when Corporal Marcellus dashed up into the attic of a house for a look, he was shot in the mouth.[43]

With 'C' Company quickly clearing houses, the Germans started trying to escape the village. Their lines of retreat were either along the seaward side of the dyke to the front of 'A' Company or out into the fields where 'B' Company was. The latter company was taking heavy fire from a farmhouse to its west, but attempts to storm the place were driven back. Finally, with darkness falling, the company dug in with instructions to block any withdrawal by the Germans in the village. 'C' Company was well positioned within the village and 'A' Company remained pinned in front of the bunkers. 'D' Company had been held in reserve back at the beach.

Most of 'A' Company was still using the ditch for cover. "Much of the time we just had our heads out of the water," Howarth remembered. "If you got up, you were a goner. Since it was fall, it was cold that time of year... It was starting to get dark and the Germans started to shell us." Everyone was in for a long, hard night.[44]

But with all of 9 CIB successfully through the back door of the Breskens Pocket, the tide of battle was slowly turning in First Canadian Army's favour. News of the landings near Hoofdplaat offered a glimmer of hope for 7th Canadian Infantry Brigade mired in the grim bridgehead on the Leopold Canal. On the morning of October 9, the situation there had been marginally improved when the Royal Winnipeg Rifles managed to close the gap between the Regina Rifles and Canadian Scottish Regiment to create a coherent brigade front. Conditions remained dreadful, however, with casualties continuing to mount steadily.

Because the ground beyond the bridgehead was badly flooded, Brigadier Jock Spragge decided that wresting the initiative from the Germans would only be possible if the regiments shifted slightly westwards to gain the Maldegem–Aardenburg road crossing of the canal. The bridge here had been blown, but Spragge hoped his engineers might be able to launch a Class 40 Bailey bridge across that could be used by tanks. The farmland west of the road was also not as inundated as that to the east.[45] Spragge's plan was a modest one, but even achieving this limited objective would strain the diminished regiments to the maximum. Yet the fact that the bridgehead had survived this long was encouraging. Heartened by 9 CIB's achievement, he could see hope for his own brigade.

PART THREE

TIGHTENING THE RING

[15]

Of First Importance

II CANADIAN CORPS'S OCTOBER bid to break the German stranglehold on the West Scheldt coincided with a showdown between General Dwight G. Eisenhower and Twenty-First Army Group commander, Field Marshal Bernard Law Montgomery. An October 5 Supreme Headquarters Allied Expeditionary Force meeting in Versailles starkly concluded that "access to Antwerp must be captured with the least possible delay" or the Allied army in western Europe would grind to a standstill—literally starved of supplies.

In addition to Eisenhower, his army group commanders, the naval and air commanders-in-chiefs, and other senior SHAEF staffers, Chief of the Imperial General Staff, Field Marshal Sir Alan Brooke had also flown into Versailles from London. Despite general agreement regarding Antwerp's importance, Montgomery still considered its opening secondary to a drive into the Ruhr Valley. He wanted American divisions from the United States First Army put under his command to achieve this. Given adequate forces and overall command, Montgomery argued, he could seize the Ruhr without worrying about Antwerp.

Montgomery's proposal was met by a verbal broadside from Naval Commander-in-Chief Admiral Sir Bertram Ramsay. "I...lambasted him for not having made Antwerp the immediate objective of highest priority, and I let fly with all my guns at the faulty strategy we had allowed. Our large forces were practically grounded for lack of supply, and had we now got Antwerp and not the corridor [Nijmegen bridgehead] we should be in a far better position for launching the knockout blow. CIGS Brooke told me after the meeting that I had spoken his thoughts, and it was high time someone expressed them."[1]

In his diary, Brooke commented: "I feel that Monty's strategy for once is at fault. Instead of carrying out the advance on Arnhem he ought to have made certain of Antwerp in the first place... Ike nobly took all the blame on himself as he had approved Monty's suggestion to operate on Arnhem."[2]

Despite general agreement that Antwerp must have first priority, the moment the meeting broke up, Montgomery set off on the course he had advocated. On October 8, he told Twelfth Army Group's General Omar N. Bradley and United States First Army commander, Lieutenant General Courtenay Hodges that he would continue playing what in "cricketing parlance" was a "two-eyed stance." The following day, Montgomery outlined three priorities. First, the Nijmegen bridgehead "must be securely held and maintained." Second, the area west of the Maas "must be cleaned up, and the enemy pushed back eastwards over the river." Third was the need to "open up Antwerp quickly. The use of Antwerp is vital to the Allies... operations to open the port must have priority as regards troops, ammunition, and so on." For the latter, Montgomery would strengthen First Canadian Army with an American infantry division moving from Cherbourg to near Brussels in a week's time. The 52nd British (Lowland) Division, deploying from England to Oostende on October 13, could also be committed.

Eisenhower reiterated the "supreme importance of Antwerp" by telegram on October 9. "I must repeat, we are now squarely up against the situation which we have anticipated for months; our intake into Continent will not support our battle. All operations will come to a standstill unless Antwerp is producing by the middle of November. I must emphasise that I consider Antwerp of first importance of all our endeavours on entire front from Switzerland to Channel. I believe your personal attention is required in operation designed to clear entrance."[3]

Unmoved, Montgomery countered with an appreciation entitled: "Notes on Command in Western Europe: 10 October, 1944." Mentioning Antwerp not at all, he declared the Ruhr "a definite and clear-cut military objective" that could only be won if one commander controlled both British and American forces. Either he or Bradley should command and the other be subordinate. "It may be that political and national considerations prevent us having a sound organization," he closed. "If this is the case I would suggest that we say so. Do not let us pretend we are all right, whereas we are very far from being all right in that respect."[4]

Eisenhower responded at length. "The questions you raise are serious ones and I will discuss them later in this letter. However, they do not constitute the real issue now at hand. That issue is Antwerp." The parlous supply state was "why I keep reverting again and again to the matter of getting Antwerp into a workable condition. I have been informed, both by the Chief of the Imperial General Staff [Brooke] and the Chief of Staff of the United States Army [George C. Marshall] that they seriously considered giving me a flat order that until the capture of Antwerp and its approaches were fully assured, this operation should take precedence over all others." Ever since the failure of Market Garden, "I have been... ready to furnish additional troops from U.S. sources for the purpose, provided only that you desired them, and that they could be gotten up to you and supplied... I do not mean to be repeating myself about something that is well known to us both. The reason for re-stating it, however, is that the Antwerp operation does not involve the question of command in any slightest degree. Everything that can be brought in to help, no matter of what nationality, belongs to you."[5]

Army group commanders, he argued, were adequately empowered for battlefield operations, while Eisenhower's job was to adjust the larger boundaries between army groups, assign air, ground, or airborne forces, and set supply priorities. As for the Ruhr, Eisenhower agreed a single commander should control those forces involved. But with Twenty-First Army Group's commitments shifting westwards to help open Antwerp, it would fall to Bradley's Twelfth Army Group to carry the main burden on this front.

Montgomery folded. "You will hear no more on the subject of command from me. I have given you my views and you have given me your answer. That ends the matter and I and all of us up here will weigh in one hundred percent to do what you want and we will pull it through without a doubt. I have given Antwerp top priority in all operations in 21 Army Group and all energies and efforts will be now devoted towards opening up that place. Your very devoted and loyal subordinate, Monty."[6]

During this debate—ended only on October 16—First Canadian Army saw little change in its situation. It continued the Scheldt campaign with the meagre and ever diminishing strength of a single corps—II Canadian Corps. Meanwhile, I British Corps on the right wing remained directed northeast in support of British Second Army, which was not immediately turned towards opening Antwerp.

ON THE LEOPOLD CANAL, 7th Canadian Infantry Brigade headquarters staff looked less for relief from Montgomery and his superiors than to faint hopes that the German will to fight was crumbling. On October 10, captured artillerymen had claimed "their officers held them to their gun positions at the point of a pistol and that reprisals would be inflicted on their families by the Gestapo if they surrendered. These reports left us wondering whether their high morale at the commencement of the operation had decreased, but reports from any of our people forward of [battalion] HQ very emphatically denied the fact." Other prisoner reports held that some German forces had been withdrawn from the bridgehead area to meet 9th Canadian Infantry Brigade's beachhead near Hoofdplaat.[7]

Although the Canadian hold on the Leopold Canal bridgehead was precarious, it had taxed 64th Infantry Division's Generalmajor Knut Eberding's resources to the limit—forcing commitment of the reserve battalions of his three infantry regiments. Impressed by "the bravery and determination of the Canadian soldiers" there, he had still remained confident that the bridgehead could be contained indefinitely. The lull in September before First Canadian Army began its operations against the Breskens Pocket had provided time to identify potential crossing points and prepare strong fortifications for their defence. The entire canal had been ranged in by artillery so that instant and accurate fire could be ranged on any point. On October 6, 7 CIB had paddled into the heart of a well-prepared kill zone that stopped it cold. Since then, Eberding had calmly fed in reserves as needed to keep the bridgehead bottled up.

9 CIB's amphibious operation, however, presented a crisis. Only commitment of his divisional reserve—held back to counter disasters—had limited the assault's initial success.[8] Eberding was a seasoned veteran. He had joined the army at nineteen in September 1914, fought in both Russia and Flanders during the Great War, and gained the rank of company commander. Discharged in 1920, he had returned to service in 1923 and by 1943 was a generalmajor. He was a tough, no-nonsense leader, and his men followed suit. Fully indoctrinated in the Hitler Youth, most had served on either the Russian, Italian, or Norwegian fronts before being rounded up (while on furlough) to join this new division's ranks in June and July of 1944 in response to the Normandy invasion. Arriving just as the Falaise Pocket collapsed, the 64th had joined Fifteenth Army's retreat until ordered to hold the Breskens Pocket in September.[9] They had so far performed this task competently and in a manner that surprised Allied intelligence staff.

Sustaining the Breskens Pocket defenders' will to fight was an equal measure of training, sense of duty, fanatical patriotism, and fear of retribution. Their commanders invoked whatever combination of motivators seemed strongest at a given time. On October 7, for example, Fifteenth Army's General der Infanterie Gustav von Zangen appealed to patriotism and duty when he stated that "overrunning the Scheldt fortifications" would enable the Allies to "land great masses of material in a large and completely sheltered harbour. With this material they might deliver a death-blow at the North German plateau and at Berlin before the onset of winter... The enemy knows that he must assault the European fortresses as speedily as possible before its inner lines of resistance are built up and occupied by new divisions. For this reason he needs Antwerp. And for this reason, we must hold the Scheldt fortifications to the end. The German people are watching us... Each additional day you deny the port of Antwerp to the enemy and to the resources that he has at his disposal will be vital."[10]

Von Zangen had sought not only to rally the troops on the Leopold Canal front, but also those garrisoning the increasingly waterlogged Walcheren Island. Unable to stem seawater flowing through the breach in the Westkapelle dyke, conditions for Germans and Dutch alike had steadily deteriorated. Then, even as von Zangen had issued his statement, an RAF formation of 120 Lancasters led by four Mosquitos struck at Vlissingen. Five waves of twelve bombers each bombed the Nolledijk west of the city. Spaced ten minutes apart, the waves unleashed a mixed load of explosives that included many 1,000-pound bombs fused with time-delay detonators. A second group of 60 Lancasters, meanwhile, struck a dyke about a mile east of the dockyards. A total of 730 tons of explosives rained down on these targets.[11]

Seventeen-year-old Ad van Dijk and his father, Vlissigen's financial officer, were among only about 3,000 of the city's population of 22,000 still living in the small city. The rest had fled or been ordered to leave. Ad's father remained full-time to see to his municipal responsibilities, while the rest of the family had relocated to a farm near Veere on Walcheren's northern coast. On October 7, Ad had bicycled—as he regularly did—to Vlissingen and had seen the bombers leaving. He found his father on the flat-topped roof of their home near the harbour. Despite the danger presented by the exploding bombs, the man had remained here throughout the raid. At first, Ad thought the dykes little damaged. Then a slow, steady series of massive explosions rapidly widened the breaches. The delayed-action bombs, buried deep into the dyke by their massive weight, continued to detonate for about six hours.[12] Soon the breach west of Vlissingen was 150 feet wide and the one to the east a gaping 1,000 feet.[13]

Before dusk, Ad cycled out to the Nolledijk. Seawater surged through and into the fields. He could see logs, lumber, even a section of a German guardhouse rushing along in the water. Peddling back through the city in the dark, exploding bombs still sending huge balls of red flame high overhead, he marvelled at the lack of panic displayed by the Dutch civilians. Stalwartly, they moved furniture and other belongings from the ground floor to the upstairs, or nailed boards across the bottoms of doors in an effort to prevent the inflow of water. Surprisingly, there had been no Dutch casualties in this raid.[14]

The bombers that struck the Nolledijk also attacked the nearby West Battery. One large coastal gun here was destroyed by a direct hit, a second jammed and thrown out of balance, but the other two remained operational. One soldier was killed, another missing and presumed dead, and four were wounded. When the ammunition bunker's roof blew in, about four thousand shells were destroyed and the place was flooded by three feet of water. All bicycles—the battery's only means of transportation—were destroyed, as were the cookhouse, recreation room, canteen, and some barracks.[15]

Conditions throughout Walcheren Island rapidly worsened after the raid. The van Dijk home, like all others in lower Vlissingen, flooded twice daily at high tide to a depth of three feet. Four days after the Vlissingen raid, RAF bombers again struck Walcheren—breaching the coastal dyke near Veere. Henceforth, water spread relentlessly until the entire saucer-like interior below sea level became a mucky floodplain. Only the slightly higher bands on the outer edges remained. While the Dutch knew that the floodwaters would rise and fall according to the tides, Ad van Dijk realized that the Germans did not understand this. "They were very demoralized and didn't feel at home. They went from the houses they were staying in to their gun positions by walking barefoot with their pant legs rolled up. I learned that they were all men from inland parts of Germany, who had no knowledge of the sea. They didn't like the seawater."

"What do you think?" one asked the boy. "How high will the water come?"

"You know Middelburg and the big tower there?" When the men gathered around all nodded, van Dijk added, "Just at the top. That will be the level." The Germans noticeably paled, apparently believing the water could rise to the peak of a tower so tall that it could be seen from anywhere on the island. The youth happily sowed fear in their souls and was rewarded to hear several confide that they had lost all hope. The floodwaters would either claim them or they would be killed by the Allies. None would survive, for their orders were to fight to the last man.[16]

The last-stand order, Eberding believed, emanated from Hitler personally. The 64th Infantry Division in the Breskens Pocket and the 70th Infantry Division guarding Walcheren Island and South Beveland were to mount an "obstinate defence," the October 7 order declared. Such orders had become common on the Russian front and had always been the Führer's work. In German battle doctrine, "obstinate defence" called for extreme sacrifices, if merited. Eberding considered the tactic unwarranted here. Consequently, he substituted "holding defence" before distributing the order through his division, while 70th Division's Generalleutnant Wilhelm Daser kept the original wording. By "holding defence," Eberding meant that his men should surrender no ground without his personal instruction.[17] Given the situation on the Leopold Canal, the general had been confident the division could hold so long as supplies and manpower permitted.

That had changed two days later. The "possibility of an Allied waterborne assault at the Braakman inlet had been dismissed [by Eberding] on the assumption that the opponent did not have the requisite equipment in the area."[18] After throwing his divisional reserves against the beachhead at Hoofdplaat, Eberding sought assistance from Fifteenth Army. To his good fortune, a mist blanketed the West Scheldt between Walcheren and the port of Breskens, enabling von Zangen to send reinforcements from the 70th Division by boat on October 9. By nightfall, Eberding could deploy three and a half battalions against the beachhead and declared it "sealed off," although the "situation [was] still tense."[19]

FROM THE CANADIAN perspective, 3rd Division's Major General Dan Spry believed the beachhead anything but boxed in. 9 CIB's Brigadier John Rockingham's reports encouraged him to completely reverse its importance to Operation Switchback, and order 8th Canadian Infantry Brigade to reinforce the beachhead. On the evening of October 9, Spry consequently directed Lieutenant Colonel Thomas Cripps Lewis to attack south of the beachhead in the Isabellapolder area near Boekhoute to establish a land link to 9 CIB.[20] The two brigades would then advance on the port of Breskens. Seizing the port would sever any chance of supply or escape for 64th Infantry Division, ensuring its destruction.

Spry realized that the intensity of fighting in the beachhead meant 9 CIB needed reinforcement, but sending an infantry regiment seemed impossible. 7 CIB was completely tied down on the Leopold, and 8 CIB was committed to the breakthrough. That left only his reconnaissance unit, so he ordered it moved by Buffaloes into the beachhead on the night of October 10. Its armoured cars being too large, each troop was equipped with four Bren carriers and would fight as mounted infantry.[21]

Despite shifting the division's main weight away from the Leopold Canal, Spry never considered abandoning the bridgehead. Its role in pinning the major German strength in place was too valuable, and exploitation from here remained a key component of Operation Switchback. But the bridgehead would never become usable unless 7 CIB gained the Maldegem–Aardenburg crossing west of the bridgehead. A sixteen-foot-square pillbox that bristled with machine guns set behind two-foot-thick walls blocked any advance in this direction.

The Regina Rifles were ordered to take it out, with 'C' Company kicking off the attack on October 10 at 0250. Halfway to the pillbox, 'A' Company would leapfrog into the lead.[22] Major Ronald Shawcross was still dragging the leg that had been injured when the house collapsed on him during the October 6 crossing operation. His back also hurt like hell. He was dispirited, but not by physical pain. The loss of so many men during the past days crushed his shoulders. No question that tonight more good men must die.[23]

'C' Company's Lieutenant Bob Gray also expected a rough night. Even after being reinforced with two officers and thirty other ranks, the company remained badly depleted. Both new officers were artillerymen, who had been given a crash course in infantry fighting. Gray lined the company up, put the gunners in the midst of an experienced section, and "instructed them to follow the veteran other ranks as the fighting progressed... they were to be learners, not leaders."

Just before Gray led his men forward, the company's second-in-command, who had been on leave, ran up and announced that he was taking the reins and the lieutenant was ordered Left Out of Battle. In every attack, a certain number of officers and men were held back as an experienced nucleus around which a company could be rebuilt in the event the unit was shredded. Gray briefed the officer and "then departed in an exhausted state." Crossing the kapok bridge, he proceeded to the Reginas' rear echelon area and promptly "slept the clock around. It was my first sleep of any kind since 6 October."[24]

'C' Company fought through to its objective by 0345. 'A' Company then moved through its lines and was almost immediately cut to ribbons by a heavy mortar barrage that reduced it to single platoon strength.[25] 'C' Company rushed a platoon forward, and during the course of this move, one of the gunners-turned-infantry officers excitedly ran too far ahead of his section and was killed.[26]

Shawcross and his mixed 'A' and 'C' Company force managed to reach the pillbox, and cleared it in vicious hand-to-hand combat that netted thirty-five prisoners. The regiment's war diarist noted that although the Germans were from a grab bag of infantry units, they were all "the real Nazi type, [that] have no idea of surrender, and still think Germany will win the war."[27] Two hundred yards away lay the blown bridge, but the Reginas were spent. Controlling the dyke's water side along the stretch of ground won was sufficient challenge. The deadly grenade exchange game with the Germans began.

As Shawcross had feared, 'A' Company had been destroyed. Only twenty of his men still stood. It was also the end of the line for this D-Day veteran. Lieutenant Colonel Foster Matheson ordered him to see the medical officer, who discovered he had "extensive bruising, internal injuries of some kind, shock and my right foot was dragging." Shawcross was evacuated to hospital in Bruges. "It hurt a little being pulled out of battle in this fashion after this long period of comradeship and fighting, but in the end I realized I needed to go. I was tired, worn out and like most, confused with the horror of death, the bloated bodies of all the animals, humans and the general horror of the whole thing... all [those] days and nights of fear and dread." On D-Day, Shawcross had weighed 220 pounds. Now he was 165. Eventually, it was discovered that among his other injuries, Shawcross had a broken back—a compression fracture of the third and fourth lumbar vertebrae probably inflicted during the building collapse. He would be hospitalized for the rest of the war.[28]

Within hours of sending the major to see the medical officer, Matheson too was ordered out of the line. When the lieutenant colonel had come to brigade headquarters on the afternoon of October 10, Brigadier Jock Spragge recognized that Matheson was verging on a complete breakdown.[29] The popular commander was replaced temporarily by Lieutenant Colonel G.H. Gilday, who had no connection to the Reginas. Hardly an original officer remained.

THE ROYAL WINNIPEG RIFLES also received a new battalion commander on October 10, but its men and officers knew him well. As with Matheson, Lieutenant Colonel John Meldram had been ordered out for a rest. Both knew their combat days were over. They had landed together on Juno Beach and led their regiments through months of desperate battle. The responsibility of command over such a long and intense period had taken its grim toll on the physical and psychological health of many First Canadian Army senior officers. The time had come for younger, fresher men. The Winnipegers' new commander was just twenty-seven.

Major Lockhart Ross "Lochie" Fulton was also a D-Day veteran, who had won the Distinguished Service Order during the Normandy campaign. Fulton had just returned to the regiment from leave granted after Calais fell. He and two other 7 CIB company commanders had spent the past couple of days chasing after the brigade. Knowing they were overdue, they had rotated turns driving the jeep, and none of them had slept during the forty-eight-hour pursuit. Fulton walked into brigade headquarters shortly after Matheson's departure, only to be scolded by the adjutant for being a day late and then told the brigadier wanted to see him immediately. Presenting himself, he offered no excuses while the brigadier tore a strip off him. Then Spragge said, "Well, you're now commanding the Winnipegs. John Meldram has been returned to England. I want you to get moving. You've got companies across the canal and we've got to get a breakthrough there."[30]

Spragge wanted the Winnipegs to drive a mile north from the canal to seize first the small hamlet of Graaf Jan and then the larger village of Biezen.[31] As the Winnipegs increased the bridgehead's depth, Spragge would pull the Canadian Scottish Regiment away from Moershoofd on the extreme right flank preparatory to a move through the Regina front on October 12 to seize the bridge crossing and capture Eede. Fulton was taken aback. He had expected to return as the battalion's second-in-command and be able to catch up on the lost sleep. Now he was promoted to acting lieutenant colonel pending rank confirmation, replacing a man he respected, and being told to lead the regiment into an attack "as quickly as I could get it organized."

Fulton rushed to the canal and started across the kapok bridge to check on his rifle companies. No sooner had he stepped on the bridge than the Germans began dropping shells into the water. Fulton sprinted across and threw himself into a slit trench beside Major Dave Campbell, who commanded 'D' company. Campbell reported the companies all down to about platoon strength. Between the heavy shelling and the Germans dug in on the opposite side of the dyke, both men thought "the possibility of any attack succeeding was almost out of the question." But Fulton had orders.[32]

At 1400 hours on October 11, he threw 'C' Company towards Graaf Jan. Some of the ground they must cross was flooded, the streets of the hamlet itself transformed into canals, and the yards awash. At first, the men sank up to their knees, then waists. In places, they lurched into water neck deep, desperately holding weapons above their heads to keep them dry. Little fire came from Graaf Jan until the Winnipegs closed on the buildings and a strong German force stormed out of Biezen to meet them. A bitter struggle ensued as soldiers fired on each other at point-blank range. Ammunition almost exhausted, 'C' Company finally withdrew to the narrow front by the canal. The Germans smothered the position with artillery fire and pushed infantry up to where they could harass it with small-arms fire. Movement became impossible "except by crawling on the semi-flooded ground or in water-filled ditches, both of which were littered with German and Canadian dead," reported the war diarist.[33]

Determined to succeed, Fulton ordered 'C' Company forward the next morning at 0530 hours, with a platoon from 'A' Company beefing its ranks. He personally led the attack, preferring to be at the front of his troops. Again the men wallowed through the flooded ground, gaining the village by 0620. This time, they had most of the village in hand before the Germans counterattacked from Biezen, but were unable to gain the northerly houses. It became "a house to house battle and in some cases room to room."[34]

'C' Company's commander was pressed against the outside of a house, with Germans holding the second storey. His runner was beside him. Overhead, a German kept poking his rifle out a window, but if he leaned over to shoot the two Canadians, they would be able to engage him with their guns. It was a deadly standoff. The officer knew they must get a grenade through the window or the German would soon drop one on their heads, so he yelled at the runner to do the job. "I don't know how to do it," the man replied. A new reinforcement, the man just stared apprehensively at the grenade. The officer snatched it from his hand, pulled the pin, held it a few seconds, and then stepped out far enough from the wall to allow a clean pitch into the window. One more building was secured.[35]

'C' Company's Sergeant Kelly decided the battle by rushing his section into the open so they could throw grenades freely into the windows of the enemy-held houses. "The exploding grenades were too much for the Germans and leaving many dead and wounded [they] withdrew to Biezen. Casualties among the [Winnipegs] were also heavy and included Lt. D.L. Riesberry and one section of 'A' Company who were killed or captured when they were surrounded and had used up all their ammunition. The battalion snipers were brought forward and succeeded in killing Germans who risked exposing themselves. The remainder of the day was devoted largely to reinforcing the walls of occupied houses and in bringing up food and ammunition."[36] The body of thirty-year-old Donald Leach Riesberry of Brandon, Manitoba was soon discovered, along with those of most of his men.

With Biezen obviously strongly garrisoned, Fulton held his badly depleted force at Graaf Jan. The hamlet stood parallel to the southernmost part of Eede, and its seizure served to somewhat protect the right flank of the Canadian Scottish fighting to take the bridge crossing. That was the best the Winnipegs could manage.

THE CANADIAN SCOTTISH attack had kicked off at 0100 hours on October 12 with 'C' Company, commanded by Lieutenant Jack Gallagher, striking out from where the Regina Rifles' 'A' Company held the pillbox. Lieutenant Royce Marshall's No. 15 Platoon led, as the Can Scots "crept cautiously through the sloppy, sucking mud" along the water side of the dyke.[37] Marshall's men reached the Maldegem–Aardenburg road and set up on its right-hand side. Lieutenant Peter MacDonnel then jumped No. 14 Platoon silently across the road and consolidated to its left. The Can Scots began "burrowing into the canal side of the dyke," Marshall later recounted. "Soon we found the Germans were burrowed in on the other side...when grenades started to fall amongst us. We, of course, retaliated and all night and the next day we exchanged grenades to such a degree that the RSM [Regimental Sergeant Major] was complaining that the battalion reserve was nearly exhausted."[38]

While the Germans facing No. 15 Platoon seemed content to pin them in place, once the sun rose, No. 14 Platoon fended off one counterattack after another. Gallagher organized a carrying party to "bring up grenades as fast as they could and after we used approximately twenty-five boxes we managed to drive them off." About ten men were wounded, and MacDonnel's platoon was forced to give up about a hundred yards—crowding in close to the road.[39]

Normally, 'C' Company would have dealt with the Germans by driving over the canal to gain control of the other side, "but to put one's head over the level of the dyke was to cause the top of the dyke to be swept by enemy machinegun fire. Artillery fire could not be laid on owing to the close proximity of our troops to the enemy which was about five yards."[40]

At about 1400 hours, Major David Pugh brought a platoon from 'D' Company up to reinforce No. 14 Platoon. This enabled the

Can Scots to regain some lost ground, and soon the rapid grenade exchange slowed to a desultory trickle. In the late afternoon, a German first-aid man slipped into No. 15 Platoon's position and asked for a twenty-minute truce to allow him to evacuate twenty-five men immobilized by wounds. Marshall realized that the Type 36 grenade, which was more explosive and produced a greater spread of shrapnel than the German potato-mashers, was inflicting "a harvest of shrapnel wounds and burns." Gallagher agreed to the truce, using the time to evacuate his own wounded and resupply with grenades.[41]

According to plan, the rest of the battalion was supposed to have attacked towards Eede from the front line held by 'C' and 'D' Companies at midnight. But it was obvious that before this could happen the Germans immediately across the dyke had to be driven off. Pugh and Gallagher conferred with the Regina Rifles and agreed on a joint attack along the length of their line. Once the Germans were driven off, Can Scots' Major Earl English's 'B' Company would move up the road before veering left to seize the southern outskirts of Eede, while 'A' Company struck out on a northwesterly angle alongside two parallelling hedgerows to enter the village from the east.[42]

At 2200 hours, just as a brief artillery and mortar bombardment lifted, 'C' and 'D' Companies went over the top of the dyke "after making a barrage of our own with...grenades." The attack seemed to stun the defending Germans, many of whom immediately surrendered. Despite numbering only fourteen men, Sergeant T. Byron's No. 13 Platoon rounded up thirty prisoners. When Byron was wounded, Corporal A.H. Palmer took over without the platoon suffering any loss of momentum. Private P. Colman, leading Palmer's section, skillfully ferreted the Germans out of their positions on the side of the dyke. Although wounded in both arms, Private E.G. Shannon "carried on until the fight was over...These are men who were mentioned to me," Gallagher later wrote, "but there were many more, and every man did an excellent job."[43] In all, the two companies took more than 150 prisoners—a remarkable feat considering 'C' Company had just thirty-five men left and 'D' Company was little better off.[44] By 2230 hours, they reported the "last resistance had been cleaned out and we had established ourselves firmly on both sides of the dyke and as far out as a group of buildings 100 yards to our front."[45]

This set the stage for 'A' and 'B' Companies' push for Eede, which they began at 0030 hours on October 13. Eede stood west of the main road astride a secondary road, while the highway was itself bordered by closely packed farmhouses. The village was a long straggle of interspersed houses rather than a tightly knit community. 'B' Company made good progress into the village, coming to a halt about two hundred yards from the canal in order to avoid being separated from the rest of the Can Scot front. 'A' Company, under Major J.D.M. Gillan, also met no resistance as it slipped alongside the hedgerows to where they intersected the main road. Moving out ahead of the rest of the company, No. 7 Platoon returned a report that the houses west of the road were clear. Captain Gillan then moved the company up and spread the platoons among the houses to consolidate its hold.

Unwittingly, Gillan established company headquarters inside a house where a group of Germans under command of a sergeant was hiding in the basement. Plopping down on some sandbags in the kitchen, the captain propped his feet against the cellar door just as someone tried pushing it open. Thinking one of his men was searching the place, Gillan gently eased the door closed when the person trying to open it abruptly stopped. A moment later, someone shoved hard, compressing Gillan's knees up around his neck. Then an arm clutching a stick grenade appeared. The thrown grenade collided with Gillan's helmeted head and spun across the room, while the arm, wearing a grey uniform marked with sergeant's stripes, disappeared amid much crashing of a body tumbling down stairs. The grenade exploded, wounding both Gillan and his second-in-command, Captain S.L. Chambers. No. 7 Platoon, responding to the explosion, quickly rounded up the German sergeant—a bit battered from his tumble—and his men.[46]

While the Can Scots had not cleared all of Eede for simple want of manpower, they had pushed the bridgehead far enough from the canal to give the engineers breathing space to launch a Bailey bridge. 7 CIB's trial by fire on the Leopold Canal was not yet over, but things were markedly improved. "For an entire week," the Can Scot regimental historian later wrote, "the brigade had had to claw its way forward in a battle reminiscent of the First World War, with no tanks, no carriers, and no vehicles of any sort to help it. With the bridge complete, and the engineers and pioneers busy clearing the road of mines, the armour could be brought in to blast the enemy from his entrenched positions around Eede."

In the morning, the Germans seemed to sense this. After a spate of counterattacks repelled with help from the artillery, opposition noticeably slackened.[47] While the Germans continued pounding the bridgehead—particularly where the engineers worked on the bridge—only the occasional sniper tried infiltrating the position. "As the strain has been relieved now," wrote the Regina Rifles war diarist, "thirty men are sent out for a rest for 24 hours, the plan being to give all the men in the line a rest in this way. On their way out they get cleaned up at the mobile bath. The balance of the men are getting their baths throughout the day. Blankets have been brought in and distributed to the [companies]."[48]

[16]

The Toughest Yet

ON OCTOBER 9, the day after 9th Canadian Infantry Brigade's amphibious assault across the Braakman Inlet, Generalmajor Knut Eberding recognized that 64th Infantry Division was losing control of the Breskens Pocket, with the most serious threat the "Canadian forces [that] took Hoofdplaat after bitter fighting." His counterattack attempts "were delayed by air attacks and damaged roads."[1] Given the pressure on his front, Eberding mistakenly concluded that he faced two full divisions—3rd Canadian Infantry Division and 4th Canadian Armoured Division—and feared the latter would unleash an unstoppable armoured juggernaut despite the polders being so ill-suited to tanks.[2]

Major General Dan Spry, meanwhile, had his own concerns, not least being 9 CIB's failure on October 10 to widen the beachhead. It had been a cloudy, showery day and the brigade's war diarist noted "no lull in the enemy's continuous efforts to dislodge us." Vlissingen coastal battery's shelling was increasingly more accurate and deadly. Any advance was met by "small arms and mortar fire from carefully sited positions along the roads and canals," causing heavy casualties.[3]

Spry planned to have 8th Canadian Infantry Brigade reinforce the beachhead by driving through the Isabellapolder south of the

Braakman Inlet. On October 10 at 0300 hours, 4th Canadian Armoured Division's Algonquin Regiment attempted to open a hole in the German front lines there. The Algonquins attacked behind the covering fire of artillery and the medium machine guns of the Cameron Highlanders of Ottawa. 'B' Company was immediately pinned down by fire from strongpoints and quickly withdrew after taking many casualties, including the wounding of its commander, Captain W.F. Grafton. 'D' company got through a network of barbed wire only to be "pretty well cut up as the obstacle was covered by enemy [light machine guns] and grenade fire." Lieutenant Colonel Robert Bradburn ordered it back. When 'A' and 'D' Companies tried again in the afternoon, they "met with no better success... and another withdrawal had to be effected." Casualties for the day tallied twenty-one.[4]

Well west of the Algonquins, the Argyll and Sutherland Highlanders had also tried to penetrate the German defences by sending a four-man patrol across the Leopold Canal south of Watervliet in two reconnaissance boats. Lieutenant Kerrigan Milne King and the others surprised a machine-gun post and killed its crew with grenades. But the single burst the gunners fired mortally wounded King. Sergeant Mooney and the other two men picked up the dying officer and slithered down the slippery bank to their boats. The patrol escaped despite being illuminated by flares and subjected to a rain of grenades and rifle grenade volleys. The severity of the German response to the patrol showed that no easy opening existed along the Argyll front.[5]

Realizing that 8 CIB would be unable to advance overland, Spry changed plans again. This brigade, along with the 7th Reconnaissance Regiment, would land on the beachhead. The North Shore (New Brunswick) Regiment and the reconnaissance troops would move in on October 11, and the rest of 8 CIB the day after.

In the beachhead, the immediate concern during the night of October 10–11 was the gaps developing in the front line. The Highland Light Infantry near Biervliet and the adjacent North Nova Scotia Highlanders were not tied together. The North Novas also had lost direct contact with the Stormont, Dundas and Glengarry Highlanders to their west. This gap could only widen further as the

Glens were moving away from the Novas in an attempt to seize the western part of Hoofdplaat.[6]

Immediately south of this village, the Glens' 'B' Company was still harassed by heavy fire from 20-millimetre flak guns hidden among a clutch of farmhouses. It was also being fired on from positions in the gap between the Glens and North Novas. On Hoofdplaat's seaward side, 'A' Company remained pinned in front of the bunker system covering the dyke. Only 'C' Company, in Hoofdplaat's centre, enjoyed limited freedom of movement.

While the North Novas controlled one side of a dyke east of the Glens, the Germans were dug in opposite, resulting in the routine grenade exchange. With the dawn, the North Novas' 'D' Company—its thirty-five men bolstered by a 'C' Company platoon commanded by Sergeant Andy Cannon and the battalion's three Wasp Bren carriers—had attempted to eliminate the Germans. The moment the Wasps finished releasing a salvo of flame over the dyke, the infantry charged with the carriers close behind. Any German dugouts that refused to surrender were burned out by the Wasps. A thirty-minute action won the dyke, for the loss of only one damaged Wasp.[7]

The North Novas now pushed southwest towards Driewegen, which lay two and a half miles away across open polder. 'A' Company made good progress until being "stopped by very heavy machine gun fire and [having] to go to ground about 100 yards in front of the enemy position." The men remained trapped there the rest of the day, unable to evacuate their ever growing number of wounded. Nightfall brought no respite, for shelling had set several nearby farm buildings alight and the fires illuminated the battlefield. The company had nearly exhausted its ammunition when Company Sergeant Major Dave Smith assembled a small party that carried ammunition forward on stretchers and brought out the wounded. The CSM kept this shuttle force going all night, each trip made through withering fire.[8]

While the battalion's main effort had been directed at Driewegen, the North Novas also slipped a company to the right to establish contact with the Glens' 'B' Company. This enabled the Glens to attack the gun positions hidden in the farm buildings. Without regard for its own casualties, 'B' Company punched through a storm of shells from the 20-millimetre guns. One platoon was cut to only ten men. Although the position was taken by mid-morning, no sooner had it been cleared than the Germans counterattacked. But the Cameron Highlanders of Ottawa, who had been supporting the Glens, broke the attack with long-range fire from their machine guns. This was considered "a great sight for the tired, wet riflemen."[9]

From Hoofdplaat, 'C' Company struck the flank of the bunkers pinning 'A' Company down. Captain B.G. Fox and the antitank platoon pushed their six-pounders forward manually to support this attack. The large bunkers were heavily reinforced and fitted with steel doors, so Fox ordered the guns fired from a range of just fifty yards. The combined infantry and antitank gun assault silenced the 20-millimetre guns, and fifty Germans surrendered.[10]

As 'A' Company advanced into the bunker system in the early afternoon, it found that each contained two or three rooms separated by internal steel doors. In one bunker, a section of Glens discovered an adjoining room full of Germans. They could hear someone talking on a wireless set, and realized that he was directing artillery fire against the battalion. Unable to break the door down or to gain a safe firing angle for a PIAT, the pioneer platoon was summoned. They blew the door in with an explosive charge. Thirty more Germans were dragged out as prisoners and the wireless set was secured.[11]

Still facing heavy opposition, the three companies advanced in line, with 'B' Company on the southern outskirts of Hoofdplaat, 'C' Company in its centre, and 'A' Company on the seaward side of the dyke. Artillery fire stalked them, prompting the war diarist to note that "the SDG are being badly cut up... and have suffered quite a few casualties." Despite the low ceiling, brigade kept an artillery spotter plane codenamed Skylark overhead, and the forward observation officer aboard directed counterbattery fire against the German guns. The moment the plane was forced to land, however, the volume of incoming fire surged, driving the Glens to ground. "Skylark was over," Lieutenant Colonel Roger Rowley signalled brigade. "He seems to keep the big guns quiet. If possible we'd like to keep that fellow overhead. Every time he buggers off the guns open up." He warned that "we will soon need reinforcements as we are gradually being eaten away."

Late in the afternoon, Skylark was grounded permanently, the battlefield obscured by rain and mist. The Germans counterattacked, fighting "practically hand to hand." Two captured Germans had flamethrowers strapped on their backs. Night fell with Hoofdplaat still disputed. The Glens found about fifty civilians cowering in basements and evacuated them to the beach for shipment out of the battle zone. In the darkness, they could see the flashes of the Vlissingen coastal guns.[12]

ON THE BEACHHEAD'S opposite flank, the Highland Light Infantry's 'A' Company had driven west from Amber Beach to close the gap between their battalion and the North Novas, while Major J.C. King's 'B' Company assaulted across the main dyke on the left flank. 'B' Company was supported by the battalion's Wasps, and after several bursts of flame, the Germans surrendered. Many, in the words of the HLI war diarist, were "badly scorched." Although the HLI now controlled the dyke, German snipers across the facing polder posed a deadly hazard. Forward Observation Officer Captain John Lawrence Murdoch was shot dead. The thirty-six-year-old 19th Field Regiment officer had always been right out front, despite the wireless set's telltale whip antenna marking him clearly for snipers.[13]

Major Tom Prest's 'C' Company pushed out from the main dyke to increase the depth of the beachhead. Initially, gains were measured in yards, but by afternoon the situation loosened, and the advance became so rapid that a couple of wagons loaded with German wounded were overrun. Leaving the wounded Germans to be taken in by stretcher-bearers, Prest and his men had gone only a short distance beyond when gunfire broke out behind them. Spinning around, the men watched shells from a German 20-millimetre gun riddle the carts. Some of the wounded tried to escape, but were cut down as they crawled or hobbled away. Prest was shocked by this cold-blooded murder. When the guns turned on 'C' Company, it was forced to pull back to a more defensible position just ahead of the carts. During the withdrawal, several dead Glens had to be left behind, including twenty-nine-year-old Company Sergeant Major Johnny McDonald. On September 2, his brother

Donald Russell McDonald—three years younger, and also a CSM with the Highland Light Infantry—had been killed.[14]

With three companies engaged, a steady stream of wounded flowed into the farmhouse on the south side of the main dyke that served as the Regimental Aid Post. "An awful lot of the lads were getting wounded," Padre Jock Anderson recalled. "I think there were more wounds there than any other battle because it was Small Arms fire. Usually in a battle... there was a lot of SA fire when you got into the village, but a lot of casualties were before they ever got in sight of the enemy. There were the mortars and the shellings and a lot were killed outright. But in close-in fighting, when there was Small Arms, they might get wounded in the arm or leg, or a chin blown off."[15]

Hearing of the 'C' Company deaths, Padre Anderson set out by jeep with his driver Mitch to retrieve the bodies. Passing the carts, he noticed "all kinds of German dead lying around them." Reaching Prest's position, Anderson asked where McDonald was. When the major said the body was too exposed to recover until after dark, Anderson decided to return later. Heading back to the RAP, Anderson saw a German lurch out of a ditch beside the carts and collapse. "I slammed on the brakes and told Mitch, 'We've got to get him. He's still alive.'

"Mitch looked at me and said: 'You're not stopping here?' I told him, 'Sure, why not?' So I backed up and we ran into the ditch and picked him up and all the time we were putting him on a stretcher on the jeep there was a German sniper out in the field trying to get us. I think I almost lost my head that time.

"Then we went over and felt all the bodies in the other cart and there was one still alive so we got him on a stretcher and took both of them down to our RAP."[16]

With nightfall, 7th Reconnaissance Regiment (17th Duke of York's Royal Canadian Hussars) took over part of the HLI front so it could reorganize for a breakout to Biervliet in the morning. Nobody was sorry to leave the embattled front. "Fighting today has been hard and the men are having a grim time. So far this operation is the toughest yet," the war diarist concluded.[17]

The 7th Reconnaissance Regiment completed relieving the HLI just before dawn on October 12. First light "broke and, as the degree of visibility increased, the men, peering out of the trenches which lined the dyke they had taken over, looked with interest on their new battle-ground. The polders seemed to stretch for miles in front of them broken only by the separating dykes and the smashed structure of what had been a farmhouse. Water lay everywhere and, half submerged in it, cattle—some dead and bloated; others alive and miserable. Everything looked dead and, if not so, doomed... The light had hardly increased enough to see 200 yards when the air was filled with the chatter of the enemy machine guns and the slower throb of the 20mm, whose explosive shells burst on the front of the dugouts. The Germans, quite obviously, were close at hand. This sort of thing kept up all day with both sides firing point-blank at each other but no advances being made either way."[18]

At Hoofdplaat, the Glens spent the day clearing the last buildings. In a bizarre twist, an enemy gunboat opened fire from just offshore. Before artillery could be summoned to counter this threat, two Spitfires dropped out of the low clouds and left it "blazing bow to stern."[19]

The North Novas tried again for Driewegen, and 'C' Company initially gained ground. But acutely accurate artillery fire forced the men to relinquish their gains or be killed. 'A' and 'D' Companies formed up next, looking up a perfectly straight dyke road that led to the village eight hundred yards away. Just on the village outskirts, a crosswise-running dyke offered good cover to regroup for a final push. The infantry were to advance with one company hugging either side of the dyke, while two Wasps commanded by Corporal C.V. Thomas chugged straight up the road. The carriers roared into the "face of intense fire, including the shelling from an anti-tank gun." One carrier took a direct hit—killing its crew—but Thomas's Wasp gained the other dyke and helped eliminate the Germans there. Lieutenant Colonel Don Forbes, a "get it done but not in a reckless manner" kind of officer, decided the North Novas had done sufficient. He pulled 'A' Company back to reorganize, and arranged to borrow a second Wasp from the Glens for another attempt the next day.[20]

Also on the offensive, the HLI had gone for Biervliet with 'A' Company advancing up a dyke on the left and 'D' following a parallelling one to the right. Sandwiched between was an open polder. To the battalion's surprise, it met little resistance, and by late afternoon the village was taken. Then, belatedly realizing what had happened, the Germans saturated it with artillery. Caught in the open southwest of the town, 'D' Company was reduced to only forty men. At 2300 hours, German infantry infiltrated its perimeter. Several positions were overrun and regained in hand-to-hand fighting before the company fell back to the edge of town and dug in. With 'A' company to its left and 'C' Company to the right, the three companies were tight in a rough triangle.[21]

While the HLI had been securing Biervliet, their acting commander, Major G.A.M. Edwards—slightly wounded in the action—was called back to brigade and evacuated. The brigade major, Phil Strickland, took over the battalion's command and was promoted to lieutenant colonel. Brigadier John Rockingham considered Strickland—a long-time HLI officer before brigade assignment—intelligent, courageous, and capable.[22] "This is good news to all," the HLI war diarist agreed. "We are happy to have Major Strickland back as C.O. of the unit."[23]

Ill pleased with 9 CIB's overall progress so far, Rockingham hoped to shake things up. Major General Don Spry was also unhappy and ordered Rockingham to consolidate the brigade's hold on ground won, establish a land link around the Braakman Inlet to the beachhead, and then crack westwards to capture Breskens and Schoondijke.[24] This breakthrough was progressing too slowly. But, with 8th Canadian Infantry Brigade unloading from Buffaloes, Spry expected to have doubled his strength on the ground by the morning of October 13. Already, the North Shore (New Brunswick) Regiment was behind the HLI, establishing a protected supply line back to the beach.[25]

IN THE MORNING, the North Shores' 'A' Company had moved right to link up with the North Nova Scotia Highlanders, only to walk straight into a German counterattack. Under a grey, colourless sky, men in mud-splattered grey and khaki engaged each other at point-blank range with rifles, machine guns, and grenades. No manoeuvre, no good cover, no supporting artillery, just a deadly shootout. It lasted scant minutes before the Germans broke and fled, but thirteen North Shores were wounded and one was missing. Still, the Germans had yielded. Nobody bothered counting the number of their dead floating in the polder or sprawled on the muddy dyke.

The Germans retaliated with artillery, scoring a direct hit on the company headquarters building, which began to burn. As Major F.F. "Toot" Moar beat out the fire, a second shell exploded, and flying debris knocked him unconscious. He was evacuated, and Captain Andy Woodcock took the reins.

Because 8 CIB headquarters was not yet ashore, the North Shores were temporarily under command of Brigadier Rockingham, who urged them to get through to the North Novas. "We were told that no enemy opposition was expected," Woodcock recalled. "All we had to do was move over to a group of Dutch farm houses and relieve the troops stationed there. It sounded simple enough." But the shootout left Woodcock suspicious. Would the Germans be so reckless if their flank was exposed to Canadians in the houses?

Putting his men into tactical formation, he sent 'A' Company off along the dyke leading to the farm. Machine guns and rifles opened up from within the buildings, the sheet-ripping screech of German MG 42s unmistakable. Woodcock called for artillery, but was refused because "we were asking our guns to fire on friendly troops." Lieutenant Murray Quinn and a veteran platoon sergeant were both killed trying to direct Bren gun fire while Woodcock argued with headquarters.[26] Finally, 'B' Company of the Camerons brought up its 50-calibre Vickers and No. 15 Platoon the heavy mortars. With their support, 'A' Company cleared the buildings.[27] The North Novas were soon located in another group of farmhouses farther away. Woodcock was "very bitter over the fact that we had lost a very fine officer and men through such wrong information."[28]

All along the Canadian front, small gains were won that day. At Hoofdplaat, the Glens swept up isolated pockets of Germans, and 'D' Company pushed out to control the dyke it had been forced off the previous night.[29] The Highland Light Infantry gained a facing dyke south of Biervliet at 1520 hours that had given them "a great deal of trouble with small arms fire and reducing our movement to a minimum. We are now to sit tight and hold our ground. Our companies are spread out along the... dyke."[30]

Right of the HLI, the North Novas by late afternoon were leapfrogging companies along the dykes towards Driewegen while artillery hammered it. Their path passed regularly spaced farms that would have been prosperous before being reduced to ruins by shelling. Each had to be wrested from defending Germans. Once the lead company achieved this, the one behind jumped past to attack the next farm. 'A' Company had initially led, taken one farm, and then 'B' Company took over. Captain Jock Grieve having been wounded, Captain Doug Eastwood was in charge. The company advanced through shellfire to the next farm, where the owners had taken refuge in slit trenches roofed over with bales of hay. Most everyone had been killed or wounded by shells.

As the North Novas cleared the buildings, a German sergeant major stepped out of one and demanded in English that the company surrender. Lieutenant Fitch shot him dead. Eastwood encountered four Germans at the corner of a dyke, who promptly surrendered when he shouted without thinking, "You're under arrest." One man reported that there were some Germans farther along wanting to surrender, so Eastwood sent a prisoner to bring them in. As soon as the man started off along the dyke, a 'B' Company soldier, thinking he was trying to escape, killed him with a rifle shot. After this, the Germans on the dyke refused to answer calls to surrender, but also abstained from fighting. 'B' Company had reached its objective, but was still short of Driewegen, with night falling. The company mustered just forty-two men.[31] How confused the situation was became clear when Captain J.W. Campbell "pulled the hat trick by capturing 25 Germans [while] recceing a position for his anti-tank guns" well behind the attacking companies.[32]

Throughout the day, 8 CIB had continued landing and started "pushing south to attempt to link up with the 10th Canadian Infantry Brigade" holding the east side of the Isabellapolder, the North Nova war diarist wrote. "Once the road is opened we will be able to get more supplies and possibly armour, which will make a great improvement."[33]

OCTOBER 13 WAS a Friday, yet in the beachhead the hard battle was taking a turn that perhaps dispelled superstitions on the Canadian side. German artillery, particularly from the coastal guns, remained fierce. But the German infantry were noticeably less determined. Driewegen was taken in an attack supported by rocket-firing Typhoons that added more to the village's destruction and thoroughly demoralized the exhausted German defenders. The North Novas war diarist regretted that there were "still numerous fires burning in the area and the barns and houses are mostly total wrecks. The little town of Driewegen is totally wrecked. It seems a shame that this little country has to be shelled to such an extent."[34]

While 9 CIB focused on securing the beachhead, 8 CIB hastened towards the Isabellapolder, where 4th Canadian Armoured Division's 10th Canadian Infantry Brigade waited. The North Shores moved from Biervliet, with 'B' Company leading, followed by 'C' and 'D' Companies. Progress was good, with many Germans opting to surrender. By day's end they bagged 236 prisoners, including four officers. The cost to the Canadians was one man killed, Lieutenant T. Galatizine, and thirteen other ranks wounded, as well as one man missing.[35]

The Queen's Own Rifles, meanwhile, had relieved the HLI at Biervliet and then pushed south. To their left, closely following the Braakman Inlet's shore, was Le Régiment de la Chaudière. Its 'D' Company was forced to dive for cover when suddenly shelled. Already nervous about this grim, wet landscape, some of the men were more shaken by the event than normally would be the case. One poked his head out of a ditch and asked if the shells were German or Canadian. Unsmiling, his officer replied: "Don't worry, lad, they're ours." By then, the company commander had managed to get the friendly fire lifted and the advance resumed.[36]

Two large polders separated 8 CIB from 10 CIB. For weeks, the latter had faced the heavily fortified Isabellapolder. Behind it stood the Angelina Polder. There was every reason to expect a hard fight through fortifications guarding this badly flooded ground. Despite weeks of failures, 10 CIB was ordered to make an all-out effort the morning of October 14. Given past experience, the Algonquins risked only a tentative patrol from 'A' Company the night before that soon reported tantalizingly that the defensive works were abandoned. More patrols returned the same news from other sectors.[37]

Farther south, the Argyll and Sutherland Highlanders Lieutenant Colonel J.D. Stewart had ordered the scouts and pioneers to cross the Leopold Canal by improvising a bridge, and then to proceed north to Watervliet—the town denied them for weeks. "Jaws of the people involved dropped at this bland pronouncement," the regimental historian recorded. But the soldiers duly set off and at noon were indeed in Watervliet. They had thrown a rope bridge across the canal next to a blown-out concrete one and gone over unopposed. Slowly they progressed one thousand yards up the road, lifting mines en route and encountering only a few seemingly bewildered Germans who meekly surrendered. Stewart pushed 'A' Company across, and by the end of that lucky Friday, the entire battalion was anchored around Watervliet.[38] None of the Canadians understood why the Germans had fled such strong positions.

To try and contain 9 CIB in its beachhead, Generalmajor Knut Eberding had steadily siphoned men out of the 64th Infantry Division's frontage with 10 CIB. He had gambled that the weary Canadian battalions would fail to realize how weak his units there were. When 8 CIB pushed southeastward out of the beachhead, he had little to meet it with, so ordered the area abandoned.[39] Due to the heavy fighting, Eberding reported to Oberkommando der Wehrmacht (OKW), his division "had been reduced in some cases to one third of earlier strength."[40]

On the Isabellapolder, meanwhile, the Algonquins were awed by the dauntingly intricate fortifications they searched. Deep "concrete dugouts connected by underground tunnels...skillfully sited weapons positions," and sophisticated "intercommunication methods. The area was full of booby traps and mines...The engineers lifted 150 Teller and box mines in a stretch of dyke about 200 yards long. A frontal assault on a position of this nature was foredoomed to failure." In the late afternoon, an Algonquin patrol encountered one from 8 CIB's Queen's Own Rifles carefully picking its way southwards.[41] The battle for the beachhead was won.

Establishment of a land link meant the amphibious operation by the British 5th Assault Regiment, Royal Engineers closed that evening. This first tactical use of amphibians in the European theatre had been an all-round success. The Buffaloes and Terrapins had moved 880 loads consisting of two full infantry brigades and about 600 guns and vehicles. Protected by smokescreens from the coastal guns on Walcheren Island, it suffered only four men killed and twenty-two wounded or injured. Three Buffaloes had been destroyed: one sunk after a nighttime collision, one riddled by shrapnel after bogging in mud and being targeted by the coastal guns, and another blown apart by a direct shell hit.[42]

THE LEOPOLD CANAL, so long unassailable, no longer posed an obstacle to 3rd Canadian Infantry Division. On the afternoon of October 13, engineers from 4th Canadian Armoured Division's 8th and 9th Field Squadrons completed construction of a Bailey bridge at the Maldegem–Aardenburg crossing behind 7th Canadian Infantry Brigade's narrow bridgehead. "At last the great day has arrived," the 9th Field Squadron war diarist wrote. The bridge was 120 feet long with 10-foot ramps on either side. With the Germans offering no resistance other than light shelling, the engineers had started the bridge at 1210 hours and opened it to traffic at 1605.[43] The 8th Field Squadron suffered two men slightly wounded in the operation, while the 9th had no casualties.[44]

On the morning of October 14, the British Columbia Regiment sent four Shermans to support a Canadian Scottish Regiment raid on Eede.[45] The tanks encountered stiff opposition, but knocked out several pillboxes and dugouts. Working with the tankers, 'A' Company rounded up forty-five prisoners. Although the Germans still held Eede, Lieutenant Colonel Desmond Crofton was sufficiently encouraged to tee up a major attack.

To gain information on the German defences, Crofton ordered 'A' Company and the scout platoon to probe various parts of Eede. A three-man patrol under Corporal A.E. MacDonald crept north through the village to a crossroad running east to the Maldegem–Aardenburg highway. After gathering a good appreciation of German defences in this area, MacDonald sent the other two men back to report. He then cut across country to explore a pillbox facing 'D' Company's position that was so camouflaged it had previously gone undetected. Prowling through the bushes concealing the pillbox, MacDonald was spotted by a sentry. Instantly, a machine gun raked the ground near him and several grenades came flying in. Frantically, MacDonald crawled into the darkness. His route of escape brought him to the canal well beyond 7 CIB's bridgehead. Knowing he was unlikely to slip through the German lines undetected, MacDonald instead swam the canal and then returned to battalion headquarters with precise map coordinates for the pillbox. At dawn, a heavy artillery concentration was brought down and the position destroyed. MacDonald's solo patrol earned a Military Medal.[46]

Although the British Columbia Regiment squadron had remained in the bridgehead overnight, Crofton wanted more tanks to cross the bridge in the morning. Unluckily, a chance hit by one of the large coastal guns blasted a hole in the decking before the tanks came forward, and Crofton decided to delay the attack to October 16. It was well he did, as the fight that developed in Eede became a hard slugging match, with only the presence of tanks and three Wasp carriers enabling the Can Scots to carry the day. At the same time as Eede was taken, the Regina Rifles had unsuccessfully attempted to advance west to Middelburg. On the far right flank, however, the Royal Winnipeg Rifles patrolled about four miles northeastwards from the bridgehead to discover Saint Kruis undefended.[47]

On October 18, 7 CIB learned it was to be relieved by 157th Infantry Brigade of the 52nd British (Lowland) Division. The Canadians wearily crossed the bridge that afternoon, turning the bridgehead and its muddy polders over to a division specially trained for mountain warfare.

During the worst period of fighting between October 6 and 12, 7 CIB had suffered 553 casualties—111 fatal. The Regina Rifles, with 'B' Company of the Royal Montreal Regiment under command, had been the worst mauled, with 51 dead and 229 wounded.[48] Except for twenty-four-year-old Private Harold Rodrigue Patrick Watts, who had been on patrol with a section of the Reginas' 'D' Company, the

RMR had withdrawn on October 10. Watts was to be sent out when the patrol returned, but the private never showed. On October 11, Lieutenant C.W. Smith returned to the canal and learned that Watts had been killed. The Reginas told Smith that Watts "had located an enemy sniper. He took aim and fired but the rifle jammed and the sniper returned the fire killing [Private] Watts instantly."[49] Including Watts, the Montreal regiment's casualty roll tallied six dead, 35 wounded, and 21 missing.[50] Its combat christening on the Leopold Canal had proved painful. For all three 7 CIB battalions, the canal had devastated their ranks. Not a man was sorry to turn his back on the place.

To the northeast, the Argyll and Sutherland Highlanders and the Algonquins felt the same on October 15, when they withdrew from their grim vigil. The Argylls had been elated just before pulling out to encounter a North Shore carrier patrol ahead of their position, and then a unit from the 7th Reconnaissance Regiment had arrived. Having picked up their armoured cars after engineers pushed a road through the Isabella and Angelina polders earlier that day, the Recon unit spent the rest of October 15 and the next day clearing German stragglers from the flooded ground between the beachhead and Watervliet.[51] October 17, it pushed west along the northern flank of the Leopold Canal, headed for a linkup with 7 CIB's bridgehead. To the immediate north, 8 CIB parallelled its advance, with Le Régiment de la Chaudière on the south flank, Queen's Own Rifles in the centre, and North Shores the north. Sticking close to the West Scheldt coastline, 9 CIB parallelled this advance. Because of the width of the front, the battleground remained quite porous.

On October 17, confusion about safe lines resulted in Lieutenant Colonel Thomas Cripps Lewis—8 CIB's acting commander—driving into a German ambush while en route to meet the Chaudière commander. Lewis and his driver were travelling alone, the officer seeking a vantage from which he could locate the French-Canadian regiment. About two hundred yards from a farm, the jeep suddenly drew fire from Germans hidden in its buildings. Both men dived into a ditch, but were pinned by machine-gun fire. Moments later, an artillery concentration landed square on their position and Lewis was killed instantly by shrapnel. Once the shelling lifted, Germans took the driver prisoner, locking him in one of the farm buildings. Lewis's body was stripped of personal effects and left where it had fallen.

After nightfall, the Germans withdrew, leaving the driver behind. He was picked up the morning of October 19 and Lewis's body was then recovered. The farm was subsequently discovered to have been subjected to a Canadian defensive fire mission close to the time the driver believed they were shelled, leading to the conclusion that Lewis had been killed by friendly fire. Lieutenant Colonel P.C. Klaehn, commander of the Cameron Highlanders of Ottawa, had taken over the brigade when Lewis went missing. He would retain this position until a permanent brigadier could be appointed.[52]

October 17 brought the Queen's Own Rifles to the town of Ijzendijke. To deny the Canadians access to a good road running northwest to Schoondijke, the Germans resisted fiercely. Rifleman Jack Martin was having the usual problem firing a mortar in the polders. Fire a round; dig the base plate out of muck. His section sergeant, Carl Warnick, was directing the fire towards a little wood where some Germans were milling about. The sergeant had initially told Martin to toss a bomb into the woods to see what response it elicited. The bizarre result saw the Germans all shuffle leftwards as if they were in some chorus line. "Go and throw another bomb down," Warnick called. Another leftwards shuffle ensued, taking the Germans just beyond the last zone of fire. Then Martin saw a German running along the dyke to the right, swivelled the tube to range in on him, and fired. As soon as the bomb left the mortar, Martin ran to the top of the dyke behind which the platoon was emplaced. He came up on the dyke just as the round struck the German square in the chest. The enemy soldier disappeared in a red mist of gore mixed with grey smoke. Mortars seldom hit men directly and Martin had never seen a man killed by his fire.[53]

'A' and 'B' Companies bulled their way into Ijzendijke despite tough opposition. Closing on the town square, Major Dick Medland's 'A' Company came under heavy machine-gun fire from a sandbagged house on the opposite side, and No. 7 Platoon was pinned down. The two companies had been moving quickly along the streets to this point, but now Medland knew he would have to slow down and organize a company-scale attack. Actions over the past few days had tended to be short, sharp affairs fought at the platoon or even section level: a lot of crawling, dashing, and rolling across distances of three to five hundred yards to wipe out German positions set up inside haystacks, houses, barns, pigpens, chicken coops, or greenhouses with the overhead glass generally blown out, but the three-foot-high brick walls providing a perfect firing step for machine guns. Men died or were wounded in these piecemeal engagements that warranted not even a mention in the regiment's war diary. Consequently, 'A' Company reached Ijzendijke's main square with only half its allotted strength, each platoon section numbering six to seven men.

Medland ordered No. 7 Platoon, hunkered inside a house on the east side of the square, to bring the fortified building under fire. No. 8 Platoon would move left to gain a position from which it could cover No. 9 Platoon's swing around to the right to get behind the German position. Like the others, No. 9 Platoon was in rough shape. It had lost two officers in a row, was short a couple of sergeants, and low on riflemen. Before being promoted company sergeant major prior to D-Day, Charles Martin had been No. 9 Platoon's sergeant—a role he had reverted to because of the leadership shortage. Martin arranged for the battalion's mortar platoon to fire behind the building for fifteen minutes to force any Germans under cover while he slipped one section in for an attack.

Martin and six men loaded up with firepower. Each carried four grenades. One had the company's two-inch mortar and smoke rounds in case they had to throw out a screen for the rush on the house. Riflemen Jack Morgan and Drew Kehoe packed Bren guns. Martin and Rifleman Bob Dunstan had Stens. The section moved as quietly as possible around the buildings facing the square, taking advantage of every concealing feature while the mortar rounds exploded behind the house. Finally, they were looking at its back, seeing no sign of Germans. Taking out a fortified house was always dangerous work. Martin and Dunstan decided they would go in first through the single window facing the back. Morgan and Kehoe would then kick in the back door.

Smoke was dropped and the four men charged. Dunstan chucked a grenade through the window and the moment it exploded, Martin dove through. He rolled left and came up spraying the Sten in an arc across that section of the room, while Dustan rolled right and worked that side over. The door flew open. Morgan and Kehoe burst in with Bren guns blazing from the hip. Everyone fired until their magazines were dry and then reloaded. The room was full of smoke, drifting bits of plaster, and dust. Several men were shouting, "Kamerad." When the smoke cleared and the debris settled, Martin saw only three Germans. Except for a few minor flesh wounds, they had amazingly been unhurt by the grenade explosion and the shooting spree. Sometimes it went that way. Kehoe rustled up a white sheet, and carefully unfurled it out a window facing the square to let the rest of the company know the house was taken. Then Martin fired a green flare as a signal to Medland. Only after the adrenaline stopped pumping did he notice that a sliver of shrapnel had pierced his left shoulder. He had the company stretcher-bearer put a bandage over the wound. Nobody bothered going back to the Regimental Aid Post for minor wounds anymore. Almost everyone had a bandage covering some injury.[54]

Ijzendijke was taken. From cellars, civilians emerged "who all wanted to shake our hands, feed us and to see the 'Kanadeesh' or some such name," wrote the battalion's war diarist. "However Jerry whistled a few shells in and we had a magical disappearing act." The shells caused several large fires. When 'C' Company's No. 15 Platoon led the battalion out of the town, it came under intense mortar fire from a position on the outskirts. With night falling, it was decided to hold tight inside the battered town until dawn.

Next morning, 'C' Company raided the mortar position and found "six very forlorn Germans who were only too willing to surrender. We used them to peel potatoes back at rear [battalion headquarters]. The Jerry's are very good at that job. They peel very fine, not like our boys, who just cut the peel off."[55]

[17]

A Godsend

THIRD CANADIAN INFANTRY DIVISION broke the German lockhold on the Leopold Canal before Field Marshal Bernard Law Montgomery issued an October 16 directive that finally gave opening Antwerp "complete priority over all other offensive operations in 21 Army Group without any qualification whatsoever." The "whole of the available offensive power of Second Army" was to support First Canadian Army. Previously, 1 British Corps had been moving northeast away from the Scheldt to assist British Second Army. Now that army was to shift northwestwards and guard First Canadian Army's right flank. This would allow Lieutenant General John Crocker to clear the ground to the north and east of 2nd Canadian Infantry Division, which was still attempting to sever the South Beveland isthmus north of Antwerp.

To provide Crocker with sufficient strength, 4th Canadian Armoured Division had already begun moving from its guard position along the Leopold Canal to a concentration area northeast of Antwerp. The division came under Crocker's control on October 17. Crocker announced his intention to prevent German interference with 2 CID's efforts to capture South Beveland. He planned to commit 4 CAD on October 20 to an advance towards Essen and then Bergen op Zoom. Right of 4 CAD, the 49th (West Riding) Infantry

Division would move north from Brecht to seize Roosendaal. Clearly signalling the importance that General Eisenhower put on freeing Antwerp, the 104th U.S. Infantry Division was also under Crocker's command, and would clear the country east of the 49th Division's right flank, while farther east still, 1st Polish Armoured Division's job would be to drive through to Breda and then gain control of the mouth of the Maas River.[1] If successful, this operation—codenamed "Suitcase"—would bring all southwestern Holland into Allied hands.

While the redirection of 1 British Corps to closely support 11 Canadian Corps sounded significant, the 49th Division had seen hard fighting and was understrength. And by mid-October, 1st Polish Armoured Division was recognized as close to becoming "ineffective." On October 12, Lieutenant General Guy Simonds had sent Crocker a note stating that the division remained under his command only for use "to hold a quiet sector... but I do not think you should count on them being used offensively until they have had a chance to reorganize and properly train and absorb reinforcements."[2]

An appended report by Brigadier E.O. Herbert of Simonds's general staff stated that the division was short 90 officers and 750 other ranks, having taken about 600 casualties in the first six days of October while driving northeastwards from the Antwerp–Turnhout Canal from Merksplas to Alphen. Reinforcements would not be available until the second part of November, and consisted of about 250 Poles who had been found serving with British Royal Armoured Corps and 600 Polish conscripts taken prisoner while serving in German units. The latter had become the primary source for Polish divisions, whether serving in northwest Europe or Italy. But Herbert recognized that such prisoners "are NOT fighting well. They are NOT well trained, often bomb-shy, and very frightened of being captured. As a result much more leadership is necessary; this in turn results in more [officer casualties,] and the best [officers] at that." Herbert recommended the division be withdrawn for rebuilding, coinciding with 4 CAD's coming under 1 British Corps command.[3]

Crocker was not of a mind to wait until mid-November to commit the division again to operations. It must reorganize and integrate troops as well as possible, while remaining in readiness to carry out securing the mouth of the Maas River whenever the divisions operating west of it made this possible.

Operation Suitcase came into being as 2 CID was almost as much at the breaking point as the Poles. The past week had yielded both tragic failures and near pyrrhic successes. Fifth Canadian Infantry Brigade had gained control of Hoogerheide immediately east of Woensdrecht, but had been so badly cut up that it desperately needed relief. Meanwhile, 4th Canadian Infantry Brigade's Royal Regiment of Canada had by October 11 established itself out in the polders west of this village. The narrow isthmus linking South Beveland to the mainland had been successfully blocked by Germans manning positions astride a raised railway embankment.

As Montgomery had not yet agreed to redirect Twenty-First Army Group away from British Second Army's front near Nijmegen, the division's right flank was critically overextended, considering its depleted manpower. Recognizing this, Simonds had sent what reinforcements he could to guard the division's right and free its fighting battalions for the offensive needed to capture Woensdrecht and cut off the isthmus. The South Alberta Regiment—4 CAD's armoured reconnaissance unit—and one rifle company from the Algonquin Regiment took over the front near Brecht to the north of the Antwerp–Turnhout Canal. This freed the Fort Garry Horse Regiment's tanks to support the Woensdrecht attack. The 3rd Light Anti-Aircraft Regiment was also temporarily given rifles and put into the line as infantry with the 2nd Canadian Anti-Tank Regiment, in a long line that stretched all the way from near Hoogerheide to Brecht. It was a desperate gamble, 2 CID's Brigadier Holly Keefler literally crossing his fingers that the Germans would not discover the fragility of his defences there. To give the illusion of strength, tanks and other armoured vehicles regularly cruised the front's length.

Earlier, on October 9, Keefler had attached the South Saskatchewan Regiment from 6th Canadian Infantry Brigade to 4 CIB. The battalion made a night move from Brecht, and deployed near the highway leading from Putte to Woensdrecht, with orders to advance up the Abdijlaan, a dirt road running on a northeasterly axis to join the Huijbergseweg at the midway point between Hoogerheide and

Huijbergen. Here, a thickly wooded area identified on maps as Het Eiland (The Island), lay north of the road. As a German advance from these woods or Huijbergen via the Abdijlaan would threaten the division's rear, Keefler wanted the South Saskatchewans to establish a blocking position.[4]

Meanwhile, on October 11, Keefler relieved 5 CIB in Woensdrecht with 4 CIB's Royal Hamilton Light Infantry and the Essex Scottish. Although the Black Watch was pulled out of Hoogerheide that afternoon, it was not being offered a rest. Instead, this 5 CIB regiment was to tee up an attack from out of the Royal Regiment's positions in the polders to seize the railway embankment near Woensdrecht Station.[5]

Major General Charles Foulkes, temporary commander of II Canadian Corps, delivered the order for the Black Watch attack personally to Keefler and 5 CIB's Brigadier Bill Megill that night. His intention was "to plug the neck" of the isthmus. Once the Black Watch gained the railway embankment, the rest of the brigade would pass through to seal the approaches to the isthmus from Korteven to the east and Bergen op Zoom to the north. Megill protested the order. He believed the Germans too strong and well dug in to be defeated by a head-on assault. As for his men, they needed rest, not another battle. Like all of 2 CID, the brigade had lost many veterans, and over the past two weeks, reinforcements had been fed in haphazardly without much thought to proper integration.

Foulkes remained adamant. Montgomery was still focused on Nijmegen, so the corps commander believed that 2 CID must fend for itself. Although the 52nd (Lowland) Infantry Division and the 104th U.S. Divisions had been promised, the former was slated to assist 3 CID and the latter would not be available for about ten days. First Canadian Army was to get Antwerp open, and to do that the isthmus had to be cut now. He promised Megill all the artillery and mortar ammunition needed. Foulkes wanted the attack that coming morning, but the brigadier convinced him to delay it to October 13. That was the only compromise. There was no question that the Black Watch would have to carry the day. Le Régiment de Maisonneuve was short two hundred men and the Calgary Highlanders had faced the worst of the fighting in Hoogerheide.⁶ Keefler, Megill, and their staffs got to work developing an artillery support plan.

Lieutenant Colonel Bruce Ritchie was dismayed. The Black Watch had hardly enjoyed a field day in Hoogerheide. It had taken two hundred casualties between October 6 and 8. This, after Ritchie had only completed rebuilding the battalion after taking command in the third week of September, and then had led it through stiff fighting on the Antwerp–Turnhout Canal. Morale was poor. When Ritchie sought intelligence from brigade on the German defences, the intelligence staff had nothing to offer. He was reassured that they were nothing special. Ritchie believed none of it.⁷

EVIDENCE OF BOTH the growing number and fighting quality of German units facing 2 CID was demonstrated when the South Saskatchewan Regiment advanced at 1500 hours on October 11 up the Abdijlaan. The initial objective was a position along the track that 4 CIB's Brigadier Fred Cabeldu instructed Lieutenant Colonel Vern Stott must be "held at all costs." 'A' Company led the way, and the South Saskatchewans were soon on the objective without meeting any opposition. Emboldened, Stott decided to push to the intersection with the Huijbergseweg. 'B' Company led, with the other rifle companies behind.

Night was falling as No. 11 Platoon under Lieutenant W.L. Brown closed on the crossroads. Brown, who had been badly wounded at Verrières Ridge in Normandy, had just returned to duty that morning. As the platoon reached the Huijbergseweg, heavy machine-gun fire hit it from both flanks. Brown and his men "immediately went to ground and became the fire platoon, opposing fire with fire." Despite the fight being lopsided in favour of the Germans, who had overwhelming fire superiority and had allowed the platoon to walk into the middle of a carefully prepared killing zone before tipping their hand, only a few of Brown's men were hit.

Captain Fraser Lee, a Chinese Canadian from Saskatoon, responded quickly by ordering No. 10 Platoon to move leftwards to occupy three houses directly across the road from Het Eiland. From here, it was able to cover No. 11 Platoon as it cleared several houses closer to the crossroads. But when Brown tried to push a section across the road itself, the men were driven back by withering machine-gun fire. Clearly, the Germans were willing to cede the south side of the road, but determined to lose no ground within the forest opposite. Lee set up an all-round defensive perimeter centred on the string of houses, with No. 10 and No. 11 Platoon facing the road and No. 12 Platoon covering the company's rear. The carrier platoon, serving as a reserve, was sheltered near the house he took over for a tactical headquarters. Even though separated only by the narrow road, neither side fired at the other, not wanting the tracers and gun flashes to betray their positions.

Shortly after midnight, Lee had No. 12 Platoon slip a fighting patrol across the road with instructions to find and destroy the machine guns that had fired on No. 11 Platoon. The patrol failed, neither drawing fire nor tripping over the German gunners in the inky blackness. Lee figured the "Germans were holding their fire" to avoid detection and had just let the patrol walk by.[8] The patrol was tracked back to 'B' Company's perimeter, and minutes later, heavy mortar and artillery fire started coming in.[9]

The company's radiomen, Riflemen Chic Goodman and Ted Exchange, had been close to the headquarters when the shelling started and took cover in a ditch. The other man had been carrying the radio, Goodman trying to puzzle out by the faint starlight the words in a letter he had just received. He was an eighteen-year-old kid looking for news from home and still trying to read the letter when something struck him hard in the back of the neck with numbing force. A hand to the neck came away with something thick and wet. Goodman said softly, "I've really had it. I'm badly hit on the back of the neck." His friend took a look and then chuckled. A clod of mud, oozing dirty black water, had struck him. When the shelling momentarily eased, the two men dodged into the company headquarters.[10]

First light found Lieutenant Brown and No. 11 Platoon crawling along a ditch next to the road, headed for a point where a muddy track crossed it. Their intent was to clear another three buildings there. A machine gun opened up ahead, but the leading section quickly knocked it out. Across the road, a German soldier popped to his feet and cried, "Kamerad!" This being what Germans surrendering often hollered, two of Brown's men stood up and waved for him to come in. The German ducked down and suddenly a 20-millimetre anti-aircraft gun opened fire. As the platoon tried to crawl clear, the gun's fire "grazed the top of the ditch, exploding on both sides, causing nine casualties." The platoon escaped, dragging their dead and wounded, and the battalion's mortar platoon pounded the forest where the gun had been sited.

The presence of the anti-aircraft gun confirmed that the woods were held in a strength the South Saskatchewans were unable to match. Stott ordered 'B' Company to hold firm for the day, while the battalion sent patrols out on its flanks to contact the 108th Anti-Tank Battery operating to the right and Le Régiment de Maisonneuve, which had come up on the left. The Germans seemed content with this arrangement, confining themselves to sniping at anybody moving in 'B' Company's perimeter and periodically mortaring it.[11]

The identity of the Germans in the woods remained a mystery. In fact, they were paratroopers who had deployed in Het Eiland early October 11, and spent the entire day and night digging fortifications and establishing lines of fire. Supporting them were the remnants of the 252nd Composite Flak Section and the 14th Machine Gun Battalion. Concentration of this force in the woods was part of a general regrouping that day by Kampfgruppe Chill. Oberstleutnant Friederich von der Heydte also moved paratroop formations into previously prepared defensive positions at Zandfort, immediately north of Hoogerheide, and along the rail embankment running out onto the South Beveland isthmus.[12] By end of the day on October 11, Kampfgruppe Chill had been ready to hit 2nd Canadian Infantry Division hard wherever it might try an advance—precisely what the South Saskatchewans had discovered.

As the day wore on in 'B' Company's perimeter, however, there was no sign that the Germans contemplated offensive action. The battalion signallers ran a telephone line out to the company, which tended to happen only when things were quieting down. Consequently, with nightfall and no resumption of the heavy shelling and mortaring of the previous night, a sense of calm settled in and thoughts turned to getting some badly needed sleep. Adding to the sense of security was the arrival of the company carrier from battalion headquarters with a hot meal for everyone. At the house serving as company headquarters, the Company Sergeant Major was feeling so sanguine after this unexpectedly pleasant meal that at about 1930 hours, he announced there would be no need to stand watch for another thirty minutes. A few minutes later, Lee kicked off his sodden boots, put his feet into a pair of Dutch wooden shoes, tucked a pistol in his back pocket, and walked contentedly towards an outhouse in the back yard.

Goodman was just checking the time at 1950 hours when a stick grenade came through the window into the room he, the other signaller, and a company runner occupied. Nobody was hurt when it exploded. But a grenade simultaneously thrown into the room opposite that contained the CSM, two stretcher-bearers, and the other runner blinded one of the stretcher-bearers. Panicked, the man started screaming. The CSM, who carried a U.S. Army .45-calibre Colt pistol, drew his gun and opened the outside door, only to stand face to face with a German paratrooper gripping a submachine gun. The sergeant quickly closed the door before either man could fire. Somebody had doused the Coleman lanterns, plunging the place into darkness. A stretcher leaning against the wall next to the door fell at such an angle that it was wedged shut. That was good, because the Germans were now trying to kick it in.

Outside, the carrier driver and company quartermaster had been spotted and fired on. They rolled under the carrier and stayed put. Lee could do nothing but hide in the outhouse.[13] The platoons were all engaged in separate fights with paratroopers. Everyone had been taken by surprise, the first warning of a counterattack being "a series of grenades... thrown through the windows of the houses they were occupying."[14]

After discovering that the land line had been cut, Rifleman Ted Exchange was trying to raise battalion headquarters on the wireless. Goodman scooped up a Sten gun just in time to open fire on a paratrooper trying to come through the window on the heels of a grenade. His ears were ringing from the concussion of exploding grenades and crack of the Sten firing in the confined space. The German fell back outside, but the rifleman didn't know if he had been hit.

Goodman started putting measured bursts out the windows to keep the Germans from getting close enough to throw more grenades in. He was only partially successful, somewhere between six and ten more grenades coming through the windows and exploding. Amazingly, nobody was hurt. Goodman, the only man with a useful gun, lost his night vision with each explosion and was forced to fire blind. Occasionally, he caught glimpses of furtively moving shadows and tried to hit them. A German kept shouting for the Canadians to come out and surrender. The wounded stretcher-bearer was still screaming. Ted Exchange shouted into the wireless that he had no idea what was happening with the platoons, while battalion couldn't decide whether to send reinforcements into the confused situation or not.

To Goodman, the fight was interminable, hours dragging by. Soon just one 9-millimetre magazine remained. The CSM was considering taking the German up on the surrender demand. Goodman flailed around in the darkness, searching for more ammunition. He found a Jerry can riddled by shrapnel that was gushing water, which explained the soaking wet floor. Then he found a web belt with pouches bulging with 9-millimetre rounds. "A God send," he thought, and started loading magazines. The CSM pronounced they would stand firm. As soon as Goodman resumed shooting, the German ceased demanding their surrender. A few minutes later, the sounds of gunfire faded away and the night grew still.

Everyone in the house waited; even the wounded man stopped screaming. "Sergeant-Major, are you there?" Lee called from softly from outside. The CSM whispered, "Don't answer. He's been captured. It's a trick to make us surrender." Lee began calling out the names of each man inside the house. Then he asked, "Anybody alive in there?"

"Don't answer," the CSM cautioned.

Goodman muttered, "Maybe he's not captured. One way we can let them know it's us. I'll fire a burst of Sten gun fire and they'll know it's a Canadian weapon." He did so and for a long moment there was only silence.

Outside, someone whispered, "They've been captured or they're dead."

Then Lee said sternly, "If you don't answer, we're going to blow down this door with a PIAT."

Goodman and the others shouted that they were indeed there, alive, and not prisoners. Surprisingly, there had been few casualties. In the morning, Goodman saw that he had shot the outhouse full of holes, fortunately missing Lee huddled on the floor. There were no German dead, but plenty of blood trails indicated that he had done some damage. Also a casualty was Lee's newly acquired raincoat purloined from British stores. "It was a jazzy raincoat with epaulettes and so on. Very military looking," Goodman noticed. "He'd worn it that day because it had been raining and he had hung it outside on a clothesline. And some of the Germans I had seen moving back and forth that night were in fact his raincoat and he had a nicely perforated raincoat with a few dozen Sten holes in it."

Lee decided to move the company headquarters in with one of the platoons for added security. Exchange carried the radio, Goodman providing cover with the Sten. As they closed on the platoon, one of its corporals stood up in a slit trench and was hit by a burst of gunfire from outside the perimeter. Everyone dived for cover. Seeing that nobody else was going to the wounded man's aid, Goodman covered the intervening ground in three long leaps and a bound that put him in the slit trench. The man was in a bad way. A string of slugs had opened his torso to expose most of his stomach and some lung. Knowing he had to do something, Goodman pushed the organs back inside gently without knowing how to arrange anything correctly. Extracting a shell dressing, Goodman wrapped the man up carefully. Then the carrier driver rolled the vehicle in between the slit trench and the German line of fire. Goodman dragged the soldier to the carrier and lifted him into the back. He figured the man would die for sure. (In fact, Goodman encountered him after the war doing perfectly fine.)[15]

AFTER SOME INDECISION about whether to reinforce 'B' Company during the night, Lieutenant Colonel Stott ordered two platoons of 'C' Company forward. Before the men could move out, however, heavy machine-gun, mortar, and 20-millimetre anti-aircraft fire streamed in from about six hundred yards to the west and pinned the entire company down. This fire lifted at about the same time as the counterattack on 'B' Company broke off.[16]

October 13 dawned on a confused situation. German units had used the cover of darkness to move out of Het Eiland and cross the Huijbergseweg, but their strength and positions were unknown. Artillery and mortar fire was striking all the South Saskatchewan companies with unnerving accuracy. To the southeast, the commander of 108th Anti-Tank Battery, Major D. McCarthy, set off in a jeep with Lieutenant K.L. Murray to get a sense of things. They were pushing up a narrow track next to where Groote Meer—a muddy bog that reputed until recently to have been a lake—met the Dutch border. A group of soldiers wearing camouflage fatigues and "British steel helmets complete with nets and shell dressings" suddenly appeared ahead. Too late, the two officers realized it was a German trick and were taken prisoner. Murray managed to escape shortly after and reported what had happened, while McCarthy was taken to Essen for interrogation. When he was searched, the Germans found a map indicating the precise location of the South Saskatchewan battalion headquarters. This intelligence in hand, Kampfgruppe Chill staff began preparing an attack.[17]

During the afternoon, Stott received permission from 4 CIB to withdraw the badly exposed 'B' Company. It moved back about two miles to a position east of the Abdijlaan that was known as Staartse Heide—an area of woods and sand dunes—a short distance north of Groote Meer. Captain Lee's men were still on the move at 1700 hours when 'A' Company's Major Ken Williams sent an s.o.s. to battalion that his position on the western edge of Staartse Heide was being counterattacked.

Shortly thereafter, a German self-propelled gun and paratroops from the Hermann Göring Ersatz Regiment cut around 'A' Company's right flank in a carefully executed manoeuvre that brought it to within a half-mile of the South Saskatchewan battalion's tactical headquarters, which was in a house on the eastern side of the highway running from Putte to Woensdrecht. The SPG began pounding the building with its 75-millimetre gun and quickly scored five direct hits. Stott and his staff bailed out, while Lieutenant Cecil Law's mortar platoon blinded the SPG with smoke rounds. Stott moved to a new farmhouse where the highway intersected with the Abdijlaan.[18]

The mortar fire had a surprising effect—convincing the German force it was being counterattacked. Consequently, the SPG and paratroops retreated. 'A' Company, however, remained cut off, while the battalion was holding such a wide front that assaulting to relieve Williams's beleaguered group was impossible. Stott was forced to tell Williams this to his face when the major slipped through to his new tactical headquarters. Making such a relief effort even more difficult, Stott had been informed by divisional artillery staff that the supporting guns were limited to only fifteen rounds each for the day in order to free ammunition for the Black Watch attack—which had priority. Williams headed back to 'A' Company but was captured en route.

When 4 CIB was advised of the situation facing 'A' Company, Brigadier Fred Cabeldu sent two companies of Le Régiment de Maisonneuve, temporarily placed under his command, to the rescue. But by the time they moved into the area, night had fallen, so the French Canadians set up south of 'A' Company to await the morning and locate the South Saskatchewan positions. With Williams missing, Company Sergeant Major Don S. Allan took command of 'A' Company. He ordered the men to hunker down and stay quiet to avoid detection by the Germans prowling in the darkness. Stott, meanwhile, teed up an attack for the morning of October 14 by a company of Essex Scottish and the South Saskatchewans' 'C' Company, with support from a squadron of Fort Garry Horse tanks.

At 1100 hours, this attack kicked off behind a heavy artillery barrage and was so ferociously carried out—with the tanks growling close behind the infantry and firing their main guns—that the Germans surrounding 'A' Company were caught by surprise. Two officers and 104 paratroops were taken prisoner. An officer from 185th Artillery Regiment was also captured, and the maps he carried showed all of Kampfgruppe Chill's positions in and around Huijbergen. Soon after 'A' Company's relief was affected, Major Ken Williams reappeared. He had taken the onset of the artillery barrage as an opportunity to escape. The Essex Scottish company dug in alongside 'A' Company for most of the day until ordered to return to its battalion area in exchange for two companies of the Royal Regiment of Canada.

Neither of these companies, however, had arrived when Kampfgruppe Chill counterattacked 'A' Company's position at 1700 hours.[19] About a hundred troops of the 1053rd Grenadier Regiment supported by four SPGs crashed in, catching Williams and his men completely by surprise. Stott immediately halted the Royals' move towards 'A' Company, and had it establish a firm fire base with several tanks in support. He then ordered 'A' Company to withdraw to this position. Williams brought his men back in an orderly fashion, bringing the wounded with them. They had been roughly treated, with fifteen men wounded and eight missing.

This was the third and final counterattack against the South Saskatchewans. A patrol sent at 0200 hours on October 15 found 'A' Company's original position in German hands and accurately pinpointed the enemy positions. A major artillery concentration was brought against it by all three of the division's field regiments and two medium artillery regiments of 1 Corps. After that battering, Kampfgruppe Chill showed no further interest in testing the division's left flank.[20]

[18]

Black Friday

THE SOUTH SASKATCHEWAN REGIMENT had run up against Kampfgruppe Chill prior to the Black Watch's planned attack west of Woensdrecht, to cut off the isthmus to South Beveland. Yet nobody at divisional, corps, or army command concluded from the resistance met that the Germans facing 2nd Canadian Infantry Division were well organized, heavily entrenched, and offensively minded. The timer kept winding down to the morning of October 13 and zero hour. As Major General Charles Foulkes had only ordered the attack late on October 11, there was little time for planning. Both Lieutenant Colonel Bruce Ritchie and Brigadier Bill Megill knew they were to send the Black Watch into a hell like those the battalion had experienced in the Great War, where men marched out behind bagpipes with officers swinging walking sticks only to be slaughtered by machine guns. But there the orders lay.

An extensive fire program was organized that entailed two of the division's field regiments and one corps medium regiment, the Toronto Scottish Regiment's 4.2-inch mortars and Vickers heavy machine-gun units, and a troop of Fort Garry Horse tanks. There was no question of the Shermans advancing with the infantry, because the fields were so open that a single antitank gun could pick them off at its leisure. Instead, they would provide main-gun fire from nearby positions of cover. The 3.7-inch guns of a Royal Marine heavy anti-aircraft regiment were also on call, although this unit was short on ammunition. Weather permitting, No. 84 Group, RAF promised the cover of Typhoons and Spitfires. Targets from the railway embankment back to Korteven were to be plastered with fire. In the afternoon of October 12, Ritchie went aloft in an artillery spotter plane to further study the ground.[1] Then Megill convened an O Group at 1500 hours in the 5th Canadian Infantry Brigade's tent headquarters near Hoogerheide to "discuss the latest plan."[2]

As the Royal Hamilton Light Infantry was supposed to secure the Black Watch start line, Lieutenant Colonel Denis Whitaker attended. "Why make the attack in broad daylight over open and saturated polders against a strongly defended enemy position?" he wondered. Even Ritchie considered it "a funny sort of battle plan—crazy." It was codenamed Angus and there were three objectives "coinciding with intersections along the dyke and railway embankment running northeast." The first was Angus 1, where five roads converged from various points of the compass next to the Caters Polder. Angus 2 was the railway embankment directly north of Angus 1. From here, the Black Watch would swing northeast along the railway to Angus 3—Woensdrecht Station. Total advance was a little more than two miles. Visually, Ritchie considered it to be like taking "four posts, four areas roughly in the form of a square with a 1000-yard side." 'C' Company would advance to Angus 1, where 'B' Company would pass through and take Angus 2, with 'A' Company then leading the way to Angus 3. Zero hour was set for 0615 hours.[3]

Whitaker left the O Group deeply troubled. As a professional quarterback, he knew the value of simple game plans. Absentmindedly walking back to his unit through the rubble of Hoogerheide, Whitaker imagined a playing field with too many players packed into one small area and saw people getting tangled up with each other and a complicated plan falling into confusion. Whitaker expressed his concerns to 4th CIB's Brigadier Fred Cabeldu. He told his brigade commander the attack was doomed, there would be many casualties, and he would not order his men "into this debacle." Cabeldu agreed with Whitaker and ordered the Rileys removed from the plan. But Cabeldu had no authority over the Black Watch, so he could not prevent its being sent forward.[4]

The Black Watch was billeted in a string of farmhouses south of Hoogerheide, and it was here that Ritchie briefed his officers at 1930 hours. Each company commander then set out the plan to his men. Captain Nick Buch told 'C' Company it would advance with fixed bayonets and grenades strapped to web belts. The grenades were to throw across the dykes when Germans were encountered on the opposite side. Corporal John Dubetz listened attentively. He had just returned to the battalion on October 10 after five weeks convalescing from a wound suffered in August. Dubetz was disheartened to find that all but five of the men he had known in his platoon had been either killed or wounded. In Canada, Dubetz had been an advanced infantry instructor and he immediately concluded that most of the replacements had little training. Yet the men seemed ready, even eager to fight. Everyone turned in early.

In the morning, as they were forming up at 0500 hours, Buch came over and told Dubetz to take a Bren gun from one replacement. He took the gun and got in line right behind his section leader. On his way out of the billet, Dubetz had lifted a knitted scarf and pair of gloves from a rack by the door. Now he felt guilty, and feared the theft would bring bad luck. Wrap the scarf around his neck, he reasoned, and likely get his head blown off. Dubetz ran back and replaced the scarf, but kept the gloves. He could live with the risk of losing his hands, but not his head.

The company marched single file through darkness for a couple of hours, to the edge of a low ridge overlooking the polders from the east. Descending towards the fields, Dubetz passed a group of officers. It was too dark to see their insignias, but the corporal read the worry on their faces. Not a good sign. As they moved out onto the polders, Dubetz had the impression that they were going into the attack without artillery support. Nobody had told the men, either, where they should expect to meet German resistance. The company seemed to be just walking blindly forward.[5]

In fact, 'C' Company had been thirty minutes late reaching the start line, but nobody had thought to delay the artillery program.

Lieutenant Colonel E.H. Dobell, 2 CID's artillery commander, wrote later that the late arrival put "the fire plan...way ahead of infantry all during the attack."[6]

The polder that 'C' Company entered consisted of wide beet fields that had not been harvested. Dubetz judged that the tops of the beets were about two feet high, and each platoon moved single file between two big leafy rows. They were about a half-mile out when a bright flare arced from the northern dyke and hell broke loose. Along the length of the dyke, machine guns opened fire.[7] Buch fell severely wounded. Mortar bombs poured down, some exploding overhead to spray men with shrapnel.[8] The Germans fired tracer rounds, and Dubetz "could see the bullets coming at us like a shower of rain; we were being massacred. Immediately I hit the ground between two rows of beets. The beets gave me some protection from sight but this was no protection from bullets... most of the new recruits panicked. They ran in all directions firing their rifles... I could see them being toppled like rabbits, by the German fire. I heard one of them hollering, 'Corporal, help.'"

Dubetz ignored the call. He was looking for targets. About five hundred yards off, he saw three German officers standing beside a trench, calmly pointing towards the company and directing their men's fire. "These officers were heavily dressed in long winter coats and they wore high brown boots. I studied the situation and was about to turn my Bren gun on them, when suddenly, I felt a hot, sharp pain through my arm. A rifle bullet pierced my arm and knocked the Bren gun out of my hands. At the time my head was resting on my arm. I thought about the scarf that I had left behind in the house that morning. With my arm shattered I could not do anything; my fighting was over."[9]

'C' Company was being torn apart and 'B' Company—moving forward to take over the lead—was also taking heavy mortar fire. Major Douglas Chapman fell mortally wounded. Ritchie, meanwhile, had got the Toronto Scottish mortar platoon pumping out bombs to support the attack. The platoon fired 264 rounds against the well-entrenched German positions without measurable effect. Both companies were hopelessly pinned down.[10]

Dubetz pulled himself into the cover of some beets, but bullets kept striking all around him, dicing the beets into pieces. Lying in a large pool of blood, Dubetz knew he would bleed to death unless a tourniquet was applied quickly. Both the man ahead of him and the one behind seemed dead. Neither one moved, nor responded to his calls. Desperate, he squeezed his upper arm above the wound as hard as possible, and that seemed to slow the bleeding. Dubetz figured he was going to die.

Then he heard shells exploding practically on top of him and was sure this was the end, but smoke began to drift over the area. He thought friendly artillery was laying a smokescreen to cover a withdrawal. Dubetz lay watching the smoke for awhile, and then suddenly thought, "Get out of here, John." Dubetz began crawling, dragging himself with his good arm. At first, he tried pulling the Bren gun along, but soon abandoned it. He went past and sometimes over an endless parade of corpses. Pausing to catch his breath, Dubetz wondered why he was crawling. The smokescreen was still thick. Dubetz walked, cradling his arm protectively.

He went slowly, picking a path around the dead. Soon he came out of the smoke, and saw soldiers on the hill they had descended waving at him, cheering him forward. Bullets were cracking through the air, but it was as if he could hear them hitting a wall behind him and falling harmlessly to the ground. Still, he expected to die. Finally, after collapsing once or twice, Dubetz reached the crest of the hill. He stumbled past the soldiers, who cheered and applauded as if a marathoner had just crossed a finish line. As he collapsed, a stretcher-bearer rushed to help.

Dubetz was loaded into a carrier, where he promptly passed out. Hours later, he awoke to find himself being carried into No. 8 Canadian General Hospital in Antwerp's sprawling Belgian Veterans Hospital. Several nurses taking a smoke break outside had been on the ward where he had been treated for the last wound. "Look, Curly's back," one said. Curly was a nickname they had given him because of his closely shorn hair that had only just started growing back when he was hospitalized. They teased him for a few moments, like young girls might while waiting for a slightly injured athlete to be carried off a high school playing field. But their eyes betrayed their familiarity with the day-to-day parade of shattered, often dying, soldiers that passed through their care.

One of the nurses came to his cot soon after. Dubetz still had four grenades attached to his waist web belt. She removed them, and his mud- and blood-crusted uniform. The arm was so swollen that getting the jacket off was impossible, so she scissored it into pieces. When the doctor came to check the injury, Dubetz said he was hoping it was just a flesh wound and he could get back to his buddies soon.

The next morning, a doctor showed him an X-ray. There were bones in his arm missing one-inch pieces where the bullet had gone clean through. Two days later, he was flown to England and underwent an extensive operation. As he was being put on the plane, Dubetz could hear massive explosions nearby.[11] On October 13, Hitler had ordered Antwerp subjected to v-1 and v-2 attack in an attempt to destroy port facilities and disrupt their use by the Allies. The first rockets fell that day.

While the v-1—a jet-powered flying bomb that carried a one-ton warhead at a speed of four hundred miles per hour—could be detected and sometimes shot down by anti-aircraft guns or fighter planes, the v-2 was undetectable and impossible to counter. The v-2 was a liquid fuel–powered rocket, forty-six feet long, weighing thirteen tons, and carrying a one-ton warhead. It reached Mach 1 in less than thirty seconds, and barrelled down upon its target from previously unimagined altitudes of fifty to sixty miles at 3,500 feet per second just five minutes after launch. The force of impact meant that the missile often penetrated deep into the ground before exploding, creating great holes. But this also meant that much of its destructive power was harmlessly absorbed. Still, the damage and casualties were great, because there was no warning of a v-2 approach and so no time to take cover.

Next to London, Antwerp was to endure more v-1 and v-2 attacks than any other city. At No. 8 Canadian General Hospital, Nursing Sister Harriet J.T. Sloan realized that Antwerp had become a deadly place. Day and night, "with monotonous regularity at about half hour intervals, the diabolical machines crashed into the city... there was no warning, only the terrible impact and great explosion.

"Gradually we had no windows left and we learned to leave all the doors open so they were not torn from their hinges by concussion. And to the hospital now came hundreds of tragic civilians—men, women, and children. Flying glass is one of the more deadly missiles one can encounter."[12] There would be more than 30,000 civilian casualties during the city's long siege, with 3,700 fatalities. Not until March 1945 would the bombardment cease.[13]

IN THE POLDER west of Woensdrecht, the survivors of 'B' and 'C' Companies had not withdrawn behind the smokescreen as Dubetz had thought. The smoke instead was covering a renewed assault towards Angus 1, and the men still on their feet had gone forward. From the roof of a barn, Black Watch intelligence officer Lieutenant W.J. Shea watched a tiny clutch of men in khaki make it to the dyke. Then he saw them pinned down. The Germans were throwing stick grenades from across the dyke. It was 0900 hours. "The companies are being annihilated," he reported to headquarters.[14]

Ritchie, too, watched the tragedy play out. The Germans had the situation so in hand that they were jumping up, waving their arms, and obviously taunting the trapped Canadians. When a soldier fired on them, the paratroops quickly dropped back into cover and shot with deadly accuracy. Sickened, Ritchie ordered the two companies to withdraw without first seeking authority from either brigade or divisional command.[15]

Not everyone could get away. Shea watched helplessly as survivors of the lead platoon from 'C' Company that had reached the dyke were forced to surrender. He counted sixteen lost as prisoners. Then German stretcher-bearers moved into the field and began taking wounded out.[16] Just twenty-five men from 'C' Company escaped unwounded, and forty-one from 'B' Company.[17]

The Black Watch failure on this Friday the thirteenth morning was not the end of the battalion's ordeal. Ritchie was ordered to renew the attack at 1500 hours. In the meantime, RAF carried out three separate attacks against the German defences. At 1145, eight

Typhoons from No. 263 Squadron struck a 105-millimetre artillery position north of Korteven, but failed to score any hits. Soon thereafter, ten Typhoons of No. 197 Squadron divebombed the paratroops dug in along the railway embankment without noticeable effect. At 1300, No. 74 Squadron struck targets near Woensdrecht Station, with eleven Spitfires each dropping a 500-pound bomb. Despite the pilots reporting nine hits, damage was minimal. The German defences remained as strong as before.[18]

Ritchie abandoned any thought of advancing all the way to Angus 3. Instead, the Black Watch would just attempt to take Angus 1, with 'A' Company advancing right of the road leading from the start line to the dyke while 'D' Company was on the left. This time, the tanks would try to go along. 'C' Company's survivors and the antitank platoon would provide covering fire, as would two 2nd Anti-Tank Regiment batteries. The battalion's three Wasp carriers would engage the dyke with their flamethrowers.

'A' Company's Captain William Ewing studied the ground he was to cover, and decided the "concept of the attack was fundamentally cockeyed." Before him lay 1,200 yards of beet fields bisected by a ditch that was too wide to jump, and traversed by only a single narrow bridge surely covered by machine guns. The attack was to start at 1700 hours, and Ewing wondered why not delay it another hour or two, and at least go in under cover of darkness. As for the dyke objective, it seemed about twenty feet high—hard to climb and requiring a bloody good arm to throw grenades over.[19]

Despite his reservations, Ewing went forward behind a hail of machine-gun and artillery fire. The carriers trundled along, and once in range, opened up with the flamethrowers. When they flamed out, the carriers withdrew. One bogged in mud on the way back. Two reported a couple of misfires. It appeared that their fire had no effect, Lieutenant Shea noted, as "the enemy resistance stiffened, and by 1820 the situation was very sticky."[20]

Ewing's 'A' Company was being slaughtered by machine-gun fire. The men were throwing grenades up the dyke, but most were rolling back down on them. 'D' Company was faring little better. Major Alex Popham, a Normandy veteran, managed to reach the railway embankment with one platoon, but his other two were pinned down in the polder. Although darkness had now closed in, German flares denied the men any concealment. When Popham was severely wounded, Lieutenant Lewis took over 'D' Company after convincing the major to go back before the wound killed him. Popham went grudgingly. Soon after, Ewing walked into headquarters nursing a wound. Ewing told Ritchie that 'A' Company had failed to reach its objective, "casualties had been extremely heavy, and that few of the Company would come out alive." The Black Watch had now lost every company commander. Young lieutenants were in charge.[21]

Some of the men were breaking, going back without orders. "When you lose all your key people, all your senior NCOS, even down to corporal, which is really what happened," Ewing said later, "you never really recover from it."[22]

Unlike earlier, Ritchie would not order a withdrawal on his own authority. Not until 0100 on October 14 did Brigadier Megill agree to one. The evacuation took the rest of the night, and it was after sunrise when the last man reportedly returned to the lines. Many, however, still lay in the beet fields. Most were dead, but others were unrescued wounded. The Black Watch had been horribly mauled. Only nine men of 'A' Company walked out.[23] Initially, casualties were estimated at 183, but the final tally was 145—56 fatal, 62 wounded, and 27 taken prisoner.[24] It was not just the casualty count that was tragic, but the extremely high percentage of men killed. Normal casualty ratios were about three or four wounded to every fatality. October 13, 1944 would be remembered by the regiment as Black Friday. Nothing had been gained. The Germans lost not an inch of ground, and 1st Battalion, 6th Parachute Regiment recorded just one man killed.[25]

"The weary and nearly exhausted men rode back in carriers and jeeps to the positions they had left barely twenty four hours earlier, though to them it had seemed days." They were given a hot meal and allowed to sleep the day away. That night, after supper, the Knights of Columbus showed a movie. The war film, *We Die at Dawn*, had been scheduled, "but this was hurriedly changed and the film substituted therefore was in much lighter vein."[26]

ON OCTOBER 14, 2nd Canadian Infantry Division regrouped. The Black Watch was now incapable of battalion-scale combat and would have to be rebuilt—a process expected to take four months due to reinforcement shortages and the loss of so many officers and non-commissioned officers. In the polders west of Woensdrecht, the Calgary Highlanders relieved the Royal Regiment of Canada, which went into reserve behind the South Saskatchewan Regiment. Le Régiment de Maisonneuve was split in half—one guarding the sluice gates on the Völckerpolder about 2,500 yards south of the German-held railway embankment and the other moving into reserve at Ossendrecht. The Essex Scottish took over the Royal Hamilton Light Infantry's positions near Hoogerheide, so that battalion could attack Woensdrecht.[27]

Even as the Black Watch had been slaughtered, a new offensive plan was born. Now that it was obvious any attempt to outflank Woensdrecht with an advance in the polders or by moving north from Hoogerheide was doomed, division ordered the town taken. At 0900 hours on October 14, Brigadier Fred Cabeldu summoned Lieutenant Colonel Denis Whitaker. Whitaker was given forty-eight hours to attack Woensdrecht.[28]

The principal mistake that led to Black Sunday, he believed, had been dangerously underestimating the Germans. Even now, divisional and brigade intelligence reports claimed Woensdrecht was defended by one infantry company commanded by a seventy-year-old officer. Bunk, Whitaker thought, and ordered a series of reconnaissance patrols to probe the German lines that night. The Germans who slaughtered the Black Watch had proven themselves tough, brave, skilled, and canny. It was also clear that those holding Woensdrecht knew the Canadians were coming, for the Red Cross reported the town being evacuated of civilians. Although ordered north to Bergen op Zoom, many slipped south through the Canadian lines for Ossendrecht. They said there were at least one hundred Germans dug into gardens of the houses on the south side of the town. Between Woensdrecht and Bergen op Zoom, some reported, two thousand paratroops were deployed. Whitaker figured their role was to counterattack any move against the town.[29]

Assuming the Germans were expecting them, Whitaker knew that surprise was only possible with a night attack. Such attacks were fraught with problems, particularly the likelihood of companies getting lost. The lack of ambient light in the Scheldt guaranteed a black night. But, as Whitaker planned a massive artillery program, the darkness would be lit by explosions that could serve as guides. His most "extravagant" artillery plan ever, Whitaker called it.[30] "For the first time in many weeks a 'full dress' fire plan... complete with a barrage, [concentrations,] and [defensive fire] tasks," 2 CID's artillery commander wrote.[31]

A total of 168 guns would be involved. All seventy-two 25-pounders of the division's three field regiments and forty-eight 4.5-inch and 5.5-inch guns of the 7th Medium Regiment, Royal Canadian Artillery and 84th and 121st Medium Regiments, Royal Artillery. The 115th Heavy Anti-Aircraft Regiment, Royal Artillery provided an additional forty-two 3.7-inch guns.[32] Also weighing in would be the Toronto Scottish machine-gun and mortar units and a squadron of Fort Garry Horse tanks.

Whitaker intended his men to go right to Woensdrecht behind a creeping barrage, while simultaneously forcing the Germans to ground with a relentless series of concentrations dropped on their positions. When the artillery stopped firing, the Rileys should overrun the Germans before they recovered from the trauma of being shelled. Sufficient veterans remained, he thought, to carry the day. These were tough soldiers, proud of their reputation for always gaining their objective and never being forced off it by counterattack. They knew how to lean into a barrage, getting to within twenty-five yards of each of the timed lifts, and then to jump ahead the moment the guns moved their fire forward. The plan consisted of three vital components—good troops, a good fire and movement scheme, and a chance of gaining surprise by attacking at night. But, Whitaker thought, a fourth component—luck—would determine the final victor.[33]

Regimental pride is important to building a battalion's fighting prowess, but it can also lead to overestimation of ability. Unlike the Black Watch, the Rileys were led by veteran officers, had many experienced men in the ranks, and enjoyed consequent high morale. But, as with all the First Canadian Army infantry battalions, the reinforcements taken in over the past weeks were largely untrained. Even as the battalion prepared for battle, some of these new men were "quietly taken aside for... a short course in how to shoot a rifle and stay alive in battle." Section leaders walked others through a "sad spectacle of... crawling on barn floors to demonstrate movement under fire. Elementary section and platoon tactics were explained. There were men who could not strip a Bren."[34]

That afternoon, Whitaker convened a preliminary O Group in the badly damaged Hoogerheide town hall. The main room was crowded with Riley officers and representatives of all the supporting units. Using maps and aerial photographs, Whitaker explained his plan.[35] H-Hour would be 0330 on Tuesday, October 16, and the Rileys would attack in a box formation. Everyone, including his tactical battalion headquarters, would cross the start line—a track midway between Hoogerheide and Woensdrecht—and advance to the objective. The pace would be 100 yards every four minutes, and the leading companies had about 1,500 yards to travel. These companies would be Major Jack Halladay's 'A' Company on the right flank and Major Louis Froggett's 'D' Company to the left. Major Joe Pigott's 'C' Company would follow Halladay's men, mopping up bypassed pockets of resistance, while Major H.A. "Huck" Welch's 'B' Company did the same behind 'D' Company.[36]

The reconnaissance patrols went out soon after the O Group broke up and returned with reports that confirmed Whitaker's suspicion that intelligence staff underestimated the German defence. So, too, did the aerial photograhs. Although many seemed unoccupied, the area was riddled with slit trenches and bunkers.

By Sunday morning, a sandbox contour model showing the topography around Woensdrecht was in place at the Hoogerheide town hall, and the company commanders spent hours examining it. Along with Whitaker, each man also went up in an artillery spotter plane to take a look at the actual ground. Each commander took pains to ensure that his men also understood the plan. Briefings at company level were extensive and detailed. Whitaker was confident the Rileys would take the objective. What worried him were the civilian reports about the paratroops deployed north of the town. If the estimates were correct, the regiment could be outnumbered four to one when the inevitable counterattack came. That made the chances of victory in Woensdrecht pretty slim.

But nothing could be done about that. So everyone concentrated on preparing his personal fighting kit. At 2359 hours, a hot meal and a rare four-ounce rum ration were served. As the calendar turned to October 16, the Rileys settled down to wait for the order to move to the start line.[37]

A clear example of how even best-laid plans can go awry at the last moment came just minutes before H-Hour when 'A' Company's second-in-command, Captain Lyn Hegelheimer, called Whitaker to report that Halladay had fallen asleep and for the past hour all efforts to awaken him had failed. Having landed at Dieppe and fought through Normandy, Halladay was the battalion's senior major, but he had succumbed literally to battle exhaustion. Whitaker quickly ordered Hegelheimer to take over. Having been designated Left Out of Battle, Hegelheimer had not participated in any attack briefings. Whitaker quickly briefed him on his tasks and the timings. Then the artillery opened fire right on schedule at 0330 hours, and the Rileys attacked.[38]

WHITAKER HAD COUNTED on darkness giving an element of surprise, but at 0230 hours Oberstleutnant Friederich von der Heydte received a report from Woensdrecht of unusual movement. Throughout the day, his sumptuous headquarters in the Mattemburg country house had been subjected to repeated bombing by Spitfires from 127 Squadron, RAF and he had suspected this meant a major attack was forming. Woensdrecht was the obvious candidate. Therefore, he directed two companies of 6th Parachute Regiment's 1st Battalion to move from the railway embankment towards the town.

Now, he was even more certain the attack was coming. Jumping into his motorcycle's sidecar, von der Heydte was driven to Woensdrecht. Previously, he had established a defensive plan whereby the German units would immediately withdraw to a prearranged second resistance line on the northern outskirts of Woensdrecht. Here, they would await reinforcement and begin counterattacking. By pure coincidence, this second resistance line was precisely astride the Rileys' final objective. When von der Heydte arrived at 0300 hours, the town was undergoing a preliminary bombardment. He immediately ordered the withdrawal and sped back to Mattemburg to organize a counterattack.[39]

Despite his last-minute briefing, Captain Hegelheimer got 'A' Company moving on time. Ahead, the "fields heaved and trembled under the weight of exploding shells." The gunners drenched a 1,200-yard square with shells, with Woensdrecht at the centre. To keep the men on track, every fifteen seconds, anti-aircraft guns fired a rapid, fiery trail of tracers overhead towards the objective.[40] Hegelheimer advanced on a northwesterly axis that would take his company through the hamlet of Nederheide along the main road leading to his objective, "a line running through houses on the northern fringe" of Woensdrecht. Moving closely behind the creeping barrage, 'A' Company made good progress and met no opposition. At 0515, he thought his men were on the objective. They had suffered only two casualties.

'D' Company followed another northwesterly running road to its objective of a reverse slope on Woensdrecht's outskirts, and at 0445 hours, Major Froggett reported being on the objective. Major Pigott's 'C' Company was tasked with clearing any Germans out of Nederheide. His men quickly rounded up forty-five dazed Germans at a cost of only three men wounded. 'B' Company, under Major Welch, had a harder time carrying out its clearing task in Woensdrecht. A skirmish erupted as the company was engaged by Germans firing from slit trenches dug behind a number of buildings. Then the platoon moving east through the town came under fire and started tripping booby traps. With casualties mounting and the situation confused by darkness, Welch consolidated until daylight made it easier to renew the mopping-up operation. So far, the attack seemed on track.[41]

Major Pigott had set up headquarters in a cottage on the western edge of Woensdrecht, beside a road that ran along a narrow finger-like ridge pointing towards South Beveland before descending to the polders. The quiet front and lack of strong German forces disquieted him. Pigott knew German tactics. A favourite was to pull back "when the heat was on," and then counterattack before the opponent could set up proper defensive positions. He feared the Rileys were being set up for a sucker punch, and warned his men they were "going to catch hell first thing in the morning." He was worried, too, about his platoon disposition. Groping in the dark, Pigott had set each in place by feel and guesswork. 'A' Company was out somewhere ahead of 'C' Company, but an intervening rise of ground blocked it from sight. Not until first light at 0615 hours would Pigott be able to get a clear sense of his position. His unease grew with every passing minute.[42]

[19]

Dominate the Situation

Just after dawn on October 16, Lieutenant Colonel Denis Whitaker moved the Royal Hamilton Light Infantry headquarters into a white stucco farmhouse on Dorpstraat—a main street running west to east through the southern part of Woensdrecht. From here, he could see Major Huck Welch's 'B' Company a few blocks to the west, and Major Louis Froggett's 'D' Company on a rise holding the battalion's western flank. Back of the rifle companies, Captain Bob Wright's pioneer platoon was barricaded in a house on the northwest corner of the street to guard against an attack along Dorpstraat from this direction. Whitaker's most forward companies, 'A' and 'C', were on the other side of a slope to the north and out of sight.

Within minutes of Whitaker's headquarters section moving into the farmhouse, his men had taken ten paratroops prisoner who were discovered hiding in the cellar and pits in the backyard. That these men were all paratroopers greatly concerned Whitaker. When he tried questioning one, the man spat in his face. "Even in captivity, the beast could snarl," he thought.[1]

Dawn brought unpleasant realizations for his company commanders. Pigott discovered one platoon so out of place it could neither support nor be supported by the other two. He got busy repositioning the company so each platoon could interlock fire with the others. Froggett's 'D' Company was 150 yards short of its objective, but when he sent two platoons up the hill to rectify the problem, they were pinned down by Germans holding the summit. Froggett threw his reserve platoon into a vigorous attack that convinced the paratroops to fall back so quickly they left burning candles in their dugouts. The situation restored, Froggett began to relax.

In Woensdrecht itself, 'B' Company had started clearing the town, only to run up against many well-emplaced snipers hiding in houses and barns near the main crossroads. Welch reported his men taking casualties, but determined to control the situation.

Over at 'A' Company, Captain Lyn Hegelheimer was struggling to properly position his men. Contrary to his initial report that the company had gained its objective, the young captain had overshot it. Turning everyone around, he led them back up the hill. Coming upon two paratroopers from the rear, he took them prisoner at pistol point. The ground was more rugged than Hegelheimer had expected, and the inexperienced officer decided that the only way to defend it was to cast his platoons far and wide, to cover every possible line of approach. But this left gaps between each platoon, meaning they were unable to support each other. Hegelheimer also put his company headquarters section so far back, he was unable to exert proper control.[2]

The company was still digging in when the paratroops counterattacked at 1000 hours with three self-propelled guns of the 255th Sturmgeschutz Company supporting. Hegelheimer sent a runner to Whitaker warning that 'A' Company was being overrun. In setting up his platoons, Hegelheimer had given no thought to meeting an armoured attack. Too late, he realized he should have pulled his company in tight among the buildings around the crossroads that lay in the centre of his position. From these positions of cover—all close enough for voice communication—the SPGs could have been effectively engaged.[3] Such hindsight could not save 'A' Company, which was badly shot up in a matter of minutes. When Hegelheimer ordered it to fall back on 'C' Company's position, many of the men bolted.

Pigott had just brewed a cup of tea in his stone cottage headquarters when the Germans struck 'A' Company. Looking out a window, the 'C' Company commander saw some of Hegelheimer's men "running down the hill. We got them stopped—some were crying and panic-stricken—and they told us that they'd been wiped out. I could hardly believe it."[4] Not all the men were stopped. Some ran back to battalion headquarters, where Whitaker halted them with a drawn revolver.[5]

'A' Company had been shredded, and about thirty men taken prisoner. No sooner had its survivors poured through 'C' Company's lines than Pigott saw the paratroops come over the hillcrest. "You could tell they were crack troops just by looking at them, by the way they moved and used the ground." Close behind was an SPG that rumbled to within fifty yards of the cottage and opened fire with a combination of armour-piercing and high-explosive shells. Pigott's driver, Private Harry Gram, had his chest and face flayed by shrapnel and stone chips. The wounds looked bad, so Pigott ordered him to the rear. Half stunned, weakened by blood loss, the short, stocky driver tried to leave the normal way—in his jeep. When it failed to start on the first crank, Gram kept pumping the starter and wiggling the gear shift, despite the fact that the SPG was sitting there with the jeep in its sights. Any moment, Pigott expected Gram to be blown to bits. But the gun remained quiet. Then the SPG commander stood up so that he was exposed to the waist, and motioned impatiently towards Gram as if brushing aside a pesky fly. Whether Gram saw the gesture or not, he dismounted from the jeep and trudged off. Once he was out of the line of fire, the SPG commander ducked down and the 75-millimetre gun resumed methodically hammering the cottage apart.[6]

Pigott's situation was desperate. 'C' Company was going to face the same fate that had befallen 'A' Company if the paratroopers got in among his men. Grabbing his wireless handset, Pigott told Whitaker that he needed artillery immediately right on his position. Whitaker never hesitated. Pushing aside the thought that his friend was asking him to be "his executioner," Whitaker yelled to Major Jack Drewery, his artillery representative from 4th Field Regiment, that he wanted a Victor Target, Scale Ten concentration fired on the coordinates of 'C' Company's headquarters. Drewery responded instantly. Pigott was yelling and shouting for his troops to get low in their slits when the first shells started whistling down.[7]

A Victor Target drew fire from all artillery in range. In this case, that consisted of the three divisional artillery regiments, three medium regiments, and three heavy anti-aircraft regiments—a total of 312 guns firing ten rounds per minute. Pigott figured as the Germans were "on their feet and attacking and our men dug in, they'd probably lose 90 per cent to our 10 ... The first salvo was right on. It came over like 70 or 80 express trains pulling into Union Station at the same time."

In little more than a minute, about four thousand shells bearing fifty tons of high explosive turned this small patch of Holland into a slaughterhouse. The paratroopers were literally torn asunder, the attack shattered. Those who survived the salvo reeled in shock towards their lines. Pigott, who had been wounded in the scalp by fire from the SPG moments before, headed out of his battered cottage towards a six-pounder antitank gun and its crew. Getting there required dodging across a hundred yards of open ground still cut by machine-gun fire and exploding shells. He directed the gun crew to push it to where they could fire on the still unscathed SPG. Several shots later, the SPG was destroyed, its crew dead. An eerie silence fell over the battleground, wreathed in smoke and small fires. Miraculously, only one Canadian had been killed by the artillery concentration. For his bravery, Pigott received an immediate Distinguished Service Order citation.[8] 'C' Company had suffered badly, though, with Pigott reporting initially that he had only twenty men left, but soon after, he managed to round up another twenty to bolster the ranks to forty.[9]

Although the threat to 'C' Company had been alleviated, the battle for Woensdrecht raged on. Welch's 'B' Company, supposedly the battalion reserve, was snarled in a relentless firefight with snipers for control of the town. Sergeant Ernie Dearden, leading No. 11 Platoon, was shot in the arm and wounded in both legs by shrapnel. But he refused evacuation, leading his men onwards until the majority of the Germans were dead or captured. As he staggered into the Regimental Aid Post, Dearden fainted from loss of blood. His actions resulted in a Military Medal.[10] Around noon, Welch consolidated his company in the town centre, and an hour later detached a platoon to help 'C' Company, which was now being heavily shelled and mortared. The platoon no sooner reached Pigott's position than its commander, Lieutenant Arthur Cairns, was killed.[11]

The Rileys were hanging on to most of their original objectives, but only just. Major Froggett's 'D' Company had been doing all right until noon, when they received an urgent call from 4th Field Regiment Forward Observation Officer, Captain Douglas McDonald, that he was surrounded on the left flank and needed help breaking out. Froggett sent a section of men, but they were all killed by fire from the same machine gun pinning down the FOO. Some time later, McDonald managed to get through to the company.[12] 'D' Company was soon forced off the top of the slope and into a pocket about a hundred yards in diameter, centred on a farmhouse in which a shell-shocked goat was hiding. Froggett was headquartered inside, his men spread out in slit trenches on either side of the building.[13]

All the antitank guns had been knocked out or lost, but 'B' Squadron of the Fort Garry Horse had moved into the town and was providing fire support. At 1410, Whitaker radioed 4th Canadian Infantry Brigade headquarters regarding "our thinness on the ground." 'A' Company had just one officer and eighteen men, 'B' Company two officers and thirty-nine other ranks, 'C' Company two officers and forty men, 'D' Company only Froggett and sixty other ranks. Less than an hour later, Lieutenant D.R. Brown, commanding the battalion mortar platoon, was trying to set the tubes up behind 'C' Company's position when a shell fragment broke his leg. He finished deploying the mortars before going to the RAP for treatment.[14] The Rileys were being ground away.

Earlier, at 1415 hours, the first evidence of Field Marshal Montgomery's sudden resolve to give First Canadian Army's efforts to open Antwerp priority had revealed itself in one of the heaviest air attacks launched in its support. A complete wing of four Spitfire squadrons from No. 84 Fighter Group struck German positions to the immediate north of Woensdrecht. The 132 Norwegian Wing roared down upon a wide range of targets, dropping about fifty tons of bombs. Two hours later, thirty-six Spitfires returned for a second series of attacks.[15]

Whitaker, meanwhile, had ordered Froggett to regain the top of the slope earlier relinquished to the paratroopers. With a troop of Fort Garry Shermans alongside, Lieutenant G.P.J. Des Grosseilliers led his No. 16 Platoon up the slope and gained a toehold at 1600 hours. All around, Typhoon fighter-bombers swooped down to strafe and rocket German positions close to Woensdrecht, but that did nothing to slow the rate of mortar and artillery fire pounding the Rileys. At 1700, this fire intensified, and all companies reported casualties. The medical officer, Captain J.W. Weinstock, informed Whitaker that he had evacuated more than ninety wounded through the RAP. Then No. 16 Platoon was overrun by paratroops counterattacking from the northeast. Only six men escaped to join the rest of 'D' Company. Des Grosseilliers was among those taken prisoner. No. 17 Platoon was struck soon afterwards from three sides and reduced to only seventeen men. Froggett ordered his company to withdraw down the slope to concentrate around the farmhouse.[16]

The Rileys were so thin on the ground that Whitaker told Brigadier Fred Cabeldu he doubted they could hold their current positions through the night. Cabeldu ordered 'B' Company of the Essex Scottish up from Hoogerheide to take position to the rear of 'C' Company. The Essex Scottish settled in place just as night fell at 1800 hours, strengthening the Canadian hold on Woensdrecht.[17]

In the dark morning hours of October 17, Company Sergeant Major K.C. "Casey" Lingen, who had just reported to the Rileys' 'D' Company for duty the day before, decided to check his men. He asked Froggett to point out each platoon's position, so the two men crawled from the farmhouse. "The sniping was hellish," Froggett noted. "Run as fast as you can," he advised Lingen. The CSM went out safely and stayed with the platoons for awhile. Froggett waited where he lay for Lingen's return. "I saw him running back to me, and then he fell, dead."[18]

MORNING BROUGHT NO RELIEF from the vicious sniping of 'D' and 'C' Companies. Deciding to fight fire with fire, Whitaker ordered Lieutenant J.A. Williamson to unleash the snipers in his scout platoon. Williamson sent three men—Corporal Joe Friyia, and Privates

Wilbert Jacob Ludwig Kunzelman and J.S. Whitehead—who soon managed to whittle away the snipers sufficiently to ease the pressure.[19]

The Canadians clinging tenuously to their part of Woensdrecht and the Germans facing them spent a long day on October 17 pounding each other with artillery and mortar fire. But neither side could mount serious infantry attacks. The Rileys were still unable to gain control of the town centre, although they were within a hundred yards of it. "We did not have enough bodies on the ground to completely control the Woensdrecht feature and it was possible for the enemy to infiltrate," the battalion war diarist wrote late that day. "The enemy appeared to suffer very heavy casualties from our arty fire which was used unsparingly, but he continued to reinforce his [positions.] We were prevented from probing forward as the average coy strength was forty-five and the casualties amongst our [officers] and NCOS and older men were very heavy. The bulk of the men in the [battalion] at the present time had not had very much inf[antry] training, but had been remustered from other branches of the service. At this time 'D' Coy had one [officer], Major E.L. Froggett. 'B' Coy had Major H.A. Welch and Lt. D.A. Bonnallie, 'C' Coy [having had a missing lieutenant find his way home] had three officers including Major J.M. Pigott. 'A' Coy had one officer, Capt. H.L. Hegelheimer."[20]

That evening, the regiment recorded having suffered 161 casualties in two days of fighting, with 21 fatal. Reinforcements on October 17 totalled just 39, and almost none had infantry training.[21] The Rileys were ordered to hang on to their gains until they could be relieved by a fresh unit, but nobody knew when this might occur.

After a comparatively quiet night, October 18 dawned with renewed shelling and mortaring. Paratroopers had also used the darkness to gain positions from which light machine guns could be ranged on the front lines. Whitaker called an O Group at 0900 to give his officers the welcome news that 1 British Corps was finally shifting westwards to secure 2 CID's right flank, and that 4th Canadian Armoured Division should soon be in position to swing north past Woensdrecht in a right-flanking movement, around the base of the South Beveland isthmus, to seize Bergen op Zoom and cut off the lines of escape for the Germans facing them. That was the good news. The bad news was that the battalion would likely have to remain in place for another seven days.[22]

Whitaker had received all this news from Brigadier Fred Cabeldu during a briefing earlier that morning at the latter's headquarters. For his part, Whitaker had told Cabeldu that his battalion was "very weak in men and lacking in training for the type of fighting necessary in that area. The Hun is battling most bitterly and seems to have no shortage of weapons. It is close, hand to hand fighting—the enemy is not giving up here the way he has in the past." Whitaker said it was the artillery support, particularly the massive concentration fired on Pigott's position on October 16, which had turned the battle in the Rileys' favour.[23]

The relentless shelling kept disrupting the battalion's internal communications by ripping up telephone wires soon after they were laid. Lieutenant A.M. Tedford and his signals platoon prowled back and forth between the companies and battalion headquarters repairing lines around the clock. Corporal Sam Nutt and Private T. Lashkivich were fixing wire in 'B' Company's perimeter when the paratroops attacked at about noon. Nutt, an old-timer, was killed, while Lashkivich scooped up a Bren gun and proved instrumental in driving the Germans off. Another signaller, Private J.R. Bulmer, was taken prisoner while assisting some wounded Rileys.

After their previous success relieving the pressure of snipers, the intrepid sniping team of Corporal Friyia and Privates Kunzelman and Whitehead swung back into action at about 1400 hours. Friyia ambitiously led the others on a patrol sixty yards to the front of 'D' Company, while a Sherman tank stood by to offer fire support. The team surprised and captured eight paratroopers, and thought they killed about the same number. That foray having gone so well, they decided to go out again, only to get tangled in a firefight. Friyia's Sten jammed and he was shot in the foot. Seeing the trouble the men were in, Major Froggett rushed to the rescue and helped get Friyia back, with Whitehead covering the withdrawal. Back in the Canadian lines, everyone realized Kunzelman was missing. His body was discovered the next day. Friyia was awarded a Military Medal for his actions.

Nowhere in Woensdrecht was safe. At 2000 hours, Captain Walter James Williamson, the twenty-seven-year-old second-in-command of 'C' Company, and its Company Quartermaster Sergeant, forty-three-year-old Lawrence Arthur Gendron, were killed by a mortar bomb a hundred yards from Whitaker's headquarters. Early that evening while on reconnaissance, Whitaker had to hunker down for fifty minutes within sight of the white farmhouse until a heavy shell and mortar bombardment lifted. The next day, at 1630 hours, a shell scored a direct hit on the house where the pioneer platoon was positioned. Five men were buried under a collapsed section of the building and all required hospitalization.[24]

Whitaker was nonplussed on October 19 when divisional command suggested that he go over to the offensive to clear the rest of the high ground. Good soldier that he was, Whitaker called his company commanders and those from the supporting artillery and tank units together at 1000 hours on October 20 to discuss the notion. Everyone was emphatically opposed. Only one company could be freed for an attack, and it was so short of men that there was no chance of success. While the paratroopers were no longer fighting tenaciously, they still had the greater numbers. Whitaker informed Cabeldu the idea was "not a practical one."

Four hours later, Cabeldu advised that the Rileys would be relieved the following day. At 1315 on October 21, Whitaker held another O Group. The relief would be carried out that evening with 6th Canadian Infantry Brigade's Queen's Own Cameron Highlanders taking over the Riley positions. But there would only be a twenty-four-hour rest period. And they would spend that time incorporating largely untrained reinforcements into the companies in preparation for "an attack on the neck of the Scheldt."

The takeover by the Camerons began at 2200 hours. With the Germans lurking and harassing the lines with mortar fire, great care was made to transfer men in and out in "absolute quiet." But the takeover went smoothly, completed by 0100 hours.

At 0900 on October 22, Whitaker and his intelligence officer attended a briefing at brigade for Operation Vitality—the planned attack on South Beveland and Walcheren Island. Meanwhile, the battalion received another 200 reinforcements to add to the 150 taken on three days earlier. Both drafts had few or no men with any infantry training, so the battalion's non-commissioned officers started providing bare-bones instruction in how to stay alive on a battlefield while not endangering those around you.[25]

SECOND CANADIAN INFANTRY DIVISION's operations between October 15 and 20 had convinced LXVII Corps's Chief of Staff, Oberst Elmar Warning, that the campaign to prevent Antwerp's opening had entered an end-game the Germans could not win. Although the Canadians had failed to cut the South Beveland isthmus entirely, by October 15, German forces could no longer move between the mainland and the peninsula. That same day, Oberkommando der Wehrmacht, West concluded that "a permanent recapture of the land connection with Walcheren can no longer be expected" and consented to flooding as much of this area as possible to deny the Canadians free movement.[26] Then came the assault on Woensdrecht and Kampfgruppe Chill's subsequent failure to dislodge the Rileys, leading Warning to believe First Canadian Army's next move would, "after broadening, extending, and securing his approach to the isthmus, to get possession quickly of the whole area south of the Maas." He worried 711th Infantry Division immediately west of Kampfgruppe Chill was in danger of being enveloped, a development that would cause "a collapse of the whole front."

Warning knew it was just a matter of days before the Breskens Pocket and Walcheren Island were lost. When I British Corps started shifting westwards, with 4th Canadian Armoured Division coming into play on 2 CID's flank, he realized this division's arrival indicated that "the enemy was able to throw in new, fresh, and victory-conscious divisions against the exhausted and battle-weary German units, for which there was no possibility of rehabilitation or relief. There were no German reserves in the corps area; and [Fifteenth] Army had none in view of the tense situation on its whole front. The complete mastery of the air by the enemy air force made itself felt more from day to day."

But Warning detected one silver lining. If the West Scheldt was lost, "there no longer existed the two missions of defence which had been essential up to this time, namely, control of the mouth of the

[Scheldt] and direct influence on Antwerp harbour to prevent its exploitation by the enemy. Because of the strength ratio mentioned, everyone knew that the area south of the Maas could not be held for long. It was also to be foreseen that, after our forces were withdrawn over the Maas...a rather long lull in the fighting would begin." He did not believe the Allies could immediately attack "across this strong natural obstacle into the southern Netherlands area, with its numerous large cities, an area which he could traverse only with great difficulty because of the numerous canals and flood areas."

The job now was consequently "to fix strong enemy forces as long as possible in the area south of the mouth of the Maas." But no more German forces should be moved into the area. At the corps level, Warning wanted to withdraw all support troops south of the Maas River to prevent chaos when operations there had to be abandoned, and a mad scramble began for the few undestroyed bridge crossings. The fighting units to the south, meanwhile, should cease defending every scrap of ground and move to a "fluid operation, a battle to gain time." Fifteenth Army headquarters concurred and presented this argument to OKW, which responded that Hitler demanded "obstinate holding on to every foot of ground south of the Maas."

Recognizing that Hitler's directive was ludicrous, LXVII Corps, with Fifteenth Army's complicit approval, "decided now to act independently," and began withdrawal of support units and preparation of a defensive line north of the Maas.[27] Still, there was no intention of surrendering the line running from Bergen op Zoom east to Roosendaal without a major fight. To strengthen Kampfgruppe Chill, 245th Infantry Division was moved to positions south of Bergen op Zoom, completed on October 20.[28]

As for 70th Infantry Division defending South Beveland and Walcheren Island and 64th Infantry Division trapped in the Breskens Pocket, these two units were considered doomed. Generalleutnant Wilhelm Daser's 70th Infantry Division had as yet seen little fighting, but it was under heavy pressure from Allied aerial bombardment directed at silencing the coastal guns and systematically flooding Walcheren. From the small fishing port of Veere, an irregular ferry service was able to move limited troops and supplies to North Beveland and then across the East Scheldt. But this was a tenuous link, likely to be severed any time by the Allied navy and air forces. Daser had little confidence in his division of men plagued with stomach problems, when the time came to meet the Canadian drive across the isthmus into South Beveland.

In the Breskens Pocket, Generalmajor Knut Eberding could only delay the inevitable. His division had no reliable link to other German forces beyond the occasional boat slipping in from Vlissingen to bring supplies and evacuate wounded at Breskens, Cadzand, and several well-fortified coastal batteries northwest of Cadzand. OKW had contemplated airlifting two parachute battalions on October 15 to eliminate the beachhead won by 9th Canadian Infantry Brigade, but by the time this scheme was hatched it was already too late and so was scrubbed. The division would fight and die alone. The pressure from the Canadians against the ever shortening eastern flank was continuous.

On October 19, 64th Infantry Division withdrew to a new defensive line anchored on the north at Breskens, which extended in a westward arc through Schoondijke, Oostburg, Sluis, and thereafter followed the Leopold Canal to the North Sea. Here, Eberding hoped to stand for several days. The division had suffered heavy losses—3rd Canadian Infantry Division had reported taking three thousand prisoners. Many others had been killed or wounded. Only the greatly narrowed defensive front made it possible to offer any organized resistance.[29]

THE GERMAN WITHDRAWAL in the Pocket was discovered by 52nd British (Lowland) Division's 157th Infantry Brigade patrols on October 19, which found Eede and Middelburg abandoned. Shortly thereafter, the 7th Canadian Reconnaissance Regiment entered Aardenburg without incident.[30] It was the same across the entire line of 3rd Canadian Infantry Division's advancing battalions. Where the Germans had previously stood and fought for every little village or defensible position, they had now melted away. Major General Dan Spry pushed forward rapidly to control the surrendered ground, and began planning an assault on Breskens.

Although 9th Canadian Infantry Brigade was badly worn by the hard fighting since the October 9 amphibious landing near Hoofdplaat, Spry required it to carry out this last attack before gaining a rest. The brigade was to simultaneously capture Breskens and Schoondijke, about three miles to the south. Once these objectives were taken, 7th Canadian Infantry Brigade—returning to duty after a short relief period—would pass through and clear the entire coastal area northeast of Cadzand. Simultaneously, 8th Canadian Infantry Brigade would seize Oostburg, Sluis, and then Cadzand itself. From Cadzand, 8 CIB would then swing south, and with the coast to the right and the Bruges–Sluis Canal to the left, march to the Leopold Canal, eliminating any German resistance it met.

To give the offensive armoured teeth, First Canadian Army had secured the services of 79th British Armoured Division's specialized tanks—nicknamed "Hobart's Funnies" in homage to their eccentric creator and commander, Major General Percy Hobart. These included what was called either the Crab or Flail, a tank fitted with a rotating cylinder to which long chains had been attached that churned up the ground ahead to detonate mines. There was also the Petard, a turretless Churchill tank chassis mounting a short-barrelled 12-inch demolition gun that fired a 40-pound, square-shaped round. The Petard was a fortification-buster. Other modified Churchills carried an array of specialized bridging systems for quickly establishing crossings over waterways and trenches. The Crocodile was a Churchill with its machine gun replaced by a flamethrower. A Conger could detonate whole swaths of mines by launching a 300-foot canvas hose in a straight line with a five-inch rocket. The hose was then pressurized with liquid nitroglycerine and detonated, creating an eighteen-foot wide corridor. All of these "Funnies" were made available.

The capture of Breskens was assigned to the Stormont, Dundas and Glengarry Highlanders, while the Highland Light Infantry would advance on Schoondijke. The North Nova Scotia Highlanders were in reserve. Artillery consisting of four field regiments, four medium regiments, and two heavy regiments was assembled. Air support would be extensive, with major raids against the coastal gun positions across the West Scheldt at Vlissingen and Typhoon fighter-bombers attacking targets throughout Breskens.[31]

At an October 20 morning O Group, Lieutenant Colonel Roger Rowley broke the news to the Glens that an expected rest was out. Nothing, he said, "could be further from the truth. We have to get Antwerp. The decision has been made on a high level that Breskens will be taken this week... regardless of Flushing [Vlissingen], Schoondijke." He went on to describe the overall Allied strategic situation, with the conclusion "that we are in a critical position, worse in some ways than the situation in 1918," when manpower and supply shortages almost broke the Allied back. "We can not break through the Germans at the rate we are going," Rowley warned. "We can 'dominate' the situation, but little more. It is a matter of supply and material." Antwerp had to be unlocked and seizing Breskens would be a major step in that direction.[32]

Not that Rowley thought the task easy. He described Breskens as a heavily fortified city, surrounded by an antitank ditch, an extensive network of minefields, tangles of barbed wire, and pillboxes. Rowley and Spry put together a complex attack that wove the Funnies intricately into individual company assaults. Each platoon was provided with a man-packed flamethrower called a Lifebuoy for additional punch. Even with all this added firepower, Rowley thought the operation likely to fail and that casualties would be terrific.[33]

Then came terrible news. The 284th Squadron, Royal Engineers tasked with supporting 9 CIB had harboured for the night in a farmyard near Ijzendijke on October 19. In the morning, a convoy from the Royal Canadian Army Service Corps joined it to deliver supplies of food, ammunition, petrol, and highly volatile liquid nitroglycerine. Shortly after 1300 hours, while the engineers and truckers unloaded cargo from the trucks, the farmyard was shattered by a tremendous explosion. The farmhouse and outbuildings collapsed, tanks and trucks were engulfed in flames and exploded, an adjacent orchard was set afire, and men were torn asunder or turned into human torches.

Thrown twenty feet into the air by the blast, Engineer Sergeant Harry Prince had clawed wildly for any kind of purchase as he soared towards the farmhouse. Then the building disintegrated and he whacked hard onto the ground in front of it. Two women stumbled out of the ruin, one with clothes shredded and blood pumping out of a wound in her breast. Prince staggered over to her and applied a shell dressing. The devastation was horrendous. Three tanks and seven trucks were wrecked. No trace of the truck carrying the nitroglycerine remained. Sixteen Canadians and thirty British died outright or were mortally wounded, the bodies of seven of the Canadians and nine Britons having been completely vapourized. Another thirty-eight men were injured. Miraculously, no civilians were killed. Although six tanks remained operational, and the surviving engineers offered to form ad hoc crews, 79th divisional command ordered the squadron withdrawn from the operation.[34]

Rowley learned the news hours later. He immediately went to Spry, who agreed that the attack must be delayed until the devastated squadron could be replaced. While Spry sought approval from II Canadian Corps commander Major General Charles Foulkes, Rowley went to a dinner that more resembled a wake. At 2100 hours, while still eating, news came that the operation was postponed twenty-four hours. Rowley relaxed, and for about half an hour everyone "had a hell of a good time" before another signal came in announcing "the operation is now on." Rumours flew that the order emanated from corps, others that it was made at army level, while some even saw the personal hand of Winston Churchill at play. Rowley spent most of the night jiggering his plan into one that could be carried out by infantry alone.[35]

RAIN FELL FROM a slate-grey sky the morning of October 21 as the Glens formed to attack Breskens. At 0930 hours, the massed artillery opened up on the little port town with a terrific bombardment. At the same time, the sky began slowly clearing, reassuring Rowley that the promised air support should be available. No sooner did he begin to think this, however, than he received a signal that the bombers tasked with attacking Vlissingen would be delayed and so would the Typhoons aimed at Breskens and its harbour area. The artillery kept firing, though, and at 1000 hours, 'A' and 'C' Companies moved forward. Immediately, the coastal guns at Vlissingen began ranging on the advancing infantry. The two heavy regiments instantly shifted their guns towards Walcheren Island, which caused the German gunners to forget about the Glens and enter into an artillery duel. Twenty minutes later, the Vlissingen batteries fell silent.

By that time, RAF had Spitfires over Breskens, but it looked to Rowley as if they were just strafing with machine guns. There were no Typhoons. Rowley bluntly messaged that he "would like to see rockets in use." After ten minutes, the fighters roared off, leaving him "of the opinion that...the air programme...was a farce." He was reassured by 9 CIB headquarters that Typhoons would "be over with rockets in a few minutes."

Despite the haphazard air support, the leading companies progressed well, reaching their first objective to the front of the antitank ditch that ringed Breskens. It was a formidable obstacle—thirty feet wide and filled with water twelve feet deep.[36] The warming air had created a ground mist, so when the Typhoons appeared at about 1050, it was difficult to accurately engage any targets. But the mist also frustrated German attempts to zero in on the Glens. Intermittently, the Vlissingen batteries sent over salvos and the heavy artillery regiments quickly responded with counterbattery fire.[37]

'B' Company passed through 'A' Company, and headed for a bridge crossing the antitank ditch that allowed entrance into the town. Although standing, the bridge was heavily damaged—its deck riddled with holes and draped in aprons of barbed wire. A German machine gun in a farmhouse to its left raked the approach.[38] As the gun position was well south of the direction of the attack, brigade ordered the North Nova Scotia Highlanders to take it out. The North Novas' 'B' Company quickly silenced the gun and took four prisoners, but in moving towards the farmhouse, it was caught by friendly artillery fire that wounded six men.[39]

It was now 1145, and Rowley was urging the Glens' 'B' Company "to get across the bridge." All the companies were slowing down, at times having to wait for teams of engineers to clear paths through dense thickets of mines. 'C' Company managed to get over the antitank ditch by throwing a kapok bridge across. The company made the crossing single file and up close to the seawall that sheltered the main harbour, a move that caught the Germans by surprise.

'B' Company was soon on the damaged bridge, but reported it "useless. It is heavily mined and fortified with obstacles. The engineers can do nothing with it." Like 'C' Company, it got across using a kapok bridge. After clearing the houses on one short street, 'B' Company came under heavy fire from a 20-millimetre anti-aircraft gun that pinned one platoon down. Sergeant Francis Keilty and Private Val Perry were killed by its first salvo, while Sergeant Begg and a couple of men from his section were trapped inside a pillbox they had just cleared. Every time they tried to slip out, the gun spattered the concrete position with fire that forced them back inside.

Corporal "Frosty" Campbell, experiencing his first day of combat, was moving towards the pillbox, unaware that Begg and his men had already taken it. With mortar bombs landing all over the place and the flak gun drenching the area with deadly fire, he had little idea where anyone other than his five-man section was situated. Figuring the pillbox still in German hands, Campbell told his men to fix bayonets, and they charged the position. They got inside without a scratch, and fortunately neither group of Glens inflicted any casualties on the other. Inexplicably, the moment Campbell's men reached the pillbox, the anti-aircraft gun fell silent and was not heard from again. Soon every section of 'B' Company reported itself inside one of the many pillboxes strung across their line on the edge of Breskens. They were deluxe affairs, one so large that a horse was tethered inside. The Glens tried chasing it out to make room, but it kept barging back in to avoid the thick fire cutting the air. Nobody had the heart to shoot the animal. In another pillbox, a section reported finding it outfitted with running water, modern toilet facilities, six bicycles, and six "healthy Germans" who had meekly surrendered.[40]

At 1245, RAF medium bombers appeared over Vlissingen and pounded the batteries with explosives. Rowley was finally satisfied, deeming it a "lovely show. The place is going up like a hot cake." Typhoons, too, were doing good work now that the ground mist had lifted. They swooped down out of the sunny sky and "shot up three guns and hit an oil dump," along with other targets.

Brigadier John Rockingham arrived at battalion headquarters at 1410 to discuss the progress. He and Rowley agreed that, although behind schedule, Breskens was being taken faster than might have been expected, given the fortifications. The biggest problem was the bridge. Until the engineers—working under intermittent fire—could remove the mines and patch the deck, there was no way to get the antitank platoon across, or a troop of 79th Armoured Division Crocodiles that had arrived.

At 1440, the Germans pulled a favourite trick on the Glens when two antitank guns opened up from positions to the rear of the rifle companies. Positioned inside well-camouflaged concrete bunkers, their crews had allowed the infantry to go past before opening up on the units operating in the rear. With the bunkers impervious to artillery fire and considered too close to friendly forces to have the Typhoons strafe them, Rowley was forced to pull two platoons back from 'D' Company, which had moved up to strengthen the attack shortly after noon, to silence the guns. At 1625 hours, 'D' Company reported the guns taken care of.

Sporadic skirmishing persisted throughout Breskens and the harbour area, but it was clear by nightfall that the Glens had carried the day. 'D' Company had complete control of the harbour, its platoons strung along the pier. 'B' Company had taken the hardest hit in the fighting, reporting twenty-two casualties. About 150 prisoners had been taken, and an undetermined number of Germans killed.

The engineers reported the bridge open at 2150 hours, and the antitank platoon moved to take up positions in Breskens. In the morning, the Crocodiles would cross. Soon after the bridge opened, both Major General Dan Spry and Brigadier Rockingham congratulated Rowley on his battalion's performance.[41]

Everyone was surprised that the Germans had failed to detonate an extensive array of demolition charges spread throughout the port facilities. The port remained functional. Rowley could only think that the heavy artillery fire throughout the day had prevented the German sappers from igniting them. In fact, it seemed by the nature of the opposition that everything had been put into the "shop window" of the antitank ditch, and once that was defeated, organized resistance had largely collapsed.

Despite Rowley's initial dissatisfaction with the air support provided, by the end of the day RAF's fighter squadrons had flown 232 sorties in support of 3 CID—most directly backing up the Glens. There had also been heavy bomber strikes on Vlissingen, similar attacks by medium bombers against the coastal batteries near Cadzand, and Typhoon strafing runs against Fort Frederik Hendrik, immediately west of Breskens.[42]

"It has been a good day," wrote the Glens war diarist. "Night finds the boys in good heart, tired, but pleased... despite the fact that they haven't managed to have much to eat all day."[43]

[20]

To the Last Cartridge

MORNING OF OCTOBER 22 found the Stormont, Dundas and Glengarry Highlanders cautiously clearing the streets of Breskens and meeting little resistance. Occasionally, a German anti-tank gun tried taking them on, but the infantry just dodged into cover and left it to the Crocodiles to burn the gunners out. Mines and booby traps were plentiful, keeping the engineers busy. While tedious, sometimes dangerous work, none of it was especially taxing—what the men found more difficult was the sight of Breskens itself. The town was "utterly destroyed, perhaps the most complete destruction of any town we have yet passed through. The destruction wrought by the heavy bombers and the arty of both sides is terrific."

West of Breskens remained Fort Frederik Hendrik. Built by Napoleon in the early 1800s, the Germans had modernized its defences while taking advantage of the historically thick earthen walls and ramparts, surrounding moat, and excellent firing positions. Strategically positioned, Breskens harbour could not be used until it was taken. As First Canadian Army's plan for assaulting Walcheren Island hinged on using the harbour as a launch point for an amphibious assault against Vlissingen, Lieutenant General Guy Simonds had ordered the fort taken as quickly as possible. Patrols from the Glens' 'C' Company warily approached the outer defensive works at

1100 hours and reported no opposition, which nurtured hopes that it might have been abandoned.

Actually taking the fort fell to the North Nova Scotia Highlanders. Around noon, Lieutenant Colonel Don Forbes had his driver take the jeep right through Breskens and practically to the edge of the moat. Standing there, calmly smoking his pipe, Forbes looked the place over and liked nothing he saw. No shots were fired in his direction, and a Red Cross flag flapping in the breeze above one building signalled that it was a hospital. But scouts said the flag had only gone up earlier in the day, so Forbes decided the supposed hospital would be his first objective, and sent 'D' Company towards it, with 'C' Company in reserve. The lead platoon under twenty-five-year-old Lieutenant Gordon Ross Creelman almost made it to the building before being forced back by heavy machine-gun and mortar fire. Creelman was fatally wounded. A cautious and thorough leader, Forbes drew his men back. He would arrange heavy fire support and try again the next day. Urgent demands from army headquarters aside, Forbes saw no need to recklessly waste lives.[1]

South of Breskens, 9th Canadian Infantry Brigade's third battalion tossed caution entirely away with a direct assault on Schoondijke at 1530 hours. Knowing the village had been heavily fortified, the Highland Light Infantry hoped to bounce it by hitting hard and fast. 'B' Company met heavy opposition, but put its flamethrowers to work, and the Germans either surrendered or were burned to death in their dugouts. By 1800 hours, the HLI controlled the town centre, and despite heavy shelling, reported "remarkably light" casualties. To bring vehicles into the town, a bulldozer had to first push the streets clear of tons of rubble from collapsed houses. At 2100 hours, Lieutenant Colonel Phil Strickland reported the town "almost completely in our hands."[2]

Seizing Schoondijke was the second-last task Major General Dan Spry had set for 9 CIB before it would be withdrawn for a deserved rest. Fort Frederik Hendrik was the final job. The North Novas tried again with another attack by 'D' Company on October 23, but were stopped cold by fierce artillery and mortar fire and what seemed a maze of machine guns spread across the line of advance. Forbes pulled the company back and put in place a plan to subject the fort to a massive air and artillery bombardment. The main problem was the German artillery, which, the battalion war diarist noted, "he throws at us wherever we go." There seemed no end to the guns the Germans could call.

October 24 dawned a grey, dank day with heavy overcast. "Poor day for bombing," the war diarist remarked. The rifle companies hunkered inside battered buildings on the edge of Breskens, trying to sleep, waiting for the fire program. 'A' Company would lead the attack and Forbes had arranged for it to be supported by Flails, Petards, and Crocodiles. The ceiling remained low, however, and the job was put off to the next day.

Everyone was ready to finish the matter that morning, but just as Forbes got ready to give the signal that would bring down a storm of hellfire upon Fort Frederik Hendrik, word came that the Glens had taken some prisoners who claimed that its garrison had withdrawn and only fifty men, eager to surrender, remained. A patrol soon came back with all the Germans in tow. The Novas' 'A' and 'B' Companies went in, combed the fortress works, and came out without finding anybody or firing a single shot. The job done, Spry told Forbes to prepare his men for a move to Ijzendijke for a short rest. 9 CIB was relieved.[3]

THE GERMANS HAD been forced to abandon Fort Frederik Hendrik to avoid encirclement by an unexpectedly rapid Canadian advance cutting across its flank to the south. On October 23, 7th Canadian Infantry Brigade had returned to the fray, after travelling by truck from its rest areas around Biervliet along badly potholed dirt roads running along the tops of the dykes. "Occasionally," recorded the Canadian Scottish Regiment's war diarist, "we would pass through an area where bodies had still not been buried. The sickening smell of dead humans and animals would form a vision of slaughter in our mind's eye as we hurried on. Villages which crowded the edges of the dykes were often found to be completely uninhabitable. The few civilians who were seen poking about disconsolately in the ruins of their homes would only sometimes wave. They had been left with nothing. So different from the wide parts of France and Belgium relatively untouched by War's ravages."[4]

During the few days away from the front, 7 CIB had received many reinforcements and was almost back to full strength. The Can Scots, for example, reported having 805 men, which put it just 45 below normal. Although quality remained low, morale was surprisingly high, with the return to combat seen as positive because "every advance means that the pocket of enemy resistance is decreasing and Antwerp's harbour facilities are soon to be used."[5]

Not that anyone expected clearing the rest of Breskens Pocket to be easy, but there was a sense that keeping the pressure on could prevent development of another stout defensive line. Major General Dan Spry had correctly concluded that Generalmajor Knut Eberding's last-ditch plan was to use Oostburg as a pivot upon which he could slowly swivel a fighting withdrawal of 64th Infantry Division's units on the left flank back from one system of concentric dykes to another, until he was forced into the heavy fortifications at Cadzand. Executed well, this would force 3 CID to mount an endless series of frontal attacks that would grind its strength down while costing the Germans little.

Spry had no intention of giving Eberding time to implement this plan. No sooner was Breskens in hand than 8 CIB struck hard against Oostburg to knock the Germans off their pivot and then punch through to Sluis and Cadzand. At the same time, 7 CIB passed through 9 CIB to advance along a two-mile-wide front west along the coast from Breskens. Spry believed the many coastal fortifications were directed towards the sea, and that if 7 CIB hugged the shore closely, it could outflank the Germans and quickly gain Cadzand. With Cadzand threatened by two pincers, the Germans would be unable to mount an effective defence.[6]

The 64th Division might be badly cut up, but its troops had repeatedly demonstrated resilience and determination to fight to the end, so a tough fight was expected. Leading the way for 7 CIB, the Royal Winnipeg Rifles crossed the Breskens–Schoondijke road on October 23 at 0930 hours, with 'A' Company on the left and 'B' Company on the right. 'A' Company came under immediate fire from an antitank gun and numerous snipers that slowed it to a crawl.

No. 7 Platoon finally took cover in a small building across from a solid brick structure crawling with snipers. Rifleman John Hayward stuck his Lee Enfield out the window "to try for a shot, and immediately a sniper shot a bullet through the forestock of the barrel."

Hayward's lieutenant told him to hit the building with the PIAT gun. The soldier lay on the floor facing a door, while Rifleman Hank Grant loaded the two-and-a-half-pound hollow-charge bomb. "When they opened the door, I aimed at the snipers' area and fired, but the bomb just landed in front of us in the street. Hank had neglected to hook the retaining ring in the clip. The door was slammed shut and the PIAT reloaded. This time I delivered a bomb into the brick building and we heard no more from the snipers."

The company started moving. "We were running and shooting and I jumped over a low wall," Hayward recalled. "When I was still in the air, I knew I was going to land on a dead German. In a flash of time, I noticed several things about him. He was lying on his back with his mouth open, and had a perfect set of white teeth. He was a fine looking chap, with features similar to those of my uncle back in New Brunswick. He had several wounds and his arm had been blown off just below the elbow. I managed to scramble off him as soon as I landed.

"I ran between some buildings and saw a German run into a small building, and I ran behind him with my rifle. He gave me a look as if to impart that he was superior to me, and was not about to surrender. I threatened to lay the bayonet into him, and he changed his mind." The German was a lieutenant, "not much older than I was, and he had a flesh wound in his upper arm. I took his pistol and waited until he bound his wound with a black scarf to stop the bleeding. I then marched him out and turned him over to some other boys who were guarding a bunch of prisoners."[7] 'A' Company kept pushing, but its advance was painfully slow, and by 1400 hours little ground had been won because of the constant fire from the antitank gun. After nightfall, Lieutenant Colonel Lochie Fulton had 'C' Company outflank its position, and after a stiff firefight the gun was captured.

'B' Company had begun its advance by moving through the hamlet of Kruisdijk west of the road and heading north towards the village of Boerenhol, only to have to fight for control of every farmhouse in its path. Manned dugouts and slit trenches were everywhere. Both sides took heavy casualties, but the Winnipegs ended the day with about fifty prisoners from the 1037th Grenadier Regiment. And, by day's end, 'B' Company was on the village's outskirts.[8]

Right of the Winnipegs, the Can Scots had an easier time—more troubled by Vlissingen's coastal batteries than German infantry. Only one man was wounded on October 23. Morning brought an unusual problem when the quartermaster was unable to get rations up to the rifle companies, less because of the artillery than the mud. "Truly it is a deep mud," complained the war diarist, "that bogs a carrier." The troops advanced hungry.[9]

The day mirrored the previous one, with the Can Scots meeting little resistance, while the Winnipegs found every house in Boerenhol had to be cleared in bitter fighting that kept 'B' Company tangled up for the entire day. 'A' Company, meanwhile, advanced at noon due west towards Groede. Rifleman Hayward's section had a new man, nineteen-year-old Leslie Frank Bull of Penticton, British Columbia. Although Hayward was only three years older, he found himself treating Bull like a younger brother. Yet Bull proved himself resourceful, producing eggs scavenged from a henhouse. "We'll cook these later on," he said, carefully putting them into his mess tin.

"They'll probably be scrambled after this do," Rifleman Bob Chisamore replied, as he passed around a tin of bully beef that served as the section's lunch. Forming up in an extended line, 'A' Company started running across a mucky field behind a thin smokescreen laid down by the company's two-inch mortars. Beside Hayward, Bull was panting. "I'm not going to make it," he gasped. Hayward grabbed a Bren gun from his hands to lighten the young man's load. Even carrying a Sten in one hand and the Bren in the other, he outdistanced Bull, and threw himself into some cover just as an 88-millimetre shell whistled in behind. Looking back, Hayward saw Bull fly twelve to fifteen feet off the ground. He and Chisamore both felt terrible. They had been trying to look after "this young fellow" and still he got killed.[10]

Soon after the advance towards Groede began, a German medical officer approached and told a Winnipeg rifle company commander that there were many civilian refugees in the town, and a military hospital that contained both Canadian and German casualties. Blindfolded, he was taken to a crossroads to meet Brigadier Jock Spragge. Through an interpreter, the German asked that the town be evacuated through the Canadian lines. Spragge didn't like this idea because it "would necessitate a truce and would play into the enemy's plans of stalling." He countered that Groede should be "considered an open town. It would not be attacked nor would any tanks enter it. If our advance is resisted," Spragge warned, "it will be dealt with most severely." The two officers agreed with a handshake. The Can Scots then advanced north of the town while the Winnipegs slipped past to the south.[11]

Night found the Winnipegs' 'A' Company hunkered down behind a nameless dyke. Hayward wrapped himself inside a musty-smelling German greatcoat for a blanket. There had been a couple of close calls. A small chunk of shrapnel had cut through the tongue of one boot and lodged in the top of his foot. Then a bullet had chipped the boot heel off. Chisamore broke open a box of rations, and Hayward ate a can of cold rice before trying to get some sleep.

Reveille came at 0100 hours on October 25, and the company was soon walking single file along the dyke until it reached another one that angled off to the right. Hayward's platoon commander told him to take his section up close to some buildings and then clear them at first light. Once his men were in place, he was to come back and report. Hayward and his men crept through the darkness until the buildings loomed ahead of them. Once he was sure everyone was under good cover, Hayward went back. The officer said, "You're not nearly close enough yet."

"I can see the buildings quite plainly," Hayward shot back.

The platoon sergeant, A.F. Richardson, didn't like his tone. "Take your section right in close, Hayward."

Not liking the order, Hayward returned to his men and they crawled forward another fifty yards. From twenty yards to their front, a German sentry rose up in a slit trench and hissed a challenge. Hayward cut him down with a Sten gun burst. Chisamore was there at his shoulder as the two men charged the German position. Together, they chucked four grenades and then blazed away with their Stens. Both men were yelling, trying to terrify the enemy by sounding like Comanches. Chisamore burned through his two magazines, so Hayward passed him one of his remaining five. From somewhere behind them, Sergeant Richardson was shouting: "Give them hell, Hayward." A bullet tore through Hayward's pants and opened a gash above his left knee. He swivelled, firing his last magazine. Something hit hard, knocking him flat. There was an "awful flash and a terrific explosion right near me. 'Bob, I'm hit,'" he called.

Next he knew, Rifleman Elmond Joseph Choquette was applying a field dressing to a deep wound in his left thigh. The twenty-six-year-old Choquette told Hayward, "It's alright, kid, you're going to be okay." Hayward was soon having another three wounds bandaged in the Regimental Aid Post, and that was the end of his war. Choquette was killed three days later, and Murray Hector Robert Chisamore on April 7, 1945.[12]

There was little in those days of 7 CIB's advance along the coast to make one stand out in memory from the rest. Just a seemingly endless network of concrete pillboxes, dugouts, fortified houses, and reinforced emplacements behind the cover of dykes that all had to be cleared in turn. The approaches were always "covered with numerous minefields and liberal amounts of barbed wire and anti-personnel mines. Farther inland, the flat, open, flooded polder country again restricted armoured support to a secondary role. So far the fight had been, and was to continue to be, one where infantry was pitched against infantry," the Can Scot regimental historian wrote. "It was a case of constant prodding and patrolling, seeking ways through, over or around minefields and flooded areas, and enduring shelling from the enemy's supporting and coastal guns."[13]

WELL SOUTH OF 7 CIB, 8th Canadian Infantry Brigade's Queen's Own Rifles struck Oostburg on October 26, following unsuccessful attempts to gain a toehold there the previous day. 'A' and 'B' Companies led, going up an open road behind a heavy smokescreen. One of the Wasps supporting 'A' Company struck a mine and two of its crew died.[14] Lieutenant Jack Boos's No. 8 Platoon was out ahead, with the other two platoons providing covering fire from the flanks to help it cross the open ground and get into the buildings. About a hundred yards short of the town, Boos's platoon took control of the farm. No. 9 Platoon jumped forward to secure the two-acre spread of buildings, fields, and hedges, and sent a runner back to the company's tactical headquarters to report. Company Sergeant Major Charlie Martin returned with the runner to the platoons to tell them to make for Oostburg with two platoons out front and No. 7 Platoon providing covering fire from the farmyard.

He got there just in time to see Nos. 8 and 9 Platoons attacking without orders. Lieutenant Boos was right up front with No. 8 Platoon, and Lieutenant Jackie Bland's No. 9 Platoon was spread out across the road and in the parallelling ditches laying down cover fire. There was nothing Martin could do, so he and the runner became spectators watching "a moment out of the war... in fascination." He thought the attack "a wonderful example of an assault, with our men supporting each other in a clever coordination of movement, fire and flanking fire... They had crossed halfway to the houses when the enemy opened up. Then we saw men in action at a speed that was unbelievable. Nobody moved straight ahead. It was left and right. Up and down. Down and roll right. Fire. Then up again. Roll left. Fire. The action was perfect in its timing." In short order, the company was inside the town and white flags were appearing in various upstairs windows. 'A' Company had suffered only a few minor casualties getting into Oostburg.[15] Boos received a Military Cross for this exploit.[16]

But no sooner did they control a good part of the town than the Germans retaliated with heavy artillery fire. Twenty-year-old Rifleman James Barrett was standing next to a brick house with Rifleman Norm Mennard when a shell smashed into the wall. Barrett was killed and Mennard, steel helmet sent flying, suffered shrapnel wounds to his legs and arms. As he reached to retrieve the helmet, the wall collapsed and a brick struck his head. Mennard lost consciousness the moment after he put the helmet back on. When he woke up, CSM Martin and a stretcher-bearer were digging him out of the bricks. Mennard, unaware that he was badly wounded, complained about how much being struck by bricks hurt. The stretcher-bearer retorted, "The government saved the cost of the first shot of morphine thanks to a brick; now here's a real one for you just in case there are no more bricks."[17]

Le Régiment de la Chaudière had supported the QOR attack, its 'D' Company moving into the southern outskirts in the early morning hours by leapfrogging platoons up a three-foot-deep ditch, with the men doubled over to prevent detection. This enabled the company to get in among the buildings unscathed and they quickly cleared the area of surprised Germans. Expecting to be counterattacked, Major Michel Gauvin set up an all-round defence. At 0300 hours, his fears were realized as numerous flares turned night into day and many Germans charged his lines. As the Germans came on, they yelled, "Kamerad, Kamerad," but Gauvin and his men were not fooled into believing these madly running soldiers sought to surrender. 'D' Company's machine-gunners opened fire with long bursts that cut the Germans down in swaths. Then the flares went out, and the battlefield descended into darkness.

A few minutes later, about a dozen Germans were detected inside the French-Canadian perimeter and they began yelling back and forth loudly in an obvious attempt to lure the Chauds into betraying their positions. Gauvin quietly instructed his men to lay low in their slit trenches, and then calmly called a concentration of artillery down on 'D' Company's position that shredded the German infiltrators caught in the open. The few who survived fled to their lines.[18]

Losing Oostburg dealt 64th Infantry Division a hard blow, as 8 CIB pushed southwest towards Sluis and then the coast. With 7 CIB advancing along the coast, the two pincers were on a path to converge around Cadzand. About two miles southwest of Oostburg, 7th Reconnaissance Regiment was also making good progress, having secured a crossing for engineers to construct a bridge over the Uitwateringskanaal to enable its armoured cars to advance on Sluis.[19] On October 26, the Regina Rifles secured the coastal area directly north of Nieuwvliet, forcing abandonment of a large coastal battery and bringing 7 CIB to within two and a half miles of Cadzand.

WITH THE CANADIANS crowding the Germans into an increasingly tight corner from which there was no hope of escape, even the most fanatical Nazi had to question whether dying in these miserable polders served the Fatherland. Many decided there was no purpose, and each battalion reported dramatic daily increases in men taken prisoner. But 64th Infantry Division's orders remained to hold out to the last man and bullet. On the night of October 25–26, the defenders had received welcome support when a fishing cutter and two flat-bottomed motorboats slipped into Cadzand harbour and offloaded 130 tons of ammunition. The following night, four hundred casualties were successfully evacuated by boat to Vlissingen.[20]

The nature of German resistance was increasingly erratic. When the Canadian Scottish passed through the Reginas on October 27 to carry the brigade to within a mile of Cadzand, the advance went well, with thirty-six prisoners taken and a three-quarter-mile gain in the face of scant opposition. 'A' Company was leading, with 'D' Company in trail and the rest of the battalion prowling some distance behind, in case it became necessary to outflank German positions. The wireless hummed with one successful advance reported after another until noon, when suddenly a hellstorm of shells ranged in on 'A' Company from every coastal battery in the Breskens Pocket and even the guns at Vlissingen. Fortunately, the company had just cleared an area riddled with slit trenches and dugouts into which the men dived, but the attack still caused heavy casualties.

When the shelling eased in the mid-afternoon, 'A' Company moved carefully forward with Lieutenant E.W. Schneider's No. 9 Platoon out front. As the platoon edged along a road at the base of a dyke, it was struck by machine-gun fire from all sides. Schneider realized that some Germans had allowed the platoon to pass their positions in order to surround it. The platoon runner, Private Bowling, managed to slip past the gunners to the rear and warn company headquarters. Caught in an uneven contest, No. 9 Platoon resisted fiercely. "They gathered into coordinated groups and answered the enemy with a hail of Bren and rifle fire. But the uneven battle could not last. Their ammunition was soon exhausted, their position on the open below the muzzles of the German machine guns untenable." Twelve men managed to escape, but Schneider and the rest were either killed or taken prisoner. At nightfall, 'D' Company took the area without incident, rounding up thirty-five prisoners. The battalion had taken its heaviest casualties since the Leopold Canal, four killed, five wounded, and forty-one missing.[21]

Just before dark, 'C' Company had pushed out to the left to gain the village of In de Vijf Wegen and outflank the strongpoint that blocked 'A' Company. Night fell when it was still halfway to the objective, so the company dug in to wait for morning. In the predawn of October 28, Lance Corporal Cox led a three-man patrol to the front of No. 14 Platoon to locate the nearest enemy. Fifty yards out, they crept up on a dugout in the side of a dyke and took four sleeping Germans prisoner. Sergeant MacDonald of No. 14 Platoon went forward with a larger patrol to an anti-aircraft position about four hundred yards away, and surprised the crews there, taking them all captive.

The company's subsequent advance to the village turned up no further Germans, and the place itself was abandoned. But within minutes of entering the village, coastal guns brought it under fire. A massive shell blew apart a building that a section from No. 13 Platoon had been searching and wiped it out. Nineteen-year-old Privates James Stanley Myhon and Paul Reiger died, and the others were all wounded. Despite the fact that the road to the village was under the sights of an 88-millimetre gun, Company Sergeant Major C.J. Smith came forward with a jeep and took the wounded to safety.[22]

By mid-morning, 7 CIB was advancing across a broad front, with the Regina Rifles hugging the coast, the Can Scots in the middle, and the Royal Winnipeg Rifles farther inland. The Winnipegs sent patrols to the south and established contact with the North Shore (New Brunswick) Regiment, which was on the northern flank of 8 CIB's advance and closing on Zuidzande, two and a half miles southeast of Cadzand. Resistance was crumbling. The six Canadian battalions each took well over a hundred prisoners this day, and overran several coastal batteries.

In the evening, the "fixed guns of Battery Cadzand were demolished" when it became clear they would be lost the next day. Only a single battery of two 15-centimetre guns manned and defended by nine officers and 243 men of the 203rd Naval Coast Artillery Battalion south of Cadzand remained. When its commander reported by wireless that the battery's ammunition was low, higher command reiterated that "the bridgehead was to be defended to the last cartridge."[23] That night, Generalmajor Knut Eberding moved his headquarters to Knokke-aan-zee, three miles west of Cadzand, in Belgium. Cadzand was abandoned to the Canadians, but several well-fortified positions northwest of the town remained garrisoned by troops determined to offer a final stand. A Regina patrol entered the town the morning of October 29 and learned of the pullout from civilians. Then 7 CIB's battalions turned to eliminating the strongpoints, a task that took three days.[24] Eager to close the Breskens Pocket at last, Major General Spry threw 9 CIB back in on October 31, the Stormont, Dundas and Glengarry Highlanders and the Highland Light Infantry moving through 7 CIB's lines in a drive on Knokke-aan-zee.

The Canadians were now in the odd circumstance of backtracking from Holland into Belgium to clear up the remnants of 64th Infantry Division. Blocking 3 CID's path about midway between Cadzand and the border was a major canal running from the coast inland to the Sluis area. The Glens put 'A' and 'B' Companies across in boats, while engineers spanned the water with a Bailey bridge. On the opposite shore at Fort Hazegras, the Germans were in complete confusion, their communication systems collapsing.

'A' Company quickly seized the ancient fort by following a German two-man patrol across the lowered drawbridge before it could be raised. Most of the garrison was asleep, and when wakened, meekly surrendered. Soon a motorcycle with a sidecar pulled up, and the officer and driver aboard were captured. When a heavily armed platoon marched towards the fort, the Glens allowed the troops to get within twenty yards of the gates before appearing all along the battlements with guns at the ready. The Germans dropped their equipment and entered the fort as prisoners. "A horse-drawn ration wagon that came bringing a meal for the garrison suffered the same fate."[25]

To the south of 9 CIB, Le Régiment de la Chaudière had been ordered to establish a temporary crossing of the canal by jury-rigging a bridge capable of bearing the weight of a Bren carrier. The pioneer platoon tackled the job under fire, fastening together tree trunks and other material scrounged from near the crossing site until they had something that appeared strong. A Bren carrier rolled onto it and promptly crashed through the centre of the deck to settle on the canal bottom while its crew scrambled to safety. The sunken carrier, however, provided a stout support upon which the pioneers piled more trees and timbers, and soon the battalion was able to send men over on foot. At 1300 hours, three companies moved out from the improvised bridge to create a bridgehead wide enough for engineers to come forward and erect a proper Bailey bridge. By evening, this bridge was operational and Le Chaudière had taken 106 prisoners.[26]

The rest of 8 CIB had spent the day clearing the area around Sluis and establishing more bridgeheads across the canal. Sluis itself, with its formidable fortifications, was to be tackled by the North Shores on November 1. 'B' Company led the attack at 0645 hours. The only approach was directly up a road on top of a dyke with flooded polders on either side. Lieutenant Blake Oulton's platoon led, expecting to be hit any moment. The Germans had knocked all the trees lining the road down with explosives, so it was a matter of scrambling over one after the other.[27] Little resistance was offered, however, and the town was secured by 0810. The battalion accepted the surrender of five officers and 312 other ranks.[28]

That night, the Queen's Own Rifles moved into Sluis and formed for an early morning attack that would carry them about five miles forward on a line passing through Westkapelle, to gain the Leopold Canal. At the same time, 9 CIB's Glens and HLI were to envelop Knokke-aan-zee, and then the North Nova Scotia Highlanders would pass through and drive for the last objective to close the Breskens Pocket—Heist, just west of Knokke-aan-zee. Knokke proved a tough nut. It was "honeycombed with strongpoints, pillboxes, and machine gun and anti-tank emplacements." The Glens fought their way up the streets, knocking out one position after another while trying not to rack up unnecessary casualties. This close to the end of a difficult operation, everyone hoped to survive. Although losses in the street fighting were few, the battalion took a hard blow when its headquarters was hit by a high-velocity shell that caused twenty-five casualties. Also wounded were three adult civilians and a five-year-old boy. Five Glens lost their lives that last day.

The HLI also met tough fighting, particularly to the east of Knokke-aan-zee at a strongpoint the Germans had dubbed Little Tobruk. When attempts to negotiate this position's surrender were rebuffed by its commander, an attack was teed up. The main problem was reaching the defenders, well ensconced behind a maze of barbed wire. There was only one solution and Corporal Norman E. Tuttle provided it by spending twenty minutes under fire cutting a gap through the wire, and then leading his platoon through. Tuttle's heroism garnered a Distinguished Conduct Medal. Once the attackers got inside the fort, the Germans surrendered.

Such was not the case, however, when the QOR came up against a pillbox with three-foot-thick walls encircled by concertina wire piled ten feet high and at least three feet deep. Mines rigged with tripwires had been woven through the concertina, and the obstacle itself was ringed by a minefield. When 'A' Company's Company Sergeant Major Charlie Martin saw the position, his instinct was to bypass it and let the Typhoons blast the pillbox apart with bombs. But the order was that the company must take it. Major Dick Medland considered the job suicidal. No way could a team cut a path through that wire without being cut to ribbons by the booby traps and certain machine guns ready to fire out of the pillbox's many apertures. Then someone noticed that the Germans had left a wire gate blocking a paved road leading up to the pillbox unfastened. Studying the road surface, Medland could see that it was free of mines. The major decided that one eight-man section from No. 7 Platoon would lead the attack, and assigned it to Sergeant Jack Meagher. CSM Martin decided to accompany the men.

On the heels of a heavy artillery concentration, the section charged in two small files up the sides of the road. The men went through the gate just as the artillery lifted, and headed for the nearest gun ports with grenades pulled and ready. They were still dangerously distant and might easily have been gunned down. Then, from every opening, white flags began to flutter. The section banged up against the concrete wall, panting for breath and dripping sweat despite the wintery chill. Martin and the others looked at each other and started to laugh. It was over; the "damned Pocket" was closed.[29]

The end had come quickly. About noon of November 1, the North Nova Scotia Highlanders had isolated Eberding's headquarters on the southern edge of Knokke-aan-zee. After four hours' negotiation, the general and his staff surrendered. The last remaining fortification at Heist fell the next day. At noon that day, a final signal emanated from the tattered remnants of 203rd Naval Coast Artillery Battalion. "Have terminated resistance," a voice said. "Scheldt Fortress South had fallen," OKW soon concluded.[30]

Closing the Breskens Pocket had been 3 CID's hardest and most drawn-out battle, one that led Canadian reporters to nickname its men "the Water Rats" because so much of the fighting had taken place in flooded polders. It had been fought against what the division's intelligence staff deemed "the best infantry division we have met." During the long slugging match from October 6 to November 1, 12,707 prisoners had been taken and the German dead were estimated simply as "many." Only a few hundred German wounded were successfully evacuated from the Pocket. Canadian casualties were calculated at 2,077, with 314 fatalities. Another 231 were listed as missing and presumed dead.[31]

Within twenty-four hours, the division was on the move, heading south to Ghent. The new mission was codenamed Operation Relax. Everyone was exhausted, both physically and mentally. With a sense of dazed wonder, the men aboard the convoys entered the city to be greeted by throngs of Belgians cheering and waving flags. Divvied into small groups, each soldier was housed in a private home. For the next five days, everybody was mostly free to carouse in whatever way he pleased in Ghent's many bars and restaurants. Most of the civilian hosts opened their doors willingly, and made a point of preparing sumptuous meals to try to put some meat on the gaunt frames of these weary young soldiers. After an all too brief five days, the division moved again on November 7 for a new battlefront near Nijmegen, about a hundred miles to the east on the Waal River.

At 0950 hours on November 2, a notation had been entered in 3 CID's operational log. "Operation Switchback now complete," it read. In the margin beside, somebody scribbled, "Thank God!"[32]

[21]

Foot-Slogging Jobs

WHEN 3RD CANADIAN Infantry Division kicked off the final leg of closing the Breskens Pocket on October 22 by clearing the port town itself, 2nd Canadian Infantry Division had been still trying to gain control of Woensdrecht. Until the town and height of ground it occupied was taken, cutting the South Beveland isthmus remained impossible. The division was in a bad way after trying to advance across a far too broad front for so long against determined, capable opposition. Had 4th Canadian Armoured Division not come up on its right flank on the morning of October 20, as part of Field Marshal Bernard Law Montgomery's agreement to shift 1 British Corps and British Second Army westward, the advance would have stalled completely. The Royal Hamilton Light Infantry in Woensdrecht had been ground down to a skeletal regiment when the Queen's Own Cameron Highlanders took over on October 22. This battalion had in turn been relieved by 4 CAD, now covering the long front that 6th Canadian Infantry Brigade had been guarding in the area of Kamp van Brasschaat.

As 4 CAD took over this area, 2 CID was able to cease its piecemeal operations and develop a cohesive strategy. Its efforts would now be concentrated against South Beveland, with 6 CIB cutting the isthmus and securing the division's hold on the Brabant Wall "in order to prevent any enemy move to interfere with the clearing of that neck of land." Once this was achieved, 4th Canadian Infantry Brigade would drive across the South Beveland peninsula. 5th Canadian Infantry Brigade would stand in readiness to either pass through 4 CIB to continue the advance or, if "resistance met by 4 [CIB] was too great... make a landing on the peninsula" to outflank the German defenders.[1]

While 2 CID reorganized, 4 CAD starred in the opening act of 1 British Corps's Operation Suitcase—intended to drive the Germans out of the coastal area west of the mouth of the Maas River. To the right of 4 CAD, the 49th British (West Riding) Infantry Division parallelled its advance. As the front loosened, the 104th U.S. Infantry Division and 1st Polish Armoured Division would be committed to clear the area east of Roosendaal to the Maas's mouth.

Major General Harry Foster's plan was classically simple. The division had only two brigades—the 10th Canadian Infantry and the 4th Canadian Armoured—so each would go north about nine miles side by side to Essen, in a knife-like thrust across a narrow front. The armoured brigade would follow the Antwerp–Roosendaal railway and a roughly parallelling road, passing west of Kalmthout, and pausing just north of that town at a crossroad identified as Dorp to establish a firm base. Staying east of Kalmthout, the infantry brigade would have its right flank guided by a second north-south–running road and establish its firm base at the crossroads at Achterbroek, east of Dorp. From these positions, the two brigades would then move on Essen.

Seizing Essen would sever a road the Germans used to move reinforcements and supplies west to the Huijbergen-Woensdrecht area. Once 4 CAD controlled this objective, 49th Infantry Division would take over. This would free the armoured division "to forge ahead to the northwest without delay" in order to capture Bergen op Zoom, on the East Scheldt coast.

Although Foster's operational plan indicated the two brigades advancing independently, the division's composition made the situation less tidy. The armoured brigade consisted of three tank battalions with one infantry battalion attached, while the infantry brigade fielded three battalions of foot-sloggers. Intended to match the pace of tanks during a rapid breakout, The Lake Superior Regiment (Motor) was equipped with an extensive fleet of Bren carriers and other armoured personnel carriers. But Operation Suitcase would be no motorized race across open country. Foster knew the tank brigade needed additional infantry to win the ground, so the Argyll and Sutherland Highlanders were shifted from 10 CIB to 4 CAB. Each infantry battalion would be supported by a Canadian Grenadier Guards squadron. The Superiors would be on the left, the Argylls the right. Meanwhile, 10 CIB Brigadier Jim Jefferson would advance the Lincoln and Welland and Algonquin regiments, with the tanks of the British Columbia Regiment supporting the former and those of the division's reconnaissance regiment (the South Alberta) the latter. The Lincs would move along the western edge of the woods north of Kamp van Brasschaat, while the Algonquins forged through the woods to the right of the road.

Having moved earlier from the Breskens Pocket to lend its armoured teeth to 2 CID, the division's remaining tank battalion—the Governor General's Foot Guards—was to protect 4 CAD's left flank with an advance north from Putte. A squadron of flame-throwing Crocodiles manned by the British 2nd Fife and Forfashire Yeomanry, and Flail tanks from the 22nd British Dragoons would support the offensive. The attack would be preceded by a heavy artillery barrage and, weather permitting, rocket-firing Typhoons and Spitfires would be on call.[2] The 5th Canadian Anti-Tank Regiment would also have three batteries equipped with self-propelled guns advancing behind the infantry and tankers.[3]

While it was a relief to have left the polders and dykes behind, the "land ahead was covered with small woods, sand dunes, and grassy fields. The terrain was flat and there were no great water barriers... However, should the rains be heavy, there would be mud, and plenty of it," the Superiors' regimental historian wrote.[4] "It was country in which one might once more expect to encounter the deadly anti-tank weapons of the enemy, innumerable mines, frequent craters and road blocks, and plenty of opposition should the enemy be disposed to offer it." The ground through which the attack would first pass was mostly dense deciduous woods choked with brambles and saplings.

On the division's left, 4 CAB would face a more complex situation. Kamp van Brasschaat had been a Belgian military training ground with a small airfield. The brigade would have to first advance through the camp's many firing ranges, laced with concrete bunkers that the Germans had transformed into defensive positions. Any open ground could be considered a well-prepared fire zone, while the thick woods—suspected of being riddled with mines—promised to impede movement and separate tanks from infantry.[5]

October 20 dawned cloudy, rainy, and with a ground mist reducing visibility to a few hundred yards. Infantry and tankers formed up on their start lines while artillery fired on predetermined targets for thirty minutes.[6] At 0730 hours, the guns fell silent and the attack went in. On 4 CAD's western flank, the Lake Superior Regiment advanced with 'B' Company leading, followed by 'A' Company. The other two companies remained in reserve. Resistance was light, confined to occasional pockets of infantry that had to be rooted out. As well, the companies were continually harassed by mortar and artillery fire, and slowed more than anticipated by mines.

'A' Company's scout platoon learned the hard way what happened when sandy soil transformed into mud, as two of its Bren carriers slid into a roadside ditch and became hopelessly mired. Even stripping the transmissions out failed to lighten the carriers enough so the platoon could wrestle them free. Finally Corporal A.G. Johnson reported the situation to his platoon commander. On his way back to the carriers, Johnson was cutting through a wood when a German pointing a rifle stepped from behind a tree. Another rifle prodded his back and he was ordered to get marching, one of the Germans holding him by an arm. Although his rifle was back at the carrier, Johnson had a German pistol in the pocket of his greatcoat. Managing to extricate it, he fired a shot at the man beside him, then whirled and shot at the second German, who had lagged well behind. Both men dropped to the ground, and Johnson fled without knowing whether he hit either of them.[7]

For the Superiors, the day was one of frustration. Their advance was slowed to a crawl by the mud that resulted in little distance gained, dampening the spirits of a regiment that prided itself on rapid mechanized operations.

The Argylls to their east hit trouble from the start—moving into an area strewn with mines, and under mortar fire that grew more intense with every passing hour. On the right, Major Alex Logie's 'B' Company entered a dense wood that blocked all wireless transmissions. Most worrisome for Logie was losing contact with a small part of the company operating independently on the right flank in concert with the scout and carrier platoon.

Commanded by Captain Peter Blaker, this section found the crossroads marking its start line not only heavily mined, but covered by German positions in buildings at the intersection. The men immediately went to ground in the woods south of the crossroads. Exploding mortar rounds were shattering trees, and branches and wooden splinters whirred through the air. Casualties mounted fast. Blaker was unable to raise battalion headquarters, talk to the supporting tankers, or get advice from Logie. Recently made 'B' Company's second-in-command, Blaker felt terribly inexperienced and uncertain. "How the hell are we going to get out of this?" he wondered.

Just then, some Flail tanks came up and lashed the road with their great chains. Mines exploded like firecrackers on a string. Blaker knew he could get across the road now, but on the opposite side was a field of scrubby brush probably also sown with mines. His men waited for instructions, but the young officer had frozen, fearing that if he ordered them forward many would die. Then he was listening to the longest whirr of an incoming mortar round he had ever heard. When it struck, Blaker was wounded.[8] Sergeant Earl McAllister was killed soon thereafter.[9]

Blaker realized later that he had been undone by caution and the fear of losing men. What he should have done was to lead his troops in a dash into that field, taking the chance with mines, in an effort to outflank the Germans while having the supporting tanks pound their positions. Men likely would have been killed or wounded, but the whole situation would have been better.

Meanwhile, the carrier and scout platoons farther on the right had stalled when a mine knocked out a Flail tank ahead of them. The carrier platoon commander, Lieutenant Ed Brook, hesitated to have his men cut around it. Taking advantage of this momentary stop, the Germans fired on stationary targets, wounding Brook and Sergeant

Douglas A. Boulton. Later, Brook often wondered "if it was lack of initiative on our part or my part that we didn't proceed more quickly."[10]

'B' Company was badly bogged down, making very slow progress. To its left, however, Major John Farmer's 'D' Company had bypassed several pockets of resistance, and by 1325 hours was a thousand yards ahead. Facing the small hamlet of Kapellenbosch—about midway between Kamp van Brasschaat and Kalmthout—Farmer realized that one company would be insufficient to clear the place, and informed Lieutenant Colonel Dave Stewart that he was waiting for 'B' Company to come abreast. About an hour later, 'B' Company managed to reach 'D' Company, and together they started clearing Kapellenbosch under intensive mortar and sniper fire.[11] The Canadian Grenadier Guards were little help, as the sniper fire forced the tank commanders to keep tightly buttoned up inside their turrets or almost certainly get shot. Captain W.D. MacDonald and Lieutenant J.A.S. Milne were both wounded in this manner, while Guardsman Robert Maskell was killed when he dismounted from his Sherman to check damage from a mine explosion.[12]

Late in the afternoon, Lieutenant Harold Place of 'B' Company was in a trench near one occupied by Logie. The two men were planning, talking back and forth. Logie, who shunned helmets, was wearing an Argyll balmoral. It was something he did often, something other officers had warned him against. The balmoral tempted sniper fire. Today it proved a fatal affectation, for a sniper round struck Logie in the head and he died instantly.[13] Alexander Chisholm Logie was the thirty-eight-year-old son of Major General W.A. Logie, who had helped found the Aryglls in 1903 and been its first commander.

By evening, the Argylls consolidated midway between Kappellenbosch and Kalmthout. It had been a difficult, frustrating day with little ground gained at a cost of thirty casualties. The expectation was that worse would follow in the morning.[14]

THE ADVANCE BY 10th Canadian Infantry Brigade on October 20 had also been at first touch-and-go. On the eastern flank, Lieutenant Colonel W.T. Cromb of the Lincoln and Welland Regiment and British Columbia Regiment commander Lieutenant Colonel C.E.

Parrish decided to steer clear of a triangular wood through which the infantry had originally been to advance, and proceed instead across open country immediately to the west. Once they got past the woods, the force would veer east to anchor its right flank alongside the Algonquins and clear a large hangar on the airstrip before advancing to a position near Groote Heide—a village next to the north-south–trending highway. 'A' Company under Captain Herbert Lambert led off with the Shermans from Captain James Tedlie's 'B' Squadron in support. 'B' and 'C' Companies were in line behind.[15]

Lambert hailed originally from Cincinnati, Ohio, and was considered flamboyant by some, eccentric or even crazy by others. He had taken over 'A' Company on October 9. Normally a gentleman in manner, when provoked he could swear like the roughest dockyard worker. Eschewing a helmet, Lambert went into battle this day wearing a beret and a heavy white woollen scarf around his neck to keep away the chill.

Despite small-arms fire from the woods, 'A' Company made good progress through the open country. But when Lambert reached the prescribed turning point, he kept going straight ahead. Realizing that Lambert was lost, Tedlie hailed him with a correct map reference. This prompted an argument that Lambert reported to Cromb by wireless. Believing that tankers were generally better map readers than infantry officers, Cromb replied that Lambert was wherever Tedlie said.[16] At that point, battalion headquarters lost all ability to talk to 'A' Company, although they could receive its signals and heard Lambert report being on his objective.

Following behind, 'B' Company's Major M.J. McCutcheon and 'C' Company's Major J.L. Dandy recognized Lambert's error and turned at the northern edge of the woods. Unassisted by the tanks, which had remained with Lambert, 'B' Company entered a stiff fight for control of the hangar. No. 11 Platoon engaged in a twenty-minute grenade duel that finally ended with the German defenders driven off. Once the hangar fell, McCutcheon and Dandy both tried unsuccessfully to raise Lambert on their wirelesses to get him moving in the right direction. As they also were unable to contact Cromb, Dandy went back to brief him on the situation. Finally, after repeated efforts, Cromb got through to Lambert and ordered 'A' Company to "repair its error by going to its proper objective."[17]

Lambert's men were spread out single file, trudging steadily northwards with a ten-foot gap between each soldier, when he acknowledged Cromb's order. The officer decided to rectify the situation through an unorthodox manoeuvre by ordering the men to stop where they were and swivel so they faced east towards where 'B' and 'C' Companies were located. He then spaced the tanks at regular intervals along the line and ordered everyone to advance line abreast across the lightly overgrown fields, in which Germans, were dug into a number of positions. As the men advanced, they fired into any likely thickets that could contain Germans, while their commander moved up and down the line inexplicably yelling, "Peanuts, popcorn, and programs." The combined effect of gunfire and ballgame vendor-hailing elicited an unexpected response as one German after another emerged with hands raised. Those who opted to flee from the advancing line were brought under deadly fire by 'B' Company's Sergeant Major Campbell, who had set up a Bren gun to cut off the German line of retreat.[18]

Although 'B' Squadron had one tank disabled by a mine, none of its crew was injured. The tankers were suitably impressed by the stream of prisoners taken, mostly identified as members of 346th Infantry Division, supplemented by some artillery troops fighting as infantry.[19] 'A' Company passed through the other companies and advanced up the road to its Groote Heide area objective. 'B' Company, now supported by the tanks, proceeded another two thousand yards along the road before digging in at 1730 hours. It took about forty prisoners along the way.

The tanks withdrew, as night had fallen and they needed to replenish fuel and ammunition. 'C' Company moved north along the road alone, only to meet strong resistance. To avoid a firefight in the dark, Dandy fell back on 'B' Company's position. Patrols sent out that night established contact with elements of the Algonquins who had succeeded in advancing north to Kruisstraat.[20] During the course of the day, the Lincs had taken about 170 prisoners in exchange for five killed and twenty-three wounded.[21]

In heavy October rain, Calgary Highlanders pass a knocked-out German self-propelled gun in Hoogerheide after they finished clearing the Lindonk on October 27, 1944, in the last stage of the Canadian campaign to free the Woensdrecht-Hoogerheide area. Ken Bell photo. LAC PA-138422.

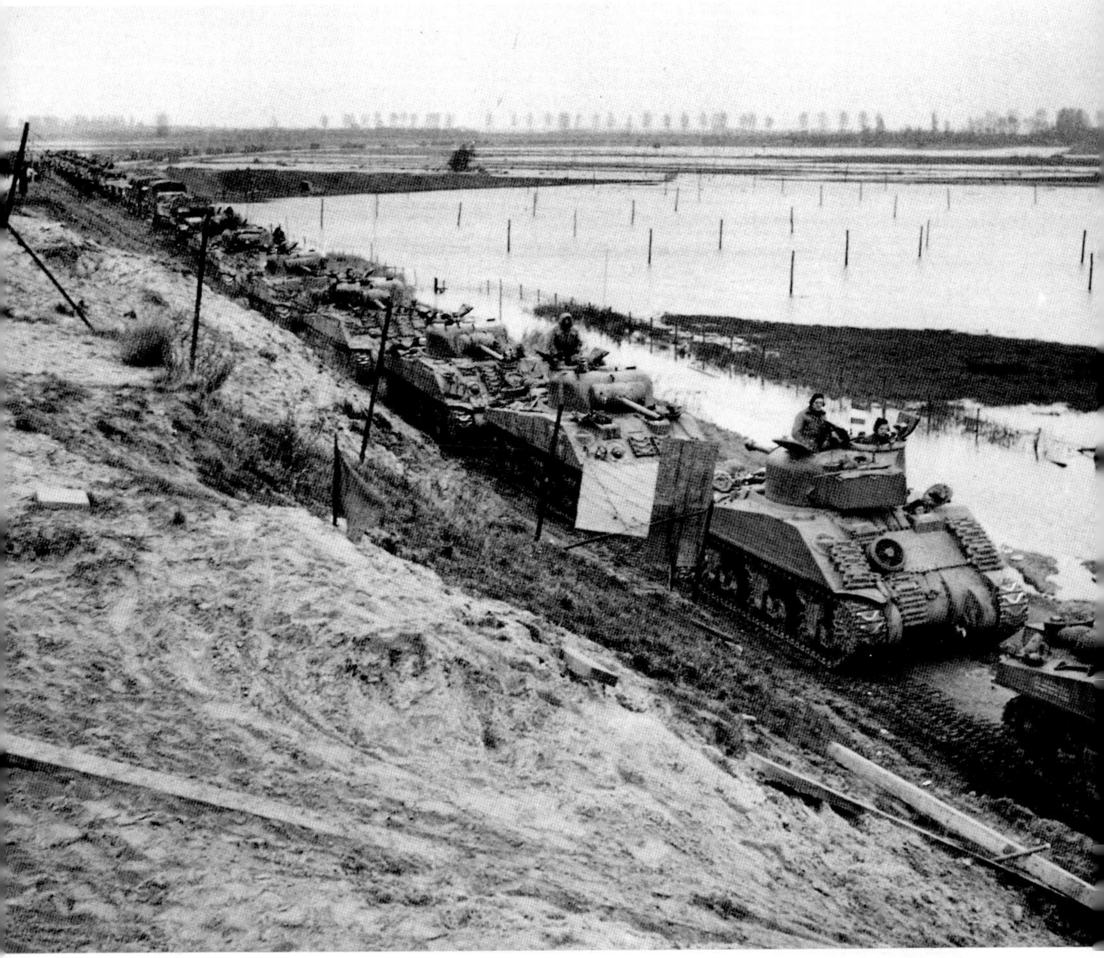

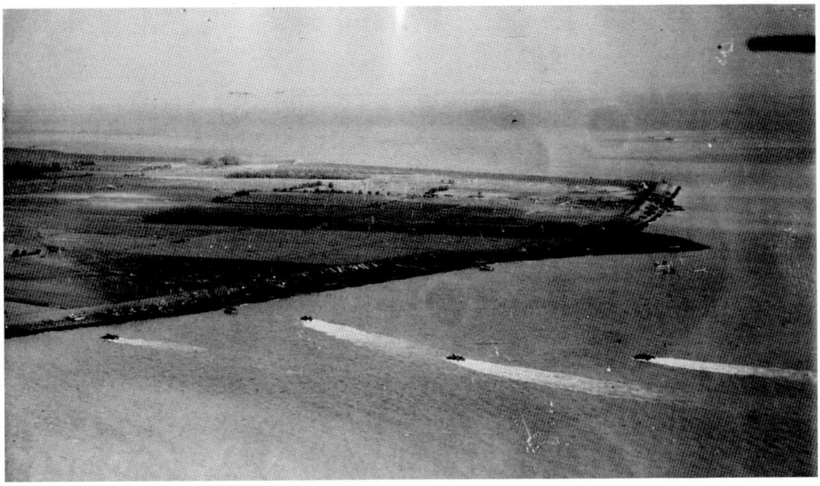

top left · A column of Fort Garry Horse 'C' Squadron tanks, with the South Saskatchewan Regiment following in trucks, advances across South Beveland towards the city of Goes. In the first tank is Sergeant Gregory John Eno (left), who earned a Military Medal in an earlier engagement during the campaign. Next to him is Corporal Weeks. Riding high in the turret of the second tank is Captain J.G. Robson, Eno's squadron commander. Ken Bell photo. LAC PA–138429.

left · Landing craft carry 156th Brigade of the 52nd British (Lowland) Infantry Division across the Scheldt estuary towards beaches on South Beveland. Photographer unknown. LAC E004665474.

above · A dead German lies where he fell in a dugout near the western end of the South Beveland isthmus. Ken Bell photo. LAC PA–138424.

above · A section of men from the Highland Light Infantry waits on one side of a dyke for supporting artillery to cease fire prior to an attack during the advance from Hoofdplaat towards Schoondijke. Hugh H. McCaughey photo. LAC PA–142104.

top right · The Sloedam, or causeway, between South Beveland and Walcheren Island. Ken Bell photo. LAC PA–137151.

right · Privates G.M. Godere and H. Couture administer tetanus anti-toxin shot to Private W.R. Van Horne of the Calgary Highlanders at the Casualty Clearing Post of 18th Canadian Field Ambulance at Lewedorp. Van Horne was wounded in the fighting for the causeway linking South Beveland and Walcheren Island. Ken Bell photo. LAC PA–131260.

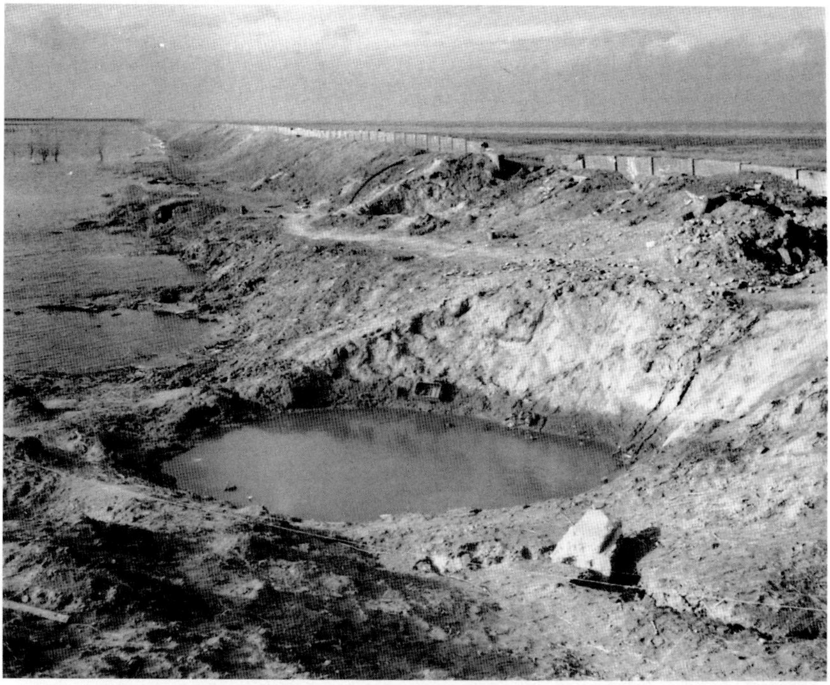

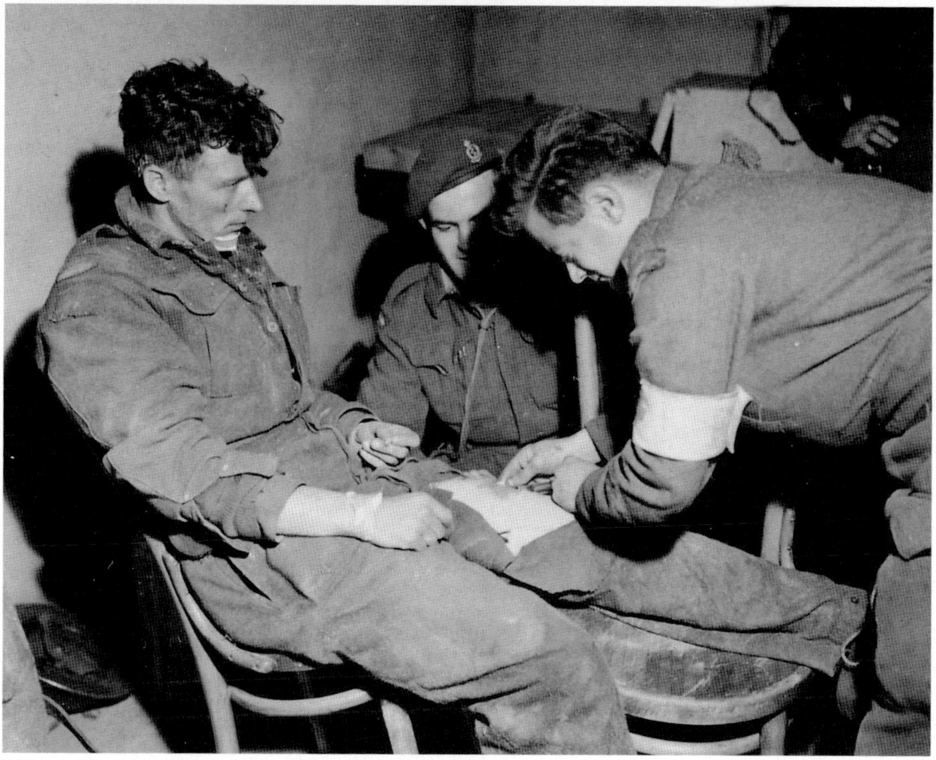

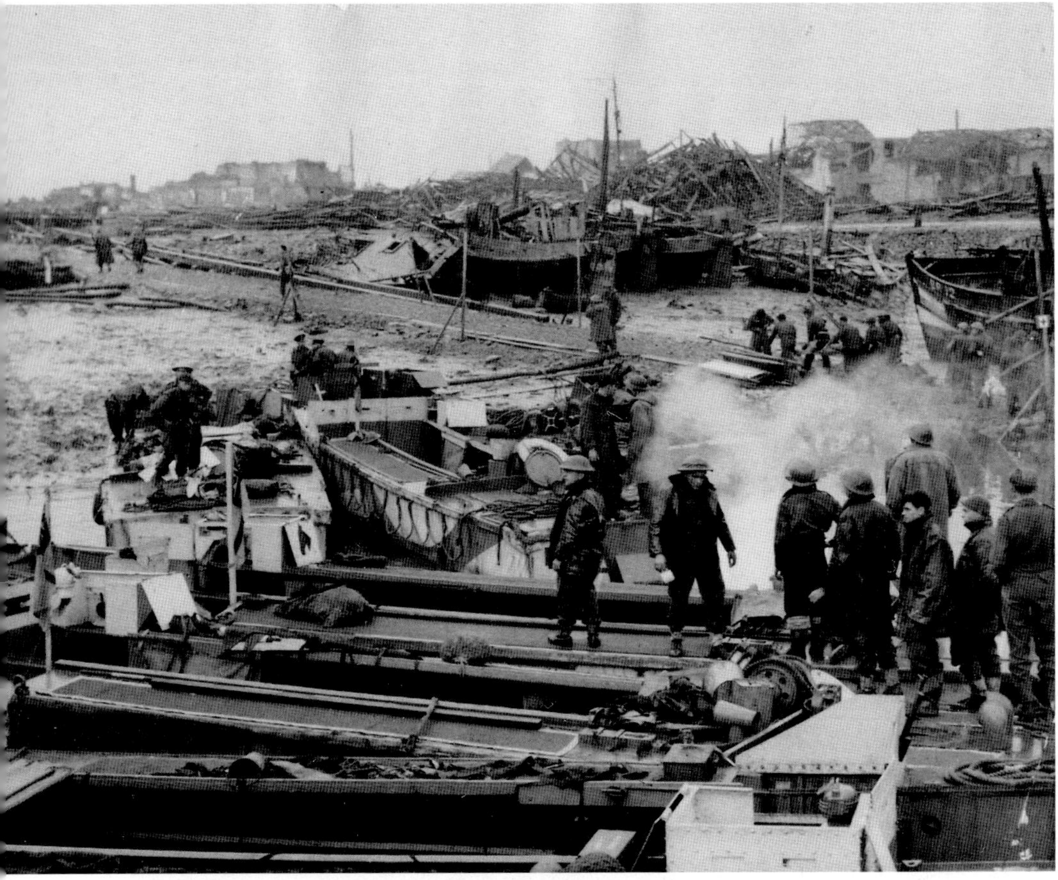

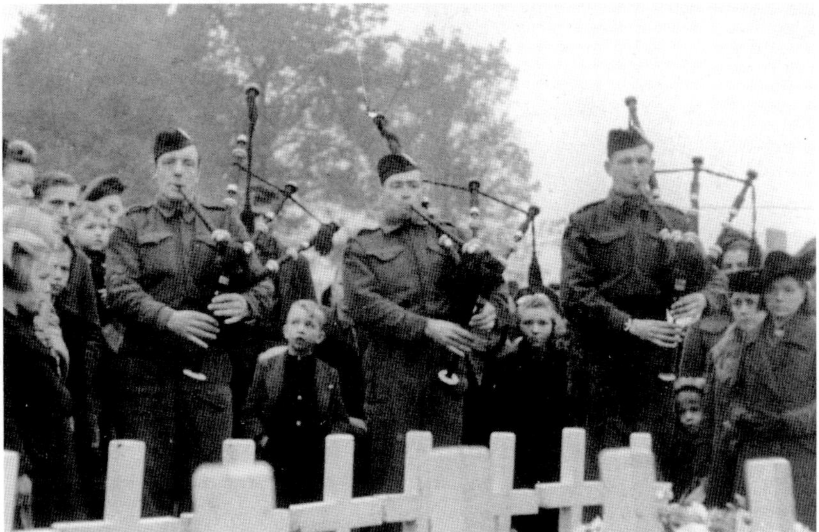

top left · British troops work to ready landing craft for No. 4 Commando's amphibious assault on Vlissingen. Note the extensive damage shelling and bombing have caused to Breskens harbour. Photographer unknown. LAC E004665473.

left · Pipers from the Black Watch play a lament during a burial of the regiment's dead from the disaster of Black Friday, October 13, 1944, at the local cemetery of Ossendrecht on October 26, 1944. L.E. Weekes photo. LAC PA–142112.

above · Sherman tanks and other vehicles from the South Alberta Regiment of 4th Canadian Armoured Division gather in the main square of Bergen op Zoom. Harold G. Aikman photo. LAC PA-138411.

Back home in Canada, Black Watch Corporal John Dubetz (right) with cousin Bill Smithaniuk in naval uniform (centre), and brother Steve Dubetz in the air force uniform (left). The gridlike apparatus close to Dubetz's left hand is part of a special sling supporting his arm, which was badly damaged on Black Friday. Photo courtesy of Al Dubetz.

The Algonquins had struck out from the Maria-ter-Heide Château, about a mile and a half northeast of Kamp van Brasschaat, with 'B' Company going for a set of bunkers right of the road just before the artillery ceased firing. This enabled the troops to get almost on top of the position before the Germans recovered. A sharp firefight ensued that ended with the company in control of the bunkers, but Private John Redden was killed and several others wounded.[22]

'A' Company had been on the move left of 'B' Company and, meeting no resistance, was entering a small wood when a nearby antitank gun fired from a bunker and shells started detonating in the overhead branches. Ahead lay an open field that would provide a perfect killing ground if the company entered it, so the troops were trapped in the deadly wood with casualties mounting by the moment. Realizing that something had to be done, Lieutenant Charles Ratte led a two-man Bren gun team and three riflemen in a direct attack. Charging across the open ground, the men suddenly became mired in deep mud and were struck by fire from a machine gun protecting the antitank gun. Ratte, who had only recently joined the regiment, and Private Joseph Henry were killed instantly. The others were all wounded, Private William John Cosens mortally. Although the team failed to carry out their intention, the boldness of their action so alarmed the Germans that they soon abandoned the gun.[23]

When 'A' and 'B' Companies tried to renew the advance, sniper fire from "all points of the compass" forced them to take cover in the captured bunkers. An attempt by the carrier platoon to clean out the snipers to their rear was thwarted when the lead carrier blew up on a mine. Sergeant Bob McWhirter and Private Roy Duff were killed by the explosion.

'D' Company, heading for a château almost directly behind the positions of the two leading companies, was passing a large tangle of gorse on its right when snipers hidden in its cover opened fire. Sergeant Howard Turner immediately swung a section towards the snipers only to be killed by a bullet. The company went to ground while its commander teed up an artillery concentration on the sniper position. When the shells stopped falling, the company was able to advance another seven hundred yards before running into crossfire from either side of the road. With night falling, Lieutenant Colonel Robert Bradburn ordered the three companies to dig in where they were. 'A' and 'B' Companies scraped out slit trenches in the marshy fields around the bunkers, while 'D' Company slipped into the edge of the forest to get out of the open.

As these three companies had advanced along the road, 'C' Company had been sent to support 'C' Squadron of the British Columbia Regiment in a probe out on the Algonquin left flank that met little resistance. The tankers thought it possible to drive through to Kruisstraat and outflank the Germans blocking the rest of the battalion. It went off as hoped, but not without loss. Nineteen-year-old infantryman Private Edward Dalton Chisholm was killed.[24] So, too, were tankers Lieutenant Ken Clarke and Trooper Clarence Sharrard when their tank was knocked out by an antitank gun.[25]

THE FLANK ATTACK that seized Kruisstraat proved a mixed blessing for 10th Canadian Infantry Brigade because the Algonquins were now divided, with one company up in the village and the other three blocked by strong German forces between. Assessing the situation, Brigadier Jim Jefferson decided to disengage the Algonquins from their current front and pass them through the Lincs to Kruisstraat, and then renew the advance north along the road to Achterbroek. From there, the battalion was to continue towards a rather mysterious watercourse, identified by divisional intelligence as the Roosendaal Canal, that they thought posed a major obstacle. The sooner the canal was secured so that engineers could bridge it, the better.

'D' Company, which had been least heavily engaged during the day, would lead. At 0100 hours on October 21, the company began to carefully extricate itself from the position it had established in the woods. Groping through the darkness, two of its men, Sergeant A.G. Smith and Corporal J.P. Kelly, triggered wooden box mines loaded with just sufficient explosive to tear a foot off. The other two companies were able to pull out without incident, and by dawn the Algonquins were ready to begin their advance.[26]

While the Algonquins were to push through to Achterbroek, the task for the Lincs was now to secure the area behind by patrolling extensively for lingering Germans. Throughout the day, the Lincs gathered more prisoners, mostly men who had deliberately stayed behind to surrender. The biggest impediment was mines—more than the Lincs had ever encountered. By 1430 hours, the mopping-up was deemed complete and the battalion set off for Foxemaat, a village less than a mile south of Achterbroek, which the Algonquins were to have cleared en route to their objective.[27]

From day's outset, divisional command had been relentlessly urging both brigades to hasten the pace to Roosendaal Canal. While the Algonquins pushed hard for the objective, 4th Canadian Armoured Brigade's Lake Superior Regiment had initially balked at orders to get moving at first light with 'A' and 'B' Companies leading. The previous day's hard fighting had taken the men by surprise, especially as they had gone into it as standard infantry rather than aboard their armoured vehicles. Perhaps, confessed the regimental historian later, "the Lake Superiors, who prided themselves on being a motor battalion, just did not like the footslogging jobs that belonged to the run-of-the-mill infantry battalions... as if by common agreement, both companies moved off half an hour late in the general mood, 'well, if the higher-ups want us to move earlier, why don't they come here and move us themselves.'" Not surprisingly, a furious Brigadier Robert Moncel appeared at the regiment's command vehicle and "expressed his extreme annoyance at the failure of the Lake Superiors to move with the speed expected."[28]

Neither the Superiors nor Argyll and Sutherland Highlanders met much resistance, being held up more by roadblocks created by fallen trees and seemingly endless mines. The Algonquins, meanwhile, had first searched Kruisstraat and found it abandoned. With divisional headquarters demanding that the battalion pick up the pace, 'D' Company mounted carriers and the squadron of supporting tanks—the idea being to race up the road to the canal in a single-file armoured column. But as they exited Kruisstraat and approached a sharp bend, Germans armed with Panzerfausts opened fire. The lead tank was knocked out, and another round barely missed a Bren carrier. A hasty attack was organized, and with support from the artillery called in by 15th Canadian Field Regiment's Major Noel

Rutherford, who was serving as the forward observation officer, the enemy position was soon cleared.

Fearing that more infantry armed with antitank weapons lurked in the bordering woods, the tankers "were burning everything in sight, proceeding on an overwhelming barrage of shell and co-axial gunfire," Major George Cassidy, who had recently switched from 'A' Company to command 'D' Company, later wrote. "As the column raced along at about twenty-five miles an hour, over on the far right, we could see the heavy Churchill tanks of 49 British Div. converging on our axis, tossing off huge smokescreens on their own right flank. Nearing the road junction in front of the canal, another enemy outpost was bumped, and a brisk firefight developed."

Lieutenant L.G. Dirassar and Private W.J. Walker were both wounded in this sharp engagement. But as the Algonquins and tankers were slugging it out with the Germans, the wireless was crackling with edicts from division to get on to the canal and send back immediate reports on where a crossing could be constructed, as well as an estimate of how much bridging material would be required. Having cleared out the Germans, the officers near the head of the column were puzzling over where precisely "this most important canal was. The only body of water in the area was a large ditch, perhaps ten feet across, which ran under the road through a culvert." The Germans had not even tried to destroy the culvert with demolitions, so eventually the Algonquins reported that they had in fact secured the assigned canal.[29]

To the left of 10 CIB's line of advance, the Argylls failed to even note when they crossed the canal. The Superiors came across it at 0930 hours, and what "a disappointment it proved to be. The Roosendaal was no Leopold or even [Bruges–] Ghent Canal; it was not much more than a good-sized ditch, about ten feet across and with no more than three feet of water in it." Crossing it easily, the regiment pushed patrols out to the north and found the area largely abandoned.[30]

While 4th Canadian Armoured Division's main thrust towards Essen encountered little determined resistance, the Governor General's Foot Guards advancing on the extreme left flank near Putte had been ambushed when they entered a defile that provided the only means for tanks to pass through a thick wood. No. 2 Squadron commanded by Major G.T. Baylay led the way in, with Lieutenant Collins's troop on point. Moments later, they came under fire from German paratroops armed with Panzerfausts, but were able to keep them at bay with fire from the 75-millimetre guns and machine guns. An antitank gun was also spotted and destroyed before it could open fire, but a second gun went undetected until it fired a round that knocked Collins's tank out of action.

The entire squadron moved up in support. Under their protective fire, Collins and his men were able to crawl back without casualties. No. 2 Squadron poured "devastating fire into the woods," but failed to silence the antitank gun. Lance Corporal Lloyd Arthur Jennett's tank was disabled, and he ordered the crew to abandon it. Outside the tank, Jennett realized that Guardsman Evan Cameron MacMillan had not bailed out and went back for him. As he climbed aboard, a second armour-piercing round tore into its hull, and Jennett was killed. The twenty-two-year-old was the eldest son in a family of twenty from Vasey, Ontario. Thirty-seven-year-old MacMillan from New Liskeard, Ontario also died.

Realizing that trying to bull through the narrow defile only invited disaster, Lieutenant Colonel E.M. Smith ordered No. 2 Squadron to disengage. He then sought to bypass the German strongpoint by moving No. 3 Squadron under Major Robert Fernand, with Lieutenant Hanway's troop on point, through the woods by following a strip of high ground where the vegetation thinned. "Progress was slow and difficult, many tanks being bogged in the marshy ground," recorded the regimental historian. "Proceeding to the west, in an attempt to pass the obstacle, Lieutenant Hanway suddenly became aware that two of his tanks had been knocked out behind him. One of these blocked both his withdrawal and the forward advance of the Regiment. His tank took cover in a clump of woods further to the west and was immediately attacked by infantry whom the crew succeeded in driving off."

A self-propelled gun opened up from a concealed position and punched a hole through the turret of Sergeant T.B. Murray's tank. Guardsmen Reuben Erland Young and Dan Alexander Kozar were killed and Murray was wounded. Although he had successfully bailed out of the tank, the driver, Guardsman J.M. Levasseur, realized that the tank blocked the line of advance for the others. Despite heavy machine-gun and rifle fire, Levasseur climbed back inside the tank, and ignoring the fact that the tank could again be struck by the SPG, managed to back and fill until he had the Sherman turned around. He then drove to safety.

A stiff engagement followed as the other troops of No. 3 Squadron entered the fray, while at least one antitank gun and two more SPGs weighed in on the German side. The antitank gun was knocked out, but one of the SPGs punched a hole in Lieutenant Adams's tank. Although the crew successfully escaped, Corporal John Allan Weatherson was mortally wounded when the Germans started shelling the area with high-explosive rounds. Eventually, both the Germans and the tankers broke off the action by withdrawing several hundred yards. A standoff ensued, with the Foot Guards ordered to hold and the paratroopers lurking menacingly in the woods a thousand yards distant.[31]

DESPITE THE AMBUSHES that had caught the Governor General's Foot Guards, 4th Canadian Armoured Division's good progress led Major General Harry Foster to call an Orders Group at 1900 hours to outline a bold move that would conform with instructions from Twenty-First Army Group. On October 22, Field Marshal Montgomery planned to unleash British Second Army's XII Corps westwards from the Nijmegen corridor towards Breda, with its right flank brushing the Maas River and its left extended about ten miles south of Tilburg.[32] Montgomery's intention was to spring a trap on the Fifteenth Army divisions south of the Maas. Accordingly, Foster told his brigadiers and assembled staff officers, 4 CAD's mission was not only to provide right flank protection for 2nd Canadian Infantry Division in its operations to clear South Beveland and Walcheren Island, but also to bring pressure to bear in their area—the southwest corner of the trap.[33]

Capturing Essen and its strategically important crossroads was of utmost importance, Foster said, so rather than wait for morning they would go forward tonight, with 10th Canadian Infantry Brigade's Lincoln and Welland Regiment on the left and the Algonquin Regiment on the right.[34] Seizing the town would be the responsibility of these two battalions, but the Lake Superior Regiment and Argyll and Sutherland Highlanders operating under 4th Canadian Armoured Brigade's command would also make a night move to come up on Essen's western flank.[35]

Foster hoped that the night advance would both fulfill the Twenty-First Army Group demands and deny the facing Germans an opportunity to regroup during the night and dig in along a new defensive line. Everyone present knew the gamble. Throughout the day, there had been a high percentage of troops from the 6th Parachute Regiment among the prisoners, which appeared to have been leavened in among the less elite units to stiffen their backbone. "Their presence," the Algonquins' Major Cassidy believed, "indicated that we could expect more violent opposition from now on, as the Germans tried to prevent the total outflanking of the Beveland Causeway battle area."[36]

Back at their respective brigade headquarters, Brigadiers Moncel and Jefferson got their battalions underway before midnight. Nobody knew how many Germans, particularly paratroopers, lurked in the woods through which they were to move. Nor did they have any idea what minefields and other booby traps might exist. Losing direction was another concern, one the Algonquins countered by having Captain R.A. Scott lead the advance with a navigation party equipped with a compass and the most accurate maps available. Every man in the battalion carried extra ammunition and food, for it was uncertain when supporting tanks or supply vehicles might be able to reach Essen. All the battalions moved in single file, maintaining absolute silence in the hope that they could quietly bypass any Germans. To avoid wireless traffic betraying the movement, radio silence was enforced.[37]

"Every man," the Lake Superior regimental historian recorded, "was tense, doubly tense because of the darkness, the uncertainty, and their own fears of detection. There was no moon. Only the flash of gun fire from time to time revealed the dusky forms of the

Canadians moving through the trees. They were aided, fortunately, by the noises of the night. This was no silent night in the north country of Canada; it was a night of war in Belgium. And the crash of the artillery, the rattle of vehicles, the bursts of small arms fire, and the bawling of wounded cattle could be heard everywhere and pinned down nowhere. So the Canadians got through. It was a daring thing to attempt; and it succeeded because of its very boldness and unexpectedness."[38]

The Argylls bumped the occasional German position that fired on them, but 'C' Company in the lead ignored the fire and kept moving, while 'A' Company in trail overran the opposition. "It was a thoroughly nervewracking experience for everyone concerned, but there was as yet no evidence that the Germans had any real idea of what was going on, and the absence of really organized opposition in itself lent a measure of confidence to the troops." The Argylls arrived on schedule at the crossroads they were to hold, and captured three Germans equipped with a British antitank gun. Turning the weapon around, the battalion dug in and prepared for a fight in the morning.[39]

'C' Company, on point for the Lincs, silently tiptoed past the German defences until they came upon a dirt track a hundred yards north of the hamlet of Zandstraat at 0130 hours, and detected what seemed to be a strong force dug in on the opposite side. Unable to find a way to bypass the position, the company quietly pulled back to the hamlet and set in for the night among its abandoned houses. Less than two miles from Essen, Lieutenant Colonel Bill Cromb believed his men could reach the objective quickly and go into the attack not far behind schedule once dawn came.[40]

The Algonquins' Major Cassidy initially wondered if it would be possible for the battalion to reach Essen before dawn even if it didn't trip any German ambushes. Essen lay four miles north of the start line, but in order to bypass known positions, the route to be followed was almost six miles long. "The pace was very slow. Every two or three minutes the entire column had to halt while the wire fences were cut. These eventually totalled forty-three. Splendid discipline was evident, both in maintaining silence, and in staying together."

At about 0130 hours, the column approached a river that intelligence predicted was five to six feet deep, a tough obstacle to cross under the weight of all the equipment. Suddenly, a challenge was shouted, followed by a shot fired. The entire battalion hit the dirt, while the lead company carried out a hasty attack on the spot where the muzzle flash had been spotted, but the sentry had fled. Pushing on, the Algonquins discovered that the river was a mere eight inches deep and easily forded.

At 0300 hours, they quietly entered a barnyard. The farmhouse door opened and two Germans stepped outside. Blinded by the light from inside, they walked right into the Canadians. "In a second, a hail of fire came from all directions, and many thought that we had walked into a set ambush. But the firing was all our own, and the two Germans were left riddled with bullets from five or six Brens. In the mix-up, it was very lucky that we had suffered no casualties from our own fire, which was pretty indiscriminate in the darkness. Again we feared that the firing would alert the enemy, but there apparently was no means of communication from their troops out on the flank, and the main body remained blissfully ignorant of our approach in force."

Soon after, the Algonquins reached a château near Kleynen Schriek, less than a mile south of Essen, and paused here to regroup for the dawn. Already, prearranged artillery concentrations were pounding the town. The officers gathered in an abandoned German trench and held an O Group, with a blanket overhead to prevent the glow of a flashlight escaping. The Algonquins planned to hit the town by sending some companies around its eastern flank to come in from the north, while also striking from the south, where they believed most of the German defenders would be concentrated. Captain Scott's 'B' Company would enter the town from the north, near a hospital. Major Cassidy's 'D' Company would go for the area north of the main square, while 'A' Company under Captain R.B. Stock took the square itself. 'C' Company, commanded by Major Stirling, would strike from the south in company with the battalion command group. This latter company would go in once the tank support arrived.

With dawn streaking the sky, the companies headed off. To Cassidy's amazement, 'A' and 'D' Companies were able to dash across a two-hundred-yard swath of open ground to gain the town's outer buildings without detection. Within minutes, three companies were inside the town, quietly searching one house after another and finding no sign of Germans or civilians. Soon, gunfire erupted to the south and it was clear that 'C' Company had met the main German defences as expected. The sound of 75-millimetre guns firing also indicated that 'A' Squadron of the British Columbia Regiment was joining the battle.

It proved a short, sharp engagement—the town was in hand by 0900 hours.[41] The success of their surprise became clear an hour later when a convoy of twenty-two trucks bearing supplies drove into the town and was captured. In all, the division had taken about 450 prisoners during the advance and fight for Essen. By noon, the Canadians were irreversibly ensconced, and already reorganizing to swing westwards on Bergen op Zoom.[42]

PART FOUR

FIGHT TO THE FINISH

---

[22]

Troops on the Ground

FOURTH CANADIAN ARMOURED DIVISION's rapid breakthrough to Essen had fallen on the weakest point in LXVII Corps's General der Infanterie Otto Sponheimer's defensive line. His initial response was to seek permission for 711th Infantry Division to conduct a limited withdrawal, but Oberkommando Wehrmacht, West refused. Meanwhile, Sponheimer had also ordered a counterattack against 49th British (West Riding) Division near Wuustwezel, to the east of Kalmthout, which so weakened the corps's artillery and depleted its supply resources that he was powerless to oppose 4 CAD's advance. Consequently, Essen and its vital crossroads were lost.[1] Worse, the Wuustwezel counterattack had been broken by artillery and flame-throwing tanks, so despite several "gallant attacks," the town had remained in British hands. Sponheimer recognized that with this failure the writing was on the wall, and "an end would have to be made to this process of attrition if any worthwhile forces were to reach the area north of the Maas."[2]

On Fifteenth Army's western flank, Kampfgruppe Chill had shortened its lines to the east to meet the renewed attempts by 2nd Canadian Infantry Division to clear Woensdrecht and the adjacent heights.[3] This forced 346th Division to stretch its thin forces across an even wider front, but also enabled the Germans to strengthen defences near the South Beveland isthmus.

These were precisely the defensive positions 2 CID attacked on October 23. Clearing Woensdrecht and then advancing north through Nederheide and Zandfort to Korteven fell to 6th Canadian Infantry Brigade, with the Queen's Own Cameron Highlanders given the first task. The South Saskatchewan Regiment formed the brigade's right flank, advancing east of Zandfort, while Les Fusiliers Mont-Royal headed up the brigade's centre for Korteven. The Calgary Highlanders of 5th Canadian Infantry Brigade, meanwhile, assaulted across open polders towards Woensdrecht Station to clear the paratroopers off the railway embankment following the northern edge of the isthmus.[4]

The advance was preceded by heavy artillery fire from the 6th Canadian Field Regiment, which fired fifty rounds per gun.[5] Frost lay on the ground as Les Fusiliers Mont-Royal crossed the start line at 0700 hours. The sky was overcast, grounding 2nd Tactical Air Force. Because of its high casualty rate and the desperate shortage of French-speaking reinforcements, the Fusiliers fielded only three rifle companies rather than four. Captain Elmo Thiebeault's 'B' Company was on the left and Captain D.H. Ouimet's 'C' Company on the right, as the battalion advanced on either side of the main road from Woensdrecht to Bergen op Zoom. 'A' Company was close behind with the battalion's support platoons. A Fort Garry Horse squadron was strung out in column on the road because the mud elsewhere prevented spreading out.

Thiebeault's men moved alongside a hedge that covered their advance for about five hundred yards, but the moment they stepped beyond this screen, machine-gun fire drove them to ground. Although one platoon found shelter in an abandoned casemate, another was caught in the open. When two tanks tried to come to its aid, they were knocked out by mines. Lieutenant Réal Liboiron, at the head of the lead platoon, was wounded. Despite mounting casualties, Thiebeault sought to regroup and renew the advance.

'C' Company had been without cover from the outset, moving across a heavily mined field of muddy gumbo, into which the men's boots sucked deeply, making every step a struggle. On the road, the tanks were stalled by roadblocks of fallen trees. Ouimet's 'C' Company was soon pinned down in a roadside ditch.

Despite being in trail, 'A' Company's casualties were mounting because of accurate artillery and mortar fire. Wondering what was holding things up, Major Georges White crept up to 'C' Company and Ouimet in the ditch with the lead platoon. Nobody knew where the machine-gun fire pinning them down was coming from, so White tried to pinpoint the enemy positions. Although Ouimet warned the veteran officer this was an unhealthy location, the twenty-seven-year-old from Rockland, Ontario climbed a wall next to the ditch in order to see better. A burst of fire toppled him dead.

Thiebeault realized that the only possible place where an advance might be possible was on the left flank, where a string of buildings offered slight cover. He ordered Lieutenant Joseph Morrissette's platoon to weave from house to house to a nearby crossroads, while covered by the other 'B' Company platoons and a couple of tanks firing from behind a small rise that sheltered them from antitank guns. When the supporting fire was unleashed, it was directed against each building's second storey rather than the ground floor, so the moment Morrissette led his men out beyond the hedge, a machine gun in the lower level of the first building ripped into them. Half the men were cut down and Morrissette was killed as the attack collapsed.

By 1100 hours, the Fusiliers' acting commander, Major Jacques "Jimmy" Dextraze, realized there was no prevailing against the strong positions without additional support from brigade. He requested reinforcements and ordered the two leading companies to dig in, while 'A' Company occupied a small wood right of 'B' Company to guard that flank. The Fusiliers and Germans began a steady exchange of gunfire, but neither showed any intention of giving way. In the late afternoon, a heavy anti-aircraft battery that had been providing fire support miscalculated its range and shelled 'B' Company. Eight men were wounded. A volunteer Belgian medical unit ran through intense German fire to evacuate the injured soldiers. In the course of the successful evacuation, several stretcher-bearers were wounded and a female nurse was killed.[6] The Fusiliers could do little after this but hunker down and hope that brigade eventually sent reinforcements.

TO THE FUSILIERS' right, the South Saskatchewan Regiment had run into "stiff opposition" in the form of machine-gun, rifle, and mortar fire immediately after crossing the start line. 'A' and 'B' Companies "fought their way forward foot by foot, suffering a number of casualties." The battalion's war diarist noted that the terrain "was not the kind you dream about to make an attack in as it was partially wooded and partially open and it had many buildings, ditches, and O Pip posts in the trees. The country was ideal for snipers and they inflicted a number of casualties."[7]

Lieutenant Cecil Law, commanding the battalion's mortar platoon, was stalked by a sniper when he tried to link up with 'A' Company in order to control the mortars from the front via wireless. The company's start line had been about a mile from his departure point at battalion headquarters. To look less like an officer, he carried a rifle and because of the distance had left his No. 38 wireless, its operator, and his runner behind. Instead, he planned to use the company's No. 18 set for communication. A deep ditch to the right of the road provided good cover but was sloppy with water, and his old, deteriorating boots were soon saturated. That was hardly new; they had rarely been dry since they had entered this godforsaken country in September. Law stopped thinking about his feet when he came to a culvert passing under a narrow track leading to a field. It was too narrow to crawl through and full of water anyway. "Nothing for it but to make a quick dash across. So I gathered myself, charged out of the ditch, ran across the road, and jumped into the other side, just before a shot cracked behind my head. Bullets don't whistle or whine; they're supersonic, and crack most viciously as they pass close by." Law was grateful the German seemed a poor shot.

But soon he reached another culvert. "Resolving to really run fast this time, and zig-zag twice as much, I did, and he did! Once again the shot cracked behind me as I jumped into the ditch. But I still had nearly 100 yards to go.

"Naturally, I almost immediately came to another culvert. This was getting tough." Law again dashed out, only to be presented with two culverted side roads. Redoubling his speed and zigzagging frantically, he hurtled across and dove into the ditch as another bullet cracked past. About twenty yards ahead, he saw the house where 'A' Company was headquartered. Soaking wet from a mixture of rain and sweat, Law took a long pause that he hoped would trick the sniper into believing he had been hit, and then madly dashed out. "I grabbed for the gate post to swing myself around into the side, which was slightly angled. Just as I did so, the sniper fired. His bullet sliced through most of my belt, and broke the tapes holding my gas cape on my back. My bully beef lunch was also wrapped in that gas cape. The damned thing tripped me up and I sprawled onto the sidewalk, luckily behind the angle of the wall.

"A familiar voice drawled out, 'Hey, that was great running. Lucky he missed.'" Another voice commented that Law was fortunate the German sniper was slow. Having been an 'A' Company platoon commander before being assigned to the mortar platoon, Law recognized the voices of the company sniper, "Gunny" Powell, and his observer, Corporal George Grandbois. "Why don't you just go out again for a second, and this time I'll be ready and get him," the sniper suggested. "Just give me a few minutes to climb into my blind, and I'll get him long before he can shoot. He was always at the side of a little wall before, now he'll have to peek over the top." Law didn't want to do this, but he knew that if he was going to spot for the mortars, the German had to be taken out. "I didn't feel very brave, but I had to do my job too." Grandbois signalled that the sniper was ready. "With my heart in my mouth I bobbed out on the street and then back. Powell's rifle cracked and he said, 'Got him!'"

Later, the three went out to retrieve the German's rifle. "Behind the wall was a young German paratrooper, dead. He was in nearly new uniform, with new calf high jump boots, beautiful, soft, pliable, lovely, *waterproof* jump boots, and just my size. Obviously this poor devil didn't need boots anymore, but I certainly did. Plus he had a new black leather belt around his jump smock, and my belt was half shot away. I took his belt too, and lo and behold, the boots were a perfect fit."[8]

The elimination of one sniper did little to enable the battalion to gain its objective. Despite a persistent effort, the battalion had only advanced half the distance assigned by 1500 hours, when Brigadier

Guy Gauvreau ordered it to consolidate for the night. Two officers and twenty-nine other ranks had been killed or wounded.[9]

While the South Saskatchewans and Fusiliers Mont-Royal had pushed north towards Korteven, the Queen's Own Cameron Highlanders had undertaken clearing elements of 6th Parachute Regiment out of the western part of Woensdrecht. The Royal Hamilton Light Infantry had earlier failed to do this because it had been seriously depleted just gaining a toehold in the town. Having spent most of the past two weeks guarding the right flank near Kapellen, the Camerons had seen relatively little fighting, and consequently, Lieutenant Colonel Ernest Thompson, who at twenty-three was First Canadian Army's youngest battalion commander, was confident that he had the manpower to succeed.

'A' Company, under Major Art Cavanagh, advanced along a westerly running street towards a crossroads on the edge of the town, while 'B' Company followed behind with two tanks in support to carry out the actual house clearing.[10] The Camerons were soon on the crossroads with forty paratroopers in the bag, but suddenly the area was plastered by German artillery and mortar fire. Casualties mounted quickly, particularly among Lieutenant James F. Hayman's platoon, which had led the attack. By 1430 hours, the shell and mortar fire reached such a furious crescendo that 'A' Company was forced to fall back to its starting point. Hayman was among the dead. 'B' Company had fared no better, and the entire battalion was back where it had started.[11]

About the time 6th Canadian Infantry Brigade's battalions dug in for the night after a day of successive failures, 5th Canadian Infantry Brigade's Calgary Highlanders crossed the start line to clear the remaining German-held polders below Woensdrecht. Despite the fact that German movement between South Beveland and the mainland via the isthmus had been rendered impossible by 2 CID's previous advances here, a strong force of paratroopers remained dug in along the railway embankment, around Woensdrecht Station, and to its west, in the Hoogerwaardpolder north of the railway tracks that separated the polder area from the marshy beaches of the East Scheldt. Laced with typical drainage ditches and narrow canals, the polder was partially flooded, and the rest saturated. Across its centre, atop a dyke, ran the main highway to Walcheren Island. Rectangle-shaped and stretching two miles east to west and a half mile north to south, the ground held by the Germans roughly resembled a coffin—leading the Calgarians to dub the operation "the coffin show."[12]

The plan was to attack on a three-company-wide front. Rather than going forward shoulder to shoulder, however, the two companies on the flanks would swing wide, and once past the railway embankment, turn and hook back towards the centre company. 'A' Company was to go out on the left, 'D' Company on the right, while 'C' Company butted up the middle. 'B' Company was in reserve. The 5th Field Regiment fired on known and then on suspected German positions, and the Toronto Scottish Regiment (MG) directed heavy machine-gun and 4.2-inch mortar fire on the railway embankment as the attack went in at 1500 hours. With an icy rain falling, the troops advanced across the sodden ground through tendrils of light fog.

'A' Company managed to creep to the railway without being detected. Major Wynn Lasher gave the signal and the entire company lunged across the tracks. But when they started the hook right towards the centre, an MG 42 opened up with its distinctive sheet-ripping sound, and No. 7 Platoon was cut off. Private Sanford Ross began shuttling through the fire to carry messages between the platoon and headquarters. On each return trip, he lugged back ammunition. Lasher decided the best way to relieve this platoon was to outflank the gun position by heading for the highway, then turning east to clear out the paratroopers dug in behind. The move worked like a charm, and soon 'A' Company was on its objective and waiting for the other two companies to come alongside.[13]

'C' and 'D' Companies, however, had advanced straight into the maw of the same network of heavy machine-gun emplacements that had cut the Black Watch to pieces ten days earlier. Captain H.J. "Sandy" Pearson's 'D' Company had been pinned down only three hundred yards out. Pearson was wounded at 1526 hours, and Lieutenant Amos Wilkins took over.[14] When the lead platoon appeared to be making no effort to advance, Private William C. Brown left his section and crawled forward to see what was happening. He discovered that Wilkins and all the non-commissioned officers had been hit. With no other takers, Brown took command of the platoon. Managing to crawl to the top of a dyke, he directed the platoon's Bren guns onto several German positions, and this relieved the pressure enough to enable the company to advance a little farther.[15] But it remained well short of the objective, with Brown in charge of one platoon and two corporals the others.[16]

Captain Dalt Heyland's 'C' Company managed to advance to within a hundred yards of their dyke's intersection with the railway before machine-gun fire forced it to ground, with Nos. 13 and 14 Platoons on the west side of the dyke and No. 15 the other. Everyone started digging in. Sergeant Ken Crockett, the hero of the Antwerp–Turnhout Canal battle, was pressed against one side of the dyke and engaged in a duel with a German sniper. Every time the sniper popped up to loose a round, Crockett snapped off a rifle shot. When his Lee Enfield's magazine ran dry, Crockett leaned against the dyke to reload, and the German fired a single round that struck Crockett in the knee. It was a serious wound that ended his soldiering days.[17]

With darkness falling and the three forward rifle companies all badly cut up, Major Ross Ellis ordered Major S.O. Robinson to take two platoons of 'B' Company and not only reinforce 'D' Company, but take over its command. The carrier platoon hustled up to strengthen 'C' Company, and 'A' Company was reinforced with two platoons drawn from the Black Watch. Everyone dug in where they were for the night.[18] It had been another bitter day, but due to 'A' Company's success, the Calgarians had achieved every task except the capture of Woensdrecht Station itself.[19]

The cost had been high: eighteen dead and fifty-one wounded. Only nine paratroops had been taken prisoner. Because they often continued firing from a machine-gun position until just before it was overrun and then hastily surrendered, the low prisoner count indicated the ferocity of the fighting—many preferring to fight to the end. Although not a complete success, the regiment's war diarist felt justified in stating: "Once again the Calgary Highlanders 'did it.' Supporting arms contributed a large part of the deciding factors but in the long run it took the [infantry] with men on the ground to take and hold the ground."[20]

WHILE 2ND CANADIAN INFANTRY DIVISION spent October 23 trying to gain control of the entrance to South Beveland, 4th Canadian Armoured Division had struck westwards from Essen towards Bergen op Zoom. The plan was for 4th Canadian Armoured Brigade to seize the three-mile-distant Dutch village of Wouwse Plantage with a phased assault. Phase one entailed the 10th Canadian Infantry Brigade's Argyll and Sutherland Highlanders—temporarily under 4 CAB command—with two tank squadrons of Canadian Grenadier Guards, advancing a mile to secure a road and woods just inside Holland. From here, the Lake Superior Regiment and a squadron of Governor General's Foot Guards would advance to the village. If the village proved heavily defended, this formation would establish a firm base to provide fire support for the Argylls to pass into Wouwse Plantage. When the village fell, 10 CIB's other regiments would advance north through 4 CAB to cut the main road between Bergen op Zoom and Roosendaal.[21]

At 0800 hours, 'B' and 'D' Companies of the Argylls and the Grenadiers' No. 1 and No. 3 Squadrons were moving out from covering woods when they were caught by a series of German artillery salvos. 'B' Company got off lightly, moving forward on schedule, but 'D' Company became disorganized. For almost thirty minutes, the latter company was pummelled by one concentration after another. Major John Farmer and one of the company's two lieutenants were badly wounded by shrapnel.[22] Private Sidney Webb, one of Farmer's signallers, was hugging the dirt like everyone else. On only his second day of combat, Webb was terrified, and watched in awe as a sergeant walked calmly up and down the company line amid the exploding shells repeatedly advising, "Lookit, it's alright." Although so crippled by wounds to his lower body he could barely walk, Farmer initially refused evacuation until Lieutenant Colonel Dave Stewart came forward to personally reorganize the unit.[23] Lieutenant Ecclestone, a reinforcement who had arrived the day before, was the only unhurt officer. Stewart told him he had command. Most of the men were as green as the young lieutenant. With Stewart's help, Ecclestone formed the survivors up, and 'D' Company headed out.[24]

The Argylls encountered little direct resistance, but continual artillery and mortar fire took its toll. Snipers also posed a threat, particularly to the tankers whenever they emerged from the safety of their Shermans. A new Grenadier officer, Lieutenant Simeon Besen, was shot dead. So was Guardsman Donald George Hewitt. Lieutenant J.R. Fergusson and three other tankers were wounded.[25] It took three gruelling hours for the force to work its way across the border into Holland and secure the road to begin the second phase. The cost to the Argylls was four killed and twenty-five wounded, mostly due to the initial shelling.[26]

'A' Company of the Lake Superior Regiment and the Foot Guards' No. 1 Squadron passed through the Argylls' position and advanced up the Mariabaan, a road that arced gently northwest towards Wouwse Plantage. In support was a troop of Flail tanks. When this phase had been teed up, Major General Harry Foster and Brigadier Robert Moncel had envisioned it as "a run across the two-mile approach to the town. But once again tanks were roadbound by ten-foot ditches and soft muddy fields. The ground was devoid of contour and wide open for several hundred yards on each side of the main axis of advance, except where clusters of wood and farm yards dotted the panorama."[27]

Lying in ambush, several self-propelled guns opened fire from positions in the woods and behind well-concealed concrete bunkers. The first troop of three tanks commanded by Lieutenant Dan Crocker was knocked out within three minutes, as was the Superiors' leading Bren carrier. While the infantry scattered off the road, the Shermans were trapped on it by the deep ditches. Crocker and his men all escaped their tanks, got into one of the ditches, and headed towards the rear. Major A.G.V. Smith's No. 1 Squadron was down to eight tanks that ground carefully around the three wrecked Shermans and the carrier, their main guns blasting blindly at the still undetected antitank guns.

An armour-piercing round cracked into the rear idler on Smith's tank, and ball bearings spewed in all directions. Coming to a drive that accessed a farmyard, the tankers turned in and deployed among the buildings, which afforded scant cover. 'A' Company soon joined them, and Smith jumped down to discuss the situation with the Superiors' Major Malach. With German artillery and the SPGs systematically demolishing the buildings, the farm was not a healthy place to remain for long.

Despite the incoming fire, Smith decided to set up there with the two tanks of his headquarters section, while the rest of No. 1 Squadron would continue along the road. One platoon of Superiors remained to provide security for the tanks.[28] Leading the first troop onto the road was Lieutenant E.J. Canavan. Within minutes, German antitank fire blew one of his Sherman's tracks off, but he ordered his crew to keep on fighting despite its being unable to move. The Sherman commanded by Lance Sergeant Aldege Tessier was holed, and he and Guardsman Robert Parent were killed. The other tank in Canavan's troop was also knocked out.[29]

One by one, the remaining tanks were "reduced to hunks of tangled steel, blood-spattered and useless."[30] The Flails had also been destroyed, so the Superiors proceeded alone. Canavan and his crew stayed in the fight for three hours, benefiting from a smoke screen boiling around them from the nearby burning tanks and carriers, and managed to knock out one SPG that rolled up onto the road and presented a perfect target. Its burning hulk ended up crosswise on the road, creating an effective roadblock. When Canavan exhausted his ammunition, he ordered the Sherman abandoned.[31] It was 1400 hours, and the squadron was reduced to just three tanks gathered at the devastated farm.

The Superiors edged "from bush to bush, and from outbuilding to outbuilding, clinging to the ground and crouching behind every miserable little hollow," until they were about a mile from the town. Blocked by a deadly rain of machine-gun and small-arms fire and without tank support, there was no possibility of fighting through.[32]

Back at the farmyard, Major Smith was following the progress on his tank's wireless. Realizing the situation, he decided to try breaking through to the infantry. But the moment the Shermans turned out of the farmyard, they came under fire from an SPG sheltered behind a concrete bunker that the Superiors had bypassed. The tankers returned fire. Then a shell pierced one Sherman's turret, and Lance Corporal Lionel Lalonde and Guardsman Joseph Bordeleau were both killed. Another round struck Smith's tank a glancing blow that caved in one side of the turret, seizing it up. The Sherman of his battle captain, who had been maintaining the wireless link to regimental headquarters, was knocked out, and Lance Corporal Roland St. Amand died inside.

Only Smith's tank, with a damaged idler and a main gun rendered useless because the turret would not swivel, remained semi-operational. At 1800 hours, Smith ordered it driven from the field. As the tank rolled into the regimental headquarters, the idler burst into flames, causing a fire that was difficult to extinguish. The rest of the surviving guardsmen of the wiped-out No. 1 Squadron trickled in on foot. A little after midnight, tragedy struck once again when a Browning machine gun accidentally discharged towards the headquarters tank of No. 3 Squadron. Major Robert Fernand Major was killed by the burst and Captain E.F. Mooers seriously wounded.[33]

At 2300 hours, Brigadier Moncel ordered the Argylls to break through to the Superiors and carry Wouwse Plantage. Two troops of Canadian Grenadier Guards and five Bren carriers borrowed from the Superiors would be boarded by 'A' and 'C' Companies. The "tanks would lead along the road with all lights on, shooting up any area that looked as if it might hide enemy or enemy weapons. A speedy break-through was expected." It soon became evident that the attack force, slated to begin advancing at 0100 hours, could not possibly be ready until just before dawn because the night had turned bitter. Heavy rain was falling, and the dirt tracks that the tanks followed to gain the start line had been transformed into deep mud bogs. One tank after another mired and had to be hauled free by others. Waiting in the woods, the Argylls spent a cold, wet, miserable night.[34]

ALTHOUGH FAILING to seize Wouwse Plantage, 4th Canadian Armoured Division's limited advance on October 23 warned Fifteenth Army's General der Infanterie Gustav von Zangen that time was running out to safely extract 6th Parachute Regiment from the Woensdrecht area. He could not indefinitely keep the Canadians pushing towards Bergen op Zoom at bay. LXVII Corps's General der Infanterie Otto Sponheimer had been urging such a withdrawal for days, and now von Zangen consented.

The paratroops began quietly withdrawing under cover of darkness. At the same time, the rest of Kampfgruppe Chill pulled out from around Huijbergen.[35] The battle to open the Scheldt had just taken a dramatic turn, as Fifteenth Army effectively abandoned 70th Infantry Division on South Beveland and Walcheren Island to its fate, and began a fighting withdrawal to the Maas.

6th Canadian Infantry Brigade patrols that night returned reports that the Germans had withdrawn. In the morning, the South Saskatchewan Regiment and Les Fusiliers Mont-Royal advanced towards Korteven, while the Queen's Own Cameron Highlanders moved down from the heights of Woensdrecht to clear the Prins Karel Polder to the northwest. Bulking up the ranks of the understrength Fusiliers was a detachment of Flemish Belgian resistance fighters. Only light resistance was encountered, and Korteven fell without a fight that evening.[36] In contrast to previous days, 6 CIB recorded only one casualty on October 24. Cameron Highlanders Lieutenant William French, who had earned a battlefield commission, died after stepping on a mine.[37] That evening, 6 CIB was relieved by 5th Canadian Infantry Brigade and withdrawn to Hoogerheide for a brief forty-eight-hour regrouping, preparatory to its joining 2 CID's advance into South Beveland.

Not all the Germans had pulled back, however, and the Calgary Highlanders had faced a stiff fight along the railway embankment to gain control of Woensdrecht Station. This mission achieved, the Calgarians were assigned the task of clearing a rectangular-shaped height of ground, about half a mile wide by a mile and a half long, to the north of Woensdrecht, called the Lidonk. Fighting from the cover of dugouts and concrete pillboxes with mortars emplaced to their rear and firing on fixed lanes down the gentle slope the Calgarians were ascending, the Germans had every advantage and were determined to hold this ground as long as possible to prevent Canadian movement on the isthmus.

For three days, the Calgarians fought yard by yard for mastery of Lidonk. October 25 was the worst day, with seven men killed and twenty-five wounded. During the afternoon, the gunfire exchange became so intense that the rifle companies used ammunition faster than it could be replenished. Despite this, little ground was gained. The next day, six soldiers died and another six were wounded, while the situation remained deadlocked. Backed by a full Fort Garry Horse squadron, the Calgarians tried again on October 27 and found the paratroops had abandoned Lidonk during the night. Brigadier Holly Keefler, commanding 2 CID, commented: "The Calgary Highlanders have done a damn fine job for the division."[38] Almost five days of constant combat cost the regiment 140 casualties, 31 being fatal.[39]

Kampfgruppe Chill's Oberstleutnant Friederich von der Heydte had decided to pull the elements of 1st Battalion, 2nd Parachute Regiment out of Lidonk in order to shorten his lines and strengthen the German forces heavily engaged by 4 CAD. This coincided with a general contraction of LXVII Corps's front by several miles to recover from a 49th (West Riding) Infantry Division breakthrough of the 346th Infantry Division's lines at Nispen on October 23.[40]

DESPITE HEAVY CASUALTIES and increasingly foul weather that favoured the defence, 4th Canadian Armoured Division relentlessly pursued its drive towards Bergen op Zoom—badly straining Kampfgruppe Chill's resources. When the Lake Superior Regiment failed on October 23 to capture Wouwse Plantage, Brigadier Robert Moncel immediately ordered the Argyll and Sutherland Highlanders and the Canadian Grenadier Guards forward. After being postponed several hours because of difficulty forming up, the attack went in at 0445 hours, with the infantry and tanks moving along the same stretch of the Mariabaan where No. 1 Squadron of the Governor General's Foot Guards had been destroyed the day before. The Argylls had two companies up front, 'A' in the ditch on the left side of the road and 'C' in the one on the right. No. 3 Squadron provided the Shermans, with No. 1 Troop in the van.[41]

It had rained so heavily that the road was awash, the tanks wallowing through mud so deep they could barely make headway. The column had advanced just four hundred yards when the lead tank came up against the self-propelled gun knocked out by the Foot Guards' Lieutenant Canavan. Trying to creep around it, the troop leader's Sherman slid into the ditch. The rest of the squadron carefully picked past, and No. 4 Troop, commanded by Sergeant Samuel Hurwitz, headed towards the first objective—a low rise overlooking Wouwse Plantage.[42]

The tanks bypassed a couple of small pockets of infantry, quickly rounded up by the Argylls. These were from the Hermann Göring Division's 1st Battalion.[43] When opposition stiffened, the Shermans opened up on likely positions. A number of farm buildings were soon burning fiercely, with the unfortunate effect of silhouetting the tanks on the road.[44] A German hiding in a slit trench popped up and fired a Panzerfaust at the second tank in No. 4 Troop. Although the Argylls immediately cut him down, the charge struck the rear of the turret. The Sherman burst into flames and halted square in the middle of the road. When the crew bailed out, they were taken prisoner by the Germans. The road was too narrow for the rest of the tanks to work around the destroyed one, and the ground on either side too boggy to bear a Sherman's weight. Except for Sergeant Hurwitz's tank, which had been in front, No. 3 Squadron was effectively stalled. Hurwitz headed towards the high ground alone.[45]

Dawn was breaking, and the Argylls were taking heavy fire, but still trying to gain the heights and the village beyond. Both 'A' Company's Captain J.D. "Pete" McCordic and 'C' Company's Major Bob Paterson sent a platoon to their flank, in an attempt to loop behind the German positions while the other platoons provided covering fire. The platoons staying put attempted to dig in, but the first shovel strike came up dripping water, so the men lay behind whatever surface cover they could find and began shooting.[46]

Hurwitz, meantime, had gained the high ground, which was really only a few feet above the surrounding country, only to find Germans with Panzerfausts on every side. He and his crew fought a frantic engagement for a few minutes until the tank was knocked out. The mortally wounded Hurwitz and his crew were taken prisoner.[47]

Meanwhile, Brigadier Keefler had ordered a company of the Lincoln and Welland Regiment advanced from near Nispen up the northwest-running Bergse Baan towards the Bergen op Zoom–Roosendaal highway. If successful, the Lincs would outflank Wouwse Plantage about a mile and a half to the north and cut off the Germans defending the village. Major J.L. Dandy's 'C' Company, with a troop of British Columbia Regiment tanks and two troops of Crocodile flamethrower tanks from the 79th British Armoured Division in support, undertook this task at 1345 hours. The force moved across open country towards a wood two thousand yards distant. In short order, Dandy reported reaching an intermediary objective of a crossroads five hundred yards short of the wood. Here, however, the tanks mired in mud and could go no farther, and the infantry came under intense machine-gun and antitank fire from the woods.[48]

One platoon under Lieutenant W.E. Edwards, who had returned to the regiment only three hours before the attack, fought through to the woods, only to be overrun. Edwards and ten men were taken prisoner. Caught in the open, the rest of 'C' Company was pinned down by relentless fire, and Dandy requested either reinforcements or permission to withdraw. Finally, at 1645 hours, he was permitted to pull out, and the company retreated to the start line under cover of a smokescreen. Of the hundred men in the attack, nine had died and thirty-five had been wounded.[49]

The Argylls' flanking attempt also came to misfortune when supporting Bren carriers from the Lake Superiors spotted the soldiers moving in the distance. Mistaking them for Germans, the crews opened up with their Bren guns and forced the Argylls to ground. Both platoons returned to their companies and the infantry hunkered down alongside the line of tanks. Attempts by the Grenadiers to hook cables onto the destroyed tank and drag it aside resulted in nothing more than a few wounded tankers. In an attempt to restart the attack, Lieutenant Colonel Dave Stewart ordered 'B' Company forward. But the moment Captain Raymond George McGivney led his men out of the woods, they were caught by a heavy mortar concentration. McGivney was killed, and Company Sergeant Major Charles McDonald lost a foot. The loss of these key leaders threw the company into disarray.

Stewart tried again at 1600 hours to get 'A' and 'C' Companies and the Grenadiers going, with the Argylls' Wasps up behind the tanks. Heavy mortar fire immediately tied the infantry down, and an antitank gun ranged in on the Grenadiers, which still faced a blocked road. The tanks backed towards the rear. Heavily outmatched by the massive Shermans coming their way, the crews aboard the Wasps drove into the ditches to avoid being crushed. The attack collapsed. "It is useless, of course, to attempt to assess reasons for the failure," observed the Argylls' regimental historian. "Probably fatigue, cold and wet played as great a part as any. The battalion had been pushed to the limit."[50]

When Moncel radioed Stewart with fresh instructions, the latter officer's headquarters was under a rain of mortar and artillery fire. "Push on! I can't even get out of my headquarters!" Stewart snapped and held the handset of his radio out the window so the brigadier could hear the explosions shaking the building. The attack order was scrubbed. That sort of behaviour endeared Stewart to his men. He stood up for them when things turned bad, and October 24 had been rough indeed, with thirteen killed and another twenty wounded.[51/52] That night, two companies from the Lincoln and Welland Regiment came under 4 CAB's command and took over the forward position from the Argylls.

In the morning, with two Governor General's Foot Guard squadrons in support, the Lincs and Superiors launched a joint assault. The Superiors' 'C' Company was to work through a brickyard on the southern outskirts to gain Wouwse Plantage, while 'A' Company provided covering fire. 'A' and 'B' Companies of the Lincs were to drive directly up the main road "regardless of the cost."[53] Brigadier Moncel had even issued a deadline—the village must be taken by 1400 hours.[54]

Under covering fog, the companies slunk close to the German lines and, as it lifted, struck the village from three sides. A vicious firefight ensued, each company with supporting tanks advancing "through the bursting shells and flying fragments. It was fighting of the fiercest kind," the Superiors' regimental historian recorded. "The Germans were tough and persistent, and worked with frenzy as they fed shells and bombs into their guns and mortars. They had to hold this, the key to their defences in the whole area, and so they used their weapons with savage ferocity."[55]

The Superiors tore a path through the brickworks, bypassing enemy strongpoints, then drove the Germans from the village cemetery and gained the village itself. 'A' Company's Major Malach was wounded in the cheek. Lieutenant James Kallethe Brown, commander of the scout platoon, took over, but was killed when the Bren carrier he was aboard took a direct hit from an antitank gun. Casualties mounted so alarmingly in 'A' Company that it had to be reinforced by thirty men drawn from the battalion's support echelon.[56]

Major M.J. McCutcheon's 'B' Company led the Lincs into the village and Captain Herbert Lambert's 'A' Company was also soon fighting through the houses. With Wasps borrowed from the Superiors, the Lincs burned many defenders out of their fortified houses. At 1530 hours, Wouwse Plantage was declared taken. For his leadership during the gruelling action, McCutcheon received a Military Cross. His company had been shredded, thirty of the fifty men in the two forward platoons killed or wounded.[57] During the three-day battle for the village, about 80 Canadians had died and another 230 had been either wounded or taken prisoner. An estimated 70 Germans died in the fighting and another 100 had been captured.[58]

While the battle for Wouwse Plantage raged, divisional command had been visited by Field Marshal Bernard Montgomery. He emphasized the urgent need to take Bergen op Zoom. Foster accordingly assigned 10th Canadian Infantry Brigade the task of attacking the city, with 4th Canadian Armoured Brigade charged with protecting its right flank.[59] The British 49th Division would shift its left flank slightly westwards to maintain contact with 4 CAD—a move made possible by 104th U. S. Infantry Division's joining the operation immediately east of the 49th.

By mid-afternoon on October 25, 4 CAD began probing the German lines with 29th Reconnaissance Regiment (South Alberta) patrols advancing north from Huijbergen. Major Dave Currie's 'C' Squadron drove up a dirt track identified as the Huijbergsche Baan, warily eyeing the forestry plantation woods after which Wouwse Plantage was named that pressed in on either flank. The squadron was down to just three troops, but the lead troop under Lieutenant Danny McLeod surprised and captured about twenty-six Germans from 6th Parachute Regiment and the Hermann Göring Regiment.

At 1830 hours, however, the squadron suddenly came under deadly Panzerfaust and antitank fire from the rear. Currie realized that the

Germans had allowed it to pass through the first line of defence and were now springing an ambush. Lieutenant Don Stewart's troop fended off Panzerfaust-packing paratroopers and Lieutenant Harold Kreewin's troop went to his aid. In the furious exchange of fire, Kreewin's tanks eliminated six Panzerfaust positions but lost two of four tanks. Up front, Lieutenant McLeod was running out of ammunition when the tank commanded by Corporal Frank Moan took a tremendous hit and began to burn. His crew escaped, but Moan died.

The squadron fought its way back to Huijbergen. It lost four tanks and four men wounded in an action the war diarist declared "unsuited to tanks." More galling, he believed, "if the higher command had been quick enough to exploit this initial breakthrough by 'C' Squadron there would have been little difficulty in dislodging the enemy completely from this area and pushing on to Bergen op Zoom."[60]

[23]

The South Beveland Race

WITH THE CAPTURE of Wouwse Plantage imminent and Woensdrecht cleared, the long-anticipated clearing of South Beveland and Walcheren Island had begun early on the morning of October 24. South Beveland was shaped rather like a turkey drumstick; its tip, the isthmus linking it to the mainland. In planning this operation, Lieutenant General Guy Simonds had appreciated that once 2nd Canadian Infantry Division advanced to the Beveland Canal—where metaphorical leg joined thigh—it would face a formidable obstacle cutting north to south across the peninsula. Mirroring Operation Switchback, Simonds intended to outflank the canal with an amphibious operation out of Terneuzen, which would land between Hoedekenskerke and Baarland at precisely the same moment the other brigades reached the canal.[1] When it became clear that 2 CID would have its hands full with the initial assault, Simonds assigned the amphibious phase to the 52nd British (Lowland) Division's 156th and 157th Brigades.[2]

The land assault across South Beveland to Walcheren Island was codenamed Operation Vitality. It constituted the first prong of a complex operation to overcome the island's formidable defences. The second prong—Operation Infatuate—would require two separate amphibious assault landings on Walcheren itself, one at Vlissingen and the other at Westkapelle. These landings would coincide with the land attack from South Beveland. By striking the Germans on three fronts, Simonds hoped to avoid a drawn-out battle for mastery of Walcheren.

But first South Beveland had to be taken. The plan was "to get forward rapidly, by-passing opposition, and seize crossings over the Beveland Canal." The first line of the 70th Infantry Division's defences was to be cracked by 4th Canadian Infantry Brigade's Royal Regiment of Canada. Then, two mixed columns composed of Fort Garry Horse tanks, armoured cars of 8th Reconnaissance Regiment (14th Canadian Hussars), and Essex Scottish infantry companies riding in Kangaroos—the converted Priest 105-millimetre self-propelled guns that Simonds had redesigned to carry infantry in Normandy—would dash to the canal.[3]

The isthmus was narrowest where it met the mainland, barely fifteen hundred yards wide. Consequently, only one battalion could operate here. The Royals' Lieutenant Colonel R.M. Lendrum had studied this small patch of ground for three days and knew the task was a tough one. The start line was immediately behind a fourteen-foot-high dyke, in front of which lay salt marsh, bordered on the left by a narrow raised road that hugged the coast of the West Scheldt. To the right, the railroad and main highway ran atop a causeway towards Walcheren. About a mile ahead stood their objective, another dyke. The Germans were dug in there, but they were also positioned along the causeway and the road to the south. Trying to cross the marsh exposed men to three-sided crossfire. Knee-deep coarse grass covered the marsh and concealed a crisscrossing network of ten-foot-deep drainage ditches. Deep ditches also bordered the road and causeway. Through binoculars, Lendrum could see that the facing dyke bristled with brick and concrete bunkers. Out in the marsh were a few cottages the Germans had fortified.[4]

Obviously, one company must move straight along the side of the road to the south and another along the causeway to the north, eliminating German strongpoints as they were encountered. The Royals would go as far as they could at night because Brigadier Holly Keefler was convinced that a daylight attack would be suicidal.[5] Even at night, artillery support would be critical, and a total of seven field and medium regiments were committed. A creeping barrage would precede the company attacking along the southern flank, while a series of timed concentrations would protect the one following the causeway. Heavy mortars would keep German heads on the facing dyke down, while anti-aircraft guns firing tracer overhead kept the infantry on line. Major Hank Caldwell's 'A' Company and Major Bob Suckling's 'D' Company would lead the assault, with 'C' Company moving up the centre of the marsh later to clear whatever Germans lurked there. 'B' Company would be in reserve.

At 0430 hours on October 24, the guns began firing and the Royals attacked. "The soldiers," recorded the regimental historian, "had almost to feel their way along in the inky darkness; and as they surged determinedly forward through the noisy night, they bumped successive German posts along the dykes. These were cleared, although often only after bitter hand-to-hand fighting."[6] Five hundred yards from the facing dyke, 'A' Company ran out of steam. 'B' Company leapfrogged it and pushed on to the objective.[7] By 0700 hours, the dyke was secure and the battalion turned to clearing out bypassed pockets. Suckling's men rounded up fifteen prisoners and put them in a sheltered position behind the safety of the dyke, only to see them killed minutes later when one of the first salvos of German mortar fire fell directly on top of the men. The Royals by comparison got off amazingly lightly for such a hard-fought and dangerous attack—six men dead and nineteen wounded.[8]

The roads were so mud-drenched that the armoured columns bearing 'A' and 'C' Companies of the Essex Scottish only managed to reach the start line by fitting the vehicles with chains. To gain the highway, engineers had to first cut a gap in the railway and bulldoze a grade that the tanks, armoured cars, and Kangaroos could claw up.[9] Three armoured cars from 'A' Squadron of the 14th Canadian Hussars led the way, followed by three 'A' Squadron Fort Garry Horse tanks and several Kangaroos, all maintaining "regular, neat-looking intervals."[10] Less than six hundred yards out, a German antitank gun tore into the column, and the leading armoured cars and tanks were knocked out. "So the armoured thrust ended there," noted the Essex war diarist, "and the marching troops were ordered to march once again."[11]

Brigadier Keefler's conclusion that a daytime attack across the salt marsh would be suicidal applied equally to an advance along the raised highway up the isthmus. The Essex Scottish headed for another dyke codenamed "Mary," which was a short distance east of Krabbendijke. One officer soon commented over the wireless that "Mary" was proving "a very tough girl."[12] Raked by machine-gun fire and pounded by mortars, the two companies made little progress. Lieutenants Stewart Jones and Harold Lindal were killed and another lieutenant wounded as the officers dangerously exposed themselves. Finally, Lieutenant Colonel John Pangman ordered a withdrawal to the start line of the dyke won by the Royals, and "the artillery plastered all suspected positions and Typhoons were also called in."[13] The 4th Canadian Field Regiment directed the firing and controlled the Typhoons, while its guns alone fired five hundred rounds against targets to soften them for a second attack under cover of darkness.[14]

"Mounted on a cold, clear, moonless night," this attack succeeded as 'A' and 'D' Companies dashed forward, with the artillery "pouring fire on the two crossroads which were the [battalion] objective, the troops with pluck and determination pushed ahead. The enemy, when our men got to close quarters, gave in easily." By 0600 on October 25, "Mary" was taken, and about 120 Germans marched into captivity. "The tough shell of the defences at the narrowest point of the peninsula had been broken," observed the Essex war diarist, "making matters easier for everyone. The armoured thrust in which none of us had much faith had failed but the infantry had carried through as usual and to them much credit is due."[15]

The Royal Hamilton Light Infantry had also been moving that night to the left of the Essex Scottish towards the village of Rilland. Major "Huck" Walsh's 'B' Company led, reaching the objective at dawn and surprising the Germans. By 0800 hours, the village fell and the Rileys bagged 150 prisoners.[16] 4 CIB's war diarist proclaimed the attack "most successful. The enemy seemed most confused and unable to cope with our enveloping moves."[17]

Now well past the chokepoint of the isthmus and about halfway to the Beveland Canal, the gains won were sufficient to encourage Simonds to order the 52nd British (Lowland) Division to launch the planned amphibious assault to outflank the Beveland Canal on the night of October 25–26. 156th Brigade's Royal Scots Fusiliers and 6th Cameronians with the 5th Highland Light Infantry also under command, and a squadron of the Staffordshire Yeomanry in support, crowded the quays of Terneuzen's port to board a vast assemblage of Buffaloes and amphibious vehicles. First Canadian Army's naval liaison officer, Royal Navy Lieutenant Commander Robert Franks, once again played navigator. The armada sailed at 0245 hours in two flotillas. Several amphibious duplex-drive Shermans were present, carrying out the longest sailing ever asked of this complex tank—five miles for those supporting the 6th Cameronians, nine for the ones accompanying the Royal Scots. The latter flotilla was bound for Green Beach, midway between Baarland and Hoedekenskerke, while the former would land on Amber Beach, south of Baarland.

Each flotilla arrived at its respective beach at 0450 hours on October 26. The Cameronians went ashore at Amber Beach unopposed, but the Royal Scots came under artillery fire that damaged several vehicles. The battalion commander, Lieutenant Colonel A.N. Gosselin, suffered burn injuries when his craft was sunk. Otherwise, the landing at Green Beach went well. On neither beach were the duplex-drive tanks able to climb the steep dykes bordering the shore, so they trekked back to Terneuzen. Within two hours, the two forces had linked up, established a bridgehead a couple of miles deep, taken the village of Oudelande, and were meeting only light resistance from an obviously surprised enemy. The 52nd's combat christening was deemed a great success, its task now to drive west towards the causeway linking South Beveland and Walcheren Island.[18]

Fully converted to night attacks, meanwhile, 4 CIB's Essex Scottish had leapfrogged through the Rileys at 0400 hours on October 26, "in an attempt to swing behind the enemy at Krabbendijke" by passing south through Gawege. The Rileys had inadvertently failed to advance as far as the assigned start line, which led to some surprise for the carrier platoon leading the advancing column when it "began to pick up prisoners right and left on the home side of the start line. Germans began to appear from every stump and hollow and before the attack had ever really begun over 70 prisoners were in the bag."

Brimming with confidence, the Essex had all four companies deployed. 'D' Company was on the northern flank headed directly for Gawege, 'A' and 'B' Companies marched in the centre, and 'C' Company moved along the marshy ground bordering the West Scheldt. Another eighty prisoners were swept up in this broad net before 'D' Company was brought up sharply by heavy machine-gun and mortar fire in front of Gawege. Lieutenant Colonel Pangman ordered 'C' Company to outflank the hamlet, but it "was almost trapped by an enemy force which lay low instead of giving up." Taken aback that the Germans were suddenly putting up a fight, 'C' Company withdrew "after wading through deep marshes and with the men filthy and tired."

Realizing that 4 CIB was running out of steam, Keefler ordered 6th Canadian Infantry Brigade to take over. At nightfall, the Essex pulled back to Rilland only to find the village "already jammed with troops" from the other two 4 CIB battalions. Eventually, a dry roof was found for everyone and "the men were given a good meal, a chance to clean up and rest." [19]

FOURTH CANADIAN INFANTRY Brigade had carried the division almost halfway to the Beveland Canal, and Brigadier Keefler hoped another night advance on October 26–27 would gain the eastern bank and finish this "urgent task." Keefler was less worried about reaching the canal than crossing it. The six-mile-long waterway was designed to pass ships between the two Scheldts without their having to venture into the North Sea. Twenty-one feet deep, about two hundred feet wide, with banks rising five feet higher than average water level, the canal was also flanked by twenty-foot-wide drainage ditches. There were three possible crossings—"two through the locks located at the northern and southern ends of the Canal, and one in the centre where the main highway to Goes crossed... Both of the lock crossings presented possibilities of 'jumping' them—that is, obtaining crossings before the enemy was able to destroy them."

But Keefler wanted the highway and adjacent railway crossing if possible, so decided that 6 CIB would advance its battalions at once, with each heading for a specific crossing point.[20]

The brigade spent much of October 26 aboard Kangaroos and other vehicles, creeping along the muddy South Beveland roads to reach 4 CIB's forward positions. Not only mud, but a profusion of mines and roadblocks of fallen trees also hampered progress. Nobody cared for the new battlefield. All the polders had been flooded and were knee to waist deep, so movement was constricted to the boggy dykes.[21]

Lieutenant Cecil Law was on point for the South Saskatchewan Regiment's column. His mortar platoon rode their open-topped Bren carriers, thinking the drivers could more easily spot mines than those driving Kangaroos. Behind his platoon, the Fort Garry Horse's 'C' Squadron clawed up the track, and then came the rest of the South Saskatchewans in one long, tightly packed line. As the column rumbled along, a jeep with three soldiers aboard persistently edged past the vehicles on the right side until it finally passed Law's carrier. Moments later, an explosion lifted the jeep into the air, and the beret of the man riding in the front passenger seat sailed about thirty feet skyward before falling onto the carrier's front end.[22] The jeep's occupants were identified as Brigadier Guy Gauvreau, his intelligence officer, Captain Maurice Gravel, and a driver. The latter man was dead. Gauvreau was seriously wounded. Both Gravel's legs had been broken and he was in shock.[23] Engineers determined that the jeep had triggered three Italian box mines loaded with a total of twenty-one tons of TNT.

Following this debacle, Lieutenant Colonel Vern Stott ordered his men to dismount and continue on foot. The tanks were obviously useless in this terrain, and it would soon be dark, so Stott told Law to help the Shermans turn around on the narrow road and guide them to a harbour area.[24] Temporary command of 6 CIB passed to Lieutenant Colonel Ernest Thompson, while Major J.J. Gagnon assumed the helm of the Queen's Own Cameron Highlanders.

By about 1500 hours, 6 CIB's three battalions had all passed through 4 CIB's lines. Les Fusiliers Mont-Royal moved along the southern flank of South Beveland towards the village of Waarde, the South Saskatchewans were in the centre on the main road, and the Camerons were to the north bound for Yerseke. Opposition was generally light, indicating that the Germans were prepared to yield the ground east of the canal and only conducting a delaying action. The Fusiliers were hindered more by the "especially wet and treacherous" ground they had to cross than enemy fire, and by midnight had cleared Waarde.[25] Meeting stiffer resistance than the other battalions, the South Saskatchewans were slowed even more by the endless mines blocking its route. Advancing on the right flank via a winding dyke, the Camerons made good progress. Once night fell, the pace quickened all across the front—the tactic once again surprising the Germans.

At midnight, the Fusiliers set sights on the crossing in front of Hansweert at the canal's southern mouth. Wading across one polder after another, it was a miserable trek. But after a couple of hours they climbed over a dyke and pushed into Kruiningen without a fight. A deep antitank ditch delayed their exit from the other side, but once across, the battalion was back in polders—the only opposition deep mud and icy water that all too often was waist deep. Dawn found the battalion just four hundred yards short of the canal. Caught in the open of the Kruiningen Polder, they were driven to ground by fire from the opposite bank. Lieutenant Colonel Jacques Dextraze ordered his men to dig in, where they endured a long, gruelling day under fire. Going on in daylight would be suicidal, so the Fusiliers lay doggo waiting for nightfall.[26]

The Camerons entered Yerseke at first light, passed through without incident, and held up north of the town with the canal in sight. Gagnon could see a small footbridge spanning the canal, and he planned to put the battalion across it one company at a time in the early morning hours of October 28. As with the Fusiliers, moving closer in daylight would just invite needless casualties.[27]

Not as lucky, the South Saskatchewans remained far enough from the canal at dawn that they pushed on in the face of mortar and small-arms fire, only reaching their objective short of the eastern bank by mid-morning. As the lead companies closed in, the

Germans blew both bridges. At 1040 hours, Stott held an O Group and laid out a new plan. The battalion would cross yet another canal in assault boats. 'A' Company would secure the launchpoint, then 'D' Company would go over with eighteen men per boat and establish a bridgehead. The other three companies would follow, with 'B' first in line, then 'C,' and finally 'A' Company. H-Hour was set for 1600 hours.[28]

Because the highway provided the only means for moving heavy vehicles west from the canal, Keefler decided the attack here would be the main one. The other two attacks would, however, force the Germans to spread thin to meet each threat and thus improve the odds. But Keefler also believed it vital for the Fusiliers and Camerons to prevent the Germans blowing the locks that controlled the respective canal entrances. Were the locks destroyed, the canal would become tidal, and even the dykes and other raised ground nearby would be inundated, perhaps cutting the Canadian line of advance.[29]

While the South Saskatchewan attack was being assembled, Stott and the rifle company commanders had conducted a brazen reconnaissance that convinced them the crossing might meet no resistance. Immediately south of the crossing point lay the village of Schore, and the fortifications in front of it showed no signs of life. When Stott and his party strolled back and forth along the dyke without drawing fire, their confidence grew.[30]

'A' Company's efforts to secure the canal bank were delayed by mines and the increasingly "miserable weather," so the launch was delayed to 1915 hours.[31] As 'D' Company began sliding down the bank with the boats, the positions that had appeared abandoned spat gunfire. 'C' Company's Major Victor Schubert sent an immediate wireless message back to the 6th Canadian Field Regiment for a heavy prearranged bombardment on Schore and the German fortifications. Schubert was sorry to see the little red-roofed village torn apart, but knew it was necessary.[32]

The gunners kept firing as 'D' Company paddled across the canal. The men scrambled up the banks while the boats were ferried back for the next company. In short order, the other three companies were across and widening the bridgehead, while the artillery kept pouring shells down until the preset fire plan concluded at 0100 hours. Through the rest of the night, 6th Field continued "harassing anything and everything that looked like a possible enemy hideout."[33]

Much of the artillery was directed towards assisting the Camerons, who made a run for the footbridge just after dark, only to find it well covered by mortars and an antitank gun positioned near the other end. After losing six men wounded and two killed, Major Gagnon scrubbed the attempt and called for assault boats. By 2230, the boats were in position, with 'B' Company providing the paddlers and 'C' Company the landing force. Paddling alongside the northern lock, the Camerons were forced by heavy fire from the opposite shore to land on a small island in the middle of the canal that served as an anchoring platform for the lock.[34] The estimated sixty Germans defending the western bank sank nine of the ten assault boats at this point, and only with extreme difficulty were the two companies able to escape in small packets to the eastern bank aboard the remaining boat.[35] Lieutenant Joseph David Trail Hailey and twenty other ranks were killed during the failed attack, and another twenty-one wounded.[36]

At the southern end of the canal, the Fusiliers' 'B' Company carefully groped its way out onto the lock in the early hours of October 28, and managed to gain the opposite shore undiscovered at 0500 hours. Surprise was complete, and the bridgehead expanded rapidly as the rest of the battalion poured across. Hansweert fell with hardly a shot fired as the French Canadians rousted 121 prisoners.[37]

WITH TWO BATTALIONS on the western side of the canal by daybreak, 6 CIB had broken the back of the German defences on South Beveland. A desperate counterattack against the South Saskatchewan bridgehead in the early morning was shattered by fire from the 6th Field Regiment that reduced its ammunition supply to ten rounds per gun.[38] By the end of this action, the South Saskatchewans had recorded a surprisingly light casualty total of sixteen killed or wounded. The bridgehead was consolidated during the morning when Schore was cleared and engineers began constructing a bridge next to the blown highway crossing.

In light of this progress, Keefler decided to scrub the plan for the Camerons to force a crossing in their area, after receiving reports that the pillboxes facing it were heavily defended. When the bridge opened for traffic at 1430 hours, 4 CIB—having come forward from Rilland— began crowding onto it, with orders to pass through the South Saskatchewan front and charge towards the causeway linking South Beveland to Walcheren Island. The Royal Hamilton Light Infantry led the brigade's advance by moving towards Biezelinge, while 6 CIB finished clearing the western shore of the canal, reporting that its three battalions bagged a total of 285 prisoners by day's end.[39]

'B' Company, leading the Rileys' advance, had reached the canal while the bridge was still being completed, and so shuttled across aboard five assault boats. In the middle of this undertaking, German artillery ranged in and "the shrouds of driving rain seemed filled with shrapnel. The boats bucked and rolled and the men clung grimly to the gunwales and to each other. But the barrage fell for an hour and ended as suddenly as it started when the sodden and shaken Rileys advanced beyond the canal. Mercifully, there had been only a few casualties." Brushing aside occasional pockets of resistance, the Rileys pushed through to Biezelinge by nightfall and took about ninety prisoners.[40]

The Essex Scottish had been delayed when they arrived at the bridge and found the road "packed with vehicles" waiting to cross. Piling out of their Kangaroos, the rifle companies moved across one after the other in single file. Heading up the north side of the highway, the Essex reached Kapelle by 2000 hours. They found the inhabitants of this "pleasant little town...very glad to see us." Battalion headquarters was quickly established in a large house that had ceased only the previous morning serving the same purpose for a German unit.[41]

South of the bridge, the Royal Regiment had used assault boats to put the leading rifle companies onto the western bank. Marching through darkness, 'D' Company reached the outskirts of Gravenpolder just after midnight. A tentative probe revealed that it was still heavily defended, so an attack with supporting artillery was teed up for the morning. After the town was heavily shelled, the Royals easily cleared the Germans out.

Also early in the morning of October 29, the Royals linked up with the right flank of the 157th Infantry Brigade, and sent their Bren carrier platoon patrolling the area behind Gravenpolder to clean up any bypassed German forces. Finding the carriers bogged down on some of the dykes, Captain Tom Wilcox and some of his men purloined bicycles to move about more easily. All of his "men were desperately tired and in a filthy, wet, muddy condition" when they came upon a small boat unloading some British soldiers. "Then forth from the boat onto shore stepped what seemed to me to be the finest soldier I had ever seen in my life, a fine figure of a Scottish gentleman, carrying the shepherd's crook affected by some senior Scottish officers in place of a cane or swagger stick. He had a small pack neatly adjusted on his back. (I had absolutely no idea where mine was and couldn't care less.)... He had his pistol in a neatly balanced web holster. (I had mine in my hip pocket.) He had a neatly kept map case. (I had mine stuck in my breast pocket.) He was a Colonel and I was a Captain. His boots were neatly polished and I was wearing turned-down rubber boots. I did manage to salute, although I think it must have been haphazard. He politely enquired if we were Canadians. (Although who else could have looked as we did?)" When the officer asked direction to his battalion headquarters, Wilcox personally escorted him there, "taking no chances on losing such a beautiful specimen of a soldier to the German Army."[42]

During the day, a 'D' Company patrol ambushed an enemy column bound for Gravenpolder. They took twenty-eight prisoners along with four 75-millimetre guns, fourteen horses, seventeen ammunition wagons, and several heavy mortars. The horses were turned loose, the wagons overturned, and the ammunition dumped into the water below the dyke.[43]

October 29 was a rare, clear, sunny day that enabled Lieutenant Colonel John Pangman and his Essex headquarters staff to spend the morning studying the countryside and town of Goes—South Beveland's largest—from the steeple of Kapelle's church. Pangman decided "the enemy was pulling back as rapidly as possible."[44] His assessment was correct, for a general withdrawal to the Walcheren causeway was underway and what resistance there was "seemed to be of a most disjointed nature."[45]

Nipping at 70th Infantry Division's heels, the Canadians and British made good progress, with the latter advancing on 2 CID's left flank. Upon entering the wide western part of the peninsula, Keefler put two Canadian brigades up front to avoid leaving pockets of Germans behind to threaten the divisional rear. 4 CIB advanced to the south of Goes with its left flank against that of 157th British Infantry Brigade, while the newly arrived 5th Canadian Infantry Brigade joined the chase at 0530 hours, with the Black Watch making a beeline for Goes. The 14th Canadian Hussars reconnaissance regiment covered the division's right flank by advancing along the northern coastline.

At this moment, Brigadier Holly Keefler, in an attempt to ensure that each brigade advanced as quickly as possible, declared a horserace with a grim penalty to the loser. Whichever brigade failed to gain the Walcheren Island causeway first would draw the expected bloody task of forcing a crossing.[46] In reality, this was a joke and a rather cruel one, because should 5 CIB—having crossed the start line later than 4 CIB—win, Keefler had no intention of awarding it the prize. He was sure that 4 CIB would win, though. Spurred on by their respective brigadiers, however, the battalions gamely entered the race.[47]

After fighting through several pockets of resistance that cost the battalion thirty casualties, of which only one was serious, the Black Watch entered Goes in the early afternoon. "The reception we received," recorded the war diarist, "was tumultuous. Orange flags were being flown everywhere. The people clambered all over our vehicles, and the riflemen had to fight their way through the civilians to get to their areas of the town. When they heard that the men had had nothing to eat since early morning they brought out tea, coffee, hot chocolate, bread, biscuits, cake, and all sorts of fruit. One old lady brought out a bottle of 'OLD MULL' and handed it to the boys telling them that she had been saving it for four and a half years for this day. The people knew we were coming but had not expected us until the following day, so perhaps the element of surprise had a bearing upon the spontaneity of their welcome. The men had to kiss babies and sign autographs all the way through town. No sooner were we established than the White Brigade started rounding up their collaborators." The town's German commandant was found to have fled so quickly he had left a half-written letter on his desk.[48]

Such was the pace that by the afternoon of October 30, Keefler urged Brigadier Fred Cabeldu to push 4 CIB all the way through to the causeway, get across it, and establish a bridgehead on Walcheren Island. Cabeldu called a meeting of his battalion commanders at Nieuwdorp, which the Essex Scottish had liberated followed a gruelling twelve-mile march from Kapelle that the brigadier believed had been executed so rapidly it left "the enemy stupefied."[49] Such advances, Cabeldu learned, had left 4 CIB's infantrymen too worn out "to force a passage over the causeway." He took the argument to Keefler, who agreed that 4 CIB needed only to clean "up as much of the enemy as possible at this end of the causeway." It would then fall, as he had earlier planned, to 5 CIB to bull across and form a bridgehead through which 157th Brigade would pass.[50]

BY LATE AFTERNOON, the Royal Regiment was within a half-mile of the causeway. When Lieutenant Colonel R.M. Lendrum ordered Major Ralph Young and Captain Tom Wilcox to get an estimate of enemy strength, they reported about two hundred Germans "squeezed into a quarter circle that had the end of the causeway as its apex. The two radii forming the sides of the quadrant were the sea-dykes of that corner of the peninsula, while the arc of the quadrant was a line of mined and wired posts, well-manned and mounting machine-guns and anti-aircraft guns employed in a ground role. Along the sea wall opposite Walcheren a line of concrete shelters had been sunk into the dyke and protected in front by a line of concrete fire-positions. All in all, it was a formidable defensive locality."[51]

Lendrum scrubbed plans for a hasty attack, and teed up an operation for October 31. He decided to hit the Germans with a pincer by having a company move along each sea dyke and converge at the end of the causeway, while the other two companies struck directly at the quadrant's arc with a feint intended to keep the enemy in their forward positions. Moving swiftly in from the flanks, the two companies coming along the dykes might be able to cut the causeway before the Germans realized that the Royals were behind them. Lendrum hoped to prevent any of the defenders escaping. The attack would be supported by the 4th and 5th Canadian Field Regiments, a Toronto Scottish Regiment mortar platoon, and two of its machine-gun platoons laying down fire on identified German positions, on the causeway to prevent movement of reinforcements along it, and against suspected artillery and mortar positions on Walcheren that were within range.

At 0200 hours, 'A' Company under Captain John Ellis Stothers moved north along the dyke opposite Walcheren, while 'B' Company came down the other dyke and 'C' and 'D' Companies began pressing towards the German front. 'A' Company's attempt at stealth failed almost immediately, as the Germans opened with heavy fire that pinned down Lieutenant Maurice Berry's No. 7 Platoon. While Stothers got on the wireless and called in mortar fire, Berry crawled forward alone to a pillbox protecting a heavy machine gun, and silenced it by throwing grenades through the apertures.

Realizing that 'A' Company was in a dogfight, Lendrum pulled a couple of platoons away from 'C' Company's feint to reinforce it. The attack was renewed, with the men cutting paths through heavy barbed-wire barriers and working past mines and other booby traps. Finding one pillbox too well sited to overrun and knowing it was critical to cut the causeway quickly, Stothers dropped a platoon to keep it under fire while he pressed on with the rest of the company. Fifty minutes after going into the attack, 'A' Company reported that it controlled the causeway entrance. The defiant pillbox was eliminated about the same time by burning the defenders out with a flamethrower.

With the other companies pressing in on the Germans from every flank, the garrison surrendered. Two officers and 153 other ranks were taken prisoner.[52] Stothers's subsequent Military Cross citation noted that he "employed his own and supporting weapons with such skill and aggressiveness that his company [was] successful in consolidating the end of the causeway, cutting the enemy communications and capturing almost the entire garrison, including three 75-millimetre guns, several flak guns, and their small arms. This brilliant attack ensured the success of the battalion operation which gave the division the firm base from which the attacks on Walcheren were launched."[53] Berry also earned a Military Cross for bravery. Having cleared the objective, the Royals dug in and sat tight through a rainstorm of mortar fire in order to secure the start line for 5 CIB's causeway assault.

While the Royals had been eliminating the last opposition on South Beveland, a squadron of the 14th Canadian Hussars embarked on an impromptu amphibious invasion of North Beveland, undertaken when their commander, Major Dick Porteous, learned from residents that the island was ripe for picking. North Beveland, which measured about seven miles long and three miles wide, was separated from South Beveland by a narrow channel called the Zandkreek. Loading the Daimlers of 'A' Squadron aboard a barge and an array of fishing boats and other small craft, Porteous ferried it over in the afternoon. Lieutenant E.G. McLeod led his troop in a rapid dash to Kamperland, the island's largest village, with such verve that it garnered him a Military Cross and netted about two hundred prisoners. Over the next two days, the squadron ranged across North Beveland until declaring it secure on November 2, with a final prisoner tally of 450.[54]

The clearing of South Beveland buttoned 70th Infantry Division inside its defences on the mostly flooded Walcheren Island. But because its coastal batteries remained intact and no Allied shipping could safely pass them to gain Antwerp, the West Scheldt was still effectively closed. Only a major offensive would wrest this last piece of Zeeland real estate from German hands. In concert with 5 CIB's assault on the causeway, the amphibious landings that comprised Operation Infatuate must proceed despite the great inherent risks.

On October 31 at 0930 hours, Lieutenant General Guy Simonds put Infatuate into motion and notified 11 Canadian Corps's Major General Charles Foulkes. Foulkes messaged Brigadier Keefler tersely to "get on with it." Simonds wanted 2nd Canadian Infantry Division to hit the causeway hard in the hopes of convincing 70th Infantry Division's Generalleutnant Wilhelm Daser to concentrate his forces on blocking this attack, which would improve the odds for successful landings at Vlissingen and Westkapelle. Initially, Foulkes considered having the 157th Brigade's fresher and full-strength Glasgow Highlanders put in this assault rather than the worn-down troops of 5 CIB. But the British advance on South Beveland had been slow, the untested brigade tentatively feeling its way, so that it was too far from the causeway to arrive before morning on November 1. Foulkes needed an attack now, so Keefler told Brigadier Bill Megill to send his men forward.[55]

[24]

Let's Take the Damned Place

WHILE 2ND CANADIAN INFANTRY DIVISION had been securing South Beveland, 4th Canadian Armoured Division had advanced from Wouwse Plantage towards Bergen op Zoom. The deadly ambush 6th Parachute Regiment had sprung on the South Albertas' 'C' Squadron late October 25 had proven that Kampfgruppe Chill was well entrenched in the forest plantation through which the division must pass, so these piney woods would have to be cleared. On the morning of October 26, 'C' and 'D' Companies of 10th Canadian Infantry Brigade's Lincoln and Welland Regiment and the South Albertas' 'C' Squadron headed back towards the ambush site.[1]

Simultaneously, the Algonquin Regiment advanced out of the settlement of Centrum, which lay literally in the middle of the densely wooded Wouwse Plantage, supported by the South Albertas' 'B' Squadron. Two Algonquin companies were to clear the brickworks the Lake Superior Regiment had bypassed the day before during its charge into the Wouwse Plantage village, while the other two companies pushed west along a dirt road to Zoomvliet.[2] Between the Lincs and Algonquins, the Argyll and Sutherland Highlanders sent 'A' and 'B' Companies into the dense forest from a point two miles south of Centrum, with 'A' Squadron helping.[3] North of Wouwse Plantage village, 4 CAB was to guard 10 CIB's flank.

The Argylls had awakened to learn they had taken a hit on the jaw during the night. Private Robert van Luven of the carrier platoon had been in battalion headquarters when Brigadier Jim Jefferson phoned Lieutenant Colonel Dave Stewart with the attack order. "Look, my people are tired," he heard Stewart say. "They've been in there for three weeks now. And I'm getting tired. I'm getting tired being nursemaid to the rest of the Division. We're not going in."[4] Stewart was promptly summoned to brigade, his deputy Major B. Stockloser assuming command. Officially, his recall was so that he could receive minor surgery, but the rumour mill held that Stewart had been pulled—everyone hoped temporarily—for defying orders.[5]

Major Gord Armstrong agreed the regiment was exhausted. Having suffered a football injury before the deployment to the continent in July, he had just returned to active duty. Arm still in a cast, he first had to get the medical officer to okay his commanding a rifle company. At the Regimental Aid Post, Armstrong walked with Padre Charlie Maclean to where twelve bodies awaited burial. Among them were Major Alex Logie and Captain Raymond McGivney, who had both died leading 'B' Company. Seeing his predecessors soon to be interred beneath muddy Dutch soil gave him an appreciation of what battle meant. Cleared by the MO, Armstrong took command of 'B' Company. He didn't care for the look of the men; they were all unshaven, their skin a yellowish hue. "They looked like a bunch of ragamuffins." He and the also-just-arrived company sergeant major ordered a shave and parade inspection. Hoping this re-instilled some discipline, Armstrong then led them towards the woods.[6]

A terrific mortar and artillery bombardment preceded the Argylls' advance. Both the woods and road were riddled with mines. Four 'A' Squadron tanks were knocked out, and one brewed up. Trapped inside, its driver, Trooper James Foster, burned to death. When a mine crippled Corporal Charles Smith's Sherman, he and the co-driver began clearing mines by hand. Seeing the road laced with tripwires running to mines, several other tankers joined in. The men carefully tied long strings to the networks of wires, then detonated the mines with a hard yank from behind the shelter of their knocked-out tanks. Although Flails were called, the mine-clearing tanks bogged in mud short of the road.[7] When a couple of Crocodiles tried going forward anyway, they struck mines, and their hulks blocked the road entirely. By mid-afternoon, having got nowhere, 'A' Squadron withdrew to the start point. Lacking tank support, the Argylls advanced only one thousand yards before an antitank ditch guarded by highly accurate mortar fire blocked their path and night closed in.[8]

To the north, the Algonquins met trouble on the road to Zoomvliet. The previous day, 'B' Company had advanced with 'B' Squadron's No. 4 Troop to just past a crossroads a mile and a half north of Centrum before dark, and dug in for the night. Using the cover of darkness, German paratroopers infiltrated behind their position to heavily mine the road and prepare several ambush sites. Company Sergeant Major E. Burns, with two privates, was outbound from battalion headquarters to 'B' Company when his party was ambushed and everyone taken prisoner. When a patrol from 'D' Company tried to contact 'B' Company, it was driven back, with two casualties.[9]

'B' Company was effectively cut off, a fact realized when the morning advance led by 'D' Company and 'B' Squadron's No. 3 Troop moved along the road bordered by "Minen" signs. Just before a small clearing, one tank struck a mine and another was knocked out by a Panzerfaust. That halted the advance, freeing the Germans to concentrate on tightening the noose around 'B' Company and No. 4 Troop.

While pounding 'B' Company's perimeter with artillery and mortar fire, the paratroops manhandled an antitank gun to a building a few hundred yards to the west. Although Corporal Chuck Fearn spotted the enemy gun, it knocked his tank out before the gunner could unsafe his 75-millimetre to fire. In rapid order, the remaining three tanks in Lieutenant Leaman Casey's troop were damaged or knocked out. The infantry were also hard-pressed. An exploding shell badly wounded 'B' Company Commander Captain Robert Scott. When Private Orville Reeves attempted to run the gauntlet in the company Bren carrier to carry the captain to the RAP, it struck a mine and blew "end-over-end for thirty yards."[10] Reeves perished and Scott, having suffered a second serious injury, died soon after, despite efforts by German medical personnel to save him.

As the only surviving officers besides himself were Casey and an Algonquin lieutenant, 15th Canadian Field Regiment's FOO Captain Jack Forbes took command. Using the radio in a tank, Forbes calmly directed artillery fire against any paratroops he saw massing for an assault even as the Sherman took three antitank-gun hits.[11] The artillery, Forbes knew, was the only thing keeping the Germans at bay. If the wireless in the tank was knocked out, the little force would be doomed.

At 15th Field's headquarters, "small groups gathered around the earphones to hear how the battle progressed." With Forbes and his three-man crew out there, "the battle... became a matter of personal interest. Artillery support was supplied on a generous scale, and, spurred on by reports telephoned from the command posts, the gunners sweated with a will as target after target was engaged."[12]

Efforts were being made to rescue 'B' Company. When the attack on the brickworks was successfully concluded, 'A' and 'C' Companies had started working into the woods north of 'B' Company's position. But with few remaining hours of daylight left, Lieutenant Colonel Robert Bradburn realized they were unlikely to reach the embattled force before nightfall. He and 'B' Squadron's Major T.B. "Darby" Nash decided to evacuate the position with the Algonquin Bren carrier platoon.[13] Nash ordered the three remaining tanks of Lieutenant Jean Marc "Johnny" Guyot's troop to provide covering fire. When Guyot told his men to saddle up, he learned that one of the tanks had electrical problems. He led the other two Shermans forward.

Crawling around one of the tanks disabled in the earlier advance, Guyot drove into an ambush. A Panzerfaust bomb struck his tank, which exploded into flames. Guyot and Trooper Melvin Danielson were badly wounded and taken prisoner. Although the paratroopers administered first aid, the twenty-eight-year-old Guyot bled to death. Under a flag of truce, they then allowed an ambulance to fetch Danielson, but the nineteen-year-old Stockholm, Saskatchewan farmer died during surgery to amputate a leg.[14]

The Algonquins' 'C' Company, meanwhile, had managed to secure an antitank ditch across which a bulldozer constructed a crude crossing for the carrier platoon. At 1600 hours, the platoon barrelled cross-country through a hail of small-arms and mortar fire to gain

'B' Company's position. Quickly gathering infantrymen, tankers, and artillerymen aboard, the platoon dashed back without casualties.[15]

Returning to 15th Field Regiment's headquarters, Captain Forbes dryly declared that his continuous wireless performance had convinced him to become a radio announcer when the war was over. He was awarded a Military Cross, for undoubtedly saving many Canadian lives.[16]

While 'A' and 'B' Squadrons of the South Albertas had taken serious losses on October 26, 'C' Squadron had fared better on the Huijbergsche Baan, where the Germans had caused it such grief the day before. Working along the verges beside the tanks, the Lincs' Major Jim Swayze of 'D' Company had stared at the trees pressing in on either flank and wondered, "When the hell are we going to get out of here?"

Lieutenant Don Stewart of 'C' Squadron had been so apprehensive about re-entering the woods that he solemnly shook the hand of another troop officer, sure neither would see the other again. Stewart's troop was second in line behind Lieutenant Danny McLeod's troop. Initially, progress was encouraging and the combined force soon moved past Helmolen, little more than a mile from Bergen op Zoom's outskirts. Then a Panzerfaust bomb sliced across the bow of McLeod's Sherman in a close miss. Seeing that the fire came from a concrete bunker, McLeod called up a Crocodile manned by the Fife and Forfarshire Yeomanry Regiment of 79th British Armoured Division. Two Crocodiles bore right past McLeod's tank troop. McLeod yelled at the British tankers to flame out the bunker, but they seemed to think he was just cheering them forward. A Panzerfaust blasted the lead Crocodile and it spun off the road into the right-hand ditch, while the second quickly burned out the bunker.[17]

'D' Company caught up to the tanks at this point to provide flank protection, but with the mines thickening whenever the troops went farther into the woods, Swayze had to keep his men within twenty-five yards of the road on either side. Even the presence of Captain Percy Easser's pioneer platoon armed with mine detectors little speeded the advance, because the disarming mechanisms were generally booby trapped, so each mine had to be lassoed with a long rope and detonated at a distance.[18]

When the surviving Crocodile was knocked out by a Panzerfaust, Major Dave Currie decided there was no point in continuing an advance that could not be reinforced. He ordered McLeod to pull everyone back to the crossroads near Helmolen, dig in for the night, and to personally attend an o Group at his headquarters. As McLeod walked back along the road, puzzling over why the force had been called all the way back to Helmolen rather than reinforced, he saw through the intervening trees that fires burned on the nearby roads. Everywhere, he realized, tanks were burning. Walking into Currie's headquarters, he asked, "What the hell happened?" Currie told him what had befallen the squadrons supporting the other infantry battalions.[19]

NORTHWEST OF WOUWSE PLANTAGE village, 4th Canadian Armoured Brigade had attempted a one-mile advance to cut the Bergen op Zoom–Roosendaal highway—along which Kampfgruppe Chill was evacuating heavy equipment from the coastal city. Beyond the village, a wide, heavily defended, antitank ditch barred the way. 'B' Company of the Lake Superior Regiment was ordered to clear it, but as its two motor platoons numbered no more than fifteen men each, 'C' Company was added to the task. Together, the two companies managed to breach the obstacle and establish a narrow bridgehead. Despite repeated German attempts to throw the small force back, it clung tenaciously to the position until night fell and the enemy withdrew. Four men had been killed and another seven wounded, including Major Murray and Lieutenant J.A. Brown.

With the antitank ditch surmounted, 4 CAB's Brigadier Robert Moncel decided to launch an all-out drive towards the highway in the morning, with each Superior company supported by one tank regiment. 'A' Company would have a squadron of the British Columbia Regiment, 'B' one from the Governor General's Foot Guards, and 'C' one courtesy of the Canadian Grenadier Guards.[20] A troop of Flail and Crocodile tanks would also accompany each column. "Push on," was the general tenor of Moncel's instruction at the Brigade O Group.[21]

In forcing the antitank ditch, the Superiors had taken twenty-three prisoners, all from Hermann Göring Regiment or 6th Parachute Regiment. "The individual German soldier fights very stubbornly and at times brilliantly when controlled by his superior officer. When left alone he surrenders with alacrity," commented the 4th CAB war diarist.[22] The Germans had, however, pinned the Canadian brigade in place for another day, gaining more time for an orderly withdrawal from Bergen op Zoom.

The situation in the city was chaotic, with heavy Canadian artillery fire pounding it throughout October 26. Its normal population of about thirty thousand had doubled with refugees from the south. People were sheltered in any available cellar or basement to escape the shelling, while others had dug trenches in backyard gardens and roofed them with doors and timbers that were then covered with sod and sand. Summoned to German headquarters, Burgomeister Lijnkamp was instructed to evacuate all civilians within twenty-four hours. Realizing that the Germans might intend a last stand in the city streets, Lijnkamp refused. Instead, he argued that, given the many refugees, evacuation was impossible. Finally, the Germans agreed not to defend the city, but imposed four conditions. Anybody hampering German movement would be shot, there would be no public gatherings, all German matériel was to be surrendered by noon the next day, and if there was any unrest, the city would be set ablaze by an incendiary bombardment.

Throughout October 27, there were increasing signs that the Germans were pulling out, but they did not go quietly. The sound of demolitions thundered throughout the city, as three church towers that could be used for observation points were blown down. Radio transmission towers were also toppled, the telephone exchange destroyed, railcars overturned, rail lines ripped up, and the quayside wharves damaged with explosives. As the Germans moved across the Zoom—the ancient canal that cut through the city's northern outskirts to the sea and had been used for centuries to ferry peat moss from the inland marsh country—they rigged the bridges with demolitions.[23]

The German decision to surrender most of Bergen op Zoom without a fight was little motivated by humanitarian concerns. It was rather a response to LXVII Corps's rapidly deteriorating situation.

Across a broad front, 1 British Corps was pushing northward, with 49th British (West Riding) Infantry Division putting pressure on 346th Infantry Division south of Roosendaal. The German division was so exhausted, noted LXVII Corps's Chief of Staff, Oberst Elmar Warning, "that it could not hold out long." Only the intercession of elements of Kampfgruppe Chill on its left enabled the division to hang on. East of Roosendaal, Breda was also imperilled and its loss expected, as the 104th U.S. Infantry Division closed in from the west and 1st Polish Armoured Division from the east. The 711th Infantry Division was suffering heavy losses trying to delay the city's fall. Elements of 719th Infantry Division east of Breda were withdrawing rapidly into the lines of 711th Division as British Second Army's 7th Armoured Division collapsed its left flank with a drive along the southern bank of the Maas River.[24]

Despite a phone call from Oberkommando der Wehrmacht Operations Chief, Generaloberst Alfred Jodl, to OB West's Chief of Staff, General der Kavallerie Siegfried Westphal, at 0215 hours on October 27 reminding him "that the Fuehrer wanted the withdrawal movements of Fifteenth Army to be carried out as slowly as possible... German forces from Bergen op Zoom to s'Hertogenbosch were being speeded on their way by strong Allied pressure."[25]

That the Germans were withdrawing was soon recognized when the Canadians renewed the advance that morning. During the night, 4 CAD's Major General Harry Foster had informed his commanders that Field Marshal Montgomery wanted the city taken that day. Already British Broadcasting Corporation had mistakenly reported it liberated several times, and Foster's divisional headquarters was being swarmed by correspondents eager to cover First Canadian Army's freeing its first major Dutch city. While 10 CIB would carry out the main thrust from the south, 4 CAB would advance a smaller force from the east.[26]

The South Albertas' 'A' and 'C' Squadrons and 'C' and 'D' Companies of the Lincoln and Welland Regiment put in the attack from the south. It was a cold, dull day with intermittent showers that only made the infantrymen's lot more miserable. At first the advance was cautious, but as "only slight opposition was met" the pace quickened.[27] By noon, 'A' Squadron was through the woods and nearly in

Zoomvliet, while 'C' Squadron was well past Helmolen. South Alberta Lieutenant Colonel Gordon "Swatty" Wotherspoon and his Lincoln counterpart, Lieutenant Colonel Bill Cromb, had moved their tactical headquarters forward to a dirt road south of the latter village.[28]

Tanks and infantry were being met by civilians, who all reported the Germans gone. At 1345 hours, 'C' Squadron's Lieutenant Danny McLeod was a mile and a half from Bergen's centre and being inundated with civilian reports. Some held that German tanks were massing north of the Zoom and about two hundred infantry had dug in along its northern bank, so Wotherspoon and Cromb directed several artillery concentrations on the suspected positions. There was a grave risk that if the force bulled into the city, it would get caught in a deadly street fight. Bergen was a medieval city, its centre a maze of narrow streets where tank movement would be restricted. Finally, Wotherspoon turned to Cromb and said simply, "Hell, Bill, let's take the damned place." Cromb nodded agreement.

To speed things, the infantry mounted the Shermans, Major Jim Swayze taking a moment to explain to his wet, exhausted men that the Germans were "in there and they're nice and dry. We're out here and we're getting soaked. Are we going to stay out here and get soaked?"[29] On the outskirts, McLeod dropped his infantry to proceed on foot, so the tanks could go faster. His orders were to make for the main square—the Grote Markt—and secure it. Left to his own navigating, McLeod would probably have got hopelessly lost in the winding, narrow streets, but Dutch resistance fighter Ad de Munck hopped on the fender of McLeod's tank and guided the Shermans to the square. People poured out of houses, waving towels and orange flags. Clogging the streets, they slowed the tanks to a crawl. At about 1615, McLeod's troop reached the square.

Soon, the infantry and other tanks were in the city. Swayze's men deployed around the square, and suggested the tankers put a Sherman at the head of each street running northwards to meet any German counterattack. Shortly thereafter, the two lieutenant colonels entered the city and set up headquarters in the elegant Hotel de Draak (Dragon Hotel), which at 547 years old was one of Europe's oldest hostelries. McLeod, meanwhile, was already on the move again and closing on the Zoom to test whether the Germans were on the north bank. Seeing the main bridge still standing, he edged towards it, only to have an armour-piercing round crease one of the tanks in a narrow miss. The tankers hastily withdrew behind a covering screen of smoke shells.[30]

The Germans on the Zoom would have been in a difficult position had 4 CAB's thrust towards Bergen succeeded. The Governor General's Foot Guards No. 2 Squadron and 'B' Company of the Lake Superior Regiment had struck out on a northwesterly angle to gain the Bergen op Zoom–Roosendaal Highway and gain the city. All had gone well as the force reached the highway and proceeded west along it until being blocked by a blown bridge just before Vijfhoek. Here, the road was heavily mined, and Germans were well emplaced with antitank guns on the opposite bank of the bridge crossing.

The tank commander, Major G.T. Baylay, reported the situation to Lieutenant Colonel E.M. Smith, who sent the reconnaissance troop patrolling for other routes to Bergen. When Lieutenant J.W. Devitt reported all other roads equally blocked, Smith advised Brigadier Moncel that the force could only get to Bergen by plowing right into the position at Vijfhoek. Moncel replied that it was more important for his brigade to push north rather than west to Bergen, so the force should turn about and take over the advance on Heerle from the Canadian Grenadier Guards.[31] The Guards, meanwhile, would advance from Wouwse Plantage on a northwesterly axis to cut the highway at Vijfhoek.

Midway between Wouwse Plantage and the highway, the little village of Wouwse Hill stood to the right of a vital intersection. It was towards this intermediate objective that the Grenadiers' No. 2 Squadron and the Superiors' 'C' Company had advanced the morning of October 27. As the column closed on the village, it came under heavy antitank fire. One Sherman was disabled, while another remained in the fight despite being hit ten times. Rushing to the front with his headquarters section, Major C.A. Greenleaf personally directed his squadron's return fire, and a total of eight German guns were knocked out. With this antitank screen eliminated, the village was easily taken, along with about thirty prisoners.

Half a mile to the west, however, the hamlet of Westlaar proved a thornier obstacle. Attempts to approach it from Wouwse Hill were repelled by antitank fire, so at 1600 hours, Greenleaf sent Sergeant W.M. Irvine's No. 4 Troop around on a secondary road to attack it from the south, with a platoon of Superiors in support. Five hundred yards short of the hamlet, this force was met by antitank fire to which Irvine's troop replied with their 75-millimetre guns. With antitank guns and tanks locked in a furious duel, the infantry went to ground to await a victor. Unimpressed, Irvine jumped out of his tank and organized a combined tank and infantry assault that broke into the village and ended the firefight. Another fourteen prisoners were taken.

Westlaar posing no further threat, Greenleaf renewed the advance towards the highway at midnight.[32] Covered by artillery concentrations against Vijfhoek, tanks and infantry rolled through a night illuminated by the many fires sparked by Canadian and German guns. With orders from the Grenadiers' Lieutenant Colonel W.W. Halpenny to be in position to attack the village at first light, Greenleaf ensured that the advance proceeded steadily while keeping noise to a minimum—the sounds of tanks and Bren carriers were muffled by the regular detonations of artillery shells—in hopes of achieving surprise. At dawn, tanks and infantry stormed and captured the German antitank positions that had blocked the Governor General's Foot Guards. Vijfhoek was quickly cleared and the highway cut. More than forty German prisoners were rounded up, including fifteen who Sergeant Hubert bluffed into surrendering with an empty Bren gun. The other two Grenadier squadrons came up, and a major blocking position was created astride the highway.[33]

Having cut the Germans' eastward escape route from Bergen op Zoom, 4 CAB spent October 28 tightening its grip on the highway, while beginning to prepare for a drive northwest towards Steenbergen, six miles away. Ahead lay the usual Dutch countryside—a collage of farms, villages sprouting church towers, windmills, muddy marshes, and small woods. The ubiquitous mud confined the brigade's vehicles and tanks to roads, making it impossible to outflank German blocking positions.

The Superiors' 'B' Company ran into problems navigating road demolitions en route to the forming-up position for the attack towards Heerle on October 29. Only a single platoon had arrived by the time the Foot Guards were ready to start. Major Baylay's No. 2 Squadron was to lead, but after a personal reconnaissance, he realized that the village overlooked a wide stretch of fields so sodden, a spread-out frontal assault would only bog down with the tanks stranded and exposed to antitank guns. He decided to send a single tank troop and the Superior platoon up the narrow road to test the defences. Lieutenant Liddell's troop moved out under heavy mortar and shell fire that slowed the advance to a painful crawl. Beset by heavy sniping that exacted a heavy toll on the infantry, Liddell reported there was no chance Heerle could be secured with so small a force, and Baylay told him to fall back on the squadron.[34]

At 1400 hours, Brigadier Moncel ordered a renewed effort, with the main tank thrust to turn more westwards in an attempt to cut the Bergen op Zoom–Steenbergen road south of the latter town.[35] Clearing Heerle would be left to the remaining Superiors. The Foot Guards accompanied by the Superiors' 'B' Company headed northwest towards Moerstraten—about three miles away—at 0900 on October 30 with Baylay's squadron again leading. Aerial reconnaissance had led First Canadian Army's intelligence staff to declare the ground north of Heerle "impassable to tanks," and it "was appreciated that stubborn resistance might block this attempt and its success was expected to be limited." The only decent road passed through Heerle, so the Foot Guards' Lieutenant Colonel E.M. Smith gambled by sending the tanks out on a cross-country run. Immediately after the Shermans crossed the start line, they came under heavy shelling and mortaring. One tank bogged down, and the others were wallowing on the verge.[36] The intelligence appreciation seemed forebodingly prescient. As the tanks bypassed Heerle and struck out westwards, 'B' Company split off to clear the village. Heerle fell quickly, and the company dashed a short distance north to secure Hazelaar before jinking west to reunite with the tanks.[37]

To everyone's surprise, the Shermans managed to keep clawing their way forward. No. 2 Squadron had two troops abreast, with Baylay and the other troop following close behind, a tactical formation the tankers had not been able to use for a long time because of their confinement to roads. Other than incessant shelling, they encountered no opposition until closing on Diefhoef about a mile from Heerle, where several antitank guns opened up. Able to manoeuvre, the tankers responded smartly, with the Shermans commanded by Sergeant H.S. Slater and Corporal Romeo Tremblay attacking one gun that the corporal knocked out with a shell. The rest of the squadron deployed and rolled up on the flanks of the lead troop to join the firefight. When a second antitank gun was eliminated, the Germans broke off the engagement. One Sherman had been holed by an armour-piercing round, but its crew escaped unscathed.

Baylay continued, one troop screening the other two with smoke shells, moving in bounds to close on Moerstraten. Known to be strongly held, Baylay's instructions were to bypass the village and leave its clearing to the Superiors. Commanding the lead troop, Lieutenant Middleton-Hope realized that the ground around Moerstraten was so mucky a bypass would be impossible. So his troop went "down the main street with all guns blazing in a confusion of dust and flying tracers while shells fell, and the enemy hurled grenades from the buildings lining the route." The tanks broke free on the western side and Middleton-Hope deployed on the open ground to await the rest of the squadron. Jockeying for position, both Slater and Tremblay's tanks mired in quagmire. The lieutenant moved his tank to provide protective fire for the two stuck Shermans, whose crews buttoned up because of the airburst shells exploding overhead.

Behind the tank troop, a fierce battle was underway for control of Moerstraten, as the tanks exchanged fire with concealed antitank guns and the Superiors shot it out with German paratroopers. A shell whacked into the cargo box on the back of Lieutenant Liddell's tank, sending the contents of a flour sack spewing into the air. Baylay got into a duel with an antitank gun, which his gunner won on the third shot by lining his sights up with the fall of the incoming rounds smashing against the Sherman. Shrapnel from the last German shell riddled the rear cargo box, however, and the squadron's rum issue gushed onto the ground. With dusk falling, the Germans pulled out. But they also used the covering darkness to push an antitank gun into range of the two bogged-down Shermans on the western flank. Both tanks were knocked out. Tremblay and Guardsmen

R.R. Burns, L.R. Kirker, and J.D. Stronach died, while Slater and Guardsmen A. Draper and B.A. Maloney were seriously wounded.[38]

Moerstraten was slightly higher than the ground to the west, so the tankers were able to observe and range in on the Bergen op Zoom–Steenbergen highway. But Lieutenant Colonel Smith's orders had been to cut it and this he intended to do. Major G.C. Lewis's No. 3 Squadron, which numbered only eight tanks instead of the normal fifteen, set out in the dark across very difficult ground. Lewis split his force into two echelons, with three tanks right, four left, and his tank serving as a tactical headquarters. From in front of Moerstraten, No. 2 Squadron lay down a heavy bombardment ahead of the advancing tanks. Groping across treacherously marshy ground illuminated only by the fires of farmhouses set afire with 75-millimetre incendiary rounds, each echelon soon lost a tank to the muck. The rest carried on until blocked by an impassable canal one thousand yards short of the road. Lewis ordered his remaining six tanks to deploy in line to dominate the road with their main guns and soon managed to knock out an antitank gun firing from a position fifteen hundred yards off.

No. 2 Squadron, leading the rest of the Foot Guards, descended from Moerstraten, and the night advance continued by circumnavigating the canal on a wide sweep. To avoid one tank chewing up the path in front of the others, Lieutenant Colonel Smith had the regiment advance widely spaced as it ground over a mile of marshes cut by deep ditches. Although many Shermans bogged down, the regiment's three specialized recovery tanks were able to pull most free. First light found the regiment close to the highway and No. 1 Squadron came astride it at 0830 hours on October 31. Quickly rolling north on the good road, the squadron overran the village of Oude Molen, about two and a half miles north of Bergen op Zoom.

The regiment firmed up inside this village, while No. 1 Squadron continued north on the road with a company of Superiors towards Steenbergen. But this force was brought up short south of Lepelstraat—midway between Bergen op Zoom and Steenbergen—by a partially destroyed canal bridge that proved impassable. Attempts to force a crossing were blocked by heavy German opposition, and by nightfall there had been no further progress.[39] That evening, Major

General Harry Foster, realizing that Steenbergen would be strongly defended and that 4 CAB's "limited infantry resources" were "worn out from lack of rest," ordered the brigade to hold in place until 10th Canadian Infantry Brigade could come from Bergen op Zoom to take over.[40]

IN BERGEN OP ZOOM, an unexpectedly bitter battle along the Zoom had developed on October 28. During the night, the Lincoln and Welland Regiment had established a defensive line along the southern bank to prevent German infiltration into the city. The morning passed fairly quietly, each side harassing the other with only desultory artillery and mortar exchanges, while 10 CIB waited for the Argyll and Sutherland Highlanders to arrive to carry out the attack.

At noon, the Argylls unloaded from trucks and their officers considered the problem ahead. Rather than blowing the main bridge, the Germans had cratered it with explosives and dumped a huge concrete cylinder square in the centre that effectively barred tanks or carriers getting across. Major Stockloser was not overly concerned, because he believed that the canal had terraced sides ensuring easy passage, was only a few feet wide, and that the water running in it was shallow. The Zoom, he declared, "constituted no great obstacle," and little heeded Brigadier Jim Jefferson's suggestion that where it flowed through a culvert to gain the sea, the narrow neck of land "offered some chance for an outflanking movement."

Stockloser decided to bull straight ahead, to pound the Germans senseless with artillery and have 'C' Company establish a secure crossing point on the canal bank. Then, with 'C' Company providing covering fire, 'D' Company would dash across the Zoom and seize the buildings around the bridge intersection, "thus making a firm bridgehead beyond which the other two companies would exploit."[41]

"You don't like me, do you?" Stockloser had growled at 'C' Company's Major Bob Paterson earlier that week. Paterson offered no reply. What he wanted to ask today, however, as Stockloser set out his intentions, was, "Why couldn't they hit with three companies forward instead of one?" Time and again, the same drill prevailed. Advance one company with the rest behind. "Shit, you didn't have a hope in hell," Paterson figured, particularly when a company mustered barely fifty or sixty men.

More officers than Paterson mistrusted Stockloser. Carrier platoon commander Captain Hugh Maclean considered him careless and forgetful. He was unsurprised when summoned that morning only to find that the acting battalion commander could not recall the intended mission. Then suddenly Stockloser pointed at a map and told Maclean to patrol way off on a flank to a point nobody had any information about. "Jesus, I don't think Stewart would have done this," he thought, as he headed off on a reconnaissance of the narrow neck of ground that Jefferson had proposed using for the attack.[42]

At 1400 hours, the battalion started advancing through the streets towards the Zoom, and immediately the Germans struck with accurate 88-millimetre artillery firing airburst rounds, quickly joined by heavy mortaring. The men in the lead companies hunched against this deadly rain as some fell wounded or killed. Civilians, who had been crowding around, scattered. A few minutes later, the Canadian barrage opened up, but several 5.5-inch medium gun battery shells fell short, adding to the casualty toll.[43] One landed in front of the headquarters of the South Albertas' 'C' Squadron, killing one man and wounding six others.[44]

When Paterson led his men from the line of buildings into the park that bordered the Zoom, the Germans opened fire from the opposite bank. Men dodged and jigged to gain the protection of trees and other vegetation, and by 1445 hours, having gained control of the canal's southern bank, were trading bullets with the paratroopers. 'D' Company plunged out from the buildings, only to be driven to ground immediately by machine-gun and sniper fire. The men started crawling. Private Philip Kazimir's helmet kept falling off, and he found it better to throw his rifle out ahead and then belly forward to retrieve it rather than cradling it across his arms as trained. At the edge of the canal was a tangle of wire, the banks steeper and the narrow channel full of more water than they had been told to expect. Nobody was going to cross the Zoom here alive. 'D' Company pulled back to some buildings behind the bridge, and the two companies dug in while the Germans pounded them with artillery and mortar fire. Exhausted, Kazimir lay down in a barn and rolled into his ground sheet. "I didn't care... because you got to that stage you didn't care."[45]

Frontal attack having failed, Stockloser decided to follow Jefferson's advice and attack across the coastal neck. Maclean had patrolled it earlier and gone two hundred yards east along the north bank without encountering any enemy. While the Argylls crossed the neck, the Lincs would put on a diversionary assault to gain some factory buildings across the Zoom east of the bridge that might serve as a firm base for further advances.

The Argylls' 'A' Company went forward at about 2130 hours. The lead platoon managed to cross undetected before Lieutenant Johnny Gravel and another man from the second platoon were wounded when they stepped on mines. At once, German machine guns began raking the area and the lead platoon frantically withdrew to safety. "The neck of land was too narrow to permit... a large scale advance under such fire," the regimental historian noted, "so the attempt was abandoned."[46]

The Lincs, meanwhile, had launched the diversionary assault with Captain Herbert Lambert's 'A' Company leading. Some of his fellow officers were convinced that the eccentric company commander had been "half tight" during the battalion O Group. But he went into the attack right on the sharp end of the company. Coming to an elevated railway track, the men became badly exposed to heavy fire. Some fell wounded, while everyone else hit the dirt. Bullets were spanging off the steel rails. At least three machine guns poured fire in their direction.

Lambert never halted, skidding down the side of the canal and shouting, "Are you coming with me or am I going alone?" Some followed, more didn't. Those who did splashed into the canal and swam to the other side. Then it was up the other bank, cross a narrow park, clamber over a fence, and pause in front of a factory. Lambert did a tally. He had thirteen men. Breaking into the factory, the Canadians chased the German defenders out into an alley. Next moment, the Germans were chasing the Canadians in what became a surreal roundabout where the pursued soon turned into pursuer. Eventually, the two groups took cover in alternate ends of a factory and exchanged insults and epithets as often as bullets. Lambert managed to get a report back that he was cut off and needed reinforcement.

Lieutenant Colonel Cromb told 'C' Company to break through, but a concentration of friendly medium artillery fire fell short and threw it into disarray. So Major Jim Swayze's 'D' Company took over. Knowing that the Germans had likely pulled back in anticipation of an artillery concentration, he scrapped the program in hopes of getting over before the paratroops realized the Canadians were coming and returned to their positions. Swayze had a barn door torn off its hinges and skidded down into the canal to provide a springboard the men could use to dash across without having to swim. Easily gaining the other side, 'D' Company got into the cover of a factory and then called in the artillery. When it lifted, they cut down the Germans rushing to firing positions, taking about fourteen prisoners.[47] The Lincs had a toehold across the Zoom, and Lambert's dash garnered him a Military Cross.[48]

To the west, Major Stockloser decided that the Argylls' 'B' Company should give the frontal crossing a go. Major Gord Armstrong led his men forward warily and quietly, slipping down to examine the Zoom closely. Fifty feet wide, he judged, and full of water easily higher than a man's head. Sending his men back to facing houses, Armstrong slipped down the bank and—still with his arm in a cast—breast-stroked through the icy cold water to the other side. The opposite bank had a well-maintained path running along its edge that would allow rapid movement by infantry. If all his men could swim over undetected, the bridge would be his, but Armstrong knew that would be impossible.[49] So he swam back and told Stockloser that, given four of the pioneer platoon's rubber reconnaissance boats, the company could cross. These were quickly supplied, but found to have been punctured.

Stockloser was in no mood to give up, and dawn was fast approaching. Either the Argylls got across before first light or they would have to wait until the next night to try again. So 'A' Company was ordered to give the land route another try, with 'B' Company behind. This time, the Germans apparently not suspecting that anyone would try such a suicidal-seeming approach twice, the Argylls picked carefully through the mines and gained the other side in full strength. Staying below the crest of the canal bank, the men moved towards the bridge, but eventually were spotted and the Germans began sniping and mortaring the column. As the Argylls closed on the bridge, the German positions were close enough to the edge of the canal that they could throw stick grenades down at them. Most exploded harmlessly in the water, but casualties rose. The situation was critical because the Argylls were unable to look over the edge of the bank without drawing enemy fire, so they could only respond by blindly throwing grenades.

In an attempt to relieve the pressure on the two companies working along the Zoom, Stockloser had 'D' Company attempt to cross the bridge itself. A small number of men managed to get through the heavy fire and took up position in two houses on the right-hand side of the intersection. 'A' and 'B' Companies had now run out of options. Either they went over the top in an attack towards the left-hand side or were trapped. 'A' Company went first, with one platoon that made the dash relatively unscathed except for its lieutenant being wounded. But the second platoon "was heavily engaged as soon as it emerged into the open and had several casualties," including Sergeant Victor John Mann, who was killed.

Major Armstrong and Captain Pete McCordic, acting commander of 'A' Company, decided it was time for personal action. Armed with a rifle and Sten that soon jammed so it only fired a single round at a time, the two officers provided covering fire from the lip of the bank. This tipped the balance, and most of the two companies were soon in among the buildings, beginning the tiresome and deadly task of house-to-house fighting for control of the Zoom frontage. By 1630 hours on October 29, the three companies had forced the Germans back two hundred yards, creating sufficient protection to enable engineers to remove the concrete cylinder and open the bridge to traffic. The Lincs were similarly engaged to the right of the bridge. Having lost the Zoom, the Germans resorted to heavy artillery and mortaring that made movement on either side of it deadly. But the Argylls and Lincs clung to their positions, widening them wherever possible through the night.

In the morning, the Algonquin Regiment relieved both battalions. When the three Argyll companies that had breached the Zoom moved back to the south shore, they numbered only 125 men, barely more than one company's normal strength. For his leadership during this operation, Armstrong received the Distinguished Service Order.[50] The Lincs, too, had been roughly treated, with thirty-eight casualties, eleven fatal.[51] For the Algonquins, the only real problem came in gaining the north side of the Zoom. Shellfire inflicted fourteen casualties during the crossing.[52] By late afternoon October 30, the battle was over and the Germans were withdrawing to escape being cut off by 4th Canadian Armoured Brigade, now astride the Bergen op Zoom–Steenbergen highway.

[25]

The Damned Causeway

THE CLEARING OF the Zoom canal was concluded on the same day 2nd Canadian Infantry Division gained control of the South Beveland entrance to the causeway to Walcheren Island. At first, 5th Canadian Infantry Brigade's Bill Megill had understood that the 52nd (Lowland) Division's 157th Infantry Brigade would be responsible for seizing the causeway. Then Brigadier Holly Keefler declared that, come the morning, 5 CIB must undertake clearing "that part of Walcheren which is not yet flooded, with Middelburg and Flushing [Vlissingen] our two main objectives." The brigade war diarist captured Megill's sentiments, writing: "This comes as an unpleasant order as we were definitely informed that we were to go no further than the WEST end of ZUID BEVELAND and in fact had been promised a week's rest once we had done this job."

A few hours later, this order was countered: "The show was off and we would come out of the line and get our rest after all as there is no forecast of future ops." Everyone relaxed, only to learn during the early hours of October 31 that the "plan has been changed again and we are now to... cross the causeway and secure a [bridge]head on Walcheren Island to enable 157 Bde... to pass through." Megill's staff scrambled to retrieve maps, aerial photos, and other information they had turned in as no longer relevant. These had to be redistributed to the battalion officers during a series of hastily held O Groups.[1]

One look at any of the relevant maps or photos confirmed that the causeway was a perfectly engineered killing ground. The Canadian army's official historian later described it as "singularly uninviting. It was some 1200 yards long and only about 40 yards wide, with sodden reed-grown mud-flats on either side. It was as straight as a gun-barrel and offered no cover except bomb-craters and some roadside slit trenches dug by the Germans in accordance with their custom. The line of spindly trees fringing its southern edge had been badly blasted. The causeway carried the railway line (a single track, the second track having been removed) and the main road; also the characteristic Dutch bicycle-path. At its western end, although it abutted upon one of the few dry areas of Walcheren, there was a wide water-filled ditch on each side of the embankment. The German engineers had been unable to cut the causeway completely, but they had cratered it very heavily just west of its centre, creating a transverse 'furrow' which filled with water armpit-deep. This made the causeway impassable to tanks or other vehicles. The Germans' artillery had certainly registered carefully upon it. They had infantry positions dug into the eastern dyke of Walcheren on either side of the causeway; the road at its western end was heavily blocked; there was a tank or possibly a self-propelled gun dug into the railway embankment just west of the block, and in addition there are reports of a high-velocity gun firing straight down the road."[2]

Megill wanted to avoid sending his men out there entirely. He planned to invade Walcheren via an amphibious operation whereby the Calgary Highlanders paddled across in storm boats. Once they secured a toehold, Le Régiment de Maisonneuve would be ferried over. Meantime, Megill wanted to test the German defences by having the Black Watch "push a strong fighting patrol on to the other side" in a "quick operation."[3] By the time a Brigade O Group was held at 1040 hours, a more ambitious scheme had been hatched. "It is the intention that this brigade shall form a bridgehead across the causeway, on Walcheren Island, 1000 to 1500 yards deep." This was to be achieved by a full-scale battalion attack, with 'C' Company leading, followed in line by 'A', 'B', and 'D'.[4]

That the most battered battalion in the division would be sent into this kill zone struck the Black Watch's Lieutenant Colonel

Bruce Ritchie as "monstrous."[5] Still reeling from the slaughter it had suffered eighteen days earlier on Black Friday, the battalion was barely fit for combat. "The morale of the Battalion at rest is good," Ritchie wrote in a summary to close the October War Diary. "However it must be said that 'Battle Morale' is definitely not good due to the fact that inadequately trained men are, of necessity, being sent into action ignorant of any idea of their own strength, and after their first mortaring, overwhelmingly convinced of the enemy's. This feeling is no doubt increased by their ignorance of field-craft in its most elementary form."[6]

In the past four months, the Black Watch had suffered more than 1,400 casualties. This was a loss rate surpassing those common to infantry battalions in the Great War. Officers and non-commissioned officers had been particularly hard hit, seriously diminishing the number of experienced hands that normally guided new soldiers through their first combat.[7] Each company was still at half-strength, mustering only fifty to sixty men, including several designated Left Out of Battle.[8]

A little past noon, Captain H.S. Lamb led 'C' Company onto the causeway and into an immediate storm of artillery and mortar fire. Hiding in the marshy grass on the causeway's edges, snipers opened up with deadly fire.[9] Only 5th Canadian Field Regiment's guns were firing in support of the Black Watch, the division's other two field regiments having been sent to new firing stations near Breskens to support the next day's landing by British troops at Vlissingen.[10] The 5th Field fired a thirty-round-per-gun Mike Target bombardment to force the Germans to ground, but to negligible effect. Repeated concentrations of the same degree little slowed the rate of deadly fire.[11]

From a slit trench just back of the causeway, Royal Regiment of Canada's Lieutenant Maurice Berry—a former Black Watch officer—watched with a mixture of horror and admiration 'C' Company's gallant but doomed drive into the maelstrom. "The Germans, of course, had the whole place taped and they simply plastered it with shells, mortar bombs and MG fire. They even put the odd AP shot down the road and very unpleasant it sounded when it bounced off the road and went [w]hirring over our heads. They do this for its demoralizing effect, but it never checked the BW. Our boys were very impressed with the way the first two Coys went through, and it made me proud that I had once worn the Hackle."[12]

One heavy German gun was dropping shells that "raised plumes of water 200 feet high when they fell short," but had devastating effect when they struck the causeway. The ricocheting armour-piercing rounds, contrary to Berry's observation, "was hard on the morale of the men." At the midway point, what was left of 'C' Company plunged through the armpit-high water in the crater and clawed their way across. But the attack was coming apart, the Canadian shellfire failing to disrupt the German defences. Only No. 13 Platoon under Lieutenant J.P. Jodoin managed to keep going until it was stopped seventy-five yards short of the end by fire from four MG 42 gun positions. Unable to send a runner back with map coordinates for artillery fire, Jodoin and his men went to ground. Lamb's company started digging in wherever they were pinned down.

Captain William Ewing's 'A' Company was out on the causeway right behind 'C' Company. Ahead, he could see that the artillery fire was striking five to six hundred yards wide. "I don't know what the hell they were trying to do," he said later. Investigation afterward determined the 5th Field this day was calibrating its gun support on a faulty 75-millimetre field piece that resulted in the shells going wide.[13]

Hearing that 'B' Company was preparing to move onto the causeway, Ewing got on the wireless and advised that it stay put. There were already too many people lying in terribly exposed positions and nothing to be gained by putting more at risk. A lot of the causeway was surfaced with bricks or rocky ground, and even to dig a six-inch-deep trench meant hacking away with shovels or knives. His wireless knocked out, Ewing left Company Sergeant Major Alan Turnbull temporarily in command and crawled to the rear to impress the futility of the situation on Ritchie. Turnbull felt as if the company were lying in the middle of a bowling alley, with his men the ten pins and 88-millimetre AP rounds the balls. Nobody was getting anywhere at digging a decent hole. Finally, Ewing returned with permission to get out. Whereas 'A' Company extricated itself easily enough, 'C' Company was so strung out and burdened with wounded that it was hard pressed to fall back.[14] Captain Lamb was wounded, but a couple of men managed to carry the officer to the end of the causeway and load him onto a jeep.

Some of 'C' Company withdrew safely to the concentration point about two hundred yards west of the South Beveland causeway entrance, but more crawled into German slit trenches well to the front and hunkered down. Everyone knew that the plan was for artillery to hammer the rest of the causeway once the Black Watch had withdrawn. Jodoin and four of his men, two of whom were wounded, had worked forward to within twenty-five yards of the causeway's western end when the withdrawal order came. Knowing they could not possibly get back before the artillery arrived, the five men went to ground in a German slit trench.[15] Few of the other wounded in 'C' Company could be evacuated either, for "at the slightest sound of movement the enemy plastered the roadway with shells and mortar, and [MGS] firing on fixed lines." The thirty-minute artillery concentration started at 2340 hours, so for many of 'C' Company's men—wounded or not—the month closed as "the red fire of Bofors laced the dark sky, mortar shells could be seen bursting on the far bank, and the sound of our heavier artillery was everywhere."

From the day after Black Friday to October 31, the Black Watch recorded eighty-five casualties, the majority of those suffered on the causeway. During the last week of October, the battalion had received only thirty-four reinforcements. This all too common attrition-versus-replacement ratio kept chipping the battalion closer to the bone.[16]

THE ARTILLERY CONCENTRATION was to support the Calgary Highlander attack. Major Ross Ellis and his 'B' Company commanders had spent the day anxiously working out the details for Megill's proposed amphibious crossing next to the causeway. As 'B' Company was to lead the effort, Major Francis H. "Nobby" Clarke drew the duty of boat captain. He and his sergeants, all trained in amphibious operations, sketched the outlines of assault craft in sand and then walked the men through boat-handling procedures. All the time, Clarke "couldn't believe the storm-boat idea." He had asked Ellis if he was joking after being told what they were to do. As his men dutifully clambered in and out of the sand-sketch boats, he kept "praying that sanity would return to someone in a position and prepared to stop it before too late."[17]

Launch time was midnight because intelligence predicted the Sloe, as the channel was called, would be fourteen feet deep.[18] This and the fact that the quarter-inch-to-a-mile map at brigade headquarters showed a half-mile strip of nice blue water had convinced Megill and his staff that the assault boat scheme was practicable. Then in the early afternoon, Megill and Brigade Major George Hees were finally able to look at the channel itself. They stared at a mud flat. Elsewhere, the Sloe perhaps could be crossed by boat, but not near the causeway. And there was no time to reconnoitre the channel for a different crossing. If a bridgehead was to draw Germans away from Vlissingen and Westkapelle before the amphibious landings on November 1, it had to be won that night.

Megill and Hees realized the only possible way across would be "on the damned causeway." The brigade commander hoped that he could still keep the operation limited to a "quick and easy in-and-out," with the British taking over the bridgehead soon after 5 CIB won it. The men were exhausted and he wanted to limit casualties. Frankly, the brigadier reminded himself, nobody in the brigade was "really interested in fighting at [this] point at all."[19]

Megill broke the news to Ellis, who in turn informed his battalion at 1830 hours that there would "be no 'boating.'" Instead, Clarke's 'B' Company would lead the way onto the causeway, with 'D', 'A', and 'C' following in line. 'B' Company, Ellis said, "would traverse the Causeway and fan out North, South, and West" to form a narrow bridgehead. 'D' Company would pass through and thrust southward. 'A' and 'C' Companies would then push the bridgehead out farther, with 'B' passing through 'C' at first light to carry the village of Arnemuiden, a little over a mile west of the causeway. An impressive support fire program was prepared that included the 52nd (Lowland) Division's artillery regiments, 5th Canadian Field Regiment, a medium artillery regiment, the 40-millimetre Bofors of an anti-aircraft regiment, 4.2-inch mortars of the Toronto Scottish Regiment's 'A' Company, and the Black Watch's mortar platoon. Once the Calgarians had attained their objectives, Le Régiment de Maisonneuve would expand the bridgehead even farther. As the O Group broke up, one wag boasted that "Jerry would not forget the Halloween party... the Calgary Highlanders calculated to put on for [his] benefit!"[20]

It was a clear, cold night as Major Clarke's 'B' Company moved towards the causeway just before midnight in single file, with five yards distance between each man. Signaller Private Frank Holm dogged Clarke, a No. 18 set strapped to his back. Holm had only one earphone on so that he could hear sounds around him. All seemed quiet, calm. Then the artillery opened up as the company came onto the causeway, and immediately the Germans responded with intensive shelling along its entire length. The same type of high-velocity shells that had rattled the Black Watch ricocheted off the hard road in a shower of sparks and screeched overhead. Shrapnel sang through the air.[21]

'B' Company was about a hundred strong, Lieutenant Walter Lafroy at the head with No. 12 Platoon. Despite the intensity of incoming fire, Lafroy and his men got to the midway point before a major concentration of mortar caught them. Everyone piled into the massive crater for cover. When the firing eased, the platoon slithered out along the southern edge. Most of the German machine-gun fire was high, but men were still getting hit. Private John Morrison caught some shrapnel seconds after a rifle grenade explosion killed a man just behind. Lafroy had a chest wound and a bullet had gone through Corporal D.H. Richardson's arm. Finally, the platoon came up against a roadblock made out of steel railroad tracks anchored with cement. They could hear a lot of Germans chattering on the opposite side, far too many for a platoon as badly chewed up as No. 12 to take on.[22]

Behind the platoons, Clarke and signaller Holm had taken cover in a German slit trench. Holm was impressed to see it was nicely brick-lined, an impressive shelter that had obviously been constructed at leisure. Telling Holm to stay put, Clarke took off towards the front with his runner, Private David Maxwell. The Germans were now pounding the causeway with what Holm figured had to be Walcheren's coastal guns. Each explosion sent a shock wave coursing through his body, leaving his nervous system so jarred Holm feared he was going to crack up. "I swore that if I ever got out of this hellish place alive I wouldn't mind eating dirt for the rest of my life."[23]

Suddenly, two men plunged into the trench and Private Maxwell was panting in Holm's ear that "Clarke was a hard man to keep up with."[24] The captain grabbed the microphone and asked Ellis for permission to withdraw. Ellis contacted Megill, who consented. Slowly the men started pulling back, taking with them their wounded and those Black Watch soldiers—including Lieutenant Joidin and his four men—who had been stranded on the causeway earlier. By 0300 hours, everyone was clear.[25]

The withdrawal was but a brief respite, Ellis and Megill working frantically to draft another artillery fire plan to support a renewed attempt at 0530 hours. Major Bruce MacKenzie's 'D' Company would lead, followed in line by Major Wynn Lasher's 'A' Company, Major Clarke and 'B' Company, and lastly Major Frederick Baker's 'C' Company. The new fire plan called for two field artillery regiments to concentrate across a 750-yard-wide frontage to catch any snipers positioned out on the mud flats either side of the causeway, with fifty-yard lifts every two minutes to keep just ahead of the infantry. Delays teeing up the artillery pushed the attack back first to 0545, and then to 0605.[26]

As they formed at the head of the causeway, 'D' Company glimpsed in the starlight what they were to enter. A lot of the troops were replacements that twenty-five-year-old Private George Teasdale thought of as young kids, and he could see them "getting upset." Despite the creeping barrage, the Germans were still replying with heavy artillery and mortaring, as well as a lot of machine-gun and sniper fire coming in.

MacKenzie suddenly stepped to the front and yelled, "Come on, you sons-of-bitches!" Teasdale and the others started running, glancing nervously at the Canadian corpses strewn across their path.[27] Leaning on the barrage, at 0652 hours, 'D' Company reached the roadblock that had stopped 'B' Company's leading platoon, and came under intense machine-gun and 20-millimetre cannon fire that drove the men to ground. From a slit trench twenty-five yards short of it, MacKenzie glared at the roadblock. The only way past was by direct assault, right into the teeth of that fire.

"Shit," he growled to Sergeant Emile John "Blackie" Laloge, and then called for a two-minute heavy barrage on top of the obstacle.

When the last shells exploded, the company charged into withering MG 42 fire that punched one man after another down. Then the survivors were on the roadblock, some clambering over, while others sprayed Sten and Bren guns through gaps into the chests and faces of the defending Germans. Moments later, they had fourteen prisoners and the lead platoon was darting off the causeway onto Walcheren Island.[28]

At 0933 hours, MacKenzie reported that he was past the causeway and had a platoon creeping south along the dyke bordering the Sloe. The prisoners taken at the roadblock were being sent back, and MacKenzie wanted another company brought up pronto, although he warned that "care should be taken because of the high velocity gun firing down the road." 'D' Company was too badly torn up to silence the thing.

'A' Company began crawling along the north side of the causeway, while 'B' Company did the same on the south flank, with 'C' Company following it. Reaching the other side, Major Wynn Lasher turned 'A' Company north against "light opposition."[29] Major Clarke soon had 'B' Company past the 'D' Company platoon on the southern dyke and headed towards some farm buildings about six hundred yards off. The company was hugging the bank facing the channel, moving in single file. Soon it was directly opposite the farms, but Clarke realized that the ground between the dyke and the buildings was too exposed and wide for the company to cross without artillery fire. He had no means of calling up such support, for his wireless had been damaged and Holm had gone back across the causeway for a replacement. So Clarke lay there on the muddy edge of the dyke looking with "despair and exasperation" first at the objective and then out across the Sloe, where he could plainly see battalion headquarters set up and monitoring the operation. Knowing it was a ridiculous hope, he thought perhaps they would see 'B' Company's predicament and provide artillery on their own initiative.

Major Ellis and his headquarters staff believed all was going well. So much so that at 1210, his reports to brigade prompted Brigadier Megill to alert Le Régiment de Maisonneuve to be ready to cross at 1305 hours. In fact, it was about this time that the Calgary assault began to fall apart. 'B' Company was still stalled on the dyke for want of a wireless set. To the north, 'A' Company had been stopped cold when it came face to face with a bunker complex. Lasher, with Lieutenant Howard O. Schoening in tow, dashed forward to try getting things going again. The officers paused to discuss the situation with two men in a slit trench, and a bullet hit Schoening in the right arm with such force that he was spun around before being thrown to the ground. Lasher was also down, a bullet in his back. When the German fire paused, the two men helped each other crawl to the rear. That single German burst of fire had taken out the last of 'A' Company's officers.

Ellis and Brigade Major George Hees crossed the causeway at 1545 hours to assess the situation personally. Moving from one front position to another, Ellis calmly stood on the edges of the slit trenches chatting with the men in them. Shells exploded all around, bullets whipped the air, but Ellis seemed unconcerned. Discovering that 'A' Company was leaderless, Hees—a staff officer who had never been in combat—volunteered to take command. As Hees was from brigade, permission had to be secured from Megill. Once that came in, he traded soft cap for steel helmet and Sten gun. Captain Bill Newman, an artillery forward observation officer, volunteered to act as company second-in-command. The two men set off on their new assignment. Ellis thought it "took a lot of guts for a guy who had never been in action to go into a hell-hole like that one."[30]

Out on the causeway, the engineers had a bulldozer filling in the crater to open the way for tanks, but it was soon driven off by heavy fire. Even the arrival of a squadron of Typhoons, which rocketed and strafed German positions at about 1545 hours, and two Spitfire squadrons soon after, failed to dampen the resistance. Instead, the Germans counterattacked, concentrating their fury at the axis where 'B' and 'D' Companies' lines joined.

The Germans came in supported by men carrying flamethrowers. 'B' Company's Lieutenant Johnny Moffat and No. 10 Platoon out on the far flank were caught in a fiery fray that wiped out the forward section. Moffat was shot dead. The company was strung in a long line along the dyke, and with 'D' Company behind it also under attack there was no going back or forward. In 'D' Company's sector, Sergeant Laloge was up with No. 18 Platoon throwing German grenades back at the charging enemy. When a Bren gunner was cut down, Laloge picked up his gun only to find it damaged. Calmly taking the time to repair it, Laloge then opened fire.

Over at 'B' Company, Lance Corporal Richard G. Wolfe volunteered to stay behind with his two-inch mortar while the rest fell back on 'D' Company's position. With Wolfe punching out rounds, Clarke pulled the men back. Wolfe's fire held up the German advance, but the soldier was captured. (He would be returned by the Germans two days later bearing a note asking that artillery stop firing on a position that housed a field hospital.) His bravery was rewarded with a Military Medal.[31]

'B' Company reached 'D' Company's lines just as it began falling back to the causeway. Clarke found Sergeant Laloge "swearing something fierce and returning Gerry grenades as fast as they arrived over the dyke." The two companies worked their way back in line. Laloge's actions garnered a Distinguished Conduct Medal. 'A' Company was also being pushed towards the causeway, Hees wounded in the arm but still leading his new command.

The remnants of 'B' and 'D' Companies led the way back along the causeway to take a position about three hundred yards from the Walcheren end. But as both counted barely twenty men apiece, Ellis ordered them to come right out. 'A' and 'C' Companies dug in near the crater to hold a forward start line, should the Maisonneuve be sent into the grinder. Nineteen men were dead, another forty-five wounded.[32] Megill told Ellis the Calgarians must stay on the causeway until "division decided what to do." So there the two companies remained, continuing to be mortared and shelled. As night fell, the regiment's war diarist reflected on the hellish operation and wrote that "words are inadequate to express all the difficulties that had to be surmounted to make an advance along the... narrow Causeway. The memory of it will live long in the minds of the Calgary Highlanders."[33]

WHILE TWO CALGARY companies clung to the causeway, corps and divisional commanders puzzled over next steps. Brigadier Keefler waffled. Major General Charles Foulkes at 11 Canadian Corps grasped at straws to justify throwing the last 5 CIB regiment into the cauldron. At 1630 hours, a message from corps advised Keefler of a wireless intercept indicating that the Walcheren garrison was "ready to surrender." He therefore ordered 5 CIB "to push on and establish a bridgehead as soon as possible."[34] In doing so, Foulkes ignored the intelligence summary prepared by corps intelligence staff for his Chief of Staff, Brigadier Elliott Rodgers, that concluded: "In spite of many reports to the contrary there is as yet no definite indication that the garrison at Walcheren is packing up."[35]

Foulkes and Keefler dangled a carrot before Brigadier Megill. Le Régiment de Maisonneuve was to pass through the Calgary Highlanders, gain Walcheren, and establish a tight bridgehead in the early morning hours of November 2. Then "only one hour after they start their push," the 157th British Brigade's 1st Battalion, Glasgow Highlanders would relieve them at 0500 hours. Immediately, the two Calgary companies would withdraw, quickly followed by the Maisies, and then 5 CIB could have a well-deserved rest. Because of the attack's short duration and the causeway's narrow passage, the Maisonneuve would send only two companies forward.[36]

In truth, the men in Captain Camile Montpetit's 'D' Company who mustered at 0400 hours to lead what the regimental history later declared "une odyssée incroyable" numbered just forty—a single platoon's normal strength—and included five Belgian White Brigade volunteers.[37] Montpetit was blessed with two experienced platoon leaders, so split the little force into two sections. Lieutenant Charles Forbes led No. 18 Platoon and Lieutenant Guy de Merlis No. 16.[38] With three medium regiments firing counterbattery missions and three field regiments laying down a barrage, Montpetit led his men into a maelstrom of German fire. Sticking close to Montpetit's heels was the 5th Field Regiment's Lieutenant Donald Innes with five signallers lugging the vital wireless sets needed to direct the gunnery. In minutes, Innes was wounded, three of his signallers were also casualties, and shellfire had destroyed the radios. Taking over Montpetit's wireless and ignoring his injuries, Innes continued directing the artillery.[39] Despite the fierce opposition, 'D' Company was within two hundred yards of the western end of the causeway in fifteen minutes.

It seemed as if every German artillery piece, mortar, anti-aircraft gun, and machine gun on Walcheren had zeroed on the causeway, but 'D' Company kept going. 'B' Company was close behind, with the other two companies hovering at the entrance to join in if ordered.[40] Forbes and de Merlis struggled to maintain control of their men in darkness illuminated only by explosions, streams of tracer, flares, and small fires burning on the causeway and its entrance to Walcheren.

Forbes, at the head of the lead platoon, could hardly make sense of the confusion, and believed what they were doing was "madness." Wounded in the left wrist, he led his men out onto the mud-soaked island and blundered forward. In a wild melee, they managed to knock out the antitank gun that had been skipping armour-piercing rounds up the causeway. Getting his bearings was impossible in the blackness, but somehow Forbes found a farmhouse beside a railway underpass about five hundred yards beyond the causeway. Montpetit established his headquarters here, with the platoons deployed back to back on either side of the underpass.[41]

'B' Company, meanwhile, had been driven to ground midway across. Montpetit's men were cut off and surrounded. At least three 20-millimetre anti-aircraft guns fired at the house. It was 0500 hours, but looking around, the captain saw no sign that the Glasgow Highlanders or any other relief was coming.

In the rear, bitter arguments were underway. Major General Edmund Hakewill Smith, the 52nd British (Lowland) Division's commander, opposed Foulkes's plan to bounce the causeway— believing such a frontal attack doomed from the outset. Instead, while 5 CIB had fed each of its battalions in turn onto the causeway, Hakewill Smith had ordered 202nd Field Company, Royal Engineers to survey the Sloe to find a route across for a clandestine assault.[42] Foulkes, knowing that the immediate task was to draw forces away from Westkapelle and Vlissingen, had argued there was no time for feasibility studies and so ordered 5 CIB's attack. Shortly before midnight on November 1, the two men had wrangled again for more than an hour before Foulkes bluntly ordered the British general to commit his division to forcing the causeway. Hakewill Smith thrust a piece of blank paper at Foulkes, demanding that he issue the order in writing. Foulkes blinked, and then gave the general precisely forty-eight hours to make an alternate attack or be sacked.[43] Meantime, the Glasgow Highlanders were to relieve the Maisonneuve and hold whatever bridgehead had been won.

At 5 CIB headquarters, a new argument ensued as a Canadian brigadier locked horns with his British counterpart. Brigadier J.D. Russell disliked the idea of sending the Glasgow Highlanders across the causeway as much as did his superior. Acting in accordance with Hakewill Smith's instructions, he had set the engineers searching for alternatives and hoped to avoid the classical military blunder of "reinforcing failure." For plainly the causeway attacks had been failures, three battalions battered to a halt with nothing to show for the losses suffered. But Megill was insistent and had the backing of Foulkes. Megill flatly stated that if the British didn't relieve the Maisonneuve, he would be forced to bring back his exhausted battalions and do the job himself. There would, of course, be all hell to pay in the aftermath of such direct disobedience of an order from corps.

This time, the British side blinked. At 0520 hours, Russell told the Glasgow commander that the relief was to be made, but that he was to commit only as many men as there were Maisies on the other side "after deducting casualties." A dispirited Lieutenant Colonel Julien Bibeau advised that he believed only about forty of his men were alive on Walcheren itself, so the British agreed to send one platoon to relieve them. At 0610, that platoon set out, their progress slowed by snipers and shellfire harassment.[44]

Across the causeway, Montpetit and his embattled force knew nothing of these disputes. As a dirty dawn lit the battleground, they fought for survival. Looking to the east, Forbes was stunned to see an entire column of Germans marching along a road in a brazen withdrawal towards Middleburg. The Canadians opened up with small-arms fire and scattered them. With daylight, some welcome assistance arrived in the form of an RAF Typhoon, which blew the turret off a tank bearing down on the farmhouse, with a well-placed rocket salvo.[45] Although wounded, Private J.C. Carrière crawled along a water-filled ditch with a PIAT to knock out a 20-millimetre gun. This successful action garnered a Military Medal.[46]

For six hours, 'D' Company stood its ground, fighting with ever lessening hope that relief would come. Remarkably, while many men were wounded, only Private Paul Emile Fortier's injury proved fatal. With Megill hectoring, the Glasgow commander gradually fed more than the one platoon into the operation, and at 1155 hours a small relief force got through to Montpetit's men. But the situation remained so critical that it was another two hours before a withdrawal could be undertaken, and then only because Lieutenant Innes was able to call in a covering smokescreen. For his actions throughout, Innes was awarded a Military Cross.[47]

Jacques Cantinieaux, one of the Belgians with the Canadians, later described the withdrawal, which was anything but orderly. "At the first shell burst, a dash—a desperate escape across the road—a jump into icy water that paralyzed the limbs and blurred the sight. Some stumbled in the barbed wire. Death whistled its little song in our ears. We reached the railroad, then climbed the side of the dyke to safety. After several minutes we walked. It didn't matter if we were fired on; we followed the road in a dream. It was unreal. Life floated and danced in front of our eyes. Time after time, we stumbled in a shell hole like a blind man."[48]

'D' Company's return marked the end of 2nd Canadian Infantry Division's long ordeal in the campaign to open the West Scheldt and Antwerp. The Maisonneuves reported twelve men in 'D' Company as casualties, which meant a third of its strength.[49] In three days, 135 men in 5 CIB had been killed, wounded, or lost missing. For the division, since crossing the Antwerp–Turnhout Canal in late September, 207 officers and 3,443 other ranks had become casualties.[50]

The division turned its back on Walcheren Island, and "a long line of weary, muddy infantrymen plodded slowly back down the road to meet the vehicles that would take them to the new area... The men were indescribably dirty. They were bearded, cold as it is only possible to be in Holland in November, and wet from living in water-filled holes in the ground for 24 hours of the day. Their eyes were red-rimmed from lack of sleep, and they were exhausted from the swift advance on foot under terrible conditions. Yet all ranks realized with a certain grim sense of satisfaction that a hard job had been well and truly done."[51]

[26]

A Fine Performance

WHEN 5TH CANADIAN INFANTRY BRIGADE was withdrawn from winning a bridgehead, there was no clear intelligence to indicate whether or not the effort had achieved its purpose. And by last light on November 2, the Glasgow Highlanders grimly clung to a tenuous hold on the causeway itself, without knowing if the price paid to draw the Germans away from Vlissingen and Westkapelle had yielded good value. What they did know was that the only hope for a renewed advance from the causeway rested with 157th British Infantry Brigade's plan to send its other battalions across the Sloe to the south in the early morning hours of November 3.[1]

Already, though, the German fortress on Walcheren was doomed to elimination by the success of the November 1 Vlissingen and Westkapelle assaults. Codenamed respectively Operations Infatuate I and Infatuate II, planning these assaults had preoccupied First Canadian Army's headquarters staff, that of 4th British Special Service Brigade, and to a lesser extent a variety of air and naval staffs for many weeks. Everyone appreciated that the landings were against "some of the strongest defences in the world."[2] This was the reason that Walcheren had first been flooded and then its defences subjected to protracted aerial bombardment, until finally it was agreed that the "desired degree of 'softening-up' had been attained."[3]

Never before had the Allies attempted a landing "on a coast where opposition encountered [would be] both from casemated coast guns and strong beach defences," concluded one report. "In Normandy there were no enemy coast artillery batteries in action in the sectors assaulted. The enemy opposition came from infantry and anti-tank beach defences." At Westkapelle, the "opposition was... coast batteries and their local defence weapons and some subsidiary gun positions."[4]

The general plan called for three commando units in amphibian vessels to assault through the breach made earlier in the coastal dyke at Westkapelle. At the same time, another commando would land immediately east of Vlissingen. Ideally, this latter landing would be reinforced by the 52nd British (Lowland) Division's 155th Infantry Brigade. However, if resistance proved too severe, the brigade would be redirected to Westkapelle.[5]

As the flooding had effectively divided the island into three non-inundated parts—a strip of dunes and woods to the northwest of Westkapelle, a dune strip to its southwest extending almost to Vlissingen, and the slightly higher ground east of Middelburg that bordered the Sloe Channel—German movement was greatly restricted and some gun batteries had been drowned.[6] Still, the batteries at Westkapelle were largely intact and formidable. The most powerful and well-positioned batteries were: the four 8.7-inch-gun W17 just west of Domburg, four 4.1-inch-gun W19 on Walcheren's northwest tip, and three batteries, each mounting four 5.9-inch guns, that were closer to Westkapelle. These were W15, just north of Westkapelle and one of the landing beaches; W13, southeast of Westkapelle and adjacent to another landing beach; and W11, midway between Zoutelande and Vlissingen. These guns were so positioned that they posed a greater threat to the Westkapelle landing force than the guns at Vlissingen. As well, numerous smaller gun positions and anti-aircraft batteries were scattered along most of Walcheren's shoreline.[7]

About 9,000 German troops were believed still deployed on Walcheren, mostly part of 70th Infantry Division, and about a third of these were concentrated around Vlissingen. But there was little to no intelligence regarding the actual deployment of these forces. The nature of the Vlissingen shoreline greatly concerned the planners, for an assault was constricted to a very narrow frontage. If the Germans were well dug in and numerous, the likelihood was that the first wave would be annihilated or forced to retreat. This was the fear that kept 155th Brigade on standby for a possible shift to Westkapelle.[8]

The most obvious landing point was a bathing beach directly in front of the grand Hotel Britannia in the city's centre, but aerial photography indicated that it was heavily defended. There was also a high seawall on top of which a wide promenade ran, and behind this a depression that had been flooded. Progress off the beach consequently would "be confined to the sea road, a very narrow strip swept by fire from a large number of strongpoints all along its length."

Realizing that a landing here would fail, the decision had been to land east of where the seawall ended and was replaced by a sloping dyke directly beneath the distinctive landmark of a large brick windmill—the Oranje Molen. Next to the windmill, which stood on the edge of a promontory, was a small bay that had once served as a harbour. As the bay was clogged with anti-landing obstacles, the decision was made to set the first assault wave down directly on the promontory below the windmill. This meant a small force of 550 men, mostly drawn from No. 4 Commando. They would land from twenty Landing Craft, Assault (LCA) that would sail from Breskens.[9]

The landings at Westkapelle would be on a larger scale, calling "for three Troops of No. 41 (Royal Marine) Commando to go ashore on the north shoulder of the gap to cover the main landings by clearing the area between the dyke and the western edge of Westkapelle village. The remainder of the Commando, strengthened by No. 10 (Inter-Allied) Commando were then to land from Buffaloes and Weasels, launched from tank landing craft, clear Westkapelle and push north. No. 48 (Royal Marine) Commando, carried to battle the same way, was to land south of the gap and move south as far as Zouteland; and No. 47 (Royal Marine) Commando, landing in the same place, was to push towards Flushing [Vlissingen] until they met with No. 4 Commando...To support the advance of No. 41 (Royal Marine) Commando, tanks and flail tanks were to land in the first flight."[10]

Although all of the 4th Special Service Brigade commando units were technically British, they contained a great diversity of nationalities. No. 4 Commando had about one hundred Frenchmen, while one No. 10 Troop was Belgian and the other Norwegian. Leavened throughout was also a troop of Dutch soldiers, providing local knowledge. First Canadian Army—always the most multinational Allied army—was, at least temporarily, undeniably cosmopolitan.[11]

As the landing forces had mustered either in Breskens or at Oostende, from which Infatuate II would be launched, 2nd Tactical Air Force spent October 28–30 pounding German defences with a total of 646 sorties. Between September 17 and October 30, Bomber Command, meanwhile, had—albeit often under protest and not to the extent the assault planners desired—flown 2,219 sorties against Walcheren and dropped 10,219 tons of bombs. Extensive bomber support was also to be provided on November 1.[12]

Sandwiched on the northern bank of the West Scheldt, in the closest concentration any of the gunners could recall, stood a total of 314 guns—96 field, 112 medium, 48 heavy anti-aircraft (3.7-inch), and 58 heavy and super-heavy. The heavy regiments, such as the 59th (Newfoundland) Heavy Regiment, Royal Artillery, fired 155-millimetre "Long Toms," while the super-heavy regiments had 8-inch and 240-millimetre guns. Only medium regiments and above could range on Westkapelle, some from nine miles away. II Canadian Corps's Commander, Corps Royal Artillery, Brigadier Bruce Matthews, had spent weeks developing an elaborate artillery program.[13]

Because of the artillery range limits, the landings at Westkapelle would also be supported by the battleship *Warspite* and monitors *Erebus* and *Roberts*. Between them, the monitors mounted ten 15-inch guns and *Warspite* had six of its eight 15-inch guns available, two having been damaged in the Mediterranean. Closer in would be twenty-seven craft of various types mounting an array of weaponry—most powerful of which were large and medium Landing Craft, Gun, which respectively carried 4.7-inch and 17-pounder guns—dubbed Support Squadron, East Flank.[14]

All this planning very nearly came to nought as October 31 turned into a foul, nasty day with low ceilings making flying difficult.

Timing the landings for November 1 had not been arbitrary. It was guided by consideration of tides, which provided two ideal windows of opportunity. Not until November 14 would conditions again be right. A two-week delay in opening the Scheldt was something Lieutenant General Guy Simonds was determined not to allow. Meeting with Admiral Sir Bertram Ramsay, the Naval Commander-in-Chief, and II Canadian Corps's Major General Charles Foulkes in Bruges that morning, the decision was made to order Force T, as the vessels carrying 4th Special Service Brigade were designated, to sail. By midafternoon, with the weather deteriorating rapidly, Simonds and Ramsay delegated responsibility for going ahead with the actual assault to Captain A.F. Pugsley and Brigadier B.W. Leicester, respectively the naval and army commanders.[15] In the early morning hours, Force T sailed from Oostende.

No. 4 Commando formed up in Breskens at 0315 hours on November 1 and moved down to a long wooden jetty where the LCAS waited.[16] Still, an air of indecision hung over the whole adventure. Heavy mist blanketed the airfields in Britain and the tactical fighter-bomber fields in Belgium. This meant the bombing program that was to have preceded the landings was cancelled and also that spotting aircraft would be unable to direct the fire from the naval ships standing off Westkapelle. Aboard Force T's flagship frigate HMS *Kingsmill,* Pugsley and his army counterpart Brigadier B.W. Leicester decided to continue, but the naval officer was prepared to cancel if the initial advance towards the coast met too stiff resistance.[17]

AT 0440 HOURS, the first LCAS packed with No. 4 Commando slipped their moorings and sailed towards Vlissingen. Five minutes later, the southern sky erupted in a false sunrise as every artillery piece fired simultaneously, kicking off a two-and-a-half-hour pounding of Walcheren. The diarist for one of the two 2nd Canadian Infantry Division field regiments involved was so awed by the immensity of shot going out that he described his own unit as being "just a small voice in the roar of cannon around us."[18]

From their craft, the commandos saw Walcheren "silhouetted against the flickering muzzle flashes of three hundred guns... all we could see were the sudden bright pinpoints of light all along the waterfront which were our own explosions." Numerous fires soon burned throughout the town and sometimes "shells struck the steel anti-landing stakes and then there was a shower of red sparks reminiscent of a firework display." The German guns, which they had feared, "remained silent."

"Gradually the fire in the town was gaining hold, and suddenly the unmistakable silhouette of the windmill—the ORANJE MOLEN—was thrown into relief against the glare. We could have had no clearer indication of our chosen landing point."[19]

The commandos were arrayed in three flights, and at 0545 the reconnaissance party in the lead wove past anti-landing stakes, from which shells and mines rigged with contact detonators dangled, to make a perfect landing on the promontory tip below the windmill. Before a shot was fired, the commandos overran the immediate defenders, cut the wire on the dyke, and set about clearing the promontory. In quick order, the first two flights got ashore and the immediate beachhead was won, with about eighty-five prisoners taken and several artillery pieces captured intact.

At 0630 hours, however, the third flight met more opposition as it closed on the beach and came under machine-gun, 20-millimetre antitank gun, and small-arms fire. One LCA was hit just as the bow dropped. As it began sinking, the men scrambled out, having to abandon some heavy equipment. One man was shot dead as he came up on the beach.[20]

The commandos advanced into the heart of the old town of Vlissingen, fighting their way along narrow streets that sloped gradually upwards, giving the Germans the advantage of better lines of sight. Shells were exploding throughout the town, and some buildings collapsed as the heavy and super-heavy rounds caused the earth to rattle as if struck by an earthquake. Each commando troop worked to a plan, its advance directed towards a predesignated objective rather than just winning ground. When the streets proved too laced with fire for safe movement, the commandos used explosive charges to breach the interlocking walls of the row houses, mouseholing forward. At one point, "half a dozen Commando soldiers were... seen on the roof of a building hanging head downwards and flinging grenades through the window of a room beneath them."[21]

Two hours after the commandos landed, the 155th Brigade's 4th Battalion of the King's Own Scottish Borderers joined the fray. Its sister battalion, the 5th King's Own, was timed to arrive at 1400 hours, but the beachhead was judged too insecure, and it returned to Breskens with orders to land under cover of darkness. Into the night the bitter fight raged. Ultimately, the battle for Vlissingen would draw all three battalions of 155th British Infantry Brigade into a bloody contest that, although the outcome was foretold from the time the commandos gained their first toehold, would not be won until the early morning hours of November 4.[22]

Meanwhile, at Westkapelle, with no advantage of surprise, Force T had faced a harder fight made more so by failure of aerial support. Throughout the night, Captain Pugsley and Brigadier Leicester, aboard *Kingsmill,* had struggled with their decision. Britain remained fog-shrouded, the heavy Lancaster bombers and fighter-bombers grounded. Neither would there be any spotter planes to direct the fire from the naval vessels forced to stand thirteen miles offshore to avoid the mine-strewn waters closer in. About 0700 hours, the two men decided and signalled First Canadian Army headquarters: "Nelson." The assault was on, and the armada of 150 craft turned towards Walcheren, eleven miles distant. Soon Westkapelle's tall lighthouse became visible, then the ridgelike outline of the sand dunes. From far out to sea came rumbling thunder as the warships fired.[23]

Aboard *Warspite,* correspondent Martin Chisholm of the British weekly magazine, *Picture Post,* had his tin hat blown off by the concussion of three 15-inch guns firing the opening salvo at 0800. As those gun crews reloaded, the other three fired a salvo. "At each salvo the wind blows into our faces whiffs of ugly-brown cordite smoke. As the smoke clears, we hear the shells screaming towards their mark. Sometimes you can even see them for a second... Just before they fire maybe you duck, hands to ears, against the blast. I am doing this when the captain sees me and grins. 'Better take your pipe out of your mouth next time,' he says. 'It's much worse if it catches you with your mouth closed.'"[24] From its first salvo to 1800 hours, when the ceasefire order came, *Warspite* fired 353 rounds, mostly directed at coastal battery w17, which attempted to engage it in a duel. It proved an uneven contest, *Warspite* not even noticing that the battery's 4.1-inch guns were firing upon it. Lacking the help of a spotter plane, *Warspite* failed to score a direct hit. But wear and tear on the battery's guns led one to develop a pull to one side, while another twisted on its mounting. As a bomb had earlier disabled a third, by early afternoon only a single gun remained operational. Meanwhile, *Roberts* and *Erebus* had engaged other batteries, with the only success coming when *Roberts* scored three hits on w15 at Westkapelle that silenced two guns.[25]

Closer in, Support Squadron, East Flank's array of small combat ships under command of Commodore K.A. "Monkey" Sellar drenched the beach and German batteries with fire as the landing craft bearing the commandos headed for shore. On June 6, Sellar had noticed that German gun batteries inclined to engage craft firing upon them rather than unarmed landing craft, something clearly evident this cold November morning. As one after another of his vessels was sunk, Sellar calmly noted that the commando landing was progressing "satisfactorily," therefore "so long as the Germans made the mistake of concentrating their fire at the Support Squadron, close action was justified and losses acceptable."[26] Sellar maintained that stance until 1230 hours, by which time only eight of the twenty-seven vessels remained operational. Nine of the others had been sunk and ten so damaged they were no longer capable of combat. Casualties were very heavy, with 172 killed and 286 wounded, or one out of every four men. But this "gallant attempt at a task far beyond its powers" was a sacrifice that enabled the commandos to get ashore with comparatively light casualties.[27]

It still proved a hard undertaking, as Lieutenant Colonel J.B. Hillsman, commander of 8th Canadian Field Surgical Unit—part of the Canadian medical force serving with the commandos—had observed from aboard the craft carrying him to the beach. Ahead, the Landing Craft, Tank that was to serve as the hospital ship turned out of line because "we didn't want her in the muck yet. As it passed us, it struck a sea mine. There was a tremendous explosion and the entire ship was hurled into the air. It settled rapidly. Men jumped into the sea. Some were picked up by the following craft. Others floated face down in their lifebelts."[28] In addition to 8th Canadian Field Surgical Unit, No. 17 Canadian Light Field Ambulance, 9th Canadian Field Surgical Unit, No. 5 Canadian Field Transfusion Unit, and No. 10 Canadian Field Dressing Station were all aboard vessels waiting to go ashore once the beachhead was established.[29]

Two LCAS bearing commandos were hit just offshore, but No. 41 (Royal Marine) and No. 48 (Royal Marine) both got their lead troops landed on opposite sides of the breach in the dyke. From the edge of Westkapelle village, No. 41 was soon firing at w15 with small arms. The rest of this commando unit fought its way into the village and, supported by tanks of the 1st Lothian Regiment, reported it taken at 1115 hours. No. 41 then began a slow march north towards Domburg, along a road bordered by sand dunes on one side and flooded polders the other—progress hindered more by Germans wanting to surrender than those wanting to fight.

No. 48 Commando found the first objective, a row of concrete pillboxes on the gap's southern flank, undefended. So, too, was the second objective, a radar station. Both were secured by the first flight of troops landed before the rest of the commando reached shore. But heavy shellfire caught the Buffaloes and Weasels carrying the follow-on forces and several were destroyed, resulting in heavy casualties. Despite this, the commando quickly reorganized and began an advance against w13, which was wreaking havoc among the support craft offshore.[30]

Major Derek de Stacpoole and his 'Y' Troop rushed the wire perimeter, only to be driven to ground by fire from the battery, killing the major and almost wiping out his unit. No. 48 Commando's Lieutenant Colonel J.L. Moulton realized that a more coordinated effort would be required. The problem was the narrow frontage. w13 stood on a long spit wide enough for only one troop to advance at a time. There was, however, a spur of sand dunes poking into the flooded polders and so he established one troop there to lay down flanking fire. He then arranged for a timed fire program by 3rd Canadian Medium Regiment from the south bank of the West Scheldt, and was promised a strafing run by Typhoons that had managed to come on station as the weather improved marginally over Britain. The fire mission started at 1545 hours, and the moment it lifted, 'B' Troop charged, followed by 'X' and 'Y' Troops. It was over in minutes, the battery taken, and about eighty prisoners rounded up.[31]

By nightfall, 4th Special Service Brigade had secured about six miles of coastal dunes and all its commandos were ashore. Next day, No. 41 Commando continued its push on Domburg, but the village did not fall until November 3. Meanwhile, No. 47 Commando fought a hard battle to eliminate battery w11 south of Zoutelande that cost it many casualties over two days. But by the end of the day on November 3, all resistance between Westkapelle and Vlissingen had ceased. Although a good deal of cleaning up remained before Walcheren Island could be declared cleared, it no longer posed any obstacle to shipping entering the West Scheldt.

Although still under orders to fight to the last, the Germans on Walcheren had been written off by Oberkommando der Wehrmacht. South Holland's German naval commander, Captain Aschmann, realized this on November 2 after receiving a personal signal from Grosseadmiral Karl Dönitz. "For the past four weeks my whole heart has been with you in your brave struggle," he said. "If ever a fight to the finish is of strategical importance, it is so in your mission to keep the enemy from using Antwerp. Give my greetings to your brave men. You are not fighting alone, with you are the whole Navy, nay, the whole German nation which you are protecting with your tenacious resistance."[32] But the Germans on Walcheren were alone and, surrounded on three sides, being forced inland towards Middelburg.

BY THE TIME the ground between Vlissingen and Westkapelle was cleared on November 3, the 52nd (Lowland) Infantry Division's 157th Brigade had executed its small amphibious crossing of the Sloe Channel. The previous night, two sappers, Lieutenant F. Turner and Sergeant Humphrey, had conducted an extensive reconnaissance of the Sloe south of the causeway, where the 1st Battalion, Glasgow Highlanders grimly clung to a tenuous bridgehead. They returned with a route worked out.

But the proposal was not an easy or even a normal amphibious crossing. The Sloe Channel was just "a muddy and ambiguous creek," which became a salt wash three hundred yards wide at high tide. At low tide, it contracted to half the width, "leaving on both sides stretches of grey and glutinous mud... Above high-water mark on the Walcheren side a salt marsh, green but treacherous, stretches more than 1,000 yards before firm ground is reached. This in turn is criss-crossed in herringbone pattern by muddy creeks, just wide and deep enough to stop an armed man from either wading or swimming across... As the Lowlanders painfully discovered," wrote the divisional historian, "the mud could take an armed man more than waist-high."[33]

Into this quagmire, 6th (Lanarkshire) Battalion of the Cameronians (Scottish Rifles) ventured at 0330 hours on November 3. Slithering down the bank to board assault boats that were then paddled across the short stretch of open channel, the lead company piled out into muck and began a trek of 1,500 yards through deep mud. At times, heavily burdened soldiers were trapped, and had to be hauled out with ropes by their companions. For the last six hundred yards, the mud was often four feet deep. But they made it, the first ten-man section surprising the German defenders and taking 250 prisoners without a shot fired.[34]

Daybreak, however, saw a stiffening of resistance and little ground gained throughout the day. At dusk, 5th Battalion, Highland Light Infantry crossed, and in the morning this tipped the balance, the German defence crumbling rapidly as it became clear that Walcheren Fortress was being overrun. A few hours later, the HLI broke across to the Glasgow Highlanders, and the unflooded ground on the eastern flank of the island was quickly cleared.[35]

Walcheren's complete fall was now just a question of time. On November 6, 155th Infantry Brigade sent 'A' Company of the 7th/9th Royal Scots aboard Buffaloes from Vlissingen to the water-surrounded Middelburg. About two thousand Germans were concentrated in the city, and nobody knew whether they would make a stand. But none was offered. Generalleutnant Wilhelm Daser instead insisted that he would surrender to nobody but an officer of equal rank. Whereupon Major R.H.B. Johnston, commanding

'A' Company, borrowed a "subaltern's pips to add to the crown on his shoulder," to masquerade as a colonel, and convinced Daser this rank was sufficient to preserve the man's honour. With that, two thousand Germans surrendered to two hundred Scots and Walcheren Island was cleared. Two days previously, the first minesweepers had entered the West Scheldt to begin the "most extensive and intricate sweeping operations ever undertaken by any navy" to open Antwerp.[36]

ON THE SAME day that minesweepers entered the West Scheldt, a small Canadian force raced northwest from Steenbergen along a road leading into St. Philipsland. The St. Philipsland peninsula was the last objective given 4th Canadian Armoured Division as part of I British Corps's push to the Maas River. The peninsula itself was of little importance, but intelligence believed the Germans were using the narrow Zijpe Channel between it and the island of Schowen en Duiveland to ferry troops out of Zeeland. Cutting this escape route was the urgent mission of the Lake Superior Regiment (Motor) and a troop of British Columbia Regiment Shermans from 'C' Squadron. The road was strewn with obstacles, craters, and mines, a fact that prompted acting commander Major Parker to swap the battalion's Bren carriers for more manoeuvrable rear echelon jeeps. Tops removed, machine guns and mortars piled in, these were soon "bristling with firepower."[37]

Surprising all of 4 CAD's battalions advancing north on November 4 was the lack of German resistance after the stiff fight in front of Steenbergen around the village of Welberg. Not knowing that Steenbergen had been one of the last anchors in the final defensive line south of the Maas, the Canadians had expected to continue their slugging match for every modest gain.

The dust-up at Welberg had reinforced that notion. Instead of continuing to withdraw, the tattered remnants of 6th Parachute Regiment and two battalions of Hermann Göring Regiment had been dug in and ready to fight. Intelligence had estimated the defenders, anchored in Steenbergen but extending their defences a mile to the south to encompass Welberg, at about five hundred infantry supported by several 75- and 88-millimetre self-propelled guns.[38]

The night of October 31, the Algonquin Regiment had tried to bounce Steenbergen, with 'B' company assaulting up a road a mile west of Welberg, while 'A' and 'C' Companies cleared the forward village by coming in on a northwesterly angle. Although Welberg had been reached, a German counterattack had quickly overrun the two companies in a confused battle. Both 'A' Company's Major Don Atkinson, who had taken a bullet in the leg, and 'C' Company's Major A.K. Stirling, along with several other men, were taken prisoner in the early morning hours of November 1. The survivors retreated to the attack's start line. 'B' Company had also been forced back, its Major J.S. McLeod seriously wounded in the chest by shrapnel.[39]

On November 2, 10th Canadian Infantry Brigade had struck again with a more organized attempt that had the Lincoln and Welland Regiment out on the left taking the route of the Algonquins' 'B' Company, while the Algonquin Regiment was to the right in a concentrated attack on Welberg. A typical Dutch village, the houses and shops of Welberg straggled off the main road to Steenbergen along an eastward-running street. Where the street intersected the road, a small square centred on a church. Once Welberg fell, the Argyll and Sutherland Highlanders would pass through to clear Steenbergen.

The Lincs had 'A' and 'D' Companies forward. Their commanders both designated Left Out of Battle, the second-in-commands Captain W.H. Barkman and Captain R.F. Dickie led the men across the start line at 1900 hours. There was virtually no cover, just wide, flat fields through which the troops ducked and dodged in a frenzied effort to avoid the heavy artillery and mortar fire. A little over an hour later, however, they reached their objective immediately west of Welberg and started digging in. Both companies had suffered heavy casualties. During the night, an SPG pushed in and banged away at their lines incessantly until driven off by a self-propelled 17-pounder gun of the 5th Anti-Tank Regiment.[40]

To the right, the Algonquins had attacked with three companies. 'A' and 'B' Companies had gone in line up a tree-lined road that led to the square, while 'D' Company put in a right hook along a dyke road to hit Welberg from the east. 'C' Company, standing in reserve, would then come up on the inside of 'D' Company to clear the village's centre. Captain R.B. Stock commanded 'A' Company, Captain

J.M. "Johnny" Jewell 'B', Captain A.R. Herbert 'C', and Major George Cassidy 'D'.

An earlier reconnaissance had indicated that the road was undefended, but instead 'A' Company—mustering just thirty-three men—immediately came under heavy small-arms fire.[41] Things went from bad to worse when one of the M10 self-propelled guns mounting a 17-pounder of 5th Canadian Anti-Tank Regiment's 'B' Troop, which was supporting the advance, was knocked out by grenades thrown into the turret and began to burn.[42] At 2100 hours, Stock reported a second M10 destroyed "and the situation was very confused due to heavy shelling of their positions by enemy SPs." Stock soon appeared at battalion headquarters to personally report that some of his company, newly arrived reinforcements "lacking in battle experience had run away when the SPs opened fire." He headed back to reorganize the company, promising to be ready to go again shortly.[43]

Major Cassidy's 'D' Company, meanwhile, had fared better. From the top of the dyke, Cassidy could see Welberg and Steenbergen both erupting "in red, angry flashes" as the artillery worked them over. The terrific noise and "milky haze of smoke" thickening the air covered his company's approach until they were opened up on by a single machine gun about three hundred yards short of the village. Corporal Wes Callander and his lead section immediately hit the dirt, and replied with a volley of gunfire that killed the lone gunner with two bullets to the head.

Within minutes, the company was in among the buildings. The company Bren carrier and M10s of 'C' Troop under Lieutenant J.C. Hooke came forward, clustering in the narrow roadway. Suddenly a Panzerfaust round narrowly missed Hooke's SPG, struck a wheelbarrow loaded with turnips, ricocheted up into the air, and exploded harmlessly overhead. After this, the night passed with little further fighting, and 'C' Company came forward to gain control of the village centre. Out on the left flank, however, 'A' and 'B' Companies were heavily engaged and made little progress.

With the dawn, the Germans counterattacked 'D' and 'C' Companies with infantry supported by an SPG and a tank. A well-planned affair, the Germans "sliced in between 'D's position and where 'C' Coy was working through the buildings on the north central part of the town." The foremost infantry platoons were forced to take cover inside buildings, as the tank and SPG hammered away. Adding to the confusion were Dutch civilians, who, thinking Welberg liberated, poured out of cellars into the midst of the firefight. Cassidy and some other Algonquins frantically waved them back into their hiding places, then began trying to figure out how to drive the Germans off. Finally, despite the Germans being only one hundred yards from the closest Canadian platoons, an artillery concentration was brought to bear, and the streets soon boiled with smoke and flames.[44]

While the shells were hammering down, 'C' Troop's Lance Sergeant Hedley Arthur Honey had manoeuvred his M10 around to find an angle of fire on either the German SPG or tank, only to have it bottom out crossing a deep ditch. Dismounting, Honey went forward on foot and discovered the SPG was separated from his position only by a wooden barn. Returning to the M10, Honey slammed a 17-pound shell through the barn to score a direct hit. As the SPG began burning, the tank retreated towards Steenbergen. Having lost their support, the infantry quickly followed on the run.[45] Welberg was soon cleared, but when Honey poked his M10 out onto the road leading to Steenbergen, it was struck by a shot from a hidden SPG and the twenty-one-year-old from Dewberry, Alberta was killed. For his actions this day, he was Mentioned in Despatches, while a Military Cross was awarded to Lieutenant Hooke.[46]

Having been driven out of Welberg, the Germans resorted to pounding it with highly accurate artillery. This hampered the Argylls forming up to assault Steenbergen, and also caused a number of Algonquin casualties, the worst being an entire section of Cassidy's company all killed or wounded when a shell struck a building where they had gathered for a meal.[47] Finally, at nightfall, the shelling unexpectedly and abruptly ceased.

At 0500 hours on November 4, the Argylls attacked Steenbergen, and in less than an hour were inside the battered town. The reason for the cessation of artillery fire the night before became clear, as they met virtually no opposition. "During the night," wrote the Argyll war diarist, "the Germans had evacuated the entire area between us and the water far to the north."[48] The regiment suffered just two casualties, both killed by a lone sniper. Captain John Shirley Prugh and

Private Ronald Dennis McPherson were killed by single shots.[49] At 1000 hours, Major B. Stockloser ventured into the town and then signalled brigade that the *Battle of Steenbergen* was over." That afternoon, the Argylls having passed out of the town to establish defensive positions facing north, the Provost Corps arrived and declared Steenbergen out of bounds to all ranks, unless on duty, "which was inclined to dim the romantic and alcoholic ardour of the men."[50]

The Algonquins remained in Welberg that day. They had suffered the most in the somewhat misnamed Battle of Steenbergen—eleven killed and twenty-one wounded. In the late afternoon, they were once again moving north, towards Dinteloord, but after carrying out a brilliant textbook crossing of the Steenborgsche Canal on a partially destroyed bridge, were ordered to hold fast in order to avoid a friendly-fire meeting between the Canadians and the 49th (West Riding) Infantry Division closing on the town from the east. That brought to an end 4 CAD's advance towards the Maas River.

To the east, 104th U.S. Infantry Division and 1st Polish Armoured Division closed in on the river's mouth. The bridges at Moerdijk over which hundreds of Germans streamed in long columns were under artillery fire and soon pinched off entirely. Most of Fifteenth Army had, however, managed to escape—thus assuring that the Allies would spend a long winter watch on the Maas as they regrouped and prepared for further offensive action.

All that remained was for the Lake Superiors and 'C' Squadron of the British Columbia Regiment to close the Zijpe Channel at St. Philipsland. Entering the little town bearing the peninsula's name, the Canadians learned that several German vessels were harboured at Zijpe on the island of Schowen en Duiveland. When this information was relayed back to 4th Canadian Armoured Brigade headquarters, it prompted Brigadier Robert Moncel to come forward on November 5 to personally assess the situation. He and the Superiors' acting commander, Major Parker, climbed a water tower near the coast and surveyed the harbour that lay just across the narrow channel. "Enemy boats could easily be seen, also marines carelessly walking around in the area. Apparently they were unaware of our presence."[51] Moncel ordered every weapon possible brought to bear on the boats.

The troop of Shermans, commanded by Lieutenant R.H. Goepel, opened fire with a 17-pounder Firefly and two 75-millimetre tanks, while the Superiors weighed in with their six-pounder antitank guns and mortars. Although it appeared that the mortars scored two direct hits, the high breakwaters protecting the little harbour so obscured the view that it was impossible to tell what damage was inflicted. The German ships responded with some desultory, badly aimed fire.

Unsure whether they were going to have to take Zijpe by storm, a two-platoon fighting patrol commanded by 'A' Company's Captain Styffe rounded up a fishing boat and a police cutter and crossed on the afternoon of November 6. Meeting no opposition, the force entered the harbour and discovered that three of the German vessels had been sunk and the fourth was listing. Lieutenant Black slipped aboard the damaged one and found its commander and three other officers dead on the deck. He returned bearing the vessel's signal flags and Iron Cross naval pennant. The BCR's Lieutenant Goepel was along to carry off the ship's bell to hang in the regiment's mess. When someone handed Styffe the ship's log, he looked out at the slowly settling vessel, and jotted a final entry: "Gersunken by Lake Superior Regiment and British Columbia Regiment—Canadian Army."[52] And so First Canadian Army fired its last shots of the Battle of the Scheldt.

FIELD MARSHAL BERNARD LAW MONTGOMERY wrote Lieutenant General Guy Simonds to "express to you personally and to all commanders and troops in the Canadian Army, my admiration for the way in which you have all carried out the very difficult task given to you. The operation was conducted under the most appalling conditions of ground—and water—and the advantage in these respects favoured the enemy. But in spite of great difficulties you slowly and relentlessly wore down the enemy resistance, drove him back, and captured great numbers of prisoners. It has been a fine performance, and one that could have been carried out only by first class troops. The Canadian Army is composed of troops from many different nations and countries. But the way in which you have all pulled together, and operated as one fighting machine, has been an inspiration to us all. I congratulate you personally. And I also congratulate all commanders and troops serving under your command. Please tell all your formations and units how very pleased I am with the splendid work they have done."

To this, Lieutenant General Harry Crerar, returning from convalescence to reclaim the army's reins, added his congratulations on bringing the campaign to a successful conclusion. "As a result," he wrote, "the battle reputation of First Canadian Army has never stood higher."

The Germans suffered heavy losses in their efforts to keep Antwerp closed. Between October 1 and November 8 when the Moerdijk bridges were closed, First Canadian Army took 41,043 prisoners. No attempt was made at the time to estimate German dead and wounded, but a Dutch historian later meticulously tabulated these figures by place of incident for the entire campaign. He determined that 4,079 Germans had been killed in action and 55 died later in hospitals. Using the standard one-to-four ratio, he then estimated that over 16,000 Germans were wounded.[53] As the war scythed through their lands, leaving vast destruction in its wake, many civilians also lost their lives. A recent tabulation by a team of Belgian and Dutch historians found that, excluding fatalities resulting from the v-1 and v-2 campaign, about 2,100 to 2,200 Dutch and 700 to 750 Belgian civilians were killed during the fighting to open Antwerp. Almost all these casualities resulted from Allied artillery or aerial bombardment.[54]

Victory came to First Canadian Army at a terrible price. From October 1 to November 8, it recorded 703 officers and 12,170 men killed, wounded, or missing. Of these, almost exactly half, 355 officers and 6,012 men were Canadians.[55] This statistic, however, failed to include the many casualties suffered in the opening phase of the campaign, which began with the ill-fated attempt by the Algonquins to force a crossing of the Leopold Canal on September 13 and rapidly escalated to the end of the month. First Canadian Army weekly casualty estimates for September 13 through October 4—including the divisions in 1 British Corps—listed a total of 3,768 men killed, wounded, or missing, of which 624 were fatal.[56] This, however, included 3rd Canadian Infantry Division casualties suffered clearing Boulogne and Calais, as well as all casualties during the first four days of October. While it is impossible to clarify the period of overlap, 3 CID's casualties in opening the two Channel ports totalled 676.[57] So it is not unreasonable to estimate that it cost First Canadian Army close to 15,000 casualties to open Antwerp.

THROUGH NOVEMBER, MORE than one hundred minesweepers laboured to clear the West Scheldt of mines. It took more than sixteen passes each along the entire seventy-five-mile length to finally declare the job done after removing 267 mines. On November 28, the first eighteen-ship convoy sailed into Antwerp. Montgomery was there, and Allied Naval Commander, Admiral Bertram Ramsay, as well as many other top brass from the U.S. and British armies.

No Canadians were invited, but happenstance put a Canadian Military Headquarters historical officer, Major W.E.C. Harrison, on the scene. "The band struck up with 'Hearts of Oak,' he recorded. "The ship made fast. The time was 2:30 p.m. The various national anthems were played. All stood in salute. The photographers took their pictures. The correspondents made their notes. The rain poured off the canvas stand in a steady stream. Then the ship's master came ashore with his mate and both were introduced to [Ramsay], who gave a warm welcome...The Canadian Army was not represented... Actually, the principal participant in the ceremony was a Canadian. I refer to the ship. She had been built in a Canadian yard and bore the local and historic name of *Fort Cataraqui*."[58]

Antwerp was now out of bounds to military personnel not on official business, so Captain George Blackburn's presence was made possible by his having purloined an "official pass." The point of his mission was to purchase a supply of liquor for the 4th Canadian Field Regiment officers. It was impossible to ignore the incoming V-1 and V-2 rockets hurtling in, engaged by the anti-aircraft guns ringing the city. This day, they numbered thirty-five, and of the fifteen not shot down one landed in a busy intersection and killed eleven civilians.[59] Unaware of the momentous ceremony taking place down at the port, he loaded cases of booze into a jeep and began the journey along muddy roads back to the cold, misty Nijmegen salient where First Canadian Army had settled for a bleak, brutal winter in what seemed a war without end.

[EPILOGUE]

The Scheldt in Memory

I STAND ON A ridge of the Brabant Wall south of Woensdrecht, looking out over an expanse of ground that remains dead level far to the west until a line of haze marks where land meets sea. Immediately below, stand several tidy, prosperous-looking farms. The buildings are modern, the crops varied, so that some fields have just been broken for spring planting while others are already lush with green hay. Beyond the farms, the A58 linking Antwerp and Rotterdam streams with traffic. On the highway's western flank is a large polder. Standing next to me, Johan van Doorn points solemnly to different landmarks in the polder country, some obscured now by the highway. "Angus One, Angus Two, Angus Three," he says. "The Black Watch came from there. They did not get further than that point there," Johan gestures to a spot just short of the ground he has identified as Angus One.

Black Friday, October 13, 1944—the day the Black Watch was torn asunder in beetfields awash with mud and the blood of young men dying for no good purpose. "The paratroopers were there," Johan says. "They had an unlimited field of fire. They had the MG 42s, they had the mortars. They were completely dug in. The attack was doomed from the start."

Looking at the ground, even as it has changed over the decades, it's impossible to imagine how anyone could have believed that a single understrength battalion of infantrymen advancing across such open ground in broad daylight might succeed. And, of course, the Black Watch did fail. Fifty-six men died in that polder, sixty-two others were wounded, and twenty-seven were taken prisoner.

For two weeks, Johan and I have been meticulously visiting each and every battleground where Canadians fought a grim campaign from September to November 1944, that ended with the opening of the Scheldt estuary enabling Allied shipping to access Antwerp's vast port. We have stood on the banks of the Leopold Canal, where the Algonquin Regiment came to sorrow in front of Moerkerke on September 13–14. Walked along the dyke to examine the concrete bunker that protected German machine guns as they inflicted so many casualties on the Regina Rifles when they crossed the Leopold in canvas boats on October 6. Stood on the seawall overlooking where 9th Canadian Infantry Brigade carried out its end-run amphibious landings west of the Braakman Inlet on October 9. Crouched next to another German bunker dug into a dyke on the southern flank of the Walcheren Causeway, and again been struck by how nakedly exposed the Canadians advancing towards these positions would have been to their deadly fire.

I have visited the battlefields of Normandy, toured most of those in Italy and Sicily, and consider the terrain in which the Battle of the Scheldt was fought unparallelled in its unsuitability to military operations. Yet it was here that First Canadian Army fought its most important and costly campaign of the war. Antwerp was essential to the Allies, and ultimately the Canadians made its use possible.

It was, of course, a campaign that need not have been fought. Had the British Second Army, after it rumbled triumphantly into Antwerp on September 4, kept going and cut the isthmus to South Beveland, a great victory would have been won at little cost. But in arguably his biggest blunder of the war, Montgomery failed to realize the opportunity. So the British paused, a German army escaped, and First Canadian Army had to save the day. The result was a terrible victory because of its cost, but a great Allied victory nonetheless.

Inherent in that cost, and often forgotten, is the destruction wrought on the land. Most villages, towns, and farms were seriously damaged or all but destroyed by shellfire and aerial bombardment. Vast areas were deliberately flooded with seawater. While most of this flooding was conducted by the Germans to hamper and funnel Allied movement, Walcheren Island was inundated by us to equally inhibit the Germans. The deliberate sinking of this island remains a topic of debate in Zeeland and to a lesser extent in Canada and the United Kingdom. It took more than a year for the civilians to finally reseal the breaches in the dykes to stem the influx of tidal water, and then more years for the soil to be desalinated. Today, however, Walcheren is completely recovered and once again a thriving agricultural area.

But was the inundation necessary? Touring the island with a mind to its defence by the Germans, I am struck by the many bunkers and fortifications that still stand in farm fields well inland from the coast—constructed and positioned so that the Allies would be forced to overwhelm one position after another. It seems clear that without the flooding the battle for Walcheren would have been far more protracted, and likely to have required commitment of additional troops—drawn either from the badly worn-out 2nd Canadian Infantry Division or the equally weary "Water Rats" of 3rd Canadian Infantry Division. More than two thousand Germans surrendered at Middelburg, which had been reduced to a walled island encircled by the sea. Had the surrounding ground not been flooded, these same troops would have been able to offer stiff resistance across a wide front instead of being trapped within the city. Such an extended battle would have delayed Antwerp's opening even longer, seriously hampering Allied operations and, in particular, the ability to meet the Germans' December offensive aimed at Antwerp, which became known as the Battle of the Bulge. Flooding Walcheren was not embarked upon lightly by First Canadian Army's Lieutenant General Guy Simonds or his planning staff—they well understood the civilian suffering that would result. Even in hindsight, though, it seems a decision rightly made.

For those who fought it, the Scheldt is usually considered the worst of what were always bad experiences. In the face of that, many responded by carefully secreting their memories into parts of the mind that need never be visited. "Think I just blacked it out of my mind ever since because it was one of the worst encounters I'd ever seen," one veteran said. Many others put the same thought only slightly less succinctly. "We were wet, always wet, always cold. The shelling never let up, the fighting just went on day after day without let up. I thought it'd never end," remembered another. The wet, they all remember that. Days and nights spent in mud, uniforms perpetually soaked through. And more than one mentions the brutality of the fighting. How up close and personal the combat was. More men killed or wounded by gunshot and grenades thrown at close range than normal. A drenched battlefield that they came to think of as hell.

In researching this book, I had more veterans say that they could remember nothing useful than ever before. At first, I thought that it was a matter of age and fading memory, but discussing other battles with these veterans, it soon became apparent that it was a result of how deeply buried were their memories of the Scheldt. Even more than sixty years later, many still preferred not to remember.

Little wonder then that the Scheldt is not well known in Canada. Dieppe, and more recently Juno Beach and Ortona, are names many Canadians recognize. But the Scheldt has no such resonance.

This is not, however, the case in Belgian Flanders and Dutch Zeeland. In addition to visiting the battle sites and the two Canadian military cemeteries where most of those who died during the campaign lie, Johan and I tracked down each and every memorial that has been erected to commemorate Canada's role in liberating this land. There are many, some created in cooperation with Canadian regiments, but an equal number the result entirely of work by dedicated Dutch or Belgian citizens. And while few Canadian books have documented this battle, Dutch and Belgian works abound. Most, however, examine the campaign with a tight focus on the towns close to them—giving largely equal attention to the experiences of Canadian and other soldiers of First Canadian Army, the Germans, and the civilians whose homelands provided the field of battle.

Johan is such a writer, his *Slag om Woensdrecht* covering 2nd Canadian Infantry Division and 4th Canadian Armoured Division operations near this town. Together, we meet other writers and amateur historians who spend countless hours studying the battle that raged near their homes. They vary greatly in age. The youngest I meet is Wally Schoofs, who is in his twenties. Wally spends much of his free time armed with a metal detector scouring the woods near Brecht, unearthing bits and pieces of weaponry and other equipment and scraps of military kit. Twice he has discovered the remains of lost German soldiers and participated in exhumations that have led to their identification and removal to military cemeteries.

There is also Francis Huijbrechts and Luc Cox. They bundle Johan and I into the tight confines of Luc's car for a daylong tour of the battlefield that begins in Antwerp and follows the fighting around the Antwerp–Turnhout Canal. It is in their company that we visit what for me proved the most powerful memorial. At Wijnegem, where Calgary Highlander Sergeant Ken Crockett led a section of 'C' Company across the canal, a single cement marker, shaped like a headstone, lies inside a tiny triangular patch of grass. The memorial is bordered by the road running along the canal on one side and a lane fronting the row of houses that the Calgarians fought fiercely for on the night of September 21–22. The stone is badly worn now, the Flemish inscription hard to make out. Francis translates: "Here died and is buried here"—the name is obscured and looks possibly like Langwell, R.W.—"A Canadian soldier. Moved from here June 1947." It is unclear who created the monument, but it was soon after the soldier's body was removed. Positioned in front of it is an equally weathered concrete planter filled with good soil that, when the weather improves, will be brightened with flowers— the little plot maintained by villagers. Later, I search the Canadian Virtual War Memorial, and discover that the soldier was Private Raymond Wesley Dingwell, from Humbermouth, Newfoundland. He was thirty-two when he died on September 22. In 1947, his body was moved to Schoonselhof Cemetery in a suburb of Antwerp. His is one of only three Commonwealth soldiers buried here, but the Commonwealth Graves Commission maintains these plots as well as any of their own meticulously cared-for cemeteries.

I am struck by the stark simplicity of this small act of remembrance that is today maintained as anonymously as it was created. Obviously, some resident or residents of Wijnegem, a village much battered by war, carefully interned Private Dingwell, and when his body was later moved, decided that its first resting place warranted tribute.

Remembrance, I realize, need not be complicated or dressed in pomp and ceremony. It can be as simple as the Wijnegem monument to Private Dingwell. As simple as taking a few minutes to join other Canadians at memorial services on November 11. Or even pausing for a full minute's silence on that eleventh day of the eleventh month at the eleventh hour while thinking of those Canadians, like Private Dingwell, who died in a foreign land far from home in the service of this country.

APPENDIX A:
CANADIANS IN THE SCHELDT
SEPTEMBER 13 – NOVEMBER 6, 1944
(NOT ALL UNITS LISTED)

FIRST CANADIAN ARMY TROOPS
Royal Montreal Regiment
1st Armoured Personnel Carrier Regiment

1st Army Group, Royal Canadian Artillery:
11th Field Regiment
1st Medium Regiment
2nd Medium Regiment
5th Medium Regiment

2nd Army Group, Royal Canadian Artillery:
19th Field Regiment
3rd Medium Regiment
4th Medium Regiment
7th Medium Regiment
2nd Heavy Anti-Aircraft Regiment (Mobile)

Corps of Royal Canadian Engineers:
10th Field Park Company
5th Field Company
20th Field Company
23rd Field Company

II CANADIAN CORPS TROOPS
18th Armoured Car Regiment (12th Manitoba Dragoons)
6th Anti-Tank Regiment
2nd Survey Regiment
6th Light Anti-Aircraft Regiment

Corps of Royal Canadian Engineers:
8th Field Park Company
29th Field Company
30th Field Company
31st Field Company

2ND CANADIAN INFANTRY DIVISION
8th Reconnaissance Regiment (14th Canadian Hussars)
Toronto Scottish Regiment (MG)

The Royal Canadian Artillery:
4th Field Regiment
5th Field Regiment
6th Field Regiment
2nd Anti-Tank Regiment
3rd Light Anti-Aircraft Regiment

Corps of Royal Canadian Engineers:
1st Field Park Company
2nd Field Company
7th Field Company
11th Field Company

4th Canadian Infantry Brigade:
Royal Regiment of Canada
Royal Hamilton Light Infantry
Essex Scottish Regiment

5th Canadian Infantry Brigade:
The Black Watch (Royal High-land Regiment) of Canada
Le Régiment de Maisonneuve
The Calgary Highlanders

6th Canadian Infantry Brigade:
Les Fusiliers Mont-Royal
Queen's Own Cameron Highlanders
South Saskatchewan Regiment

3RD CANADIAN INFANTRY DIVISION
7th Reconnaissance Regiment
(17th Duke of York's Royal Canadian Hussars)
The Cameron Highlanders of Ottawa (MG Battalion)

The Royal Canadian Artillery:
12th Field Regiment
13th Field Regiment
14th Field Regiment
3rd Anti-Tank Regiment
4th Light Anti-Aircraft Regiment

Corps of Royal Canadian Engineers:
3rd Field Park Company
6th Field Company
16th Field Company
18th Field Company

7th Canadian Infantry Brigade:
The Royal Winnipeg Rifles
The Regina Rifle Regiment
1st Battalion, Canadian Scottish Regiment

8th Canadian Infantry Brigade:
The Queen's Own Rifles of Canada
Le Régiment de la Chaudière
The North Shore (New Brunswick) Regiment

9th Canadian Infantry Brigade:
The Highland Light Infantry of Canada
The Stormont, Dundas and Glengarry Highlanders
The North Nova Scotia Highlanders

4TH CANADIAN ARMOURED DIVISION
29th Armoured Reconnaissance Regiment
    (South Alberta Regiment)
10th Canadian Independent MG Company
    (New Brunswick Rangers)
Lake Superior Regiment (Motor)

Royal Canadian Artillery:
15th Field Regiment
23rd Field Regiment (Self-Propelled)
5th Anti-Tank Regiment
8th Light Anti-Aircraft Regiment

Royal Canadian Corps of Engineers:
6th Field Park Squadron
8th Field Squadron
9th Field Squadron

4th Canadian Armoured Brigade:
21st Armoured Regiment (Governor General's Foot Guards)
22nd Armoured Regiment (Canadian Grenadier Guards)
23rd Armoured Regiment (British Columbia Regiment)

10th Canadian Infantry Brigade:
Lincoln and Welland Regiment
Algonquin Regiment
Argyll and Sutherland Highlanders of Canada

2nd Canadian Armoured Brigade:
6th Armoured Regiment (1st Hussars)
10th Armoured Regiment (The Fort Garry Horse)
27th Armoured Regiment (The Sherbrooke Fusiliers Regiment)

APPENDIX B
CANADIAN INFANTRY BATTALION
(TYPICAL ORGANIZATION)

HQ COMPANY:
No. 1: Signals Platoon
No. 2: Administrative Platoon

SUPPORT COMPANY:
No. 3: Mortar Platoon (3-inch)
No. 4: Bren Carrier Platoon
No. 5: Assault Pioneer Platoon
No. 6: Antitank Platoon (6-pounder)

A COMPANY:
No. 7 Platoon
No. 8 Platoon
No. 9 Platoon

B COMPANY:
No. 10 Platoon
No. 11 Platoon
No. 12 Platoon

C COMPANY:
No. 13 Platoon
No. 14 Platoon
No. 15 Platoon

D COMPANY:
No. 16 Platoon
No. 17 Platoon
No. 18 Platoon

APPENDIX C
CANADIAN AND GERMAN ARMY ORDER OF RANKS
(LOWEST TO HIGHEST)

Like most Commonwealth nations, the Canadian army used the British ranking system. Except for the lower ranks, this system little differed from one service arm to another. The German army system, however, tended to identify service and rank throughout most of its command chain. The translations are roughly based on the Canadian ranking system, although there is no Canadian equivalent for many German ranks and some differentiation in responsibility each rank bestowed on its holder.

CANADIAN ARMY	GERMAN ARMY
Private, infantry	Schütze
Rifleman, rifle regiments	Schütze
Private	Grenadier
Gunner (artillery equivalent of private)	Kanonier
Trooper (armoured equivalent of private)	Panzerschütze
Sapper (engineer equivalent of private)	Pionier
Signaller (signals equivalent of private)	Funker
Lance Corporal	Gefreiter
Corporal	Obergefreiter
Lance Sergeant	Unteroffizier

CANADIAN ARMY	GERMAN ARMY
Sergeant	Unterfeldwebel
Company Sergeant Major	Feldwebel
Battalion Sergeant Major	Oberfeldwebel
Regimental Sergeant Major	Stabsfeldwebel
Second Lieutenant	Leutnant
Lieutenant	Oberleutnant
Captain	Hauptmann
Major	Major
Lieutenant Colonel	Oberstleutnant
Colonel	Oberst
Brigadier	Generalmajor
Major General	Generalleutnant
Lieutenant General (No differentiation)	General der (service arm) General der Artillerie General der Infanterie General der Kavallerie General der Pioniere General der Panzertruppen
General	Generaloberst
Field Marshal	Generalfeldmarschall
Commander-in-Chief	Oberbefehlshaber

APPENDIX D
THE DECORATIONS

Canadian military personnel won many military decorations during the Scheldt campaign. The decoration system that Canada used in World War II, like most other aspects of its military organization and tradition, derived from Britain. A class-based system, most military decorations can be awarded either to officers or to "other ranks," but not both. The Canadian army, navy, and air force also have distinct decorations. Only the Victoria Cross—the nation's highest award—can be won by personnel from any arm of the service or rank.

The decorations and qualifying ranks are:

VICTORIA CROSS (VC): Awarded for gallantry in the presence of the enemy. Instituted in 1856. Open to all ranks. The only award that can be granted for action in which the recipient was killed, other than Mentioned in Despatches—a less formal honour whereby an act of bravery was given specific credit in a formal report.

DISTINGUISHED SERVICE ORDER (DSO): Army officers of all ranks, but more commonly awarded to officers with ranks of major or higher.

DISTINGUISHED SERVICE CROSS (DSC): Navy officers ranging in rank from commander down to lieutenant.

MILITARY CROSS (MC): Army officers with a rank normally below major and, rarely, warrant officers.

DISTINGUISHED FLYING CROSS (DFC): Air Force officers and warrant officers for acts of valour while flying in active operations against the enemy.

AIR FORCE CROSS (AFC): Air Force officers and warrant officers for valour while flying, but not while in active operations against the enemy.

DISTINGUISHED CONDUCT MEDAL (DCM): Army warrant officers and all lower ranks.

CONSPICUOUS GALLANTRY MEDAL (CGM): Navy chief petty officers, petty officers, and men.

DISTINGUISHED SERVICE MEDAL (DSM): Navy chief petty officers, petty officers, and men.

MILITARY MEDAL (MM): Army warrant officers and all lower ranks.

DISTINGUISHED FLYING MEDAL: Air Force non-commissioned officers and men for valour while flying in active operations against the enemy.

AIR FORCE MEDAL: Air Force non-commissioned officers and men for valour while flying, but not in active operations against the enemy.

NOTES

INTRODUCTION: A SIMPLE PLAN

1. Col. C.P. Stacey, *The Victory Campaign: The Operations in North-West Europe, 1944–1945*, vol. 3 (Ottawa: Queen's Printer, 1960), 361.
2. "Memorandum on Operations of 4 Cdn. Armd. Div. on Leopold Canal, 13–14 Sep. 44," vol. 10936, RG 24, Library and Archives Canada, 1.
3. Terry Copp, "The Liberation of Belgium," *Legion Magazine*, November/December 2000.
4. G.L. Cassidy, *Warpath: The Story of the Algonquin Regiment, 1939–1945* (Toronto: Ryerson Press, 1948), 138.
5. Ibid., 138–39.
6. Karel Aernoudts, *Waar de rode klaproos bloeit* (Osstburg: Uitgeverij W. J. Pieters, 1972), n.p.
7. Cassidy, 139.
8. "Memorandum on Operations of 4 Cdn. Armd. Div. on Leopold Canal, 13–14 Sep. 44," 1.
9. Cassidy, 140.
10. R.L. Rogers, *History of the Lincoln and Welland Regiment* (n.p., 1954), 175.
11. Cassidy, 140.
12. A.B.J. Goossens, *West-Zeeuws-Vlanderen 1939–1946, Deel 2: Vlucht en bevrijding* (Apeldoorn: n.p., 1997), 101.
13. Cassidy, 140–45.
14. Report No. 69 Historical Section Army Headquarters: "The Campaign in North-West Europe, Information from German Sources—Part III: German Defence Operations in the Sphere of First Canadian Army (23 Aug.–8 Nov. 44)," Directorate of Heritage and History, Department of National Defence, 30 July, 1954, para.76.
15. Stacey, 362.
16. Algonquin Regiment War Diary, September 1944, RG24, Library and Archives Canada, n.p.

17 Cassidy, 145–46.
18 Roger Morre, *De slag om 't Molentje: Moerkerke 1944* (Eeklo, Belgium: n.p., 1981), n.p.
19 Cassidy, 145.
20 Stacey, 362.
21 Cassidy, 146–47.
22 Stacey, 363.
23 Cassidy, 147–49.
24 Ibid., 149–52.
25 Stacey, 363
26 "Memorandum on Operations of 4 Cdn. Armd. Div. on Leopold Canal, 13–14 Sep. 44," 3.
27 Johan van Doorn, correspondence with author, Sommelsdijk, Holland, June 6, 2006.
28 Cassidy, 149–51.
29 10th Canadian Infantry Brigade War Diary, September 1944, RG24, Library and Archives Canada, p. 5.
30 Stacey, 362.
31 Ibid., 363.

I: BEGINNING OF THE END

1 Forrest C. Pogue, *Supreme Command* (Washington, DC: U.S. Government Printing Office, 1954), 244–45.
2 Chester Wilmot, *The Struggle for Europe* (London: Collins, 1952), 434–35.
3 Hubert Meyer, *The History of the 12. SS-Panzerdivision "Hitlerjugend"* (Winnipeg: J.J. Fedorowicz Publishing, 1994), 204.
4 Reginald Roy, *1944: The Canadians in Normandy* (Toronto: Macmillan of Canada, 1984), 315.
5 Ibid., 315–16.
6 Col. C.P. Stacey, *The Victory Campaign: The Operations in North-West Europe, 1944–1945*, vol. 3 (Ottawa: Queen's Printer, 1960), 270–71.
7 Ibid., 181.
8 Ibid., 266.
9 Ibid., 267–68.
10 George Blackburn, *The History of the 4th Field Regiment* (n.p., 1945), n.p.
11 Stacey, 291–94.
12 Ronald Gendall Shawcross, *What Was It Like? A Rifleman Remembers: Some Memories of World War II, 1939–1945* (Victoria: Trafford Publishing, 2004), 192–93.
13 Blackburn, n.p.
14 n.a., *History of H.Q., R.C.A. 2 CDN INF DIV From 1 Nov 44 to 5 May 45, World War II* (Ottawa: n.p., 1945), 8.
15 Dominick Graham, *The Price of Command: A Biography of General Guy Simonds* (Toronto: Stoddart, 1993), 178.
16 Jeffrey Williams, *The Long Left Flank: The Hard Fought Way to the Reich, 1944–1945* (Toronto: Stoddart, 1988), 33.

17 J.L. Granatstein, *The Generals: The Canadian Army's Senior Commanders in the Second World War* (Toronto: Stoddart, 1993), 112–13.
18 Williams, 34.
19 Granatstein, 112.
20 Ibid., 110–11.
21 Graham, 60–62.
22 Ibid., 178.

2: THE JEWEL

1 Chester Wilmot, *The Struggle for Europe* (London: Collins, 1952), 470.
2 Brian Horrocks with Eversley Belfield and H. Essame, *Corps Commander* (London: Sidgwick & Jackson, 1977), 69.
3 Ibid., 71.
4 R.W. Thompson, *The Eighty-Five Days: The Story of the Battle of the Scheldt* (London: Hutchinson & Co., 1957), 48.
5 Horrocks, 74.
6 Ibid., 80.
7 W. Denis Whitaker and Shelagh Whitaker, *Tug of War: The Canadian Victory that Opened Antwerp* (Toronto: Stoddart, 1984), 18–39.
8 J.L. Moulton, *Battle for Antwerp: The Liberation of the City and the Opening of the Scheldt, 1944* (New York: Hippocrene Books, 1978), 34.
9 B.H. Liddell Hart, *The Tanks: The History of the Royal Tank Regiment, vol. 2: 1939–1945* (London: Cassell, 1959), 414.
10 P.K. Kemp, *The History of the 4th Battalion King's Shropshire Light Infantry (T.A.) 1745–1945* (Shrewsbury, England: Wilding & Son, 1955), 119.
11 Whitaker, 39–40.
12 Horrocks, 81.
13 B.H. Liddell Hart, *History of the Second World War* (New York: G.P. Putnam's Sons, 1970), 567.
14 Whitaker, 40.
15 L.F. Ellis with A.E. Warhurst, *Victory in the West: Volume II: The Defeat of Germany* (London: Her Majesty's Stationery Office, 1968), 9–10.
16 Charles B. MacDonald, *United States Army in World War II: The European Theater of Operations—The Siegfried Line Campaign* (Washington: Office of the Chief of Military History United States Army, 1963), 207.
17 Forrest C. Pogue, *Supreme Command* (Washington, DC: U.S. Government Printing Office, 1954), 255.
18 Bernard Law Montgomery, *The Memoirs of Field Marshal The Viscount Montgomery of Alamein, K.G.* (London: Collins, 1958), 275.
19 Ellis, 5.
20 Ibid., 72.
21 Wilmot, 494.
22 Ibid., 472.
23 Arnold Warren, *Wait for the Waggon: The Story of The Royal Canadian Army Service Corps* (Toronto: McClelland & Stewart, 1961), 310.

24 Warren, 308.
25 Ibid., 309–10.
26 Col. C.P. Stacey, *The Victory Campaign: The Operations in North-West Europe, 1944–1945*, vol. 3 (Ottawa: Queen's Printer, 1960), 300.
27 Ellis, 131–32.
28 MacDonald, 207.
29 Ibid., 10.
30 Ibid., 10–11.
31 Report No. 69 Historical Section Army Headquarters: "The Campaign in North-West Europe, Information from German Sources—Part III: German Defence Operations in the Sphere of First Canadian Army (23 Aug.–8 Nov. 44)," Directorate of Heritage and History, Department of National Defence, 30 July, 1954, para. 50–51.
32 Ibid., 55.
33 Ibid., 51–52.
34 Wilmot, 480.
35 "The Campaign in North-West Europe, Information from German Sources—Part III," 66–79.

3: THE STREETCAR WAR

1 L.F. Ellis with A.E. Warhurst, *Victory in the West: Volume II: The Defeat of Germany* (London: Her Majesty's Stationery Office, 1968), 12–15.
2 Col. C.P. Stacey, *The Victory Campaign: The Operations in North-West Europe, 1944–1945*, vol. 3 (Ottawa: Queen's Printer, 1960), 356.
3 Ibid., 330.
4 Ibid., 327.
5 Ellis, 19.
6 Stacey, 331.
7 Ibid., 359–60.
8 Jean Bouchery, *The Canadian Soldier in North-West Europe, 1944–1945*, trans: Alan McKay (Paris: Histoire & Collections, 2003), 14.
9 1 Battalion, Royal Regiment of Canada War Diary, September 1944, RG24, Library and Archives Canada, n.p.
10 Essex Scottish Regiment War Diary, September 1944, RG24, Library and Archives Canada, 6.
11 George Blackburn, *The History of the 4th Field Regiment* (n.p., 1945), n.p.
12 Essex Scottish War Diary, 6.
13 Ken M. Hossack, *Mike Target* (Ottawa: n.p., 1945), 23.
14 Essex Scottish War Diary, 6.
15 Johan van Doorn, correspondence with author, Sommelsdijk, Holland, June 3, 2006.
16 Headquarters 2nd Canadian Infantry Division, G Branch, War Diary, September 1944, RG24, Library and Archives Canada, 6
17 W. Denis Whitaker and Shelagh Whitaker, *Tug of War: The Canadian Victory that Opened Antwerp* (Toronto: Stoddart, 1984), 139.

18 4th Canadian Infantry Brigade War Diary, September 1944, RG24, Library and Archives Canada, 13–15.
19 D.J. Goodspeed, *Battle Royal: A History of the Royal Regiment of Canada, 1862–1962* (Toronto: The Royal Regiment of Canada Assoc., 1962), 488.
20 Hossack, 21.
21 Whitaker, 135–36.
22 Hossack, 24.
23 Blackburn, *History of the 4th Field Regiment*, n.p.
24 Hossack, 24.
25 Ibid., 25.
26 Goodspeed, 489.
27 2nd Canadian Infantry Division, G Branch, War Diary, September 1944, 7.
28 Ibid.
29 Kingsley Brown, Sr., Kingsley Brown, Jr., and Brereton Greenhous, *Semper Paratus: The History of The Royal Hamilton Light Infantry (Wentworth Regiment), 1862–1977* (Hamilton: The RHLI Historical Assoc., 1977), n.p.
30 Royal Hamilton Light Infantry War Diary, September 1944, RG24, Library and Archives Canada, 12
31 Essex Scottish War Diary, September 1944, 7.
32 George Blackburn, *The Guns of Victory: A Soldier's Eye View, Belgium, Holland, and Germany, 1944–45* (Toronto: McClelland & Stewart, 1996), 30.
33 Essex Scottish War Diary, September 1944, 7.
34 4th Canadian Infantry Brigade War Diary, September 1944, 16.

4: A VERY HEAVY PROGRAM

1 Report No. 188 Historical Section Canadian Military Headquarters: "Canadian Participation in the Operations in North-West Europe–Part VI: Canadian Operations, 1 Oct–8 Nov, The Clearance of the Scheldt Estuary," Department of National Defence, 7 April, 1948, 6.
2 Col. C.P. Stacey, *The Victory Campaign: The Operations in North-West Europe, 1944–1945*, vol. 3 (Ottawa: Queen's Printer, 1960), 364.
3 "1st Polish Armoured Division Operational Report," RG24, vol. 10942, Library and Archives Canada, 31.
4 Ibid., 30.
5 Połozyński Antoni, *10 Pułk Strzelców Konnych* (Nürnberg, Germany: F. Willmy GmbH, 1947), n.p.
6 Report No. 69 Historical Section Army Headquarters: "The Campaign in North-West Europe, Information from German Sources—Part III: German Defence Operations in the Sphere of First Canadian Army (23 Aug.–8 Nov. 44)," Directorate of Heritage and History, Department of National Defence, 30 July, 1954, para. 89.
7 "1st Polish Armoured Division Operational Report," 30.
8 Ibid., 26.
9 Ibid., 31.
10 "The Clearance of the Scheldt Estuary," 6.

11 L.F. Ellis with A.E. Warhurst, *Victory in the West: Volume II: The Defeat of Germany* (London: Her Majesty's Stationery Office, 1968), 59.
12 Stacey, 369–73.
13 "Polders and Waterways of the Netherlands," Crerar Papers, MG30, vol. 3, Library and Archives Canada, 1–12.
14 "Report on the Islands of South Beveland and Walcheren and the Mainland Opposite the Islands to the South of the River Scheldt," RG 24, vol. 10539, Library and Archives Canada, 1.
15 "The Clearance of the Scheldt Estuary," 8–9.
16 Stacey, 392.
17 "The Clearance of the Scheldt Estuary," 9.
18 Chester Wilmot, *The Struggle for Europe* (London: Collins, 1952), 501.
19 Ibid., 408–22.
20 Bernard Law Montgomery, *Normandy to the Baltic* (London: Hutchinson, 1947), 186.
21 Bernard Law Montgomery, *The Memoirs of Field Marshal The Viscount Montgomery of Alamein, K.G.* (London: Collins, 1958), 294.
22 Ibid., 297.
23 Stacey, 336–43.
24 Ibid., 352.
25 Ibid., 352–54.
26 Ibid., 392.
27 Ibid., 364.
28 "The Clearance of the Scheldt Estuary," 7–8.
29 Stacey, 370.
30 "The Clearance of the Scheldt Estuary," 11–15.
31 Ibid., 9–10.

5: ILLUSION OF VICTORY

1 "Simonds to Crerar, 21 September 1944," Crerar Papers. MG30, vol. 2, Library and Archives Canada, 1–4.
2 Col. C.P. Stacey, *The Victory Campaign: The Operations in North-West Europe, 1944–1945*, vol. 3 (Ottawa: Queen's Printer, 1960), 371–72.
3 Crerar handwritten notes on "Simonds to Crerar," Crerar Papers, MG30, vol. 2, Library and Archives Canada, 3–4.
4 Stacey, 373.
5 Ibid., 374.
6 "Notes for Conference on Operation 'Infatuate,'" 22 September 1944, Crerar Papers, MG30, vol. 2, Library and Archives Canada, 1–4.
7 "Conference: Operation Infatutate, 1430A hrs 23 Sep," Crerar Papers, MG30, vol. 2, Library and Archives Canada, 1–3.
8 "Extract from R.A.F. Narrative: The Liberation of North-West Europe, The Assault on Walcheren," 570.013 (D3A), Directorate of Heritage and History, Department of National Defence, 3.
9 "Conference: Operation 'Infatuate,'" 3–4.
10 "Extract from R.A.F. Narrative," 3.

11 Report No. 188 Historical Section Canadian Military Headquarters: "Canadian Participation in the Operations in North-West Europe—Part VI: Canadian Operations, 1 Oct–8 Nov, The Clearance of the Scheldt Estuary," Department of National Defence, 7 April, 1948, 36.
12 Terry Copp, *The Brigade: The Fifth Canadian Infantry Brigade, 1939–1945* (Stoney Creek, ON: Fortress Publications, 1992), 126.
13 Headquarters 2nd Canadian Infantry Division, G Branch, War Diary, September 1944, RG24, Library and Archives Canada, 6.
14 1st Battalion, The Black Watch (RHR) of Canada War Diary, September 1944, RG24, Library and Archives Canada, n.p.
15 Calgary Highlanders War Diary, September 1944, RG24, Library and Archives Canada, 29.
16 Copp, 37.
17 Headquarters 2nd Canadian Infantry Division War Diary, 6.
18 Calgary Highlanders War Diary, 31–32.
19 The Black Watch War Diary, n.p.
20 Copp, 126–27.
21 Paul P. Hutchison, *Canada's Black Watch: The First Hundred Years, 1862–1962* (Montreal: The Black Watch (RHR) of Canada, 1962), 228.
22 Calgary Highlanders War Diary, 33.
23 David Bercuson, *Battalion of Heroes: The Calgary Highlanders in World War II* (Calgary: Calgary Highlanders Regimental Funds Foundation, 1994), 143.
24 Ibid., 144–45.
25 "Sergeant Clarence Kenneth Crockett, DCM," http://www.calgaryhighlanders.com/history/crockett.htm, July 6, 2006, 2.
26 Bercuson, 146.
27 Ibid., 149.
28 Ibid., 147–48.
29 Stacey, 366.
30 Bercuson, 148–49.
31 Report No. 69 Historical Section Army Headquarters: "The Campaign in North-West Europe, Information from German Sources—Part III: German Defence Operations in the Sphere of First Canadian Army (23 Aug.–8 Nov. 44)," Directorate of Heritage and History, Department of National Defence, 30 July, 1954, paras 93–94.
32 G.L. Cassidy, *Warpath: The Story of the Algonquin Regiment, 1939–1945* (Toronto: Ryerson Press, 1948), 159–60.
33 Report No. 183 Historical Section Canadian Military Headquarters: "Canadian Participation in North West Europe, 1944, Part IV: First Canadian Army in the Pursuit (23 Aug–30 Sep)," Directorate of Heritage and History, Department of National Defence, para 253.
34 Cassidy, 60.

6: POOR DEVILS

1 Report No. 69 Historical Section Army Headquarters: "The Campaign in North-West Europe, Information from German Sources—Part III: German

Defence Operations in the Sphere of First Canadian Army (23 Aug.–8 Nov. 44)," Directorate of Heritage and History, Department of National Defence, 30 July, 1954, paras 95–96.
2. Gustav von Zangen, "Ops of 15th German Army," RG24, vol. 20522, Library and Archives Canada, 67.
3. Ibid., 65–66.
4. Ibid., 68.
5. "The Campaign in North-West Europe, Information from German Sources—Part III," 92.
6. Ibid., 104–20.
7. Report No. 183 Historical Section Canadian Military Headquarters: "Canadian Participation in North West Europe, 1944, Part IV: First Canadian Army in the Pursuit (23 Aug–30 Sep)," Directorate of Heritage and History, Department of National Defence, para 276.
8. Ibid., 277.
9. Ibid.
10. Ibid., para 265.
11. 6th Canadian Infantry Brigade War Diary, September 1944, RG24, Library and Archives Canada, 12.
12. Alex McQuarrie, English translation in possession of author from *Cent ans d'histoire d'un régiment canadien-français: les Fusiliers Mont-Royal, 1869–1969* (Montréal: Editions Du Jour Montréal, 1971), n.p.
13. South Saskatchewan Regiment War Diary, September 1944, RG24, Library and Archives Canada, 17.
14. Cecil Law, "Lochtenberg—23 Sep 44 to 2 Oct 44," unpublished memoir, in possession of author, 3.
15. "South Saskatchewan Regiment Field Return of Officers, 16 September 1944," Appendix to South Saskatchewan War Diary, n.p.
16. Cecil Law, correspondence with author, 14 April 2006.
17. Cecil Law, correspondence with author, 10 May 2006.
18. Ibid.
19. Law, "Lochtenberg—23 Sep 44 to 2 Oct 44," 3–4.
20. Les Fusiliers Mont-Royal War Diary, September 1944, RG24, Library and Archives Canada, n.p.
21. South Saskatchewan War Diary, 1944, n.p.
22. Ibid.
23. Cecil Law, correspondence with author, 14 July 2006.
24. Saskatchewan War Diary, September 1944, n.p.
25. Cecil Law, 14 July 2006.
26. Charles Goodman, interview by author, Saanichton, BC, 2 June 2006.
27. Cecil Law, 14 July 2006.
28. Goodman interview.
29. Cecil Law, 14 July 2006.
30. Goodman interview.
31. Cecil Law, 14 July 2006.

32 Law, "Lochtenberg—23 Sep 44 to 2 Oct 44," 4–6.
33 Les Fusiliers Mont-Royal War Diary, September 1944, n.p.
34 Ibid.
35 6th Canadian Field Regiment War Diary, September 1944, RG24, Library and Archives Canada, n.p.
36 6th Canadian Infantry Brigade War Diary, 12.
37 Charles E. Goodman, interview by David Gantzer, 1, 5 December, 1979, 16 January 1980, University of Victoria Special Collections.
38 6th Canadian Infantry Brigade War Diary, 12.
39 Law, "Lochtenberg—23 Sep 44 to 2 Oct 44," 7.
40 Ibid., 6.
41 Cecil Law, 14 April and 14 July 2006.
42 "The Campaign in North-West Europe, Information from German Sources—Part III," 98–100.
43 "Report No. 183 Historical Section Canadian Military Headquarters—Canadian Participation in North West Europe, 1944, Part IV: First Canadian Army in the Pursuit (23 Aug–30 Sep)," para 261.
44 Oberst G. Elmar Warning, "Battles of LXVII Inf Corps Between the Schelde and the Maas, 15 Sep–25 Nov 44," RG24, vol. 20523, Library and Archives Canada, 9–11.
45 John Benson, "Belgium," http://fourthlincolns.tripod.com/page5/html, July 18, 2006, 5.
46 N.a., "Fact Sheet No. B21: World War 2–2nd Battalion South Wales Borderers," http://www.rrw.org.uk/museums/brecon/fact_sheets/21.htm, July 18, 2006, n.p.
47 H.M. Jackson, *The Sherbrooke Regiment (12th Armoured Regiment)* (n.p., 1958), 150.
48 "The Campaign in North-West Europe, Information from German Sources—Part III," 101.
49 Ibid., 13–14.
50 Jackson, 150–51.
51 Warning, 14.

7: SIMONDS TAKES COMMAND
1 Forrest C. Pogue, *Supreme Command* (Washington, DC: U.S. Government Printing Office, 1954), 297.
2 Bernard Montgomery, "21 Army Group, General Operational Situation and Directive," Crerar Papers, MG30, vol. 2, Library and Archives Canada, 1–3.
3 Col. C.P. Stacey, *The Victory Campaign: The Operations in North-West Europe, 1944–1945*, vol. 3 (Ottawa: Queen's Printer, 1960), 373.
4 Ibid.
5 N.R. Rodgers, Personal Diary, George Metcalf Archival Collection, Canadian War Museum, n.p.
6 J.L. Granatstein, *The Generals: The Canadian Army's Senior Commanders in the Second World War* (Toronto: Stoddart, 1993), 174–75.
7 Dominick Graham, *The Price of Command: A Biography of General Guy Simonds* (Toronto: Stoddart, 1993), 183.
8 David Bercuson, *Battalion of Heroes: The Calgary Highlanders in World War II*

(Calgary: Calgary Highlanders Regimental Funds Foundation, 1994), 152.
9 6th Canadian Infantry War Diary, September 1944, RG24, Library and Archives Canada, 13.
10 South Saskatchewan Regiment War Diary, September 1944, RG24, Library and Archives Canada, 23.
11 Cecil Law, "Compilation of South Saskatchewan Regiment Casualties," in possession of author.
12 Cecil Law, "Lochtenberg—23 Sep 44 to 2 Oct 44," unpublished memoir, in possession of author, 7.
13 Le Régiment de Maisonneuve War Diary, September 1944, RG24, Library and Archives Canada, n.p.
14 N.a., *Vanguard: The Fort Garry Horse in the Second World War* (Doetincham, Holland: Uitgevers-Maatschappij, C. Misset, NV, n.d.), 77.
15 Fort Garry Horse War Diary, September 1944, RG24, Library and Archives Canada, n.p.
16 *Vanguard*, 77.
17 Fort Garry Horse War Diary, n.p.
18 Gérard Marchand, *Le Régiment de Maisonneuve Vers la Victoire, 1944–1945* (Montréal: Les Presses Libres, 1980), 142.
19 Le Régiment de Maisonneuve War Diary, n.p.
20 Fort Garry Horse War Diary, n.p.
21 1st Battalion, The Black Watch (RHR) of Canada War Diary, September 1944, RG24, Library and Archives Canada, n.p.
22 *Vanguard*, 77.
23 Black Watch War Diary, n.p.
24 South Saskatchewan War Diary, 23–24.
25 Major J.H.D. Barrett, "11 Field Company, RCE: From Seine to Scheldt, 1 Sep/31 Oct 44," 143.3F11011(D1), Directorate of Heritage and History, Department of National Defence, n.p.
26 Bercuson, 153–54.
27 HQ 2nd Canadian Armoured Brigade War Diary, September 1944, RG24, Library and Archives Canada, 2.
28 Fort Garry Horse War Diary, September 1944, n.p.
29 HQ 2nd Canadian Armoured Brigade War Diary, September 1944, 2–3.
30 Report No. 188 Historical Section Canadian Military Headquarters: "Canadian Participation in the Operations in North-West Europe–Part VI: Canadian Operations, 1 Oct–8 Nov, The Clearance of the Scheldt Estuary," Department of National Defence, 7 April, 1948, 39.
31 W. Denis Whitaker and Shelagh Whitaker, *Tug of War: The Canadian Victory that Opened Antwerp* (Toronto: Stoddart, 1984), 115.
32 "The Clearance of the Scheldt Estuary," 39–40.
33 Brian A. Read, *No Holding Back: Operation Totalize, Normandy, August 1944* (Toronto: Robin Brass Studio, 2005), 84.
34 "The Clearance of the Scheldt Estuary," 41–42.
35 Ibid., 42.

8: OFF OUR BACKSIDES
1. Calgary Highlanders War Diary, September 1944, RG24, Library and Archives Canada, 50.
2. Calgary Highlanders War Diary, October 1944, RG24, Library and Archives Canada, 1.
3. Ibid.
4. Col. C.P. Stacey, *The Victory Campaign: The Operations in North-West Europe, 1944–1945*, vol. 3 (Ottawa: Queen's Printer, 1960), 191–92.
5. "Lieutenant Colonel Donald MacLaughlan (sic), DSO," http://www.calgaryhighlanders.com/history/mac.htm, July 6, 2006, 1.
6. Calgary Highlanders War Diary, October 1944, 2.
7. 1st Battalion, The Black Watch (RHR) of Canada War Diary, October 1944, RG24, Library and Archives Canada, 1.
8. Arthur K. Kember, *The Six Years of 6 Canadian Field Regiment Royal Canadian Artillery: September 1939–September 1945* (Amsterdam: Town Printing, 1945), 73.
9. Black Watch War Diary, 1.
10. Fort Garry Horse War Diary, October 1944, RG24, Library and Archives Canada, 1.
11. Black Watch War Diary, 1.
12. Ibid., 4.
13. Calgary Highlanders War Diary, October 1944, 2.
14. David Bercuson, *Battalion of Heroes: The Calgary Highlanders in World War II* (Calgary: Calgary Highlanders Regimental Funds Foundation, 1994), 156.
15. Fort Garry Horse War Diary, Appendix, October 1944, n.p.
16. Calgary Highlanders War Diary, October 1944, 3.
17. Major J.H.D. Barrett, "11 Field Company, RCE: From Seine to Scheldt, 1 Sep/31 Oct 44," 143.3F11011(D1), Directorate of Heritage and History, Department of National Defence, n.p.
18. 4th Canadian Infantry Brigade War Diary, September 1944, RG24, Library and Archives Canada, n.p.
19. D.J. Goodspeed, *Battle Royal: A History of the Royal Regiment of Canada, 1862–1962* (Toronto: The Royal Regiment of Canada Assoc., 1962), 488.
20. Ibid., 492.
21. Royal Regiment of Canada War Diary, October 1944, RG24, Library and Archives Canada, 2.
22. Goodspeed, 492.
23. W. Denis Whitaker and Shelagh Whitaker, *Tug of War: The Canadian Victory that Opened Antwerp* (Toronto: Stoddart, 1984), 156.
24. Goodspeed, 492–94.
25. George G. Blackburn, *The Guns of Victory: A Soldier's Eye View, Belgium, Holland, and Germany, 1944–45* (Toronto: McClelland & Stewart, 1996), 45.
26. Royal Regiment of Canada War Diary, October 1944, 2.
27. Goodspeed, 494.
28. Royal Regiment of Canada War Diary, October 1944, 2.
29. Goodspeed, 494.
30. Johan van Doorn, correspondence with author, Sommelsdijk, Holland, 16

September 2006.
31 Goodspeed, 494.
32 Essex Scottish War Diary, October 1944, RG24, Library and Archives Canada, n.p.
33 George Blackburn, *The History of the 4th Field Regiment* (n.p., 1945), n.p.
34 Whitaker, 153–54.
35 Jean Bouchery, *The Canadian Soldier in North-West Europe, 1944–1945*, trans: Alan McKay (Paris: Histoire & Collections, 2003), 102.
36 Blackburn, *The Guns of Victory*, 280.
37 Royal Hamilton Light Infantry War Diary, October 1944, RG24, Library and Archives Canada, n.p.
38 Kingsley Brown, Sr., Kingsley Brown, Jr., and Brereton Greenhous, *Semper Paratus: The History of The Royal Hamilton Light Infantry (Wentworth Regiment), 1862–1977* (Hamilton: The RHLI Historical Assoc., 1977), n.p.
39 Ibid.
40 2nd Canadian Anti-Tank Regiment, RCA War Diary, October 1944, RG24, Library and Archives Canada, 2.
41 Whitaker, 154.
42 Kingsley Brown, n.p.
43 Whitaker, 154.
44 Kingsley Brown, n.p.
45 Royal Hamilton Light Infantry War Diary, n.p.
46 Whitaker, 154.
47 South Saskatchewan Regiment War Diary, October 1944, RG24, Library and Archives Canada, 2.
48 Ibid., 2.
49 Ibid., 2–3.
50 Fort Garry Horse War Diary, October 1944, n.p.
51 R.W. Queen-Hughes, *Whatever Men Dare: A History of the Queen's Own Cameron Highlanders of Canada, 1935–1960* (Winnipeg: Bulman Bros., 1960), 136–37.
52 Queen's Own Cameron Highlanders of Canada War Diary, October 1944, RG24, Library and Archives Canada, 3.
53 G.B. Buchanan, *The March of the Prairie Men: A Story of the South Saskatchewan Regiment* (n.p., n.d.), 41.
54 N.a., *Vanguard: The Fort Garry Horse in the Second World War* (Doetincham, Holland: Uitgevers-Maatschappij, C. Misset, NV, n.d.), 80.

9: CLOSE TO THE DANGER LINE
1 Hen Bollen, *Worsteling om Walcheren, 1939–1945* (Netherlands: Uitgeverij Terra Zuthphen, 1985), 137.
2 W. Denis Whitaker and Shelagh Whitaker, *Tug of War: The Canadian Victory that Opened Antwerp* (Toronto: Stoddart, 1984), 118.
3 Bollen, 137.
4 Ibid., 134.
5 Andrew Rawson, *Walcheren: Operation Infatuate* (South Yorkshire: Pen & Sword Books, 2003), 28.

6 "Extract from RAF Narrative: The Liberation of North-West Europe, The Assault on Walcheren—preliminary air operations," 570.013(D3A), Directorate of Heritage and History, DND, 4.
7 "Extract from RAF narrative," 4.
8 Bollen, 134–35.
9 Ibid., 145.
10 Whitaker, 122.
11 Bollen, 147.
12 Ibid., 144.
13 Ibid., 148.
14 "Extract from RAF narrative," 3.
15 Bollen, 147.
16 J.L. Moulton, *Battle for Antwerp: The Liberation of the City and the Opening of the Scheldt, 1944* (New York: Hippocrene Books, 1978), 95.
17 Col. C.P. Stacey, *The Victory Campaign: The Operations in North-West Europe, 1944–1945*, vol. 3 (Ottawa: Queen's Printer, 1960), 374.
18 Ibid., 377–78.
19 Whitaker, 126.
20 Stacey, 379.
21 Report No. 188 Historical Section Canadian Military Headquarters: "Canadian Participation in the Operations in North-West Europe–Part VI: Canadian Operations, 1 Oct–8 Nov, The Clearance of the Scheldt Estuary," Department of National Defence, 7 April, 1948, 47.
22 Stacey, 425.
23 J.L. Granatstein, *Canada's Army: Waging War and Keeping the Peace* (Toronto: University of Toronto Press, 2002), 292.
24 E.L.M. Burns, *Manpower in the Canadian Army, 1939–1945* (Toronto: Clarke, Irwin & Company, 1956), 6.
25 Bill McAndrew, *Liberation: The Canadians in Europe* (Montreal: Éditions Art Global, 1995), 63.
26 Ibid.
27 1st Battalion, The Black Watch (RHR) of Canada War Diary, October 1944, RG24, Library and Archives Canada, 23.
28 George G. Blackburn, *The Guns of Victory: A Soldier's Eye View, Belgium, Holland, and Germany, 1944–45* (Toronto: McClelland & Stewart, 1996), 49.
29 Black Watch War Diary, October 1944, 12.
30 McAndrew, 62.
31 "Miscellaneous Papers, 1944–1979 Regarding a Chaplain's Role," MG 31, vol. F18, Library and Archives Canada, n.p.
32 Burns, 115.
33 Charles Goodman, interview by author, Saanichton, BC, 2 June 2006.
34 Burns, 167.

10: A HARD FIGHT

1 Oberst G. Elmar Warning, "Battles of LXVII Inf Corps Between the Schelde and the

Maas, 15 Sep–25 Nov 44," RG24, vol. 20523, Library and Archives Canada, 19–20.
2. Report No. 69 Historical Section Army Headquarters: "The Campaign in North-West Europe, Information from German Sources—Part III: German Defence Operations in the Sphere of First Canadian Army (23 Aug.–8 Nov. 44)," Directorate of Heritage and History, Department of National Defence, 30 July, 1954, paras 124–26.
3. Johan van Doorn, *Slag om Woensdrecht: bevrijding van de Zuidwesthoek, Oktober 1944* (Willemstad: n.p., 1995), 39.
4. Col. C.P. Stacey, *The Victory Campaign: The Operations in North-West Europe, 1944–1945*, vol. 3 (Ottawa: Queen's Printer, 1960), 381.
5. W. Denis Whitaker and Shelagh Whitaker, *Tug of War: The Canadian Victory that Opened Antwerp* (Toronto: Stoddart, 1984), 167.
6. Warning, 17.
7. Ibid., 18.
8. Essex Scottish War Diary, October 1944, RG24, Library and Archives Canada, n.p.
9. Ibid.
10. Ken M. Hossack, *Mike Target* (Ottawa: n.p., 1945), 25.
11. 4th Canadian Field Regiment War Diary, October 1944, RG24, Library and Archives Canada, 1.
12. Essex Scottish War Diary, October 1944, n.p.
13. Ibid.
14. George G. Blackburn, *The Guns of Victory: A Soldier's Eye View, Belgium, Holland, and Germany, 1944–45* (Toronto: McClelland & Stewart, 1996), 53.
15. Hossack, 26.
16. Essex Scottish War Diary, October 1944, n.p.
17. N.a., *VIII CDN Recce Rgt. 14 CH: Battle History of the Regt.* (n.p., n.d.), 29.
18. Blackburn, 54.
19. Essex Scottish War Diary, October 1944, n.p.
20. Royal Hamilton Light Infantry War Diary, October 1944, RG24, Library and Archives Canada, n.p.
21. Fort Garry Horse War Diary, October 1944, RG24, Library and Archives Canada, 3.
22. Royal Hamilton Light Infantry War Diary, October 1944, n.p.
23. D.J. Goodspeed, *Battle Royal: A History of the Royal Regiment of Canada, 1862–1962* (Toronto: The Royal Regiment of Canada Assoc., 1962), 496.
24. Blackburn, 56–61.
25. 1 Battalion, Royal Regiment of Canada War Diary, October 1944, RG24, Library and Archives Canada, 6–7.
26. George Blackburn, *The History of the 4th Field Regiment* (n.p., 1945), n.p.
27. Hossack, 26–27.
28. David Bercuson, *Battalion of Heroes: The Calgary Highlanders in World War II* (Calgary: Calgary Highlanders Regimental Funds Foundation, 1994), 161.
29. 1 Battalion, The Black Watch (RHR) of Canada War Diary, October 1944, RG24, Library and Archives Canada, 4.
30. N.a., *Vanguard: The Fort Garry Horse in the Second World War* (Doetincham, Holland: Uitgevers-Maatschappij, C. Misset, NV, n.d.), 81.

31 Fort Garry Horse War Diary, October 1944, Appendix, n.p.
32 *Vanguard*, 81.
33 5th Canadian Infantry Brigade War Diary, October 1944, RG24, Library and Archives Canada, 4.
34 Bercuson, 161–62.
35 Fort Garry Horse War Diary, October 1944, Appendix, n.p.
36 Ernest Teagle, interview by Mark C. Hill, 20 June 1985, University of Victoria Special Collections.
37 Calgary Highlanders War Diary, October 1944, RG24, Library and Archives Canada, 22.
38 Warning, 20–21.
39 "The Campaign in North-West Europe, Information from German Sources—Part III", 130.
40 van Doorn, 39–40.
41 Bill McAndrew, *Liberation: The Canadians in Europe* (Montreal: Éditions Art Global, 1995), 53.
42 Ibid., 54.
43 II Canadian Corps War Diary, October 1944, Appendix, Intelligence Summary No. 64, RG24, Library and Archives Canada, 1.
44 6th Canadian Infantry Brigade War Diary, October 1944, RG24, Library and Archives Canada, 5–6.
45 Ibid., 6.
46 van Doorn, 38.
47 *Vanguard*, 82.
48 van Doorn, 38.
49 Warning, 21.
50 6th Canadian Infantry Brigade War Diary, October 1944, 8.

II: WITH DEVASTATING EFFECT

1 D.J. Goodspeed, *Battle Royal: A History of the Royal Regiment of Canada, 1862–1962* (Toronto: The Royal Regiment of Canada Assoc., 1962), 499.
2 Goodspeed, 499–500.
3 Terry Copp, *The Brigade: The Fifth Canadian Infantry Brigade, 1939–45* (Stoney Creek, ON: Fortress Publications, 1992), 139.
4 1st Battalion, The Black Watch (RHR) of Canada War Diary, October 1944, RG24, Library and Archives Canada, 5.
5 Johan van Doorn, *Slag om Woensdrecht: bevrijding van de Zuidwesthoek, Oktober 1944* (Willemstad: n.p., 1995), 39.
6 Black Watch War Diary, October 1944, 5.
7 van Doorn, 39.
8 David Bercuson, *Battalion of Heroes: The Calgary Highlanders in World War II* (Calgary: Calgary Highlanders Regimental Funds Foundation, 1994), 164.
9 Oberst G. Elmar Warning, "Battles of LXVII Inf Corps Between the Schelde and the Maas, 15 Sep–25 Nov 44," RG24, vol. 20523, Library and Archives Canada, 21.
10 Black Watch War Diary, October 1944, 5.

11 Bercuson, 165.
12 Calgary Highlanders War Diary, October 1944, RG24, Library and Archives Canada, 23.
13 5th Canadian Infantry Brigade War Diary, October 1944, RG24, Library and Archives Canada, 5.
14 van Doorn, 39–41.
15 Black Watch War Diary, October 1944, 6.
16 Calgary Highlanders War Diary, October 1944, 24.
17 Black Watch War Diary, October 1944, 5.
18 Harold MacDonald with M.A. MacDonald, "The Long Wait (Part 1): A Personal Account of Infantry Training in Britain," *Canadian Military History*, vol. 14, Spring 2006, 37.
19 Black Watch War Diary, October 1944, 5.
20 Calgary Highlander War Diary, October 1944, 25.
21 Bercuson, 166.
22 Calgary Highlander War Diary, October 1944, 25.
23 Ibid., 26.
24 Ibid., 26–27.
25 van Doorn, 41.
26 Black Watch War Diary, October 1944, 6.
27 Fort Garry Horse War Diary, October 1944, RG24, Library and Archives Canada, 5.
28 Bercuson, 170.
29 Calgary Highlanders War Diary, October 1944, 28.
30 Bercuson, 170.
31 Ibid.
32 5th Canadian Infantry Brigade War Diary, 6.
33 Ibid.
34 Calgary Highlanders War Diary, October 1944, 28.
35 Bercuson, 170–71.
36 Johan van Doorn, correspondence with author, 1 November 2006.
37 Bercuson, 171–72.
38 Calgary Highlanders War Diary, October 1944, 29.
39 Black Watch War Diary, October 1944, 6.
40 5th Canadian Infantry Brigade War Diary, October 1944, 6.
41 Black Watch War Diary, 6.
42 5th Canadian Infantry Brigade War Diary, October 1944, 7.
43 Bercuson, 172–73.
44 Bercuson, 173.
45 Copp, 142.
46 van Doorn, correspondence.
47 Goodspeed, 500.
48 van Doorn, *Slag om Woensdrecht*, 44.
49 1st Battalion, Royal Regiment of Canada War Diary, October 1944, RG24, Library and Archives Canada, 9.
50 Goodspeed, 500.

51 Royal Regiment of Canada War Diary, 10.
52 4th Canadian Infantry Brigade War Diary, October 1944, RG24, Library and Archives Canada, 8.
53 Goodspeed, 500.
54 van Doorn, *Slag om Woensdrecht*, 45.
55 Goodspeed, 501.
56 4th Canadian Infantry Brigade War Diary, October 1944, 8.
57 Royal Regiment of Canada War Diary, 12.
58 Goodspeed, 502.
59 van Doorn, 47.

12: DID OUR BEST

1 "21st Army Group, Clearing of the Scheldt Estuary, Oct–Nov 1944," Crerar Papers, MG30, Library and Archives Canada, 4.
2 "Operation 'Switchback': The Clearing of the South Bank of the Schelde (Battle Narrative Prepared by Historical Officer, 3 CDN INF DIV," Canadian Operations in North-West Europe: October–November 1944, Extracts from War Diaries and Memoranda (Series 18), 018.(D2), Directorate of Heritage and History, Department of National Defence, 3.
3 "21st Army Group," 4.
4 Col. C.P. Stacey, *The Victory Campaign: The Operations in North-West Europe, 1944–1945*, vol. 3 (Ottawa: Queen's Printer, 1960), 393.
5 Brig. P.A.S. Todd, "Artillery in Operation 'Switchback': Account by Brig. P.A.S. Todd, DSO, OBE, ED, CCRA, 2 CDN CORPS, given to Historical Officer 3 CDN INF DIV, 9 Dec. 1944," Appendix 'A,' Canadian Operations in North-West Europe: October–November 1944, Extracts from War Diaries and Memoranda (Series 18), 018.(D2), Directorate of Heritage and History, Department of National Defence, 18.
6 "Operation Switchback," 4.
7 Ibid.
8 H.M. Jackson (ed), *The Argyll and Sutherland Highlanders of Canada (Princess Louise's), 1928–1953* (n.p., 1953), 128.
9 "Some Aspects of the Technique of Flame Throwing: 'WASP' and 'Lifebuoy' (Account by Lt. George Bannerman, Sask L.I. (M.G.), Tech Offr (Flame), First Canadian Army, Given to Historical Officer, 2 CDN INF DIV, 26 Nov 44), Canadian Operations in North-West Europe: June–November 1944, Extracts from War Diaries and Memoranda (Series 17), 018 (D2), Directorate of Heritage and History, Department of National Defence, 1–2.
10 Jackson, 128.
11 G.L. Cassidy, *Warpath: The Story of the Algonquin Regiment, 1939–1945* (Toronto: Ryerson Press, 1948), 160.
12 Ibid., 160–63.
13 Algonquin Regiment War Diary, October 1944, RG24, Library and Archives Canada, 3–4.
14 Jackson, 128–29.
15 Canadian Scottish War Diary, October 1944, RG24, Library and Archives Canada, 5.

16 Reginald H. Roy, *Ready for the Fray: The History of the Canadian Scottish Regiment (Princess Mary's), 1920 to 1955* (Vancouver: Evergreen Press, 1958), 325.
17 Ronald Gendall Shawcross, *What Was It Like? A Rifleman Remembers: Some Memories of World War II, 1939–1945* (Victoria: Trafford Publishing, 2004), 209–10.
18 Gordon Brown and Terry Copp, *Look to Your Front... Regina Rifles: A Regiment at War, 1944–45* (Waterloo, ON: Laurier Centre Military Strategic Disarmament Studies, 2001), 146.
19 Shawcross, 211.
20 Canadian Scottish War Diary, October 1944, Appendix 9: Personal Accounts of Battle, Capt. B. Fraser, "WASPS–Flame Throwing Carriers," 1.
21 Roy, 325.
22 Canadian Scottish War Diary, Appendix 9: Fraser, 1.
23 Shawcross, 211.
24 R.C. Fetherstonhaugh, *The Royal Montreal Regiment, 1925–1945* (Westmount, QC: The Royal Montreal Regiment, 1949), 184.
25 First Canadian Army HQ Defence Company (RMR) War Diary, Appendix 5, October 1944, RG24, Library and Archives Canada, 1.
26 Ibid.
27 First Canadian Army HQ Defence Company (RMR) War Diary, Appendix 12, 1–2.
28 First Canadian Army HQ Defence Company (RMR) War Diary, Appendix 5, 2.
29 Fetherstonhaugh, 185–86.
30 "The Bridgehead over the Leopold Canal: Account by Maj. A.L. Gollnick, 2 IC and Capt. C.M. Rehill, Adjt. Regina Rif, Given to Historical Officer, 13 Nov 44," 145.2R11011(2), Directorate of Heritage and History, Department of National Defence, 2.
31 Evert M. Nordstrom, "1989 account," *The Recollections of the Regina Rifles: N.W. Europe World War 2, June 6, 1944–May 8, 1945* (n.p., n.d.), 4.
32 "The Bridgehead over the Leopold Canal," 2.
33 Ken Bergin, "The Experiences of One Regina Rifle John as a POW of the Germans and the Russians," *The Recollections of the Regina Rifles: N.W. Europe World War 2, June 6, 1944–May 8, 1945* (n.p., n.d.), 2.
34 Stewart A.G. Mein, *Up the Johns! The Story of the Royal Regina Rifles.* (North Battleford, SK: Turner-Warwick Publications, 1992), 128.
35 Bergin, 2.
36 Ibid., 2–10.
37 First Canadian Army HQ Defence Company (RMR) War Diary, Appendix 5, 3.
38 Bert Adams (originally Adamoski), "Personal Account," *The Recollections of the Regina Rifles: N.W. Europe World War 2, June 6, 1944–May 8, 1945* (n.p., n.d.), 4.
39 Eric Luxton (ed), *1st Battalion, The Regina Rifle Regiment, 1939–1946* (Regina, SK: The Regiment, 1946), 53.
40 Mein, 129.
41 Shawcross, 212.
42 "The Bridgehead over the Leopold Canal," 2.
43 T.J. Bell, *Into Action with the 12th Field* (Utrecht: J. van Boekhoven, 1945), 92.

44 12th Canadian Field Regiment War Diary, October 1944, RG24, Library and Archives Canada, 2.
45 First Canadian Army HQ Defence Company (RMR) War Diary, Appendix 12, 3.

13: A HELL OF A WAY TO GO

1 Reginald H. Roy, *Ready for the Fray: The History of the Canadian Scottish Regiment (Princess Mary's), 1920 to 1955* (Vancouver: Evergreen Press, 1958), 326.
2 Royce Marshall correspondence with Reginald Roy, 28 Jan. 1957, Reginald Roy Collection, Special Collections, University of Victoria, 2.
3 Roger Schjelderup correspondence with Reginald Roy, 16 July 1957, Reginald Roy Collection, Special Collections, University of Victoria, 6.
4 Canadian Scottish War Diary, October 1944, Appendix 9: Personal Accounts of Battle, 'B' Coy: 1 Bn, C. Scot. R., Lieut. L. Hobden, RG24, Library and Archives Canada, 2.
5 L. Hobden correspondence with Reginald Roy, 8 May 1957, Reginald Roy Collection, Special Collections, University of Victoria, 5.
6 Earl English correspondence with Reginald Roy, 12 April 1957, Reginald Roy Collection, Special Collections, University of Victoria, 1.
7 L. Hobden correspondence, 5.
8 Marshall correspondence, 1.
9 Schjelderup correspondence, 2.
10 Marshall correspondence, 2.
11 Schjelderup correspondence, 5–6.
12 Marshall correspondence, 2.
13 Roy, 328.
14 Schjelderup correspondence, 2.
15 Thomas William Lowell Butters, interview by Tom Torrie, 19 August 1987, University of Victoria Special Collections.
16 Schjelderup correspondence, 2.
17 Roy, 328–29.
18 7th Canadian Infantry Brigade War Diary, October 1944, RG24, Library and Archives Canada, 3.
19 Royal Winnipeg Rifles War Diary, October 1944, RG24, Library and Archives Canada, 2.
20 Report No. 188 Historical Section Canadian Military Headquarters: "Canadian Participation in the Operations in North-West Europe–Part VI: Canadian Operations, 1 Oct–8 Nov, The Clearance of the Scheldt Estuary," Department of National Defence, 7 April, 1948, 56.
21 John Beer interview, interview by David Gantzer, 26 & 28 Nov. 1979, University of Victoria Special Collections.
22 12th Canadian Field Regiment, RCA War Diary, October 1944, RG24, Library and Archives Canada, 3.
23 1st Battalion, Regina Rifles War Diary, October 1944, Appendix 5, RG24, Library and Archives Canada, 3.
24 Marshall correspondence, 2.

25 "Personal Accounts of Battle, Canadian Scottish, Jun 44–May 45, 'Two Came Back,'" 145.2C4009 (d11), Directorate of Heritage and History, Department of National Defence, 1.
26 Schjelderup correspondence, 3–4.
27 Ibid.
28 Canadian Scottish War Diary, Appendix 9, 'B' Coy: 1 Bn, C. Scot. R., Lieut. L. Hobden, 2
29 Marshall correspondence, 3.
30 Schjelderup correspondence, 4.
31 "Personal Accounts of Battle, Canadian Scottish, Jun 44–May 45, 'Two Came Back,'" 4–9.
32 Bruce Tascona and Eric Wells, *Little Black Devils: A History of the Royal Winnipeg Rifles* (Winnipeg: Frye Publishing, 1983), 176.
33 Will R. Bird, *North Shore (New Brunswick) Regiment* (Fredericton, NB: Brunswick Press, 1963), 437–39.
34 Jim Parks, interview by Ken MacLeod, Vancouver, BC, November 1997.
35 "The Bridgehead over the Leopold Canal: Account by Maj. A.L. Gollnick, 2 IC and Capt. C.M. Rehill, Adjt. Regina Rif, Given to Historical Officer, 13 Nov 44," 145.2R11011(2), Directorate of Heritage and History, Department of National Defence, 3.
36 Gordon Brown and Terry Copp, *Look to Your Front... Regina Rifles: A Regiment at War, 1944–45* (Waterloo, ON: Laurier Centre Military Strategic Disarmament Studies, 2001), 146–47.
37 "Tom Odette letter," *The Recollections of the Regina Rifles: N.W. Europe World War 2, June 6, 1944–May 8, 1945* (n.p., n.d.), 2.
38 Eric Luxton (ed), *1st Battalion, The Regina Rifle Regiment, 1939–1946* (Regina, SK: The Regiment, 1946), 53.
39 Roy, 334.
40 Bob Gray, "Life and Death on the Leopold," *The Recollections of the Regina Rifles: N.W. Europe World War 2, June 6, 1944–May 8, 1945* (n.p., n.d.), 1–5.
41 Canadian Scottish War Diary, October 1944, 10.
42 Col. C.P. Stacey, *The Victory Campaign: The Operations in North-West Europe, 1944–1945*, vol. 3 (Ottawa: Queen's Printer, 1960), 395–96.

14: IN THE BACK DOOR

1 N.a., *1st Battalion, The Highland Light Infantry of Canada: 1940–1945* (Galt, ON: Highland Light Infantry of Canada Assoc., 1951), 66.
2 The Highland Light Infantry of Canada War Diary, October 1944, RG24, Library and Archives Canada, 2.
3 "The Amphibious Operation Against the Rear of the 'Breskens Pocket,' 9 Oct 44: (a) Account of the Landing of 9 CDN INF BDE, given to Hist Offr 3 CDN INF DIV by Major R. T. Wiltshire, O.C. 80 Sqn, 5 Aslt Regt, R.E., 16 Oct," Canadian Operations Northwest Europe, MG30, vol. 8, E157, Library and Archives Canada, 7.
4 "Combined Operations Headquarters–Bulletin Y/43: 'Amphibians in Operation 'Switchback,'" MG30, vol. 8, Library and Archives Canada, 2–7.

NOTES / 497

5 "The Amphibious Operation Against the Rear of the 'Breskens Pocket,' Wiltshire," 4.
6 North Nova Scotia Highlanders War Diary, October 1944, RG24, Library and Archives Canada, n.p.
7 "Amphibians in Operation Switchback," 1.
8 Ibid., 6.
9 Ibid., Appendix E.
10 Ibid., 2.
11 North Nova Scotia Highlanders War Diary, October 1944, n.p.
12 Jean E. Portugal, *We Were There: The Navy, the Army and the RCAF—A Record for Canada*, vol. 4 (Shelburne, ON: The Battered Silicon Dispatch Box, 1998), 1765.
13 North Nova Scotia Highlanders War Diary, October 1944, n.p.
14 "The Assault Across Savojaards Plaat, 8–9 Oct. 44," RG24, vol. 10908, Library and Archives Canada, 6.
15 *1st Battalion, The Highland Light Infantry*, 66.
16 "Amphibians in Operation Switchback," 3.
17 North Nova Scotia Highlanders War Diary, n.p.
18 Ibid.
19 Portugal, 1765.
20 9th Canadian Infantry Brigade War Diary, October 1944, RG24, Library and Archives Canada, 3.
21 "The Amphibious Operation Against the Rear of the 'Breskens Pocket,' 9 Oct 44: (b) Account by Lt.-Cdr. R. D. Franks, R. N. (Naval Liaison Officer, H.Q. First CDN Army) Given to Hist Offr, H.Q. First CDN Army," Canadian Operations Northwest Europe, MG30, vol. 8, E157, Library and Archives Canada, 8.
22 Ibid.
23 "The Amphibious Operation Against the Rear of the 'Breskens Pocket,' Wiltshire," 6.
24 Ibid., 5.
25 "The Assault Across Savojaards Plaat, 8–9 Oct. 44," 8.
26 *1st Battalion, The Hamilton Light Infantry*, 67.
27 "The Amphibious Operation Against the Rear of the 'Breskens Pocket,' 9 Oct 44, Franks," 8.
28 Will R. Bird, *No Retreating Footsteps: The Story of the North Nova Scotia Highlanders* (Hantsport, NS: Lancelot Press, 1983), 246.
29 North Nova Scotia Highlanders War Diary, October 1944, n.p.
30 The Hamilton Light Infantry War Diary, October 1944, 5.
31 *1st Battalion, The Hamilton Light Infantry*, 67.
32 Portugal, 1765–66.
33 *1st Battalion, The Hamilton Light Infantry*, 68.
34 Bird, 249–50.
35 Ibid., 250.
36 Brig. P.A.S. Todd, "Artillery in Operation 'Switchback': Account by Brig. P.A.S. Todd, DSO, OBE, ED, CCRA, 2 CDN CORPS, given to Historical Officer 3 CDN INF DIV, 9 Dec. 1944," Appendix 'A,' Canadian Operations in North-West Europe: October–

November 1944, Extracts from War Diaries and Memoranda (Series 18), 018.(D2), Directorate of Heritage and History, Department of National Defence, 18.
37 "The Amphibious Operation Against the Rear of the 'Breskens Pocket,' 9 Oct 44, Franks," 8–9.
38 William Boss, *Up the Glens: Stormont, Dundas and Glengarry Highlanders, 1783–1994* (Cornwall, ON: Old Book Store, 1995), 224–25.
39 Ibid., 225.
40 W. Denis Whitaker and Shelagh Whitaker, *Tug of War: The Canadian Victory that Opened Antwerp* (Toronto: Stoddart, 1984), 292.
41 Jean E. Portugal, *We Were There*, vol. 3, 1347.
42 Boss, 226.
43 Ibid.
44 Portugal, *We Were There*, vol. 3, 1347–48.
45 Reginald H. Roy, *Ready for the Fray: The History of the Canadian Scottish Regiment (Princess Mary's), 1920 to 1955* (Vancouver: Evergreen Press, 1958), 336–37.

15: OF FIRST IMPORTANCE
1 W.S. Chalmers, *Full Cycle: The Biography of Admiral Sir Bertram Home Ramsay, KCB, KBE, MVC*, vol. 2, (London: Hodder & Stoughton, 1959), 252.
2 L.F. Ellis with A.E. Warhurst, *Victory in the West: Volume II: The Defeat of Germany* (London: Her Majesty's Stationery Office, 1968), 83.
3 Ibid., 85.
4 Ibid., 86–88.
5 Ellis, 88–89.
6 Col. C.P. Stacey, *The Victory Campaign: The Operations in North-West Europe, 1944–1945*, vol. 3 (Ottawa: Queen's Printer, 1960), 389.
7 7th Canadian Infantry Brigade War Diary, October 1944, RG24, Library and Archives Canada, 4.
8 "Conversation GOC 3 Cdn Inf Div with Maj-Gen Eberding, GOC 64 German Inf Div–1 Nov 44," 19830036.001, Canadian War Museum, 1.
9 Report No. 69 Historical Section Army Headquarters: "The Campaign in North-West Europe, Information from German Sources—Part III: German Defence Operations in the Sphere of First Canadian Army (23 Aug.–8 Nov. 44)," Directorate of Heritage and History, Department of National Defence, 30 July, 1954, paras 210–13.
10 J.L. Moulton, *Battle for Antwerp: The Liberation of the City and the Opening of the Scheldt, 1944* (New York: Hippocrene Books, 1978), 149.
11 Hen Bollen, *Worsteling om Walcheren, 1939–1945* (Netherlands: Uitgeverij Terra Zuthphen, 1985), 153.
12 Ad van Dijk, interview with author, Vlissingen, 17 May 2003.
13 Bollen, 153.
14 van Dijk interview.
15 Bollen, 156.
16 van Dijk interview.
17 W. Denis Whitaker and Shelagh Whitaker, *Tug of War: The Canadian Victory that Opened Antwerp* (Toronto: Stoddart, 1984), 267.

18 "The Campaign in North-West Europe, Information from German Sources—Part III," 210.
19 Ibid., 209.
20 8th Canadian Infantry Brigade War Diary, October 1944, RG24, Library and Archives Canada, n.p.
21 Walter G. Pavey, *An Historical Account of the 7th Canadian Reconnaissance Regiment (17th Duke of York's Royal Canadian Hussars)*, (Gardenvale, QC: Harpell's Press, 1948), 77–78.
22 1st Battalion, Regina Rifles War Diary, October 1944, RG24, Library and Archives Canada, 7.
23 Ronald Gendall Shawcross, *What Was It Like? A Rifleman Remembers: Some Memories of World War II, 1939–1945* (Victoria: Trafford Publishing, 2004), 211–13.
24 Bob Gray, "Life and Death on the Leopold," *The Recollections of the Regina Rifles: N.W. Europe World War 2, June 6, 1944–May 8, 1945* (n.p., n.d.), 5–6.
25 Regina Rifles War Diary, October 1944, n.p.
26 Gray, 6.
27 Regina Rifles War Diary, October 1944, n.p.
28 Shawcross, 212–19.
29 Gordon Brown and Terry Copp, *Look to Your Front... Regina Rifles: A Regiment at War, 1944–45* (Waterloo, ON: Laurier Centre Military Strategic Disarmament Studies, 2001), 143.
30 Lochie Fulton, interview by Ken MacLeod, Victoria, BC, 9 February 1998.
31 Royal Winnipeg Rifles War Diary, October 1944, RG24, Library and Archives Canada, 4.
32 Fulton interview.
33 Royal Winnipeg Rifles War Diary, October 1944, 4.
34 Ibid.
35 Fulton interview.
36 Royal Winnipeg Rifles War Diary, October 1944, 4–5.
37 Reginald H. Roy, *Ready for the Fray: The History of the Canadian Scottish Regiment (Princess Mary's), 1920 to 1955* (Vancouver: Evergreen Press, 1958), 337.
38 Royce Marshall correspondence with Reginald Roy, 28 Jan. 1957, Reginald Roy Collection, Special Collections, University of Victoria, 3–4.
39 Canadian Scottish War Diary, October 1944, Appendix 9: Personal Accounts of Battle, Report on 'C' coys Attack on the Bridge Across the Leopold Canal October 12 44, RG24, Library and Archives Canada, 1.
40 Marshall correspondence, 4.
41 Canadian Scottish War Diary, October 1944, Appendix 9: Personal Accounts of Battle, Charlie Coy's Activities October 6–13 1944, Reported by Lt. R. S. Marshall, P.C. 15 Pl., 3.
42 Roy, 339.
43 Ibid.
44 Canadian Scottish War Diary, October 1944, RG24, Library and Archives Canada, 16.
45 Canadian Scottish War Diary, October 1944, Appendix 9: Personal Accounts of Battle, Report on 'C' coys Attack on the Bridge Across the Leopold Canal October 12 44, 1.

46 Roy, 340–41.
47 Ibid., 342.
48 Regina Rifles War Diary, October 1944, n.p.

16: THE TOUGHEST YET

1 Report No. 69 Historical Section Army Headquarters: "The Campaign in North-West Europe, Information from German Sources—Part III: German Defence Operations in the Sphere of First Canadian Army (23 Aug.–8 Nov. 44)," Directorate of Heritage and History, Department of National Defence, 30 July, 1954, paras 214–15.
2 "Conversation GOC 3 Cdn Inf Div with Maj-Gen Eberding, GOC 64 German Inf Div–1 Nov 44," 19830036.001, Canadian War Museum, 1.
3 9th Canadian Infantry Brigade War Diary, October 1944, RG24, Library and Archives Canada, 4.
4 Algonquin Regiment War Diary, October 1944, RG24, Library and Archives Canada, 7.
5 Argyll and Sutherland Highlanders War Diary, October 1944, RG24, Library and Archives Canada, n.p.
6 Col. C.P. Stacey, *The Victory Campaign: The Operations in North-West Europe, 1944–1945*, vol. 3 (Ottawa: Queen's Printer, 1960), 397.
7 Will R. Bird, *No Retreating Footsteps: The Story of the North Nova Scotia Highlanders* (Hantsport, NS: Lancelot Press, 1983), 252–53.
8 Ibid., 253.
9 William Boss, *Up the Glens: Stormont, Dundas and Glengarry Highlanders, 1783–1994* (Cornwall, ON: Old Book Store, 1995), 226.
10 Stormont, Dundas and Glengarry War Diary, October 1944, RG24, Library and Archives Canada, 5.
11 Boss, 227.
12 Stormont, Dundas and Glengarry War Diary, 5–6.
13 Highland Light Infantry War Diary, October 1944, RG24, Library and Archives Canada, 5.
14 Jean E. Portugal, *We Were There: The Navy, the Army and the RCAF–A Record for Canada*, vol. 4 (Shelburne, ON: The Battered Silicon Dispatch Box, 1998), 1767.
15 Ibid., 1766.
16 Ibid., 1768.
17 Highland Light Infantry War Diary, 6.
18 Walter G. Pavey, *An Historical Account of the 7th Canadian Reconnaissance Regiment (17th Duke of York's Royal Canadian Hussars)*, (Gardenvale, QC: Harpell's Press, 1948), 78.
19 9th Canadian Infantry Brigade War Diary, 4.
20 Bird, 253.
21 N.a., *1st Battalion, The Highland Light Infantry of Canada: 1940–1945* (Galt, ON: Highland Light Infantry of Canada Assoc., 1951), 69–70.
22 W. Denis Whitaker and Shelagh Whitaker, *Tug of War: The Canadian Victory that Opened Antwerp* (Toronto: Stoddart, 1984), 292.
23 Highland Light Infantry War Diary, 6.

24 9th Canadian Infantry Brigade War Diary, 5.
25 8th Canadian Infantry Brigade War Diary, October 1944, RG24, Library and Archives Canada, n.p.
26 Will Bird, *North Shore (New Brunswick) Regiment* (Fredericton, NB: Brunswick Press, 1963), 442–43.
27 Richard M. Ross, *The History of the 1st Battalion Cameron Highlanders of Ottawa (MG)*, (n.p., n.d.), 71.
28 Bird, *North Shore (New Brunswick) Regiment*, 443.
29 Boss, 70.
30 Highland Light Infantry War Diary, 7.
31 Bird, *No Retreating Footsteps*, 254–55.
32 North Nova Scotia Highlanders War Diary, RG24, Library and Archives Canada, n.p.
33 Ibid., n.p.
34 Ibid., n.p.
35 North Shore (New Brunswick) Regiment War Diary, October 1944, RG24, Library and Archives Canada, 5.
36 Jacques Castonguay and Armand Ross, *Le Régiment de la Chaudière* (Lévis, PQ: n.p., 1983), 303.
37 G.L. Cassidy, *Warpath: The Story of the Algonquin Regiment, 1939–1945* (Toronto: Ryerson Press, 1948), 164.
38 H.M. Jackson, ed. *The Argyll and Sutherland Highlanders of Canada (Princess Louise's), 1928–1953* (n.p., 1953), 130.
39 "Conversation Maj-Gen Eberding, 1.
40 "The Campaign in North-West Europe, Information from German Sources—Part III", 218.
41 Cassidy, 164.
42 "Combined Operations Headquarters–Bulletin Y/43: 'Amphibians in Operation 'Switchback,' Appendix F'" MG30, vol. 8, Library and Archives Canada, n.p.
43 9th Canadian Field Squadron, RCE War Diary, October 1944, RG24, Library and Archives Canada, 3.
44 8th Canadian Field Squadron, RCE War Diary, October 1944, RG24, Library and Archives Canada, 6.
45 Report No. 188 Historical Section Canadian Military Headquarters: "Canadian Participation in the Operations in North-West Europe–Part VI: Canadian Operations, 1 Oct–8 Nov, The Clearance of the Scheldt Estuary," Department of National Defence, 7 April, 1948, 57.
46 Reginald H. Roy, *Ready for the Fray: The History of the Canadian Scottish Regiment (Princess Mary's), 1920 to 1955* (Vancouver: Evergreen Press, 1958), 343.
47 Ibid., 343–44.
48 Stacey, 395.
49 First Canadian Army HQ Defence Company (RMR) War Diary, October 1944, RG24, Library and Archives Canada, 5.
50 R.C. Fetherstonhaugh, *The Royal Montreal Regiment, 1925–1945* (Westmount, QC: The Royal Montreal Regiment, 1949), 189.
51 7th Reconnaissance Regiment (17DYRCH) War Diary, October 1944, RG24, Library and Archives Canada, 9–10.

52 Ibid., 10–12.
53 Jack Martin, interview by John Gregory Thompson, Scarborough, ON, 1 October 2003.
54 Charles Cromwell Martin, *Battle Diary: From D-Day and Normandy to the Zuider Zee* (Toronto: Dundurn Press, 1994), 91–92.
55 Queen's Own Rifles War Diary, October 1944, RG24, Library and Archives Canada, n.p.

17: A GODSEND

1 Col. C.P. Stacey, *The Victory Campaign: The Operations in North-West Europe, 1944–1945*, vol. 3 (Ottawa: Queen's Printer, 1960), 389–90.
2 Lieutenant General Guy Simonds Correspondence, 12 Oct 44, Crerar Papers, MG30, vol. 2, Library and Archives Canada, 1.
3 E.O. Herbert, "Polish Armd Div, 7 Oct 44," Crerar Papers, MG30, vol. 2, Library and Archives Canada, 1.
4 Johan van Doorn, *Slag om Woensdrecht: bevrijding van de Zuidwesthoek, Oktober 1944* (Willemstad: n.p., 1995), 51–52.
5 van Doorn, 51.
6 Terry Copp, *The Brigade: The Fifth Canadian Infantry Brigade, 1939–45* (Stoney Creek, ON: Fortress Publications, 1992), 147–48.
7 W. Denis Whitaker and Shelagh Whitaker, *Tug of War: The Canadian Victory that Opened Antwerp* (Toronto: Stoddart, 1984), 172–75.
8 South Saskatchewan Regiment War Diary, October 1944, RG24, Library and Archives Canada, 17–18.
9 van Doorn, 52.
10 Charles E. Goodman, interview by David Gantzer, 1 & 5 December 1980, University of Victoria Special Collections.
11 South Saskatchewan Regiment War Diary, October 1944, 18–19.
12 van Doorn, 51.
13 Charles Goodman, interview by author, Saanichton, BC, 2 June 2006.
14 South Saskatchewan Regiment War Diary, October 1944, 19.
15 Charles Goodman interview.
16 South Saskatchewan Regiment War Diary, October 1944, 19.
17 van Doorn, 52.
18 South Saskatchewan Regiment War Diary, October 1944, 20.
19 Ibid., 20–21.
20 van Doorn, 52–55.

18: BLACK FRIDAY

1 Terry Copp, *The Brigade: The Fifth Canadian Infantry Brigade, 1939–45* (Stoney Creek, ON: Fortress Publications, 1992), 148.
2 5th Canadian Infantry Brigade War Diary, October 1944, RG24, Library and Archives Canada, 8.
3 "The Action at Woensdrecht, 8–14 Oct 44: Account by Lt. W. J. Shea, I.O., R.H.C., given to Historical Officer, 2 CDN INF DIV, 15 Oct 44," 145.2R14011(1), Directorate

of Heritage and History, Department of National Defence, 1.
4 W. Denis Whitaker and Shelagh Whitaker, *Tug of War: The Canadian Victory that Opened Antwerp* (Toronto: Stoddart, 1984), 174–75.
5 John Dubetz, "Friday, October 13, 1944, 'Black Friday,'" http://www.smokylake.com/history/other/blackfriday/htm, December 7, 2007, 1–2.
6 HQ RCA 2nd Canadian Infantry Division War Diary, October 1944, RG24, Library and Archives Canada, n.p.
7 Dubetz, 2.
8 1st Battalion, The Black Watch (RHR) of Canada War Diary, October 1944, RG24, Library and Archives Canada, 8.
9 Dubetz, 2–3.
10 Johan van Doorn, *Slag om Woensdrecht: bevrijding van de Zuidwesthoek, Oktober 1944* (Willemstad: n.p., 1995), 57–58.
11 Dubetz, 3–5.
12 Jean Portugal, *We Were There: The Navy, the Army and the RCAF–A Record for Canada*, vol. 5 (Shelburne, ON: The Battered Silicon Dispatch Box, 1998), 2282.
13 T.D. Dungan, "Antwerp, City of Sudden Death," www.v2rocket.com/start/chapters/antwerp.html, n.p.
14 "The Action at Woensdrecht," 1.
15 van Doorn, 59.
16 "The Action at Woensdrecht," 1.
17 Black Watch War Diary, 9.
18 van Doorn, 59–60.
19 Whitaker, 175–76.
20 Black Watch War Diary, 10.
21 Ibid.
22 Whitaker, 176.
23 "The Action at Woensdrecht," 2.
24 Col. C.P. Stacey, *The Victory Campaign: The Operations in North-West Europe, 1944–1945*, vol. 3 (Ottawa: Queen's Printer, 1960), 384.
25 van Doorn, 61.
26 Black Watch War Diary, 11.
27 van Doorn, 61.
28 Royal Hamilton Light Infantry War Diary, October 1944, RG24, Library and Archives Canada, n.p.
29 "RHLI Operation Order No. 1, Woensdrecht Feature 15/16 Oct 44," 145.2R14011(1), Directorate of Heritage and History, Department of National Defence, 1.
30 Whitaker, 181.
31 HQ RCA 2nd Canadian Infantry Division War Diary, October 1944, 4.
32 Stacey, 384.
33 Whitaker, 181.
34 Kingsley Brown, Sr., Kingsley Brown, Jr., and Brereton Greenhous, *Semper Paratus: The History of The Royal Hamilton Light Infantry (Wentworth Regiment), 1862–1977* (Hamilton: The RHLI Historical Assoc., 1977), n.p.
35 Ibid., 182.

36 "The Capture of Woensdrecht: Accounts by Officers of R.H.L.I. Given to Historical Officer, 2 CDN INF DIV, 22 Oct 44," 145.2R14011(1), Directorate of Heritage and History, Department of National Defence, 1–2.
37 Whitaker, 184–88.
38 Kingsley Brown, n.p.
39 van Doorn, 68–69.
40 Kingsley Brown, n.p.
41 "The Capture of Woensdrecht," 1–4.
42 Whitaker, 190.

19: DOMINATE THE SITUATION

1 W. Denis Whitaker and Shelagh Whitaker, *Tug of War: The Canadian Victory that Opened Antwerp* (Toronto: Stoddart, 1984), 192–93.
2 Kingsley Brown, Sr., Kingsley Brown, Jr., and Brereton Greenhous, *Semper Paratus: The History of The Royal Hamilton Light Infantry (Wentworth Regiment), 1862–1977* (Hamilton: The RHLI Historical Assoc., 1977), n.p.
3 "The Capture of Woensdrecht: Accounts by Officers of RHLI. Given to Historical Officer, 2 CDN INF DIV, 22 Oct 44," 145.2R14011(1), Directorate of Heritage and History, Department of National Defence, 2.
4 Kingsley Brown, n.p.
5 Whitaker, 194.
6 Kingsley Brown, n.p.
7 Whitaker, 195.
8 Kingsley Brown, n.p.
9 "The Capture of Woensdrecht," 2.
10 Kingsley Brown, n.p.
11 "The Capture of Woensdrecht, 2–3.
12 Ibid., 3.
13 Kingsley Brown, n.p.
14 Royal Hamilton Light Infantry War Diary, October 1944, RG24, Library and Archives Canada, 16.
15 Johan van Doorn, *Slag om Woensdrecht: bevrijding van de Zuidwesthoek, Oktober 1944* (Willemstad: n.p., 1995), 72.
16 "The Capture of Woensdrecht, 3.
17 Royal Hamilton Light Infantry War Diary, October 1944, 17.
18 Kingsley Brown, n.p.
19 Ibid., n.p.
20 Royal Hamilton Light Infantry War Diary, October 1944, 17–18.
21 Ibid., 17.
22 Ibid., 18.
23 4th Canadian Infantry Brigade War Diary, October 1944, RG24, Library and Archives Canada, 14.
24 Royal Hamilton Light Infantry War Diary, October 1944, 18–19.
25 Ibid., 18–20.
26 Report No. 69 Historical Section Army Headquarters: "The Campaign in North-West

Europe, Information from German Sources—Part III: German Defence Operations in the Sphere of First Canadian Army (23 Aug.–8 Nov. 44)," Directorate of Heritage and History, Department of National Defence, 30 July, 1954, paras 147.
27 Oberst G. Elmar Warning, "Battles of LXVII Inf Corps Between the Schelde and the Maas, 15 Sep–25 Nov 44," RG24, vol. 20523, Library and Archives Canada, 27–29.
28 "The Campaign in North-West Europe, Information from German Sources—Part III," 149.
29 Col. C.P. Stacey, *The Victory Campaign: The Operations in North-West Europe, 1944–1945*, vol. 3 (Ottawa: Queen's Printer, 1960), 398.
30 Ibid.
31 Ibid.
32 Stormont, Dundas and Glengarry Highlanders War Diary, October 1944, RG24, Library and Archives Canada, 20–21.
33 Whitaker, 302.
34 Karel Magrey, "The Ijzendijke Explosion," *After the Battle*, No. 99, 1998, 44–53.
35 Whitaker, 303.
36 Report No. 188 Historical Section Canadian Military Headquarters: "Canadian Participation in the Operations in North-West Europe–Part VI: Canadian Operations, 1 Oct–8 Nov, The Clearance of the Scheldt Estuary," Department of National Defence, 7 April, 1948, 69.
37 Stormont, Dundas and Glengarry Highlanders War Diary, October 1944, 23.
38 William Boss, *Up the Glens: Stormont, Dundas and Glengarry Highlanders, 1783–1994* (Cornwall, ON: Old Book Store, 1995), 232.
39 North Nova Scotia Highlanders War Diary, October 1944, RG24, Library and Archives Canada, n.p.
40 Boss, 232–33.
41 Stormont, Dundas and Glengarry Highlanders War Diary, October 1944, 25–26.
42 "Canadian Participation in the Operations in North-West Europe–Part VI," 69.
43 Stormont, Dundas and Glengarry Highlanders War Diary, October 1944, 26.

20: TO THE LAST CARTRIDGE
1 North Nova Scotia Highlanders War Diary, October 1944, RG24, Library and Archives Canada, n.p.
2 Highland Light Infantry War Diary, October 1944, RG24, Library and Archives Canada, 11.
3 North Nova Scotia Highlanders War Diary, October 1944, n.p.
4 Canadian Scottish Regiment War Diary, October 1944, RG24, Library and Archives Canada, 24–25.
5 Ibid., 26.
6 Col. C.P. Stacey, *The Victory Campaign: The Operations in North-West Europe, 1944–1945*, vol. 3 (Ottawa: Queen's Printer, 1960), 398–99.
7 Jean E. Portugal, *We Were There: The Navy, the Army and the RCAF–A Record for Canada*, vol. 6 (Shelburne, ON: The Battered Silicon Dispatch Box, 1998), 3008–9.
8 Royal Winnipeg Rifles War Diary, October 1944, RG24, Library and Archives Canada, 8.

9 Canadian Scottish Regiment War Diary, October 1944, 29.
10 Portugal, *We Were There*, vol. 6, 3011.
11 Canadian Scottish Regiment War Diary, October 1944, 29.
12 Portugal, 3011–12.
13 Reginald H. Roy, *Ready for the Fray: The History of the Canadian Scottish Regiment (Princess Mary's), 1920 to 1955* (Vancouver: Evergreen Press, 1958), 347–48.
14 Queen's Own Rifles War Diary, October 1944, RG24, Library and Archives Canada, n.p.
15 Charles Cromwell Martin, *Battle Diary: From D-Day and Normandy to the Zuider Zee* (Toronto: Dundurn Press, 1994), 93–95.
16 W.T. Barnard, *The Queen's Own Rifles of Canada, 1860–1960* (Don Mills, ON: Ontario Publishing Co., 1960), 236.
17 Martin, 95.
18 Jacques Catonguay and Armand Ross, *Le Régiment de la Chaudière* (Lévis, QC: n.p., 1983), 310–11.
19 Walter G. Pavey, *An Historical Account of the 7th Canadian Reconnaissance Regiment (17th Duke of York's Royal Canadian Hussars)*, (Gardenvale, QC: Harpell's Press, 1948), 83–84.
20 Report No. 69 Historical Section Army Headquarters: "The Campaign in North-West Europe, Information from German Sources—Part III: German Defence Operations in the Sphere of First Canadian Army (23 Aug.–8 Nov. 44)," Directorate of Heritage and History, Department of National Defence, 30 July, 1954, paras 232–33.
21 Canadian Scottish Regiment War Diary, October 1944, 34.
22 Roy, 349.
23 "The Campaign in North-West Europe, Information from German Sources—Part III," 234–35.
24 Stacey, 399.
25 William Boss, *Up the Glens: Stormont, Dundas and Glengarry Highlanders, 1783–1994* (Cornwall, ON: Old Book Store, 1995), 234.
26 Catonguay and Ross, 312–13.
27 Will Bird, *North Shore (New Brunswick) Regiment* (Fredericton, NB: Brunswick Press, 1963), 464.
28 North Shore (New Brunswick) Regiment War Diary, November 1944, RG24, Library and Archives Canada, 1.
29 Martin, 96–98.
30 "The Campaign in North-West Europe, Information from German Sources—Part III," 241.
31 Stacey, 399–400.
32 Stacey, 400.

21: FOOT-SLOGGING JOBS

1 6th Canadian Infantry Brigade War Diary, October 1944, RG24, Library and Archives Canada, 13.
2 Report No. 188 Historical Section Canadian Military Headquarters: "Canadian

Participation in the Operations in North-West Europe–Part VI: Canadian Operations, 1 Oct– 8 Nov, The Clearance of the Scheldt Estuary," Department of National Defence, 7 April, 1948, 89.
3 J.M. Savage, *The History of the 5th Canadian Anti-tank Regiment, 10 Sept., 1941–10 June, 1945* (Canada: 4th Canadian Armoured Division, 1945), 39.
4 George F.G. Stanley, *In the Face of Danger: The History of the Lake Superior Regiment* (Port Arthur, ON: The Lake Superior Scottish Regiment, 1960), 208.
5 G.L. Cassidy, *Warpath: The Story of the Algonquin Regiment, 1939–1945* (Toronto: Ryerson Press, 1948), 170–71.
6 Headquarters, RCA, 4th Canadian Armoured Division War Diary, October 1944, RG24, Library and Archives Canada, 11.
7 Stanley, 209.
8 Robert L. Fraser, *Black Yesterdays: The Argyll's War* (Hamilton: Argyll Foundation, 1996), 299.
9 H.M. Jackson, ed. *The Argyll and Sutherland Highlanders of Canada (Princess Louise's), 1928–1953* (n.p., 1953), 135.
10 Fraser, 299–300.
11 Argyll and Sutherland Highlanders War Diary, October 1944, RG24, Library and Archives Canada, n.p.
12 A. Fortescue Duguid, *History of the Canadian Grenadier Guards, 1760–1964* (Montreal: Gazette Printing Co., 1965), 303.
13 Fraser, 300.
14 Jackson, 135.
15 R.L. Rogers, *History of the Lincoln and Welland Regiment* (n.p., 1954), 195.
16 Geoffrey Hayes, *The Lincs: A History of the Lincoln and Welland Regiment at War* (Alma, ON: Maple Leaf Route, 1986), 59.
17 Rogers, 195–96.
18 Ibid., 196.
19 28th Canadian Armoured Regiment (British Columbia Regiment) War Diary, October 1944, RG24, Library and Archives Canada, n.p.
20 Rogers, 196.
21 Hayes, 59.
22 Cassidy, 170.
23 Ibid.
24 Cassidy, 171–72.
25 Douglas E. Harker, *The Dukes: The Story of the Men Who have Served in Peace and War with the British Columbia Regiment (DCO.), 1883–1973* (The British Columbia Regiment, 1974), 269.
26 Cassidy, 172.
27 Rogers, 197.
28 Stanley, 210.
29 Cassidy, 172–73.
30 Stanley, 210.
31 N.a. *The Regimental History of the Governor General's Foot Guards* (Ottawa: Mortimer, 1948), 154–57.

32 L.F. Ellis with A.E. Warhurst, *Victory in the West: Volume II: The Defeat of Germany* (London: Her Majesty's Stationery Office, 1968), 123–24.
33 G Branch, 4th Canadian Armoured Division War Diary, October 1944, RG24, Library and Archives Canada, 22.
34 10th Canadian Infantry Brigade War Diary, October 1944, RG24, Library and Archives Canada, 7.
35 4th Canadian Armoured Brigade War Diary, October 1944, RG24, Library and Archives Canada, 21.
36 Cassidy, 173.
37 Ibid., 174.
38 Stanley, 211.
39 Jackson, 136.
40 Rogers, 197.
41 Cassidy, 174–177.
42 "The Clearance of the Scheldt Estuary," 91.

22: TROOPS ON THE GROUND

1 Johan van Doorn, *Slag om Woensdrecht: bevrijding van de Zuidwesthoek, Oktober 1944* (Willemstad: n.p., 1995), 93.
2 Report No. 69 Historical Section Army Headquarters: "The Campaign in North-West Europe, Information from German Sources—Part III: German Defence Operations in the Sphere of First Canadian Army (23 Aug.–8 Nov. 44)," Directorate of Heritage and History, Department of National Defence, 30 July, 1954, para. 156–58.
3 van Doorn, 93.
4 Col. C.P. Stacey, *The Victory Campaign: The Operations in North-West Europe, 1944–1945*, vol. 3 (Ottawa: Queen's Printer, 1960), 391.
5 6th Canadian Field Regiment, RCA War Diary, October 1944, RG24, Library and Archives Canada, n.p.
6 N.a. *Cent ans d'histoire d'un régiment canadien-français : les Fusiliers Mont-Royal, 1869-1969* (Montréal: Editions Du Jour, 1971), n.p.
7 South Saskatchewan Regiment War Diary, October 1944, RG24, Library and Archives Canada, 31.
8 Cecil Law, "Sniper," unpublished account, in possession of author, 28 May 2004.
9 South Saskatchewan Regiment War Diary, 31.
10 van Doorn, 80.
11 The Queen's Own Cameron Highlanders of Canada War Diary, October 1944, RG24, Library and Archives Canada, 9.
12 David Bercuson, *Battalion of Heroes: The Calgary Highlanders in World War II* (Calgary: Calgary Highlanders Regimental Funds Foundation, 1994), 176–77.
13 Ibid., 177.
14 Calgary Highlanders War Diary, October 1944, RG24, Library and Archives Canada, 67.
15 Bercuson, 177.
16 van Doorn, 83.

17 Bercuson, 177–78.
18 Calgary Highlanders War Diary, 67.
19 van Doorn, 83.
20 Calgary Highlanders War Diary, 67–68.
21 4th Canadian Armoured Brigade War Diary, October 1944, RG24, Library and Archives Canada, 22.
22 Argyll and Sutherland Highlanders War Diary, October 1944, RG24, Library and Archives Canada, n.p.
23 Robert L. Fraser, *Black Yesterdays: The Argyll's War* (Hamilton: Argyll Foundation, 1996), 303.
24 H.M. Jackson, ed. *The Argyll and Sutherland Highlanders of Canada (Princess Louise's), 1928–1953* (n.p., 1953), 138.
25 A. Fortescue Duguid, *History of the Canadian Grenadier Guards, 1760–1964* (Montreal: Gazette Printing Co., 1965), 303–4.
26 Argyll and Sutherland Highlanders War Diary, October 1944, n.p.
27 G.M. Alexander, ed, *Europe, July 1944–May 1945: A Brief History of the 4th Canadian Armoured Brigade in Action* (Mitcham, England: West Brothers, 1945), 23.
28 N.a. *The Regimental History of the Governor General's Foot Guards* (Ottawa: Mortimer, 1948), 159.
29 Ibid.
30 George F.G. Stanley, *In the Face of Danger: The History of the Lake Superior Regiment* (Port Arthur, ON: The Lake Superior Scottish Regiment, 1960), 213.
31 21st Canadian Armoured Regiment (Governor General's Foot Guards) War Diary, October 1944, RG24, Library and Archives Canada, 14.
32 Stanley, 214.
33 *The Regimental History of the Governor General's Foot Guards*, 159–61.
34 Jackson, 138–39.
35 "The Campaign in North-West Europe, Information from German Sources—Part III," 157–60.
36 6th Canadian Infantry Brigade War Diary, October 1944, RG24, Library and Archives Canada, 17.
37 R.W. Queen-Hughes, *Whatever Men Dare: A History of the Queen's Own Cameron Highlanders of Canada, 1935–1960* (Winnipeg: Bulman Bros., 1960), 142.
38 Calgary Highlanders War Diary, 72–75.
39 Bercuson, 179.
40 van Doorn, 96.
41 Jackson, 139.
42 Duguid, 304.
43 4th Canadian Armoured Brigade War Diary, October 1944, 24.
44 Jackson, 139.
45 Duguid, 304.
46 Jackson, 139.
47 Duguid, 304–5.
48 Lincoln and Welland Regiment War Diary, October 1944, RG24, Library and Archives Canada, n.p.

49 Geoffrey Hayes, *The Lincs: A History of the Lincoln and Welland Regiment at War* (Alma, ON: Maple Leaf Route, 1986), 62.
50 Jackson, 140.
51 Ibid., 150.
52 Fraser, 304.
53 Stanley, 215.
54 R.L. Rogers, *History of the Lincoln and Welland Regiment*, (n.p., 1954), 199.
55 Stanley, 215–16.
56 1st Battalion, Lake Superior Regiment (Motor) War Diary, October 1944, RG24, Library and Archives Canada, 15–16.
57 N.a., "The Battle of Bergen Op Zoom," www.army.forces.gc.ca/Land_Force_Central_Area/31_Canadian Brigade_Group/Lincoln_Welland_Regiment/History.asp.
58 van Doorn, 96.
59 4th Canadian Armoured Division War Diary, October 1944, 27–28.
60 29th Reconnaissance Regiment (South Alberta) War Diary, October 1944, RG24, Library and Archives Canada, 36–37.

23: THE SOUTH BEVELAND RACE

1 Report No. 188 Historical Section Canadian Military Headquarters: "Canadian Participation in the Operations in North-West Europe–Part VI: Canadian Operations, 1 Oct–8 Nov, The Clearance of the Scheldt Estuary," Department of National Defence, 7 April, 1948, 96–97.
2 George Blake, *Mountain and Flood: The History of the 52nd (Lowland) Division, 1939–1946* (Glasgow: Jackson, Son & Co., 1950), 83.
3 Col. C.P. Stacey, *The Victory Campaign: The Operations in North-West Europe, 1944–1945*, vol. 3 (Ottawa: Queen's Printer, 1960), 401.
4 D.J. Goodspeed, *Battle Royal: A History of the Royal Regiment of Canada, 1862–1962* (Toronto: The Royal Regiment of Canada Assoc., 1962), 505–6.
5 "The Capture of Zuid Beveland: Account by Brigadier R.H. Keefler, E.D., A/Comd, 2 CDN INF DIV, Given to Historical Officer, 2 CDN INF DIV, 11 Nov. 44," RG24, vol. 10897, Library and Archives Canada, 1.
6 Goodspeed, 506–7.
7 Royal Regiment of Canada War Diary, October 1944, RG24, Library and Archives Canada, 19.
8 Goodspeed, 507.
9 Essex Scottish War Diary, October 1944, RG24, Library and Archives Canada, 13.
10 N.a., *Vanguard: The Fort Garry Horse in the Second World War* (Doetincham, Holland: Uitgevers-Maatschappij, C. Misset, NV, n.d.), 84.
11 Essex Scottish War Diary, October 1944, 13.
12 George Blackburn, *The History of the 4th Field Regiment* (n.p., 1945), n.p.
13 Essex Scottish War Diary, October 1944, 14.
14 Blackburn, n.p.
15 Essex Scottish War Diary, October 1944, 14.
16 Kingsley Brown, Sr., Kingsley Brown, Jr., and Brereton Greenhous, *Semper Paratus: The History of The Royal Hamilton Light Infantry (Wentworth Regiment), 1862–1977*

(Hamilton: The RHLI Historical Assoc., 1977), n.p.
17 4th Canadian Infantry Brigade War Diary, October 1944, RG24, Library and Archives Canada, 21.
18 Blake, 84–86.
19 Essex Scottish War Diary, October 1944, n.p.
20 "The Capture of Zuid Beveland," 1–3.
21 R.W. Queen-Hughes, *Whatever Men Dare: A History of the Queen's Own Cameron Highlanders of Canada, 1935–1960* (Winnipeg: Bulman Bros., 1960), 142.
22 Cecil Law, "South Beveland Peninsula Battles," unpublished account, in possession of author, 1.
23 6th Canadian Infantry Brigade War Diary, October 1944, RG24, Library and Archives Canada, 18.
24 Law, 1.
25 "The Clearance of the Scheldt Estuary," 100.
26 N.a. *Cent ans d'histoire d'un régiment canadien-français : les Fusiliers Mont-Royal, 1869–1969* (Montréal: Editions Du Jour, 1971), n.p.
27 The Queen's Own Cameron Highlanders War Diary, October 1944, RG24, Library and Archives Canada, 10.
28 South Saskatchewan Regiment War Diary, October 1944, RG24, Library and Archives Canada, 36–37.
29 "The Capture of Zuid Beveland," 1.
30 W. Denis Whitaker and Shelagh Whitaker, *Tug of War: The Canadian Victory that Opened Antwerp* (Toronto: Stoddart, 1984), 253.
31 South Saskatchewan Regiment War Diary, October 1944, 37.
32 Whitaker, 254.
33 Arthur K. Kembar, *The Six Years of 6 Canadian Field Regiment, Royal Canadian Artillery: September 1939–September 1945* (Amsterdam: Crown Printing Office, 1945), 80.
34 "The Crossing of the Beveland Canal at Wemeldinge: Account of Major J.J.D. Gagnon, A./C.O., Camerons of C., Given to Historical Officer, 2 CDN INF DIV, 6 Nov. 44," 145.2R14011(1), Directorate of Heritage and History, Department of National Defence, 1.
35 6th Canadian Infantry Brigade War Diary, 18.
36 The Queen's Own Cameron Highlanders War Diary, October 1944, 11.
37 Les Fusiliers Mont-Royal War Diary, October 1944, RG24, Library and Archives Canada, 5.
38 Kembar, 80.
39 6th Canadian Infantry Brigade War Diary, October 1944, 19.
40 Kingsley Brown, n.p.
41 Essex Scottish War Diary, October 1944, 16.
42 Goodspeed, 509–10.
43 Ibid., 510.
44 Essex Scottish War Diary, October 1944, 16.
45 4th Canadian Infantry Brigade War Diary, October 1944, 25.
46 Stacey, 402.

47 Jeffrey Williams, *The Long Left Flank: The Hard Fought Way to the Reich, 1944–1945* (Toronto: Stoddart, 1988), 134.
48 The Black Watch (RHR) of Canada War Diary, October 1944, 19.
49 "The Clearance of the Scheldt Estuary," 105.
50 4th Canadian Infantry Brigade War Diary, October 1944, 27–28.
51 Goodspeed, 511.
52 Ibid., 511–12.
53 Captain John Ellis Stothers citation, from Johan van Doorn archive, in possession of author.
54 N.a., *VIII CDN Recce Rgt 14 CH Battle History of the Regt* (Victoria, BC: 8th CDN Recce Assoc., 1993), 34.
55 Terry Copp, *The Brigade: The Fifth Canadian Infantry Brigade, 1939–45* (Stoney Creek, ON: Fortress Publications, 1992), 156.

24: LET'S TAKE THE DAMNED PLACE

1 Lincoln and Welland Regiment War Diary, October 1944, RG24, Library and Archives Canada, n.p.
2 G.L. Cassidy, *Warpath: The Story of the Algonquin Regiment, 1939–1945* (Toronto: Ryerson Press, 1948), 180.
3 Argyll and Sutherland Highlanders War Diary, October 1944, RG24, Library and Archives Canada, n.p.
4 Robert L. Fraser, *Black Yesterdays: The Argyll's War* (Hamilton, ON: Argyll Foundation, 1996), 305.
5 Argyll and Sutherland Highlanders War Diary, October 1944, n.p.
6 Fraser, 305.
7 Donald E. Graves, *South Alberta's: A Canadian Regiment at war* (Toronto: Robin Brass Studio, 1998), 227.
8 Argyll and Sutherland Highlanders War Diary, October 1944, n.p.
9 Algonquin Regiment War Diary, October 1944, RG24, Library and Archives Canada, 17.
10 Graves, 224–25.
11 15th Canadian Field Regiment, RCA War Diary, October 1944, RG24, Library and Archives Canada, 7.
12 Robert A. Spencer, *History of the Fifteenth Canadian Field Regiment, Royal Canadian Artillery: 1941 to 1945* (New York: Elsevier, 1945), 177.
13 Cassidy, 182.
14 Graves, 225–26.
15 Cassidy, 182.
16 Spencer, 177.
17 Graves, 223.
18 Geoffrey Hayes, "Where Are Our Liberators?" The Canadian Liberation of West Brabant, 1944," vol. 1, 1995, *Canadian Military History*, 64.
19 Graves, 223–24.
20 George F.G. Stanley, *In the Face of Danger: The History of the Lake Superior Regiment* (Port Arthur, ON: The Lake Superior Scottish Regiment, 1960), 216–17.

21 G.M. Alexander, ed, *Europe, July 1944–May 1945: A Brief History of the 4th Canadian Armoured Brigade in Action* (Mitcham, England: West Brothers, 1945), 24.
22 4th Canadian Armoured Brigade War Diary, October 1944, RG24, Library and Archives Canada, 26.
23 Hayes, 15.
24 Oberst G. Elmar Warning, "Battles of LXVII Inf Corps Between the Schelde and the Maas, 15 Sep–25 Nov 44," RG24, vol. 20523, Library and Archives Canada, 34–35.
25 Report No. 69 Historical Section Army Headquarters: "The Campaign in North-West Europe, Information from German Sources—Part III: German Defence Operations in the Sphere of First Canadian Army (23 Aug.–8 Nov. 44)," Directorate of Heritage and History, Department of National Defence, 30 July, 1954, para. 169.
26 Graves, 227–28.
27 29th Reconnaissance Regiment (South Alberta) War Diary, October 1944, RG24, Library and Archives Canada, 39.
28 Graves, 228.
29 Hayes, 64.
30 Graves, 228.
31 Robert M. Foster, et. al. *Steady the Buttons Two by Two: Governor General's Foot Guards Regimental History, 125th Anniversary: 1872–1997* (Ottawa: Governor General's Foot Guards, 1999), 207.
32 A. Fortescue Duguid, *History of the Canadian Grenadier Guards, 1760–1964* (Montreal: Gazette Printing Co., 1965), 306.
33 22nd Armoured Regiment (Canadian Grenadier Guards) War Diary, October 1944, RG24, Library and Archives Canada, 4.
34 N.a., *The Regimental History of the Governor General's Foot Guards* (Ottawa: Mortimer, 1948), 165.
35 21st Canadian Armoured Regiment (Governor General's Foot Guards) War Diary, October 1944, RG24, Library and Archives Canada, 19.
36 *The Regimental History of the Governor General's Foot Guards*, 165.
37 1st Battalion, The Lake Superior Regiment (Motor) War Diary, October 1944, RG24, Library and Archives Canada, 18.
38 *The Regimental History of the Governor General's Foot Guards*, 166–67.
39 Ibid., 168–72.
40 Alexander, 25.
41 Argyll and Sutherland Highlanders War Diary, October 1944, n.p.
42 Fraser, 306–7.
43 H.M. Jackson, ed. *The Argyll and Sutherland Highlanders of Canada (Princess Louise's), 1928–1953* (n.p., 1953), 142–43.
44 South Alberta Regiment War Diary, October 1944, 42.
45 Fraser, 307–8.
46 Jackson, 143.
47 Hayes, 65–66.
48 R.L. Rogers, *History of the Lincoln and Welland Regiment* (n.p., 1954), 201.
49 Fraser, 309.

50 Jackson, 145–46.
51 Hayes, 68.
52 Cassidy, 185.

25: THE DAMNED CAUSEWAY

1 5th Canadian Infantry Brigade War Diary, October 1944, RG24, Library and Archives Canada, 20.
2 Col. C.P. Stacey, *The Victory Campaign: The Operations in North-West Europe, 1944–1945*, vol. 3 (Ottawa: Queen's Printer, 1960), 403.
3 Terry Copp, *The Brigade: The Fifth Canadian Infantry Brigade, 1939–45* (Stoney Creek, ON: Fortress Publications, 1992), 158–59.
4 1st Battalion, The Black Watch (RHR) of Canada War Diary, October 1944, RG24, Library and Archives Canada, 20.
5 W. Denis Whitaker and Shelagh Whitaker, *Tug of War: The Canadian Victory that Opened Antwerp* (Toronto: Stoddart, 1984), 324.
6 Black Watch War Diary, October 1944, 23.
7 Jeffrey Williams, *The Long Left Flank: The Hard Fought Way to the Reich, 1944–1945* (Toronto: Stoddart, 1988), 135.
8 Whitaker, 322.
9 Black Watch War Diary, October 1944, 20.
10 George Blackburn, *The History of the 4th Field Regiment* (n.p., 1945), n.p.
11 5th Canadian Field Regiment War Diary, October 1944, RG24, Library and Archives Canada, n.p.
12 Lt. Maurice Berry, "letter November 20, 1944 to Lt. Col. W.E. MacFarlane," http://blackwatchcanada.com/en/archives.htm, 7/11/2006.
13 Whitaker, 322–23.
14 Ibid., 323–24.
15 1st Battalion, The Black Watch (RHR) of Canada War Diary, November 1944, RG24, Library and Archives Canada, 1.
16 Black Watch War Diary, October 1944, 20–21.
17 Williams, 136.
18 Calgary Highlanders War Diary, October 1944, RG24, Library and Archives Canada, 83.
19 Whitaker, 321–25.
20 Calgary Highlanders War Diary, October 1944, 85–86.
21 Frank Holm, "Personal Narratives-Walcheren Causeway," http://www.calgaryhighlanders.com/history/walch.htm, 7/6/2006.
22 David Bercuson, *Battalion of Heroes: The Calgary Highlanders in World War II* (Calgary: Calgary Highlanders Regimental Funds Foundation, 1994), 185.
23 Ibid., 185.
24 Holm, "Personal Narratives."
25 Bercuson, 186.
26 Calgary Highlanders War Diary, November 1944, RG24, Library and Archives Canada, 1.
27 David Kaufman and Michiel Horn, *A Liberation Album: Canadians in the*

Netherlands, 1944–45 (Toronto: McGraw-Hill Ryerson, 1980), 39.
28 Williams, 138.
29 Calgary Highlanders War Diary, November 1944, 1.
30 Bercuson, 186–87.
31 Ibid., 187–88.
32 Ibid., 188–89.
33 Calgary Highlanders War Diary, November 1944, 2.
34 HQ 2nd Canadian Infantry Division War Diary, November 1944, Appendix: "Message Log," RG24, Library and Archives Canada, n.p.
35 II Canadian Corps War Diary, November 1944, "Intelligence Summary No. 77, Nov. 2, 1944," RG24, Library and Archives Canada, 3.
36 5th Canadian Infantry Brigade War Diary, November 1944, RG24, Library and Archives Canada, 1.
37 Gérard Marchand, *Le Régiment de Maisonneuve Vers la Victoire, 1944–1945* (Montréal: Les Presses Libres, 1980), 163.
38 Copp, 161.
39 Donald George Innes Award Citation, Directorate of Heritage and History, Department of National Defence, 1.
40 Le Régiment de Maisonneuve War Diary, November 1944, RG24, Library and Archives Canada, 1.
41 Whitaker, 334–35.
42 Gerald Rawling, *Cinderella Operation: The Battle for Walcheren 1944* (London: Cassell, 1980), 83.
43 Whitaker, 341–42.
44 Stacey, 405.
45 Williams, 140.
46 Stacey, 405.
47 Ibid., 405–6.
48 Whitaker, 339.
49 Le Régiment de Maisonneuve War Diary, November 1944, 1.
50 Stacey, 406.
51 D.J. Goodspeed, *Battle Royal: A History of the Royal Regiment of Canada, 1862–1962* (Toronto: The Royal Regiment of Canada Assoc., 1962), 513.

26: A FINE PERFORMANCE

1 George Blake, *Mountain and Flood: The History of the 52nd (Lowland) Division, 1939–1946* (Glasgow: Jackson, Son & Co., 1950), 92.
2 Col. C.P. Stacey, *The Victory Campaign: The Operations in North-West Europe, 1944–1945,* vol. 3 (Ottawa: Queen's Printer, 1960), 407.
3 Captain J.C. Dorward, "The Westkapelle Assault on Walcheren," RG24, vol. 20339, Library and Archives Canada, 9.
4 Ibid., 3.
5 Ibid., 9.
6 Ibid., 10.
7 Ibid., 12.

8. "Report on No. 4 Commando in Flushing Area," 693.013(D1), Directorate of Heritage and History, Department of National Defence, 5–9.
9. Ibid., 5–6.
10. Hilary St. George Saunders, *The Green Beret: The story of the Commandos, 1940–1945* (London: Michael Joseph, 1951), 298.
11. Report No. 188 Historical Section Canadian Military Headquarters: "Canadian Participation in the Operations in North-West Europe–Part VI: Canadian Operations, 1 Oct–8 Nov, The Clearance of the Scheldt Estuary," Department of National Defence, 7 April, 1948, 109.
12. Stacey, 411–12.
13. G.W.L. Nicholson, *The Gunners of Canada*, vol. 2 (Toronto: McClelland & Stewart, 1972), 374.
14. Stacey, 417.
15. Ibid., 413–14.
16. J.L. Moulton, *Battle for Antwerp: The Liberation of the City and the Opening of the Scheldt, 1944* (New York: Hippocrene Books, 1978), 179.
17. Kenneth Edwards, *Operation Neptune* (London: Collins, 1946), 281–82.
18. Nicholson, 375.
19. "The Clearance of the Scheldt Estuary," 128.
20. James Dunning, *The Fighting Fourth: No. 4 Commando at War, 1940–45* (Phoenix Mill, UK: Sutton Publishing, 2003), 175–76.
21. St. George Saunders, 306.
22. Stacey, 416.
23. John Forfar, *From Omaha to the Scheldt: The Story of 47 Royal Marine Commando* (East Lothian, Scotland: Tuckwell Press, 2001), 197–98.
24. Martin Chisholm, "A Battleship Fires Her Heavy Guns," *Picture Post*, vol. 25, no. 8, November 8, 1944, 12–13.
25. Dorward, 28.
26. Stacey, 417.
27. Gerald Rawling, *Cinderella Operation: The Battle for Walcheren 1944* (London: Cassell, 1980), 122.
28. St. George Saunders, 300.
29. W.R. Freasby, ed., *Official History of the Canadian Medical Services, 1939–1945*, vol. 1: *Organization and Campaigns* (Ottawa: Queen's Printer, 1956), 262.
30. St. George Saunders, 301–2.
31. Moulton, 204–6.
32. Report No. 69 Historical Section Army Headquarters: "The Campaign in North-West Europe, Information from German Sources—Part III: German Defence Operations in the Sphere of First Canadian Army (23 Aug.–8 Nov. 44)," Directorate of Heritage and History, Department of National Defence, 30 July, 1954, para. 278.
33. Blake, 93.
34. C.N. Barclay, *The History of The Cameronians (Scottish Rifles)*, vol. III, *1939–1946* (London: Sifton Praed, n.d.), 194.
35. Blake, 98.

36 Ibid., 113–14.
37 1st Battalion, The Lake Superior Regiment (Motor) War Diary, November 1944, RG24, Library and Archives Canada, 2.
38 H.M. Jackson, ed. *The Argyll and Sutherland Highlanders of Canada (Princess Louise's), 1928–1953* (n.p., 1953), 147.
39 G.L. Cassidy, *Warpath: The Story of the Algonquin Regiment, 1939–1945* (Toronto: Ryerson Press, 1948), 188–90.
40 Lincoln and Welland Regiment War Diary, November 1944, RG24, Library and Archives Canada, n.p.
41 Cassidy, 194.
42 J.M. Savage, *The History of the 5th Canadian Anti-tank Regiment* (Canada: 4th Canadian Armoured Division, 1945), 42.
43 Algonquin Regiment War Diary, November 1944, RG24, Library and Archives Canada, 1.
44 Cassidy, 196–97.
45 Ibid., 197.
46 Savage, 41–42.
47 Cassidy, 198.
48 Argyll and Sutherland Highlanders War Diary, November 1944, RG24, Library and Archives Canada, 3.
49 Jackson, 148.
50 Argyll and Sutherland Highlanders War Diary, November 1944, 3–4.
51 The Lake Superior Regiment (Motor) War Diary, November 1944, 3.
52 George F. G. Stanley, *In the Face of Danger: The History of the Lake Superior Regiment* (Port Arthur, ON: The Lake Superior Scottish Regiment, 1960), 219–20.
53 Johan van Doorn, "German casualties in the Battle of the Scheldt, 14th September–8th November 1944, compiled 22/02/2007," unpublished document, in possession of author.
54 Johan van Doorn, Francis Huijbrechts, et al., "Dutch & Belgian casualties in the Battle of the Schedlt, Compiled 29/03/2007," unpublished document, in possession of author.
55 Stacey, 424.
56 Terry Copp, *Cinderella Army: The Canadians in Northwest Europe, 1944–1945* (Toronto: University of Toronto Press, 2006), 299–303.
57 Jeffrey Williams, *The Long Left Flank: The Hard Fought Way to the Reich, 1944–1945* (Toronto: Stoddart, 1988), 72–78.
58 Stacey, 422–23.
59 George G. Blackburn, The Guns of Victory: A Soldier's Eye View, Belgium, Holland, and Germany, 1944–45 (Toronto: McClelland & Stewart, 1996), 175.

BIBLIOGRAPHY

BOOKS

Aernoudts, Karel. *Waar de rode klaproos bloeit*. Oostburg: Uitgeverij W.J. Pieters, 1972.

Alexander, G.M., ed. *Europe, July 1944–May 1945: A Brief History of the 4th Canadian Armoured Brigade in Action*. Mitcham, England: West Brothers, 1945.

Barclay, C.N. *The History of the Cameronians (Scottish Rifles). Vol. 3: 1939–1946*. London: Sifton Praed, n.d.

Barnard, W.T. *The Queen's Own Rifles of Canada, 1860–1960: One Hundred Years of Canada*. Don Mills, ON: Ontario Publishing Co., 1960.

Bell, T.J. *Into Action with the 12th Field*. Utrecht: J. van Boekhoven, 1945.

Bercuson, David. *Battalion of Heroes: The Calgary Highlanders in World War II*. Calgary: Calgary Highlanders Regimental Funds Foundation, 1994.

Bird, Will R. *North Shore (New Brunswick) Regiment*. Fredericton, NB: Brunswick Press, 1963.

———. *No Retreating Footsteps: The Story of the North Nova Scotia Highlanders*. Hantsport, NS: Lancelot Press, 1983.

Blackburn, George. *The Guns of Victory: A Soldier's Eye View, Belgium, Holland, and Germany, 1944–45*. Toronto: McClelland & Stewart, 1996.

Blake, George, *Mountain and Flood: The History of the 52nd (Lowland) Division, 1939–1945*. Glasgow: Jackson, Son & Co., 1950.

Bollen, Hen. *Worsteling om Walcheren, 1939–1945*. Netherlands: Uitgeverij Terra Zuthphen, 1985.

Boss, William. *Up the Glens: Stormont, Dundas and Glengarry Highlanders, 1783–1994*. 2nd ed., Cornwall, ON: Old Book Store, 1995.

Bouchery, Jean. Trans: Alan McKay. *The Canadian Soldier in North-West Europe, 1944–1945*. Paris: Histoire & Collections, 2003.

Brown, Gordon and Terry Copp. *Look to Your Front... Regina Rifles: A Regiment at War, 1944–45*. Waterloo, ON: Laurier Centre Military Strategic Disarmament Studies, 2001.

Brown, Sr., Kingsley, Kingsley Brown, Jr. and Brereton Greenhous. *Semper Paratus: The History of The Royal Hamilton Light Infantry (Wentworth Regiment), 1862–1977*. Hamilton: The RHLI Historical Assoc., 1977.

Buchanan, G.B. *The March of the Prairie Men: A Story of the South Saskatchewan Regiment* n.p., n.d.

Burns, E.L.M. *Manpower in the Canadian Army, 1939–1945*. Toronto: Clarke, Irwin & Co., 1956.

Cassidy, G.L. *Warpath: The Story of the Algonquin Regiment, 1939–1945*. Toronto: Ryerson Press, 1948.

Castonguay, Jacques and Armand Ross. *Le Régiment de la Chaudière*. Lévis, QC: n.p., 1983.

Chalmers, W.S. *Full Cycle: The Biography of Admiral Sir Bertram Home Ramsay, KCB, KBE, MVC*. Vol. 2. London: Hodder & Stoughton, 1959.

Copp, Terry. *The Brigade: The Fifth Canadian Infantry Brigade, 1939–1945*. Stoney Creek, ON: Fortress Publications, 1992.

———. *Cinderella Army: The Canadians in Northwest Europe, 1944–1945*. Toronto: University of Toronto Press, 2006.

———. and William McAndrew. *Battle Exhaustion*. Montreal: McGill-Queen's University Press, 1990.

———. and Robert Vogel. *Maple Leaf Route: Caen*. Alma, ON: Maple Leaf Route, 1983.

Duguid, A. Fortescue. *History of the Canadian Grenadier Guards, 1760–1964*. Montreal: Gazette Printing Co., 1965.

Dunning, James. *The Fighting Fourth: No. 4 Commando at War, 1940–45*. Phoenix Mill, UK: Sutton Publishing, 2003.

Edwards, Kenneth. *Operation Neptune*. London: Collins, 1946.

Ellis, L.F. with A.E. Warhurst. *Victory in the West. Vol. II–The Defeat of Germany*. London: Her Majesty's Stationery Office, 1968.

Fetherstonhaugh, R.C., *The Royal Montreal Regiment, 1925–1945*. Westmount, QC: The Royal Montreal Regiment, 1949.

1st Battalion, The Highland Light Infantry of Canada: 1940–1945 Galt, ON: Highland Light Infantry of Canada Assoc., 1951.

Forfar, John. *From Omaha to the Scheldt: The Story of 47 Royal Marine Commando*. East Lothian, Scotland: Tuckwell Press, 2001.

Foster, Robert M. et. al. *Steady the Buttons Two by Two: Governor General's Foot Guards Regimental History, 125th Anniversary: 1872–1997*. Ottawa: Governor General's Foot Guards, 1999.

Fraser, Robert L. *Black Yesterdays: The Argyll's War*. Hamilton: Argyll Foundation, 1996.

Freasby, W.R., ed., *Official History of the Canadian Medical Services, 1939–1945. Vol. 1: Organization and Campaigns*. Ottawa: Queen's Printer, 1956.

Goodspeed, D.J. *Battle Royal: A History of the Royal Regiment of Canada, 1862–1962*. Toronto: The Royal Regiment of Canada Assoc., 1962.

Goossens, A.B.J. *West-Zeeuws-Vlanderen 1939–1946. Deel 2: Vlucht en bevrijding*. Apeldoorn: n.p., 1997.

Graham, Dominick. *The Price of Command: A Biography of General Guy Simonds*. Toronto: Stoddart, 1993.

Granatstein, J.L. *Canada's Army: Waging War and Keeping the Peace*. Toronto: University of Toronto Press, 2002.

———. *The Generals: The Canadian Army's Senior Commanders in the Second World War*. Toronto: Stoddart, 1993.

Graves, Donald. *South Alberta's: A Canadian Regiment at War*. Toronto: Robin Brass Studio, 1998.

Harker, Douglas E. *The Dukes: The Story of the Men Who have Served in Peace and War with the British Columbia Regiment (D.C.O.), 1883–1973*. The British Columbia Regiment, 1974.

Hayes, Geoffrey. *The Lincs: A History of the Lincoln and Welland Regiment at War*. Alma, ON: Maple Leaf Route, 1986.

Hoebeke, R.E. *Slagveld Sloedam*. Nieuw-en Sint Joosland, Holland: n.p., 2002.

Horrocks, Brian with Eversley Belfield and H. Essame. *Corps Commander*. London: Sidgwick & Jackson, 1977.

Hutchison, Paul P. *Canada's Black Watch: The First Hundred Years, 1862–1962*. Montreal: The Black Watch (RHR) of Canada, 1962.

Jackson, H.M. *The Argyll and Sutherland Highlanders of Canada (Princess Louise's), 1928–1953*. n.p., 1953.

———. *The Sherbrooke Regiment (12th Armoured Regiment)*. n.p., 1958.

Kaufman, David and Michiel Horn. *A Liberation Album: Canadians in the Netherlands, 1944–45*. Toronto: McGraw-Hill Ryerson, 1980.

Kember, Arthur K. *The Six Years of 6 Canadian Field Regiment Royal Canadian Artillery: September 1939–September 1945*. Amsterdam: Town Printing, 1945.

Kemp, P.K. *The History of the 4th Battalion King's Shropshire Light Infantry (T.A.) 1745–1945*. Shrewsbury, England: Wilding & Son Ltd., 1955.

Kuppers, Alex, ed. *Perspectives*. Royal Winnipeg Rifles Assoc., British Columbia Branch, 2003.

Liddell Hart, B.H. *History of the Second World War*. New York: G.P. Putnam's Sons, 1970.

———. *The Tanks, The History of the Royal Tank Regiment. Vol. 2: 1939–1945*. London: Cassell, 1959.

Luxton, Eric, ed. *1st Battalion, The Regina Rifles Regiment, 1939–1946*. Regina: The Regiment, 1946.

McAndrew, Bill. *Liberation: The Canadians in Europe*. Montréal: Éditions Art Global, 1995.

———, Donald Graves and Michael Whitby. *Normandy 1944: The Canadian Summer*. Montreal: Éditions Art Global, 1994.

Macdonald, Charles B. *United States Army in World War II: The European Theater of Operations–The Siefried Line Campaign*. Washington, DC: U.S. Government Printing Office, 1954.

Marchand, Gérard. *Le Régiment de Maisonneuve Vers la Victoire, 1944–1945*. Montréal: Les Presses Libres, 1980.

Marteinson, John and Michael R. McNorgan. *The Royal Canadian Armoured Corps: An Illustrated History*. Toronto: Robin Brass Studio, 2000.

Martin, Charles Cromwell. *Battle Diary: From D-Day and Normandy to the Zuider Zee*. Toronto: Dundurn Press, 1994.

Mein, Stewart A.G. *Up the Johns! The Story of the Royal Regina Rifles*. North Battleford, SK: Turner-Warwick Publications, 1992.

Meyer, Hubert. *The History of the 12. ss-Panzerdivision "Hitlerjugend."* Winnipeg: J.J. Fedorowicz, 1994.

Montgomery, Bernard Law. *The Memoirs of Field Marshal The Viscount Montgomery of Alamein, K.G.* London: Collins, 1958.
———. *Normandy to the Baltic.* London: Hutchinson, 1947.
Moore, Roger. *De slag om 't Molentje: Moerkerke 1944.* Eeklo, Belgium: n.p., 1981.
Moulton, J.L. *Battle for Antwerp: The Liberation of the City and the Opening of the Scheldt, 1944.* New York: Hippocrene Books, 1978.
Nicholson, G.W.L. *The Gunners of Canada. Vol. 2.* Toronto: McClelland & Stewart, 1972.
Pavey, Walter G. *An Historical Account of the 7th Canadian Reconnaissance Regiment (17th Duke of York's Royal Canadian Hussars).* Gardenvale, QC: Harpell's Press, 1948.
Pogue, Forrest C. *Supreme Command.* Washington, DC: U.S. Government Printing Office, 1954.
Położyński, Antoni. *10 Pułk Strzelców Konnych.* Nürnberg, Germany: F. Willmy GmbH, 1947.
Portugal, Jean E. *We Were There: The Navy, the Army and the RCAF—A Record for Canada. Vol. 1–7.* Shelburne, ON: The Battered Silicon Dispatch Box, 1998.
Queen-Hughes, R.W. *Whatever Men Dare: A History of the Queen's Own Cameron Highlanders of Canada, 1935–1960.* Winnipeg: Bulman Bros. 1960.
Rawling, Gerald. *Cinderella Operation: The Battle for Walcheren 1944.* London: Cassell, 1980.
Rawson, Andrew. *Walcheren: Operation Infatuate.* South Yorkshire: Pen & Sword Books, 2003.
Read, Brian A. *No Holding Back: Operation Totalize, Normandy, August 1944.* Toronto: Robin Brass Studio, 2005.
The Regimental History of the Governor General's Foot Guards. Ottawa: Mortimer, 1948.
Rogers, R.L. *History of the Lincoln and Welland Regiment.* n.p., 1954.
Ross, Richard M. *The History of the 1st Battalion Cameron Highlanders of Ottawa (MG).* n.p, n.d.
Roy, Reginald, *The Canadians in Normandy.* Toronto: Macmillan of Canada, 1984.
———. *Ready for the Fray: The History of the Canadian Scottish Regiment (Princess Mary's), 1920 to 1955.* Vancouver: Evergreen Press, 1958.
Ruffee, G.E.M. *The History of the 14 Field Regiment Royal Canadian Artillery, 1940–1945.* Amsterdam: Wereldbibliotheek, NV, 1945.
St. George Saunders, Hilary. *The Green Beret: The Story of the Commandos, 1940–1945.* London: Michael Joseph, 1951.
Savage, J.M. *The History of the 5th Canadian Anti-tank Regiment, 10 Sept., 1941–10 June, 1945.* Canada: 4th Canadian Armoured Division, 1945.
Schofield, B.B. *Operation Neptune.* London: Ian Allan, 1974.
Schoofs, Wally. *De Slag om Brecht: 1940–1945. Wereldoorlog II in Brecht–Sint-Lenaarts–Sint-Job-in-'t-Goor.* Baarle-Nassau, Belgium: n.p., 2005.
Service, G.T. *The Gate: A History of the Fort Garry Horse.* Calgary: n.p., 1971.
Shawcross, Ronald Gendall. *What Was It Like? A Rifleman Remembers: Some Memories of World War II, 1939–1945.* Victoria: Trafford Publishing, 2004.
Spencer, Robert A. *History of the Fifteenth Canadian Field Regiment, Royal Canadian Artillery: 1941 to 1945.* New York: Elsevier, 1945.

Stacey, C.P. *The Victory Campaign: The Operations in North-West Europe, 1944–1945.* Vol. 3. Ottawa: Queen's Printer, 1960.
Stanley, George F.G. *In the Face of Danger: The History of the Lake Superior Regiment.* Port Arthur, ON: The Lake Superior Scottish Regiment, 1960.
Tascona, Bruce and Eric Wells. *Little Black Devils: A History of the Royal Winnipeg Rifles.* Winnipeg: Frye Publishing, 1983.
Thompson, R.W. *The Eighty-Five Days: The Story of the Battle of the Scheldt.* London: Hutchinson & Co., 1957.
van Doorn, Johan. *Slag om Woensdrecht: bevrijding van de Zuidwesthoek, Oktober 1944.* Willemstad: n.p., 1995.
Vanguard: The Fort Garry Horse in the Second World War. Doetincham, Holland: Uitgevers-Maatschappij, C. Misset, NV, nd.
Warren, Arnold. *Wait for the Waggon: The Story of the Royal Canadian Army Service Corps.* Toronto: McClelland & Stewart, 1961.
Whitaker, W. Denis and Shelagh Whitaker. *Tug of War: The Canadian Victory that Opened Antwerp.* Toronto: Stoddart, 1984.
Whitsed, Roy. *Canadians: A Battalion at War.* Mississauga, ON: Burlington Books, 1996.
Williams, Jeffrey. *The Long Left Flank: The Hard Fought Way to the Reich, 1944–1945.* Toronto: Stoddart, 1988.
Wilmot, Chester. *The Struggle for Europe.* London, Collins, 1952.

MAGAZINES, NEWSPAPERS, ARTICLES

Chisholm, Martin. "A Battleship Fires Her Heavy Guns." *Picture Post,* vol. 25, no. 8: Nov. 8, 1944.
Copp, Terry. "The Liberation of Belgium." *Legion Magazine.* Nov./Dec. 2000.
MacDonald, Harold with M.A. MacDonald. "The Long Wait (Part 1): A Personal Account of Infantry Training in Britain." *Canadian Military History,* vol. 14: Spring 2006.
Magrey, Karel. "The Ijzendijke Explosion." *After The Battle,* no. 99: 1998.

WEBSITES

"The Battle of Bergen Op Zoom." http://www.army.forces.gc.ca/Land-Force_Central_Area/31_Canadian Brigade_Group/Lincoln_Welland_Regiment/History.asp. Dec. 19, 2006.
Benson, John. "Belgium." http://fourthlincolns.tripod.com/page5/html. July 18, 2006.
Berry, Lt. Maurice. "letter November 20, 1944 to Lt. Col. W.E. MacFarlane." http://blackwatchcanada.com/en/archives.htm. Nov. 11, 2006.
Dubetz, John. "Friday, October 13, 1944, 'Black Friday.'" http://www.smokylake.com/history/other/blackfriday/htm. Dec. 7, 2006.
Dungan, T.D. "Antwerp: City of Sudden Death." http://www.v2rocket.com/start/chapters/antwerp.html. Dec. 8, 2006.
"Fact Sheet No. B21: World War 2–2nd Battalion South Wales Borderers." http://www.rrw.org.uk/museums/brecon/fact_sheets/21.htm. July 18, 2006.
Holm, Frank. "Personal Narratives–Walcheren Causeway." http://www.calgaryhighlanders.com/history/walch.htm. July 6, 2006.

"Lieutenant Colonel MacLaughlan (sic), DSO." http://www.calgaryhighlanders.com/history/mac.htm. July 6, 2006.

"Sergeant Clarence Kenneth Crockett, DCM." http://www.calgaryhighlanders.com/history/crockett.htm. July 6, 2006.

UNPUBLISHED MATERIALS

Algonquin Regiment War Diary, Sept–Nov 1944. RG24, Library and Archives Canada.

"The Amphibious Operation Against the Rear of the 'Breskens Pocket,' 9 Oct 44: (a) Account of the Landing of 9 CDN INF BDE, given to Hist Offr 3 CDN INF DIV by Major R.T. Wiltshire, O.C. 80 Sqn, 5 Aslt Regt, R.E., 16 Oct," and, "(b) Account by Lt.-Cdr. R.D. Franks, R.N. (Naval Liaison Officer, H.Q. First CDN Army), given to Hist Offr, H.Q. First CDN Army." Canadian Operations Northwest Europe, MG30, vol. 8, E157, Library and Archives Canada.

Argyll and Sutherland Highlanders War Diary, Sept–Nov 1944. RG24, Library and Archives Canada.

"The Assault Across Savojaards Plaat, 8–9 Oct 44." RG24, vol. 10908, Library and Archives Canada.

Bannerman, Lt. George. "Some Aspects of the Technique of Flame Throwing: 'WASP' and 'Lifebuoy' (Account by Lt. George Bannerman, Sask L.I. (M.G.), Tech Offr (Flame), First Canadian Army, Given to Historical Officer, 2 CDN INF DIV, 26 Nov 44)." Canadian Operations in North-West Europe: June–November 1944, Extracts from War Diaries and Memoranda (Series 17), 018(D2), Directorate of Heritage and History, Department of National Defence.

Barrett, Maj. J.H.D. "11th Field Company, RCE: From Seine to Scheldt, 1 Sep/31 Oct 44." 143.3F11011(D1), Directorate of Heritage and History, Department of National Defence.

Blackburn, George. *The History of the 4th Field Regiment.* n.p., 1945.

"The Bridgehead over the Leopold Canal: Account by Maj. A.L. Gollnick, 2 IC and Capt. C.M. Rehill, Adjt. Regina Rif, Given to Historical Officer, 13 Nov 44." 145.2R11011(2), Directorate of Heritage and History, Department of National Defence.

Calgary Highlanders War Diary, Sept–Nov 1944. RG24, Library and Archives Canada.

Cameron Highlanders of Ottawa (MG) War Diary, Sept–Nov 1944. RG24, Library and Archives Canada.

Canadian Scottish Regiment, 1st Battalion War Diary, Sept–Nov 1944. RG24, Library and Archives Canada.

"The Capture of Woensdrecht: Accounts by Officers of R.H.L.I. Given to Historical Officer, 2 CDN INF DIV, 22 Oct 44," 145.2R14011(1), Directorate of Heritage and History, Department of National Defence.

"Combined Operations Headquarters–Bulletin Y/43: 'Amphibians in Operation 'Switchback.'" MG30, vol. 8, Library and Archives Canada.

"Conversation GOC 3 Cdn Inf Div with Maj-Gen Eberding, GOC 64 German Inf Div–1 Nov 44." 19830036.001, Canadian War Museum.

Crerar Papers. MG30, vol. 2, vol. 3, Library and Archives Canada.

Donald George Innes Award Citation. Directorate of Heritage and History, Department of National Defence.

Dorward, Capt. J.C. "The Westkapelle Assault on Walcheren." RG24, vol. 20339, Library and Archives Canada.
8th Canadian Field Squadron, RCE War Diary, Sept–Nov 1944. RG24, Library and Archives Canada.
8th Canadian Infantry Brigade War Diary, Sept–Nov 1944. RG24, Library and Archives Canada.
VIII CDN Recce Rgt. 14 CH: *Battle History of the Regt.* n.p., n.d. Canadian War Museum.
Essex Scottish War Diary, Sept–Nov 1944. RG24, Library and Archives Canada.
"Extract from R.A.F. Narrative: The Liberation of North-West Europe, The Assault on Walcheren." 570.013 (D3A), Directorate of Heritage and History, Department of National Defence.
15th Canadian Field Regiment, RCA War Diary, Sept–Nov 1944. RG24, Library and Archives Canada.
5th Canadian Field Company, Royal Canadian Engineers War Diary, Sept–Nov 1944. RG24, Library and Archives Canada.
5th Canadian Infantry Brigade War Diary, Sept–Nov 1944. RG24, Library and Archives Canada.
1st Battalion, The Black Watch (RHR) War Diary, Sept–Nov 1944. RG24, Library and Archives Canada.
1st Battalion, The Lake Superior Regiment (Motor) War Diary, Sept–Nov 1944. RG24, Library and Archives Canada.
1st Battalion, Royal Regiment of Canada War Diary, Sept–Nov 1944. RG24, Library and Archives Canada.
First Canadian Army HQ Defence Company (RMR) War Diary, Sept–Nov 1944. RG24, Library and Archives Canada.
"1st Polish Armoured Division Operational Report," RG24, vol. 10942, Library and Archives Canada.
Fort Garry Horse (10th Canadian Armoured Regiment) War Diary, Sept–Nov 1944. RG24, Library and Archives Canada.
14th Field Regiment, Royal Canadian Artillery War Diary, Sept–Nov 1944. RG24, Library and Archives Canada.
4th Canadian Armoured Brigade War Diary, Sept–Nov 1944. RG24, Library and Archives Canada.
4th Canadian Armoured Division War Diary, Sept–Nov 1944. RG24, Library and Archives Canada.
4th Canadian Field Regiment War Diary, Sept–Nov 1944. RG24, Library and Archives Canada.
4th Canadian Infantry Brigade War Diary, Sept–Nov 1944. RG24, Library and Archives Canada.
G Branch, 4th Canadian Armoured Division War Diary, Sept–Nov 1944. RG24, Library and Archives Canada.
Headquarters, RCA, 4th Canadian Armoured Division War Diary, Sept–Nov 1944. RG24, Library and Archives Canada.
Headquarters 2nd Canadian Infantry Division, G Branch, War Diary, Sept–Nov 1944. RG24, Library and Archives Canada.

Highland Light Infantry of Canada War Diary, Sept–Nov 1944. RG24, Library and Archives Canada.
History of H.Q., R.C.A. 2 CDN INF DIV *From 1 Nov 44 to 5 May 45, World War* II. Ottawa, n.p., 1945.
Hossack, Ken. *Mike Target*. Ottawa: n.p., 1945.
HQ 2nd Canadian Armoured Brigade War Diary, Sept–Nov 1944. RG24, Library and Archives Canada.
HQ RCA 2nd Canadian Infantry Division War Diary, Sept–Nov 1944. RG24, Library and Archives Canada.
Keefler, Brig. R., "The Capture of Zuid Beveland: Account by Brigadier R.H. Keefler, ED, A/Comd, 2 CDN INF DIV, Given to Historical Officer, 2 CDN INF DIV, 11 Nov 44." RG24, vol. 10897, Library and Archives Canada.
La Régiment de la Chaudière War Diary, Sept–Nov 1944. RG24, Library and Archives Canada.
Law, Cecil. "Compilation of South Saskatchewan Regiment Casualties." In possession of author.
———. "Lochtenberg–23 Sep 44 to 2 Oct 44." Unpublished memoir, in possession of author.
———. "Sniper." Unpublished account, in possession of author.
———. "South Beveland Peninsula Battles." Unpublished account, in possession of author.
Le Régiment de Maisonneuve War Diary, Sept–Nov 1944. RG24, Library and Archives Canada.
Les Fusiliers Mont-Royal War Diary, Sept–Nov 1944. RG24, Library and Archives Canada.
McQuarrie, Alex English trans. in possession of author from *Cent ans d'histoire d'un régiment canadien-français: les Fusiliers Mont-Royal, 1869-1969*. Montréal: Editions Du Jour Montréal, 1971.
"Memorandum on Operations of 4 Cdn. Armd. Div. on Leopold Canal, 13–14 Sep. 44." Vol. 10936, RG24, Library and Archives Canada.
"Miscellaneous Papers, 1944–1979 Regarding a Chaplain's Role." MG31, vol. F18, Library and Archives Canada.
19th Field Regiment, Royal Canadian Artillery War Diary, Sept–Nov 1944. RG24, Library and Archives Canada.
9th Canadian Field Squadron, RCE War Diary, Sept–Nov 1944. RG24, Library and Archives Canada.
9th Canadian Infantry Brigade War Diary, Sept–Nov 1944. RG24, Library and Archives Canada.
North Nova Scotia Highlanders War Diary, Sept–Nov 1944. RG24, Library and Archives Canada.
North Shore (New Brunswick) Regiment War Diary, Sept–Nov 1944. RG24, Library and Archives Canada.
"Operation 'Switchback': The Clearing of the South Bank of the Schelde (Battle Narrative Prepared by Historical Officer, 3 CDN INF DIV." *Canadian Operations in North-West Europe: October–November 1944, Extracts from War Diaries and*

Memoranda. (Series 18), 018 (D2) Directorate of Heritage and History, Department of National Defence.

"Personal Accounts of Battle, Canadian Scottish, Jun 44–May 45, 'Two Came Back.'" 145.2C4009(D11), Directorate of Heritage and History, Department of National Defence.

Queen's Own Cameron Highlanders of Canada War Diary, Sept–Nov 1944. RG24, Library and Archives Canada.

The Recollections of the Regina Rifles: N.W. Europe World War 2, June 6, 1944–May 8, 1945. Looseleaf folder in possession of author.

"Report No. 69 Historical Section Army Headquarters: The Campaign in North-West Europe, Information from German Sources—Part III: German Defence Operations in the Sphere of First Canadian Army (23 Aug. 8–Nov. 44." Directorate of Heritage and History, Department of National Defence, 30 July 1954.

"Report No. 183 Historical Section Canadian Military Headquarters: Canadian Participation in the Operations in North-West Europe—Part IV: First Canadian Army in the Pursuit (23 Aug–30 Sep)." Directorate of Heritage and History, Department of National Defence.

"Report No. 188 Historical Section Canadian Military Headquarters: Canadian Participation in the Operations in North-West Europe—Part VI: Canadian Operations, 1 Oct–8 Nov, The Clearance of the Scheldt Estuary." Department of National Defence, 7 April 1948.

"Report on the Islands of South Beveland and Walcheren and the Mainland Opposite the Islands to the South of the River Scheldt." RG24, vol. 10539, Library and Archives Canada.

"Report on No. 4 Commando in Flushing Area." 693.013(D1), Directorate of Heritage and History, Department of National Defence.

"RHLI Operation Order No. 1 Woensdrecht Feature 15/16 Oct 44." 145.2R14011(1), Directorate of Heritage and History, Department of National Defence.

Rodgers, N.R. "Personal Diary." George Metcalf Archival Collection, Canadian War Museum.

Royal Hamilton Light Infantry War Diary, Sept–Nov 1944. RG24, Library and Archives Canada.

Royal Regina Rifles Regiment, 1st Battalion War Diary, Sept–Nov 1944. RG24, Library and Archives Canada.

Royal Winnipeg Rifles War Diary, Sept–Nov 1944. RG24, Library and Archives Canada.

Seaborn, Robert Lowder. Diary, Robert Lowder Seaborn and family. MG31, F 18, vols. 2–6, Library and Archives Canada.

2nd Canadian Anti-Tank Regiment, RCA War Diary, Sept–Nov 1944. RG24, Library and Archives Canada.

2nd Canadian Armoured Brigade War Diary, Sept–Nov 1944. RG24, Library and Archives Canada.

II Canadian Corps War Diary, Sept–Nov 1944. RG24, Library and Archives Canada.

7th Canadian Infantry Brigade War Diary, Sept–Nov 1944. RG 24, Library and Archives Canada.

7th Canadian Reconnaissance Regiment (17 DYRCH) War Diary, Sept–Nov 1944. RG24, Library and Archives Canada.

Shea, Lt. W.J. "The Action at Woensdrecht, 8–14 Oct 44: Account by Lt. W.J. Shea, I.O., R.H.C., given to Historical Officer, 2 CDN INF DIV, 15 Oct 44." 145.2R14OII(I), Directorate of Heritage and History, Department of National Defence.

6th Canadian Infantry Brigade War Diary, Sept–Nov 1944. RG24, Library and Archives Canada.

6th Canadian Field Regiment War Diary, Sept–Nov 1944. RG24, Library and Archives Canada.

South Saskatchewan Regiment War Diary, Sept–Nov 1944. RG24, Library and Archives Canada.

Stormont, Dundas and Glengarry Highlanders War Diary, Sept–Nov 1944. RG24, Library and Archives Canada.

10th Canadian Infantry Brigade War Diary, Sept–Nov 1944. RG24, Library and Archives Canada.

3rd Canadian Anti-Tank Regiment War Diary, Sept–Nov 1944. RG24, Library and Archives Canada.

3rd Canadian Infantry Division GS War Diary, Sept–Nov 1944. RG 24, Library and Archives Canada.

13th Field Regiment, Royal Canadian Artillery War Diary, Sept–Nov 1944. RG24, Library and Archives Canada.

Todd, Brig. P.A.S. "Artillery in Operation 'Switchback': Account by Brig. P.A.S. Todd, DSO, OBE, ED, CCRA, 2 CDN CORPS, given to Historical Officer 3 CDN INF DIV, 9 Dec. 1944." Appendix 'A,' Canadian Operations in North-West Europe: October–November 1944, Extracts from War Diaries and Memoranda (Series 18), 018(D2), Directorate of Heritage and History, Department of National Defence.

12th Canadian Field Regiment, Royal Canadian Artillery War Diary, Sept–Nov 1944. RG24, Library and Archives Canada.

28th Canadian Armoured Regiment (British Columbia Regiment) War Diary, Sept–Nov 1944. RG24, Library and Archives Canada.

21st Canadian Armoured Regiment (Governor General's Foot Guards) War Diary, Sept–Nov 1944. RG24, Library and Archives Canada.

29th Canadian Armoured Regiment (South Alberta) War Diary, Sept–Nov 1944. RG24, Library and Archives Canada.

22nd Canadian Armoured Regiment (Canadian Grenadier Guards) War Diary, Sept–Nov 1944. RG24, Library and Archives Canada.

van Doorn, Johan. "German casualties in the Battle of the Scheldt, 14th September–8th November 1944, compiled 22/02/2007." Unpublished document, in possession of author.

Von Zangen, Gusav. *"Ops of 15th German Army,"* RG24, vol. 20522, Library and Archives Canada.

Warning, Oberst G. Elmar. "Battles of LXVII Inf Corps Between the Schelde and the Maas, 15 Sep–25 Nov 44." RG24, vol. 20523, Library and Archives Canada.

INTERVIEWS AND CORRESPONDENCE

Beer, John. Interview by David Gantzer. Victoria, BC. 26, 28 November 1979. University of Victoria Special Collections.

Butters, Thomas William Lowell. Interview by Tom Torrie. Victoria, BC. 19 August 1987. University of Victoria Special Collections.
English, Earl. Correspondence with Reginald Roy. 12 April 1957. University of Victoria Special Collections.
Fulton, Lochie. Interview by Ken MacLeod. Victoria, BC. 9 February 1998.
Goodman, Charles. Interview by author. Saanichton, BC. 2 June 2006.
———. Interview by David Gantzer. Victoria, BC. 1, 5, December 1979 and 16 January 1980. University of Victoria Special Collections.
Hobden, L. Correspondence with Reginald Roy. 8 May 1957. University of Victoria Special Collections.
Law, Cecil. Correspondence with author, 14 April, 10 May, 14 July 2006.
Martin, Jack. Interview by John G. Thompson. Scarborough, ON. 1 October 2003.
Marshall, Royce. Correspondence with Reginald Roy. 28 January 1957. University of Victoria Special Collections.
Parks, Jim. Interview by Ken MacLeod. Vancouver, BC. November 1997.
Schjelderup, Roger. Correspondence with Reginald Roy. 16 July 1957. University of Victoria Special Collections.
Teagle, Ernest. Interview by Mark C. Hill. Victoria, BC. 20 June 1985. University of Victoria Special Collections.
Van Dijk, Ad. Interview by author. Vlissingen, Holland. 17 May 2003.
van Doorn, Johan. Correspondence with author. Sommelsdijk, Holland. 3, 6 June, 16 September, 1 November 2006.

INDEX

Ranks given for individuals are highest attained as of Nov. 6, 1944.
Aachen, 115
Aalter, 60
Aardenburg, 16, 204, 213, 225, 249, 261, 266, 282, 327
Abdijlaan, 290–92, 298–99
Achterbroek, 186, 352, 360–61
Adamoski, L. Cpl. Bert, 218
Adams, Lt., 364
Adams, Capt. Ted, 174–75
Albert Canal, 45, 47–48, 54–56, 58, 63–65, 67–69, 77, 80, 91, 93, 98, 100, 103, 116, 143, 145, 148, 172
Alexander, Pte. W.C., 131
Allan, CSM Don S., 299
Allied Expeditionary Air Force (AEAF), 133, 163
Alphen, 289
Anderson, Capt. Jock, 238, 240, 244, 275
Anderson, Lt. John, 198
Angelina Polder, 280, 284
Annable, Lt. Ted, 248
Antwerp, 1–3, 13, 20, 41–42, 53–55, 58–67, 71–72, 74–75, 79–80, 86, 91–93, 102–04, 107, 120–21, 126, 131, 133–34, 136, 139, 143, 145, 147–48, 154, 163–65, 177, 204, 288–89, 291, 306, 320, 326, 329, 405, 441, 451, 453, 459–60, 461–63, 465
British failure to secure port of, 43–50
given top priority, 253–58
Antwerp–Turnhout Canal, 93, 99, 102–04, 107, 114–15, 119, 124, 133, 139, 143, 154, 186, 198, 289–90, 292, 378, 441, 465
Armstrong, Maj. Gord, 408, 424–26
Armstrong, Pte. Malcolm Elvin Thomas, 247
Arnemuiden, 432
Arnhem, 49, 58, 74, 77–79, 92, 115, 254
Aschmann, Capt., 161, 451
Ashby, Rfn. Gordon, 213–14
Atkinson, Maj. Don, 454
Axel, 72–73

Baarland, 390, 394
Baker, Maj. Frederick "Franco," 95–96, 194, 434
Bannerman, Lt. George, 207–08
Barclay, Lt. William Noel, 212
Barkman, Capt. W.H., 454
Barrett, Rfn. James, 343
Barrick, Pte. W.J., 214
Barry, CSM Wilf, 228
Bath, 188–89
Baylay, Maj. G.T., 363, 416, 418–19
Beatty, Maj. D.S. "Tim," 188–89, 200–01
Beaudoin, Maj. Fernand, 105
Beer, Capt. John, 225–26
Begg, Sgt., 332
Bell, Spr. Cecil Amos, 143
Bennett, Lt. Col. Paul, 69
Berendrecht, 173, 175–76
Bergen op Zoom, 54, 87, 90–91, 115, 121, 134, 154, 171–72, 176, 188–89, 191–92, 196, 288, 291, 310, 322, 326, 352, 368,

372, 379, 382, 384–85, 388–89, 407, 411–18, 420–21, 426
Bergin, Lt. Ken, 217–19
Bergse Baan, 385
Beringen, 58
Berry, Lt. Maurice, 404–05, 429
Besen, Lt. Simeon, 380
Beveland Canal, 81, 390–91, 394–95
Bibeau, Lt. Col. Julien, 182, 440
Biervliet, 271, 275, 277–78, 280, 337
Biezelinge, 400
Biezen, 264–66
Bingham, Pte. Robert E., 131–32
Black, Lt., 458
Black, Lt. George, 217–18
Blackburn, Capt. George, 36–37, 63, 66, 147–48, 167, 178, 460
Blake, Tpr. Robert, 127
Blaker, Capt. Peter, 355
Blue, Pte. L., 230
Boekhoute, 261
Boerenhol, 340
Bomber Command, 82, 89–91, 124, 133–36, 162, 445
Bonnallie, Lt. D.A., 322
Booker, Sgt. Gordon, 68
Boos, Lt. Jack, 342–43
Bordeleau, Gdsm. Joseph, 381
Boulogne, 51, 53, 59, 61–62, 74, 77, 79, 87, 235, 459
Boulton, Sgt. Douglas A., 356
Bourgébus Ridge, 109–10
Bowling, Pte., 345
Bowron, Pte. John, 197–98
Braakman Inlet, 57, 76, 100, 205, 208, 234, 241–42, 246, 260, 270–71, 277, 280, 462
Brabant Wall, 176–77, 180, 192, 195, 200, 351, 461
Bradburn, Lt. Col. Robert, 14–15, 22, 25, 271, 360, 410
Bradley, Gen. Omar N., 38, 254–55
Brady, L. Cpl. E.F., 24
Brasschaat, 139, 154, 196
Brecht, 125, 130, 133, 139–43, 151, 186, 196, 289–90, 465
Breda, 54, 171, 179, 289, 364, 414
Brennan, Lt. Col. M.L., 51–52

Brereton, Lt. Gen. Lewis H., 89
Breskens, 12–13, 16, 20–21, 41–42, 47, 56–57, 73, 77, 82, 101, 205, 260–61, 277, 429, 444–46, 448
 capture of, 327–38
Brochu, Maj. Armand, 105
Brook, Lt. Ed, 355–56
Brooke, Field Marshal Sir Alan, 253–55
Brown, Lt. D.R., 320
Brown, Lt. J.A., 412
Brown, Lt. James Kallethe, 388
Brown, Lt. W.L., 292–94
Brown, Pte. William C., 377–78
Brownridge, Capt. Bob, 228
Bruges, 57, 60–61, 71, 262, 446
Bruges–Ghent Canal, 57, 59–60, 362
Bruges–Sluis Canal, 205, 328, 348
Brussels, 44, 64, 254
Buch, Capt. Nick, 303–04
Buffalo, described, 235–37
Bull, Rfn. Leslie Frank, 340
Bulmer, Pte. J.R., 323
Burch, Cpl. Lee, 243
Burgess, Maj. J.W., 147
Burns, CSM E., 409
Burns, Gdsm. R.R., 420
Burns, Lt. Gen. E.L.M. "Tommy," 166, 169–70
Butler, Lt. K.E., 21
Butters, Capt. Thomas William Lowell, 224
Byron, Sgt. T., 267

Cabeldu, Brig. Fred, 65, 70, 144, 148, 176, 201, 292, 299, 302–03, 310, 321, 323–24, 403
Cadzand, 77, 234, 327–28, 334, 338, 344–47
Caen, 32, 65, 135
Cairns, Lt. Arthur, 320
Calais, 53–54, 59, 61–62, 74, 79–80, 87, 204, 210, 235, 263, 459
Caldwell, Maj. Hank, 392
Callander, Cpl. Wes, 455
Campbell, CSM, 358
Campbell, Maj. Dave, 264
Campbell, Cpl. "Frosty," 332
Campbell, Capt. J.W., 279

Canal de Dérivation de la Lys, 12, 15, 23, 27, 60–61, 76, 80, 204, 231
Canavan, Lt. E.J., 381, 384
Cannon, Sgt. Andy, 272
Cantinieaux, Jacques, 441
Cap Gris Nez, 80, 235
Carrière, Pte. J.C., 440
Carson, Gen. James, 67
Carvell, Maj. J.T., 225
Casey, Lt. Leaman, 409–10
Cassidy, Maj. George L., 13–17, 19–20, 22–25, 27, 208, 362, 365–67, 455–56
Caters Polder, 302
Cavanagh, Maj. Art, 376
Centrum, 407, 409
Chambers, Capt. S.L., 268
Chapman, Maj. Douglas, 129, 304
Cherbourg, 254
Chill, Gen. Lt. Kurt, 172
Chisamore, Rfn. Murray Hector Robert "Bob," 340–42
Chisholm, Rfn. Denis, 232
Chisholm, Pte. Edward Dalton, 360
Chisholm, Martin, 448
Choquette, Rfn. Elmond Joseph, 342
Churchill, Prime Minister Winston, 166, 330
Clarke, Maj. Francis H. "Nobby," 431–35, 437
Clarke, Lt. Ken, 360
Clements, Lt., 129
Collins, Lt., 363
Colman, Pte. P., 267
Colson, Eugene, 46–48, 64–65
Combined Chiefs of Staff, 61
Corbett, Maj. O., 211
Cosens, Pte. William John, 359
Cosgrove, Pte. W.P., 214–15
Coté, Pte. Albert Joseph, 26
Cox, L. Cpl., 346
Craddock, Sgt. W., 212–15
Creelman, Lt. Gordon Ross, 336
Crerar, Lt. Gen. Henry Duncan Graham "Harry," 37–42, 59–61, 71, 73–76, 80, 82, 87–91, 93, 115, 121–24, 134, 162, 459
Crocker, Lt. Dan, 389

Crocker, Lt. Gen. John, 40, 53, 179, 288–89
Crockett, Sgt. Ken, 95–98, 198, 378, 465
Crofton, Lt. Col. Desmond, 282–83
Cromb, Lt. Col. W.T. "Bill," 356–58, 366, 415, 424
Crowe, Pte. Fred, 248
Currie, Maj. Dave, 388, 412

Dandy, Maj. J.L., 357–58, 386
Danielson, Tpr. Melvin, 410
Daser, Gen. Lt. Wilhelm, 102, 260, 326–27, 405, 452–53
Davies, Capt., 24–25
Davies, Lt. R.W., 147
Dearden, Sgt. Ernie, 319
de Guingand, Maj. Gen. Sir Francis "Freddie," 87–88, 164
de Merlis, Lt. Guy, 438–39
Dempsey, Gen. Miles, 38, 74
de Munck, Ad, 415
Des Grosseilliers, Lt. G.P.J., 321
de Stacpoole, Maj. Derek, 450
Destelbergen, 206
Desteldonk, 235
Devitt, Lt. J.W., 416
de Winde, Peter, 241
Dextraze, Maj. Jacques "Jimmy," 373, 397
Dickens, A/C. L.W., 133, 135
Dickie, Capt. R.F., 16, 454
Dieppe, 34, 37–39, 41, 43, 52, 90, 106, 110, 148, 313, 464
Diestel, Gen. Lt. Erich, 103, 114–15
Dinteloord, 457
Dionne, Spr. Roger Charles, 143
Dirassar, Lt. L.G., 362
Dobell, Lt. Col. E.H., 304
Domburg, 443, 450–51
Donitz, Grosseadmiral Karl, 451
Douglas, Capt. Mel, 216–17, 226
Draper, Gdsm. A., 420
Drewery, Maj. Jack, 149–51, 318
Driewegen, 272, 276, 279–80
Drill, Maj. Herman, 26
Dubetz, Cpl. John, 303–06
Duff, Pte. Roy, 359
Dunkirk, 53, 59–62, 74–75, 88
Dunning, Capt. Bill, 146

Dunstan, Rfn. Bob, 286–87
Dutcher, Lt. Thomas Clair, 17

Easser, Capt. Percy, 411
East Scheldt, 87, 327, 352, 376
Eastwood, Capt. Doug, 279
Eberding, Gen. Maj. Knut, 101–02, 256–57, 260, 270, 281, 327, 338, 347, 350
Ecclestone, Lt., 379
Edwards, Gen. Frederick "Eddie," 179–80
Edwards, Maj. G.A.M., 242, 277
Edwards, Sgt. Maj. Wally, 218–19
Edwards, Lt. W.E., 386
Eede, 77, 264, 266–69, 282–83, 327
Eeklo, 60, 80
Eindhoven, 131–33, 139, 142
Eisenhower, Gen. Dwight D., 49–51, 53, 59, 61, 89, 120, 136, 162–64, 253–55, 289
Ekeren, 68, 173
Elbeuf, 36
Ellis, Maj. Ross, 180, 195, 199, 378, 431–32, 434–37
English, Maj. Earl, 222, 224, 267
Eno, Sgt. Gregory John, 183–84
Erebus, HMS, 445, 449
Essen, 187, 288, 298, 352, 362, 364, 366–68, 371, 379
Ewing, Capt. William, 308–09, 430
Exchange, Rfn. Ted, 293, 295–97

Falaise, 32, 35, 135, 257
Falkins, Lt. O.N., 224
Farmer, Maj. John, 356, 379
Fearn, Cpl. Chuck, 409
Fedun, Cpl. William, 98
Fergusson, Lt. J.R., 380
Fernand, Maj. Robert, 363
Findlay, Cpl. G.W., 213–14
Fisher, Lt. H.C., 248
Fitch, Lt., 279
Flushing. *See* Vlissingen
Forbes, Lt. Charles, 189, 438–40
Forbes, Lt. Col. Don, 239, 276, 336–37
Forbes, Capt. Jack, 410–11
Forêt de la Londe, 36, 106
Fort Frederik Hendrik, 12, 334, 335–37

Fort Hazegras, 347
Fortier, Pte. Paul Emile, 441
Foster, Maj. Gen. Harry, 12–13, 25, 27, 60, 100, 123, 352–53, 364–65, 380, 388, 414, 421
Foster, Sgt. H.E., 201
Foster, Tpr. James, 408
Foulkes, Maj. Gen. Charles, 37, 65, 69, 93, 95, 113, 122–23, 127, 196, 240, 291, 301, 330, 405–06, 437–40, 446
Fox, Capt. B.G., 273
Foxemaat, 361
Franks, Lt. Cmdr. Robert, 240, 242, 246, 394
Fraser, Capt., 182
Fraser, Capt. E., 211
French, Lt. William, 383
Freve, Cpl. Ernest, 23
Friyia, Cpl. Joe, 321, 323
Froggett, Maj. E. Louis, 312, 314, 316–17, 320–23
Fulton, Lt. Col. Lockhart Ross "Lochie," 263–66, 339

Gabrielse, Willem, 155
Gagnon, Maj. J.J., 396–97, 399
Galatizine, Lt. T., 280
Gallagher, Lt. Jack, 266–67
Gamelin, Lt., 213
Gass, Maj. Leonard, 217
Gauvin, Maj. Michel, 344
Gauvreau, Brig. J.G. "Guy," 108, 113, 125, 130, 186–87, 376, 396
Gawege, 394–95
Geel, 58
Gendron, Sgt. Lawrence Arthur, 324
Ghent, 3, 15, 44, 56–57, 60, 62, 71, 73, 102, 115, 123, 205–06, 235, 237, 350
Ghent–Terneuzen Canal, 71–73, 76, 80, 240
Gilday, Lt. Col. G.H., 263
Gillan, Maj. J.D.M., 268
Goepel, Lt. R.H., 458
Goes, 395, 401–02
Goodall, Pte. J., 230
Goodman, Pte. Charles "Chic," 109–11, 113, 169–70, 293, 295–97
Göring, Hermann, 55

Gosselin, Lt. Col. A.N., 394
Graaf Jan, 264, 266
Grafton, Capt. W.F., 209
Gram, Pte. Harry, 318
Grandbois, Cpl. George, 375
Grant, Rfn. Hank, 339
Grave, 49, 79
Gravel, Lt. Johnny, 423
Gravel, Capt. Maurice, 396
Gravenpolder, 400–01
Graves, Capt. J., 243
Graves, Rfn. Raymond, 217
Gray, Lt. Bob, 233, 261–62
Greenleaf, Maj. C.A., 416–17
Gri, Sgt. Armando, 227, 230
Grieve, Capt. Jock, 279
Groede, 340–41
Groenendaallaan Bridge, 46–47, 144, 147
Groote Heide, 357–58
Groote Meer, 298
Grote Markt, 415
Grout, Lt. Bob, 179
Guyot, Lt. Marc Jean "Johnny," 410

Hageland, 177
Hailey, Lt. Joseph David Trail, 399
Hakewill Smith, Maj. Gen. Edmund, 439–40
Halladay, Maj. Jack B., 177, 312–13
Halpenny, Lt. Col. W.W., 417
Hansen, Pte. T., 23
Hansweert, 397, 399
Hanway, Lt., 363
Harold, Sgt. Raymond A., 96–97, 198
Harris, Sir Arthur T., 136
Harrison, Capt. Del, 198
Harrison, Maj. W.E.C., 460
Hayman, Lt. James F., 376,
Hayward, Sgt. C.S., 213–14
Hayward, Rfn. John, 339–42
Hazelaar, 418
Heerle, 416–19
Hees, Brig. Maj. George, 432, 436–37
Hegelheimer, Capt. H. Lyn, 313–14, 317–18, 322
Heist, 348, 350
Henry, Pte. Joseph, 359
Herbert, Capt. A.R., 18, 455

Herbert, Brig. E.O., 289
Het Eiland, 291–92, 294, 298
Hewitt, Gdsm. Donald George, 380
Heyland, Capt. Dalt, 378
Hillsman, Lt. Col. J.B., 449
Hitler, Adolf, 13, 32, 54–56, 115, 260, 306, 326
Hobart, Maj. Gen. Percy, 328
Hobden, Lt. L., 221–22, 228–29
Hodges, Lt. Gen. Courtenay, 254
Hodgkinson, Bmdr. Ernie, 174–75
Hoedekenskerke, 82, 88, 390, 394
Holm, Pte. Frank, 433–35
Holt, Lt., 177
Honey, L. Sgt. Hedley Arthur, 456
Hoofdplaat, 205–06, 240–41, 247–49, 256, 260, 270, 272–74, 276, 278, 328
Hoogerheide, 172, 176–77, 203, 290–92, 294, 302–03, 310, 312, 321, 383
  battle for, 180–200
Hoogerwaardpolder, 376
Hooke, Lt. J.C., 455–56
Horrocks, Lt. Gen. Sir Brian, 43–44, 48, 58, 74, 78
Hossack, Bmdr. Ken, 63, 66–67, 173–75, 179
Howarth, Sgt. Fred, 247, 249
Hubert, Sgt., 417
Hughes, Pte. L.V. "Shorty," 214
Huijbergen, 176, 291, 299, 352, 383, 388–89
Huijbergseweg, 290, 292, 298
Hulst, 72
Hulst Canal, 72
Humphrey, Sgt. 451
Hunter, Lt. Geoffrey John, 21, 26
Hurwitz, Sgt. Samuel, 385

Ijzendijke, 285–87, 329, 337
In de Vijf Wegen, 346
Innes, Lt. Donald, 438, 441
Irvine, Sgt. W.M., 417

Janisse, Cornelia, 159
Janisse, Joost, 159
Jefferson, Brig. Jim, 100, 353, 360, 365, 408, 421–23
Jennett, L. Cpl. Lloyd Arthur, 363

Jewell, Capt. J.M. "Johnny," 455
Jodl, Generaloberst Alfred, 414
Jodoin, Lt. J.P., 430–31
Johnson, Cpl. A.G., 354
Johnston, Maj. R.H.B., 452
Johnston, Maj. W.A., 18–19
Jones, Lt. Stewart, 393
Jorgenson, Sgt. Gerald, 153

Kalmthout, 186–87, 352, 356, 371
Kamperland, 405
Kamp van Brasschaat, 105, 131, 152–54, 171, 351, 353–54, 356, 359
Kapelle, 400–01, 403
Kapellen, 154, 174–75, 186, 376
Kapellenbosch, 356
Kaprijke, 246
Kazimir, Pte. Philip, 422–23
Kearns, Maj. Del, 131, 140, 194–95
Keefler, Brig. R.H. "Holly," 122, 126, 131–32, 143, 185–87, 188, 196, 199, 203, 290–92, 384, 386, 391, 393, 395–96, 398, 400, 402–03, 406, 427, 437–38
Kehoe, Rfn. Drew, 286–87
Keilty, Sgt. Francis, 332
Keller, Lt. Alexander, 182
Kelly, Pte. Gerald Reginald, 26
Kelly, Cpl. J.P., 265, 360
Kidd, Rfn. Fred, 210
Kijkuit, 72
King, Maj. J.C., 274
King, Lt. Kerrigan Milne, 271
King, Prime Minister Mackenzie, 38–39
Kingsmill, HMS, 446, 448
Kingsmill, Lt. Col. Nicol, 235, 241
Kirker, Gdsm. L.R., 420
Kitching, Lt. R., 113
Klaehn, Lt. Col. P.C., 285
Knight, Lt. Donald Trumpour, 68
Knokke-aan-zee, 205, 347–50
Korteven, 172, 181, 189–92, 199, 291, 302, 308, 372, 376, 383
Kozar, Gdsm. Dan Alexander, 363
Krabbendijke, 393–94
Kreewin, Lt. Harold, 389
Kruiningen, 397

Kruisdijk, 339
Kruisschanssluis, 46, 70
Kruisstraat, 358, 360–61
Kunzelman, Pte. Wilbert Jacob Ludwig, 322–23
Kurtz, Meester W.F.P., 160

Lacey, Lt. Iler, 130
Lafroy, Lt. Walter, 433
Laloge, Sgt. Emile John "Blackie," 434, 436–37
Lalonde, Cec, 248
Lalonde, L. Cpl. Lionel, 381
Lamb, Capt. H.S., 429–31
Lambert, Capt. Herbert, 357–58, 388, 423–24
Lange, Oscar, 124
Lapscheure, 20
Larson, CSM Harold, 191
Lasher, Maj. Wynn, 184, 377, 434–36
Lashkivich, Pte. T., 323
Law, Lt. Cecil, 105–12, 114, 126, 299, 374–75, 396
Lee, Capt. Fraser, 292–93, 295–98
Le Havre, 35, 51–52, 59–60, 71, 79, 115
Leicester, Brig. B.W., 446, 448
Leigh-Mallory, A/M Trafford, 163
Lendrum, Lt. Col. R.M., 144, 146, 200–01, 391, 403–04
Leopold Canal, 12, 15, 20, 25, 27, 57, 60–61, 71, 76, 80, 83, 87, 178, 240, 246, 249, 256, 258, 260–61, 268, 271, 281–82, 284, 288, 327–28, 346, 348, 362, 459, 462
  Algonquin assault, 17–27
  CIB assault, 204–34
Leopold III, King, 64–65
Lepelstraat, 420
Levasseur, Gdsm. J.M., 364
Lewis, Lt., 191, 309
Lewis, Maj. G.C., 420
Lewis, Lt. Col. Thomas Cripps, 260, 284–85
Liboiron, Lt. Réal, 372
Liddell, Lt., 418–19
Lidonk, 383–84
Liège, 45

Lier, 48
Lilla, 103
Lijnkamp, Burgomeister, 413
Lindal, Lt. Harold, 393
Lingen, CSM K.C. "Casey," 321
Little, Capt. Bill, 181
Livingstone, Lt., 181
Locht, 142–43, 152
Lochtenberg, 104–05, 108–09, 112, 114, 116, 125, 130–31, 139, 143, 152–54
Logie, Maj. Alexander Chisholm, 355–56
Logie, Maj. Gen. W.A., 356
Lowe, Maj. A.H., 210
Lowe, Spr. Frank Arnold, 143
Lucas, Capt. P.B., 133, 135

Maagd-van-Gent, 100
Maas River, 74, 78, 179, 254, 289–90, 325–26, 352, 364, 371, 383, 414, 453, 457
Maastricht, 54
MacDonald, Sgt., 346
MacDonald, Cpl. A.E., 282–83
MacDonald, Pte. I.P., 97
MacDonald, Pte. M.S., 248
MacDonald, Capt. W.D., 356
MacDonnel, Lt. Peter, 229–30, 266
MacKay, Capt. C.D., 68
MacKenzie, Maj. Bruce, 98, 131, 194, 197, 434–35
Mackenzie, Capt. W.F., 22
MacLauchlan, Lt. Col. Donald, 95, 132, 140–42, 191, 193, 195–99
Maclean, Padre Charlie, 408
Maclean, Capt. Hugh, 422–23
MacMillan, Gdsm. Evan Cameron, 363
Maczek, Gen. Stanislaw, 72–73
Major, Maj. Robert Fernand, 382
Malach, Maj., 380, 387
Maldegem, 204–05, 249, 261, 266, 282
Maloney, Gdsm. B.A., 420
Mann, Brig. Gen. Churchill, 38, 164
Mann, Sgt. Victor John, 425
Marcellus, Cpl., 248
Mariabaan, 380
Maria-ter-Heide Château, 359
Marshall, Gen. George C., 255
Marshall, Sgt. L.J., 26

Marshall, Lt. Royce, 221–23, 226–27, 229–30, 266–67
Martin, Pte. Adelard Roger, 214
Martin, Sgt. Maj. Charles, 286–87, 343, 349
Martin, Rfn. Jack, 285
Maskell, Gdsm. Robert, 356
Matheson, Lt. Col. Foster, 210, 216–17, 219–20, 262–63
Matheson, Cpl. "Matty," 248
Mattemburg Country House, 190, 192, 313–14
Matthews, Brig. Bruce, 445
May-sur-Orne, 140
Maxwell, Pte. David, 433–34
McAllister, Sgt. Earl, 355
McCarthy, Maj. D., 298
McCordic, Capt. J.D. "Pete," 385, 425
McCutcheon, Maj. M.J., 357, 388
McDonald, CSM Charles, 386
McDonald, Lt. Dan, 22
McDonald, CSM Donald Russell, 275
McDonald, Capt. Douglas, 320
McDonald, CSM Johnny, 274–75
McGivney, Capt. Raymond George, 386
McGuffin, Pte. A.G., 21
McLean, Capt. G., 152
McLeod, Lt. Danny, 388–89, 411–12, 415
McLeod, Lt. E.G., 405
McLeod, Maj. J.S., 18–19, 22, 24, 454
McNeil, Lt. Ronnie, 245
McPherson, Pte. Ronald Dennis, 457
McWhirter, Sgt. Bob, 359
Meagher, Sgt. Jack, 349
Medhurst, Lt. Neil, 247
Medland, Maj. Dick, 285–87, 349
Megill, Brig. W.J. "Bill," 92–95, 98, 127, 130, 133, 140–41, 193, 195–96, 199, 291–92, 301–02, 309, 406, 427–28, 431–32, 434–38, 440–41
Meldram, Lt. Col. John, 225, 263
Mennard, Rfn. Norm, 343
Merksem, 45–46, 64, 67–69, 93, 103, 131, 139, 143–48, 154, 167, 172–74
Merksplas, 119, 289
Middelburg, Leopold Canal area, 204, 283, 327

Middelburg, Walcheren, 81, 84, 156, 160, 259, 427, 443, 451–52, 463
Middel Straat, 177
Middleton-Hope, Lt., 419
Milne, Lt. J.A.S., 356
Milne, Spr. Robert Strahan, 143
Mitchell, Lt. Col. Frank, 94–95
Moan, Cpl. Frank, 389
Moar, Maj. F.F. "Toot," 278
Moergestel, 55
Moerhuizen, 204, 210
Moerkerke, 12, 14–16, 20–22, 27, 61, 71, 80, 462
Moershoofd, 204, 211, 224, 264
Moerstraten, 418–20
Model, Gen. Feld. Mar. Walter, 32, 53–54, 115
Moffat, Lt. Johnny, 436
Molentje, 16, 19, 21–22, 24, 26
Moncel, Brig. Robert, 361, 363, 380, 382, 384, 387, 412, 416, 418, 457
Montgomery, Feld. Mar. Viscount Bernard Law, 33, 35, 38–42, 43, 49–53, 58–61, 73–75, 79, 82, 120–22, 134, 140, 163–65, 179, 253–56, 288, 290–91, 320, 351, 364, 388, 414, 458, 460, 462
Montpetit, Capt. Camile, 438–41
Mooers, Capt. E.F., 382
Mooney, Sgt., 271
Mooney, Padre Tom, 22
Morgan, Rfn. Jack, 286–87
Morrison, Pte. John, 433
Morrissette, Lt. Joseph, 373
Moulton, Lt. Col. J.L., 450
Muir, Pte. Don, 142, 197
Munro, Lt. Don, 195–99
Murdoch, Capt. John Lawrence, 274
Murray, Maj., 412
Murray, Sgt. Harry Thomas, 212
Murray, Lt. K.L., 298
Murray, Sgt. T.B., 363–64
Mutse Straat, 177
Myers, Pte., 97
Myhon, Pte. James Stanley, 346

Nash, Maj. T.B. "Darby," 410
Nationale Kongsgezinde Beweging (National Movement for the King), 64
Nederheide, 194, 314, 372
Neder Rijn, 77–78
Neerpelt, 58
Newman, Capt. Bill, 436
Nieuwdorp, 403
Nieuwvliet, 344
Nijmegen, 49, 77–79, 92, 120–21, 254, 290–91, 350, 364, 460
Nispen, 384–85
Nixon, Lt. Joe, 94
No. 12 Sluiskens, 46
Nolledijk, 258–59
Noordkasteel, 63
Nordstrom, Rfn. Evert, 216
North Beveland Island, 46, 75, 82, 88, 405
Nutt, Cpl. Sam, 323

Oberkommando der Wehrmacht, 20, 55, 161, 281, 325, 371, 414, 451
Odette, Lt. Tom, 232–33
Oorderen, 68, 70, 148, 151, 154, 172–73
Oostbrecht, 124, 127–28
Oostburg, 26, 77, 205, 327–28, 338, 342–44
Oostende, 53, 254, 445–46
Oostmalle, 126, 128
Operations
  Infatuate, 87–89, 164, 390, 405
  Infatuate I, 442
  Infatuate II, 442, 445
  Market Garden, 49–51, 58–59, 61, 74, 77–79, 83–84, 92, 115, 120–21, 124, 165, 179, 255
  Relax, 350
  Spring, 140
  Suitcase, 289–90, 352–53
  Switchback, 204–06, 234, 260–61, 350, 390
  Totalize, 135
  Vitality, 324, 390
  Wellhit, 53, 77
Opstalbeek River, 173, 175
Oranje Molen, 444
Orr, Capt. John Ethelbert, 198
Ossendrecht, 176–80, 184, 188–90, 200–01, 310
Oudelande, 394

Oude Molen, 420
Ouimet, Capt. D.H., 372–73
Oxland, A/V/M R.D., 90

Page, CSM D., 213–16
Palmer, Cpl. A.H., 267
Pangman, Lt. Col. John, 147, 175, 393, 395, 401
Parent, Gdsm. Robert, 381
Parker, Maj., 453, 457
Parker, Lt. A.A.H., 151
Parrish, Lt. Col. C.E., 357
Pas de Calais, 56
Paterson, Maj. Bob, 385, 421–22
Pearkes, Maj. Gen. George, 169–70
Pearson, Capt. H.J. "Sandy," 377
Perry, Pte. Val, 332
Phillips, Sgt. Maj. George, 179–80
Picture Post, 448
Pigott, Maj. Joe M., 149–51, 312, 314–20, 322–23
Place, Lt. Harold, 356
Pleasance, Lt. L.L., 201
Pollari, Pte. T.E., 215
Popham, Maj. Alex, 191, 308–09
Porteous, Maj. Dick, 405
Porter, Capt. Bob, 197, 199
Porter, A/C/M Sir Charles, 162
Powell, P/O J.R., 192
Prest, Maj. Tom, 274–75
Prince, Sgt. Harry, 329–30
Prins Karel Polder, 383
Prugh, Capt. John Shirley, 456
Pugh, Maj. David V., 224, 266–67
Pugh, Pte. R.L., 213
Pugsley, Capt. A.F., 88, 91, 133, 446, 448
Putte, 173–76, 179, 186, 196, 290, 298, 353, 362

Quinn, Lt. Murray, 278

Radio Oranje, 155, 160
Ramsay, Adm. Sir Bertram, 50, 53, 87–88, 164, 253, 446, 460
Ratte, Lt. Charles, 359
Rawlings, Gen. John, 179
Redden, Pte. John, 359
Reed, Sgt. T.J., 183

Reeves, Pte. Orville, 409
Reid, Capt. Edward James, 153
Reiger, Pte. Paul, 346
Retranchement, 205
Rhine River, 43–44, 48–50, 77, 79, 120
Richardson, Sgt. A.F., 341–42
Richardson, Cpl. D.H., 433
Ridgway, Lt. Colin, 175
Riesberry, Lt. Donald Leach, 265
Rijkevorsel, 116–19, 124–25, 128
Ritchie, Lt. Col. Bruce R., 95, 128–29, 140–41, 189–90, 292, 301–04, 307–09, 429–30
Roberts, HMS, 445, 449
Roberts, Lt. Edward, 24
Roberts, Maj. Gen. G.P.B. "Pip," 44, 47–48
Robinson, Maj. S.O., 378
Rockingham, Brig. John "Rocky," 240, 260, 277–78, 333
Rodgers, Brig. Elliot, 122, 438
Roosendaal, 87, 90–91, 115, 121, 134, 289, 326, 352, 379, 385, 412, 414, 416
Roosendaal Canal, 360–62
Ross, Pte. Sanford, 377
Rouen, 36
Rowley, Lt. Col. Roger, 247–48, 273, 329–34
Russell, Brig. J.D., 440
Russell, Cpl. L.E., 245
Rutherford, Maj. Noel, 362
Ryall, Maj. E.J.H. "Paddy," 145, 201–02
Rylasdaam, Sgt. Andy, 153

St. Amand, L. Cpl. Roland, 382
s'Hertogenbosch, 121, 179, 414
Saint Kruis, 225, 283
St. Leonard. *See* Sint-Lenaarts
Saint-Omer, 121
St. Philipsland Peninsula, 453, 457
Sander, Gen. Lt. Erwin, 20–21, 26
Sauvé, Maj. Joseph-Mignault-Paul, 108, 113
Scheldt estuary, 12–13, 28, 41, 45–46, 48–50, 53, 55–57, 59, 62, 71–76, 79–84, 85–91, 101–02, 155–56, 165, 171, 176, 201, 205, 239–242, 245, 253, 256–57, 260, 284, 288, 311, 324–26, 329, 383,

391, 395, 405, 441, 445–46, 450–51, 453, 458, 460, 462–64
Scheldt River, 73, 103, 143, 154, 171
Schjelderup, Maj. Roger, 221–24, 226–28, 290
Schneider, Lt. E.W., 345
Schoening, Lt. Howard O., 436
Schoondijke, 205, 277, 285, 327–29, 336, 338
Schore, 398–99
Schowen en Duiveland, 453, 457
Schubert, Maj. Victor, 398
Schwob, Capt. Robert, 210, 212–15, 218–19
Scott, Capt. R.A., 365, 409
Seaborn, Rev. Robert Lowder, 168
Seine River, 32, 35–36, 43–44, 47, 51
Sellar, Commodore K.A. "Monkey," 449
Shannon, Pte. E.G., 267
Sharpe, Pte., 94
Sharrard, Tpr. Clarence, 360
Shawcross, Maj. Ronald, 36, 210–12, 219, 226, 261–63
Shea, Lt. W.J., 307–08
Shipley, L. Sgt. C.B., 213
Sijsele, 14–15, 27
Simonds, Lt. Gen. Guy, 27, 33, 40–42, 53, 59, 133, 162–64, 204–06, 289–90, 335, 390–91, 394, 405, 446, 458, 463
  Advocates flooding Walcheren, 85–90
  Commands First Canadian Army, 121–24
  Sets out Scheldt offensive plan, 133–36
Sint-Lenaarts, 3, 103, 124, 128, 130–31, 139, 142
Sint-Niklaas, 72
Sirluck, Capt. Ernie, 13
Slater, Maj., 129
Slater, Sgt. H.S., 419–20
Sloan, Nursing Sister Harriet J.T., 306
Sloe Channel, 81, 432, 435, 439, 442–43, 451–52
Sloedam, 82, 156
Sluis, 16, 26, 77, 205, 327–28, 338, 344, 347–48
Sluiskill, 240
Smith, Sgt. A.G., 360

Smith, Maj. A.G.V., 380–82
Smith, Cpl. Charles, 408
Smith, CSM C.J., 346
Smith, Lt. C.W., 284
Smith, CSM Dave, 272
Smith, Lt. Col. E.M., 363, 416, 418, 420
Somme River, 37, 44
South Beveland, 47–48, 74–75, 80–83, 85–89, 93, 102, 119, 121, 124, 131, 134, 139, 154, 156, 162, 164, 181, 185–86, 188, 200, 202, 260, 288, 290, 294, 301, 314, 322, 324–27, 351–52, 364, 372, 376, 379, 383, 390, 407, 427, 431, 462
  Clearing of, 390–406
South Beveland Canal.
  See Beveland Canal
Speck, Sgt. James Henry, 26
Spiers, L. Cpl. Vernon Everett, 24
Sponheimer, Gen. Inf. Otto, 102–03, 114, 118, 371, 382
Spragge, Brig. Jock, 224–25, 249, 263–64, 341
Spry, Maj. Gen. Dan, 123, 204, 240, 260–61, 270–71, 277, 327–30, 333, 336–38, 347
Staartse Heide, 298
Stabroek, 173–75
Stadelmier, Pte. Henry, 114
Steenberg, Lt. N.R.F., 24
Steenbergen, 176, 417–18, 420–21, 426, 453–57
Sternhoven, 143
Stewart, Lt. Don, 389, 411
Stewart, Lt. Col. J. David, 281, 356, 379, 386–87, 408, 422
Stewart, Capt. Selby, 129
Stirling, Maj. A.K., 18–19, 21, 24, 367, 454
Stock, Capt. R.B., 367, 454–55
Stockloser, Maj. B., 408, 410, 421–25, 457
Stothers, Capt. John Ellis, 404
Stott, Capt. George, 198
Stott, Lt. Col. Vern, 95, 105, 108, 114, 126, 130, 292, 294, 297–300, 396, 398
Strickland, Maj. Phil, 277, 336
Stronach, Gdsm. J.D., 420

Strooibrug, 204, 207, 213
Student, Gen. Oberst. Kurt, 54–56, 103
Styffe, Capt., 458
Suckling, Maj. R.T. "Bob," 145–46, 178, 392
Supreme Headquarters Allied Expeditionary Force (SHAEF), 31, 49, 90, 124, 136, 253
Swayze, Maj. Jim, 411, 415, 424

Taylor, Pte. N.S., 214
Teasdale, Pte. George, 434
Tedder, A/C/M Arthur, 162
Tedford, Lt. A.M., 323
Tedlie, Capt. James, 357
Tennant, Capt. Mark, 99, 191
Terneuzen, 57, 71–73, 76, 88, 101, 115, 205, 237–41, 246, 390, 394
Terrapin Mark I, described, 235–36
Tessier, L. Sgt. Aldege, 381
Theune, Jo, 158–59
Thiebeault, Capt. Elmo, 372–73
Thomas, Cpl. C.V., 276
Thomas, Cpl. Elwyn Bernard, 215
Thompson, Lt. Arthur, 126–28
Thompson, Lt. Col. Ernest Payson, 153, 376, 396
Thomson, Sgt. L.G., 215
Thornicroft, Pte. Richard Maurice, 215
Tighe, Pte. Jack, 247
Tingley, Lt., 243
Todd, Brig. Stanley, 206, 246
Toole, Lt. Ernest Arlond, 110
Tremblay, Cpl. Romeo, 419
Turnbull, CSM Alan, 430
Turner, Lt. F., 451
Turner, Sgt. Howard, 359
Tuttle, Cpl. Norman E., 349

Uitwateringskanaal, 344

Valentine, Padre W., 22
Valois, Lt. Roger, 127
van Dijk, Ad, 258–59
van Luven, Pte. Robert, 408
Veere, 161, 258–59, 326
Verrières Ridge, 292

Vlissingen, 3, 13, 54, 56, 73, 81–82, 160–61, 258–59, 270, 274, 327, 329–32, 334, 335, 340, 345, 390, 406, 427, 429, 432, 439, 442–44, 451–52
 Assault on, 446–48
Völckerpolder, 310
von der Heydte, Oberstleutnant Friederich, 172, 185, 190, 192, 294, 313–14, 384
von Runstedt, Gen. Feld. Mar. Gerd, 54, 101, 115
von und zu Gilsa, Gen. Inf. Werner Freiherr, 20
von Zangen, Gen. Inf. Gustav, 102, 172, 257–58, 260, 382

Waal River, 77–79, 115, 350
Waarde, 397
Walcheren Island, 3, 13, 46–48, 54, 56, 61–62, 73–75, 80–84, 85–91, 101–03, 119, 121, 124, 134, 136, 155–57, 160–64, 185–86, 246, 258–60, 282, 324–26, 331, 335, 364, 377, 383, 390–91, 394, 400–05, 427–28, 433, 435, 437–41, 462–63
 Invasion of, 442–53
Walker, Pte. W.J., 362
Walsh, Brig. Geoffrey, 90–91, 134
Walsh, Maj. "Huck," 393
Warnick, Sgt. Carl, 285
Warning, Oberst Elmar, 184–85, 190, 325–26, 414
Warspite HMS, 88, 91, 445, 448–49
Wasp carrier, described, 207–08
Watervliet, 281, 284
Weatherson, Cpl. John, 364
Webb, Pte. Sidney, 379
Weinstock, Capt. J.W., 321
Welberg, 453–57
Welch, Maj. H.A. "Huck," 177, 312, 314, 316–17, 319, 322
Westkapelle, 134–35, 155–57, 159–62, 258, 348, 391, 406, 432, 439, 442–46, 448–51
Westlaar, 416–17
Westmalle, 143
Westphal, Gen. Kav. Siegfried, 414

West Scheldt Estuary. *See* Scheldt Estuary
Whitaker, Lt. Col. Denis, 1, 95, 148–51, 176–77, 302, 310–13, 316–18, 320–24
White Brigade, 47, 65, 145, 403, 438
White, Maj. Georges, 105, 373
Whitehead, Pte. J.S., 322–23
Wijnegem, 93, 95, 465–66
Wilcox, Capt. Tom, 401, 403
Wilkins, Lt. Amos, 377–78
Wilkinson, Pte., 94
Williams, Maj. Harry, 109–10
Williams, Maj. Ken, 109, 153, 298–300
Williamson, Sgt., 182
Williamson, Lt. J.A., 321
Williamson, Capt. Walter James, 324
Wilmarsdonk, 68
Wilson, Lt. Col. Eric Mackay, 126–28, 132–33
Wiltshire, Maj. R.T., 236
Winters, L. Cpl. Arthur Emil, 143
Wishart, Cpl. Raymond, 214
Woensdrecht, 47, 173, 176, 178, 180–81, 184, 187, 196, 199, 202–03, 290–91, 298, 301–02, 307–08, 351–52, 371–72, 376, 378, 382–83, 390, 461
 Assault on, 310–25
Wolfe, L. Cpl. Richard G., 437
Woodcock, Capt. Andy, 278
Wotherspoon, Lt. Col. Gordon "Swatty," 415
Wouwbaan, 193
Wouwse Hill, 416
Wouwse Plantage, 379–80, 382, 384–85, 387–88, 390, 407, 416
Wright, Capt. Bob, 316
Wright, Maj. E., 245–46
Wright, Pte. George Arthur, 21, 24
Wuustwezel, 371

Yerseke, 397
Young, Maj. Ralph, 403
Young, Gdsm. Reuben Erland, 363

Zandfort, 294, 372
Zandkreek, 405
Zandstraat, 366
Zandvoort, 194

Zeebrugge, 57, 76
Zeeland, 46, 75, 160, 405, 453, 463–64
Zijpe, 457–58
Zijpe Channel, 453, 457
Zoomvliet, 407, 409, 415
Zoutelande, 162, 443, 451
Zuidzande, 346

INDEX OF FORMATIONS, UNITS, AND CORPS

CANADIAN

Army
First Canadian Army, 13–14, 28, 32–35, 37, 40–42, 51–53, 57, 59–62, 71–72, 74, 79, 82, 87, 89, 104, 115, 120–21, 124, 133, 162–66, 170, 207, 210, 240–41, 249, 254, 256, 263, 288, 291, 312, 320, 325, 328, 335, 376, 394, 414, 418, 442, 445, 448, 458–60, 462–64

CORPS
I Canadian Corps, 39, 93, 166
II Canadian Corps, 27, 33–35, 40, 53, 59–60, 74, 77, 80, 87–90, 122–24, 134, 164–65, 185, 196, 206, 240, 256, 289, 291, 330, 405, 437, 445–46
Royal Canadian Army Service Corps, 51, 247, 329
Royal Canadian Signal Corps, 93

DIVISIONS
1st Canadian Infantry, 40–41
2nd Canadian Infantry, 33, 36–37, 59, 62, 64–65, 71, 80, 86, 91–93, 122, 124, 126, 131, 133–34, 139, 143, 149–50, 154, 171, 178–79, 185, 196, 202–03, 288, 290–92, 294, 301, 304, 310–11, 322, 325, 351–53, 364, 371–72, 376, 379, 383–84, 390, 402, 405, 407, 427, 441, 446, 463–64
3rd Canadian Infantry, 33, 36–37, 51, 53, 59, 62, 77, 79, 87–88, 123, 134, 168, 204, 240, 246, 270, 282, 291, 327, 334, 338, 347, 350–51, 450, 459–60, 463
4th Canadian Armoured, 12, 20, 36, 51, 60–61, 79–80, 87, 91, 100, 123, 131, 134, 178, 196, 206–07, 241, 270–71, 280, 282, 288–90, 322, 325, 351–53, 362, 364, 371, 379, 382, 384, 388, 453, 457, 464
5th Canadian Armoured, 34, 41

BRIGADES
1st Canadian Armoured, 34
2nd Canadian Armoured, 126–27, 133
4th Canadian Armoured, 352–54, 361, 365, 379, 387–88, 407, 412, 414, 416–17, 421, 426, 457
4th Canadian Infantry, 53, 62–63, 65, 68–70, 139, 143, 148, 151, 154, 173, 176, 178, 188, 193, 199, 290–92, 298–99, 320, 352, 391, 393–96, 400, 402–03, 407
5th Canadian Infantry, 91–93, 99, 119, 124–27, 130, 133, 139, 143, 151, 178, 180, 189, 192, 195, 199, 291, 302, 352, 372, 376, 383, 402–03, 405–06, 427, 432, 437–42
6th Canadian Infantry, 104, 108, 113, 116, 125, 131, 139, 141–43, 151, 154, 186, 290, 324, 351, 372, 376, 383, 395–96, 398–400
7th Canadian Infantry, 80, 204–08, 221, 224, 231, 233–34, 240, 249, 256–57, 261, 263–68, 282–84, 327–28, 337–38, 342, 344, 346–47

541

542 / TERRIBLE VICTORY

8th Canadian Infantry, 80, 205, 210, 234, 260–61, 270–71, 277–81, 284, 328, 338, 342, 344, 346, 348
9th Canadian Infantry, 80, 205–06, 235–36, 238, 240–41, 246, 249, 256–57, 260–61, 270, 277, 280–81, 284, 327–29, 331, 336–38, 347–48, 462
10th Canadian Infantry, 15–16, 80, 100, 196, 208, 279–81, 352–53, 356, 360, 362, 365, 379, 388, 407, 414, 421, 454

ARMOURED UNITS

British Columbia Regiment, 282–83, 353, 356, 360, 368, 386, 412, 453, 457–58
Canadian Grenadier Guards, 353, 356, 379, 382, 384, 386, 412, 416–17
Fort Garry Horse, 126, 128–29, 131–32, 141–42, 152–53, 176–77, 180–83, 186–87, 189, 195, 290, 299, 301, 311, 320–21, 372, 384, 391–92, 396
Governor General's Foot Guards, 353, 362, 364, 379–80, 384, 412, 416–18, 420
Sherbrooke Fusiliers, 117–18

ARTILLERY UNITS

2nd Anti-Tank Regiment, 308
5th Anti-Tank Regiment, 353, 454–55
23rd Anti-Tank Battery, 186
4th Field Regiment, 36, 63, 67, 69, 146–47, 149–50, 173–75, 178–79, 318, 320, 393, 404, 460
5th Field Regiment, 126, 195, 377, 404, 429–30, 432, 438
6th Field Regiment, 108, 113, 152, 399
12th Field Regiment, 213
13th Field Regiment, 246
14th Field Regiment, 246
15th Field Regiment, 25, 206, 246, 361, 410–11
19th Field Regiment, 206, 246, 274
3rd Light Anti-Aircraft Regiment, 290
7th Medium Regiment, 311

ENGINEER UNITS

11th Field Company, 125, 143
16th Field Company, 230
8th Field Squadron, 20, 282
9th Field Squadron, 20, 282

INFANTRY BATTALIONS/REGIMENTS

Algonquin Regiment, 33, 61, 71, 80, 93, 100, 196, 204, 208–09, 271, 280–81, 284, 290, 353, 357–62, 365–67, 407, 409–10, 426, 454, 456–57, 459, 462
  Leopold Canal Assault, 12–28
Argyll and Sutherland Highlanders of Canada, 25, 208–09, 271, 281, 284, 353, 355–56, 361–62, 365–66, 379–80, 382, 384–87, 407–09, 421, 423–26, 454, 456–57
Black Watch (RHC) of Canada, 93–95, 124, 128–29, 133, 139–42, 166–67, 181, 189–94, 198–99, 291–92, 299, 301–03, 377–78, 402, 428–29, 431–34, 461–62
  and Black Friday attack, 307–11
Calgary Highlanders, 92, 94–95, 100, 104, 124, 130–33, 139–43, 180, 182, 189, 191–95, 199, 291, 310, 372, 376–78, 383–84, 428, 431–33, 435, 437–38, 465
Canadian Scottish Regiment, 33, 106, 144, 168, 207, 209–11, 221, 225–226, 233, 249, 264, 266–68, 282–83, 337–38, 340–42, 345–46
Essex Scottish Regiment, 62, 64, 69, 144, 147, 173–75, 186, 196, 291, 299, 310, 321, 391–95, 400–01, 403
Highland Light Infantry of Canada, 64, 235, 237–38, 241, 243–44, 271, 274–80, 328, 336, 347–49,
Lake Superior Regiment, 80, 353–54, 361–62, 365, 379–82, 384, 386–88, 407, 412–13, 416–20, 440, 453, 457–58
Le Régiment de la Chaudière, 280, 284, 344, 347–48
Le Régiment de Maisonneuve, 99, 124, 126–28, 166, 180–82, 189, 192, 291, 294, 299, 310, 428, 432, 435, 437–38, 440–41
Les Fusiliers Mont-Royal, 104–05, 108, 112–113, 125–26, 131, 166, 186–87, 372–74, 376, 383, 396–99
Lincoln and Welland Regiment, 16–17, 353, 356, 358, 360–61, 365–66, 385, 387–88, 407, 411, 414–15, 421, 423–26, 454

INDEX / 543

North Nova Scotia Highlanders, 237–39, 241–46, 271–72, 274, 276–80, 328, 331, 336, 348, 350
North Shore (New Brunswick) Regiment, 210–11, 230–31, 242, 271, 277–78, 280, 284, 346, 348
Queen's Own Cameron Highlanders, 105, 142–43, 151, 153–54, 196, 324, 351, 372, 376, 383, 396–400
Queen's Own Rifles, 280–81, 284–85, 342, 344, 348–49
Regina Rifles Regiment, 36, 207, 209–11, 213, 216, 218, 221, 223, 225–26, 230–33, 249, 261–64, 266–67, 269, 283–84, 344–47, 462
Royal Hamilton Light Infantry, 68, 70, 95, 148, 176, 180, 196, 199, 302, 310–15, 320–25, 351, 376, 393–94, 400
Royal Montreal Regiment, 210, 212–15, 218, 220, 225, 283–84
Royal Regiment of Canada, 62, 66–67, 144, 146–47, 167, 175–78, 188, 200–03, 290–91, 300, 310, 316, 391–93, 400–01, 403–05, 429
Royal Rifles of Canada, 34
Royal Winnipeg Rifles, 225, 230–31, 249, 263–66, 283, 338, 340–41, 346
South Saskatchewan Regiment, 36, 95, 104–06, 108–09, 112–13, 125, 130, 151–52, 154, 186, 196, 290–92, 294, 298–300, 310, 372, 374, 376, 383, 396–400
Stormont, Dundas and Glengarry Highlanders, 238, 247, 271–74, 276, 278, 328–34, 335, 337, 347–48
Winnipeg Grenadiers, 34

OTHER UNITS
8th Field Surgical Unit, 449–50
9th Field Surgical Unit, 450
10th Base Reinforcement Group, 95
No. 23 Field Ambulance, 247
No. 10 Field Dressing Station, 450
No. 5 Field Transfusion Unit, 450
No. 8 General Hospital, 305–06
No. 16 General Hospital, 121
No. 17 Light Field Ambulance, 450

RECONNAISSANCE
South Alberta Regiment, 25, 196, 290, 353, 388, 407, 411, 414–15, 422
14th Canadian Hussars, 104–05, 126, 173, 175, 178, 186–87, 188, 391–92, 402, 405
17th Duke of York's Royal Canadian Hussars, 205, 275

SUPPORT
Cameron Highlanders of Ottawa (MG), 247, 271, 273, 278, 285
New Brunswick Rangers, 15
Toronto Scottish (MG), 149, 186, 188, 201, 301, 304, 311, 377, 404, 432

BRITISH AND COMMONWEALTH

Air Force
2nd Tactical Air Force, 82, 124, 372, 445
No. 1 Bomber Group, 157
No. 3 Bomber Group, 157
No. 5 Bomber Group, 157
No. 8 (Pathfinder Force) Group, 157
No. 84 Fighter Group, 320
132 Norwegian Wing, 320

SQUADRONS
No. 74, 308
No. 127, 313
No. 197, 308
No. 257, 192
No. 263, 308

Army
9th Army Group, 206
21st Army Group, 33, 43, 48–49, 51, 53, 59, 65, 71, 87, 120, 124, 136, 163–64, 253, 255, 290, 364–65
Second Army, 35, 38, 49–51, 58, 62, 74, 77, 79, 120–21, 134, 164–65, 179, 256, 288, 290, 351, 364, 414, 462
I Corps, 33, 35, 40, 52, 60, 74, 79, 115–16, 119, 121, 134, 164, 178, 256, 288–89, 322, 325, 351–52, 414, 453, 459
VIII Corps, 51, 58
XII Corps, 58, 60, 364
XXX Corps, 43–44, 51, 58, 74, 77–78, 172

DIVISIONS
1st Airborne, 78
3rd Infantry, 33
6th Airborne, 33
7th Armoured, 44, 60, 414
11th Armoured, 43, 58
49th (West Riding), 33, 116–17, 119, 124, 126, 288–89, 352, 371, 384, 388, 414, 457
50th Infantry, 44
51st (Highland), 33
52nd (Lowland), 33, 254, 283, 327, 390, 394, 439, 443
53rd (Welsh) Infantry, 63, 91
79th Armoured, 236, 328, 330, 333, 386, 411
Irish Guards Armoured, 44, 58, 78

BRIGADES
4th Special Service, 445–46, 451
56th Infantry, 117
146th Infantry, 116–17
155th Infantry, 443–44, 448, 452
156th Infantry, 390, 394
157th Infantry, 283, 390, 401–03, 406, 427, 438, 442, 451

COMMANDO
No. 4, 444–48

BATTALIONS/REGIMENTS
2nd Fife and Forfarshire Yeomanry, 353, 411
4th Battalion, King's Own Scottish Borderers, 448
4th Lincolns, 116–17
5th Assault, RE, 236, 282
5th Battalion, King's Own Scottish Borderers, 448
5th Highland Light Infantry (City of Glasgow), 394, 452
6th Cameronians (Scottish Rifles), 394, 452
6th (Lankashire) Battalion, 452
7th/9th Royal Scots, 452
22nd Dragoons, 353
59th (Newfoundland) Heavy, 445
79th Reconnaissance, 118
84th Medium, 311
115th Heavy Anti-Aircraft, 311
121st Medium, 311
Essex, 118
Glasgow Highlanders, 438, 452
Royal Scots Fusiliers, 394
Royal Scots (The Royal Regiment), 452
Staffordshire Yeomanry, 394

OTHER UNITS
80th Squadron, 236
202nd Field Company, RE, 439
284th Squadron, RE, 329

NAVY

FORCES
Force T, 446, 448
Support Squadron, East Flank, 445, 449

ROYAL MARINES
1st Heavy Anti-Aircraft Regiment, 200, 302
No. 41 Commando, 444, 450–51
No. 47 Commando, 444, 451
No. 48 Commando, 444, 450

UNITED STATES

Air Force
8th Air Force, 89, 162
406th Squadron, 155

Army
First Army, 253–54
12th Army Group, 254–55
XIX Corps, 44
VII Corps, 44

DIVISIONS
82nd Airborne, 78
101st Airborne, 78
104th Infantry, 289, 291, 352, 388, 414, 457

INDEX / 545

ALLIED FORCES (OTHER THAN U.S.)

1st Polish Armoured Division, 33, 60, 103, 115, 119, 289, 352, 414, 457
10th Polish Dragoon Regiment, 72

GERMAN

Army
Army Group B, 32, 54, 115
Fifteenth Army, 28, 41–42, 48–49, 53–54, 56–57, 60, 82, 101, 115, 171–72, 260, 325–26, 364, 383, 414, 457
First Parachute Army, 54, 103, 114–15
Kampfgruppe Chill, 172, 184–85, 187, 294, 298–300, 301, 325–26, 371, 383–84, 407, 412, 414
LXVII Corps, 102, 114–15, 118–19, 171, 184, 187, 325–26, 371, 382, 384, 413–14
LXXXVIII Corps, 55, 103, 116
LXXXIX Corps, 20

Divisions
3rd Parachute, 55
5th Parachute, 55
12th S.S. (Hitlerjugend) Panzer, 32
64th Infantry, 83, 101–02, 205, 256–57, 260–61, 270, 281, 326–27, 338, 344–45, 347
70th Infantry, 56, 83, 102–03, 189, 260, 326, 383, 391, 402, 405, 443
84th Infantry, 172
85th Infantry, 172
89th Infantry, 172
226th Infantry, 83
245th Infantry, 13, 20, 26, 326
346th Infantry, 103, 114, 119, 171–72, 358, 371, 384, 414
711th Infantry, 103–04, 118–19, 151, 325, 371, 414
712th Infantry, 73, 83
719th Infantry, 92, 103–04, 116, 118–19, 414
Hermann Göring 1st Batallion, 385

Brigades/Regiments
2nd Parachute Regiment, 172, 384
6th Parachute Regiment, 172, 309, 365, 376, 382, 388, 407, 453
70th Artillery, 190
225th Assault Gun Brig, 190
280th Assault Gun Brig, 103
743rd Grenadier Reg, 99
936th Grenadier Reg, 21, 26
1018th Grenadier Reg, 103, 146, 186
1037th Grenadier Reg, 340
1053rd Grenadier Reg, 300
Hermann Göring Regiment, 388, 412, 453
Hermann Göring Ersatz Regiment, 298
Hermann Göring Training Regiment, 172

Battalions
1st Battalion, Hermann Göring, 385
1st Battalion, 6th Parachute, 313
1st Battalion, 743rd Grenadier Reg, 99
559th GHQ Heavy Anti-tank Battalion, 103

Navy
Naval Special Staff Knuth, 101

ABOUT THE AUTHOR

MARK ZUEHLKE'S CRITICALLY acclaimed series on the opening days of the Normandy Invasion, *Holding Juno: Canada's Heroic Defence of the D-Day Beaches: June 7–12, 1944* and *Juno Beach: Canada's D-Day Victory: June 6, 1944* cemented his position as the nation's leading writer of popular military history. *Holding Juno* won the City of Victoria's Butler Book Prize in 2006 and was excerpted in the Canadian edition of *Reader's Digest*. His trilogy of *Ortona: Canada's Epic World War II Battle*, *The Liri Valley: Canada's World War II Breakthrough to Rome*, and *The Gothic Line: Canada's Month of Hell in World War II Italy* is considered the definitive narrative of the Canadian army's role in the Italian Campaign. His other historical works are *The Canadian Military Atlas: Four Centuries of Conflict from New France to Kosovo* (with mapmaker C. Stuart Daniel), *For Honour's Sake: The War of 1812 and the Brokering of an Uneasy Peace* (Winner of the 2007 Canadian Authors Association Lela Common Award for Canadian History), *The Gallant Cause: Canadians in the Spanish Civil War, 1936–1939*, and *Scoundrels, Dreamers and Second Sons: British Remittance Men in the Canadian West*.

Also a novelist, he is the author of the popular Elias McCann series, which follows the misadventures and investigations of a community coroner in Tofino, British Columbia. The first in this series, *Hands Like Clouds*, won the Crime Writers of Canada Arthur Ellis Award for Best First Novel in 2000. It was followed by *Carry Tiger to Mountain* and *Sweep Lotus*—the latter a finalist for the 2004 Arthur Ellis Award for Best Novel. Zuehlke lives in Victoria, British Columbia, where he is at work on his next book on Canadians in World War II.